The Handel Letters

The Handel Letters
A BIOGRAPHICAL CONVERSATION

Sandra K. Dolby

Copyright © 2017 Sandra K. Dolby

All rights reserved.

Cover and chapter art by Alexis Stahl

ISBN-13: 9781977669179
ISBN-10: 1977669174

The Handel Letters: A Biographical Conversation is dedicated to the memory of Mr. Cloyde Slater and to all who have worked to keep Handel and his music alive, in our ears and in our hearts.

Some Brief But Relevant Biographies

George Frideric Handel (1685-1759) was a late Baroque period composer, best known for his oratorio *Messiah* and such orchestral pieces as the *Water Music* and *Music for the Royal Fireworks*. Though born in the city of Halle in Germany, Handel began a career as a composer of operas in Italy and then moved to London, his home for most of his adult life and the context for his outstanding musical career. He is most often credited with making the English-language oratorio a popular genre of classical music. He became a British citizen, was made a governor of the Foundling Hospital in London, was honored with a life-size statue on the grounds of Vauxhall Gardens, and is buried, along with other notable British exemplars, in Westminster Abbey.

Sandra K. Dolby is a folklorist, known primarily for bringing academic attention to the oral personal experience story. She taught for more than thirty years in the Department of Folklore and Ethnomusicology at Indiana University. She served as Director of the Folklore Institute for a brief time and also as an Adjunct Professor in the Department of American Studies. She continues to serve on the Faculty Committee of IU's Individualized Major Program. Publications include *Literary Folkloristics and the Personal Narrative* and *Self-Help Books: Why Americans Keep Reading Them*. She has also recorded a number of albums that include original songs, folk songs, and popular covers. Academic fellowships have taken her to Australia and to Norway. She currently lives in Bloomington, Indiana. See www.sandradolby.com.

Alexis Stahl is an artist, editor, and archivist who specializes in printmaking and has worked extensively with the preservation and archiving of art objects. She earned a BA degree from Newcomb College at Tulane University and an MFA from the University of Cincinnati. She currently lives in New Orleans and works in the Research and Design Department at Mignon Faget, Ltd. See www.alexisstahl.com.

Table of Contents

Preface··· xi
Prologue··· xv

Chapter 1   Mrs. Wainwright's Query ························· 1
Chapter 2   A Stash of Letters ····························· 20
Chapter 3   Read and Remember ····························· 34
Chapter 4   A Handel Seminar······························· 57
Chapter 5   A Letter in French ···························· 83
Chapter 6   On a Clear Day································ 100
Chapter 7   Handel in Rome ······························· 124
Chapter 8   My Dear Mr. Handel ···························· 141
Chapter 9   The Lure of London ···························· 166
Chapter 10 The Queen's Theater ·························· 187
Chapter 11 Love Song to a Tree ·························· 207
Chapter 12 And Water Music ······························ 230
Chapter 13 The Esoteric-Exoteric Factor ················· 258
Chapter 14 Mothers······································· 281
Chapter 15 Academic Acclaim······························ 304
Chapter 16 In Sickness and in Health ···················· 322
Chapter 17 Handel and Mrs. Cibber ······················· 341
Chapter 18 Getting to Know You ·························· 363
Chapter 19 The Trumpet Shall Sound······················· 393
Chapter 20 Father Confessor ····························· 418

Chapter 21 Art and Artifacts · 443
Chapter 22 A Small and Treasured Gift · 469
Chapter 23 Whatever First Meets Me · 488
Chapter 24 Leave the Thorn · 505
Chapter 25 Your Humble Servant · 524
Chapter 26 Pass the Hat · 547
Chapter 27 Us versus Them · 568
Chapter 28 Personal Proverbs · 585

    Epilogue ·591
    Acknowledgments · 595
    Bibliography · 597

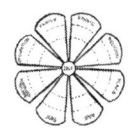

Preface

*Our topic: Learning about and from the
life of George Frideric Handel.*

FORTUNATELY FOR US, HUMANS ARE born with a great love and talent for learning. There are so many ways to learn and so many subjects, so many skills, strategies, and stores of knowledge. As an elementary school student in the 1950s, I always found the filmstrips shown in class riveting, even exciting. Usually these instructional aids were intended to show the parts of a flower or how some scientific experiment was carried out or how some animal behaved. We have much better technology now, of course, but I miss that almost clumsy attention to the process of learning, that patient unfolding of each step in our enlightenment—no matter the subject.

And so here, in this book about the composer George Frideric Handel, I explore an ancient and but underappreciated way of learning—purposeful conversation about someone's life. Conversation is how we first learn and teach. We tell stories from our own lives. We listen to others talk of their own experiences. Occasionally we set aside time to do both of these things more formally—in a discussion group or seminar. That is my model here—a topical seminar with ten or twelve participants.

And why Handel? Certainly there are many, many people interested in Handel. And there have been many books written on his life, on his music, on the times in which he lived. It is fair to guess that across the globe a high percentage of people know who Handel is and at least a little about him. Most will know of Handel's *Messiah* and maybe even have memories of singing parts of the oratorio with a community chorus. Handel is a well-known figure who has inspired many excellent biographies, but the world could easily accommodate yet another attempt to present his life story. This book is one such attempt, but it is also an attempt to tap into the process of conversation as a learning tool and vehicle for values clarification.

In the not too distant past, as a university professor, I taught graduate seminars in a department of folklore and ethnomusicology. One source I found especially helpful in presenting the generally pertinent topic of relativism was a little book titled *Who's To Say?* The author, Norman Melchert, examined the subject of relativism through a series of conversations among a group of six fictional characters, each of whom represented a particular philosophical perspective. I think my students enjoyed contemplating the topic using this conversational format, especially as they had the opportunity to play-act a bit as we read it collectively. But I also think they learned more than simply the variety of perspectives Melchert hoped to present. They also learned how emergent conversations reveal the speaker's character and values, how—each time he or she speaks—those individuals inevitably use the many frames of reference that help make them who they are.

In my own research on personal narratives, I have called this identity-based frame or constellation of sources the individual's "cultural thumbprint." If you can imagine a flower—a daisy—with a center or pseudanthium that represents the individual and the petals attached to that center as various groups that influence that person, then you have my notion of the cultural thumbprint, the range of groups that—collectively and over time—influences what a person values, thinks, or knows. In a conversation—even a conversation about Handel—the person's cultural thumbprint will show up in what he or she says in the context of that conversation. There is not simply one cultural frame that influences what a person knows or believes. There are many, and the overall constellation of influences is unique and evolving for each individual. That varying cultural and personal perspective is what I wanted to bring to my view of Handel's biography.

Contemporary folklore research welcomes just about any topic as a subject of study. That inclusiveness was part of what drew me to the field years ago. For example, I could undertake a folklore fieldwork project that examines how real people actually do respond to what is known of Handel's life, a project that asks what lessons those individuals might draw from thinking about his narrative. As a folklorist, I could carry out that fieldwork, analyze the recorded dialogues, and publish a scholarly monograph on the topic. I chose not to do that, but I think it would be a worthwhile study. Instead, I have chosen to create a fictional context loosely based on that hypothetical fieldwork design. And I have—again very loosely—drawn upon my own experience as a university professor and an American baby boomer to introduce, as seminar participants, characters who reflect something of the people I have known over the course of my life, though, to be sure, none of these fictional characters are stand-ins for any real people I have known.

Most of my information on Handel's life and music has come from the many excellent sources listed in the bibliography. I have not used the very admirable system of meticulous footnoting that we have come to expect in a piece of scholarly research. I have instead included allusions to these various resources within the conversations that comprise the content of this book. I hope readers are not disappointed with this choice. For this project, it seemed a more reader-friendly alternative to me. I should also point out that the fictional characters—though, as I say, loosely based on people I have known—are not in any way supposed to represent real individuals, living or dead. Please, if you know me, do not try to guess whether the characters are someone you know—or you, yourself. They are, for better or worse, figments of my imagination and personifications of my occasionally conflicting lines of thought.

Finally, it seemed unnecessarily pedantic to make up some fictional town and university and reference some nonexistent cultural frame for my imaginary seminar. I don't believe I have in any way defamed Indiana University or its Department of Folklore and Ethnomusicology or Bloomington, Indiana, or the Unitarian Universalist Church, though they are all named directly in the book. On the contrary, I hope all such references reflect my great ongoing delight in having been a part of each. Similarly, I reference by title and author the research on Handel that figures in the book's content, just as those works would be cited in a real conversation on the topic. I leave to my Acknowledgments page the mention of people who have contributed in a more personal and direct way to this project. Here let me simply credit the amazing field of folklore research for its central role in guiding my way of living a life of learning, teaching, and writing. "I am a part of all that I have met"—but most especially I am a part of my field of folklore research and it, an undeniable part of me.

I have always admired Handel, and I have grown to love even more of his music than I did when starting this project. People who write about historical figures are often asked what they would want to say if they could go back in time and actually meet their subjects. I am fairly certain that I would find Handel rather intimidating. But my fictional Lydia Grayston allows me to befriend Handel, and that, for me, has been the great joy that has come from writing this book. I hope you, as a reader, find that you experience some of that joy as well. I would be doubly rewarded if you do.

Prologue

Katherine took up the letter in her white-gloved hand. Deep in her body she felt that squirm of excitement that signaled, "Here it is! A piece of life from another time that thrills me in a way I scarcely understand—as though it were a part of my own life, my very heart." She traced the salutation with her finger: My Dear Mr. Handel.

KATHERINE HELEN BAKER IS A recently promoted Full Professor in the Department of Folklore and Ethnomusicology and the Department of International Studies at Indiana University. She lives in Bloomington, Indiana, and this book examines a seminar that she joined through a strange round of circumstances. I (the author) am not Katherine Baker—though I suppose I do identify with her in a number of ways. I am writing this book using materials supplied to me by a young ethnographer named Elizabeth Benfey Rhodes. Ms. Rhodes—Benfey as she prefers to be called—was hired by Professor Baker and the Seminar's co-director, Ross Wainwright, to record the meetings and discussions growing out of this Seminar. Despite signs to the contrary, this book is not intended as a piece of scholarship but rather as a kind of extended biographical and philosophical essay. I presume to be, in other words, something like a public intellectual, though time will tell whether the product becomes public or comes to be regarded as of intellectual merit. But to have the work be so regarded is my hope and my intention.

I hinted that the circumstances that sparked the formation of this Seminar were unusual. Perhaps we should start there—with the lines of recent history that brought these members of the seminar together in the first place. Where to start? One of the first pertinent incidents was, I suppose, Forella Wainwright's visit to her ophthalmologist more than a decade ago. Mrs. Wainwright—widow of successful Kingsport, Tennessee, mining executive Stanton Wainwright—was told that she suffered from the "wet" form of progressive macular degeneration and that, at that time, there were no known treatments for the disease. She would gradually lose her ability to see anything but peripheral movement. In effect, she would become blind.

We rely so heavily on our eyesight. Though she was seventy-eight years old at the time, Forella Wainwright still liked to drive her 1976 Bentley when the whim took her. She had a driver on salary, but she enjoyed getting behind the wheel herself once in a while. And she wasn't one of those worrisome elders whose driving puzzles anyone in the vicinity. No, she was a good, defensive driver—alert and always aware of the road and of her fellow travelers and their likely moves. So, this news was a blow.

And of course there was her reading, and there was her charity work. For years Forella Wainwright had been a faithful member of her reading circle, finishing a book of fiction, or more often nonfiction, at least once every other month and joining in the discussion with her own special flair—a practiced tendency to make any book she read a hidden treatise on women's rights. And the Women's Shelter of Greater Kingsport really did depend on her to contribute her time at the phones and desk—along with her generous contributions of money and pantry items. All that would go by the way if she could no longer see the ledgers or printed pages, let alone people's faces. Something had to be done.

Forella Wainwright and her son Ross were enviably close and fond of each other. No perverse Oedipal problems here—but instead a warm mutual respect and pleasure in each other's company. Ross was troubled when he heard of his mother's failing eyesight. Obviously no one ever would wish such a thing on anybody, and he was sorry at the prospect of watching her draw away from the many activities she clearly enjoyed, the things that kept her so surprisingly young and vital.

Ross was—at that time—busy with film projects in Nashville, Los Angeles, and New Delhi. He was used to flying from one location to another, and his own home was recently dissolved through a sadly unpleasant divorce. So, the old "where you hang your hat is home" adage was his mantra whenever Forella asked where he planned to settle down. But when his mother called him and repeated the bleak scenario her eye doctor had outlined, Ross asked to speak with him, asked, in fact, for a second opinion.

For that second opinion, Forella Wainwright's ophthalmologist referred mother and son to an unusual treatment center attached to the cyclotron at Indiana University. It seems that the IU Cyclotron Facility—originally built to support nuclear physics research—had adapted its equipment to offer proton radiation therapy specifically for Age-Related Macular Degeneration (AMD) and had established an experimental clinic there for selected cases that met their screening tests. Ross traveled with his mother to Bloomington, Indiana, for the admission interview, and when Forella Wainwright was accepted as a patient, Ross decided to look for a house for his mother and himself—a restful haven that would grant Forella access to the IUCF for her therapy while, just perhaps, offering him a reliable port in the storm of his busy life.

It was no easy thing to convince Forella Wainwright to leave the town she had grown to love and in which had passed those happy years of young adulthood, motherhood, and most recently, elder stateswoman-hood. She and her husband's family had deep roots in Kingsport—though it was true that she herself had grown up in Ohio, a Yankee transplant. But Forella Wainwright had always been attracted by the possibility of adventure. Faced with the necessity of moving, she would have preferred to resettle near the ocean or even, say, in South America, but she had long since given over such impractical dreams. And the treatments at the IU

Center seemed her best hope. So, Indiana it would be—a new home in the heartland.

Forella's many friends chided her for "giving in," as they called it, to Ross's plan to move north. Hadn't she always enjoyed her connections with the city's park program, the various charities, her reading club? But Forella had an answer for her detractors: she wanted to make a different kind of contribution, and she wanted to work with her son Ross to do it. Ross himself was not especially keen on the new "contribution" plan she had dreamed up, but he loved his mother, and he saw how important it was to her. So he set his assistant to work finding a home for him and an apartment for his mother, one that would allow easy access to the Cyclotron Facility as well as the wonderful music for which the college town of Bloomington was justly famous.

The "domestic" plan was to find a substantial home—one that could house the Wainwright family treasures as well as all of the artwork and other collections Ross had recently moved to his mother's mansion in Kingsport. Ross habitually accumulated mementos that evoked stories; friends were never sure whether he saved the artifacts for the stories they recalled or whether he sought out stories to celebrate any artifact he wanted to add to his collection. But as part of the divorce settlement, these many artifacts did not go with Ross's ex-wife. They were part of his personality, and they needed a suitable home. He settled on a fine large estate on the north side of Indianapolis. Here he could fly out of Indy's international airport as his work demanded and yet be within an hour's drive of his mother's Bloomington town house. And Forella Wainwright would have a fine setting for all of the family heirlooms and beautiful antiques that had surrounded her all her life in Kingsport. This "domestic" plan addressed the *where* part of the move, and even some of the *why* part—that is, to allow ready access to the treatment Forella Wainwright needed for her failing eyesight.

The other *why* part of the package involved the "contribution" plan that Mrs. Wainwright insisted must be central to the move. This more complicated plan was the one that eventually came to include Katherine

Baker and the other members of the Seminar mentioned earlier. And it all started with Forella Wainwright's purchase of some putative "letters to Handel" recently discovered at a British farmhouse in West Woodhay, on the road between London and Bath. How those letters came to light is part of our story.

CHAPTER 1

Mrs. Wainwright's Query

"Ich kann nicht umhin allhier meine Thränen fliessen zu lassen." –From Handel's letter to his brother-in-law, Michael Michaelsen in February 1731, thanking him for burying the composer's recently deceased mother according to her wishes: "Here I cannot stop my tears," Handel writes. Why are there so few such published letters from or to the Maestro?

FORELLA WAINWRIGHT'S TREATMENTS AT THE Cyclotron Facility were, sadly, not effective in staving off the loss of central vision characteristic of AMD. Within a discouragingly short time she found it impossible to drive and increasingly difficult to read, even with the help of special glasses or the most up-to-date computerized readers. Still, being the generally optimistic and energetic person she was, she put in place a plan that would bring her as much active engagement as possible. This project—for reasons definitely not the norm—involved delving into the life of late Baroque-era composer George Frideric Handel. To more effectively carry out this project, Forella Wainwright hired a young research assistant who could serve as her eyes and, happily, bring a new kind of companionship into her life as well.

Angela Houser had finished her BA degree in English some few years earlier and had, until very recently, worked as a research assistant for a professor whose never-ending self-assigned task was to compile a bibliography of all books and articles ever written about the parables of Jesus. She had found the project itself interesting enough, but she did not really enjoy working as this professor's assistant. He was inclined to appreciate only her skills in retrieving, organizing, and summarizing; he had little regard for either her accompanying creative flair or her characteristic straightforward manner of questioning. When Angela saw Mrs. Wainwright's ad on the department's website bulletin board, therefore, she immediately called and agreed to come for an interview in the spacious townhouse that served as Forella Wainwright's Bloomington residence.

Even though Mrs. Wainwright's Bloomington townhouse was much more modest than her previous residence in Kingsport—and certainly more modest than the sprawling estate Ross had purchased north of Indianapolis, she did nevertheless find it convenient to retain her butler/driver and general handyman, Randolph Bornes and his wife, Annie, who served as maid and cook. Thus it was Randolph who answered the door when Angela came for the interview. He offered to take Angela's hooded terry cloth jacket, which she wore over a comfortable knit dress, but she declined. He ushered her into the sitting room where Mrs. Wainwright sat waiting at a small work table, announced Angela's arrival in a congenial manner, and left the room. Angela immediately reached her hand over the table and said, "May I shake your hand, Mrs. Wainwright? I've read so much online about your involvement with the Women's Shelters here in Bloomington and in your previous home in Tennessee. I'm pleased to meet you."

Forella Wainwright smiled. Not only was she delighted to be talking with someone who knew and appreciated her work with the women's shelters, but she was even more pleased to find that her interlocutor did not abandon introductory niceties simply because the business at hand was, well, business, and that her interviewer was unable to respond to visual cues. She extended her hand, and Angela Houser took it, squeezed it warmly, and sat down in the chair opposite Mrs. Wainwright. She noticed that Mrs. Wainwright quickly consulted a computerized speaking notepad before commenting, "I understand that you currently work as a research assistant for a professor here in Bloomington, Ms. Houser. Is that correct? Are you aware that this is quite a different kind of position?"

Angela smiled, even though she knew that her interviewer would not see. Clearly, she was happy to be applying for the position. "Yes, Mrs. Wainwright, I understand that this is a different kind of position, and I appreciate your not wanting to draw me into something I would end up resenting. Actually the work I've been doing most recently is pretty much go-for tasks for a man who needs someone to read and summarize research. He hired me because he didn't have time to do the reading himself, and I guess I don't mind being the one who helps him out that way. But, to be honest, I like the idea of helping someone who needs me to bring some of my own creativity into the task—especially someone who works so hard for community causes."

Forella Wainwright looked over at her with a pleased but wistful look. "It has taken me some time to admit I needed the help," she said. "Why would you want to trade an academic research position for one that places a lot more responsibility on you for more basic things—like helping me keep my information in order and my reading materials in a form I can access? Are you sure you understand what is required here?"

Angela hesitated only briefly. She seemed to ponder the question rather than rush to a ready-made answer. "Yes," she said, "Your ad was really clear. I'd be working with you to search the internet and other sources and basically making sure you have what you need to move forward on various projects that are important to you—and have the information available in a form you can use. You'd rely on me to take advantage of all the technology out there. I think it suits me. I've always sort of liked the idea of being part of a team, of sharing different parts of a job according to what I'm good at but also knowing and contributing to the big picture. I think it comes from being part of a pretty large family as I was growing up. We all had our own tasks, and we knew each one was important. It's hard to get that sense of personal involvement working for a big corporation. I know; for a short time I actually gave it a shot, worked as a publishing assistant up in Chicago. Anyway, I thought this position—helping you as a personal assistant—sounded wonderful. And, it lets me stay here in Bloomington. I really like Bloomington, and I'd rather not leave if I can find something I enjoy doing that keeps me here."

"What is it about Bloomington that you find so appealing?" Forella asked. "It's a college town, of course, but you finished your coursework some time ago. I noticed the graduation date on your application." To explain her love for Bloomington, Angela immediately cited the fine restaurants, the excellent music, the social activism, and then concluded with praise for the many nearby state parks and abundant trees. "Most of my friends who have moved away are jealous of the fact that I'm still here. It's like a little oasis in the mostly staid and conservative Midwest. I mean, if you can't live in New York or Seattle, then it's the next best thing—unless you really need to be near the water. Lake Monroe is great, but it's not an ocean. Oh well."

Forella reflected on Angela's characterization of her new hometown. She too had found much to appreciate, especially once she had joined a number of volunteer causes she supported. Back in Kingsport, Forella Wainwright had been widely respected—but primarily as the wife, and later as the widow, of a "landed gentry" of sorts, a man whose family had owned the land that became a rich mining resource. She loved her husband, but she had never been comfortable with the sense of privilege that his family enjoyed. She always felt a little embarrassed by the great gap between the status and wealth of her family and that of the families of the women she met as part of her charity work. In Bloomington things seemed to be more evenly distributed. But there were still discrepancies. "Are you a born-again Christian?" she suddenly asked.

Angela was somewhat taken aback. She wasn't used to being queried about her religious beliefs, and she assumed that it was irrelevant, in fact, illegal to bring religion into a job interview. "Do you mean, Am

I a church-goer? I attend church sometimes, but I'm not, well, not born-again, not an evangelical. Why do you ask?"

"I should warn you that some of the things I will ask you to help me with may seem a little far-fetched, especially if you are very conservative in your beliefs. I thought it best to get this out in the open now. For example, I'm re-reading a book—well, listening to an audio CD—called *The Dancing Wu Li Masters*, by Gary Zukav. I remember reading Zukav's book twenty years ago, when I could still see well enough to read printed books. It's all about the new physics, and I remember being excited about the ideas it suggested back then. But now, especially since I've had to rely on my other senses more, I've wanted to dig a little deeper into some of the spiritual ideas I rejected out of hand earlier. And—I don't want you to be uncomfortable with what I'll be asking you to do. You don't have to accept the things I'll ask you to find for me, but, then, I wouldn't want you to misrepresent them or disparage them. I think it is hard for people to not let their own religious beliefs influence how they interpret new ideas. So, I need to know if you have religious ideas that would interfere. I don't really mean to pry, but it seems an important issue, given what I'll be asking you to do."

Angela Houser thought for a moment. She let her eyes skim the bookshelves, noting a great variety of books from classical works such as *Gilgamesh*, the Upanishads, or the plays of Aeschylus to modern works such as Thomas Moore's *Care of the Soul* or Neale Donald Walsch's *Conversations with God*. She also noticed a cabinet with more recent books on CD—works like Edmund Morgan's biography of Franklin, another one by Walter Isaacson, and Dan Brown's ubiquitous *Da Vinci Code*. Obviously Forella Wainwright had found ways to keep up on her reading, but just what kind of reading was it? And would Angela find it irksome to deal with this kind of material?

"I think I am ok with reading and reporting on almost anything," she said at last. "I have my own beliefs, but I don't expect everyone to think the same as I do about religion. I guess the only thing that would really bother me is if I'm asked to read works that seem to condone a lot of violence or mistreatment of others for any reason. Cults that encourage suicide or holding back women—things like that—I'm not eager to read their propaganda. But the New Physics—I think I can deal with that."

"Good, good, and the other part of the job . . .," said Mrs. Wainwright. Her voice trailed off, and for the first time in the interview there was evidence of some inner struggle moving across her face. "I must say that I find it difficult to ask someone to be a daily companion. I know you must have family, friends. Are you content to live in the downstairs apartment, to come in and fuss over an old woman's needs every day? It's not an exciting life for a young woman."

"You know," Angela said, "it's kind of an irony, I guess. When I was younger and just finishing high school, I remember thinking about going to a women's college or even a convent. I even read up on some of the requirements for becoming a nun. And it's not that I don't like guys or, you know, living in a family, but there's something about living a quiet, cloistered life that appeals to me. I had an older friend who became a teaching nun, but she stayed at a convent and followed the routines of the life there. I always sort of envied her that life—not the religious part of it, really, but the quiet alternative to a family. I've had a couple of serious boyfriends, and I do like to go out sometimes, but for now I'm happier without any commitments of that sort. So, yeah, I think I would be content with my life here. And having a separate apartment all to myself? That's so cool compared to the shared rental I have right now. It sounds great to me!"

It was, then, as a consequence of this interview, that Angela Houser initiated the correspondence that landed the bundle of putative letters to Handel on Forella Wainwright's attorney's desk late in the summer of 2009. Soon after taking on her role as assistant to Mrs. Wainwright, Angela had employed her considerable skills as an internet sleuth in response to her first assignment—to seek out any new materials on the much-researched but still poorly known personal life of George Frideric Handel. While 2009 was a celebrated year for Handelian research, concertizing, and festivals—it being the 250th anniversary of Handel's death on April 14th 1759, still Angela had not really expected to see her many-pronged electronic inquiry produce the volume of results that it did. Most intriguing—amid the links to blogs and Handel fanzines, references to websites, and bibliographic help with new articles and books—she found a curious old-fashioned email, sent—as the writer informed her—from a cyber café in London.

Dear Miss Houser,
I write in response to your recent inquiry which appeared in the Times. I am sending this letter by email through a London cyber café. Please respond to the email address I have listed if you are interested. I will return tomorrow at 11am to check for your reply.

A client, who wishes to remain anonymous, has asked me to contact you with an offer to sell your employer a package of letters that she believes were written to the composer G.F Handel over the course of some years while he lived in London. The letters themselves are still encased in the leather wallet in which they were found. They are in a very delicate state, and the client has not tried to extract or read them. However, they were accompanied by an identifying note that suggests why the letters were found at a farm near West Woodhay and reinforces the client's belief that the letters were indeed written to Handel.

My client was attracted by your employer's stated wish to learn information about Handel that might reflect his characteristics and specific actions as a living individual's possible "previous personality." It was in fact this line in your inquiry that led my client to make this offer. She is not eager to sell the letters through an auction house, and she prefers not to make the letters public if your employer is not interested.

If you are interested in this proposed purchase and if you agree to the limitations specified in the attachment, I will arrange for you to review photographs of the letter bundle and a FAX of the accompanying note found with the letters. Ideal would be a visit by you or your employer to a neutral site in London.

Sincerely,
R. F. Brown, Solicitor
Inkpen, Berkshire

Angela pondered this enigmatic note. It seemed likely that the writer did not normally use a computer as a means of correspondence—thus bringing into play the cyber café. Perhaps he or she was a Luddite, but then why not use overnight mail service? And why was that line about previous personality the one thing that caught the client's attention? Though she certainly had not wanted to challenge Mrs. Wainwright's wording of the inquiry that was sent out, this particular line was the one that Angela herself found most problematic. She was afraid people would see the perhaps mystical implication as reason to delete or ignore the memo rather than as reason to actually respond. Clearly the inquiry prompted many hits nevertheless, and this one from Solicitor Brown would be of special interest to Forella Wainwright.

As it turned out, Angela responded to the email address as requested and actually got up to check her email at 6am (to catch her correspondent at the unnamed London cyber café). She found the cloak and dagger atmosphere amusing and actually exciting. Mr. Brown—Robert F. Brown—as she discovered—was a retired solicitor who had left his London practice more than ten years earlier. Since retiring he preferred to walk the country lanes near the little village where he lived rather than peruse the internet. But he made frequent trips to the city and was not a Luddite. He used a computer when necessary—but only when necessary. In this instance, a neighbor down the road from his Berkshire residence had consulted him about the inquiry Angela had posted in the *London Times*. Fortunately, Angela had not confined her ad to electronic bulletins. Both Mr. Brown and the mystery client read printed papers, not blogs and websites, so it seemed.

Angela offered to set up a phone connection between Mrs. Wainwright and either Mr. Brown or the mystery client, but Mr. Brown preferred to continue with the email dialogue. He was intrigued by Angela's short notes identified as having come as messages posted from her phone, but he stuck to the mode of communication he had initiated. Through this exchange it was decided that Mr. Brown would send a photograph of the leather folio that held the letters as well as a photocopy of the faint but readable letter that was found with the package. This plan was agreed to only after Angela had faxed a signed statement to the effect that, should the negotiations fall through, the matter would be dropped with no further public notice. Mr. Brown explained that the letters had come into his client's possession some thirty years ago when she left a farmhouse located further to the east near West Woodhay. As Ross Wainwright was to discover some time later, the farmhouse had belonged to the client's former husband, and part of the veil of secrecy she insisted on was necessitated by her worry over whether the ex-husband or his family might challenge her right to the letters. Mr. Brown's professional opinion was that the artifacts were his client's fair and clear, but still his client preferred to keep her transactions private—or simply not continue the exchange at all.

The other worrisome circumstance was that the letters were extremely fragile. Perhaps something in the treatment of the leather pouch that held the letters had caused the extreme brittleness and discoloration of the contents. On the other hand, the note that was outside the leather folio—folded into a small square and encased within a beribboned envelope—was less damaged by the years of very careless storage. And more recently, the mystery client admitted that she had simply kept the package in a cedar chest along with her old laces and a few counterpanes. Still, she knew from the accompanying note that the letters might well be quite valuable, especially if they were indeed what they seemed to be. She only hoped to get them into the right hands before she passed on. That was her incentive and, interestingly, that was her reason for selecting Forella Wainwright as the person most likely to be the "right hands" she envisioned.

It seems that the mystery client and Forella Wainwright shared an interest in reincarnation. Granted, Forella Wainwright's interest was backed less by conviction and more by a strong inclination to solve puzzles and ponder philosophical questions, but it had obviously been sufficient to suggest that she include the provocative line about Handel representing a "previous personality." While Forella was willing to entertain the possibility that she might be proved wrong in her beliefs about Handel as some currently living soul's previous personality, Mr. Brown's mystery client was quite adamant in her belief that finding evidence of an individual's previous personality was every human's lifelong task, not to be taken lightly. Her desire to help her potential buyer with this important task was her prime incentive. It bolstered her own belief about her own earlier existence, and it felt to her like the right thing to do—to pass these letters on to someone who saw them as possible evidence in a specific instance of reincarnation.

Thus it was that Forella Wainwright was granted the opportunity to meet with Mr. Brown and discuss the artifacts—or rather, Mrs. Wainwright's chosen emissaries would meet with Mr. Brown. For this task, Forella called upon Peter Rowe, a friend she had met on first arriving in Bloomington and a specialist in manuscript preservation and curatorship and a kind of hobbyist in the field of "questioned document" examination. While Peter worked for the state historical museum in Indianapolis, he agreed to take on this task as a private citizen as a favor to Forella, not as a representative of the museum and not for pay. He would of course gain a wonderful trip to London as a consequence and a chance to do some of the kind of detective work he enjoyed. Peter would be meeting up with Forella's son Ross who would also be flying over from his current project in Italy to meet with Mr. Brown. Unfortunately, recording devices or even a stenographer were not allowed at any of the meetings. Ross would end up serving as the main informant in any records of this London trip.

Ross and Peter knew each other from previous small commercial projects that involved manuscript collections. They joked back and forth a bit about this latest inquiry undertaken by Ross's mother, but on the whole they agreed that the letters may well be worth whatever time and money would be involved even if, in the end, the letters failed to satisfy Forella Wainwright's curious "former life" query. In light of the potential value of the letters, Peter was reluctant to agree to the terms of purchase required by Mr. Brown's client. The client insisted that the letters—if they proved to be authentic—remain in private hands for the next twenty-five years.

Peter Rowe, it must be acknowledged, was acting as any professional curator would in such a situation. If one's life work revolves around old artifacts and whatever those artifacts can teach contemporary researchers and museum visitors, any notion of keeping new discoveries under wraps would seem perverse, dishonest, a great disservice. But Mr. Brown's client argued that twenty-five years was, after all, not so very long—just long enough, she observed, for her to have surely left this life, along with its troublesome secrets and past mistakes. Mr. Brown cautioned his correspondents not to pursue the matter.

This admonition, gentle though it was, caused some disquiet for Peter. Curators and document or artifact experts are not subject to some sort of Hippocratic Oath the way physicians are. Nevertheless, he felt a certain obligation to make the letters available to scholars if indeed the documents proved to be authentic—and not to wait twenty-five years to do so. Like most Americans, Peter knew a little about Handel—some of the floating anecdotes that cast him as the devout composer of *Messiah*, weeping openly as he finished the stirring Hallelujah chorus. But he also knew that there was actually a paucity of solid information about Handel, that scholars would be extremely eager to have anything at all new about the composer. Should he be party to an agreement that would withhold such information from scholars? Should he stand idly by and allow this perhaps misguided client to throw away a fortune by not selling the letters at auction? He hesitated to agree to the conditions before meeting with the client's London solicitor. But such was the requirement. The client would not allow the meeting unless all involved agreed to this twenty-five-year private holding provision.

Forella Wainwright and Angela were kept well-informed as Ross traveled to London from his filming project in Milan. He had connected by phone with Peter Rowe, and together they had agreed that all they could really do is meet with Robert Brown and see what came from that discussion. Both were glad for the chance to spend some time in London, and Angela had arranged for them to visit the Handel House Museum on Brook Street. Neither of the men had time to squander, but they did attend one of the many performances offered as part of the Handel Festival. Ross took time to meet with some of his own contacts in the area, and Peter made a second trip to the Handel Museum to examine the signatures and documents housed there. Angela had provided him with all of the internet materials he had requested. They would not be meeting with Mr. Brown unprepared.

When Ross and Peter met up with Robert Brown, their meeting place proved to be a quiet office rented out on an hourly basis by the same company that ran the cyber café Mr. Brown had been using in his correspondence with Angela Houser. After hurried introductions, Ross asked about the meeting place—what made it "neutral," why in fact did it have to be neutral. Was there already some controversy about the letters even though they were as yet undisclosed and putative?

"Ah, as you gentlemen must be aware, we Brits are inclined to dispute and debate even simple observations offered on the daily news," said Mr. Brown, gesturing them to seats at a small table. "Even more so when such observations have a theory attached. And this year being the semiquincentennial of Handel's death, you can imagine how invested everyone is in the latest news on the composer. But, truth be told, the raging issue amongst most pundits is whether or not Handel was homosexual. There have been several recent pieces of research asserting that he was, that he was a homosexual, and as usual there are meeting places that have come to be associated with one point of view or the other. My client has no wish to be a part of the debate, and she refuses to fuel it with even the slim promise of new fodder for either side."

On the other hand, it soon became apparent that Mr. Brown's client herself had an agenda of sorts. Both Ross and Peter were used to seeing the abundance of differing explanations attached to any piece of biographical information about well-known figures. In fact they both participated on a daily basis in projects that exploited the human need to create stories behind "the facts" about people and events—Ross in documentary films and Peter in museum displays. But Mr. Brown's mystery client, rather than grasping this seeming made-to-order opportunity to pit the gay-Handel vs. not-gay-Handel theorists against each other and sell to the highest bidder, was attracted instead by Forella Wainwright's hint that she might find the letters useful as evidence for reincarnation.

Among the many resources Angela Houser had supplied to Peter Rowe before his flight to London was a thin volume borrowed from the university library titled *The Letters and Writings of George Frideric Handel*, edited for Arno Press by Erich H. Müller. Unlike the documents at the museum, these printed texts did not include signatures. Instead they simply recorded the words written by Handel to various correspondents as preserved in the few such letters ever found. Müller, the editor, offered the following comment on why so few letters survive either to or from Handel: "These letters must form but a fraction of Handel's correspondence, and, at first sight it seems strange that so few have been handed down to us. We must remember, however, that Handel did not, like many of his contemporaries, hold any office which would occasion the collecting of his records and writings" (p. v). The letters written by Handel were in French, English, and German, and the text of his will and its codicils was in English. Peter expected to use such information in his detective work—along with the various biographies and copied manuscripts more generally available.

Over the years, in his work with documents that needed to be authenticated, Peter had learned to work with a number of sources that might not immediately come to mind. For example, he was especially delighted with Angela's discovery of an online BBC report on "How Handel played the markets." The author—Peter Day—had run across numerous signed ledgers archived by the Bank of England, ledgers that recorded dates that Handel was in town and made the trip to the Bank (as it was required that patrons be there in person). It would take piecing together probable dates and names from such sources for Peter to develop a professional opinion about the letters he and Ross hoped to see and perhaps purchase.

But it was Forella Wainwright's line about Handel as a possible "previous personality" that emerged as the first topic of discussion. Robert Brown, in his role as both host and arbitrator, reiterated that his client wanted to know more about this motivation for the purchase. It was clear to Ross that Mr. Brown personally was not comfortable with the need to address this issue. Nevertheless, he posed the question to Ross and Peter. "If the letters are indeed ones written to George Frideric Handel while he lived in London, what does Mrs. Wainwright plan to do with the letters? What is she hoping to find that would support her inquiry into this as a case of reincarnation?" Mr. Brown read the questions from a sheet of paper. With a sigh, he put the paper down on the table and looked across at Peter and Ross. "Well, gentlemen, can either of you offer anything that might satisfy this inquiry? I'll tell you this—my client seems poised to pull out of the discussion altogether unless she hears something she likes in answer."

Peter was ready to argue that the question might well be moot if the letters are frauds, but Ross took another tack. "Would your client like to talk with me? I think I know what she wants to hear, but it would be easier to talk with her directly. Could we maybe make a conference call to her or something?"

After some negotiation by phone, Mr. Brown's client agreed to talk with all three of the men so long as nothing was recorded. She suggested that Mr. Brown show the other two a copy of the short note that had accompanied the packet of letters. Peter grumbled that they had already seen a copy of that document—that Mr. Brown had sent it to Angela early on. Peter's willingness to come in the first place was sparked by the content of that note. Nevertheless, a copy was placed on the table next to the speaker phone, and the four-way conversation began.

Surprisingly, after those vaguely belligerent threats to abandon the negotiations if there were insufficient compliance with her wishes, the mystery client came across, by phone anyway, as timid, frail, and definitely village-bred. For Ross, her voice conjured up a picture of a tiny, wispy lady who used a cane to get around. He and Peter both melted and thought of grandmothers and lonely cottages in the countryside. Still, she choked out her question with some convincing passion. Clearly, she really cared about something. Ross wasn't sure what it was, but he had a good guess. With a nod from Mr. Brown, he took the lead.

"Ma'am, my name is Ross Wainwright. I believe I understand what you are asking. The person who would like to purchase these letters is my mother, Forella Wainwright. I am sure she would have preferred to talk with you herself, but it is difficult for her to travel such a distance by air. She has entrusted this mission to me and the other person who is here today, Peter Rowe, who is an expert at analyzing documents. As Mr. Brown has no doubt told you, we are not here to try and buy the letters for a museum. We agreed to your twenty-five year wait."

The mystery client simply said, "Yes." So, Ross continued, "I understand from Mr. Brown that you are especially interested in getting these letters into my mother's hands because she expressed an interest in past lives or previous personalities. I have had countless conversations with my mother about cultures and belief systems that include reincarnation. You would have to know my mother to understand that she is—I guess you would say, knowledgeable but not necessarily convinced—about various theories of reincarnation. She has read Ian Stevenson's books—the ones that examine cases of children seeming to know past lives. My mother is a very smart lady, and I've always respected her tendency to read widely and consider all kinds of ideas other people won't even look at. So, my guess is that you accept some of the ideas Stevenson and others are looking at in their studies—especially the idea that young children can remember past lives, even if they forget about it when they are older. Is that right?"

Again, all that Ross got in response was a quiet, "Yes, that's right." With a smile at Peter, Ross pushed on. "Well, my mother has this notion that I –me, her son—am a latter-day reincarnation of Handel. I've told her many times that I think this is nonsense, but I do understand why she has the idea—well, aside from the fact that she sometimes too readily accepts what she reads in books. She claims that when I was about three or four years old, I talked about having to tell some singers not to quarrel on stage and I kept saying the name Faustina—both little details that could be traced to Handel in some way. And, besides that—and this is true—I have a knack for playing the piano despite having never really studied it. She kept a record of some of the things I said as a little kid, and I think she hopes these letters will have some correspondences that she would find convincing. She isn't heart-set on finding this out, but it's what she meant by the line about Handel as a previous personality. She thinks it's possible that they might reveal something else that corresponds to some of the unusual remarks I made when I was much younger. As I said, I'm not convinced by any of this myself. But that is at least part of the reason she would like to buy the letters."

Ross was surprised at this point to see Peter signaling that he would like to talk with the client. With a shrug, Ross gestured toward the speaker phone that lay in the center of the table, and Peter moved closer to the phone to be sure the client would hear him. "Excuse me for intruding, Ma'am, this is Peter Rowe, here with Mr. Wainwright and Mr. Brown. I've examined the copy of the note that was supposedly found alongside the letters. Until we see the original, this copy exhibits several dubious features. But before we go any further, could I ask why you would care that a stranger living in the US might find something in the letters to support her belief about reincarnation. In other words, why are you interested in maybe selling these letters to Mrs. Wainwright but not putting them on the open market?"

Mr. Brown grimaced at this question, but Peter waved a hand and waited for the client's reply. In a quavering but noticeably stronger voice, she answered him. "I benefited from knowing about my own past lives. I believe this is what I need to do. I am certain that handing these letters on will bring me peace. If Mrs. Wainwright is the right person, then I will be happy. It sounds like she might be. That's all I care about."

Ross and Robert Brown both frowned and shook their heads, but Peter plowed on. "It sounds to me," said Peter, "like you have worked with someone to accomplish past life regression. Is that right?" Again, the client went back to her simple, "Yes," by way of answer. "Then I would guess," said Peter, "that you are convinced the letters really are as the note says—letters written to Handel by a Mrs. Grayston of London and brought somehow to the farm in Berkshire where they were found. Is this something you were convinced of through a PLR session?"

Again, both Ross and Robert Brown looked a bit stunned, but slowly, from the speaker phone, came the client's reply. "Yes, I was Nancy, the maid who delivered the note. I didn't do what I was asked to do, but now I have a chance to set things right."

"Thank you," said Peter. He signaled to Mr. Brown. "I'll ask Mr. Brown to finish off for now, and we will confer with him. Thank you again for talking with us." After a quick promise to get back to her soon, Mr. Brown closed the connection and turned to the two men. Ross was first to break the silence. "What the hell was that all about?!"

Peter had to laugh at the look of incredulity on Ross's face, but Robert Brown nodded knowingly and said, "I was afraid she was going to bring up this notion of being some woman from a past life. I warned her that it might just put people off and convince them that the whole thing is a fake. If you knew her, I don't think you would suspect her of making any of this up herself. But of course it's always possible that she has been duped by someone else. How did you cotton on to her ideas on this so quickly?" "Yeah, that's what I want to know," said Ross, "and what is this PLS or whatever?"

"PLR," said Peter. "Past life regression. It's a kind of therapy. Some therapists believe it—you know, believe in reincarnation—but some use it just to get people to imagine or displace ideas that bother them. As a matter of fact, Ross, your mother and I have talked about this kind of hypnotherapy. I forget exactly why it came up. But it actually fits in with her other idea of maybe using the letters as a basis for a kind of self-help seminar. Well, sort of."

Now it was Robert Brown's turn to pull a baffled expression. "What kind of seminar? Is this some sort of public conference you are thinking of? I'm sure that would be out of the question." Again, it was Ross who suggested that it would be best if they could actually talk with the client in person—this time face-to-face. From his many years of documentary film work, Ross had learned that live interviews always yield better fruits. And, he opined as Mr. Brown started to protest, that the client had softened a bit after hearing Peter's sympathetic comment about PLR. Maybe she would be less set against a visit now that they had talked.

"I'll be honest with you," said Robert Brown, "I worry that my client is likely to be easily led astray with regard to this reincarnation idea. It's my job to protect her, and I don't really see where this is going. If you try to talk her into some sort of conference that ends up making these letters public after all, her initial wishes will be undermined. I'm not eager to go beyond our agreement that we started out with."

"Well, we seem to be at an impasse," said Ross. "But how about this? First let me say that I really respect the way you are looking out for your client. I can tell that you are aware of her possible vulnerable spots, and you are making sure she is not taken advantage of. Peter and I are acting on behalf of another woman who could also be taken advantage of. That's our role here as well—to make sure that doesn't happen. It's hard to trust strangers, of course, but I think that is what is going to have to happen here. We've signed a statement that we will not make the letters public. But it would be helpful, I think, for all of us to talk it through in a face-to-face setting. And, I'd like to meet this person. She seems nice."

"All right," Robert Brown finally said with some resignation. "If you two will step outside, I will talk with her and see what we can arrange." Ross and Peter took advantage of the opportunity to check with their own contacts on various other projects, and within a short time, Mr. Brown called them back into the rented office. "Well, she agrees to meeting with you," he said. "Mr. Rowe, your seemingly positive take on past life studies is what put us over the top. I hope this isn't a mistake. Could we make the trip to her house this afternoon? It isn't far, and I can drive you there. Arranging public transport to her place isn't so easy."

"Excellent," Ross said, "Could we buy you lunch? It's nearly noon." But Robert Brown had promised to meet his granddaughter for lunch. "I'll pick you up at your hotel at one. It's only little more than an hour out of town. Bring your wellies. You might want to walk the roads, and it's been a bit damp lately. I'll see you shortly." Mr. Brown left. "Wellies?" Peter said as he walked out. "Boots—you know, or rubbers," Ross laughed. "Must be muddy. Real fieldwork, my friend." And they caught the underground to their hotel.

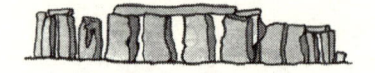

CHAPTER 2

A Stash of Letters

Ross thought of his visits to England and Stonehenge when he was a young boy. Back then visitors were allowed to touch the huge monoliths, even lie on them. And farmers, working their fields on the Salisbury Plain, occasionally turned up the distinctive inverted bell shaped pottery from Britain's bronze age. He wondered what it would be like to live here—in the land of the Beaker People.

AS THEY HEADED OUT OF London toward Newbury and on to the village where Mr. Brown's client lived, the three men talked briefly about the city of Bath and how tourists now more often visited its ancient spas rather than making the day trip to Stonehenge. Robert Brown bragged up the several examples of pottery recovered from four thousand-year-old Beaker People sites near his home village. He recommended a stop at one of the village pubs before heading back to the city. Meanwhile Ross and Peter tried to strategize a bit about how best to present their case for buying the letters—if indeed Peter seemed convinced of their likely authenticity.

Part of Peter's hesitancy arose from his perusal of the one piece of the puzzle they already had—the text of the note that accompanied the package of letters. Something about the note seemed a bit too pat. There was almost too much information, and furthermore it echoed certain facts that had been implicated in a rather notorious case of forged letters a few years earlier. And then there was the client's steering clear of any connection with professional auction houses or assessors—very suspicious. Peter pulled out his notes relating to the copied text and went over them with Ross, handing him the copy of the text they had already studied a number of times.

> Mrs. Grayston
> Sloper Hall
> Wst Woodhay
>
> London, Apr 11
> 1759
>
> Dearest Lydie
> Just as we were going to Tunbridge, came running a maid servant from Mr. Handel with a pouch of letters he had bid her give you. When I told her you had left for the country house she was most disturbed. William says this note will have to do but the poor girl was unhappy with that. Her master insisted you receive the package, that they were letters you had written him. He hoped you would destroy the letters. That was her message. The girl is Nancy. I know her from concerts at Brook street. She said Maestro wanted the letters burned if you did not receive them. She was most reluctant to give the letters to me. I promised I would bring them to you and so I shall. Handel is not well and has finished making his will. If I had time we would stop by his house to see him but we are late already. I send these on with my man John to Wst Woodhay and will see you there in another week. I hope to find you well.
>
> Yours most fondly,
> Susannah

Peter commented, "I think we must assume the writer of the note is a Mrs. Susannah Cibber, one of Handel's singers. She lived for some time in the manor house at West Woodhay. But our seller doesn't claim to be the person who wrote the note. Instead, she thinks the maid-servant—Nancy in the note—is the person she was or is—whichever."

Robert Brown chuckled as he turned the car onto a country road, "You'll have a hard time disguising your skepticism. My client is a sharp lady despite her years and frail form. But let's agree to call her by a pseudonym, shall we? She is still nervous about having anyone know she has these documents. Can we agree to calling her Mrs. Finch?"

"Ah" said Ross, "a female counterpart to Piggy in *Gentlemen Prefer Blonds*. I love it. So, are we actually going to Mrs. Finch's house, or is this meeting also at a neutral site?" Peter chimed in before an answer came, "I should say that I'm not so much skeptical of her theory of who she might have been in a past life as I am skeptical of the note itself. But then, I haven't seen the original. That will make a big difference. The hard thing for her would be—I think—finding out the note was a fake, especially if she really is convinced of its role in some past life scenario. We'll just have to see how it goes."

After driving by a large brick building that Robert Brown identified as one of the local pubs, he brought the old-model Rover to a stop in front of a cottage that appeared to be at least as old as the pub. "This is my client's house, one of the original farm cottages that once housed folks who worked the land for the owners of the old manor house a few kilometers from here. Watch your step. She needs to replace some of these flagstones."

Both Ross and Peter felt like great hulking boys stopping by grandma's house when their mystery seller opened her door and invited them in. She was, as Ross had envisioned, a small and frail-looking woman with white hair, dressed in blue gingham. She used a walker rather than a cane, but other than that detail, she was exactly as expected. Robert explained to her that they would be calling her Mrs. Finch to protect her identity. She nodded and pointed toward the sofa. From the kitchen came another, younger woman with a tray bearing tea and muffins. "Thank you, dear," said Robert Brown. "Estelle, this is Mr. Wainwright and Mr.

Rowe. Gentlemen, this is my wife, Estelle. She wanted to be sure all was in order here for our talk. It wouldn't do to miss tea. We shouldn't be more than an hour." And he handed her the keys to the Rover.

"May I?" said Peter, as he removed the tea cozy and made to pour tea into the four cups placed carefully on the tray. "This china is just like my grandmother's," he said, holding the cup up to the light. "Her family came from England—but further north, I think. She would have liked your front garden, the colorful flowers." Peter continued to play host, asking who needed sugar or milk. Ross accepted his cup with a grin and said, "Thanks, old chap."

The pseudonymous Mrs. Finch took her cup from Peter and flashed the first smile anyone had seen steal over her face the whole while. "Thank you," she said, "I *thought* you must be a tender. You sounded so on the telephone."

"A, a what?" said Peter. "A tender," she repeated, "someone who tends to others. Are you a therapist? You knew all about how important past lives can be. I thought you must be a doctor." Peter looked neither embarrassed nor cynical. "No, I'm not a doctor. But I know a little about the kind of therapy that involves past life memories or images. I've tried the technique of hypnotherapy a couple times, and sometimes that involves connecting with a past life. Is that what sparked your interest in having us look at these letters—the idea of a past life?"

With a quick look at Robert Brown, Mrs. Finch replied, "I'm getting on, and I know that menfolk especially are often disbelieving of things like this, but I feel a strong compulsion to act on what I know. And what I know is that I was led to make certain these letters were passed along to Mr. Wainwright's mother. At first I didn't know it was Mrs. Wainwright that should receive the letters. I just knew they needed to be removed from this house."

Ross leaned forward. "You mean it isn't just that the idea that in a past life I might have been George Frideric Handel that led you to respond to the inquiry in *The Times*? I'll have to say, I'm relieved—because I'm not fond of the idea myself. What convinced you that the letters needed to be removed from this house? Why are you so sure they really are letters written to Handel? As you can see, we have a lot of questions."

Robert Brown held up a hand and pointed to the clock ticking on the wall. "We don't want to take too much of your time this afternoon. Perhaps we could see the leather pouch with the letters and the note that accompanied it. You had them somewhere handy when I was here last time." Mrs. Finch pointed to a small cupboard across the room, and Mr. Brown retrieved the package while Peter cleared away the tea tray. Peter was especially eager to actually see the artifacts involved. It was apparent on first glance that the leather container was in extremely poor condition. The accompanying note in its small square envelope, on the other hand, seemed in much better shape.

As was his professional habit, Peter put on a pair of white gloves as he received the leather pouch with the letters and the accompanying note. He examined the envelope and note first. Fortunately, though the note had been folded and was now quite fragile along the creases, it was written on a sturdy rag paper. The envelope was a simple folded cover with no glue or wax—just a frayed ribbon binding it loosely. Peter could see some evidence of foxing, but surprisingly the note was neither extremely faded nor compromised by ink bleeding through. From what looked like an old-fashioned doctor's bag, Peter selected two small magnifying lenses and a number of other instruments. Everyone watched as he slowly and carefully examined the document. At last he looked up and queried Mrs. Finch. "Could you tell us a little more about how and where you found the letters and the note?"

After some false starts and furtive looks at Mr. Brown, she said, "They were hidden away in the top shelf of a built-in cupboard in the house where I lived earlier. I only found them when workers came to put heat vents in the house some years ago. They must have been there before we—before my husband and I moved into the place. I've just kept them all these years because I didn't want to have to talk with my husband about them, but Mr. Brown assures me the letters are mine to do with as I please."

It was apparent to Ross that Mrs. Finch did not want to talk about her ex-husband or even to admit that he was an ex-husband. He assumed that years ago divorce must have been a much more embarrassing event, especially for women. Peter asked her when exactly she first found the letters. "About thirty years ago," she said, "shortly after, after my husband left for Glasgow." Ross decided to steer her back to the topic of why she finally did consider selling the letters. It seemed that Peter had found nothing so far that would compel him simply to dismiss the letters or the note as counterfeits.

"Just to be clear," Ross began, "you must know that it seems odd to us that you would not want to put the letters up for auction—you know, to get as much in payment for them as possible. Museums and scholars everywhere would be eager to have these letters—if they are indeed letters written to Handel. Why are you taking this, well, extremely cautious approach to selling the letters? The price Mr. Brown quoted to us is really very low given what you would likely get at an auction house if the letters are indeed ones written to so famous a composer."

The explanation that followed avoided all mention of prices, scholarly contribution, or even some effort at proving theories of reincarnation or something similar. Instead, the client reiterated her wish to get the letters into the "right hands." She felt that Mrs. Wainwright's phrase about Handel as a possible "previous personality" was a signal, a sign that she should sell the letters to her and to no one else.

Peter Rowe set aside the note from Susannah and took up the packet of letters itself. He could easily imagine how the leather pouch might have remained untouched by human hands for so long—hidden on a little-used shelf, but he was curious about why mice had not destroyed the leather container or the letters. Nevertheless, just on the surface, he did in fact see features of the artifacts that persuaded him toward accepting their purported age and perhaps their likely source. He and Ross had agreed that Peter's intuitive assessment upon seeing the letters would be the deciding point of sway. Peter needed only to signal his positive feeling and Ross would act on it.

Peter stood up and walked into Mrs. Finch's small kitchen and looked out through the window into the surrounding countryside. His practiced guess was that the letters were real, a genuine scholarly find. As a consequence, it would be, he thought, unethical, perhaps even reprehensible, to accept the client's offer. It was really too low for such valuable artifacts. On the other hand, she seemed determined to pass them along to Forella Wainwright. The whole thing had the air of a mission or testimony for the so-named Mrs. Finch.

He had not mentioned it to Ross or Robert Brown—or even to Forella Wainwright—but Peter had, in fact, worked with other clients whose documents were alleged to be some sort of proof of former lives. Over the years, he had helped people determine the likely age and source of many letters, diaries, photographs, and other such artifacts that might affirm, for them at least, that a specific person tied in some way to the artifact could be a reincarnated personality. Peter usually accepted such detective work because he really enjoyed creating the plausible historical explanations that emerged from his research. He was also fascinated to see that often his facts were ignored or reinterpreted to fit the beliefs his clients held before they came to him with their documents.

This pattern of stubborn beliefs—despite his contrary evidence—neither surprised nor bothered Peter. In fact, he had great empathy for people who grasped at such bits of unlikely narrative. Some few years ago he had fallen in love with a woman who was married to someone else—not an uncommon occurrence. But his lover died suddenly, leaving Peter devastated but unable to grieve openly, as his affair was, so far as he knew anyway, a secret. He finally went to a therapist and there underwent the hypnotherapy he mentioned to Mrs. Finch. In his case, there was a previous personality that seemed to assure Peter that he and his lover were united at some other point, in another life. As time passed, Peter came to not really believe the reincarnation aspect of the experience, but he did recognize how helpful the supposed message was. He appreciated the value of the story, true or not. It helped him manage his grief.

When Peter returned to the room where the others were still discussing the possible purchase, he gave Ross a nodding signal and then asked Mrs. Finch to share her own stories associated with the cottage where the letters had been found. She hesitated. Fortunately, just then Mr. Brown's wife returned and knocked on the door—fortunate, because Mrs. Finch seemed more inclined to share her stories with Estelle in the room.

Both Estelle and Mrs. Finch had—independently and at some time in the past—experienced the often frightening phenomenon known locally as "being ridden by the Old Hag," the sensation of being paralyzed while half-asleep and having some sort of being sitting astride or holding the victim down. Estelle had not heard of the tradition, but when she once described the experience to Mrs. Finch, the older woman explained the source of her troubles and offered her a Holey Stone to ward off such experiences in the future. Ever since this conversation, the two women were reasonably comfortable in sharing other rather bizarre stories, which usually left Mr. Brown shaking his head in a bemused way. Still, the story-based camaraderie was useful in this instance. Mrs. Finch's reluctance to talk faded when Estelle prompted her to tell about the visit from her mother's spirit and the light in the cupboard—stories associated with her former home.

These two stories were ones that Mrs. Finch had evidently shared previously—at least with Estelle. The first story was a straightforward revenant story. Mrs. Finch was visited by her mother shortly after her mother had died. The story didn't have anything to do with the letters, but it did explain why Mrs. Finch had refused to go live with her daughter when the troubles with her husband began. The spirit of her mother warned her not to leave the cottage. So she stayed.

Her second story was more muddled. It seems that several years ago she started having dreams about a light in the cottage's built-in cupboard. An older neighbor thought she might be clairvoyant, told her to check the cupboard to see if there was something hidden there. She found nothing. It wasn't until after her husband left and she had a new heating system installed that she discovered the letters stashed behind the upper shelf.

The coincidence of the light in the cupboard and the discovery of the letters worried her, and she wasn't sure what to do with the packet of letters. She didn't want to tell her husband about them. Granted, he had turned the house over to her, but she was afraid that he would interfere.

The more she thought about the letters and what they might represent, the more depressed she became. Her apothecary recommended that she visit a doctor in Newbury. She was adamant about not taking the drugs the doctor prescribed, so he suggested she see a therapist. The therapist tried various methods that might clarify what was bothering her, but the one that Mrs. Finch responded to was hypnotherapy. The therapy led Mrs. Finch to believe that she was Nancy, the messenger in the note. For some reason, she found it reassuring to "know" why she had the letters. She kept the letters hidden away, even after she moved to the neighborhood where she now lived. When she read Angela Houser's inquiry in the Times, Mrs. Finch accepted at once that it would be best to sell the letters to Mrs. Wainwright.

This story left Peter and Ross feeling even more uneasy than before. Would it be unscrupulous to buy the letters from a little old woman whose reasons for selling them were so very odd? Then, again, she did have her reasons, and that is what they had asked to hear. Perhaps to ease his conscience, Ross asked Mrs. Finch if she thought her therapist would approve of her selling the letters. To everyone's surprise, Mrs. Finch chuckled and said, "No, I imagine she would recommend that I take them to an auction house. But, I feel good about selling them to your mother, Mr. Wainwright. I like the fact that she included the line about Handel as a previous personality in her notice. She seems like someone who will treat them as messages from beyond the grave. That's the way I view them, and I would rather they were used to improve the world—not simply put in some museum. If I were younger, I might do more with them myself, but my health isn't good any more, and . . . and besides the extra money wouldn't help my daughter now. She passed away a year ago."

"I'm so sorry," Peter said, and Ross, too, looked pained. "Losing a child is the hardest thing," Ross offered, "I hope we haven't brought up

The Handel Letters

painful memories." Mrs. Finch shook her head, "No, I miss my dear Nellie every day, just as I miss my mother. I haven't anyone now to worry over or to worry over me. Nellie never had any children herself, so it might seem I can't help anyone with what you gentlemen might want to pay for these letters. But, you see, I think that I can help the future generations by sharing these letters with your mother, Mr. Wainwright. I know it may seem far-fetched, but I've thought about it a lot. I think it is what I am supposed to do. It's my way of letting Nellie have her say. See, I think she was probably the person who wrote these letters. I think my Nellie was the Mrs. Grayston who received that note. If someone makes good use of these letters, then I think we will both be at peace."

All three men looked very uncomfortable with this comment. Even Estelle seemed surprised. Nevertheless, Ross's next observation brought everyone back to the issue at hand. "I should let you know about my mother's plan for setting up a seminar to discuss the letters if they are in any shape to actually read and copy. As I already indicated, I'm not one to hold much store by ideas about past lives, but I do think that people can benefit from hearing a variety of opinions about a shared text, especially one tied to a real person, someone who actually lived—like Handel. My mother hopes to invite several people to an ongoing seminar that will examine these letters and discuss what lessons they might have for people today. To my mind, you have suggested a similar hope. In other words, even though I personally don't hold much store by theories about past lives, I do think your wish to contribute through these letters in some way would be accomplished by selling them to my mother. I think I can assure you of that."

Mr. Brown pulled a sheet of paper from the folder he had brought along. "You will recall that we all agreed there would be no public display of these letters for twenty-five years. How can we be sure that this seminar does not infringe on that stipulation?" Ross held up his hand to stop Peter who seemed ready to respond. "Let me be very frank. My friend Peter here will be responsible for the delicate task of removing the letters from their leather container and trying to restore them for eventual display—that display to occur some twenty-five years hence. He will also take care to establish their authenticity. Obviously we are taking a risk since that process will take some time, and we need to negotiate the purchase now. He has detected enough positive signs to feel confident about the authenticity of the letters. The low purchase price allows us to take this risk. I talked of this possible scenario earlier with my mother, and she is content to move ahead."

Again he held up his hand, indicating a wish to get everything out in the open. "The second issue here is tied to what will happen with these letters over the next twenty-five years. My mother's hope is that you will find acceptable her plan to convene a seminar to discuss the letters. This is the part of the whole deal that attracted me. I like the idea of learning something more about the man Handel and then finding ways to build upon that new information in a group discussion that speculates on Handel's life and what it might teach us today. The letters themselves would remain hidden from public view though their content would be examined in this more applied context. I think I hear you saying that you would be happy with something like that outcome. Am I right about that?"

"Yes, yes," Mrs. Finch answered. She suddenly became very animated. "I want the letters to share their treasure. I am sure they are a message from those who have gone before. I'll tell you the truth. I was all set to burn the letters—just like the note carrier was supposed to do. That's when I saw the advertisement in the *Times*—the request from your mother, Mr. Wainwright. It can't be a coincidence that her request came just as I had decided to burn the letters. Now I feel good about selling them rather than destroying them. They were saved for a purpose, and this must be it. I feel much better knowing they will be used to help others. That was my role—to pass them on, but I really don't want anyone to know that I had them. I'm so glad you came to visit with me. I can be at peace now."

Ross couldn't help smiling at the happy look on the wrinkled face framed with white hair. It is such a good feeling to make someone else happy, especially people who clearly have few events that bring them such happiness. Still, he felt a twinge of conscience. Her motive seemed bizarre to him, but he couldn't argue with how pleased she seemed to be. And it is true, he rationalized to himself, that Forella Wainwright would do right by the woman's wishes. She would make sure that the letters served a positive purpose—not simply an academic one, but a real-life purpose. Snapping from his reverie, Ross responded, "Thank you, Ma'am. We will do all we can to honor the hopes you have for the letters. It has been a pleasure to meet you. I hope you continue to correspond with Mr. and Mrs. Brown and will let us know how you are doing through them. And thank you again for allowing us to visit you here in your charming home. I wish my mother could have met you and talked with you about these letters. I'm sure she would have enjoyed meeting you."

Mr. Brown took out the papers they needed to sign, and shortly after this legal ritual, they all stood and bade Mrs. Finch farewell, Peter complementing her once again on her lovely front garden. The letters and the accompanying note were placed in a special container Peter pulled from his equipment bag and quickly folded into the right proportions. With a last wave to Mrs. Finch who stood smiling at her front door, the four guests left, climbed into the Rover, and headed to the local pub. Ross insisted on treating and hearing more about the ancient Beaker artifacts found in the region. Not as healthy as a walk in the countryside would have been, but perhaps more enlightening as both Robert and Estelle Brown had many friends who showed up at the pub and regaled the visitors with stories, and even a few songs.

It was late that evening when Ross and Peter returned to the city. They agreed to meet for breakfast. Peter's plan was to send the letters ahead by special post to Mrs. Wainwright's attorney. At breakfast he and Ross talked briefly about the turn of events. Ross seemed still to be chafing under the good fortune of paying so little for the packet of letters. He was even less sanguine when Peter pointed out that they had not yet established that the letters were authentic—though he thought they very likely were. Peter hoped to set to the task of fumigating and restoring the letters as soon as possible after he returned to the US. Ross, of course, needed to complete his project in Milan before heading back home. He hoped to be in Italy only another month. They both agreed that the seminar sounded like an interesting consequence of the trip and the purchase. Ross was reasonably impressed with the young assistant his mother had hired, and he knew she had also already started lining up someone to record the seminar activities.

As they finished their coffee, Ross said, "You know, Peter, my mother will want to hear the stories our Mrs. Finch told us when we visited her—and about the cottage where the letters were found. I haven't shared any of this when I spoke with her on the phone, but I promised I would tell her what transpired here. My own inclination would be to conveniently skip over the stories of the ghostly mother and tell-tale light in the cupboard. What do you think? Is it necessary to bring all that up again?"

Peter refilled his cup and poured in some cream. As he stirred the coffee, he took out the copy of the note the long-dead servant John was supposed to deliver to the also long-dead Mrs. Grayston. "I know you don't like the Twilight Zonish stories the client shared with us," Peter began. "It's not that I don't like them," Ross interrupted. "I just don't like taking advantage of someone who believes we were somehow supposed to be here—you, know, sent by God or something. If they were just stories someone told, I'd find them pretty interesting. I'm always surprised to find out what people believe. But, I feel like some kind of bad guy here—one of those Oil Can Harry types that swindle little old ladies. You know what I mean?"

Peter laughed. "Listen, Ross, you've never been in therapy, have you? Sometimes stories aren't simply interesting. Sometimes—well, most of the time, I would argue—they carry special meaning for people. The thing about therapy is that you keep trying out various stories until one clicks, until it means something and enlightens you in a way that helps. It's not so much a matter of whether the story is really true or not—it just has to feel true for you. It has to bring you an insight into yourself that you didn't have before. I think that's what our Mrs. Finch appreciated about her series of coincidences—they helped her accept some things she didn't know how to deal with—like her divorce and her daughter dying.

We didn't take advantage of her. From one perspective, you could say we helped her. And, Ross, your idea of going to visit with her was a good one. Your instincts are good. I wouldn't worry about it. We've done what your mother wanted us to do. And, personally, I think Forella will be eager to hear the whole story—light-in-the-cupboard and all."

With that, Ross returned to his room and shortly left for the plane that would take him back to Milan. Peter stayed on in London for a couple more days, visiting the British Library and talking with some of the staff at the Handel Museum. Part of the signed agreement concerning the letters was the stipulation that no individual who learns of the letters' existence reveal anything to the general public about where the actual letters are being processed and held nor—most importantly—who had been the seller. Forella Wainwright had already agreed that anyone joining her proposed seminar would have to sign a similar statement. Peter was content that he and Ross had done all they could to be fair in their negotiations, and he felt that Robert Brown had been a good advocate for his client. All in all, it had been a satisfactory trip, and he was eager to see how things developed with the seminar. More than anything, he was eager to get to work examining and restoring the letters themselves. He was very curious to see what the mysterious Mrs. Grayston had to say to George Frideric Handel.

CHAPTER 3

Read and Remember

She recalled the visceral excitement she felt the first time she read Hurston's Mules and Men, especially the second part about Zora's experiences with Louisiana hoodoo. Katherine had always thought of ethnography as promising that kind of thrill for the researcher—something like the sensation of walking slowly over leaves and moss and wet stones in a foggy ancient forest and expecting every moment to discover amazing things that reach back into the haze of time.

AFTER SOME INITIAL RELUCTANCE, Ross had grown to like his mother's idea of convening a vaguely ethnographic seminar and recording the whole process as part of a documentary on contemporary thought or American worldview. To be sure, this last part was actually Ross's idea, not Forella's, but they were in agreement on creating a seminar, and it was definitely Forella's idea to seek out some new text that would provoke a variety of responses. The purported letters to Handel were exactly the kind of thing Forella had envisioned. Her instinct had prompted her to follow her own interest in reincarnated souls and to boldly press on with her curious intuition about a tie between her son and the renowned Mr. Handel. And, as we now know, her keen interest led to the packet of letters sent from the UK to her home in Indiana.

Ross remembered how his mother's notions on reincarnation had emerged. Until Ross's father died, Forella's readings on reincarnation were simply another part of her general background on world religions and new age thought. But when her husband collapsed suddenly and went into a coma, Forella found herself wondering where that person was, that being who used to live behind those now blank eyes. And when Stanton Wainwright never came out of his coma, she became obsessed with finding out where he had gone. Ross listened patiently as his mother invoked everything from Enkidu's dream of the house of dust to Shirley MacLaine's *Out on a Limb*. He even heard her out as she moved on from deathless souls to former lives, previous personalities. He did not laugh when she said he might have been George Frideric Handel in an earlier life. He loved his mother's passionate desire to see life go on forever. He did not believe the reincarnation explanation, but he saw no reason to quash her belief or stifle the question.

The more prevalent Christian belief that redeemed souls went to heaven in some bodily or spiritual sense had been left behind several decades earlier when Forella confronted her own strong disagreement with her husband's conversion to Mormonism. It was a lonely and often embattled self-dialogue, and Forella had few friends with whom she could raise the taboo topic of religious doubt. But Forella's clearly negative response to what she saw as an unfounded and even superstitious LDS belief in the claims of a nineteenth century prophet led her to question her own traditional Christian beliefs as well. For a period of nearly twenty years, Forella queried preachers in various faiths, read countless books, and attended innumerable retreats, seminars, and conventions. But, in the end, in addition to rejecting her husband's Mormonism, she sadly cast aside her own childhood beliefs and settled into a time of admitting she did not know what she believed. She had not really left that unsettled state when Stanton Wainwright's coma and death brought the question of an afterlife starkly before her once again.

Gradually Forella Wainwright became less desperate to find that elusive answer—less desperate, but no less ardent. And as a consequence of that compelling quest, she now had some letters supposedly written to Handel, and she hoped to use them in a way that might help others who relished life as she did—or perhaps even more, those who did not. At the back of her mind was still a vague hope that the letters might reveal something about life after death, or about how souls come to be part of our humanness, something about connections with people who had died. But more than just history. Nothing against historians, but Forella Wainwright hoped to hear more than how the Handel letters might add to historical knowledge. She envisioned a seminar of people who would treat the letters as—not a new book of Revelations, certainly, but perhaps a new basis for inspiring thought, their own wise colloquy.

Truth be told, the idea for a seminar had been growing in Forella's mind well before her purchase of the Handel letters. Like her son, she was not a one-project person but preferred instead to have several ideas and activities brewing at once. It takes a deep reservoir of energy to be involved in a really committed way with more than one or two projects. And Forella had finally admitted that her energy reserves were somewhat weaker than they used to be—and that her fading vision had imposed additional demands on her naturally high energy in any case. Still, she was excited by the idea of bringing together people intent upon discussing important issues that would arise from some new text—some historical artifact that hadn't been examined before. In her usual straightforward manner, she pondered the notion of a part-research, part-self-help seminar and wrote out a list of desiderata—or rather, she had her assistant, Angela Houser, draft the list and takes notes on their conversation.

First and foremost was a commitment on the part of seminar participants to reasoned argument rather than authority. To Forella Wainwright's mind this meant freedom from any creed or movement that would dictate how one thinks or believes. She imagined a seminar made up of people with little or no allegiances to religious doctrines or political ideologies that would put the brakes on certain lines of discussion. On the other hand, she thought that the seminar members would have to be considerate, friendly people—people who could disagree without becoming belligerent. Finally, she suggested that the seminar should be comprised of middle-aged or older people, people in their fifties, sixties, seventies, maybe even eighties or nineties. Forella promised to expound upon these notions at the first planning session.

Angela typed these suggestions onto her laptop and agreed to send a copy to Ross once the notes were in order. It was this message with its working list of seminar features that Forella, Ross, Peter Rowe, Angela, and two additions to the group met to consider when Ross returned from his work in Italy. By this time Peter had started the process of treating the fragile letters for eventual storage and display and had determined that they were indeed authentic. Forella was well-aware that Mr. Brown and the unnamed seller had bypassed this important authenticating procedure in dealing directly with Ross and Peter. Nevertheless, Peter felt that his carefully executed series of tests, scans, comparisons, and researches had produced the same high quality report that a reputable auction house would require before placing the items in a catalogue. Forella insisted on paying Peter for this time-consuming effort and expertise. She wanted this professionally prepared report to stay with the original letters in her vault. Only the scanned copies—or rather copies of their printed transcriptions—would be read and studied by the seminar.

Forella Wainwright and Peter Rowe shared a love for cataloguing and archiving. It was this compulsion to document details and organize objects that had occasioned Forella and Peter's meeting some months earlier. Shortly after arriving in Indiana, Forella had embarked on a small project showcasing coalminers' lunch buckets and their contents. Coalmining was to be the focus of a larger Indiana history display at the local library, and Forella, having noticed that it was typically the wives or mothers of the miners who packed lunches for their husbands or sons, hoped to create a smaller exhibit on that topic. Despite her late husband's connections with coal mining in Tennessee, Forella was not an advocate for the industry. She actually thought it was high time to find other kinds of fuel and energy sources, and she knew from experience that coal was a really dirty form of energy. Still, she thought that the role of women in the history of coal mining had been neglected, and she wanted to document their memorable traditions associated with lunch buckets and recipes. A new friend in Bloomington had recommended that she contact Peter, and he had helped her catalogue the bits and pieces of lunch-bucket lore she had gathered over the years. The resulting library display was an interesting one, but it lacked the kind of personal experience and narrative detail Forella would have liked. Peter had nodded and smiled and said, "My dear Forella, for that you need the services of an ethnographer."

So it was that as Forella contemplated bringing together this seminar, she decided to include a person whose task it would be to document the people, meetings, and ideas of the seminar itself. Peter had recommended an acquaintance of his who did folklore research—Dr. Katherine Baker—and she in turn suggested a young graduate assistant particularly skilled in documenting contemporary urban culture—Benfey Rhodes. Forella had met with Katherine Baker and her assistant, and she invited both to participate in the seminar, Katherine as a seminar member and Benfey as recorder and technician. Katherine was initially both amused and a little hesitant to be a subject in someone else's ethnography rather than play the role of ethnographer herself, but she soon warmed to the idea and agreed to join Forella's seminar. Benfey, on the other hand, was immediately delighted with both the invitation and the job. We could, perhaps, say a little more about Benfey Rhodes and how she came to be a part of the group.

The internationally celebrated Department of Folklore and Ethnomusicology at Indiana University attracts students from all over the world, and Professor Baker relished her abundant opportunities to work with these bright young researchers. Elizabeth Benfey Rhodes was an especially interesting admission to the graduate program. Faculty members were intrigued by her middle name and were agog with the news that she was distantly related to the Sanskrit scholar and linguistic theorist Theodor Benfey. Professor Benfey's Indo-European language theory fell into disrepute after World War II along with his bold assertion that the languages and folktales of Europe could be traced directly to a point of origin in India. Nevertheless, folklorists revered the late-nineteenth-century collecting projects inspired by Benfey's theories (and of course by the fieldwork of the Grimms, Campbell, Asbjörnsen and Moe, and other such scholars). It was always exciting to have descendants of noted forebears in the department.

Long before discovering that her namesake was famous among folklorists, Elizabeth Rhodes had asked friends and family to call her Benfey rather than Elizabeth or any of its many shortened forms. She liked the somewhat androgynous sound of the name, and she knew far too many Elizabeths to want to fight over who would be Beth, who Liz, and so on. When she arrived at IU, she was delighted to find that her middle name, the name she preferred, was an instant ice-breaker, at least among other folklorists. That, and her field experiences back in England, gave her an advantage she was happy to exploit. As a result, Katherine Baker tapped Benfey early on for the seminar project that shared at least some similarities with the latter's recent undergraduate work interviewing Morris dancers in the college town of Cambridge, England.

Ethnography is an emergent art form, a research-based performance that the practitioner molds from many tools and resources. As Benfey Rhodes contemplated taking on this new task, she knew that her audio recordings, her field notes, and her eventual interviews would provide the ingredients someone else would use to fashion the end product—a book, a journal issue, an exhibit, perhaps even a film. Despite being grateful for the exceptionally generous stipend this assignment would guarantee for most of her graduate career, Benfey could not help wishing that she would herself be the one to bring it all together in the final text, whatever it was to be. Her earlier independent project interviewing Morris dancers back home had convinced her that every step in any ethnographic study was a unique and significant part of the research in and of itself. What she chose to notice, what questions she asked, even which kind of microphone she used and where she positioned it—all would contribute to the project, and all would carry the spark of her own creativity.

The dozen Morris dancers she had interviewed back in Cambridge were remarkably varied in their attitudes toward the folk tradition that ostensibly bound them together as a group. Benfey had been careful to seek out informants who represented different self-identified performance groups (sides, they were called). What surprised her initially was the high level of education of her informants. These were definitely not backwoods rubes or village swains innocently carrying on a stiffened heritage of rustic music and dance. Instead, the dancers were often college students or even faculty who argued long and well over whether swords were required, how to tie the bells, when or if women could participate. Benfey found the task of recording each individual's take on the supposed "tradition" absolutely fascinating. In her advising chats with Professor Baker, Benfey talked with great enthusiasm about her fieldwork. When Angela followed up Peter's tip and asked Katherine to be a part of the Handel seminar, Katherine suggested Benfey as an excellent candidate for the role of ethnographer. Many applied, but one was chosen. Benfey was thrilled.

Gathered together, then, at the initial planning meeting of what would come to be known as the Handel Seminar were Benfey, Katherine, Ross, Peter, Angela, and Forella. Angela had reserved a seminar room at the public library. Benfey unpacked the new solid state memory card recorder and set it up with fifteen minutes to spare. Then she took her place in a chair situated away from the seminar table and set about noting the details of the seminar context. Her observations, notes, and audio recordings would be essential parts of the seminar's eventual contribution, whatever it might be.

Forella Wainwright was, of course, the primary instigator of this seminar, but at the first meeting she stated emphatically that she did not want to be the leader, the facilitator, certainly not the honored figurehead. In fact, to everyone's surprise, she admitted that she expected she might be absent from the discussion some of the time. "What?!" exclaimed Ross. "But this is your project, your idea. You are the one who talked Peter and me into going to England to check out that questionable claim about Handel and then called us all together for this meeting. I can't imagine you not wanting to be here when we talk about the letters."

Forella smiled and reached toward where she assumed Ross's hand would be. He took her hand and squeezed it. "As you can see," Forella said, "my son encourages my fantasy that I am still seventy years old—when in fact I am nearly ninety. I do want to be a part of the discussion—but on my own time, at my own speed. It's another reason why I wanted to have Miss Rhodes here with her recording equipment. I want to hear what you and whoever else joins you have to say about the letters, but I want the option of listening when I want to, not when a meeting is scheduled. I'll be the proverbial fly on the wall, listening to your conversation. Really, it is what I prefer. But I wanted to be here for this first meeting to see how you plan to carry it out."

Ross looked at her with some concern. She was right, of course. He did tend to forget that in another two months she would celebrate her ninetieth birthday. Over the several months that he had been away, she had become thinner and had lost some of her usual spark. She seemed tired, and yet even more determined than she had been earlier to move this project forward. Peter, ever the soul of empathy and comfort, spoke up. "Forella, that sounds like an excellent course of action. You are a wise woman to not let this character or any of the rest of us tell you how to spend your time. Well said. But, since you are here today and have supplied us with all these nice munchies and have our ethnographer all set to go, maybe you could say a little more about the suggestions you made for the seminar. Angela sent us a few notes, but she indicated that you would say more about the suggestions when we met."

Forella straightened her back a bit more and lifted her head as though she could in fact see the faces around her. Years of yoga and dance classes had instilled a kind of tall grace even despite the onset of age and osteoporosis. But her hand shook with a hint of palsy, and she was conscious of working to keep her head erect—something that used to be almost second-nature to her. She was sadly aware of the physical challenges that accompanied her loss of vision. It was increasingly hard to get the kind of exercise that would help fight off slumping shoulders and a rounded back. Still, for a woman of ninety years, she was impressively confident and engaged. This Handel seminar clearly was a project she wanted to foster with whatever energy and other resources she could muster.

"To the point, then. Thank you, Peter. I can imagine that everyone here would like to hear more about the preferences I outlined, and truthfully, I would like to share with you my reasons for wanting to start this seminar." Forella sipped the tea Angela had placed in front of her. "Some of you won't know my eccentricities as well as Ross and Peter do, so let me provide a little background about my personal incentives for funding a seminar like this—especially when there are so many good and needy causes out there I could have supported instead. Actually, twenty, thirty years ago, I probably wouldn't have wanted to create such a seminar. But times and people change. I haven't always been old, of course, and I haven't always been wealthy enough to spend money so freely. And, in fact, I haven't always been—well, what I like to think of as open-minded."

"Ross's father and I were young marrieds at the beginning of the second world war. My husband went off to fight on the European front, and I took in ironing and went to school on a loan from my aunt and uncle. Everyone skimped during the war years. I didn't think too much about it. After the war, Stanton came home and joined in with his father's business concerns. What you have to realize is that back then businessmen were eager to invest in what they thought would be good for the whole country—not just themselves or their investors. Of course there was a lot they didn't know—for example, how bad coalmining would be for the environment and for the miners who breathed in the coal dust. We were somewhat surprised to find ourselves becoming much wealthier after the war than anyone would have predicted. I would have probably remained oblivious to the growing social injustice in the United States if I hadn't talked with the women my sorority tried to help. Instead of just giving them the food we had gathered for them and their children, I sat down and talked with the women about why they needed the help. It was a real awakening for me. I had no idea that for lots of people poverty was still an issue—even with the post-war boom in jobs and productivity."

"I earned a teacher's certificate, and I would have liked to teach, but Ross was still too young for me to be away from him. My aunt had helped me take care of him while I went to school just after the war years, but she developed heart problems and diabetes. She was a wonderful nana, wasn't she, Ross?"

"Yeah, there'll never be another one like Auntie Lou. But, Mom, maybe we should skip to today's meeting. I remember when we talked about it earlier you had some pretty strong reasons for wanting to have just a small group and especially for wanting to include mostly older folks. Didn't you say something about having learned the ins and outs of seminar meetings by serving on all those boards you were a part of?"

"Ah, I didn't mean to ramble," Forella said with a smile toward Ross. Ross looked a bit chagrinned. "No, Mom, your reminiscences are always interesting. I just remember being intrigued by your reasons for wanting the seminar to have the special features you mentioned. We have time. I didn't mean to be impatient."

Everyone else in the room looked on with some amusement as Ross and his mother dithered back and forth about how the seminar should get started. Finally Peter said, "Ok, so tell us a little about these boards you were on, Forella. I knew you were on the History Museum's board, but I didn't know about any others."

"Oh, the History Museum was only the most recent. Actually I was on quite a few non-profit boards when I was younger—even my College's board of trustees. That's when I learned something about what seemed to work best when you have a goal of getting a variety of opinions expressed in a meeting. For one thing I noticed that you can't have one person dominating—as I'm doing now. Everyone has to join in. Even the Chair—or in my case, the oldest participant and the one who arranged to have the meeting—even that person has to be just one of the group. But, of course, it's hard to run a meeting without someone who keeps tabs on the rules and moves everything along as it should. I remember reading about Peter Senge's Learning Organizations and systems thinking back in the 1980s. He argued that hierarchy had to be abandoned at the door if a meeting was to accomplish what it really needs to do."

"But," continued Forella, "it was really the Quakers and their notion of 'deep listening' that got me to thinking about how to best accomplish what I wanted to see happen in a seminar like this one. And then, more recently, the Unitarian church that I attend started having what they call 'Chalice Circles.' The Chalice Circle Program is intended to help people work toward some common goal, like community service or even service to the church, but what I found interesting was the process during the meetings. Basically, they took the notion of deep listening that the Quakers used—the practice of listening to someone without interrupting or offering advice—and combined that with the kind of 'agreed upon' format that Peter Senge recommends for effective learning organizations. In other words, an ideal seminar is not a competition to see who can express the best ideas or make the most points, or even get his or her point of view accepted. No, instead, it is a matter of each person expressing his or her thoughts without fear of reprisal or the need to win out over someone else. People practice really listening and learning what others think, and they also practice putting their own thoughts into words without worrying about whether anyone else will agree or not."

Forella brought her hands together in front of her and waited. "I would hope everyone who joins our seminar would agree to something like that—a courteous and attentive time for sharing ideas. As to why older people? and why Handel?—well, to be honest, I would like to make the point that older people have some wisdom to share with the world, and I thought this seminar would be one way to do that. I don't necessarily think older people have better ideas or anything like that. I just would like to see what a group of people in their 50s, 60s, 70s, or 80s can contribute. And Handel? I'm just delighted to have found these letters, and I can't think of anything I would rather do than learn what other people might think about Handel and these letters written to him so long ago. I've always liked Handel's music. And I want to learn more, if I can, about how he lived his life, maybe even how he managed after he became blind. I have lots of personal reasons for wanting to start this seminar. But mostly I just want to see how it happens, how it develops—my last big project."

Katherine Baker noticed Ross grimacing a little, mostly to himself it seemed. She assumed he didn't like hearing his mother talk about her 'last project,' and, in fact, it was a sad and awkward moment for everyone. Peter, as seemed to be his wont, smoothed over the difficult silence with a cajoling note: "Forella, we're all excited to see this project start, but let's hear no more about it being your last one. Big it may be, but I know you will have many other irons in the fire. Still, I'm intrigued by your call for older seminar members. We've talked a little about this before. If I remember right, you said something about wanting the experience of participating to be a benefit to the seminar members, too. In other words, you thought it would be especially worthwhile for seniors to be stimulated to contribute their ideas. The seminar would be a good contribution in two ways—for people in the seminar as well as people who might eventually learn about the discussions. Myself, I think that it's sometimes good for older people to be mentoring their peers, not just younger people. That's why I liked your idea."

Katherine signaled with her hand that she had something to say. Peter grinned and said that the group would have to find some other way of indicating they wanted to speak. Raising hands is just too much like school. Katherine laughed. "Well I wasn't sure, but I did want to say that I thought your idea of talking with peers would be an important opportunity here. I often learn quite a bit from my graduate students, but I sometimes miss hearing what older colleagues would say to some of the questions we discuss. It may not seem exactly politically correct—I mean it does seem to be the opposite of 'ageist'—but I'd appreciate a chance to see what happens in such a seminar."

"That must have been Professor Baker," said Forella, turning in her direction. "I remember the first time I participated in one of the Chalice Circles at my church. I was a little disappointed that the group was mostly older people. I'm not sure why that happened, but I thought at the time that it should include some younger folks. The next one I joined did have younger folks. Both groups—the one with young people and the one made up of seniors—had their strong points, and of course it really depends on the people involved. But in any case, I did see the advantage in once in a while having a group of just age-peers talking together. Sometimes it made it easier to get to the point of a discussion, as though some things could be assumed right at the start."

"Yes, and please call me Katherine. I've studied some of the effects of group allegiances as a folklorist. In the case of age, people do tend to share quite a bit as a common frame of reference just by virtue of being roughly the same age. We usually take it for granted, but it shows up when you try to reference things that younger people know about only as history. Have you ever looked at the annual list that Beloit College publishes on the web? They list all the things that the incoming Freshman class knows or doesn't know. Sometimes it is pretty disheartening. Not only do they not know what a dial telephone or a mimeograph machine is, they expect everyone to be on some social network and text message at the drop of a hat. Religion and politics tend to separate people into culture groups, but so does age and ethnicity. It might be a good test to see what comes out of a seminar restricted by age."

Ross looked toward his mother and then back at Katherine. "I'll have to say that this suggestion was the one that I found a little troubling, and frankly surprising, coming from you, Mom. How many times have I heard you grumble about too many meetings where no one but old white men do all of the talking—or maybe it's just gender or race that was the issue there instead of age. Just saying. But seriously, I'd like to hear a little more about why you want a senior citizen seminar."

"Ok, ok," Forella laughed. "I did skirt around this issue. The truth is I want our seminar—if it can—to help people handle aging in a way that is good—both pleasing to them—that is, to you who participate—and beneficial to society. I know that sounds lofty, maybe even presumptuous. Young people find it hard to imagine being old. One of the hardest things about getting older is recognizing that you are no longer needed. Even your knowledge and experience don't count for much once you retire or send your kids off into the world. I've had to deal with that myself, and despite putting up what I think has been a pretty good front, I haven't always found it easy, especially after I started losing my sight. I've been very conscious of doing the things that would keep me engaged—my projects, my reading and research. Hardest of all was when I could tell that people might have preferred younger people with more energy, more up-to-date ideas doing the work I volunteered to do. But I knew that I was responsible for keeping myself from slipping into inertia and becoming disengaged. It's an important lesson and one I would like to share. I don't think younger people are ready to hear it, but older people need to. Older people are the ones I want to be the discussants but also the subjects in this seminar, so they won't have to struggle quite so much on their own—as I have had to."

Everyone in the group looked a bit stricken, and Angela actually had silent tears leaking from her eyes. She wiped them away. She couldn't help feeling sorry for Forella. Ross fidgeted with the bottle of water sitting in front of him. But Katherine looked almost accusingly at Peter. Her immediate thought was that she herself was hardly a senior citizen. Granted she had turned fifty only a few years ago, and that over-the-hill birthday party with the teasing black balloons and graveyard cake had given her pause, but a seminar specifically intended to help the participants with the issue of aging! Maybe in twenty years she would actually need something like this, but she was still very much engaged, and in fact needed. She had plenty of opportunity to share her knowledge and experience. And her graduate students were a source of constant stimulation. Why had Peter thought she would want to be a part of a seminar on aging—and as a participant, not as an ethnographer? Participant-observation is an excellent methodology, but this situation felt more like a self-help group, and, as Forella said, one for people like her, for Katherine, not just for Forella and people her age. Katherine had always resisted self-help groups, even on topics that seemed more appropriate, like how to manage both a family and a profession or how to find love after age forty. If she were being honest, she would have faulted Peter for misinforming her. He must have sensed her reproach. He looked ever so slightly chagrinned, but he rallied almost at once.

"Ah, well, Forella, it's true that none of us wants to suffer as much as you have—servants waiting on you hand and foot, a private jet to fly you to the Lyric Opera for the week-end, and all those Château Mouton Rothschild wines—now there's a challenge," said Peter. Forella laughed, and after an initial look of shock, even Katherine joined the seeming good cheer. "Yes, yes, I've had it easy in many ways," said Forella. "But, you know, money can't buy everything. A lot of my wealthiest friends have a hard time figuring out why they aren't happy. And, really, I suspect that a lot of people don't realize they are struggling with the demands of aging even when they are. They may think they are just a little depressed, or a little unhappy, when in fact they are in the process of transforming. And hopefully, they are changing into the kind of person we are supposed to become as we get older, someone who has finally grown up—as one of my favorite authors, James Hollis, says. Part of the reason I want the seminar to be seniors is that people who have passed fifty are—or at least should be—less intimidated by culture; they don't have to accommodate the expectations of others, of society, so much. They can afford to be more honest—if they choose to. It took me a long time to realize that. I think it is a wonderful thing, and I think our seminar should take advantage of it."

Katherine cleared her throat—having remembered Peter's remark about raising hands. Peter and Ross exchanged a look, and Ross said, "What's your thought, Katherine?"

"Well, I do have a question, or maybe just a reservation, about accepting the stipend Forella has offered—which is quite generous—if, in fact, much of the benefit from the seminar is likely to be for me—as a participant—rather than for some external audience or readership. Do you understand what I mean? It really is quite different from other seminars I have participated in, ones sponsored by, say the National Endowment for the Humanities or the Lilly Foundation. With those groups, it is clear that there has to be a public outlet and a specific end product. In this case, it is not so clear. And as I understand it, you hope to have several more people join the seminar. I guess my question is, what is our task, our function, and who decides on our goal?"

Ross looked at his mother, who smiled but seemed a bit tired. "I think," Ross started, "that is exactly the kind of question we need to answer in the collective—using something like this 'deep listening' model we just heard about—is that right, Mom? Where you go around the circle and just hear what each person wants to say? It might be a good trial run. I didn't get the feeling that there was a preset goal for the seminar. In other words, we will let a goal emerge from our discussion. Does that seem doable?"

Forella sat up straighter in her chair. "Yes, I wish there were someone else who had participated in one of the Chalice Circles and could review the process. As I recall, we did start out by setting some ground rules that everyone would agree on. After that, there was no policy that we had to come to any agreement or defend anything we might think. Everyone was expected to contribute if they wanted to, but they didn't have to. So, I guess even Ross's suggestion that a goal would emerge from the discussion isn't a given. It's hard for people who are trained to set goals and work toward consensus to abandon their usual procedure and simply have a dialogue. It may not work for us, but I think it is worth trying. I like the idea that today might be a trial run. I also like the idea that I can choose to not say anything else and just listen."

Ross grinned over at Peter. "All right, folks. You heard the woman. She's willing to pay good money to hear us chatter among ourselves. And to no good end, or at least no necessary end. Our task is to talk, to fill the time, to voice our opinions. Is that all that happens at these Chalice circles? People sit around and express opinions? Doesn't that seem kind of pointless?"

Having failed to get a rise out of Forella with this barb, Ross looked to Peter again. Peter put his hand up as though catching a ball. "Ok, ok, I'll bite. I don't think Forella intends for us to replicate what she has described as a Chalice Circle format—but instead just to adopt the underlying principle that a truthful exchange of ideas is more important than consensus and that sometimes the objective is simply to hear as many perspectives as possible. Sometimes it is better to be undecided or ambivalent rather than forcing agreement. And in this case we have the luxury of not having to hand over a conclusive report to some granting agency. The point is not to persuade each other to one side of an issue or another but rather to learn collectively and individually what we can from the discussion. And if others can learn from our dialogue as well, so much the better."

"Hear, hear," said Katherine. "I wish you were our college dean. But I suppose that is the point. Universities and corporations need to make decisions, not simply think about ideas, good or bad. I guess you are right. It is a luxury. So, maybe to rephrase my question—or to restate it as a proposition: Our task is to think together—not as in a think tank, where there usually is a goal in mind, but rather as in really hearing each other's thinking about a variety of issues, insofar as that is possible."

"I'd like to go back to this notion of not answering to a granting agency," said Ross. "We do tend to see it as a luxury if we get support for a project but don't feel obligated to push our sponsor's idea of what is good or right or important. I've had plenty of granting agencies backing my films, and there has never been a time when I didn't feel a certain amount of pressure to at least highlight what those agencies considered important. I suppose in this case, it is Forella Wainwright who is buying our votes or influencing our research—if you want to be cynical about it. Personally, I think the request that we find middle-age to older people for the seminar is a pretty manageable bribe. Really, so long as she doesn't require that I pretend to be Handel and start imagining that I once lived in eighteenth-century London, I'm content."

Katherine and Benfey looked puzzled, and Forella chuckled and shook her finger in Ross's direction. "Just you wait, you scoffer, you'll see. I'll bet we find irrefutable proof in these letters that you ARE Mr. Handel in a modern guise. Here is your real test, Katherine. Can you tolerate taking seriously the possibility that our seminar might—just might—get into the topic of reincarnation? Notice, I didn't say anything about needing to accept the idea—simply tolerate the possibility. After all, countless Hindus, Theosophists, Neo-Pagans, and such believe in reincarnation. Even Carl Sagan said we needed to study it. My son is such a skeptic."

Once again, Peter came to the rescue. "Don't worry, Katherine, this really is just an example of Forella's very admirable tendency to follow any idea where it leads. Ross just doesn't like the idea of being as fat as Handel was in his lifetime. You can see why he studiously avoids any comparisons to his present bodily make-up."

"Low blow, low blow," said Ross. "We'll explain the reincarnation connection later. But, what do you think, Katherine, about our larger issue—about the whole idea of keeping the seminar open and free of a directing agenda? Do you think it is a workable idea, a good idea, to not have a goal or set task for this seminar?"

"Well, I guess you have already stated one advantage in adopting an 'open' dialogue scheme for our seminar—no agency's agenda influencing our discussions, no expected conclusions or reinforcement of desired ideas. There is another advantage or effect. Folklorists are used to seeing traditional values or memes in any sort of day-to-day interactions. Certainly stories or songs or other creative expressions like that convey broader ideas that are maintained and fostered by the culture. The notion that 'the folk' are unlettered peasants was dropped long ago, and, really, it is no surprise that dialogues of the sort we will have in this seminar are now more often the subjects of folkloristic or sociolinguistic study. For folklorists, the fascinating thing is that so often the values expressed even by well-educated, sophisticated people are tied to basic values traditional to the culture. We'll be looking at these old letters written to Handel, but we'll be using our contemporary personal and communal values to interpret them."

Peter looked at Katherine and then pulled out the copy of the letter that had accompanied the packet of letters to Handel. "You know," he said, "when you think about these letters and the use to which we will put them, it is sort of like we are creating our own biblical text. Well, of course, if you believe that God literally dictated the Bible, then this analogy goes nowhere, but if you accept the idea that the Bible was compiled of various texts written down over many decades or centuries, sometimes from oral tradition in fact, then we are doing just as biblical scholars have done for years. We are trying to interpret a text from earlier times as a moral guide to us today. Well, maybe moral guide is too strong, but I was just thinking that Katherine's 'traditional values' are similar to the kind of guidance preachers usually offer by interpreting the scriptures. In a way, it reminds me of a book I recently read called *Jesus Was a Liberal*. As you might guess, the point of the book is that the author's or reader's own values very much influence the direction of the interpretation of the Bible. I'm sure it will be the same with our seminar and the interpretation of these letters."

Katherine watched Ross doodling on his copy of the printout Angela had given them. He seemed to be drawing some sort of elf or goblin with a little pointed hat. Obviously he was not listening in rapt attention. As she followed his pen sketching in the imp's silly grin, she thought about her graduate students—some of whom often did the same kind of fairly artistic doodling while a classmate—or even the professor—spoke during a seminar session. She had wondered whether it meant they were bored, whether they were simply too self-centered to listen to other people's ideas, whether they were ADHD, or maybe that she was not managing the class very well. She remembered the first time that she consciously tried to address the issue with students. Some said they weren't aware that they were doodling, but others said they doodled to keep from feeling angry or impatient with what was being said. Some actually said that they found the requirement of listening to other people really disturbing. For would-be folklorists, this was not a good sign.

From the very beginning of her career, Katherine had always taken a real interest in the process and skill of teaching. She had participated in countless workshops, gone to many excellent lectures sponsored by the Scholarship on Teaching and Learning program at the university, read books and articles on best practices, even taught the teaching class for graduate teaching assistants in her department. Most teaching issues revolved around undergraduate teaching, but Katherine found herself worrying more about graduate teaching. Her own graduate student years had been wonderful—but over much too quickly. Looking back she realized that part of the reason she so enjoyed her graduate school experience was that she was an exemplary student. Truth be told, she made it easy for her professors to succeed, even those few that other students found impossible. Even now, she often flashed back to her own grad school days and tried to imagine what she could do to inspire the same kind of learning behavior in her own students.

There were, of course, lots of little tricks for taking notes more efficiently, for skimming assigned readings, for keeping notes and sources organized, even for arguing forcefully and poking holes in other people's opinions. Graduate school can be a kind of internship in the forever-after practice of academic debate. Katherine had watched, both as a student and as a professor, the often painful transformation students endured as they learned to follow the well-worn path to academic success. She remembered being somewhat startled the first time she read David Damrosch's book *We Scholars* and realized that, as Damrosch said, academic institutions had long been selecting for "certain kinds of alienation and aggression on campus." In other words, grad students were trained through seminar participation to be scrappy fighters for their own opinions, their own publications, with other people's ideas used only as springboards for their better, more impressive research.

Little wonder, then, that students learned to use the time when others speak as an opportunity to think of their own rebuttal or more admirable idea—or simply to wait impatiently until the other speakers are finished, perhaps doodling to keep from rolling their eyes. But Katherine had learned, too, that quite aside from that indoctrination into grad student behavior, students were also eager to be intellectually engaged. That, in her opinion, was their saving grace, the trait that would allow them to be learners, colleagues, friends, real seminar participants. So she tried to capitalize on that trait. She tried always to guide students to hear or read the human, real-life question behind anyone else's words. What is our big question, and how is this person grappling with it in this response or this statement? She urged everyone to see a seminar as a truly collective exchange of ideas and information in answer to an important question.

Pulling herself from this reverie, Katherine noticed that everyone was looking at her as though expecting her to say something. "What, what?" she said, "Did I miss something? Sorry, Peter, did you ask me something?"

"No. It just seemed that you had something to say, so we were waiting. Ross is doodling, and you are off following your own line of thought. Maybe we need a break. What do you think?"

"A break would be nice." Katherine moved over to the corner where Benfey sat with her recording equipment. "Does your new software allow you to identify speakers and do a rough transcription?" "Yeah," Benfey answered. "I think the transcription process will go pretty smoothly. The fun part will be my notes on body language and unspoken context. I think Ross and Peter both have the usual male feelers out for your attention."

Katherine reached for Benfey's notepad. "It's not there. Just my own astute observation," said Benfey with a laugh. Then, turning serious, she said, "Really, I think the contextual notes will be a piece of cake so long as the transcription and voice identification software does its job. It might be a little harder when we add the other people, but I think it's a go. Do you know how many more people will join the group?"

When everyone reassembled, Katherine posed Benfey's question: How many more people would be invited to join them, and how would they be selected? Forella smiled in Katherine's direction. "From your experience, Katherine, what is a good number for a seminar? Are there numbers too few or too many for a good discussion? I'm happy to invite as many as we need to make for a good mix and a manageable group."

Katherine thought of the many seminars she had participated in—as a student, as a scholar, as a teacher. One seminar that stood out in her memory was actually from many years ago, from her own graduate school days. It was a seminar comprised of eight fairly seasoned students along with the professor. They were studying fairy tales. It was a wonderful class. Everyone did his or her part in researching background materials, and everyone participated in discussion. For that course, anyway, eight participants seemed ideal. But she remembered, too, that it was less successful when one or two people had to miss a session. So, perhaps eight was the minimal number. "I think a group of no less than eight or more than twelve might be best. But that's based on my experience with academic seminars, where people are expected to bring researched information into the discussion. Will we be doing that? It takes some time, and usually there is a syllabus with suggested readings on it."

Ross chuckled. "No syllabi, no assignments. I get itchy just thinking about it. But it would be good if we could come with questions and some background information from our own thinking each time. I don't think the seminar should become an onerous task added to our daily chores. I have an assistant I could draft to find materials that occur to me. I'm not trying to weasel out of doing work here, but I can only devote so much time to it. What's your thought, Peter, my friend?"

"I hadn't thought about research as part of the seminar, but I suppose as we find out more and more about Handel, we'll want to bring in relevant research. I don't have an assistant that I can legitimately ask to track down sources on this topic. It has nothing to do with my day job. I'd be happy to read something someone else suggested—like on a syllabus—sorry, Ross. What do you think, Forella?"

"Well, actually, Angela and I talked about this before coming here today. We anticipated some of this worry over researching sources that might be useful. Angela really is a treasure. She volunteered to be the go to person for any materials that you might want to bring into the discussion. I think as long as she isn't swamped with too much or asked to do something on too short notice, we should be able to have our own resource person for the seminar. Even if we expand to, say, ten people, she thought it would be something she could handle. And she has already been working on a list of names we might consider as additional members of the seminar. We're a lucky bunch to have her!"

"Thanks, Angela. That's outstanding," said Peter. "Maybe we could all look over those names and try to have a full house for our next meeting. But now I have something that I've been dying to say, and I think it will set us up nicely for that next session. As I reported to Forella, the letters we'll be reading in transcript are, in my opinion, definitely authentic.

I have run all of the tests recommended by auction houses and then some. I can't tell you how exciting it has been to work with these letters and start the preservation process. However, the big news I have for you today is that there was a surprise note inside the wallet that held the letters. It isn't a letter written by Handel—as I understand it, he was blind by the time the letters were returned to the sender. But the note does seem to have been dictated by Handel to his man-servant, Thomas Bramwell. Here is what it says:

> *Written herein by Thos. Bramwell, from Mr Handel*
> *25 Brook Street*
> *On this day 11 April 1759*
>
> *My dear Lydia,*
> *Enclosed are the letters you have sent to me over our many years of converse and kind regard. Until my eyes could no longer see, I read them as faithfully as scriptures. To me they were always as the sweetest sonnets or gladsome tunes, yet often as somber and stirring as psalms. I return them now to you as life slips away. Read and remember. I am, as always, your servant,*
>
> *G F Handel*

The signature slides down the page in what is unmistakably Handel's own hand. I must say it was very moving to find this note, to see his signature. I propose we talk about this little surprise next time we meet. And with our new members as well. I have a copy of the transcript for each of you. Enjoy!"

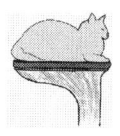

CHAPTER 4

A Handel Seminar

At Peter's request, Angela sought out information to construct a chronology of events for the date that headed the surprise note dictated by Handel—11 April 1759. Several sources reported that on that day Handel had signed and attached his seal to the fourth and final codicil to his will, leaving behind an estate of £20,000. Along with many other persons, his two man servants and two maids received bequests. There is no mention of Lydia Grayston. Handel's friend and neighbor James Smyth was the last besides his household servants to see him alive. Angela sat imagining the blind and dying composer, after his friends and attorneys had left, composing with the help of his man servant one last message—this one to a person not mentioned in his will, to his dear Lydia.

ANGELA HOUSER IMMERSED HERSELF IN the Handel Seminar project with relish. She had so longed to be useful in the way she now so clearly was. Primary among her start-up tasks was compiling a list of potential seminar members and eventually contacting those chosen, asking them to participate. Drawing up the initial long list of possible candidates was a job Angela found surprisingly fun. She knew she would have to seek out people living within a fifty- or seventy-five-mile radius since they would likely meet at least once a month. As a guide, she adopted Forella's fairly open descriptor—someone over fifty years of age, someone who might have reason to be interested in the life and times of George Frideric Handel, and someone who would bring to the seminar his or her own questions and reflections rather than any preordained by an authority. But how to ensure this last? Or how even to know? Angela felt it necessary to consult with the first rung of members before she sought to add to their number.

Forella bowed out on this advisory role, as did Peter, who said that his work with restoring and making archive copies of the letters was quite enough for him, thank you. That left Ross and Katherine. Peter suggested that Ross and Katherine be officially designated co-chairs of the seminar and that they oversee the task of choosing additional members. Angela thanked Peter profusely for making this suggestion. Despite all of the idealistic talk of non-hierarchical groups, she knew that a leader or leaders would be needed if the seminar were actually to move forward and decisions on who would join them were to be made. Katherine and Ross each separately determined to find as a new member someone who would annoy Peter, just as a punishment, but they accepted the assignment and met with Angela to further refine her list.

It was this list of potential seminar members that Angela brought along to the lunch meeting she set up near Katherine's office. Ross had started a new documentary project that would keep him in the area for several months. Meeting in Bloomington seemed a good option. Compiling a list of organizations whose members would include people described by the first two of Forella's guidelines was a fairly easy task. How to find people who would be open to new ideas and would listen without judgment to other people—that was a challenge. Angela mentioned half jokingly that Forella had asked her if she were a born-again Christian at her interview. Perhaps asking whether people held particularly strong or extreme religious or political affiliations would be a start. All agreed that it would be hard to find anyone who would actually admit to being prejudiced, closed-minded, or even simply dogmatic. And pigeonholing people by the groups they adhere to would itself be using stereotypes to sort out who might be included.

Katherine commented that—surprisingly—there were some more or less scientific tests that revealed the test-taker's psychological characteristics. Some were even especially formulated to determine whether the individual was typically responsive to authority or relatively independent. Often the tests were clearly revealing of political leanings. Ross was intrigued, but Angela cautioned that including such a test would be difficult; it would still mean that some people would be eliminated on the basis of assumptions made about them. In other words, if people tested as 'authoritative' rather than 'independent,' they would be less likely to be chosen. Katherine suggested that it might be easier to include a kind of self-evaluation in a cover letter to the people contacted. That is, they would be invited to comment on their own approach to other people and to ideas that are unfamiliar or disturbing as well as their experience with forums or seminars. Ross and Angela applauded this suggestion and voted that Katherine be the letter writer. Ouch! Benfey chuckled as she noted Katherine's grimace in her field record.

"Ok, ok," said Katherine, "I'll compose the letter, but let's get the gist of it down now. What is most important to know about a seminar member? A professor at the University of Manitoba, Bob Altemeyer, wrote an excellent study called *The Authoritarians* in which he argued that one distinguishing characteristic of people who adhere too readily to authority is simply fear—fear of people who are different, fear of new ideas, fear of change, fear of losing out. I think we need to include some line in the cover letter that asks directly whether the individual is fearful, especially of stepping out of line. What do you think?"

"Well," Ross responded, "there are lots of people who are convinced that they have the answer to anything, and they would not consider themselves fearful. You know, God on our side and all that. I think it will have to be stated in the positive, or at least in what we consider positive. For example—Do you enjoy learning new things? Are you willing to seriously entertain an opposing point of view? Do you like the idea that a good discussion might change your understanding of the world? –you know, something like that."

"So," said Katherine, "we want to elicit something about their perspective on the value of a seminar, then? Do they feel a philosophical discussion is worthwhile, do they welcome new ideas, do they think there are advantages in hearing a variety of opinions? Are they willing to consider challenges to ideas or personal beliefs without simply looking for ways to maintain what they already believe? I still think most people will respond that they are open-minded and reasonable. Few people are willing to admit they have prejudices. Most people think that sticking to your principles, no matter what, is a good thing."

"Well, I don't think we are going to find a litmus test for this," said Ross. "We are going to just have to describe what kind of seminar we are proposing and see who is attracted to participating in it. That process just by itself may weed people out. It's the more open-minded people who actually enjoy listening to other people grapple with challenging ideas. I know I'm stereotyping here, but I also think it is true."

Katherine sat lost in thought about some of the research that had been done on seminars—really on oral dialogues or congresses of any sort. She knew that historically high regard was accorded an individual's persuasive oral performance in most public domains. A thousand years ago, the old Icelandic Althing conducted its public affairs entirely by oral rather than written means, even though writing was known and practiced in other Icelandic culture contexts. They preferred to benefit from the kind of exchange fostered by verbal interactions in public. The dialogues there were performances and were taken very seriously. One needed to be skilled and careful as a performer but also truly engaged and responsive to what others were saying. All listeners were following the entire discussion, not simply waiting for sound bites with which they agreed. Each speaker was expected to pick up ideas already expressed and move them forward, much as a jazz musician does in restating yet expanding a theme. There was an expectation that the dialogue itself was the means by which new ideas emerged. Collectively building new ideas was the goal.

Angela brought Katherine out of her reverie: "Are you hoping for something like the roundtables that happen on Meet the Press or some show like that? You know, where they have people from both sides of an issue and the moderator manages the debate? I don't know whether you expect to have strong differences of opinion, but those discussions can get pretty intense."

"Public Debate for Ax Grinders?" said Ross. "I don't think so. Those shows are set up to be entertainment, and there is some expectation that one side wins the argument. We are hoping to avoid that kind of divisive showcasing. Even at the very beginning, the idea was to learn something from the Handel letters, and from the Seminar. There is a place for debate—especially in the political arena—but debaters find it hard to let themselves be educated. What's your thought, Katherine?"

"Yes, I'll admit that I find those roundtables—even the ones on PBS—more disturbing than helpful. By definition they are confrontational, and rarely does anyone let slip that they have learned anything new or seriously entertained a different perspective than the one they came with. Mostly, they reinforce for me the notion that people hold strong loyalties to ideas shared by their philosophical kin. People may not be spouting prejudices of the sort you find in ethnic jokes or other 'us versus them' expressions, but they are still reflecting a worldview that has been influenced by the groups that person thinks he or she belongs to. Or more likely, they hold worldviews taught them by groups they simply assume should be accepted as God-given, natural, or 'correct and reasonable' by everyone. It's the same issue that came up back when the notion of PC—political correctness—was front and center. Too often, people accept the idea that the dominant worldview is superior when in fact it is simply dominant and therefore powerful."

Angela entered some notes on her laptop—part of her diary of topics she promised to keep for Forella. "So this Seminar," she queried, "is somehow to avoid underscoring the dominant worldview? People are supposed to be neutral or completely nonjudgmental? Is that right?"

"I'll take this one," Ross said, waving at Katherine. "I've actually thought a lot about the question you are asking—well, really, the two questions. Let's think about your first question. You asked, in effect, are we planning to avoid or even oppose anything that represents the dominant worldview. It is an interesting question that comes up all the time, especially about religious references or activities. I know you didn't say 'oppose'; you said—what?—'avoid underscoring' the dominant worldview. But very often the people who voice this concern do actually perceive their dominant worldview as coming under attack. It's hard to see. Let me give an example."

"When I came back to Indiana after being on location in India for several months in 2007, I noticed a license plate showing up on lots of cars. It had an American flag waving and in large letters the motto: In God We Trust. I assumed it was one of the special cause, extra charge plates, like the Kids First plate, or the Support Wildlife plate. But then I wondered who was getting the donation that came with the additional fee. I was surprised to learn that it was simply an alternative plate with no extra fee. You could choose the Indiana flag plate or the In God We Trust plate—either with no extra fee. I wasn't at all surprised to learn that the ACLU challenged the legality of the plate the next year—and not really surprised to hear that they lost the case. Basically, the argument was that the majority of people approved the plate, it included a national motto—what was the problem? People could choose the other plate if they didn't like the In God We Trust one."

"Whether people like it or not, the United States, like India, is a secular society. That means it has no official religion. If the plate had said In the Buddha We Trust or In the Goddess We Trust or In Allah We Trust, there would have been an uproar. But most Americans accept that God means their god—the Christian God, or at least the God of Abraham, and that we, as a nation, agree that we all trust in that God. But the plate really only represents that dominant worldview. It is clearly NOT secular. An atheist American would not agree with the motto. Why is it accepted and even defended by the courts? Because it represents the dominant worldview. My complaint—and I suppose that of the ACLU—is that offering such a plate with no special plate charge is not simply politically incorrect, it is culturally incorrect and ethically incorrect."

"America professes to allow freedom of religion; it imposes no official religion. Allowing this In God We Trust plate as an official alternative is a hypocritical action. Clearly, the state bureau of motor vehicles cannot offer as 'unpaid alternatives to the state flag plate' specialty license plates that advocate for all of the other deities that various Hoosier might want to proclaim they believe in. So the In God We Trust plate gives an unfair promotional advantage to a religious group that happens to be dominant—unfair because the US promises equal rights of religious expression to ALL Americans. Those who hold the dominant worldview must be ever vigilant of their own actions to ensure that they do not impose their worldview on others. That is the beauty of American democracy."

"You had another question," said Ross, "something about people in the Seminar being neutral, or not having opinions. Was that it? I can just imagine my mother hearing that we expected Seminar members to be neutral. Yes, indeed, Forella Wainwright seeking out people who had no interest in expressing their opinions! Ok, ok, I'm exaggerating. I know you didn't say that. I think what you really said was something about people being non-judgmental. I appreciate the sentiment, and I think you meant it in a good way—that we wanted people who would not SIMPLY be judgmental, people who would think and evaluate things thoughtfully rather than making hasty judgments. Am I right?"

Angela looked over at Katherine with a kind of open-eyed look and grimace. Ross laughed and said, "I'm sorry. I deserved that emoticon look. Let me start over. What we want to avoid are people who take the easy way out in a serious discussion, people who jump to conclusions rather than forcing themselves to really go through someone else's thought process. Most people actually ARE judgmental; they have to be, or they wouldn't have opinions about how to do anything. But the purpose of a seminar like this one is to slow down our thought process long enough to not just say the first thing that comes to mind. What we want are people who will use reason AND be humble enough to know that they may be wrong some of the time. People who think they have nothing left to learn do not make good seminar members—even if they already know quite a lot. So, Angela, in your notes I guess you could say that we want people who try to use reason as they listen—not people who come with a lot of ready-made 'reasons' they always accept as true."

"Thanks, Ross, and you, too, Angela, for bringing up the questions," said Katherine. "I'll go to work on the letter and get back to both of you later on." What kind of description, Katherine wondered, would attract the people who would be good seminar members? A singular requirement in this case would be that the description could not really reveal the topic of the seminar. Until each seminar member signed an agreement to keep secret the relevant information about the Handel letters, the famous subject of the letters could not be shared. How do you spark the interest of people who would love to ponder new insights into the life of George Frideric Handel without actually stating that he would be the focus of the seminar?

Katherine decided that she could at least reveal that the seminar would examine new information about a prominent musical figure—but that the seminar would use this life history as a starting point for discussion of more contemporary life questions. Candidates for the seminar would have to agree to staying with the project for a period of two or three years, meeting at least once a month during the academic year and probably a couple times over the summer. There would be a small stipend for each participant as well as lunch served at every meeting. The primary requirement, Katherine emphasized in her letter, would be the individual's sincere desire to experiment with a seminar format, to practice deep listening, and to bring a learning organization approach to the discussion and interpretation of these recently discovered materials.

Katherine fussed over the wording of the letter for several days before sending it out to Ross and Angela. Ross said he thought it was excellent—except that there should be a line in it about seeking someone who knew Peter Rowe and hoped to be able to give him grief at every turn. Minus this bit of subterfuge, Angela sent the letter off to the list of candidates she had compiled earlier. Both Katherine and Ross had suggested various liberal religious groups and nonprofits as sources of people to add to the list.

Angela had already compiled a list of amateur choral societies, orchestras, and church choirs as possible contact groups. Perhaps hardest of all had been the challenge in seeking older participants without seeming to suggest that it was some sort of study on aging. Angela simply indicated that the seminar was intended for individuals well into middle age or older rather than young people. She felt no further explanation was needed as so many research projects typically involve students and younger people. This project would be a contrast to those more typical group proposals.

The most significant addition that Katherine made to the letter's outline they had created at their meeting was a list of three questions each potential seminar member should answer. Katherine drew upon her experiences on various admission committees, especially those required to select the best candidates for specialized programs, such as the Honors program for undergraduates or the fellowship nominees for her department's PhD program. Each candidate was asked to submit a typical CV or resume, to include a cover letter stating why he or she would like to participate in the seminar, and to answer the same three questions in a series of very short essays of approximately 75 to150 words. Her experience had convinced her that these answers would likely be the most useful information they would have for making their selections.

There were, of course, all kinds of questions Katherine might have posed to potential seminar members. The three she finally included were: 1) What do you feel you have to contribute to the world now that you didn't have when you were younger? 2) What is the value of music? and 3) What are you doing when you interpret a text? Candidates were asked to respond within two weeks. Ross said he himself would find responding to the questions a real challenge, but he agreed that the answers would be useful. Time to read the answers and discuss them, however, would be hard to come by. Katherine reminded him that this is what co-chairs of committees do. They agreed to meet as soon as possible after the two-week deadline to sort through and rate the submissions. Angela set up an easy online submission process and a convenient online site for Katherine and Ross to read the submissions independently and offer notes and evaluations. Ross admitted that it ended up being a more interesting task than he had imagined.

When Katherine and Ross met just a few weeks later to discuss the candidates and make their selections, they were both pleased to hear that Forella decided to join them. Angela and Benfey were present as well, so it was a convivial but serious meeting, with a clear sense that they were engaging in something like the choosing of friends for a space mission—people they would need to get along with, respect, but also learn from. They felt it was important that there be no dropouts—or worse yet, no forced expatriates. They had reviewed a goodly number of people interested in participating. Now was the time to sort the wheat from the chaff—or perhaps simply the better from the best.

Ross and Katherine had each assigned a relative valuation to each candidate. They chose the ones from each list with acceptable ratings and went over them orally both for Forella's sake and to refresh their own memories of the individuals. Angela had already compiled the working list based on responses Ross and Katherine had made earlier. Forella found it very informative to hear the responses to the three questions from each of the candidates they considered. It allowed her to ask pertinent questions. Though the process took the best part of three hours, they all felt at the end that they had made their decisions carefully and with a variety of perspectives on what might be most important when selecting members of the group. They also felt they already knew the people they had chosen—that they were, if not friends, then very familiar acquaintances.

Katherine found it a bit ironic that a few of the people on their final list were actually not, at least on the surface, the artsy type she had envisioned. In fact a couple chosen candidates were rather practical and a bit conservative for her taste. The discussion of these individuals had been pretty revealing. It was Forella, interestingly, who insisted that it would be good to include people who were well-reasoned in their conservatism, especially if they had experience to back it up. Katherine wondered, fleetingly, if Forella's willingness to welcome more conservative folks stemmed from her many years as wife to a rather conservative businessman. Katherine herself had some experience with dating men who were more conservative than she was. She ultimately came to consider it dangerous water, perhaps because it subtly invoked the vaguely appealing male-dominant perspective she had grown up with. Conservative men were, she thought to herself, like comfort food—a welcome indulgence now and then but not for daily fare.

After voicing to herself this rather catty thought, Katherine backed away from her own misgivings. She knew, in fact, that she had some issues with and felt a certain ambiguity about political and social conservatism—most of it tied to her genuine empathy with people who felt a great loyalty to the past, the beliefs and values of their families, and the need for solidarity. Often she felt that her heart was with her own conservative forebears and that it was her educated, enlightened mind that made her a liberal dissenter. She agreed, finally, with Forella that some more conservative people in the group would be useful for keeping a balance. And she wondered why Ross had offered no argument against Forella's suggestions. He seemed to support a similar desire for balance, but Katherine wondered if he had lived through conflicts of one sort or another with his conservative father. Questions for another time, she thought.

Meanwhile, they had formulated their list and sent off the invitations. Even Angela had found somewhat unpalatable the task of casting aside the profiles of the after all very fine people who had expressed an interest in the project but were not chosen. But Katherine, Ross, and Forella had disciplined themselves to include only seven more people, bringing the number of members who would usually be at each meeting to ten. In addition, Benfey would be there to record and make notes on each meeting, and Angela and Forella would be there if they chose to come or if a special reason arose for either to be there. Peter would join the group for all meetings here on out. The seven new members quickly accepted, and Angela sent each a formal contract requiring their agreement to the stipulations tied to the letters. Once she had the signed contract from each new member, Angela also sent each person an Oxford University Press version of the full vocal score of Handel's *Messiah* along with an invitation to a get-acquainted wine and cheese party at Forella's townhouse and a first assignment: plan to participate in the annual Bloomington Chamber Singers' Messiah Sing the evening after their initial get-together.

Many people who live in Bloomington know of the BCS Messiah Sing, but not all have participated. Basically people are invited to bring their own scores and sing along on all of the choruses and voice-appropriate arias in the first or Christmas part of the oratorio—as well as the Hallelujah chorus from part two. It is a food- and fund-raiser for the local food bank, and people are requested to bring canned goods along with their enthusiasm for Handel's famous piece. All of the new seminar members responded with pleasure at the "assignment." It seemed a wonderful way to begin their involvement with the celebrated subject of their seminar.

Several new members expressed surprise that their well-known musical figure was someone from so long ago. Surely in the three hundred years since Handel's heyday, everything that was going to be found about him would have long since surfaced and been archived in a museum or library. A couple new members admitted to knowing little of Handel's music besides *Messiah*, *Water Music*, the British coronation anthem, or *Music for the Royal Fireworks*. They weren't necessarily disappointed that their subject would be George Frideric Handel, but his was not a name they had included on their mental best-guess lists as they signed on to be a part of the seminar.

Though each new member was given the opportunity to back out of the seminar—having agreed when signing the contract to not reveal any information about the group or its subject if he or she chose not to participate—still, there were no drop-outs. Forella said she was not in the least surprised to see everyone staying with the group. They had chosen their cohorts carefully. The party at Forella's townhouse was the first chance they all had to speak openly about the letters and to meet the other Handel Seminar members.

Some few weeks earlier, Forella and Angela had attended one of the local gallery walks (Angela was especially good at describing artworks to Forella and critiquing them at the same time), and Forella had been intrigued by a practice that added to the walk's festival atmosphere. One of the local wine shops was invited to select a wine for each artist represented in one of the larger galleries. A knowledgeable staff person from the wine shop offered the gallery visitors a short rationale for each wine selection. The wine tasting had an added purpose, and, of course, the artist gained a bit of added interest from the tasters. Forella thought a similar scheme might enhance the first meeting of the Handel Seminar. She consulted with the wine shop owners and enlisted the services of a young staff person who happily researched wines that might come closest to being representative of what a typical early eighteenth-century British lady or gentleman might choose to drink. The young wine expert arrived with several small valises at Forella's townhouse at the Seminar's first meeting, and as an added bonus, he handed Angela a business card with his web address and the URL with a fragment identifier for three pages of information on the history of wine making, transport, and consumption in the early 1700s.

As Seminar members arrived, Forella's helpful staff, Randolph and Annie, greeted each guest, taking coats, hats, etc. and steering everyone into the large parlor where the young man from the wine shop stood. Soon Ross stepped to the center of the room and lifted one of the empty wine glasses and clinked it gently with the back of a large ruby ring on his right hand. "Hello, my friends, and good afternoon. Before we move more directly into our main event, I would like to introduce a young man who delights in researching everything wine-related—Eduardo Juan Bentley—who will tell you a little about the wines you will be invited to enjoy. "

Eduardo was a handsome young man with a smile that warmed everyone in the room. If anyone had expected his interest to be purely monetary, they were soon convinced otherwise. He clearly loved his subject. "I have chosen four wines for you based on the request Mrs. Wainwright conveyed to me. She explained that it would be good for you to experience—insofar as it is possible—the kind of wine you might have consumed as ladies and gentlemen living in London in the early 1700s. I have chosen two reds and two white wines."

As everyone gathered around the table spread with various cheeses, salmon, prawns, humus, bread, filled pastries, and vegetable trays, Eduardo uncorked the bottles of wine he had brought as samples of Handel-era potables. "This lighter red is a claret—the everyday wine one would consume with meals in eighteenth-century England," he said, lifting the bottle, pouring a small glass, and handing it to Ross, who sniffed it, smiled, and did a quick Groucho Marks eyebrow lift.

The guests were invited to try the claret before Eduardo moved on to the other wines. "A typical dinner to which guests were invited included great amounts of meat—usually venison, beef, pork, and pheasant. Though French wines were prime at the beginning of the 1700s, the ongoing War of the Spanish Succession interfered with shipments of wine from France, Spain, and the Low Countries, so a red wine from Portugal—now known as port—came to be an after dinner favorite. Because it needed to be shipped some distance, it was fortified with brandy and had a higher alcohol content. Unfortunately, it often also exhibited a high level of lead, owing to the means of bottling and transport. Not to worry. Our sample has no lead. I believe some people did suffer a disease that included paralysis and mental confusion as a result of drinking lead-tainted wine in that time period. Like gout, there were some diseases that plagued the wealthy more than the poor."

After Eduardo had introduced the other wines and answered questions from the guests, Ross stepped again into the center of the room, thanked Eduardo, and invited a round of applause for his knowledgeable presentation. Everyone was encouraged to munch, chat, and try each of the wines—or sparkling water, beer, soda, as fancy prompted them. It was a tasty and festive beginning for the Seminar, and Katherine was pleased to see that most of the new members had already confabbed with each other and put a friendly atmosphere well in place before an hour had passed.

Forella stood near the buffet table, leaning lightly on an elegant cane carved from ebony and topped with the form of a sleeping cat. The cane seemed there to steady her; she resisted Angela's suggestion that she sit in a nearby loveseat and allow Angela to guide people toward her. But at a lull in the volume of talk, Peter, Katherine, and Ross caught each other's eyes, and Ross again signaled for the conversing guests to give him their attention. "Thank you, thank you for your kind attention. If you would please find a seat. As you can see, while we were chattering away, my friend Randolph here has arranged a ring of chairs, sofas, and the like into what, in college classroom settings, passes for a discussion arrangement. I hear that some professors at IU objected to older classrooms because the seats were fixed to the floor and couldn't be moved into these chummier arrangements. But we are way ahead of the game. Good. And now, a few introductions."

Ross continued, "I get to be the MC because, as my cohort Peter says, I am used to telling people what to do. I think I managed to talk with everyone here, but just to remind you—I am Ross Wainwright. I make documentary films. My latest project—which will be released later this Spring—was a short piece based on recent research at Mount Vesuvius and the unfortunate city of Pompeii. Watch the film, then take a trip to Pompeii and surrounds. The experience was a moving one for me. We all must die, of course, but the suddenness of that annihilation really makes you realize how you can be alive one moment and dead the next. Which may sound like a really dismal way to start this Seminar. Be warned—I am inclined to find all sorts of serious issues behind the most innocent of subjects. To counter that, let me introduce the wise, charitable, and always forgiving woman who brought us all together here—Forella Wainwright, my mother and guiding light."

Forella, who had not sat down when Ross started speaking, leaned forward a bit on her cat-handled cane and nodded toward Ross. "Greetings, my friends," she said, "I am so pleased to have you here. As you were told upon signing the agreement about our little Seminar, we have the rare privilege of examining a set of letters only recently discovered—letters written to the composer George Frideric Handel. The person who had the letters and sold them to me insisted on the secrecy our agreement represents. I am sure the whole story of how we came to have these letters will emerge as time goes by, but for now I simply wanted to say that I am very excited to begin this collective discussion of these previously unseen, never before discussed and analyzed texts. I know that we could have had fruitful discussions through some electronic medium. My young friend Angela—an exceptional assistant, very well-versed in all sorts of technical jargon and procedures—Angela suggested that we might instead have a blog and invite people to comment at their leisure. But I like real face-to-face seminars, and now that my vision has faded to nearly nothing, I relish hearing real voices and the kind of interplay that can only happen in a room where people gather and talk. So, once again, I thank you for agreeing to be a part of this Handel Seminar. I look forward to getting to know more about each and everyone of you. I hope it will be an enjoyable and educational experience for you—maybe even a provocative one. I may not be here for every meeting, but I plan to listen carefully to every word. My best wishes to you all."

Everyone clapped spontaneously. Forella bowed her head graciously, and Ross, smiling, took her hand, put it on his arm, and led her to a chair next to Angela. Then he turned and signaled to Peter. "And now, let me introduce Peter Rowe, PhD, historian, archivist, curator, able-bodied sailor, and sometime banjo picker. Peter is our conservator for this project. He will be preserving the original letters and sharing their content with us. But let me turn it over to him, and he will say more about what he does with these letters. Peter."

"Thank you, Ross. And as you saw fit to bring up the banjo-playing, I'll make a point of imposing a few hours of banjo music on everyone and blaming you for it. Worse yet, I'll ask you to sing a few British pub songs. Just joking, folks. I never mix business and torture." Peter held up a few sheets of paper. "Here you have the first example of the kind of texts we will be discussing in our Seminar. As I understand it, the memo that was sent to each of you earlier contained a little of the history of these letters—how we came to have them here in Bloomington rather than back in merry old England and why we must not publicize their existence. But now I would like to give you a different kind of information—a quick overview of the process I will be going through to restore and preserve the original artifacts and make copies of their content for our Seminar."

Peter signaled Randolph to switch off the lights, and he turned to a small table holding a notebook computer and LCD projector. On a clear space on Forella's living room wall there appeared a photograph of the leather wallet Ross and Peter had first seen when they visited the little village west of London. "This," Peter said, "is the container that housed these precious letters for nearly three hundred years. You can't imagine how exciting it was to encounter this finely tooled but obviously very old leather case. You know some of the things you see on *Antiques Roadshow*? The ones that the appraiser estimates as worth many thousands of dollars? Well, this wallet alone would be worth quite a lot, especially knowing that it had been the property of so famous a person as Handel. It's actually in pretty good shape. The worn spots on the sides and ends suggest that it had been used for some other purpose prior to being pulled into service as a means of transporting the letters. But, I'm getting ahead of my story."

"What brings us together here are the letters that were in the leather case. Actually there was one letter that was outside the case, one that accompanied the case when it left Handel's house. I've already scanned a copy of that letter, and I have a printed transcription of the letter to give each of you in just a minute. But let me use it to explain the process I will go through for each of the letters. The person who sold Forella the letters stipulated that the letters not be publicly exhibited for twenty-five years, and as a consequence, each of you were required to sign a legal document agreeing not to reveal anything about these letters outside of our Seminar. Nevertheless, as the official conservator for these artifacts, I need to treat them as objects that will eventually be exhibited and that must be preserved and stored in a professional manner. In my other life, I do this sort of thing all the time—though I usually have assistants who do all the hard work. For this project, I will do all of the work myself. Don't worry. Forella is paying me handsomely, and besides it is truly a labor of love. I see it as the highlight of my career. My only regret is that, at this time, the artifacts can't be shared with the public. But that's another topic."

"So, what goes into preserving these letters and getting copies of their contents into your hands? First, I have to fumigate each letter to make sure it will not be compromised by little unseen beasties. Then, because the paper upon which the letters are written seems to be sturdy rag paper—typical of the eighteenth-century and ever so much better than the cheaper wood-based paper that came along later—because it is rag paper, I can with no damage unfold each letter and lay it flat. At that point I have chosen to scan each letter and record the contents on a small notebook computer and external hard drive, both of which will stay in the vault with the original letters along with printed hard copies of each letter. Each letter will be placed in an acid-free binder and stored in a flat file cabinet that will be kept in Forella's temperature controlled bank vault. If any letter is more than one page long, I will separate the pages with archive tissue and keep the pages together in the binder. And that's pretty much all I would do if I were just going to preserve the letters for eventual exhibition in a museum. It would take some time but could be methodically carried out over several months, and that would be the end of it."

"But for our purposes I have another task. We need to be able to discuss the content of each of these letters. Forella asked me to be responsible for making the letters readable, so we could spend most of our time actually talking about the written texts rather than trying to decipher what they say. And, to ensure that you will appreciate all my hard work and fawn over me whenever you get the chance, let me show you the scanned original of the letter I labored so diligently to make available in a readable text for you today." Peter again projected a picture on the wall—this time of a hand-written letter, the one Handel's maid had given Susannah Cibber along with the packet of letters intended for Lydia Grayston. The writing represented the cramped script of Handel's man-servant. It included a number of unusual spellings and strange capitalizations, and, to Katherine at least, the script looked rather like German gothic—spikey and slanted slightly backward.

It also included the falling signature of the maestro himself. Peter smiled as he heard several gasps from his audience. "Impressive, isn't it?" he said. "I have enhanced the contrast on this scanned copy. The original is faded but still readable. I'm sure most of you would in fact find it interesting to ponder how writing has changed over three centuries and study the peculiarities of our letter-writer. Still, Forella believes—and I agree—that the content is more important at this point than the handwriting itself. And it is apparent already, as I have examined the other letters—the ones written by Lydia Grayston, that some letters exhibit what we call "foxing"—a kind of spotting or browning that sometimes interferes with our view of the text. So I will be deciphering and transcribing each letter and printing out a modern English text for you, leaving behind the misspellings, odd capitalizations, and varying uses of "ye" as articles that are common in that period. You are welcome to come see the originals if you wish. I won't bowdlerize or censor anything, I promise. I don't doubt that each of you could become accustomed to reading the eighteenth-century script, but just as with eye-dialects, it takes some getting used to, and besides it will be best to have one text that represents just one interpretation of the script. I get to be that interpreter of the script. I hope you approve."

Once again, everyone clapped, and Peter shut down the projector and handed out the sheets of paper with his transcription of the letter they had just seen. As everyone started reading through the short letter Handel had dictated to "my dear Lydia" so long ago, Ross stepped forward yet again—this time to introduce Katherine. "We will say a little more about the letter you have there before we finish up today, but before that, let me introduce one more person who has been working to get this Seminar up and running—Professor Katherine Baker. Katherine."

Katherine stepped in front of the table where Ross had been standing. She looked around at the gathered Seminar members now looking up from the paper they had each been handed. "I'll let you finish reading that first letter, shall I? After all, it is what we are here for, isn't it?" As they returned to considering the sheets Peter had given them, Katherine looked at each new Seminar member. There sat self-made businessman Bradford Hochensmith. To Katherine's eye he looked like Clark Gable, even down to the mustache and still mostly dark hair. Next to him was Clara Sperry, at 50, the youngest addition to the group, even younger than Katherine herself who had been eligible for AARP for a few years now. Clara, a physicist at IU, played cello and sang with the Unitarian church choir. Next to Clara sat Sharon Rayette LaRose, a wonderfully intense-looking African-American woman with slightly graying dread-locks braided around the back and top of her head. Katherine knew that she sang with a church choir and also wrote poetry.

The other four new members sat on the other side of the room: Chandler Dent Jennings (CD, as he preferred to be called) was a university choir director, and next to him was a local community orchestra and chorus director and singer, Alison Jean Swift. And to the left of them, Wayne Allen Thompson, a jazz club owner from Indianapolis, and Rebecca Trent, a retired professor of anthropology and a noted feminist. Katherine felt that she knew them all well enough to jump right into a dialogue, but she realized that they still had fairly superficial information about each other—and about her, Ross, Peter, and Forella, for that matter. As the readers looked up from their papers, Katherine smiled and held up a slim paperback book with a colorfully printed title they could all read easily from anywhere in the room: A TREE IS KNOWN BY ITS FRUIT.

"Most of you seem to be finished reading, so hello, everyone. My name is Katherine Baker. You will likely remember that it was my name signed at the end of the letter you received when you were first made aware of this Seminar and were asked to send us some information about yourself. Ross and Forella and I had the happy task of selecting you as Seminar members from among the many who expressed an interest. One response that was most telling—for me at least—was your answer to the question 'What are you doing when you interpret a text?' I'm a folklorist, and one thing folklorists do is interpret oral texts—usually stories—but we also pay attention to how other people interpret the stories, songs, or sayings they share with us. So I thought, as a little warm-up exercise, I would ask you to interpret this text—the words you see on the cover of this book. What do you make of this? What do you think the book is about?"

Wayne Thompson spoke up. "Well, it seems you are not going to pass the book around so we can actually see what is inside." He paused, and a few people laughed. "That's right," said Katherine, smiling. "So, Wayne, what do you think the book is about?"

Wayne grinned. "Ok, I'll bite. I'm guessing it is NOT a book about horticulture. If this were a bible study group, I would guess it might be a book of sermons, or maybe one long sermon. Jesus says something about 'by their fruits shall ye know them,' and I think that is usually interpreted to mean that a bad upbringing produces bad people but living by the Bible leads to good people. I'm sure I have heard sermons about bringing children up in the way and so on, but this isn't a bible study group. I'll guess it has something to do with actions—what a person does. A person is known by what he does or what he produces. Maybe it's a humanist sermon—like you would hear at a Unitarian church."

"You're not far off," said Katherine. "The book itself is actually a self-help book, but what I wanted us to consider first is the title. It is an English translation of a Zulu proverb. And just like the biblical saying, it can have a number of meanings depending on how it is used. I wouldn't doubt that Jesus heard a similar Aramaic proverb and used it in his teachings. And Wayne's interpretation is pretty close to what the author of the little book wanted to convey with the title—the idea that people are known by what they actually do rather than by what they say. Actions speak louder than words. The author discusses the notion that your identity is defined by what you choose to do. And you are right—it is an existentialist 'sermon' or a humanist essay. You tell people who you are by what you do, not by what you profess to believe."

"What is particularly interesting," Katherine went on, "was Wayne's comment about how a situation or context would influence what the title might mean. And even if you didn't know the context, the proverb itself might still be interpreted differently according to the age or gender or social status of the interpreter. Proverbs are really fun that way. There is one study that asks people what they think the following proverb means—A ROLLING STONE GATHERS NO MOSS. Think about it—what do you think it means? According to the study, most of us in this room would likely interpret the proverb to mean that if you just move around all the time and don't put down roots, you will not collect the good things in life, like money—the green stuff. Younger people, on the other hand, usually take the proverb to mean that if you keep moving forward, always trying new things and being active, you won't end up stuck in place with a bunch of moldy old moss growing on you—sort of the opposite of the other interpretation. Don't take it to heart if you thought like an older person. Usually proverbs depend on the context in which they are used for meaning, but it is interesting to realize that all sorts of factors influence the way we interpret texts."

"The texts we'll be interpreting—well, after this first one that Peter gave you today—the rest of the texts will be letters written by one person to George Frideric Handel some three hundred years ago." Katherine held up the TREE IS KNOWN BY ITS FRUIT book again. "And just as with our printed title here, we will mostly depend upon what is already in our heads to help us interpret what we read. Wayne happened to know something about biblical quotes and their various meanings, so when he read the book title, he was able to suggest a possible meaning that might emerge in a Christian sermon or humanist essay. He joked that it was unlikely to be about how to grow apples or peaches, but that's because he assumed the title was a metaphor rather than literal. If you have any experience with self-help books at all, you will know they often do that—MEN ARE FROM MARS, WOMEN ARE FROM VENUS. Nobody growing up in the US takes a title like that literally, but someone just learning English in a foreign country might. But, back to the point here. What kind of background information and interpretive perspective do each of you bring to this Seminar just by being who you are?"

Rebecca Trent signaled that she wanted to comment. Since they hadn't really set any rules yet for discussions, Katherine simply nodded and Rebecca began. "Well, as I was telling Ross earlier, I have identified myself as a professor of anthropology for most of my life, so I bring a comparative and, I suppose, academic perspective to my interpretation of texts. But since I have retired, I've found that my feminist and politically liberal tendencies have influenced what I do and what interests me. For example, if you had asked us to respond to the other self-help book you mentioned—the MEN ARE FROM MARS one—I would have certainly jumped on my feminist podium and complained about its essentialist implications. I'm also fascinated by letters, so I expect I will enjoy our discussions immensely."

"Thanks, Rebecca," Katherine said. "You mentioned having recently retired. I know some of you inquired initially about the fact that we were seeking people who were middle age or older for the Seminar. The truth is we tried very hard to avoid using any stereotypes in choosing who would join our Seminar, but we had decided early on that we wanted to do a kind of affirmative action ploy in favor of older people. Basically we wanted to give older rather than younger people a chance to have their say. Lots of media and research studies focus on younger people, so we thought this Seminar would represent a counterpoint to that. But, in Rebecca's case, as she made clear, another important factor in her interpretive tool kit is her feminism—not necessarily her gender, but her feminist perspective. What other personal attributes do you think influence how we interpret texts?"

Sharon Rayette LaRose (who had explained to Katherine that, like Benfey, she preferred to use her middle name) smiled and said, "Even though Bloomington is a university town, I accept as a given that I am usually a token African-American presence on a lot of committees and other community groups. Actually, I was surprised there wasn't anyone obviously Latino or Asian chosen for the Seminar, but maybe since the number is small, only one minority was enough. I admire Handel, but that wasn't part of our application material. I suppose people assume I bring an African-American perspective to most things, but I'm not sure what that would be, especially when I am interpreting a letter that has nothing to do with my cultural background."

A couple people in the group seem to be a bit discomfited by this remark, but Katherine nodded. "Thanks, Rayette, for stating your thoughts so directly. At one point, Ross, and Peter, and I talked about whether we should try to achieve some kind of equitable mix based on cultural differences. But then we realized that there were so many cultural identities that might or might not be a factor in any one individual's life—things besides race or ethnicity or age that might—or might NOT—influence how that individual interprets things. And besides, how would we know—unless it was something an applicant volunteered? Some things, like gender, religion, education, nationality, sexual orientation, height, weight, or disabilities—any of those things can have some bearing on who a person is, what he or she brings to the table. But we decided there was no way we could reasonably take all such factors into account. So, we stuck with the one factor we mentioned—age—and looked for people of whatever backgrounds who voiced a strong appreciation for music, seemed reasonably willing to entertain new or opposing ideas, and were eager to participate in an ongoing seminar. You all fit the bill. Your answers to our three questions helped us see that."

Across the room from Rayette, CD Jennings waved his hand and said, "I suppose you could say I also represent a minority—at least I think gay men are still a minority—but as you suggested, Katherine, I'm not sure that attribute influences how I interpret a text. No doubt it does partly determine what I consider important, what I'm aware of. For example, I'll admit that I was surprised to see Handel addressing this obviously loving letter to a woman. There are several websites that clearly assume that Handel was gay. I think there is a body of research that supports that view. At least there was one book that made quite a splash a couple years ago. Not that he couldn't be gay and still have women friends, but you know he never married, and that was unusual back then. In any case, you can probably expect that I will try to bring a 'queer eye' perspective to the text. Of course these letters are from a long time ago, but if there are things in the letters that suggest to me that Handel was gay, I'll be sure to mention it. I may even do a little homework now that I know our subject. And, by the way, I'm also an organ builder and do pipe organ restoration work. Handel is known for writing dozens of organ concertos. I'll be very interested in learning more about Handel's skills as an organist. So, yeah, I'd say our backgrounds and personalities do have an influence."

Katherine looked around to see if anyone else wanted to talk. "I have the advantage of knowing a little about each of you—at least what you shared with us when you applied to join the group. I imagine much of this information will come out as we go along. My own feeling is that the various groups you belong to or that you were a part of as you grew up do have some influence on what you know, what you have been exposed to, even if you have grown away from the culture those groups gave you—or maybe even rejected it outright. Everyone in this group attended college, for example, and education is one factor that often really changes a person's worldview or perspective. I often ask my students—when they first start studying folklore—to think about their own cultural groups that might determine the kind of folklore or worldview they have learned just by growing up as they did. Your family, your ethnic group, your religion, even your region of the country probably did give you some ideas or beliefs that you wouldn't have had if you had been born into a different situation. And then there are groups you joined as you grew older—your profession, social clubs, political parties, and so on. I always think of these groups as creating a kind of cultural thumbprint—a unique set of social or cultural groups that collectively contribute to a person's repertoire of active and passive folklore. But, of course, one attribute we tried to select for when choosing members of this Seminar was a clear tendency to question all collectively held ideas—even those ideas conveyed either subtly or purposefully by your own culture groups."

Katherine looked up just long enough to see some of the glazed expressions she often saw on undergraduate faces toward the end of a lecture. "Sorry. Nothing worse than lecture mode at a cheese and wine gathering. Here's a thought. We need to head to our 'assignment'—the BCS Messiah

Sing. But before we go, I asked one of our new Seminar members—Dr. Alison Jean Swift—if she would be willing to say a little about the piece we will be hearing or singing, and she agreed. Alison?"

Alison Swift stood and held up the Oxford press score of *Messiah*. "I'm assuming most of you have heard or sung all or parts of Handel's *Messiah*. The librettist was Charles Jennens, who also wrote the librettos for Handel's *Saul* and *Belshazzar*, possibly parts of *Israel in Egypt*. But *Messiah* is Handel's magnum opus. And Handel wrote *Messiah*—at least the first version—over a period of only twenty-four days in the late summer of 1741—an amazing feat! It was first performed, not in London where he composed it, but in Dublin in April 1742. It is an oratorio, and unlike Handel's many Italian operas, *Messiah* is in English. It is Handel's most famous work. It has never been out of print, and its 'Hallelujah Chorus' is a musical icon, often parodied or adapted to various ends. You will get to sing the 'Hallelujah Chorus' today even though it is not part of the Christmas section of the oratorio. Tradition has it that everyone stands when the 'Hallelujah Chorus' is sung. We get to sing along on the arias from Part I as well. It should be great fun. Personally, I plan to move over and sing with the tenors so I can sing 'Every Valley.' So, off we go. Maybe next year we can do a flash mob of the 'Hallelujah Chorus' at the mall. Hallelujah, Hallelujah!"

"Thanks, Alison. Everyone, be sure to keep that letter Peter gave you under wraps. Bring it with you next time, and we'll begin our discussion in earnest. Enjoy the Messiah Sing!"

CHAPTER 5

A Letter in French

Ross and Peter sat in the small private antechamber near the bank vault that housed the Handel letters. Laid out before them were the first four letters from the packet Forella Wainwright had purchased and entrusted to Peter's care. As Ross looked over these letters, all written in French, the date of the fourth letter drew his attention—as did the address: January 24, 1710—to: il signor Handel, palazzo Grimani, Venezia. Ross looked over quizzically at Peter, who nodded and said, "Yeah, he was still in Italy when this whole thing started."

As co-chairs of the Handel Seminar, Ross and Katherine met for coffee and discussed the practical questions yet to be answered about the Seminar meetings—where they would meet, when they would meet, how much time to allow for each session, how to structure the discussion, and perhaps most important, what to order for the luncheons that would be provided. As this last issue came up, Ross put in a call to Angela. When Angela handed her the phone, Forella chuckled at the elaborate catering ideas Ross had suggested. "Oh, my dear, you will put everyone to sleep with meals like that," she said. "Let me speak to Katherine." Forella asked Katherine to review the plans she and Ross had discussed. It was immediately clear to Forella that Ross had simply recycled his usual work session luncheon plan in which busy participants wolfed down sandwiches, various heavy side dishes or salads, and sweets, along with a glass of wine or pale ale, all the while looking over drafts of scripts or viewing videos. Forella asked Katherine if she had suggested any alternatives.

"Well, no," Katherine admitted. "I haven't had much experience planning luncheon seminars. Actually the seminars I have participated in have been very informal. Probably the most enjoyable have been meetings held at my house, and I usually served easy snacks and drinks rather than anything catered by an outside firm. I assumed Ross knew what was typical in a situation like this. Why are you laughing?" Ross took the cell phone back from Katherine. "All right, Mom, I can see right now that you are conjuring up that infamous scene from *Back to School* where Rodney Dangerfield gathers his pudgy staff together and they all outdo each other in scarfing down edibles. So what is YOUR suggestion? Devonshire tea? Cucumber sandwiches and gazpacho? Out with it."

Forella laughed and told Ross to switch the phone to speaker mode. "Here's an idea," she said. "I like Katherine's good memories of seminars held at her house. Meeting in someone's home is just a more friendly setting. People feel more relaxed. I enjoyed having everyone here at my house for the get-acquainted meeting we had just before going to the *Messiah* Sing. How about meeting at my house rather than at a more formal meeting room downtown? Annie could prepare the lunch. She knows how to make lighter dishes—and, yes, she could make some sandwiches for meat lovers like you, Ross. Now that I have met everyone, I kind of like the idea of having everyone here for our Seminar. Even on the days I don't feel like participating, there is no reason why the Seminar couldn't meet in the back of the house—in the great room. I hardly ever use it for anything else. And it would be convenient for me or Angela to join the group on days when we want to be there. What do you think?"

"Have you asked Annie about this, Mom? That's a dozen extra people to prepare food for—at least once a month. That may be more than she bargained for."

"Well, you are right, of course. I should ask Annie first before I involve her in fixing a dozen lunches instead of two or three. But in any case, we could still meet at my house—even if we had a caterer. If I know Annie, she will scoff at the idea of a caterer, but I'll ask her. What do you think, Katherine?"

"Oh, I think meeting at your townhouse would be wonderful. It is such a comfortable place. I would certainly feel less pressured, less like I was just doing another part of my job. I think it would make our meetings a distinctly different and enjoyable part of our lives—something to look forward to. I vote yes—and thanks for suggesting it, Forella."

Ross closed off the phone connection after a few more words with his mother. "So," he said to Katherine, "we have the where, when, who, what, and why—what about the how? I'm still wondering how we can best evoke the kind of discussion we want. If I remember right, we both wanted to be sure that the letters sparked commentary on themes we might read out of the letters—not simply fact-finding about Handel and his times. I'm used to working with a film production crew to settle on issues we want to highlight in any given production. Is there any way we can do something like that? With my group, I typically take the lead on selecting themes for each project, but I usually do consult with other crew members for their ideas. What's your thought? How have you usually managed academic seminars?"

Katherine thought back over the most successful seminars she had taught—and some that were less successful. It did seem that the most successful seminar sessions usually had at least a little structure provided by an overriding question. And the questions that sparked the most invigorating discussion were usually tied to a few recurrent themes—concerns that had been of importance to her most of her life. "I think," she said, "it would be good to create a list of the themes we should try to address through our discussion. Not as a way to dictate a focus or to avoid discussing any particular topics but rather to make sure the discussions do not get bogged down in trivia or simply historical facts. It's good to have accurate facts, of course, but our purpose should always be to expand our own understanding—to really allow Handel and his letter-writing friend to help us grow in our shared insights and contemplation of humanity. I know that sounds a bit overblown, but I really do want to engage in this Seminar as a kind of intellectual, thought-provoking exercise. I want to be inspired by these letters from the past."

"Inspired, hmmm? That's a tall order, don't you think?" Ross gave Katherine a look that betrayed a hint of amusement at her idealism but yet admiration all the same. He went on, "I'm not sure our colleagues are expecting to be inspired so much as perhaps enlightened, maybe simply entertained. If we look for each letter to be soul-stirring, we'll likely be disappointed. She wasn't writing poetry, you know. I'm as eager to learn something from the letters as anyone else, but we shouldn't expect every letter to be packed with insights. That's how scriptures are born—people expecting words written by ordinary humans to bear the burden of divine inspiration. I vote for a little levity. Otherwise, we'll exhaust ourselves looking for gems of wisdom."

Katherine experienced a brief flashback—to the days when she had been scolded by much more worldly teenaged dates for being "too serious." Still, she saw Ross's fleeting sparkle of admiration and decided to respond to that instead. "I'm guessing that inspiration often comes when it isn't expected. I hope to find the letters inspiring, that's all. And I don't really mean that they have anything to do with divine messages to humankind. I do truly experience Handel's music as inspiring, so why not letters written to him by a dear friend? I'll let you in on a secret, Ross. The reason I love my discipline of folklore study is really tied to this notion of inspiration. What I find so exciting about being a folklorist is the given that everything—every common, ordinary thing that humans create—truly is, or at least can be, a source of inspiration. How could it be otherwise? If you are prepared to be impressed at an exhibition of creativity in Handel's music or Rembrandt's paintings or Shakespeare's plays, why not assume that some unknown woman's letters might inspire you as well? Well, why not?"

Ross grinned. "Ok, I see your point. So, how do we help our perhaps less easily inspired friends to follow your lead? We could hand them a list of themes we hope to discuss, but that seems pretty pedantic. On the other hand, if we just depend on the store of interests people in this group bring to the table, we'll likely become repetitive in short order. Despite our efforts to include people of differing perspectives, we are still a fairly homogenous group. But maybe we can get around that. You shared a secret with me, so let me return the favor. Believe it or not, one of the most inspiring individuals I've ever met was in fact a United Methodist minister. His name is David Owen, and he had a way of turning any small incident into an important philosophical question. I'm sure he often felt that he was literally preaching to the choir, but he always found a way to unpack some ordinary event or even some well-known scripture and make it a personally meaningful question for each listener. That's what I'd like to see happen here."

It was Katherine's turn to flash an admiring smile. "Can you give me an example?" she said. "I wasn't even aware that you attended church. How did you meet this person?"

"Well, yes, you are right. I rarely attend church—or synagogue, or mosque, or any such organized assemblage. Actually, I went to hear this man preach because a friend loaned me a book of his sermons, and I thought they were really good. This was quite a few years ago. I think he has retired since then. But, an example? Let's see. One sermon I remember was titled 'The High Cost of Knuckling Under,' and it was ostensibly based on some scripture from Saint Paul about not conforming to this world. The thing that always impressed me about David Owen's sermons was that he didn't worry too much about trying to convey an accepted theology. The scriptures were basically a jumping off point for his more philosophically or psychologically pointed essay. In this sermon he ponders this little bit of scripture along with a book he had been reading about cancer patients and concludes that it is important for everyone to 'sing his own song'—that you will be healthy and truly alive if you do what you feel is best for you rather than knuckling under to what other people want you to do with your life. I guess in that respect, this sermon was inspiring in the way you are hoping the letters will be—not necessarily in a religious sense but rather in a more personal drift, a kind of welcome, useful advice."

"He sounds like someone it would be fun to have in our group. Is he still around? Why didn't you ask him to join us? There was never any stipulation that a seminar member had to have some obvious interest in music." Katherine seemed a little put out, so not surprisingly Ross jumped back in with his defense: "I haven't kept in contact with him. I agree it would be nice to have someone like him among us, but don't worry, we have a good group. Maybe someone will have that same talent. You never know. So, how do you propose we stimulate our bunch to ask the kind of questions David Owen asked?"

"Well, that's the challenge, isn't it?" Katherine said. "I didn't mean to be disparaging, really, Ross. I guess I would simply welcome someone who could help us discover the kind of questions we want for our Seminar. Do you have a sense—from reading or hearing David Owen's sermons—of how he came up with provocative questions?"

Ross sat in thought for a while. "You know, I actually hadn't thought about that before, but now that you ask, I think I do know at least one thing he always did. He was amazingly transparent. Probably not in everything he did, but generally, I would say you knew why he did what he did. And the reason you knew is that he was careful to state the principles, beliefs, or even simply the assumptions that were at play behind his thoughts, behind what he said in his sermons. I recall one sermon that was exactly that—a short list of the principles he considered essential to living a good life—or, in fact, to giving a good sermon. His secret, I think, was to always aim his questions toward one of these principles. Just like the 'High Cost of Knuckling Under' sermon. Basically it was a question about integrity, right? That would be one of his principles."

"So, in effect," Katherine said, "he typically tried to use a scripture, or book, or some incident from real life to illuminate one of these principles or themes—is that what you are saying? But he found a way to make the question seem fresh each time he asked it. You said people felt like he directed the question specifically at them—that he was asking them to think in personal terms rather than about a general principle. How did he do that?"

Instead of answering Katherine's question, Ross stood up, walked over, took Katherine's arm firmly in hand and pulled her up from her chair. Looking straight into her eyes, he said, "Katherine, have you ever wished that you had taken a path you didn't take? Have you ever wished that you had been a little more courageous and tried to do something you were afraid to try? Have you, like me, ever thought you might have been good at some skill or talent you let fall by the way?" When Katherine looked up wide-eyed and somewhat taken aback, Ross laughed and said, "That, in effect, is what he did every time—well, not physically. But emotionally, rhetorically, he got up close and personal and asked you to think about your life. It was never boring. Sometimes disturbing. He was the best kind of mentor—even for grown-ups. I think that is why he was so effective. He led you to a place where you had to really think about your life, about your assumptions and beliefs. And he made it clear that he thought about these things with regard to his own life as well. The themes weren't new, but there were no ready-made answers." Ross let Katherine sink gently back into her chair.

"Hmm, so, well . . ." Katherine fiddled with the notebook in front of her. "Well, I doubt we can be quite that direct with people in our seminar. But you do give me an idea," she said, regaining some of her *sangfroid*. "How about if we ask each person in the Seminar to be responsible for framing a question that incorporates one specific theme and then posing that question for discussion? In other words, each person should think of a question that hones in on a given theme or principle in a personal way—just as your preacher friend did. A question that makes the letter pertinent to someone reading it today, not simply to Handel and his long-ago correspondent. That's what Forella wanted to do with these letters, after all—to make them relevant to people today—to ordinary people, not simply Handel scholars. So, what do you think, can you train our Seminarians to compose that kind of probing question?"

"Me?!" Ross exclaimed. "You're the educator here. But I like the idea of each person in the Seminar being responsible for making sure a particular theme or principle is expressed. I doubt that they would voice that theme in a question. More likely it would be in their response to a question. The real challenge would be for each person to seriously entertain a theme that isn't his or her typical interest or concern. For example, I would guess Katherine the Folklorist would feel right at home answering a question about creativity—but maybe less comfortable if you were asked to respond to a question having to do with money or, say, social class, or something like that. Am I right?"

"Hey, what do you mean? I think about money all the time," Katherine replied, with a laugh. "Yeah, I suppose we could start off letting people raise questions that come naturally to them and then compile our list of themes from there. What do you think?"

Ross frowned. "It's interesting to me how easily professors forget what they do best. Most people don't sit around thinking up good questions. That's what they pay college professors to do—and maybe good documentary filmmakers—like Ken Burns—or me. I think our folks will be eager to discuss the questions that grow out of these letters, but I'm not sure they have been trained to ask provocative questions. That may have to be our task—to create good questions that incorporate the various themes we consider important."

"Ok, so what are these mythical themes we keep talking about? You mentioned money and creativity. What else? I'd feel better about making this list if I had seen a couple of the letters first. You and Peter looked at the first few already didn't you? I'm jealous—and really eager to see the letters. And we haven't even discussed Handel's dictated note yet. Time's a-wasting." Katherine laughed and picked up her notebook.

"Well it so happens," said Ross, "that Peter agreed to meet me later today to look at the fifth letter, so I propose you come along and take a look as well. He made a real effort to rush through the process on the

The Handel Letters

first few letters. His procedure really is very time-consuming. But I agree. We need to see the letters and begin our discussions. So, shall we visit the vault?"

Ross and Katherine drove to the bank where Peter kept the original letters. Much of this early activity on Peter's part was devoted to fumigating the documents, making photocopies, and housing each letter in a drawer for safekeeping. When Ross and Katherine arrived, Peter was processing the fifth letter, as Ross had expected, and he was compiling his copies of the first four letters into reading files he could work with at home. After some fairly stringent ID checks and storage of handbags, notebooks, cases, etc., Katherine and Ross were allowed into the room where Peter had the fifth letter lightly weighted in its unfolded state. Katherine was immediately drawn to its salutation: My dear Mr. Handel. It was a very exciting moment. Putting on one of the white gloves Peter provided for handling the letters, Katherine touched the yellowed paper.

She couldn't help but speak in a whisper—though clearly there was no need. Ross and Peter both smiled at her obvious delight in seeing the actual letter. "What a treasure!" she said. "I can't wait to begin our discussions. But really, Peter, the script is awfully small and cramped. Is that typical for this time period? I was expecting a kind of large, flowery writing. Wasn't penmanship something that women—aristocratic women—were taught at that time?"

"Ah, yes, you are correct. Girls from wealthy families were taught penmanship from an early age. However, even aristocratic ladies were encouraged to confine letters to a single page. Two interesting traditions developed as a result. One was simply a smaller script, which obviously allowed more words on a single page. Remember these had to be hand delivered to the address, often weeks after being sent—especially with letters such as this one which had to find its way from London to cities far afield, we assume. Just be glad we don't have to deal with another, mostly cost saving, practice—one the wealthy usually avoided—but fairly common nonetheless. The dreaded cross-written letter. Actually they aren't that bad once you get used to reading them. Basically, the writer covers a full page and then turns the letter a quarter turn to the right and writes OVER the previous writing. Because the writing is cursive and connected, you can actually follow it pretty well. Anyway, our writer didn't do that, thank goodness. And she must have had a skilled quill pen carver in the household. Her letters so far seem uniformly clear and finely penned—if a bit cramped, as you say."

Peter showed Katherine and Ross the draft of the fifth letter—the one he was working on and entering on his laptop. "How many of the letters have you actually looked through at this point?" Katherine asked. "Do you have a sense of the general contents? Couldn't we just read them all and then go back and discuss them with that more complete background to help us get the big picture?"

Holding up his hand with a laugh, Peter, said, "Whoa—Fortunately for me, Forella specified that she wanted the letters to emerge in a more natural time scheme—slowly, in other words. I don't have time right now to process them more quickly. But, to be honest, I like the fact that we have to let the story emerge piece by piece. It's more like our own little soap opera this way, don't you think?" Peter laughed at his own analogy, but Katherine continued to look a bit grim. "Patience, Katherine," Peter said. "I'm not just rationalizing the slow process. I really do think it will be a good way to unpack these letters. I think we will pay much closer attention to details this way, AND we won't skip over points of discussion that might be ignored if we already knew what was in the next letter. It may be slow, but it will be worth it. What do you think, Ross?"

"You are our amanuensis, our scribe. Who am I to argue? Slow and steady wins the race, so says the turtle. I think Peter is right, Katherine. Let's just discover the letters as Handel did—one at a time. Though I admit I'd like to look ahead, too. But would that be fair to the other Seminar members? Besides, I always do what my mother says."

Katherine smirked, "I'll bet you do." Ross put his right hand over his heart and raised his left, "I swear, it's true." Peter started to close down his laptop. "Wait!" Katherine insisted. "Can't I at least see the first four letters you have already processed?"

"Certainly," Peter said, and he took a file from the gray cabinet in the adjacent vault. "Here is the fourth letter. It has been subjected to all my various treatments and will stay safely locked up in the vault from here on out. I dare say this one will make you appreciate my hard work, Professor Baker. Take a look."

"But this letter is in French!" said Katherine. "Wasn't Lydia Grayston British? This other one you've just shown us is in English. And look!—the address isn't French. Venezia? Ok, you two look like the cats that swallowed the canary. What's the story?"

"Damn it, man! You spoiled the surprise," said Ross. "So, yeah, she is writing to Handel in French, and Handel is in Italy—at least when he receives the first few letters. Of course Peter wants you to be impressed with his labors in not only transcribing the letters but translating them, too, at least these first ones. The fifth one—the one we looked at earlier— is the first to be written mostly in English. Just be glad it isn't German. We would have had to bring in an outsider for that. We were worried when we saw the first three letters—you, know, that they would all be in French. According to Peter, most of the few surviving letters written by Handel himself were written in French—the language of eighteenth-century diplomacy, or the upper classes. So it's no surprise that Lydia's first letters were in French, but by this letter, she had switched to English. And Peter was able to translate the ones in French. Go ahead, make Peter's day. Tell him he's the best thing since sliced bread."

"An A+ for you, Doctor Rowe—but only if you let me have copies of the first four letters. Why didn't you tell me you had already worked up these four?"

Peter looked a little sheepish. "To be honest, I wanted Ross to check over my translations before I showed them to you. I haven't had to use my grad school French much lately. I was mightily relieved that our Lydia started writing in English. Fortunately, Handel was eager to learn English, so she suggested the switch. See, there in this letter. She volunteers to be his English tutor. Anyway, I took time to get the process started here at the beginning. From now on, I should be able to just stay ahead of the seminar meetings by a letter or two. No more reading ahead. Am I forgiven?"

Katherine smiled. "Yes, IF you give me copies of the first four letters. I'm going to have a hard time hiding this from the other Seminar members, you know. They would be really annoyed if they knew we had several letters already transcribed—well, four, since you are still working on this one."

"Ah, there should be some advantage in being the organizers of this clambake," said Ross. "We'll just have to feign ignorance. Shouldn't be too hard." Katherine and Peter both threw their white gloves in Ross's face.

Out in the parking lot, Katherine looked through the copies of the first four letters. "You know, we really ought to at least contextualize the date of this first letter for our Seminar," she said. "All they have right now is the date on that touching farewell note Handel sent just before he died. If I worked something up before our first meeting, could Angela send it out to everyone? Nothing too detailed. Just a kind of timeline for Handel's life up to when the letters start. What do you think?"

"I think that is a marvelous idea, Katherine," said Ross. "I knew there was some reason besides your charm and good looks for making you co-chair of this shindig." Katherine thumbed her nose at him and went to her car.

Back in her home office, Katherine consulted some of the books she had been collecting since learning they would discuss the Handel letters. Primary among these resources was the new *Cambridge Handel Encyclopedia*, edited by Annette Landgraf and David Vickers. Like the biographies written by such Handel experts as Donald Burrows, Christopher Hogwood, Jonathan Keates, Paul Lang, and Winton Dean, the *Encyclopedia* offered a chronology of important events in Handel's life. From these various sources, Katherine composed a timeline of the most important events in Handel's life between the year of his birth and 1710, the year Handel first visited London. Handel's more recent biographers had all relied to some extent on the celebrated biography produced by

John Mainwaring in 1760, a year after Handel's death. Abundant research since then had produced surprisingly few solid facts about Handel's private life, or even about his public activities and performances. Katherine sent the Seminar members an informative letter with the biographical facts she thought most important as background before their first discussion. She included an update on where and when the first meeting would be as well as a reminder to bring the copy of the dictated letter Peter had handed out earlier.

As she worked up the timeline for Handel's first twenty-five years, Katherine reflected on the fact that Handel is rarely listed among the world's child prodigies—though by all accounts he should be. Unlike the very young Mozart or Chopin, Handel was not encouraged in his musical talent. On the contrary, the story is that his father strongly discouraged his musical interest and would not allow musical instruments in the house. Apocryphal sources claim that young Georg Friedrich secreted a small clavichord in the attic of the Handel household and practiced at stolen hours when his father was not home. Still, it must be the case that his mother or perhaps someone at the Lutheran gymnasium gave him some instruction when he was very young. At age seven he accompanied his father to the Saxon court at Weissenfels, where Duke Johann Adolf heard him playing the organ. The Duke recognized the boy's natural talent, advised the elder Handel to find a good teacher for his son, and gave him some money toward his tuition. Upon returning home, Handel began his studies with Friedrich Wilhelm Zachow, the organist of the market-place church in Halle. A child who could impress a Duke with his organ playing at age seven seemed a child prodigy in Katherine's book.

Like the hidden clavichord story, incidents that make up the sketchy narrative of Handel's early life are either guesswork or events retold from Mainwaring's biography. Though Mainwaring's book, *Memoirs of the Life of the Late George Frideric Handel*, is justly famous as the first full-length publication to treat the life and works of one musician, Katherine discovered countless more recent sources that challenge the accuracy of much of the information and many of the dates in the book. And yet, as a folklorist, Katherine was attracted to the anecdotal nature of the work. Handel's copyist, John Christopher Smith, Jr., evidently recollected most of these stories. Over the course of the last decade of Handel's life, a circle of friends and supporters brought together much of the information that would be published in Mainwaring's book. Smith's anecdotes, all gleaned from talking with Handel, comprised the biographical narrative and reminded Katherine of the genre of life stories often studied by scholars in her field. And as is often the case when a folklore genre is contrasted with oral history, the stories make up for inaccuracies in detail through their insights into character and values associated with the subject. The little we know of Handel's personality, sentiment, and humor owes much to Mainwaring's determination to record personal narratives and character anecdotes long before any folklorist thought of collecting such seeming ephemera.

Katherine decided to offer the Seminar a fairly bare bones timeline. She asked Forella if it would be all right to leave some of the books they might use as resources in the room where the Seminar would be meeting. Both Forella and Angela were enthusiastic in response. But Katherine's immediate aim was to provide some of the background that would speak to why Handel came to London late in 1710, at age twenty-five, already a star composer and performer.

Here is the timeline she developed:

1685 –February 23, 1685—Handel was born in Halle, in Saxony (Central Germany), just north of Leipzig. He was christened Georg Friederich Händel the next day at the local Lutheran church. His father, Georg Händel, a surgeon, was sixty-three years old when Handel was born. Handel's mother, Dorothea née Taust, was his father's second wife. She was in her early thirties when Handel was born. A son born two years before Handel died as an infant. Handel had two younger sisters.

1692 –age 7—Handel asked to accompany his father to Weissenfels. Handel's half-brother, Carl, lived there and worked at court. Handel's father had actively discouraged young Georg Friederich's musical interests, yet somehow Handel was accomplished enough at playing the organ to impress the Duke, who strongly advised that he be allowed to study music. Returning to Halle, Handel studied organ, harpsichord, violin, and music fundamentals with Friedrich Zachow. His first compositions were created then as part of his training. None of these survive. Zachow had an excellent library of music, some left by the previous Kapellmeister, Johann Philipp Krieger and many collected by Zachow himself as part of his teaching resources.

1697 –age 12—Handel's father died shortly before Handel's twelfth birthday. Handel wrote a poem honoring his father and signed it "George Friedrich Händel, dedicated to the liberal arts." He continued his studies with Zachow, taking on the role of apprentice organist and replacing his teacher frequently at Sunday services. At age 14 he composed a trio sonata, his earliest datable composition.

1701 –age 16—Handel met Georg Philipp Telemann and began a friendship that lasted his entire life. Telemann was four years older than Handel, studying law in Leipzig, but his primary interest was in opera, a complex musical, dramatic form he gladly introduced to Handel. In 1702 Handel enrolled at Halle University as a student of civil law, but he did not pursue a degree.

1702 –age 17—Handel was hired as organist and musical director at the main cathedral in Halle. This was a responsible paid position with housing, granted with the expectation that he would continue in the post for several years. It is unclear whether he continued with his studies at the University while carrying out his duties at the Domkirche. He evidently did not find the job to his liking. At the end of his year's contract, he resigned and traveled to Hamburg.

1703 –age 18—Handel signed on as second violinist with the opera orchestra in Hamburg, but soon he was recognized as an outstanding harpsichordist and emerging composer. While in Hamburg, he met Johann Mattheson, who was four years older than Handel and already established as a singer and composer. The two young men were friends but also professional rivals. At one point they fought a duel over who should play harpsichord and direct the orchestra at an opera composed by Mattheson. Handel was uninjured, as Mattheson's sword shattered on Handel's coat button. Though Handel benefited from Mattheson's opera connections, they did not remain fast friends.

1704 –age 19—Handel composed his first opera, *Almira*, with libretto in German and Italian. Later that year he composed a second opera, *Nero*. Both were produced in Hamburg the next year. Handel composed two more operas, *Florindo* and *Daphne* while in Hamburg. All of Handel's German operas had tenor male leads, as castrati were not popular in Germany. In 1705 he met John Wyche, a British counsel living in Hamburg, and served as music tutor to his son.

1706 –age 21—Handel left Hamburg and traveled to Italy, "on his own bottom" as Mainwaring says. Handel had saved enough money to travel to Italy and to send some money back home to his mother in Halle.

1707 –age 22—Handel had been encouraged to visit Italy by Gastone de' Medici (prince of Tuscany) as well as by friends he had met in Berlin. He went first to Florence and then on to Rome. While in Italy, he stayed with various patrons but never took on the role of house musician. In Rome, he composed Latin church music, Italian cantatas, and an early oratorio, *Il trionfo del Tempo e del Disinganno*. Later, in Florence, he composed his first Italian opera, *Rodrigo*.

1708 –age 23—Handel returned to Rome and composed the oratorio *La Resurrezione* which was performed during the Lenten season with an orchestra led by Arcangelo Corelli. Again, he composed many secular cantatas and Latin church pieces, including the outstanding *Dixit Dominus* and *Salve Regina*. It was also rumored that during this period he enjoyed the company of a lover, Vittoria Tarquini, a married singer a few years his senior.

1709 –age 24—Handel traveled to Venice, where he composed the opera *Agrippina*. The opera was immensely successful. Visitors from Hanover and London encouraged Handel to leave Italy and compose and perform in their homelands.

1710 –age 25—Handel left Italy and accepted an appointment as Kapellmeister to the Elector of Hanover. The opera house was closed in

Hanover, so Handel drew upon a clause in his contract that allowed him to be absent from his post. He traveled to London, where news of his opera *Agrippina* preceded him and made him a known figure when he first reached the city.

1711 –age 26—Within a year of arriving in London, Handel performed before Queen Anne at St. James's Palace, and his first London opera, *Rinaldo*, was performed at the Queen's Theatre, in the Haymarket.

Katherine was eager to hear how the Handel Seminar would respond to her overview.

CHAPTER 6
On a Clear Day

A half hour before the first working meeting of the Handel Seminar, Benfey arrived at Forella's townhouse and set up her recording equipment on the large table around which the Seminar would gather. Her first task would be to record a short sample of talk from each member of the seminar. She had already practiced, using Forella and Angela as the first two individual speakers to be sampled and collected into her voice dictionary. Benfey would take careful notes, of course, but the whole point of this state-of-the-art equipment was that each speaker would be identified upon speaking. The device's capacity to recognize each speaker's voice and to transcribe and attribute comments from each person would certainly make Benfey's job much easier than it would be otherwise. But she also knew that her ethnographic observations would be valuable well beyond the bare-bones transcriptions the recording would provide. Benfey set the equipment up to be as unobtrusive as possible. After Forella and Angela, Ross was the next to have his sample utterance saved to the recorder's memory, and then each of the Seminar members as they arrived. The process was new enough that everyone was intrigued. Benfey felt a bit like an Alexander Graham Bell showing off the telephone. Who would have guessed?

THE HANDEL SEMINAR GATHERED FOR its first meeting at Forella's townhouse. Annie, who wore the cook's hat along with her other duties, was happy to accommodate the extra lunch guests. She set up a buffet at the side of the dining room. Forella decided to use her large dining table as the seminar venue rather than the softer armchairs and sofas in the great room. With a laugh, she confessed to Ross that it was his snide reference to the "consuming food while having a meeting" scene in the film *Back to School* that made her think of moving to the dining room. Clearly, Rodney Dangerfield's director knew that food makes for a friendlier meeting, no matter what the subject matter. And sitting at a table created just the kind of serious interaction that Ross and Katherine hoped to encourage—an ideal seminar atmosphere.

As the Seminar members took their seats around the table, luncheon plates in hand and coffees, teas, Perriers, or other drinks before them, they greeted each other and looked expectantly toward Ross, who was cheerfully devouring a roast beef sandwich. Katherine stood up and clinked her spoon against her water glass. "We haven't established any rules for managing our Seminar, but Forella asked me to get things started as she expected Ross would be too distracted by the food to pilot this first meeting. Seems she knows him pretty well." Ross waved nonchalantly and said, "Carry on, *mon capitaine*."

Katherine suggested that it might be good to just follow Ross's lead and spend the first twenty minutes or so eating and chatting. But when talk seemed to dwindle after about fifteen minutes, Katherine asked everyone to take out the timeline she had sent and think over what they might want to say about this bit of background on their subject, the young Mr. Handel. She reminded them that they now had a set of bookends enclosing the letters they would be discussing. Peter had given them a copy of the letter Handel had dictated to Lydia Grayston shortly before he died at age seventy-four, and now Katherine had supplied a quick survey of Handel's life up to age twenty-five, just about the time he started receiving the letters in the packet Handel had sent back to Lydia with his words of farewell so long ago.

Before they moved on to this round-robin discussion, however, Brad said he had a question. "When we were contacted about this Seminar," he said, "we weren't given much information about why the letters are even here. I know we were told that we couldn't say anything about the letters to people outside the group—and we all agreed to that—but couldn't we at least know among ourselves why we have these letters to talk about? Not to be nosey, Mrs. Wainwright, but why did you end up with these letters when there are all sorts of people out there who would be happy to buy them? I'm just curious—since you don't seem to want to sell the letters—there must be some other reason. Personally, I can't see not wanting to turn the letters into some sort of profit—maybe even to support new research on Handel or something like that. But that doesn't seem to be your shtick. So, I thought I'd ask," he concluded, looking a bit apologetic, as he felt his question might be impertinent. Still he wanted to know.

Ross started to deflect the question, but Forella said, "It's all right, dear. I expected this question to come up. In fact, I would be disappointed if there weren't some question about why we are so lucky as to have these letters." She took a sip of tea and went on, "The interesting thing is that had I been interested in either buying the Handel letters as an investment or purchasing them for an institution, such as Peter's Museum up in Indianapolis, our seller has made it clear that we would not have been able to buy them. In fact, the seller would have destroyed the letters rather than make them publicly available—or so she told us. In any case, she was not looking for a purchaser. The usual order of events was reversed here. The seller had not advertised the letters for sale. She had not even had them assessed by an auction house. Instead she saw my query in a London paper and decided that I had asked the right question about the packet of letters she had kept hidden away for nearly thirty years."

"Naturally, you would like to know what that question was," Forella said. "But if you will indulge me, I'd like to share a little story first. Because, to be honest, it sometimes seems like serendipity that we ended up having these letters here in Bloomington, Indiana." Katherine saw Ross frown and lean back in his chair. She guessed that he had heard the story Forella was going to tell many times before. "When I was a young girl," Forella began, "my grandfather's sister, my Great Aunt Dorothy, died unexpectedly, and everyone gathered at what used to be the family farm to lament her passing and reminisce after the funeral. One of the cousins that I had never met started telling everyone that he expected to hear that some baby soon to be born in the family would likely carry on with Aunt Dorothy's soul and would know things only she would have known. I was just a child, so I didn't really understand what this was all about, but I do remember people looking uncomfortable and changing the subject. I assumed it was not an idea everyone shared."

"I was always pretty direct as a young person, and I'm happy to say that my parents were the kind to encourage me to ask questions rather than just assume that grown-ups always knew what was best. So, when I asked what it meant that some baby would know what only Aunt Dorothy knew, they explained that this cousin and his family were Theosophists and that many of them believed that souls of people come back as reincarnated souls and sometimes recall previous lives. I remember thinking it was a really exciting idea to me then. I wondered if I could be somebody who lived before. My mother said she didn't think so, but I was interested, and when I was a little older, I wrote to that cousin and asked more about it. He wrote back and sent various bits of information that he thought proved that, indeed, my Great Aunt Dorothy had come back as his little niece, born just a little over a year after Aunt Dorothy died. Most pieces of evidence were phrases or bits of knowledge or even visions of events that had been part of Aunt Dorothy's life. Clearly, he and his family thought that the number of correspondences between things this young child said and things associated with Aunt Dorothy were impressive enough to prove reincarnation."

"I'm sure you are wondering what this has to do with the Handel letters. I haven't forgotten your question, Mr. Hochensmith. What I wanted you to know before I answered your question—what I wanted you to feel, if you can, is how compelling I found that whole question of reincarnation. As I grew into adulthood, I became skeptical both of the concept and of the supposed evidence my cousin had shown me, but I was always attracted by the idea of souls being recycled. Wouldn't it be fun to know that your grandmother might actually come back as a child and you could get to know her all over again? Of course, the idea was disturbing, too. As an adult, I have been less attracted to the concept, but I have always been curious about it. And when Ross was born and later started talking, I just made a habit of recording things he said, or things he did that I thought might be worth checking on—especially expressions or actions that seemed to come out of nowhere."

Ross got up, went over to the wet bar, and poured himself a glass of Scotch. "The rest of this story is best taken with a grain of alcohol," he said. Forella just smiled and went on. "This cousin—actually he is a second cousin—stayed in touch with me over the years. He asked about my journal with its sayings and actions I had recorded when Ross was still a very young boy. After I shared the information with him, he did some research in an attempt to find significant correspondences. Evidently this is what he and other believers in his group often did—gather evidence to prove that someone was a particular 'previous personality.' After some study, my cousin was convinced that Ross was actually George Frideric Handel, or as he expressed it, that Handel was a 'previous personality' now reincarnated in a living person, my son. I thought Ross might be thrilled to be the possible reincarnation of George Frideric Handel, but he wasn't and isn't—thrilled, that is."

Everyone looked over at Ross, who bowed and lifted his glass. "I admit," Forella said, "that the bits of evidence were pretty skimpy—the fact that Ross plays piano with no training, a few words he said as a boy that are named figures in Handel's life. I let the idea drop by the way for many years—until I had reason more recently to wonder about reincarnation again. So, just to be completely thorough about it before I dismissed the idea entirely, I thought I would see if there was anything else about Handel's personal life out there—any resources that might shed light on whether Handel could possibly be reincarnated here in the person of my son—as my cousin had argued. My cousin and his friends had been very thorough in checking all the published sources on Handel, but they said that the best correspondences were usually found in private sources—diaries, family histories, things like that. So, I sent out an inquiry to London—where Handel spent most of his life—and asked for any sources that might be used in proving that Handel was a previous personality for a living person. And our seller saw the ad and asked her agent to contact Angela—precisely BECAUSE I had raised the possibility of Handel being a previous personality of someone living today."

As Ross had expected, everyone just looked a bit mystified, perhaps wondering if this whole performance were a joke. But Forella continued, "My cousin passed away some years ago, but I have always been curious about what it would mean if one could actually amass an abundance of convincing evidence supporting the notion that personalities are recycled. I thought it would be interesting to put my cousin's theory to the test. And if nothing came of it, well, maybe I could at least find out more about Handel in the process. I do still have an overriding interest in what defines a personality or a soul, especially a soul from the past. That will likely be a question I will come back to over and over again as we discuss the Handel letters—what can we learn through our Seminar about Handel's soul, about the concept of the soul? Is a soul or spirit the same thing as a personality? Does it remain somewhere in the cosmos after you die? It doesn't have to lead to a belief in reincarnation, but I thought it would be best to at least entertain the possibility that a person's soul—even a great soul like Handel—just might be something that doesn't die, but returns to live again. So the question that garnered these letters was really just that—did anyone have any previously unpublished information about Handel that might be useful in identifying him as some living individual's previous personality."

Brad looked at Ross, hoping to read some sign of just how this story was supposed to be taken. Ross returned a fairly good poker face, so Brad voiced his own reaction instead. "You mean reincarnation, like they believe in India or Tibet? Like the notion that the Dalai Lama is really some ancestor who lived a long time ago? I'll admit that I have pretty superficial images of reincarnation, mostly tied to the old Barbra Streisand movie *On a Clear Day You Can See Forever*. I mean, it was a cool movie, but, you know, it was a fiction—like teleportation in Star-Trek. In the movie there was this professor who looked up the 'facts' that came out when the Streisand character talked under hypnosis, but that was just part of the script. No one has ever really proved reincarnation. It was just a feel-good movie. Why would anyone in real life even think such a thing?"

Forella started to speak, but Ross walked back from the wet bar and said, "It's ok, Mom. You told the story—and very well, I'd say. I think I can give Brad some of the explanation he wants and then move things along to our discussion. Two things about the reincarnated Handel story: First, there are bound to be ideas expressed by people in this Seminar that other people consider far-fetched, illogical, or simply wrong. But actually, if you recall—those of you who have seen the movie Brad mentioned—when the president of the medical school involved—I think he is played by Bob Newhart—objects to the Yves Montand character studying reincarnation, he admits that he can't prohibit its study because, despite not liking the idea of reincarnation, his own belief that it is all just rubbish might, after all, be wrong. In other words, we should always try to keep an open mind about any idea someone expresses. And we should always be aware that the ideas we ourselves accept so easily may seem unbelievable to others. After all, is the idea of a reincarnated soul more fantastic than the idea of a soul that survives death and goes to heaven or hell? Can we in fairness dismiss the notion that the soul of a holy man from long ago returns in the form of a young boy who becomes the Dalai Lama and yet accept as true a story from two thousand years ago that a man dead for three days was resurrected, walked the earth, and ascended into heaven to sit at the right hand of God the Father?"

No one took up Ross's challenge. After a few moments' silence, he continued. "So this notion of reincarnation and what makes a person's identity," Ross went on, "will likely be a leitmotif you will hear from my mother whenever it seems relevant to her. I'm hoping each of you have some burning question or theme that we start to associate with you, too.

In fact, I'm counting on it. But to get back to Handel and reincarnation—the second thing I wanted to say. You may wonder how I feel being the subject of this story. Do I think I am Handel or that Handel has come back as Ross Wainwright? No, my mother is quite right on that. I don't believe it. But, do I believe in reincarnation? Well, I think it is an interesting question. Still—no, I don't. I'm suspicious of anything supernatural."

"On the other hand, I think it makes sense that my mother is drawn to the question. When I have talked with older relatives in my family, they have always said, 'Forella is overly sensitive. I've never known anyone as empathetic as Forella. She cries if you stub your toe. She would have made a terrible nurse. She has no sense of where someone else's feelings stop and hers begin—that woman. No wonder she weeps at sentimental stories and can't stand to watch horror movies.' That's what her relatives say. And they are right. Forella Wainwright is someone who allows herself to identify with other individuals on a regular basis. She truly does enter into other people's souls or hearts and feel what they feel. Empathy isn't the same thing as reincarnation, of course, but it is similar in some ways. It makes questions about reincarnation seem relevant to other experiences we accept as ordinary. Do you see what I mean? For some people the idea of reincarnation may not seem all that far removed from everyday experience. We need to grant each other those differences in what is perceived as ordinary, logical, or believable. We need to trust our fellow humans to be thinking rationally and acting with all best intensions, just as we are."

Clara signaled that she had something to say. Ross looked over at Katherine. It was clear he hoped to move on to the more focused discussion that was the raison d'être of the Seminar. But Katherine nodded toward Clara and sat back waiting to hear what she wanted to say. Clara grimaced slightly as she started her comment. "It's probably best that I admit this right here at the start. I am convinced that most of my fellow humans are NOT thinking rationally about a lot of things, and I see ample evidence that they do not act with what I would consider admirable intensions. Simply trusting that they are thinking logically or acting with good intensions will not make either of these so. I DO trust my own perceptions of logic—or of the lack of logic in other people's arguments, and I do trust my own perceptions of someone else's intensions—good or bad. I understand, Ross, that you were suggesting we keep an open mind and grant others the benefit of the doubt. But I can't just pretend someone is being logical if it seems to me they are being illogical. I can't imagine that you are asking us to overlook irrational arguments or misinformation and simply say 'to each his own.'"

As Ross started to respond, Katherine made one of those unmistakable hand gestures that signals time-out in sporting events—fingertips to a horizontal palm. Ross chuckled, "You think we need a time out, Katherine?"

"I suppose so," said Katherine. "Or, actually what I would prefer is to rewind (sorry, old-fashioned term—think 'scroll back') and start over. I'm afraid I muffed my task in getting our meeting started. We haven't agreed on a set of rules for discussion. That should have been the first order of business. So, let me back up and explain how this Seminar will likely differ from a typical forum. One of the things Forella wanted us to do was to incorporate the notion of 'deep listening' from practices used in the Chalice Circles she attends. Ross, Peter, Forella, and I talked about this at some length early on in the process of setting up this Seminar, but we didn't have a very clear plan for sharing our thoughts with you. So, better late than never, I hope."

"Unlike most academic or business seminars," Katherine continued, "the purpose of this Seminar really is simply to encourage everyone to think about our topic—or in this case, our texts—and to express his or her ideas freely. The objective in this kind of seminar is not to reach some conclusion or consensus but rather to spark as many thoughts as possible. If I recall from our earlier discussion, three 'rules' that seemed to emerge were: first, there should be no hierarchy—everyone is equal; second, each person should feel free to say what she or he wants to say without interruption; and, third, as in the Chalice Circles, people should refrain from commenting on someone else's thoughts, opinions, or ideas. I think it is this last that is the problem, and we may want to talk about it. But maybe it would be good to ask Forella to say something about this concept and why she felt it would be good for our Seminar."

"Oh, my," Forella sighed, "I suppose, in all honesty, what it amounts to is an agreement to not judge each other. Most adults have learned to make judgments. And of course in most parts of our lives, we must make judgments—hopefully wise ones at that. You might think of this Seminar as offering you an opportunity to abandon that habit—maybe to see what it's like to simply hear an idea without judging its merit. And, really, it is just a rule that would apply to this Seminar. It's not an attempt to change your way of interacting in the larger world. It's not even an assertion that this is somehow a morally superior way of behaving. It's just sort of an experiment. What would happen if we listen to each other but refrain from offering a critique, a comment? What would happen if we simply hear each other out—and know that we, too, can say what we are thinking without worrying about others judging us as foolish or ill informed or even simply naïve? "

Peter held up his copy of the Handel timeline. "I can tell that Ross is itching to get on with our discussion of the letters—and so am I. But I can relate to Clara's hesitation. Isn't it sort of hypocritical to simply let an illogical or incorrect statement go by without comment? Especially for an educator—isn't that like falling down on the job? I'm playing devil's advocate here, but I think it's only fair to explain why it would be good to reign in our well-oiled skills in evaluating other people's ideas. What's your thought, Professor Baker?"

Katherine sat seemingly lost in thought for several long seconds. Finally, she reached into her briefcase and took out a folder. "All of us in this Seminar have been pre-selected for liking discussions. I've been interested in the ins and outs of the discussion process for years. When Forella mentioned the UU Chalice Circles as a kind of model for our Seminar, I thought I should find out a little more about this kind of discussion. I talked with some people I knew personally who had participated in one or more Chalice Circles, and I asked them how they liked the 'rule' about not responding, not commenting on what someone else said. Obviously this wasn't a scientific study on my part or anything like that, but in general people said that they found it hard to not comment but they did see why it was important for accomplishing the objective of this kind of group—that is, to make sure everyone had an opportunity to say what he or she wanted to say without fear of judgment, as Forella said. But a few people also said that they didn't really feel a need for that kind of discussion. Basically they found discussion without commentary or response kind of pointless. They didn't feel like they were learning anything—well, other than what other people thought or had experienced in their lives."

"This notion of learning something," Katherine went on, "is the key issue, I think, and probably the reason that we cannot simply adopt the Chalice Circle as a model for our Seminar. I would guess that people in a Chalice Circle learn to be more empathetic, and that of course is a good thing. But by the rules of the game, they sacrifice learning to think critically about the topics under discussion—unless they each do that independently, in their own heads. In other words, they do not learn to think critically as part of a group. They do not really learn what it means to consider ideas collectively and bring judgment—not to the people in the group, but rather to ideas expressed in the group. That isn't their group's purpose. I think that was what I heard Clara questioning with regard to our Seminar. How can we in this Seminar learn together if we do not truthfully express our responses to ideas we hear voiced by others? How do we engage our intellect if we do not reason together? On the other hand, how can we emulate the way Chalice Circles offer a context in which people can speak without fear of being challenged or corrected or in any way made to feel stupid, bad, wrong? If you don't mind taking the time, I'd like to propose a set of practices that would, I hope, make our discussions valuable and enjoyable for everyone. Is it ok if we take a few minutes on this? Ross? Peter?"

"Well, if we can break long enough for me to get some of Annie's great cobbler," Ross said, "then I think it's an excellent idea." Rebecca Trent walked over to refill her coffee cup and said, "I second that. I have some experience with Chalice Circles, too, and I agree that the format they use would have to be modified for our group. Besides, wasn't Handel a pretty opinionated man himself? I think we owe it to him to show a little spunk and dissention."

"Hear, hear," said Peter. "So, Katherine, what do you have to propose that will bring forth both Clara's critical thinking and Forella's consideration and deep listening—and maybe some of that spunk and dissention Rebecca is looking for? We are all ears—and munching mouths. Ross wanted an excuse to keep eating anyway."

Katherine riffled through the notes in her folder. "I don't want to move into academic mode and run through a review of everything that has been written on the topic of discussions. It's amazing how much has been published on the subject—in the field of education, in business and industry, in sociology and electronic networking, and of course applications in psychology, medicine, religion, sports, journalism, entertainment, politics, even the ever popular self-help seminars. Probably one of the most influential books, especially outside the classroom, was Peter Senge's *The Fifth Discipline: The Art and Practice of the Learning Organization*. Senge's book was intended to help business managers and workers collaborate more effectively. I found Senge's book very useful in educational settings as well. But the ideas I have used in my own seminars grew out of a book written more recently as an aid for college teachers and business leaders who want to use discussions to enhance learning. The book was published in a second edition a few years ago. Its title is *Discussion as a Way of Teaching: Tools and Techniques for Democratic Classrooms*, and it was written by Stephen Brookfield and Stephen Preskill. You may wonder about that 'democratic classrooms' part, but actually that is the reason I found this book so useful. The authors were serious about using discussion as a means of fostering the kind of fairness and equality we associate with an ideal democracy. Basically they felt that a good discussion, a good seminar needed to adhere to practices we associate with a healthy democracy."

"So, what would Brookfield and Preskill have to recommend to our Seminar? In their first chapter, 'Discussion in a Democratic Society,' they discuss some of the writings that address various kinds of group talk.

My favorite quote is one that philosopher Richard Rorty borrowed from English scholar Michael Oakshott in which he characterized discussion as an 'unrehearsed intellectual adventure.' I like that definition. The authors go on, then, to outline nine 'dispositions' as they call them—basically practices that promote the kind atmosphere one could describe accurately as conducive to an 'unrehearsed intellectual adventure.' They claim there are many dispositions worth considering, but the nine they recommend and elaborate on are: hospitality, participation, mindfulness, humility, mutuality, deliberation, appreciation, hope, and autonomy. I expect most of these seem self-explanatory to people in this group, but let me pull out a few of them for comment."

Katherine wrote the nine dispositions out on a flip chart Angela had thought to set up off to the side of the buffet. "Keep in mind," Katherine continued, "that our authors were thinking of discussions in classrooms, where students are sometimes reluctant participants or perhaps simply unconvinced that discussion is an effective learning strategy. All of us here professed to enjoy discussions and likely have participated in many over the years. So, my guess is that several of these terms represent inclinations you consider givens in a good discussion." She checked off Hospitality; Participation; Appreciation; Hope. "I expect we could all agree on what these terms mean and why they are important in a seminar. But let's look at some of the other dispositions. I was surprised to see that their comments on Mindfulness, for example, evoked something very much like the thoughtful restraint Forella liked in the Chalice Circles. Here is a quote from their discussion: 'The paying of attention is what we mean by mindfulness. It involves being aware of the whole conversation—of who has spoken and who has not—and of doing what one can to ensure that the discussion doesn't get bogged down in the consideration of issues that are of concern only to a very small minority of participants.' [p.11] In other words, everyone is expected to give full attention to every speaker, as though each of us were the teacher responsible for seeing that everyone participates. I especially like the idea of making that practice of paying attention a collaborative responsibility."

Wayne Thompson signaled that he had something to say. Katherine nodded. "As I've mentioned to some of you," Wayne began, "I own a café up in Indy that books live jazz acts several nights a week. One thing I've noticed about the best combos we bring in is that they do exactly that—really pay attention to what each performer does so the whole thing makes a collective statement of the piece they are presenting, not just a jumble of individual segments. I hadn't really thought of that as mindfulness, but I think it's pretty much the same thing."

"Thanks, Wayne. I kind of like thinking of each of us as jazz performers," Katherine said. "I always associated mindfulness with some sort of philosophically heavy pondering—you know, Buddhism and meditation. In any case, I'm hoping we all agree to practice mindfulness in this more participatory way so Peter, Ross, and I don't have to take on that responsibility. What else? Another disposition they list is Humility. Their discussion of this disposition is quite short. Basically they recommend that we view all members of the group as potential teachers—and I suppose that implies that we must all also be humble enough to be students, people who seek knowledge—in this case collaboratively. They also suggest the term Mutuality. Here is their definition: 'Mutuality means that it is in the interest of all to care as much about each other's self-development as one's own.' [p.12] So both of these terms—humility and mutuality—seem to be a continuation of our collaboration motif. The Chalice Circle folks would be so proud."

"The other two dispositions—deliberation and autonomy—reverse that trend and emphasize instead our roles and objectives as individuals. These last two dispositions are potentially contentious, but they spring from the kind of integrity I think Clara was concerned to include in our procedures. To be deliberative is to think and speak carefully and thoroughly. It also requires a willingness to change one's mind if evidence warrants it. Autonomy, on the other hand, is rather like courage—being willing to take a stand. Both dispositions are desirable in our group, I think. The question is how to incorporate all of these into our rules for running the Seminar. I'd be happy to hear suggestions or thoughts on where to go from here."

Alison stood up to clear away her plate. "I liked Wayne's image of our Seminar as a kind of jazz performance," she said. "But if you think about a typical jazz ensemble, they have a lead sheet and usually at least some notes from an arranger suggesting when and how long someone plays the melody. In a discussion you won't have those elements of the music beforehand. It really is much more improvisational, and it's harder to know when someone should pick up the theme. Veteran jazz performers are good at managing the give and take, but I'm not sure the metaphor would translate to a discussion 'performance.' Everything is a lot more emergent in a discussion. That's why there usually is a moderator of some sort."

Katherine saw that CD Jennings was frowning slightly. "What's your thought, CD?" Katherine asked. "You seem perplexed." CD looked over at Wayne and Alison. "I would never have made the comparison between music and discussion," he said. "But now that you have started me thinking about it—well, here's an idea. I've thought a lot about how to teach conducting—mostly choral conducting, but orchestral, too. And the thing is, it is really difficult to get across to students how to recognize when entrances are sloppy or certain parts are off on intonation. As a conductor, you hear it, but unless you have a video with sound and play it back, it's hard to show students what was wrong. Some newer technologies are making this easier. Actually, I use some of this new software to check up on my own conducting, things like tempo and phrasing. It helps identify errors. I wonder if there might be newer audio technology that would help us know when, say, someone has talked too long or too many times, or when a set of people have dominated the discussion. Wouldn't that help us maintain some of those dispositions Katherine listed for us—at least the ones that involve sharing time and space effectively?"

Ross leaned back in his chair. "Excellent!" he said. "I think CD is right. The main thing we will have trouble with is simply being aware of when we have messed up on the more or less practical aspects of interaction, or to use Katherine's terms, when we have failed to act with mutuality or mindfulness or even hospitality. I think we all want to demonstrate the dispositions Katherine outlined for us, but it's easy to get carried away and speak too long or too often. So, Benfey, what do you think? Can your equipment help us with this?"

Everyone looked toward Benfey who was seated off to the side, entering notes on her laptop. She seemed a bit taken aback at being addressed directly, but she recovered quickly. "Well, as you know, I now have each of your voice prints recorded, and the software has already been programed to note who is talking. I'm pretty sure I can set it up to signal when any one individual has talked more than, say two minutes, or even when someone hasn't talked for some time. Just let me know what you would like me to keep track of and I think I can set things up to let us know. It shouldn't be a problem to have that ready for the next meeting."

"Thanks, Benfey," Katherine said. "And going back to what Alison suggested, I suppose it would be best to have some one person responsible for deciding when that information should make a difference—a moderator, in other words. I suppose if you can feed that information to my phone, Benfey, I can play that role. At least it takes the pressure off me to keep all that information in mind intuitively—the way I do in a grad seminar. –Unless someone else would like to volunteer for that job." As Katherine expected, everyone cheered her willingness to serve as the Seminar's "informed moderator." Katherine smiled and said, "My only stipulation is that Ross has to play the heavy if anyone gets out of line or says anything really nasty."

"Ouch," Ross winced. "Couldn't you find some other word—the disciplinarian, the enforcer? Where is this refined sensitivity, this political correctness we keep hearing about? Calling me the heavy! This ranks as the most unkindest cut of all—don't you think?!"

"Right," said Peter. "The truth always hurts. I for one am grateful that Katherine is willing to be our moderator. And Ross our Godfather. So—back to this timeline," said Peter, holding up the timeline yet again. "I'm assuming Katherine thought it would be useful for getting our discussion started. I'll have one or two of the letters ready for us to discuss next time, but I think this background information on the young Handel is a good place to start learning what each of us considers most interesting about our baroque hero. Maybe we could each formulate a question based on what most intrigues us about this timeline. What do you think, Katherine?"

"What do I think?" said Katherine. "Well, I think our Mr. Handel is just amazing! It was really fun to pull out these few bits of information about his first twenty-five years. I couldn't help comparing him to myself at twenty-five. Clearly he was much more ambitious and talented. I suppose to some extent, spending four years in Italy was sort of like going to graduate school, or maybe an internship. What most intrigues me are some of the things that—we must assume—influenced his important decisions, such as the decision to go to Italy, to study music rather than law, or eventually to go to London. We have no way of knowing the reasons for his actions, but we can speculate."

"So, yes," she continued, "I agree with Peter that having each of us formulate a question would be a good way to start. What I would really be interested to hear would be a question from each of us that speaks to our personal obsession—well, ok, maybe that is too strong. Say, instead, a question that poses a theme that sparks your curiosity. Maybe you could take the time to name that theme for us. It might be a test to see how well you know yourself. Obviously we all have many ideas that interest us, but it might be fun to hear now at the beginning of this Seminar what each of us finds most compelling as a line of inquiry. Forella already did that for us to some extent. She let us know that questions about the self and the soul—what it means, whether it survives, whether it can be reincarnated—those questions intrigue her. What are our questions?"

After several seconds ticked away, Katherine said, "Let me be the guinea pig here, and you can follow my example if you wish. As I am a folklorist, you might guess that I am intrigued by questions about culture—but also questions about creativity. So if I could resurrect the young Handel—or maybe some of the people he lived or worked with when he was young, I would want to find out what made him choose to be a musician despite the generally negative attitude in the culture of the time toward musicians. According to Mainwaring, Handel's father tried very hard to turn his son away from a career in music, or even an interest in music. There is that anecdote about Handel hiding a clavichord in the attic so he could play without his father knowing. Did he really just love music, or was there some sort of rebelliousness in his decision to go against his father's wishes? I'm sure his father was just being practical. Life can be very hard for artists—then and now. But Handel seemed to be driven to play and compose music. What was it that made that creative fire the most important thing in his life, a fire that stayed with him until the very end?"

"Creative people have to have that fire, I agree," said Rebecca. "But one of my abiding interests is education and the process of learning. What was Zachow's method of teaching Handel? He must have been an exceptional teacher. I suppose it's the old nature/nurture question again. Was Handel a genius because he was born that way, or did Zachow direct that raw talent in such a way that he became the great composer that he was? And what about Handel's friends? Did they teach him things he couldn't have learned from Zachow? Telemann went on to become a prolific composer. He probably influenced Handel in a number of ways. What kind of teacher was Handel himself? The timeline mentions his serving as tutor to the British counsel's son. I wish there were some way to know what Handel's daily routine was when he was an impressionable youngster. It must have set a pattern of practice and learning that stayed with him the rest of his life."

"I'd like to know more about Handel's friendship with Telemann," said Wayne. "One of my driving interests is social connection—basically humans as social animals. According to Katherine's outline, Handel met Telemann when Handel was just sixteen, and they remained friends their entire lives. It always amazes me that people stay friends with people they meet when they are young, people they know in high school or college. Telemann was a little older than Handel, but they must have been pretty much on the same wavelength. To be honest, I never thought of either Handel or Telemann as opera composers, so I'd be interested to learn what that shared enthusiasm was all about. And I wonder why Handel's other friend—Mattheson—resorted to fighting a duel with him. Would you actually duel with a friend? I mean, he could have injured or even killed him. Granted, we have guns and supposed friends who get killed by gunfire, but it seems that Mattheson was not the kind of friend Telemann was. Oh, and by the way, speaking of friends—most of my friends call me Wait. It started back in high school—you know, when you use your initials to identify things. My initials are WAT—Wayne Allen Thompson—but I suspect the name Wait is also because I tend to be late more times than not. Anyway, feel free to call me Wait if you wish."

CD waved his hand. "Ah, another acronymer. I think it's amusing that I actually went by Chandler Jennings all through high school and college. It wasn't until I served as graduate advisor for students in my department that people started calling me CD, and that was mostly because I signed so many forms with my initials. My husband, Alex, always calls me Chandler, and so do my siblings, but in other contexts, I've gotten used to CD. But my question—let's see. My field is choral conducting, so I have an interest obviously in Handel's evolution from an instrumentalist to someone who wrote for the voice or voices. But the question I have after reading this timeline is more about his personal life. Like Wait, I'm interested in social connections, especially in how people form sexual or intimate relationships and how society accepts or challenges those personal decisions. As I mentioned earlier, I know of several sources that claim Handel was gay. According to the timeline, he had this affair with a woman named Victoria, but he never married. And he exchanged at least some letters with his dear Lydia. Maybe these women were friends and his more intimate relationships were with men. I'm not sure what the views on marriage or homosexuality were in the 1700s. And what about these patrons he had while in Italy? Did unrelated men often live in the same household? Did the church or society in general worry about these living arrangements? I guess these are some things I would be interested in learning more about. Maybe the letters will have some answers. I'm hoping at the very least we'll find out what kind of relationship Handel had with Lydia."

There seemed to be a lull after CD's comments. Finally, Rayette spoke up. "My question goes in a different direction. I'm curious about Handel's description of himself as 'dedicated to the liberal arts.' This was when he was twelve years old. As a poet, I'm interested in how people use language. I wonder what he thought that meant. This was 1697, the year his father died. People often name the 1650s as the start of the Age of Enlightenment. Was Handel's use of language influenced by the intellectual ideas we associate with the Enlightenment? Where did he get the idea, or in fact the phrase, 'dedicated to the liberal arts?' We know he studied music with Zachow, but what other subjects did he study as part of his general education? Was he familiar with important works of literature and philosophy even though he didn't go to college? Did he know Italian before he went to Italy? Maybe that interest in opera that Wayne—I mean Wait—was curious about stemmed from Handel's liking for poetry and stories as well as music. I guess I'm eager to know more about Handel as a student and proponent of the arts and maybe expressive thinking generally."

Clara stood up and refilled her glass of water at the buffet. "Yes, I'd like to know more about that, too, Rayette. I'm curious about how or if Handel is considered an offspring of the Enlightenment. Most people assume he was a religious man, I suppose because he composed *Messiah*, but I get the feeling he was mostly an opportunist—you know, get your education and experience where you can. He didn't stick with his chance to be organist at the main church in Halle, so I figure he wasn't keen about serving God or the church. I work in applied physics, but I'm also interested in the history and philosophy of science. It's fascinating to see the inroads science made into people's view of religion and the natural world during a period like the early 1700s. While he was in Italy, Handel composed music for Roman Catholic households, and his first big oratorio there was *La Resurrezione*. We know he was raised a Lutheran, and generally there was animosity between Protestants and Catholics during that time. Did it bother him that he was composing Latin church music, especially things like his *Salve Regina*? Why didn't he just stay in Germany and become a church musician like Bach? Was Handel really a secular composer? I wonder what these letters might reveal about his own religious or philosophical beliefs."

"Beliefs are one thing, of course," Brad responded, "but sometimes the desire for money or a satisfying career is just as important. Like Katherine, I would really like to know why he decided to make music his profession. Handel is especially interesting because his music eventually became an important element in the public sphere. I mean besides *Messiah*. Didn't Handel compose the piece they use even now whenever they crown a British king or queen? He seems to have helped redefine what it means to be a professional musician. I wonder why, as a teen-ager, he left Halle? What was appealing about Hamburg? And why, after a few short years, did he leave Hamburg? Why did he leave Italy? And then, why did he abandon his position in Hanover and go to London? Each of those changes must have been in response to some incentive—money? Fame? Was it really a love of music—or maybe of musical theater? Or maybe just the excitement of being a performer. And why did he decide to buck the system of patronage that would have kept him in one place? I'm interested in his career smarts, his business sense. He seemed to know what he wanted from day one. I have a feeling he would have succeeded no matter what was thrown at him. He took a lot of chances, but he made them work. It would be great to know how he did it."

Katherine looked around to see who had yet to pose a question. Ross and Peter had held back, but Alison was another who hadn't spoken up. Katherine smiled expectantly, and Alison laughed. "Ah, a question. Honestly, I have so many questions—just from looking through this overview of Handel's life before London. We are so used to thinking of Handel as a plump, bewigged, mature man that it's hard to imagine him as a boy or a young man. I direct a choir, but I'm also a professional singer when I can fit it in. I'm probably one of the few in our group who isn't surprised to see evidence that Handel took an early and abiding interest in opera. In the last several decades, Handel's operas have been rediscovered and are actually quite popular with modern audiences. Like Clara, I'm curious why, as a young and fatherless middle-class boy from the relatively provincial district of Saxony, he didn't specialize in church music—though I guess my question is more a matter of why he chose what was then a new form of music, and one associated mostly with France and Italy rather than Germany. Handel has written some of the most beautiful arias available to operatic singers. He must have loved the sound of talented singers, the individual voice, but also great choral performances—which showed up later in his oratorios. And it's interesting that he started out playing the violin. There is a similarity in how music sounds when played well on the violin and sung well by a great singer. I would love to know why Handel found vocal music so compelling, why he wanted to create and produce operas despite the headaches that went with it. I wonder if he had a good singing voice. I suppose we'll never know."

Peter folded his copy of the timeline into a paper airplane and flew it over everyone's head and toward the window. "I wonder if Handel ever dreamed of flying," said Peter. Rebecca laughed. "And no doubt you wonder about his relationship with his mother as well," she said. Peter grinned. "Yes, indeed," he said, "I am sure Dr. Freud would have had a heyday analyzing Handel, but unfortunately he came along a couple centuries too late. I, on the other hand, can surmise all I wish—about his character, his rebelliousness, his supposed affair with Vittoria Tarquini. I am unfailingly intrigued by psychological puzzles. For example, there's the anecdote about Handel's father prohibiting any musical instruments, but what of his mother? He must have had access to music and a musical instrument through someone. And his mother was much younger than his father. Maybe she was less opposed to a career in music and doted on her talented young performer. Handel sent his mother money from Italy—or so says the timeline. Did he feel he must be the breadwinner since his father had died? And about that rumored affair with Vittoria— why would he pick a married woman? I think our young maestro is ripe for psychological scrutiny. It makes perfect sense to me that he rejected the life of a church musician in favor of the tantalizing life of an Italian dandy—at least for a while."

"Ah, Handel the international playboy," said Ross. "But I would guess he was a bit too serious to really play that role very well. For one thing, he clearly worked hard at his art, both as a performer and a composer. For Handel to be hired as organist and music director at the Dom in Halle when he was only seventeen—he must have been an exceptional musician even then. I have a hard time thinking of Handel as light-hearted, but that may just be me. I tend to be haunted by questions tied to the human condition, so I would more likely ruminate on Handel's views on death and suffering. Halle had lost half of its population to the plague just a few years before Handel was born. His father was a surgeon. Handel must have encountered death and misery even before losing his father at age twelve. I suppose my interest in the young Handel who decided to leave home and learn his art in a foreign land is what worldview sustained that passion. What gave him the courage to take the risks he took? And what gave him that sense of depth that people hear in his music? I'm convinced that Handel was a man of complex and profound emotions, truly an extraordinary artist. He must have had some of that intensity even as a young man. I expect to see glimpses of that deep humanity in the view we get of him in these letters. And I'm really eager to see how our Lydia Grayston interacts with him."

Katherine handed each person a CD that included Handel's *Dixit Dominus*, composed when Handel was still in Italy and probably not yet twenty-three years old. "Here is a recording of one of Handel's early works composed while he was in Italy. Forella wanted everyone to hear an example of the kind of music he produced before he came to London. When we gather for our next meeting, Peter has promised us the first of the letters from the packet Handel sent back to Lydia. And Angela has printed out for each of you the web address for a version of Handel's opera *Agrippina*. Both of these works would have been examples of 'new' music out of Italy that preceded Handel on his 1710 trip to London. I hope you can begin to get a feel for the kind of music Handel was composing then. He was a popular figure in Italy and fast becoming a celebrity in London. It must have been a heady time for him."

"Thank you, everyone," Katherine went on, "for your thoughtful and provocative questions here at the beginning of our venture. I look forward to our next meeting. Please stay in contact with Angela if you have any questions or concerns. See you all next time."

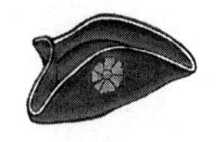

CHAPTER 7
Handel in Rome

Katherine sat listening to the recording of Handel's Dixit Dominus. That relentless Dixit, Dixit, Dixit—insistent voices that pronounce: "God spoke, spoke, spoke to my lord: Sit thou at my right hand, until I make thine enemies thy footstool." Why had Handel selected as his text Psalm 110? He was in Italy when the piece was composed, likely for a Latin vespers service. The Dixit Dominus was—and still is—an impressive, stirring, even disturbing piece. Those who first heard it must have wondered how a young man, barely twenty-two years old, could summon such mastery and such mature emotion—to imagine the voice of God. But, of course it was a chorus and soloists, simply telling the story. And yet, how clearly it conveyed that presumed power of Jehovah, the ancient Hebrew god. Already Handel had found his amazing dramatic voice.

A HALF HOUR BEFORE THE second meeting of the Handel Seminar, Benfey had set up the software that would allow her to not only identify each speaker and record his or her comments but also send a signal to Katherine whenever one of the Seminar "rules" of discussion was breached. Of course it would still be up to Katherine to decide whether to enforce the rule. Surprisingly, Katherine felt fairly confident in her ability to know when stretching the rules would be the better course. The years spent facilitating the smooth running of graduate seminars were finally having their practical real-world benefit.

Every one of the Seminar members was present at this second meeting. Even Forella and Angela were there. An air of excitement—like the first day of school—permeated the room. Most could hardly wait to read the first letter. Katherine had already read the first several letters—as had Peter and Ross. Still, Katherine felt a keen anticipation, along with those who were reading this text for the first time. After everyone had filled a plate with Annie's delicious edibles, Peter stood at his place at Forella's dining table and held up the copies of the first transcribed and translated letter.

"Hello, my friends," he said. "Well, the first of what I am sure will be many exciting moments. Here is your copy of the first letter our mysterious correspondent sent to a young George Frideric Handel. Interestingly, Handel had saved the letters in chronological order, almost as would an archivist. It seems that—as he said in his dictated note—he read through the file of letters start to finish many times over the course of his life. I have started my processing of the letters with the very earliest one, which you will see was written to Handel in 1707, while he was still in Italy. And—another point of interest, the letter is written in French. I have translated, and both Ross and Katherine gave a passing grade on the translation. So, here you are: Letter number one."

Peter handed out the copies of the letter, and everyone read eagerly as they munched lunch. Except for the sounds of chewing, all was still. Even Angela's reading aloud for Forella's benefit was quiet—almost reverent. Here is the text of Peter's translation:

To: G F Handel, Esqr.
Palazzo Pitti
Florence, Italy

23 February 1707

My Dear Mr. Handel,
I write to you in French as our lessons in English which I so enjoyed were cut short by your departure from Hamburg. And I write remembering that today is your birthday. How I miss you and cherish the

memory of the evening everyone celebrated your turning twenty. Can it be only two years ago? It seems much longer. You promised Herr Dieter that you would write with an address much before this, but he has only recently learned that you are in Florence. I hope this reaches you before you travel again.

My dear Edward continues his duties as chaplain for Sir John, and Mr. Mattheson teaches young Cyril, though his charge complains that your keyboard pieces were much more lively and rich in counterpoint exercise for him to learn. I cannot but agree. I continue my own lessons with Herr Dieter. You cannot know how barren have been my tea times now that my Robin Gif Goodfellow is no longer here to parry my reviews of concerts and new pieces of music. H Dieter thinks such comments unbecoming a lady and will not hear them. Ah, my friend, your wit and love for depth of thought are treasures I miss every day. My ailment knows no cure but to write to you.

Sir John is an excellent source of commentary on all things musical, as always. But he has so little time beyond the lovely gatherings at his home. This week past he hosted two visitors from Venice who had met you in Florence. How shameful that we must query strangers to find your whereabouts. They report that you will have a new opera in Florence early in the season. I am so envious of all who will be there. I can imagine how diligently you attend to all of the performances there in Florence and how you refine everything you take in and add to your own music. To tell the truth, Gif, that is one thing I miss above all else, seeing you grasp an idea and make it something even more striking than it was. How I wish I could follow this letter to Italy and hear what you are composing there in the heartland of opera.

I do want to share a bit of research I did in response to your question about the song I sang at that last soiree at Sir John's before you departed. I could see that you were amused at Herr Dieter's embarrassed rush to an instrumental piece after that inappropriate performance. You are right that it was not a composed aria. I could see that you were interested, as is ever your wont. The song was actually one I heard my English handmaid singing as she helped me dress. She has not had lessons, but her voice is sweet, and she says she knew the song from hearing her grandmother sing it years before. She calls it the Cherry Tree carol. I thought the story it tells was very striking. I could tell that you liked it, even though you could not understand the words.

You must continue your English lessons, if only to understand this song. I am sure you appreciate the greater value of an ode composed by a trained musician, and yet I must assume you will hear the beauty of the simple story line and refrain that makes a dramatic puzzle of Joseph's first hearing of Mary's condition. For, as I told you then, that is what the song is about. Poor Joseph learns that his betrothed is already with child, and he knows that he is not the father. I found it a wonderful task to express his anger and then, once the baby Jesus commands the tree to bend and give Mary its fruit, to take her gently on his knee and ask about the child. It is like a little opera in a single song. But of course it is heretical and simple. I believe I embarrassed Eggy in performing it, but he is a forgiving soul.

Please do write when you find an opportunity. Sir John says that he will happily accept any charge for a letter from you. Know that you are greatly missed by me and all here in Hamburg. May God keep you well.

I have the honor to be, ever yours,

Mrs. Edward Grayston
Rotth Haus, Hamburg

"So, there you have it," said Peter. "Katherine and Ross agreed that it would be good to first allow any questions to me on the physical artifact itself and my rendition of the contents. Hmm, so, yes, Brad, you have a question?"

"So this is a letter that this Mrs. Grayston—who must be the Lydia he wrote to in the note—sent to Handel while he was in Italy? But she was writing to him from Hamburg, is that right? She sent the letter to Italy from Germany?" "Yes, I think so," said Peter. Brad continued, "But you say the letter was written in French, even though this text you have given us is in English?"

"Yes," said Peter, "the letter was written in French—though the address is in a mix of Italian and English—I left that as it was. But why French? As I mentioned before, at least half of the surviving correspondence written by or to Handel was in French, not that unusual at that time. And you must remember that Handel grew up among French Huguenots who had settled in large numbers in Halle prior to Handel's birth. I think both Handel and Lydia were very comfortable writing in French. And, I'm assuming they also spoke to each other in French—at least when they first met. Edward and Lydia Grayston were English, we must assume, and may not have learned to speak or write in German as French was the, well, lingua franca of the day. Lydia hints that she had been coaching Handel in English even before he left Hamburg. But he seems not to have progressed very far."

Brad frowned a bit. "Was there something else?" Peter asked. "Well," Brad said, "I don't want to appear that I don't trust you, but since we don't have the actual letter in front of us, how do we know that this is what it really said? It doesn't sound like a letter that has been translated. I don't read French myself, but—I don't know—this sounds like a letter that was written in English. Someone help me out here."

Rayette spoke up. "I think I know what Brad means. I do read French, and I've worked with translations from the French and a few other languages. I think Brad is suggesting that the translation you have given us is maybe too polished. The translation isn't simply a literal matching of words with contemporary English meanings. It actually seems to me that you put some effort into giving us a translation that is true to the style and tone of that early eighteenth century text rather than simply a dictionary translation. Am I right?"

Peter smiled and looked over at Katherine. "They are a sharp bunch, aren't they?" said Peter. "Should I confess now, or wait until we get to the later letters?" Katherine grimaced and turned to Rayette. "Peter did initially do a very straightforward, literal translation. Frankly, it sounded very clunky in English, so, as you observed, Rayette, Peter was persuaded—by both me and Ross—to look ahead to the letters that come later, ones written in English, and try to match that tone. Peter came back with a version much closer to this text, and Ross and I added our edits as well. The issues that arise out of the art of translation are fascinating, and I'm sure some of you would love to ponder the original text and deliberate about how best to translate it. But we made a committee decision to give you this version. And, I agree that Peter did put effort and talent into giving us a translation that reflects something of Lydia's character as well as the writing style of the time. It's a good question, Brad, and a perceptive observation from Rayette, but that was the resolution we reached. We hope you are not too disappointed."

Forella led a round of applause and spoke up, "Bravo, Peter. I think it sounds wonderful. Ross has always said you had a bit of the poet in you." Peter lifted Forella's hand to his lips. "Ah, ma Cherie, merci mille fois." Peter turned back to the room at large. "I did have some fun trying to imagine myself as our Lydia and choose the English expressions she would have used, but the essential content is as true to the original as I could make it. If any of you who read French would like to see a copy of the original, let me know, and I'll bring one along next time. I think—if no one has any other questions about the artifact itself . . . yes, Clara?"

Clara held up her copy of the letter and said, "I'm eager to get to the content of the letter, too, but I'm still trying to really SEE the letter and the person who wrote it—and actually Handel himself at age twenty-two. I have a habit—well, I love the cinema—so whenever I hear of people or events from history, I try to imagine them on film, in a video. So, Lydia would have written this letter on some kind of stationery provided by her host in Hamburg—written it in French, knowing that Handel would be able to read it—and then sent it to his residence there in Florence? Did they have some sort of regular mail delivery? And was it appropriate for a married woman to be writing to a young unmarried man? I guess I am curious about just how bold this action was on her part. Would this letter be seen as a conventional kind of correspondence, or was she doing something a little out of the ordinary simply by writing to Handel?"

"Whoa, whoa, that must be about ten questions," said Peter, "and most of them beyond my area of expertise. But I can say a little about two queries you pose—what was the etiquette and procedure involved in exchanging letters in the early 1700s? and what did Handel look like when Lydia wrote to him?—this second question not exactly tied to the artifact itself, but I'll try to answer it anyway since you mentioned your cinematic interest, which I happen to share."

"So, what can we say about customs surrounding the exchange of letters in the eighteenth century? Think of the wonderful letters exchanged in the mid-to-later 1700s between John Adams—second president of the US—and his 'dearest friend,' Abigail, his wife. Their correspondence began before they were married, and most of it has now been published for our edification. The letters started out in a rather formal way but soon became playful and then, especially as the War of Independence loomed, profoundly philosophical and germane. Women—at least upper class women—were actually regarded as very good letter-writers in the eighteenth century. Granted, men rather than women usually wrote the everyday business correspondence, but women were free to engage in the expressive personal letter genre in a way somewhat at odds with the restrictions placed upon females in nearly all other contexts. So, no, it wasn't out of line for Lydia to be writing to Handel."

"Of course the real boon would be to see how Handel responded to this letter—and the ones that follow, but unfortunately we don't have any of Handel's letters to Lydia," Peter continued. "We do have, in a published collection, a few letters Handel wrote to friends or relatives—usually in French, even to German-speaking recipients, and these letters were usually rather formal, though interestingly expressive and always in proper form. Hopefully we will be able to make some assumptions about what

The Handel Letters

Handel may have written to Lydia based on responses or passing references in Lydia's letters. In any case, we can surmise that Handel and our Mrs. Grayston were fairly well acquainted, enough to warrant her being a part of Handel's social network, at least as that network was maintained by exchanging letters. And it seems she had access to some sort of mail delivery system that would connect Hamburg and Florence. I think there were packet ships that made regular trips to various European ports. And then if you want to visualize this letter writing and delivery in some sort of cinéma vérité, you can imagine Lydia in her tightly corseted silk dress sitting at a writing table in an upper class Hamburg residence penning this letter in impeccable French, sealing it, and sending it off with a man servant from the Rotth household where she was staying and posting it with the outgoing mail packet. And you could imagine Handel, perhaps several weeks later, in a cap and comfortable day coat, or banyan, composing at his harpsichord and receiving this pleasant surprise—a letter from his charming acquaintance, Mrs. Grayston."

"And," said Peter, "just to make that imagined movie moment even more effective, let me show you a painting that includes our young Mr. Handel –or Hendel, as his name was often spelled in Italy." Peter flicked on an LCD projector that Benfey had set up earlier. "I thought I might show this later, but this seems a good time." On the wall opposite, everyone could see the image of a painting depicting the front of a large urban domicile. Immediately before the façade was a line of some dozen or so people who appeared to be reviewing a battalion of soldiers who were marching by. Issuing from the large front entryway were two white horses pulling a covered carriage. Above on a balcony were several figures, likely including the nobleman who owned the house. Many people peered from windows on the two upper floors of the building. All in all, some forty people appeared to be present to review the exodus of this impressive army of soldiers. Peter waited while everyone examined the image. Rebecca and CD both left their seats and viewed the image at closer range. "All right," said Peter, "which figure do you think is Handel? He IS in the picture. It is one of the few firm records we have of where he was and what he was doing in Italy."

Alison spoke up. "I've seen a lot of pictures of Handel. He is one of the most often portrayed composers before the age of photography. But I've never seen this painting. It isn't very good, is it? If I had to guess, I'd say Handel is either the man on the far right on the balcony or the man fifth to the right of the central doorway down below. Both of these men have white or grey wigs, and Handel is usually shown wearing a wig, at least in formal settings. Most of the other men have on hats. I've never seen a picture of Handel in a hat—well other than those housecaps people wore inside. It's hard to tell from the faces."

"I think most people agree with you, Alison, that the painting isn't very good," said Peter. "But the consensus is that Handel is standing near the doorway, fourth from the right—the only man in a colorful gold outfit rather than the usual formal black. Let me show you a close-up of that portion of the painting. And, notice that the long curled wig he is wearing is a reddish brown rather than the powdered full-bottomed wig so often associated with Handel throughout most of his career. And he is holding a three-cornered hat under his arm—but not wearing it, for whatever reason. He definitely stands out as a young and dashing foreigner, happy to take an independent path, at least in terms of fashion."

"So, how did he come to be in this painting, you ask. There isn't much information on the piece, mostly because the artist is not very well known. His name is Alessandro Piazza, and he was commissioned—perhaps at the last minute—to document the march of the Marchese Ruspoli's regiment out of Rome on September 9, 1708. Handel was among the company that stood outside the palace as the soldiers marched by, as was Margherita Durastanti, a soprano known to have sung in a number of Handel's operas—the woman standing just behind Handel in the painting. So, this painting was done a year after the first letter Lydia wrote to Handel. It gives us some idea of Handel's physical appearance at that time. Actually, a bit of a rock star amid the more conservatively dressed people who appear in the scene. Even Margherita is dressed in black and sporting an old fashioned headdress. At the time, Handel was a guest at Ruspoli's residence in Rome. He must have been a popular figure—tall, slim, energetic, and good looking. I guess if we are trying to envision a cinematic representation of Handel when he and Lydia first met, we would have to cast him as a young and attractive man, full of confidence in his role as a rising composer and performer."

Peter waved a hand toward Katherine. "And now," he said, "I think I will turn our discussion over to Professor Baker. She and Ross promised to keep us in line as we dissect this letter. Carry on." Peter sat down, and Katherine picked up her copy of the letter as well as the timeline she had composed earlier. "Maybe we should review what we know about Handel's whereabouts and activities in the period when he first started receiving letters from Lydia," she said. "Now that we know what he looked like, let's consider what he was up to in Italy—well, and I suppose what we can know of his activities in Hamburg from reading Lydia's letter."

First to speak up was Rebecca. "I am surprised at how direct and informal Lydia is in writing to Handel. Granted, he is young, and possibly she is a bit older than he is, but she writes to him in a very familiar tone, as one would to a brother or sister perhaps. They must have become very good friends while he was in Hamburg. She is married, and she mentions her husband—my dear Edward, or Eggy, must be a nickname—so I don't think they were more than just friends. Still, she seems more forward, less inclined to accept the kind of secondary position women were typically expected to follow. She even compares Handel favorably against Herr Dieter who evidently did not think women should offer their commentary on music or performances. Just to be a bit anachronistic, I would say that Handel is something of a feminist. Either that, or our Lydia is a rare specimen. She doesn't appear to be the least bit intimidated by Handel, either as a rising opera composer or even simply as a man. It must be that he rather liked her informal tone and warm familiarity. Otherwise he wouldn't have kept the letters all those years. I wonder if Handel was that informal with all of the women he interacted with—or if it was just Lydia."

"That is an interesting question," said Wait. "Actually, I wonder if that directness and informality were characteristic of Handel's friendships in general. The later paintings of him always have him looking rather somber. Maybe he became more of a grouch as he got older. I'm curious—maybe in keeping with Forella's suggestion that we consider the life themes these letters raise—is it easier to make friends when you are young, harder to make friends when you are older? I'd be interested to hear what people think this letter says about friendship in a more general way."

Rayette signaled that she had something to say. "Yes, Wait, I would be interested in that as well. One thing that struck me in the letter was Lydia's use of the phrase 'Robin Gif Goodfellow.' The designation Robin Goodfellow may be unfamiliar to some of you. It's a bit archaic. English majors would probably know it—or its more common variant of 'Puck,' as in Shakespeare's *Midsummer Night's Dream*. If I remember correctly, the name Robin Goodfellow was a kind of euphemism for the trickster fairy that played pranks on people. The initials GF were sometimes used to refer to Puck or Robin Goodfellow, so it's possible that Lydia made the connection between the GF of Goodfellow and Handel's usual signature as GF Handel. I don't know. And then, of course, she inserted Gif as a middle name. Later she addresses Handel by name as Gif, and I suppose that is simply GF, his initials, adjoined into a nickname, possibly a name she heard people use in Hamburg. Still, it seems very much an intimate kind of naming, again, as Rebecca suggested, a sign that they were very good friends. In that period, men usually referred to each other by surname only. It was more often women who used nicknames or pet names. Handel must have allowed, maybe even welcomed this familiarity on Lydia's part."

"There definitely does seem to be plenty of evidence even here in this first letter that Lydia and Handel were good friends," said Katherine. "She knew when his birthday was. She had evidently been at the party for his twentieth. And her letter implies that they met often over dinner—whether just tête-à-tête or perhaps more likely with friends—to discuss music. She calls him 'my friend'—*mon ami*. And she says very directly that she misses him. She also says that she misses his wit and depth of thought—traits she would probably really notice only if she were around him quite often and in more informal situations. Maybe such friendships between men and women were rare in the eighteenth century. Maybe they still are. I think Wait's question is timely. What notions about friendship does this letter raise for us today? What ideas about friendship are we bringing to our interpretation of the letter—perhaps even unaware?"

"Well, I certainly did make some very good male friends back in graduate school and then when I had my first adjunct teaching job," said Alison. "But once I was married, I guess those friendships were mostly replaced by couples who were friends—or women, but usually not just men—and especially not men who were MY friend but not necessarily my husband's. Of course, I have friends who are actually my colleagues, men I interact with in professional and social situations growing out of my role as a choir director and singer, but that is a special kind of work friendship. I don't know about Handel and Lydia, but I think even today it would be unusual to find a really close kind of friendship between a man and a woman, especially as people get older, have families, and no longer really have time to just chat with friends. I think back then, and now, a person's age may have something to do with it."

Peter turned on the LCD projector and once more cast the Ruspoli troop review painting on the wall. "Take a look at the picture again," he said. "Notice the few women in the picture. What we tend to forget is that married women in the eighteenth century basically had no rights and were completely under their husbands' thumbs. Margherita Durastanti is there pretty much on her own because she is a singer at Ruspoli's house and unmarried—a working girl, so to speak, but the other women in the painting are likely wives or mistresses of the men standing next to them. My guess is that friendships between men and women back then would have occurred, as Alison suggests, when both parties are young or, more likely, through social events at which married couples and single men, like Handel, interact. I find it strange that even though times have changed and women, married or single, now have the same rights men have, you still rarely hear of close friendships between men and women. There are exceptions, of course, but I think the sexes still seem to be segregated in terms of friendship—except when they are young and single. How many of you know anyone who has a close opposite sex friend? What would you even call such a relationship?"

With a sort of weary signal, CD indicated that he had something to say. "Funny you should ask—what to call such a relationship, if it exits. I remember when everyone worried over what to call unmarried heterosexual couples. Should you speak of your 'significant other?' Isn't it over the top to speak of your 'lover?' More legalistic language started using 'partner'—as though this were some sort of business arrangement. But, of course, it really became an issue when speaking of gay couples. People seemed to find 'lover' especially offensive when applied to a gay lover. I remember one of the first times I referred to Alex as my 'husband.' Someone asked me if that made me the 'wife.' But more to the point here, I think the real issue is how rarely we have close friendships outside of our intimate twosomes—of whatever kind they are. Just like Alison, I have become increasingly dependent on my husband to be my best friend. It's not that I don't have friends of both sexes, but actually most of them are 'our' friends—friends Alex and I have in common. I think if I had a really close friend—either male or female—Alex would be jealous, or would at least resent the time and effort I put into that relationship. Once you make a commitment to someone, you basically promise to make that person your best friend."

Brad spoke up, with a sidelong look at Rebecca. "I'll probably ruffle some feathers here, but I think it highly unlikely that men and women—or maybe even gay men and lesbians—can be completely platonic in their relationships with people of the opposite sex or the sex that attracts them—IF that person is someone they really like. And it seems to me that Lydia really likes Handel. So, she's married. That doesn't mean she doesn't think about Handel as a potential lover—at least in her nighttime fantasies. And Handel probably really likes having this safely married woman coming on to him. He probably got all kinds of signals from her. All those things Katherine listed as signs of a great friendship between the two of them--? I'd say those are signs that she has the hots for our young Mister Handel. I don't think it is a friendship issue at all."

Ross joined in as he walked back from the buffet with a cookie and a glass of Scotch. "Love, friendship, affection, romance—some of us have trouble knowing which of these we feel toward people in our lives. Why would you say two people are 'just friends' rather than that they are 'great friends' or 'two peas in a pod?' Are people 'just friends' when a fiery romance is no longer fiery? Or is it when two people are happy to spend time together but feel no compulsion to jump into bed with one another? Why is it that we feel we must label our relationships? Or place them in a hierarchy? It seems like we see sex or lack of sex as the most important difference in defining relationships, and yet most of our relationships do not overtly involve sex. Maybe Brad is right—sex is always there, under the surface, but stifled, hidden, denied. Is this the burden of being human?"

"Ok, I warned everyone that I cannot just let things slide by that I feel need to be challenged or at least examined," said Clara. "Scientists have actually determined what kinds of chemicals in the brain and hormones in the body produce various states we associate with romantic passion or even long-lasting attachment, care, love. And not just in people—in animals, too. But it is pretty clear that the decisions we make about whether or not to follow through on these feelings is what we are really talking about here. Maybe Lydia DID feel a strong attraction to Handel, and maybe that feeling prompted her to write to him, but she knew her own situation—and probably Handel's—well enough to act as though this were just a friendship, not a romance. Handel must have known the letters were a little out of the ordinary, a bit risky, or he wouldn't have sent them back to Lydia near the end of his life and stipulated that they be burned if not given directly to her. And yet, he had kept them all those years. I think theirs was a treasured friendship on both sides—maybe unusual but really, after all, something we might all wish for. We congratulate a couple like John and Abigail Adams because they were each other's best friend AND married to each other. Why are we squeamish about celebrating the friendship of two people—a man and a woman—who are not married to each other but nevertheless great friends? I think it is our problem, not theirs."

Katherine stood up and went over to the projector Peter had used to show everyone the painting that included Handel as a young man. "Well said, Clara. Friendship is something we in this seminar have our opinions about—quite aside from what people in the early 1700s might have thought. And I can assure you we will have reason to come back to the topic many times as we read more of Lydia's letters. But I thought—before our time runs out today—that I would bring your attention to something Lydia and Handel shared by virtue of their friendship, or whatever we want to call their relationship. Remember Lydia's comment about the song she had sung at one of the gatherings at John Wyche's house before Handel left? The Cherry Tree Carol? I thought you might enjoy knowing a little more about that song. As she suggested, it is a folksong, not a composed piece of the sort usually performed at these house concerts she and Handel attended. This was well before the Romantic period, mind you, so Lydia was a bit before her time in choosing to perform this kind of piece as part of a refined evening concert. No wonder her husband was embarrassed."

Selecting another file from those on the laptop, Katherine went on: "The idea of collecting and appreciating folksongs was not to flourish until late in the eighteenth century, when Johann Gottfried von Herder published German folksongs and touted their role as carriers of the nation's 'soul.' I like to think that Lydia's decision to sing a song she had learned from listening to her maid reflects the innate instincts of a budding folklorist—or at least her ability to recognize good music when she heard it. In any case, the song she chose to sing is one that Francis James Child later included in his famous collection of English and Scottish ballads—in fact, one of the older ballads he discovered that were still being sung in America in the 1800s. Here are the words of one version; we can't know what version she might have sung nor, of course, what tune she knew. If you go to the internet, I'm sure you can find some recordings of the song from the folknik era. But, sit back now, relax, and I'll sing the version I know. Try to imagine our Lydia in a room full of Hamburg gentry."

"Joseph was and old man, and an old man was he, when he wedded Mary in the land of Galilee, when he wedded Mary in the land of Galilee," Katherine began. Everyone read along as she sang the song, closing with the yet unborn baby Jesus responding to Joseph's question of when he would be born: "On the sixth of January, the Babe said softly, on the sixth of January my birthday will be, on the sixth of January my birthday will be." Everyone clapped. Katherine smiled and turned the projector off. "I know it is hard to imagine this, but try to think of Handel hearing this song but not really knowing enough English to understand the story. Likely he would have caught the names Joseph and Mary and the place name Galilee. And he would have seen and heard how Lydia expressed anger when Joseph learned that Mary was pregnant—though, again, Handel would not know exactly who was angry about what. Lydia writes to Handel: 'I could see that you were interested, as is ever your wont.' The two of them shared some sort of sensitivity about music, some spark that Lydia must have seen in Handel's eyes as he listened. I think it tells us a little about what drew them together, maybe some of that depth Lydia saw in Handel and missed so much since he left Hamburg. I wonder if he thought more about the song—for Lydia is right—it is a little opera in miniature and a story Handel would have found fascinating, I am sure."

Ross put down his glass and looked over at Katherine. "I'm glad you sang the song. It IS very moving, isn't it?" he said. "I don't think I would have grasped the significance of the song if you had just shown us the words. Handel must have been affected by the performance itself, especially since, as you said, he did not understand the English lyrics. I suppose it was clear to him that there was some sort of story, a drama. Maybe Lydia knew how strongly Handel was drawn to a solo voice as a way to tell a story and at the same time express an emotion. And what an interesting story! As Lydia said, the song was heretical. No wonder her husband disapproved. Didn't she say he was a chaplain? I can't imagine he would have liked this folk version of Joseph's behavior. Still, the song obviously appealed to Lydia's maid—and to Lydia. I like it, too. Better than Joseph meeting up with some angel who tells Joseph not to worry about Mary being pregnant. Good song!"

"Yes, it is," said Alison, "but I'll be interested to find out if Handel ever responded to Lydia's comments in the letter. He had only recently encountered Italian opera. Lydia's offhand description of the folksong as a 'little opera' must have provoked some sort of response. After all, opera looms ahead as Handel's all-consuming passion for the next several decades. He must have heard her comment as at best naïve. Or maybe he actually DID appreciate her intuition that there was something in the emotion of performance that connected the two genres—operas and folk ballads. When will we get to see the next letter? Maybe she started a fine little argument here. Too bad there were no blogs in the eighteenth century."

"Ha, no way," said Peter. "Handel would have avoided online exchanges like the plague, I am sure—well, unless the whole internet thing started when he was a young man. There must be lots of modern innovations he would have found useful. But such speculation aside, I can promise letter number two—maybe letter three as well—at our next meeting. Thank you all for being patient as I got the processing under way. And thank you for not critiquing my translation. I guarantee you will enjoy the next round. Katherine, do we have any other announcements before we close shop?"

Katherine picked up a stack of CDs. "Our generous convener, Forella, has once again insisted that you hear something of the kind of music Handel was writing at this time. So here you have a recording of his first Italian opera, *Rodrigo*. Don't worry; it has a wordbook in English. Enjoy. See you all at our next meeting."

CHAPTER 8

My Dear Mr. Handel

From the Music Library, Peter borrowed again the small edited volume containing the few extant letters written by Handel to relatives, friends, and business acquaintances. He pondered some of the unanswered riddles posed by names and events in these letters: Who was Mademoiselle Sbülens and why did she travel with Handel from Halle to Hamburg, as alluded to in Handel's letter in German to his friend Johann Mattheson? When did Handel start to make "quelque progrés dans cette langue [English]" as he writes to a fellow German musician, Andreas Roner? Why did Handel write in French to his German brother-in-law, Michael Dietrich Michaelsen, and why always to his brother-in-law rather than to his sister, even while she was alive? The scant cache of letters, most immaterial and random as they are, offers more questions than answers.

WHEN THE HANDEL SEMINAR MET again, Angela handed around copies of a few of the earliest letters from the Arno Press collection of the *Letters and Writings of George Frideric Handel*. Peter thought the Seminar members would find it interesting to compare these examples of Handel's letters with those written by Lydia Grayston. The editor provided translations of the selected letters, which were mostly in French, with one in German and a single short business memo in English. Researchers have found no letters from the period Handel spent in Italy.

Lydia's next two letters to Handel, on the other hand, were written while Handel resided and composed in various city-states on the Italian peninsula. Lydia's first letter to Handel had been sent to the Pitti family palace in Florence. Peter was surprised to see that a year elapsed between that first letter and the second. Once everyone was settled around the dining table, luncheon plates before them, Ross stood and asked Peter to say a little about the published letters Angela had handed out and then to introduce the next two letters from Lydia.

"Well, my friends," said Peter, "in your hands you have published translations of some of the few letters ever found written by George Frideric Handel. Mr. Erich Müller, the editor of the collection of letters, provided the translations. The first one is especially interesting. It was written while Handel was still in Hamburg—written to his friend Johann Mattheson. Our purpose here is not to produce, even among ourselves, a new and better biography of Handel. We leave that task to those with time and talent necessary to the challenge. However, I think it serves our aims if we consider briefly what Handel wrote to people around the same time Lydia was writing to him."

Peter continued: "Mattheson, you may remember from Katherine's timeline, was the friend who fought a duel with Handel—supposedly over who should lead the orchestra at Mattheson's opera, but perhaps more likely over who should succeed Reinhard Keiser as the director of the Hamburg opera. This letter to Mattheson is interesting in its uncharacteristic nod to Mattheson as someone indispensible at the Hamburg opera house. Our consideration of the theme of friendship last time seems relevant here. Mattheson certainly made things easy for Handel in Hamburg. He was the sort of 'older brother' connection who introduced Handel to wealthy families in need of a good music teacher for their children, for example. And he even welcomed Handel into his family home at mealtime several times a week. But the duel suggests they saw each other as rivals, and most biographical sources say that Handel never really warmed to Mattheson again after this brief period in Hamburg."

"Another tantalizing tidbit in the letter to Mattheson," Peter went on, "is the mention of Mademoiselle Sbülens. She evidently is someone who came from Halle to Hamburg along with Handel—why, no one knows. Handel was only eighteen when he moved to Hamburg. Was this a family friend? Why do Handel and Mattheson both know her? Is she perhaps the mysterious Marie we encounter in the next letter from Lydia? Ah, I see I have aroused your curiosity with that question. So, let me give you the next two letters from Lydia to Handel, and let the games begin."

As Peter began handing out copies of the letters, Katherine stood up and took over that task. "Perhaps you should say a little about the translation of these two letters," she said. "Well, and the languages of the letters Handel wrote. I am impressed with how easily Handel switches from one language to another, but then his correspondents seem to be able to do that as well."

"That is correct," said Peter. "As you can see from the published letters written by Handel, he wrote in French or German to people in Halle or Hamburg, but by 1716, he was writing to London banking agents in English. But these two letters from Lydia were written in French. In the previous letter, she did allude to his having started learning English. But here I have translated from the French into what I like to think of as Lydia's English for the copies that I am giving you today. Handel must have learned enough Italian to read the librettos he encountered while in Italy, but there is no evidence that he ever corresponded with anyone in writing in that language. I hope the translations are satisfactory. Katherine and Ross gave me the ok."

Eager hands accepted the two translated letters, and everyone began reading. Though Katherine had read both letters earlier, she took out her pen and started circling words or sentences she wanted to mention in the discussion. Here are the translations Peter provided.

To: G F Handel, Esqr.
Palazzo Bonelli
Rome

23 February 1708

My Dear Mr. Handel,
I pray this letter does arrive at the home of your patron, the Marquis Ruspoli, there in Rome. If news from my nephew traveling there in Italy is correct, it seems neither your reply to my earlier letter nor my later one to you arrived at their destinations. These ongoing conflicts in Spain and Italy have caused everyone to be suspicious of any communications, but especially those right now that travel by mail coach through Bavaria. I am sending this letter by packet ship along the North Sea. May there be no interceptions this time. Please consider the watery route for any reply. You, my friend, must be under surveillance—a questionable Saxon in Roman lands.

But here it is your birthday once again, and I write with birthday greetings and to commend you on your many musical successes. You may wonder at the source of my enlightenment on your activities, as you have not sent messages beyond the one that was lost. Our dear, sweet Marie tells me what she hears of you from her father and brother. They come up from Halle regularly to see her. Though her Huguenot kin in Hamburg make no travels to Italy, her brother corresponds often with Signor Gasparini and learns of your latest compositions and performances. Marie expressed surprise at your composing music for Latin vespers. She thought you too staunchly a Lutheran reformist. She misses you even more than I do, and of course with greater reason.

Alain did not tell his sister news of your romance with Vittoria, but he did tell me. He believes you are a rogue and a bounder. I, on the other hand, think you are a fish and Italian opera is the net that has caught you. I saw how a dramatic soprano voice could capture your eager heart even here on the stage in Hamburg. What defense can you find against La Bombace? All the talk is that she is lovely and witty as well. A well-made net can capture even the most wary fish, my friend. Just remember that what you see and hear on the stage is a fantasy. And yet, if you are inspired to write music to match the voices you hear, I cannot complain. You are the maestro.

Mister Mattheson plays for us at Sir John's soirees, but he no longer sings on the stage. Even here in Hamburg, the cry is for the high voice of the castrato. The report is that you have written some compositions for such voices as well. What is your thought on these unnaturally high male voices? I heard one singer recently at the Gänsemarkt. He was a skilled singer, and the voice was robust, yet it was strangely disturbing. I am baffled as to why this voice is what everyone demands. Can you explain it, Gif? You are in the land of opera. I expect an erudite answer.

And now I bid you bon chance with the new work I hear you will present for the Marquis and his guests. May all go well. Please tell me about the piece. I will share with Sir John and all our friends.

I have the honor to be, ever yours,

Mrs. Edward Grayston
Rotth Haus, Hamburg

And the second translation is of a letter from a few months later.

To: G F Handel, Esqr.
Palazzo Alvito
Naples

24 June 1708

My Dear Mr. Handel,
I must thank you for sending a letter so quickly after receiving mine and for warning that your address would change for the summer

months. However, I wonder, dear Gif, why you must write to Mister Grayston as though I did not exist or could not read. Marie told me that you write even to your own sister only through her husband. I am sure this is what you were taught at the gymnasium, but you are a grown man now. One would think you and I had never met. No doubt you worry for your reputation. If it calms your fears, I will destroy your letters once I have seen them. Men have such a heavy burden. You may read that as you wish.

I, far more than the Reverend Mister Grayston, was intrigued by your report on the first performance of your new oratorio on the resurrection. I understand that the opera houses are closed in Rome, but you wrote that La Resurrezione was performed at your patron's private residence. Why, in light of this private venue, does the Pope feel compelled to offer a reprimand against a woman singing the part of Mary Magdalene? Is he still living in the time of Shakespeare, when men squeaked boyish voices on the stage rather than allow women to play their own roles? And to be replaced by a man who was never allowed to become a man? Signor Gasparini writes that a castrato sang the beautiful aria—"I have something in my heart"— Magdalene's worry that joy cannot really be hers. Sr. Gasparini sent along the words from the ornately printed libretto. How dishonest to have those words sung by a man, especially a man pretending to be a woman. I know there are times when the disguise of the character's sex is part of the plot of plays or operas, but Mary Magdalene is the consummate WOMAN! How completely ridiculous!

The only explanation you offered was that Italian opera requires the higher alto or even soprano voice for the hero, that over the last twenty years the castrato voice has supplanted the normal male voice in operas as the voice of the lead singer. No wonder poor Johann has left the stage—and he has such a fine tenor voice. And you mentioned this Arcadian Academy that seems a kind of secret guild promoted by some of your librettists and patrons. I must say I am surprised that you would even consider giving time to such diversions. I recall you stating emphatically that you were going to Italy to learn and to perform. I cannot imagine you being content to be a man of leisure who contributes now and again to musical evenings at noble households. If I know one thing about you, it is that you must be at the forefront, astonishing all others with your playing—and now, I suppose, your composing.

Who is your latest rival, I wonder. As always, you seem determined to be peerless. And not only with music—though with your music I can only agree that your efforts to be most admired means that we benefit from your ambitions. But I pity Vittoria. How could she know that your admiration would fade once you had won her away from her patron? Dear Gif, you are too young to be such a heartbreaker. Some day you will meet a woman who leaves you longing for better days, as you have those you have said you loved. Do not make your life based on the librettos you read. That is my sisterly advice. I have not asked Edward, but I am sure he agrees.

All of your friends worry that you may stay forever there in Italy. Please let us know when we may hope to see you again. Herr Brockes knew of the Arcadian Academy and commends you for staying clear of it. He says you are too independent a man to join such a group. I am not alone in my judgment, as you see. We all wish you were still here to perform and talk with us at Sir John's fine evenings. I send you my good wishes, despite my worries at your long stay in Italy. It would be so good to hear you play again.

May God keep you well.

I have the honor to be, ever yours,

Mrs. Edward Grayston
Rotth Haus, Hamburg

Katherine waited until it appeared everyone had read the letters. "Both of these letters," she said, "were written in 1708, the second year of Handel's stay in Italy. The 1708 birthday letter mentions the problems much of Europe was having with communications among countries involved in the ongoing War of the Spanish Succession. That conflict continued until 1713, and it is likely that Handel did have to watch carefully what was said even in private correspondence. Several of the letters in the little Arno Press collection are incomplete, paragraphs or closings having been cut away in the originals. So, Lydia was not wrong to guess that Handel might be under surveillance while living in Italy."

"But for us the more frustrating censorship would have to be the other paragraphs that must have followed Handel's reference to Mademoiselle Sbülens in his letter to Johann Mattheson. I was unable to find anything about this person or her family. I even asked Angela to help, but we found nothing beyond a comment by Friedrich Chrysander, a nineteenth century biographer who recorded the young woman's journey to Hamburg along with Handel in 1703. You have already heard Peter's suspicion that she is the 'dear, sweet Marie' Lydia mentions. Whether she is or is not the person Handel writes of in his letter to Mattheson, Marie is certainly someone who misses Handel and feels abandoned in light of his long stay in Italy. Her brother hopes to shield her from the news that Handel is having an affair with Vittoria Tarquini. My guess is that Marie was a girlfriend who hoped Handel would come back to her. But as we now know, Handel made no effort to return to Hamburg. He was, after all, only twenty-one when he left for Italy. And getting married didn't seem to be a priority."

Wait raised his fork, ignoring the bit of stuffed mushroom clinging to it. "You know," he said, "I'm curious about the different view of marriage they had back then. I remember reading somewhere that in Europe, in Handel's era, people actually married for the first time later than most do now—marrying then in their late twenties or thirties, maybe even in their forties. I wonder if it isn't too easy to impose our notions about marriage back onto Handel and his contemporaries rather than accepting that they might have had a different perspective."

Katherine noticed that Rebecca seemed poised to enter the discussion. Katherine nodded, and Rebecca smiled over at Wait. "Yes, perspectives on marriage certainly have changed over time, even in Western society. I've read some similar information, Wait. Several years ago I was researching the lives of governesses in Britain—you know, women like Jane Eyre in Charlotte Brönte's novel. I found some very useful sources, but one that was particularly helpful was a book titled *Marriage, a History*, by Stephanie Coontz. The book was written when the issue of gay marriage was just beginning to emerge in American society, so its focus was really on what we think of as traditional marriages. But, of course, our idea of what is 'traditional' reflects our own time and place. Europe in the eighteenth century was very different from America today."

Rebecca continued, "What I was interested in was why young women became governesses. It seems that even before the Victorian era in England, young women became governesses as a kind of stepping stone to marriage—not to the master of the house, as in *Jane Eyre*, but rather as a means to build up capitol and skills that would make the woman a good wife to a man of her own social status. It was the same for young men. Married couples were expected to join society as independent and efficiently functioning units, and usually that required that both the man and the woman work outside the home for several years—unless of course they inherited land and money. Marriage for the growing middle class in Europe was essentially an economic arrangement, even if the couple felt great affection for each other. It seems likely to me that Marie traveled with Handel to Hamburg to accept work, perhaps as a governess or a maid, and it is possible that she hoped Handel would return to Hamburg after his musical apprenticeship in Italy and marry her."

Alison joined the discussion. "I remember reading somewhere a little anecdote about Handel, and about his friend Mattheson. Supposedly, soon after Handel arrived in Hamburg, he and Mattheson traveled to Lübeck with the aim of auditioning for the post then held by none other than Dietrich Buxtehude, the noted organist and composer. It was a stipulation of the position that the person accepting the job would marry Buxtehude's daughter. Neither Mattheson nor Handel found this prospect a positive incentive, it seems, but what interests me is the notion that it would be a serious requirement. We would regard it as a joke today, but

I suppose at that time it was regarded as a reasonable arrangement. In any case, we can see that Handel was not tempted by the security of a permanent position nor the chance to marry well."

"Do we know what Buxtehude's daughter looked like?" Brad asked. "Maybe the old man thought this was the only way to marry her off. The idea of marrying the boss's daughter isn't unusual even if people do joke about it. But, you know, if she had nothing to recommend her besides connection with Papa Buxtehude, well, these guys were young—no wonder they didn't jump at the chance."

Katherine stood up and went over to the flip chart easel Angela had set up for them—a bit of old technology. She wrote three words on the blank sheet—MARRIAGE, SEXUALITY, LOVE. "There are countless themes we could draw from the letters we've read so far," she said, "but, for now, perhaps we could focus on these three related issues that seem to have already captured our interest. As Peter suggested, a Handel biographer would aim at unpacking an understanding of marriage and intimate relationships current in Handel's time. I think we want to do that as well, but an equally important question for our Seminar is what insights do we gain for our own time about relationships from our consideration of Handel's life. How do Handel's choices about his love life back in 1708 provoke changes in our thinking about love in the twenty-first century?"

Ross walked over to the easel and picked up the marker Katherine had replaced in the tray. With a flourish, he crossed out the word *marriage*, circled the word *sexuality* and put a big 'yes' beside it, and drew an arrow pointing away from the word *love*. "So far, it seems to me," he said, "Handel never does marry, but of course he doesn't know that in 1708. Or at least we assume he doesn't know that he will never marry. However, it does appear that he has decided at that time that he will not marry yet—neither Buxtehude's daughter nor the sweet Marie waiting for him in Hamburg. On the other hand, there is plenty of evidence that he was, as the Electress Sophia reported, the 'lover of Victoria.' In my book, being a lover means having sex, so I see his sexuality, at least at that time, as heterosexual and active. And finally, I think the much more complex issue of 'love' is not part of Handel's life at that time, except in his continuing support of his mother back in Halle. Most sources say that he made a point of sending money or gifts to his mother and later to his godchild, his sister's daughter, Johanna Frederica Michaelsen."

"I'm not so sure that Love with a capital L wasn't a part of Handel's life at that time," Rayette countered. "Yes, he demonstrated familial love by sending money to his mother, but it seems, in Lydia's letter, that his infatuation with Vittoria was—at least initially—truly an affaire de coeur. If we are to draw present-day wisdom from what we see happening in Handel's life, I would guess that we need to recognize young love as a viable form of love, even back in the 1700s. I do not find it surprising that he chooses not to marry, however. I agree with Rebecca that marriage in the eighteenth century was regarded as an economic necessity. Even the gentry typically chose marriage as the accepted means of establishing themselves as grown-ups in proper society. Of course, gentlemen were allowed to have mistresses, and wives were expected to look the other way. Case in point: Handel won Vittoria's affections away from Prince Ferdinando de' Medici, who was married but had kept Vittoria as his lover and sometime singer for several years before she met Handel. There may be something to that description of Handel in Lydia's letter as a rogue and a bounder. It seems he dumped Vittoria not long after he had won her away from Ferdinando. Sometimes young love is more a matter of conquest—but, of course, still la grande passione!"

Clara signaled that she had a question. "I'd like to go back to Wait's question—or an issue he sparked in my mind. He said that people back then often waited to marry until they were in their thirties or even forties. Is it possible that Handel expected to wait until he was older to marry? Maybe he just assumed that discrete love affairs were the way to go until he was securely established somewhere and had set in motion all that he wanted to as a musician and composer. I'll tell you what it reminds me of. When I was in grad school—eons ago, of course—the majority of women who went on to get graduate degrees, especially the PhD, either put off getting married or dropped out when they did get married. I was already married when I started working on my degree, and I remember the chair of my department asking whether I intended to have children. They didn't want to waste assistantship money on me if I were going to drop out and have kids. I think maybe Handel felt a lot of pressure to keep himself free from obligations and ready to go where the musical action was. At least here at the beginning of his career, that might have been a reason for his choosing not to marry."

"Lydia certainly seemed to think Handel's musical ambitions were paramount," said Katherine. "I suppose those ambitions might explain why he did not marry young, but why not later? Clara, maybe your vision of Handel accepting discrete love affairs as the way to go is something that stayed with him the rest of his life. We tend to imagine people wanting to get married if nothing stands in the way, but maybe the state of matrimony was just not appealing to him? What do you think, Peter? You are our relationship guru."

"Ah, yes, Doctor, heal thyself," said Peter. "Would that I were wise—or even lucky—about relationships. But I will say that I've read some of the research on Handel from this time period and shortly thereafter—some of the letters others wrote, not to Handel but rather to others, mentioning Handel. We have already alluded to the letter the Electress Sophia wrote to her granddaughter. A later amusing and telling comment is a note written by none other than England's King George the Third in the margin of Mainwaring's biography of Handel. I have the note here somewhere." Peter looked through a few papers and extracted a sheet with the King's words copied from Jonathan Keates' book *Handel: the Man and His Music*. Peter read aloud in his best King George accent: "Quote—'G.F. Handel was ever honest, nay excessively polite, but like all men of sense would talk all, and hear none and scorned the advice of any but the Woman He loved, but his Amours were rather of short duration, always within the pale of his own profession'—end quote (p. 15). George the Third was considerably younger than Handel, so his knowledge of Handel's actions would have come later in Handel's life. This would suggest that Handel's affairs with, we must assume, singers who worked with him reflected an ongoing pattern. Although I find it hard to imagine the pudgy, bewigged Handel of later years as a Don Juan."

"Oh, I don't know," said Katherine. "I think the painting of him by Philippe Mercier in 1730 is pretty sexy. A little five o'clock shadow, a stubble of hair, minus that huge white wig, and while he was not by any means as slender as he was in the Italian painting of years earlier, still he carried his large size well—a big man, not an obese man. This would have been when he was around forty-five. I imagine Handel's creative energy and verve attracted the attentions of many women he directed as impresario at that point in his career. But for now let us consider the consequences of his not marrying anyone, either inside or outside his profession. Some biographers argue that the life of a musician made marriage an unwise choice and that Handel was simply showing responsibility by not subjecting anyone to such a life. But I suspect that he would have married if he wanted to. I think he chose not to marry because he did not find the legal commitment of marriage necessary, or perhaps even appealing."

CD waved a hand. "I'm not sure what you mean by legal commitment," he said. "It seems that Handel was eager to be accepted as a gentleman, not simply a hireling or a working musician. Chances are, as Alison said, if he had wanted to marry with the aim of ensuring his status as a gentleman, he could have married Miss Buxtehude or some other German gentry daughter. But Handel seems not to have liked the way marriage and economic or social positions were connected. The alternative he chose was to move out of the realm of paid musician or music teacher and into the chancier career of composer and entrepreneur. It may be that even then, as a young man, he decided that love, sex, friendship—any personal or intimate relationship—should not be tied to legal or public agreements. Maybe he wanted his private life to be really, really private."

"I don't know much about what marriages were like in Handel's time," Brad said, joining in. "Like CD says, maybe Handel just did not see any advantage in getting married—in fact, maybe he saw marriage as getting in the way of what he wanted from personal relationships. He seems to have had these affairs that must have been satisfying sexually, and he had friendships that satisfied his social needs. I suppose the one thing that he did not have was the traditional 'wife and children' that most people assume a man would want, especially as he got older. Not to be cynical, but what else is marriage for besides assuring that you have progeny who will look after you in your old age, carry on your genes, and inherit your worldly goods?"

Ross stood up and walked over to the buffet. "Maybe we are getting a little ahead of ourselves," he said. "Handel was only in his early twenties when he was in Italy. If you think about the opera librettos that Handel accepted and immersed himself in, over the course of his career, well, I think it is clear that he did see the great power and attraction marriage held for the characters in his operas and the audiences who heard them. Probably he himself felt that celebrated yearning for love that most people feel, especially when they are young. How else could he dramatically represent the deeply passionate kind of love at the heart of so much of his music? I would sooner guess that he simply did not find the one person who inspired him to want to marry. I think he regarded the idealized women he showcased in his operas as goddesses, true heroines—women worthy of the deeply moving music he wrote. I wouldn't doubt that he yearned to find a real soul mate, just as, in his operas, he cast the many heroes longing for and sometimes scheming to win their ladies—and of course marrying them once they were won. When I listen to Handel's music, I hear an emotional depth that suggests the kind of longing for love he evoked in his best arias. I think he was a man with his heart on his sleeve, even when he was young. It can be just as heartbreaking to realize that your current love is not really your soul mate as it is to be rejected by someone you love. My guess is that our young Mr. Handel dumped Vittoria because she wasn't his emotional equal."

This pronouncement certainly grabbed everyone's attention. After several long moments of silence, Clara spoke up. "I don't mean this as a criticism, but—unless we see some evidence that Handel really said that, you know, Vittoria wasn't his equal or his soulmate—I think this is just an interpretation. I mean, well I suppose that would be a reason to reject her, but why that rather then some other reason? Unless we are no longer really talking about Handel here and instead just thinking generally about why people reject a lover or choose not to marry."

Ross nodded and smiled over at Katherine. "I think this is your territory," he said. With a little frown, Katherine said, "I suppose we are doing both—talking about Handel AND talking in general about why people might choose not to marry. There has been a lot written on what is involved in offering an interpretation, an explanation, a theory. When something strikes us as 'just an interpretation,' my guess is that we feel there is insufficient evidence for accepting the interpretation as a viable explanation. Clara wants to see IN WRITING the notion that Handel considered Vittoria less than his equal. Certainly that might be convincing, but how likely is it that Handel would have ever written such a statement, even if he believed it? Besides, most people don't have that kind of insight into their own motives. That's why we have therapists. No, I think we have to accept that Ross has given us an interpretation that makes sense to him. But I also think we can ask him to elaborate. How about it, Ross?"

"Elaborate, hmm?" said Ross. "Ok, let's look at the kind of music that held the strongest attraction for Handel. It wasn't church music—though most people assume so because of *Messiah* and the later biblical oratorios. What really captured Handel's passionate devotion, we must assume, was the prospect of creating operas, and operas were all about conflicted love relationships. Granted, he didn't write the librettos. Instead, he interpreted them, enhanced them, took their dramatic potential and made it live. Now, you might argue that he just liked high drama. But most biographers and musicologists agree that Handel's arias, especially those composed for his female singers, were richly empathetic. He really felt the passion and anguish of thwarted love and knew how to make those feelings obvious in the music his singers performed. Could he create that kind of deeply moving music without himself feeling the kind of fervor he was hoping to convey through his music? Maybe he could, but my take on how creative people do their thing is that they have to have a genuine passion that demands expression. So, back to my claim that Handel ditched Vittoria because she didn't match him emotionally. She was a singer. If she failed to convey the same intense passion he felt as composer, Handel would know it. And he would be disappointed. That is my view."

Across the table, CD indicated that he had a comment. He looked over at Ross with a nod but also a wry smile. "I like the idea that Handel used his music to express his own deep emotions. I'm inclined to say that is true. But we really don't know much about how musical expression happens. Humans sing, but so do birds and whales. For humans, music has become a very sophisticated kind of communication. And Handel was a very sophisticated musician. He was celebrated for his skill in performing as a harpsichordist and organist, and of course he was a composer and a conductor. But no one can say with certainty, when a performer sings or plays, that the performer is good because he or she has great emotional depth. That's really just a metaphor. We could as easily say that the performer is highly skilled. The effect is the same. So, much as I would like to think that Handel created music that allowed him to express deep driving emotions that needed expression, I think that would be more me talking about my own relationship to music than a real understanding of Handel's talent. On the other hand, as a gay man, I can completely understand why Handel would not want to marry Vittoria, or any woman for that matter, if he was attracted to men rather than women. I think it is possible that his music had nothing to do with it."

Rayette waved her sheaf of letters. "I think there is ample evidence that Handel was NOT gay. The rumormongers report him having affairs with women, not men. Gossips would have found out about homosexual affairs if he had had them. Over the course of his life, Handel had plenty of rivals or enemies who would have benefited from tarnishing his reputation if they could prove any sort of misconduct, and sodomy was considered a crime in the 1700s. On the other hand, I would agree that Handel's music has nothing to do with why he chose not to marry. Instead, I think CD's other suggestion is more likely—I think Handel was a very, very private man, so private, in fact, that he found the idea of matrimonial intimacy unappealing, maybe even frightening. It would make sense that someone who is as focused, cerebral, and creative as Handel was just might find intimate interactions with another person too invasive, too revealing. I wouldn't be surprised to find that Handel needed to be a bit drunk to allow himself the affairs he had with Vittoria or anyone else he took on as a lover. But marriage? There's no escaping into yourself there. My guess is Handel was conscientious enough to know he would not make a good marriage partner."

"Let me get this straight," said Brad. "Handel is too bashful to get married, but he plays solo organ or harpsichord performances in front of hundreds of people every chance he gets? He's not afraid to play in front of a prince or a Pope, but he has 'performance anxiety' around women? How likely is that? Peter read us the little note from King George—the one suggesting Handel was involved, shall we say, with singer after singer. It sounds to me like he just didn't want to give up his independence. I think he liked being free to love 'em and leave 'em. Sorry ladies, but there's an old saying—'Why buy the cow when you can get the milk for free?'"

A collective groan greeted this crude idiom. "Ok, ok," said Katherine, "perhaps we should wait to see if we learn anything more on the subject in later letters. I do have one concern that hasn't been voiced in our group so far. Given the, I think, convincing rumors that Handel had multiple affairs with women starting at a fairly young age, I wonder if any of his amours ever resulted in an unwanted pregnancy. I suppose that would be reason to choose married women for such affairs rather than unmarried ones. They didn't have DNA tests back then, so any child conceived by a married woman would be considered her husband's child. I've never heard anyone speculate on any illegitimate Handel children, but, still, I wonder how he avoided the possibility if he was as sexually active as it seems he was. What do you think?"

Rebecca waved a hand. "Just as a point of interest, the methods of birth control in the eighteenth century were pretty ineffective. They did, in fact, have some rather horrible sounding condoms made of animal intestines or linen cloth soaked in chemicals, and these were sold at the theaters, so Handel would have had access to them. And then there were also some very dangerous folk methods for inducing abortion, often leading to the death of the woman. Sadly, illegitimate children were often abandoned or left in the care of hospitals or orphanages. When I was doing my research on governesses, one of the disturbing things I discovered was how often couples who were waiting to marry found themselves with a child on the way. Legal systems were slow to protect women in such cases. And, just as Hardy showed us in *Tess of the d'Urbervilles*, there really was a double standard with regard to sex—still is, I would say."

Brad raised his glass and grinned. "Ok, I apologize for the rude saying. But I still think Handel was probably pretty street smart when it came to women. His father was a physician, after all. Don't you think doctors were especially quick to teach their boys how to avoid unwanted pregnancy and disease? Handel was just hitting puberty when his father died. I would guess the old man had talked with him about the birds and bees and probably in a very straightforward way. Back then, it was just as important to avoid being infected with syphilis as it was to avoid a pregnancy. I've seen Bernstein's *Candide*—Pangloss and his deformed nose. You know, they didn't have penicillin back then. Whatever advice his papa gave him must have worked. I don't remember hearing that he died of syphilis or any other STD."

Ross indicated that he had something to say to this. "I did a little research for a documentary some time back—one looking at how men were recruited into military service in the eighteenth century and earlier. It's true that syphilis and other sexually transmitted diseases came into prominence around that time in Europe. Actually the nickname for syphilis—the French disease—was a response to the primary source of the disease in the seventeenth and eighteenth centuries. Mostly, it was inflicted upon soldiers who consorted with prostitutes (in France, we must suppose) over the course of the many wars during that period. Typically, it was not suffered by middle-class couples who engaged in pre-marital sex or even by men or their mistresses who had fairly long-term relationships. In other words, syphilis, at least initially in that time period, was transmitted by prostitutes to soldiers. The real worry for people like Handel would be unwanted pregnancy, not sexually transmitted diseases."

When no one appeared to challenge this conclusion, Ross went on. "How did heterosexual lovers avoid getting pregnant back then? Mostly, I suppose, *coitus interruptus* or maybe some herbal concoction from folklore. Illegitimate children were a common consequence. In Handel's world, the Francke Foundation orphanage in Halle and later the Foundling Hospital in London were both responses to the presence of poor or often castoff children. As a point of interest, in England it wasn't until the mid-1750s that a wedding ceremony was necessary by law to bind individuals in a legal and religious contract. So, before then, the number of children born to parents not officially married to each other was very high. Handel must have remembered the establishment of the Francke orphanage in Halle. He later became a primary supporter of the Foundling Hospital in London. My guess is he saw the sorry state of many unwanted children in his lifetime and tried to improve their circumstances. I would not suggest that these children were necessarily any he fathered, but certainly many were simply an unfortunate part of the daily life Handel saw around him in that time period—before the advent of modern birth control."

Katherine looked over at Ross. "Thanks, Ross," she said, "I think it must be true that Handel felt genuine sympathy for the many poor and abandoned children he saw both in Halle and later in London. It's ironic that here in the twenty-first century, with birth control, morning after pills, and safe early-term abortions available, there is less concern for the well-being of unwanted children and greater concern for some ideological notion of potential life as de facto human life. I remember the first time I heard the ballad 'Mary Hamilton'—I think it was one that Joan Baez sang on her Child ballad album. The earliest versions of the ballad date from even a century before Handel's time, and to my mind it illustrates how worrisome it was that there was no way to avoid unwanted pregnancies other than abstinence. And if the man involved was rich or perhaps even, as in the ballad, the highest Stuart of all—the King, what recourse did the woman have? In most versions, Mary Hamilton kills the child or, as in JB's version, 'puts it out to sea.' But the whole system of shame and responsibility cast upon unwed mothers was clearly something the ballad singers wanted to bring before people in a dramatic way. I'll sing it for you if you wish. Just a moment, let me make sure I have it in mind."

Closing her eyes, she started singing the ballad. "Word is to the kitchen gone, and word is to the hall, that Mary Hamilton's borne a babe to the highest Stuart of all." She sang the dozen or so verses that told the story of Mary Hamilton's work as chambermaid to the queen, of her baby born in secret and sent to sea to "sink or swim," of her ride into Glasgow town and her journey to the gallows. The final verse brought tears to a number of eyes: "Last night there were four Marys. Tonight there'll be but three. There was Mary Seton and Mary Beaton, Mary Carmichael and me." Katherine knew that there were people—perhaps even some in their small Seminar group—who would say Mary Hamilton deserved her death by hanging. How could she set her own child out in a boat to drown? But of course the song was not a simple moralistic tale. How could the sad circumstances have been avoided? A cold shower for the King? Coitus interruptus? Pennyroyal tea to cause a miscarriage? But as it was, Mary Hamilton died for her sins, and the King lived on. Katherine was glad that Handel seemed more concerned for the welfare of abandoned children than for the need to shame or punish women who, for whatever reason, found themselves pregnant against their wishes.

"So you think the King raped Mary Hamilton, is that the message here?" asked Brad. "I mean if she took her chances and screwed around with the King, then she should have just taken her kid and left the palace. You can bet the Queen wouldn't want her around. I don't get why we are supposed to feel sorry for her. She must have known what she was getting into. And the King tells her to come down from the gallows, to come and dine with him instead. Is this story supposed to have really happened? You can see why I like blues better than ballads. Blues singers just complain about their sorry lot. It seems to me this woman should have just taken her baby and left the scene. Maybe it was unfair, but that's life."

Rebecca nearly knocked over her chair in her eagerness to answer to this comment. "Unfair is hardly the word. But really what is interesting is that some anonymous ballad singer made up a song based on some sketchy facts about royalty and an unfortunate working girl, and the song became one that listeners identified with and passed on. Something struck a chord with audiences for more than four centuries—something about how humans can't seem to sort out the tangle among sexual pleasure, power, and social commitments. Mary Hamilton is one of the Child ballads, didn't you say, Katherine? What's important isn't so much whether the exact incident really happened. It's how effective it is in making people think about things that make life difficult, painful. And maybe what we can do to make things better. Certainly effective birth control would have been a boon to people in Mary Hamilton's time, or Handel's time. I agree with Katherine that it is backward and even cruel that there are still people who stand in the way of any woman having control over whether she conceives or aborts a fetus once she discovers she is pregnant. You would think we still lived in those antiquated times. What wouldn't Mary Hamilton have given for a morning after pill?"

Across the table, Wait lifted his fork yet again. "I think I started this all with a comment about how views on marriage were different back in Handel's time. The thing is—once people start talking about marriage, it always seems to revert into a discussion about reproduction—or if not that, then economics. But—well—people get married for other reasons, even if money and having children do enter into it. I was wondering, for example, what kind of example Handel's own mother and father offered to him. Do you suppose he had a good feeling about marriage based on his experience in his own home—at least until his father died? Maybe having a father who was so much older than his mother gave Handel a skewed view of marriage. Sometimes children make a point of avoiding anything like their own parents' relationships."

"That's a good point," Peter joined in. "Handel seemed to be a smart man—someone very much aware of his own objectives and inclinations. He may have concluded that married life was not for him simply by seeing how marriage played out between the two people who were his parents. My guess is that if he liked what he saw, he would have wanted to have the same thing for himself. The only relevant anecdote about Handel that might indicate how his parents got along is the one about his hiding a clavichord in the attic against his father's wishes—but evidently with his mother's approval. While Handel benefited by having the instrument to practice on, still he may have found the necessity of keeping a secret with one parent in defiance of the other a disturbing thing. Perhaps he concluded that it is best to just be your own person, with no 'other' to whom you are answerable. What do you think, Katherine?"

Katherine started, as though pulled out of a deep thought. "Yes, I suppose we, along with Handel, must ask just what it is that marriage offers that would make it so desirable. There would have to be some advantages that outweigh the disadvantages for someone like Handel who clearly values his independence." She walked over to the flip chart where she had earlier written the words Marriage, Sexuality, and Love. "So, what might a person like Handel want if he DID in fact decide to marry? Someone he admired and wanted to spend time with, I suppose. What else?" She wrote her suggestion on the chart and added five more as others suggested them. They came up with a fine list, or so Katherine thought.

Characteristics people are seeking when they marry:

Someone you admire and want to spend time with
Someone you share a history with
Someone to care for you in illness
Someone you can trust with your weaknesses
Someone who welcomes your affection
Someone who cares and wants to see you grow

Rayette said, "You know, I like that list, but the one that really stands out for me is the one that mentions trust. I think that might have been what Handel missed in the relationship between his parents. Some people find it very hard to give or accept trust in an intimate relationship. Handel strikes me as that kind of person. That's not to say he couldn't have trusted someone that he really loved, but maybe—just as Ross said—he never found that person. I wrote a little poem while we were discussing this issue—not necessarily about Handel, but just my thoughts about what it means to want to get married, or really to not get married. Would you like to hear it?" The entire room answered, "Yes, indeed."

Reading from her notebook, Rayette shared her poem:

You are a good man.
You are not what I want.
You bring me lovely flowers.
You are not what I want.
Your house is landscaped, and the mortgage is burned.
You are not what I want.
Together we applaud fine talents and impressive performances.
You are not what I want.
We share a dinner but never drink from the same glass.
You are not what I want.

As Rayette finished reading the poem, CD smiled and said, "Yes, that's exactly why Alex and I DID want to get married. We trusted each other enough to drink from the same glass—and that's saying a lot because I'm usually pretty picky about such things. I like the poem. Sorry about that guy—whoever he is."

Rayette laughed. "No worries. Not all poems are autobiographical, you know. I think—besides the issue of trust—one thing people look for when they consider getting married is simply, to put it in the language of our list: Someone who admires you and loves who you are. But really sometimes it is just a gut feeling, not so much compatibility."

"That rounds out our list nicely," Katherine said. "I like the poem, too. But I heard it in a slightly different way than you did, CD. I suppose it's the chicken and egg thing—do you trust someone because you want him, or do you want someone because you trust him? And I think if we go back and look at Lydia's letter—her comments to Handel about his affair with Vittoria, maybe we can see one more thing that seemed to be necessary for Handel. He evidently was drawn to, enraptured, swept off his feet by women who sang in operas. Lydia chided him for surrendering to fantasies on the stage. She worried that the powerful artifice great actors and singers bring to their performances seduced him and cast real life into the shadows. Maybe he could simply not accept that mundane reality did not include people who sing their passions to each other. He wouldn't be the first person to love someone who is exciting—reason enough."

"What can we take away from our letter-enhanced peek into Handel's life so far?" Katherine asked. "It seems that women found him attractive and he enjoyed sexual intimacy. It's possible that he never found a woman who was a match for him emotionally, as Ross suggested, at least not one available for him to marry. I suppose it is also possible that he was a gay man who never really accepted his own sexual orientation, since in Handel's time homosexuality was considered sinful and illegal. Lydia seemed to think he was too attached to fantasy rather than reality in his relationships. Perhaps his quest for exciting, imaginative love affairs was what gave his music its special fire. The Byronic hero had not yet emerged on the literary stage, but perhaps Handel was a man in that mold—someone whose intensity, passion, and intelligence was flawed by poor judgment and social circumstance. My own inclination is to recognize Handel as consumed by his drive to compose, play, and help others produce the music that was his constant and dearest companion. I think anyone, any lover, would have to play second fiddle to his music. At least that seemed to be his attitude when he was young."

"Before we leave the subject," she continued, "I would like to go back to the quotation Peter shared with us—the lines British King George the Third wrote upon first reading a copy of Mainwaring's biography of Handel. The king was more than fifty years younger than Handel, but he admired Handel's music even as a young boy. His remark that Handel 'scorned the advice of any but the woman he loved' is telling. Let's say that maybe Handel and the young prince interacted in some context from which such an observation might arise. What kind of relationship would the prince have noticed that would prompt such a remark? If nothing else it would have been clear to him that Handel respected the intelligence and opinion of the woman he loved. It is possible that the prince disapproved of this favoring of a woman's opinion, but most evidence suggests that the future king admired Handel and probably accepted Handel's attitude of respect as a good thing. Personally, I am grateful to George the Third for sharing this glimpse into Handel's private life—despite George's later mistreatment of the American colonies. The king gave us a valuable insight into Handel's character and attitude. I think we can accept the insight as genuine."

Katherine turned and looked at the clock on Forella's wall. "Tempus fugit. In light of our discussion, I thought we should all listen to one of Handel's lovely duets—this one from a philosophical ode composed later when Handel was in his fifties. The duet is 'As Steals the Morn upon the Night.' Here is a recording for each of you, compliments of Forella. Think of Handel and the woman whose opinions he so valued as you listen. Enjoy. Thanks everyone for your thoughtful comments. See you all next time."

CHAPTER 9

The Lure of London

Ross ran arpeggios up and down the fine Steinway that graced the richly appointed music room in his Indianapolis home. He loved that piano, not simply for its excellent sound and glossy German finish but perhaps mostly because his grandmother had played it and introduced him to its potential for hours of musical improvisation when he was a young boy. He thought of her now, a woman very much like Forella, strong and determined. She herself had grown up playing an inexpensive old upright at the church down the street from her childhood home. When Ross's father bought the Steinway for their mansion in Kingsport, his mother-in-law was delighted. When she came for her annual visits, she and Ross spent summer afternoons "tickling the ivories." He wasn't sure then exactly what that phrase meant, but he always liked to hear her say it. He thought of her and smiled and played some Hoagy Carmichael tunes he had learned by ear, listening to her play.

WHEN EVERYONE GATHERED FOR THE next meeting of the Handel Seminar, there was a loud eruption of talk in Forella's dining room. Benfey was hard pressed to record any of it, but she did try, as the topic of conversation was the splendid Handel duet Katherine had sent home with them last time. The consensus was that "As Steals the Morn" is a delight, well worth keeping on whatever electronic device allows one to hear it over and over again. Benfey did catch Rebecca's enthusiastic snippet: "No wonder the Brits love the song. It's like a Tin Pan Alley hit—only much better."

As plates of food found their way from buffet to table, Katherine stood, raised her water glass, and smiled. "Cheers," she said. "I'm so glad you enjoyed 'As Steals the Morn.' It is a lovely piece, isn't it? One of those melodies that just stays with you—but not in an annoying way. Peter has promised a couple more letters for us today, but before we move on—and while we are distracted by Annie's inviting buffet—maybe we could learn more about this duet. I've done a little research, but if anyone else has some information for us, I'd be happy to hear it. Yes, Rayette—the floor is yours—and thanks." Katherine sat down and turned her attention to one of Annie's delicious open face sandwiches.

"Well, I will have to say that I was intrigued as much by the words as the music," said Rayette. "This isn't a piece written while Handel was in Italy. Instead it is one he and his English friends James Harris and Charles Jennens cooked up years later, during Handel's back and forth period of transition from opera to oratorio and from Italian to English language works. As I said, I was especially interested in the words of the song. So, here's a little background. The theaters were having a hard time selling opera to English audiences in the later 1730s. Librettos in Italian were falling out of fashion—at least in London. So, Handel and his two friends looked around for something to attract English listeners and suit English singers. James Harris suggested basing a musical text on John Milton's early philosophical poems 'L'Allegro' and 'Il Penseroso.' The titles were in Italian, but the poems were in Milton's impressive English verse. Handel was eager to work with Milton's texts and to collaborate with Harris and Jennens. By this time Handel's fluency in English was well-established, even if everyone claimed he still spoke with a strong German accent. He was very taken with Milton's poetry. In fact his next work was the much more famous setting of Milton's *Samson Agonistes*."

"And so," Rayette went on, "to make a long story short, James Harris outlined a libretto contrasting the two poems—'L'Allegro' presenting the happy man, or mirth and 'Il Penseroso' depicting the pensive person, or melancholy. Rather than leaving them clumped as separate poems as Milton had done, Handel felt the two moods needed to be set as a back and forth dialogue, and, in addition, he asked Charles Jennens to write a third section in which the two contrasting perspectives are reconciled to reflect a more balanced attitude rather than one extreme or the other. In response, Jennens wrote the third scene 'Il Moderato,' basing the style on Milton with a little Shakespeare for good measure. Jennens was a Shakespeare scholar. Both Jennens and Handel agreed that people who are prudent 'keep the golden mean.' In other words, both men argued for a balanced life—neither a slave to pleasure nor a moping martyr. 'All things in moderation' seemed to be their advice. Or, as Jennens wrote, God gave moderation 'mad mortals from themselves to save'—an early self-help text if ever there was one."

Peter laughed. "Of course, two best sellers—*I'm OK, You're Too Happy* and *I'm OK, You're Too Mopey*. And a sequel—*Keep to the Golden Mean.* Why not? And set to music—the easier to remember their good advice. Really, I'm surprised Handel got away with this. But then, I suppose if they could claim that they were simply giving the audience a musical Milton, who would object?"

Katherine smirked at Peter. "All right. Perhaps we should get on with the letters from Lydia. Although I do think the underlying message of the duet is relevant to this period of time in Handel's life. That's why I suggested sending the recording of 'As Steals the Morn' along with you last time. I'll come back to that in a bit. But come, Peter, rather than poking fun at Handel for composing self-help music, share the letters you have transcribed for today. What does Lydia have to say this time?"

Peter gave copies of the letters to Angela, who handed two sheets to each person at the table. "As you will see," said Peter, "Lydia switches to English in the second letter. So from now on, the transcriptions are entirely of her own words, no more translations from me. And you'll see that Handel is on the move. Happy reading! These really take the story to the next stage."

Here are the transcriptions Peter offered them:

To: G F Handel, Esqr.
Palazzo Grimani
Venice

23 February 1710

My Dear Mr. Handel,
Edward and I were so pleased to see you there in Venice in the thick of the opera season. And what a thrill to hear your Agrippina. Senora Durastanti sang the lead role excellently. Eggy could not have blessed me with a more wonderful birthday surprise than our journey to Italy and the good fortune to hear your opera and witness the great shouts of approval. "Viva il caro Sassone!" indeed. We had thought we would be in town only to hear Caldara's Partenope and perhaps be so lucky as to visit with you. Ah, my dear Gif, I could not have been more proud! You have used your time well there in the land of opera. I noticed that both the Duke of Manchester and the ambassador from Hanover were eager to talk with you. We could hardly get a word in. I regret that we could not stay longer, but Edward was committed to a meeting on behalf of Sir John in Florence, and we needed to move on. I do hope you are persuaded by either of their offers to leave Italy and continue your career in one of their homelands. In truth, I am especially hopeful that you listen most to Manchester as Eggy anticipates a need to return permanently to London within the next year or two. It would be so good to be in a city that always had your music to offer—and, of course, you there to write, play, conduct, and discuss it.

    You warned that you might be leaving to visit your mother before the start of summer. I do hope this letter reaches you. We have just returned to Hamburg from Rome. It has been a long and exhausting journey, but again I can think of little that would have pleased me more. I believe Edward felt my thirtieth birthday needed some special celebration. And you, my young maestro, here it is your birthday again. Which is it? Can you be all of twenty-five and already a star who draws audiences across the continent and among the English gentry? Even Durastanti brought with her an aria from La Resurrezione—the one the Pope would not let her sing in Rome. How wonderful—both the lovely aria and the blatant disregard for papal dictates! I was so very amused—though I must say that Mary Magdalene's words hardly fit into Agrippina's comport. Still, it is a fine showpiece for Durastanti. She must adore you for providing such a perfect song for her talents. You are a generous composer to let her carry the piece with her wherever she goes. I heard she sang it as well as an insertion in Caldara's opera.

Cardinal Grimani, your gracious host, was very kind to include us among his guests at the Saturday dinner. I was reminded once again how very much I miss having you at Sir John's informal gatherings. Your brief stay in Naples must have been an amazing adventure. I hope at a future time I will hear some of the songs you wrote as wedding music while you were there. And I would love to hear you elaborate on the notion of imagination you shared with us. Edward had not heard of your Professor Vico, but he found his ideas most interesting, as did I. To me, a strong imagination is what allows you to express so convincingly in music the feelings your heroines experience. Since you are a man, how could that empathy erupt but through a rich imagination? I think your Professor Vico is right. It is not simply the ability to critique others' work that leads to compositional competence. More important, especially in composing an opera, is the ability to imagine and empathize. And that you do so very well. Ah, my dear Gif, I miss hearing you defend these new ideas that enliven the best dinner parties. Eggy found a copy of the professor's book at a shop in Florence. He promised to help me struggle through the Latin text. I will be a more informed interlocutor next time we meet.

It is possible that such a meeting might come sooner than you would guess. If you do indeed visit your family in Halle, I may see you there. We will be going south to Hanover and Halle late in the summer. May you have safe travels wherever they may take you.

I have the honor to be, ever yours,

Mrs. Edward Grayston
Rotth Haus, Hamburg

And the second letter:

To: G F Handel, Esqr.
Kapellmeister to the Court
Hanover

27 September 1710

My Dear Mr. Handel,
Once again, Gif, I was so happy to meet your mother. She is a dear lady. It was gracious of her to speak with me in French, as my German, despite my living here in Hamburg for nearly seven years, is so rudimentary. What a wonderful, lively time we had there in Halle! Edward had heard of your decision to accept the position in Hanover but then move on to London for much of the next year. I am so glad we were able to visit you in your home city while you were there.

[Here Lydia switches from French to English]. And now, in light of this imminent journey, I shall write the remainder of this letter in English. Johann assures me that you have several English-speaking friends there in Hanover who can help you. And you will be glad to know that all of us in Sir John's retinue took up a fund to buy you Mister Kersey's new dictionary. It should arrive by the post before you leave. I expect to hear flawless English next time we meet. Truth be told, you were doing quite well before you left for Florence. And as I am sure you found in Italy, once you are in daily contact with people who speak the language you want to learn, it will come easily. Besides *you are such a linguist. I know you will tame the language just as quickly as you compose.*

I confess to being confused by your accepting the position there in Hanover. You seemed clearly so eager to try your skills in London. And Hanover's opera house is closed. Edward says you are wise to pin down a sure thing in the event that fortune does not smile upon you in London. I, on the other hand, have seen how you succeed where others would not. My sister says there is a great cry for opera in London these days, and your name is high on the list of people they hope to hear. Your Agrippina has been carried there piecemeal— the strongest arias. I think there will be great excitement when you arrive. And yet, I do know that it is a new kind of musical career you contemplate—one with few guarantees and many risks. I have always admired that boldness in you—a different kind of bravery than that seen on the battlefield.

Marie is slowly and painfully accepting the truth that you will not be returning to Hamburg nor sending for her to join you in Hanover. And Vittoria, I understand, will be in Hanover with her husband, Jean-Baptiste. It is a time of change for you, my dear young maestro. I have never known you to turn away from a challenge, and I am certain there will be many. As your mother said, "A prudent man has more than one string to his bow." I could see that she wanted you to stay in Hanover as it is closer to Halle, but she saw, as we all did, how the lure of London has captured you. Please call upon your friends if there is a need. May good fortune follow you.

I have the honor to be, ever yours,

Mrs. Edward Grayston
Rotth Haus, Hamburg

Katherine set aside her teacup and looked around to see if everyone had finished reading. "Thank you, Peter," she said. "Very interesting that in the second letter she announces her intention to write henceforth in English—AND that she and her friends have sent him an English dictionary, a relatively new kind of resource at that time. Most biographers agree that Handel really was very good with languages, just as Lydia suggests. Of course the dictionary would not be a dual language one, so it might not have been much help to him. There is an amusing anecdote shared by one of Handel's later librettists—Thomas Morell—about Handel coming by carriage to his, that is Morell's, house at five in the morning to ask what the word 'billow' meant in the libretto he was setting. When Morell answered sleepily that the word meant 'a wave of the sea,' Handel immediately left and returned to his composing without another word. Clearly Handel paid serious attention to the language of his dramatic works—and perhaps he was a bit of a perfectionist."

"So, what themes do we want to pull out of these two letters? As I was reading, I noted several topics in the margin—probably more than we want to cover today. This is roughly when our earlier timeline ends, but Lydia hints at most of the activities that occupied Handel at this time—his decision to leave Italy, the performance of his very popular *Agrippina* just as he leaves Venice, his visit to Halle to see his mother, the somewhat puzzling acceptance of a position at the court in Hanover, and the clear determination to visit London as soon as possible. There are some personal bits, such as the comments about Marie and Victoria, but the important thing, it seems to me, is the new direction his career takes as he leaves Italy. Questions about career choices certainly tie Handel to life in the twenty-first century. I think career choice will have to be one of our themes," Katherine said as she once again wrote out her suggestion on the flip chart Angela had provided.

"Yeah, I'm very interested to dig a little deeper into why he left Italy and went in this new direction," said Brad. "And I'm wondering about the whole question of the arts in society at that time. I mean, why does he even have the option of following a career in music in the first place? How could he make a living at it? It's still hard today to make a living as a musician or artist. Believe me, I've seen lots of people struggling just to have music or art as a sideline—you know, something they really love but not their day job. What were Handel's options? And why did he leave what seemed like a pretty cushy lifestyle in Italy? I've never really understood what that system of patronage was all about anyway. How does it compare with what we have—or don't have—today?"

Katherine wrote SUPPORT FOR THE ARTS on the flip chart just under her earlier theme: CAREER CHOICES. "What else?" she asked, and she was surprised to see Peter signal that he had a comment. "Yes, Peter. What do you suggest?"

"I'm not sure this really stands out in these two letters, but I see a few hints pointing to how Lydia understands Handel's character—or maybe how WE might view Handel's character. Actually, Katherine, your sending home with us that marvelous duet started me thinking about what we know of Handel's character up to this point. And maybe what motivations seem to indicate who he is, what his basic disposition is. Is he a happy-go-lucky extrovert—a happy man? Or is he a more serious, contemplative introvert? Can we tell from the choices he makes and the hints Lydia supplies in her letters? Or, is he, as Rayette explained, more likely to follow a middle path between extremes of character? What can we know about his character as we see him in these letters—at age twenty-five?"

Katherine added CHARACTER as a third theme on the flip chart. "I'm sure there are many more topics we could think about after reading these two letters, but let's start with these three," she said. "It might be good, as Brad suggested, to go back and talk a little about the system of patronage and how it affected Handel's life here at the beginning of his career. Handel must have been aware of how the system worked long before he set off for Italy. Ecclesiastical and royal patronage emerged as an especially strong force in Europe during the Renaissance and continued throughout the Baroque period. Basically priests, kings, and noblemen enlisted musicians and artists as part of their public relations team. Unfortunately, musicians and composers were often regarded as hired servants and their fortunes were tied to their patrons' varying successes and favors. This was clearly part of what prompted Georg Handel senior's desire that his son go into a profession such as law rather than one dependent on patronage. Still, it was a bit of noble patronage—the Duke of Weissenfels and his gift of tuition money—that set young Handel on the road to a musical career. The elder Handel must have been persuaded by the Duke's gift and expression of support. Patronage has both its faults and its virtues."

Wait waved his letters in an effort to get Katherine's attention. "Yes, Wait? Feel free to speak up," she laughed. "Well," Wait began, "I'm with Brad on this. I really don't understand what it means to have a patron. How is it different from, say, being hired by a restaurant to play for the dinner crowd every Friday? Or, maybe being signed to a record label or listed with a gallery if you are a painter? Isn't it just a way of getting paid for your work?"

Alison raised a hand and said, "I'll take this one." Katherine said, "Oh, thank you, thank you. This is getting out of my limited curriculum." Alison went over to the flip chart, turned over a fresh sheet, and wrote in its center the word RUSPOLI. "The Marquis, and later Prince, Francesco Maria Ruspoli," she said, "was one of Handel's patron's in Italy—probably the most significant patron over the course of Handel's stay in Italy. He was the one Handel was staying with when that painting we saw earlier was created—the one where Handel was reviewing Ruspoli's regiment. Ruspoli's primary residence was in Rome, but he had several other palaces in the countryside. His was an impressive estate. He was easily one of the richest men in all of Italy. So, let's take a look at how the patronage system brought Handel and Ruspoli together in Italy in the early 1700s."

To the left of the name RUSPOLI, Alison wrote the words OTHER NOBLES, and to the right, she wrote the word BISHOPS. She drew two double-ended arrows from these two groups in toward RUSPOLI. "These two coalitions represent Ruspoli's peers, the people he interacted with as equals and the individuals he tried to impress with his power, wealth, and sophistication. The power and wealth part he demonstrated through administrators and servants who maintained his vast estates and officers and soldiers who made up his private army." Here Alison drew arrows from the words ESTATE SERVANTS and ARMIES in toward the name RUSPOLI. She continued: "Up until the period of the Renaissance that would have been all that was required—a show of wealth and military might. However, as refined taste and leisure to indulge a love of the arts came to be associated with the nobility—whether secular or ecclesiastical, princely folk such as Ruspoli found that they needed to bring talented artists and musicians into their households as evidence of their own enlightened discernment and cultural superiority."

Alison wrote the words ARTISTS and MUSICIANS below the name RUSPOLI and drew arrows in from these two groups toward their patron—RUSPOLI. "You can see," she continued, "that the musicians and artists who benefited from the patronage system were actually there to serve the patron, much as were servants and soldiers. But there was a certain genteel quality to this servitude, at least so long as the patron felt he gained cultural capital from the arrangement. Handel was actually pretty savvy, especially for such a young man. While he did live at Ruspoli's palace, ate his food, drank his wine, and enjoyed the company of his noble friends, Handel did not contract to serve in Ruspoli's household. He wrote music for him as an honored guest and performed as a talented visitor who happened to be passing through. Handel had determined when he left Hamburg for Italy in 1706 that he would go "on his own bottom," as Mainwaring reported. He was determined even then to be as independent as was possible given the by then conventional expectation that musicians tie themselves to a specific court or church if they hope to have a successful musical career. For nearly four years, Handel managed to make the arrow from himself to his various patrons a two-way arrow. He gained as much as he gave, and in the end, he chose to leave rather than make a commitment to any one patron or church."

Brad spoke up again. "So you're saying he didn't really get paid for the composing and performing he did while he was in Italy? He was just a talented guest who enjoyed entertaining Ruspoli's rich friends? That doesn't sound like much of a deal. No wonder he left."

The Handel Letters

"Well," said CD, "it isn't all that much different than people who depend on getting grants from various sources today. Some grants pay a stipend, but some just cover expenses. Handel had his living expenses covered in a lordly way. Come to think of it, that may be why he started putting on weight. He wanted to make sure he reaped the rewards that were available to him—great quantities of excellent vittles."

"CD's right to a certain extent," said Rebecca, "but the early eighteenth century was an unusual time. What we think of as the middle class was really still emerging, and it wasn't clear how middle-class people fit into the economic and social system. The professional class—lawyers, doctors, bankers, and, of course, the educated clergy—were aiming toward the lifestyle of the nobility. Handel's father had accepted a position as surgeon at the court of Weissenfels, but he also ran a wine-selling business from his home in Halle. People not born into wealth and landownership needed to find ways to make money without assuming the role of servants. Handel had evidently learned that attitude growing up. I think it makes perfect sense that he preferred being treated as an honored guest rather than as a paid employee in the households of his wealthy patrons in Italy."

Clara stood and walked over to the flip chart, where Alison's graphic of the patronage system tied to Ruspoli and his household still silently explained itself to viewers. She wrote two more words below Alison's chart: SCIENTISTS and MERCHANTS. "There are plenty of other categories of people with growing influence during Handel's time," she said. "But the connection between these other groups and the system of patronage wasn't so clear. Just as Rebecca suggested about the professional class, there was an increasing number of people who were moving away from the lingering patronage system. After all, the patronage system harkened back to the old feudal system anathematized by the emerging middle class. But even in the age of enlightenment, scientists, for example, usually still had to have aristocratic connections if they hoped to be taken seriously, but some–people like Benjamin Franklin—managed to be accepted for their innovative ideas and intelligent commentary. And merchants—well, money talked then just as it does now. People like Ruspoli were of an era that was fading while Handel and the people he found most attractive in places like London were part of the future—even if that future wasn't quite there yet."

Ross wandered over to the chart as well, holding aloft his glass of fine bourbon in a salute. "Principe Ruspoli, here's to you and your courtly crew. Methinks you taught our young Mister Handel just as much by what you did NOT do for him as by what you did. You did not manage to train him up as a sycophant nor beat down his natural enthusiasm. Or, as Obi-Wan Kenobi would say, you did not succeed in seducing him to the dark side. You did, I think, give him a taste for the life of a gentleman, and he seems to have sought out the means to sustain that kind of life ever after. What interests me is how Handel, a fatherless boy with few connections and haling from a small town in Germany, learned the ropes of musical patronage just well enough ultimately to steer clear of them and forge a new kind of career as a composer and musical entrepreneur. Not patronage, but rather, incentive was perhaps Ruspoli's greatest gift to Handel. Like an eighteenth century Frank Sinatra, Handel was determined to do it his way. And he did."

"Methinks," said Katherine, "that we have a bit of what Clara earlier graciously identified as interpreting going on here, and—imagine that—it's Ross doing the interpreting again. But actually, Ross, I'm fine with that. We can't really know what Handel's thoughts were, but we do at least have a few hints from Lydia. She says she has already seen him succeed where others have failed. She admires his boldness in going after a career that carries many risks but represents his passion. Well, she doesn't use the word 'passion.' That's what we would say today. Like Ross, I am interested in Handel's character, but I will admit that I probably interpret his actions as evidence for the kind of character I would admire. To me, Handel seems eager to be not simply a gentleman but a good human, what we would call a mensch, an honorable person. I think Handel would have taken Polonius' advice to heart: 'To thine own self be true, And it must follow, as the night the day, Thou canst not then be false to any man.' I think Handel—even at age twenty-five—wanted to use his talent and energy to move humanity forward. I think he truly was a man of the Enlightenment."

This time it was Ross's turn to simply smile a smirky smile and nod. "Ok," he said, "nothing over the top here, is there? Well, perhaps a bit. What say you, Clara? Is it likely that a 'man of the Enlightenment' would be concerned to move humanity forward? Or is Katherine making a leap to the high road and dragging us along?"

Clara laughed and said, "Actually there was a strong belief in human progress and the worth of the individual in the early years of the Enlightenment. I would guess that Handel was immersed in such ideas in Germany. Remember his poem to his father? The one in which he described himself as 'dedicated to the liberal arts.' For the educated elite in the 1700s, the liberal arts meant an education in humanism and a celebration of human progress. I think Handel would very likely have absorbed that era's relish for learning but also a kind of Christian humanism—a concern for the suffering of children and the poor along with a desire to be wealthy and enterprising enough to help. It doesn't surprise me that later in life he became a big supporter of London's Foundling Hospital. The idea that a person should do good works and strive to live a good life was probably a part of Handel's upbringing. Wasn't his grandfather a clergyman? I expect he saw himself as both fortunate and worthy. He may not have had the language of later humanists who decried the supposed greater worth of the nobility, but I think he saw himself as an equal among men, noble or otherwise. And he seems to have had a very good education, even if he did not continue with his studies at the university. A man of the Enlightenment? I don't know. But certainly he was an independent spirit and never one to be cowed by royalty. Maybe Katherine is right—he aspired to be a mensch."

"To be honest," said Katherine, "I guess I am haunted by my own aspirations from when I was twenty-five. I suppose I was idealistic and maybe naïve, not that I consider myself jaded at this point or anything like that. But when I was younger, I wanted to do great things, and I believed I could. It seems to me that Handel saw himself writing music that would move people to be more compassionate, to be better people. I think that is why he was so attentive to the libretti he accepted and worked with—maybe even why he was interested in opera in the first place. Drama—even the unrealistic plots of operas—offers audiences a way to explore what makes a good person. Just like Shakespeare with his plays, Handel thought he had found an effective way to inspire and challenge people to feel more deeply and behave more virtuously. Dramatic poetry presented by a beautiful singing voice must surely be one of humanity's greatest sources of inspiration. Handel knew he could excel at creating the kind of music that would make the human voice a powerful instrument of emotional expression and inspiration. He found a way—a new career path—that would let him do it."

From her comfortable chair on the opposite side of the room, Forella reached forward and tapped Angela's arm, whispering that she had something to say. Seeing Angela's signal and nod toward Forella, Katherine said, "Excellent! We'd love to hear from you, Forella. Please do join the conversation."

Forella smiled and said, "Yes, I think Handel had a gift. At least that is what people of my generation would have called it. And as Katherine has suggested, such a conviction of great personal potential is something most people feel within themselves when they are very young. Handel must have known when he was a young boy that creating music was his destiny, his special gift. But unlike so many of us, he did not let those soulful stirrings slip away as he grew older, and, most importantly, he did not listen to those who would have discouraged him from following his bliss—as Joseph Campbell would have named it."

Taking a sip of tea, Forella waited for any comments, but hearing none, she went on. "For some reason, Campbell's advice always reminded me of the Wordsworth poem 'Intimations of Immortality.' I remember clearly the first time I encountered Wordsworth's 'Intimations' and realized that I had, like the poet, watched my trails of glory 'fade into the light of common day.' Like Katherine, I had hoped to do great things. I think we all do when we are young. And now we ask, Is it simply a more robust soul that manages to retain that creativity, that spark that was so exciting to us when we first came into life? The impressive evidence of that great soul is why I love our Mr. Handel—and probably why I am still convinced some of that creative energy is, one way or another, a part of Ross's constant, inborn artistic drive. Who knows what gives a person the soul of an artist? Is it luck? Determination? Good genes? Reincarnation? In retrospect we know Handel had the soul of an artist. How easy it would have been for him to be a dutiful son and become a lawyer. I wouldn't disparage lawyers, but what a waste that would have been! We can all celebrate those important decisions Handel made while still such a young man when so many distractions could have pulled him away from his destiny."

Ross grinned in the direction of his mother. "Ah, my friends, you can see why self-esteem has never been an issue for me. My mother has always been my best fan club. And she is such a perceptive woman! Thanks for the comparison, Mom, and of course since Handel isn't here to object, why not? Seriously, though, I agree—we all do hope to be 'the best that we can be,' maybe even to be one of life's exemplars, a force that moves humanity along the road to true greatness, or perhaps keeps that inborn greatness burning, as Wordsworth seemed to think. Then, again, maybe Handel simply had natural talent AND the right kind of parents—a father who instilled a bit of skepticism until proven wrong and a mother who thought he could DO no wrong. What do you think, Brad? If I remember right, you were the one who wondered about Handel's career decisions and how they came about."

Brad smiled broadly and said, "You're not going to like this, but I think Handel was just using good business sense. I suppose he must have had a natural talent for music, but most of us have some talent. And, yes, his mother probably was one of those wonderful parents who encourage instead of browbeat their kids. But I see Handel as a shrewd businessman and an intelligent innovator—sort of the eighteenth century equivalent of Steve Jobs or Bill Gates. I mean, look at his first job as organist in Halle. He knew right away that wasn't for him, and off he went to Hamburg. And in Hamburg, he had his day job as a violinist or as a music teacher just long enough to build up his reserves and head to Italy. I was sort of in the dark about what these patrons in Italy were all about, but it seems like they were again resources that Handel found a way to use toward his own ends. As Alison said, for Handel, it was a two-way arrow. So, now he's contemplating leaving Italy. He's learned a lot about opera making and has transformed from someone who played music into someone who mostly composed music for others to play or sing. So he needed to find a place where that skill would earn him money and even more possibilities than he had in Italy. Hanover seems to have been a fallback position. How he negotiated that clause in his contract that allowed him spend the next year in London rather than Hanover—and at full pay—well, as I said, I think he was a superb businessman. He saw the opportunities he wanted and went after them. And he must have been persuasive and energetic. He always seemed to land right where he needed to be to move ahead with his ideas. He didn't wait around for someone else to create a job description for him. He invented the job he wanted and convinced the necessary support groups that he was the man for the job."

"Business sense may have been a part of it," Rebecca chimed in, "but just a part—certainly not the most important part. Would you say that Elvis Presley was mostly a good businessman? Or Rogers and Hammerstein? The Beatles? These people were driven by something more than a desire for business success. And they weren't just entertainment drones who plied their craft as popular taste dictated. They learned what their culture and mentors had to teach and then went on to take whatever was current to a new level. Don't forget, Handel was himself an outstanding performer. That was his first source of fame. His teacher back in Halle had given him a deep understanding of the music of his time and the preceding century. In Hamburg and Italy, he learned what was needed to match music to voice. But it was his own ambition and fervor that drove him to become the artist we know. Handel had that compulsion to express himself that all great artists must have. If he hadn't had that, we wouldn't still be singing *Messiah* today."

"Well said," Wait agreed. "And Handel was at his best when he had a story to tell—when his music embodied strong emotions. I think people loved his music for the same reason people a few decades ago loved to hear Elvis or Ella Fitzgerald sing. A great and expressive voice can make people feel emotions they can't express themselves but can feel anyway, just because that gifted singer helps them feel the emotions they sing about. You know what I mean? Just like Lydia said to Handel—he gave his singer—what's her name—Durastanti—a great song that allowed her to move her audiences in a way other songs might not."

Clara waved a hand. "Wait, Wait—well, sorry, I mean, just a minute, Wait. Really, all of us—we are projecting our personal ideologies about creative genius unto this man from three hundred years ago. All we can really conclude from Lydia's letters so far is that Handel was eager to be on the move. Well, and that he was becoming very well known, even in England. He must have made the decision to be a musician back when he left the university. Hamburg and Italy were his two institutions of higher learning. By the end of 1710, he had written his dissertation—*Agrippina*—and was ready to find his first real job. I think Brad is right—Hanover was just a backup position. His real interest was in writing opera for London audiences. He must have researched the situation in London well enough to know that it was the context he wanted for writing the kind of opera he envisioned—still in Italian and sung by outstanding Italian singers, but for an audience he could educate on what excellent opera is all about. More than a businessman, Handel was an eighteenth century entrepreneur and in a certain light, an educator. His goal wasn't to create Microsoft or Wendy's. He wanted to create a popular tradition of opera in the heart of London."

"I won't deny that Handel did eventually act like the great trend-setter we celebrate today," said CD. "But if we are really interested in what prompted his decisions in that first decade of the 1700s, we can't look ahead and anachronistically ascribe motives from his more mature years as a composer. It's we gray-haired seniors who worry over our legacy. Like most people in their twenties, Handel probably wanted to have fun and feel a part of the exciting life he saw in the big cities. He found making music—either as a performer or as a composer—an exciting activity, and he wanted to be sure he was a part of it. So, he got the credentials that would open the path for him, and he headed for London—which must have been a very exciting place in the early 1700s. You know, 'How you gonna keep 'em down on the farm . . . ?' only in this case it was London rather than Paris that attracted Handel. London was where it was happening!"

Wait joined in again. "I agree with CD. Handel probably liked the sensation of being recognized as a celebrity. Here he had two important people fighting over who would get him to commit to his home place—the Duke of Manchester urging him to come to England, and the emissary from Hanover hoping to bring him back to Germany. The safest thing to do would have been to stay in Hanover—and it seems he did sign a contract. But Handel pretty much skipped out on that safe bet and went with what really excited him—opera productions in London. I'm sure I am projecting—just as Clara said we would—but I see Handel being turned off by the staid life of a professional musician in Hanover and instead being powerfully aroused by the prospect of life in London. And not just the opportunity to create the kind of music he liked. Don't forget, he was still a performer along with being a composer and director. Here was his chance to be front and center among the best singers and musicians of the day. I'll bet he found it a heady experience. No wonder he turned his back on the safe and secure way and moved to London."

Katherine smiled around at the entire room. "Ah, we are having such fun imagining ourselves as the young Mister Handel—I hate to bring us back down to earth. But time is running short again. Most of our comments have pointed toward a person impassioned and emboldened by his love of music but also fairly practical and maybe even calculating in his dealings with patrons and supporters. I wonder if that same personality came into play in his personal life. Lydia mentions the languishing Marie and his ex-lover Victoria, but it seems that Handel has set them both aside—whether painfully or not for him, we do not know. Unlike a young Johann Sebastian Bach who, at age twenty-two, married his cousin and took a church-related position in Germany, Handel seemed uninterested in adopting the secure life most suitable for marrying and starting a family. Many Handel biographers blame his career choice for his lifelong bachelorhood. Maybe we will take that up again next time. Meanwhile, I said I would return to the fine duet we took with us last time. "

"By the time Handel was setting the music for the Milton *cum* Charles Jennens poems—around 1740—he had decided it was good to act in moderation, but as a young man, he seemed very much 'L'Allegro,' the man of action, engaged joyfully in life around him. Could you hear the words clearly on the recording? I'll read them out for you in case you couldn't."

Ross interrupted her before she could read the poem aloud. "Just a moment, Katherine. This is for my mother. Alison agreed to help me with a little surprise. Come everyone, into the sometime library and music room over here. Mom has a fine little spinet. Alison are you ready?"

Ross sat down at the piano, and Alison stood nearby with a piece of sheet music. All Ross had was a piece of paper with the words. He began playing, and soon Alison began the duet in a clear and lovely soprano. After the first two lines, Ross joined in—obviously a baritone trying to sing tenor, but not bad. They sang through the lyrics twice, pretty much as Handel had written the closing duet.

> "As steals the morn upon the night,
> And melts the shades away:
> So Truth does Fancy's charm dissolve,
> And rising Reason puts to flight
> The fumes that did the mind involve,
> Restoring intellectual day."

When they finished, everyone clapped both loud and long. Forella had tears in her eyes. Ross and Alison grinned appreciatively at the extended applause. And Katherine looked strangely flushed as she walked over and gave Forella a hug. "Now I see what you mean," she said. "I think I understand a little more just why you have these letters." And she turned to give Ross a long look, ending in a smile.

"Thanks, Ross, Alison," Katherine said. "What a wonderful surprise!" Again, and somewhat awkwardly she said, "Thank you. I had no idea." And regaining her composure, she went on, "Well, everyone, I think we could simply let the pleasant recollection of that performance go with us as our take-away Handel music this time. However, once again Forella has provided us with a recording to whet our appetite for the next meeting. This time the piece is Handel's *Ode for the Birthday of Queen Anne.* Give yourself some quiet time to listen to the wonderful alto and trumpet duet that opens the composition. This was written when Handel first came to London. Enjoy. I look forward to seeing you all again next time with— I hope—a couple more letters from Peter. Thanks for being here. And thanks again, Alison and Ross, for 'As Steals the Morn'—it was excellent. A perfect way to end our session. Stay well, everyone."

CHAPTER 10

The Queen's Theater

As a folklorist, Katherine had studied a little about beliefs in reincarnation and the idea of past lives. It was not a popular notion in mostly Christian America, but she had encountered people who did claim to have lived before, or more often, people who claimed that someone else was a previous personality. She wondered what it must feel like to be told, especially as a child, that you are not simply yourself but instead someone who has lived before, some other person. It is hard enough to find and maintain a sense of personal identity without having that kind of burden added to the mix, she thought. On the other hand, it reminded her of the Norwegian folktale in which a giant has hidden his soul outside his body, in an egg, in a duck, in a well, near a castle, in a far away land. How could the giant be the self he felt himself to be if the thing that made him who he is was not inside him? A giant, after all, was supposed to be like a human, but not quite. And what about apes? Or those wonderful ancestral beings back in the mists of time, the ones who first experienced human consciousness. Were modern humans still reincarnating those early hominid souls? Isn't the idea that some nonmaterial part of our self survives after death simply wishful thinking? She tried to imagine some ghostlike essence that had once been George Frideric Handel taking up residence in Ross Wainwright. The whole thing seemed ludicrous. But 'there are more things in heaven *and earth, Horatio, than are dreamt of in your philosophy,' said Hamlet. Of course Shakespeare introduced a ghost into the action of his play as well. But that was fiction, literature—not real life.*

───⁂───

BRAD AND CLARA WERE EXCHANGING a few comments about Handel's "Ode for the Birthday of Queen Anne" as everyone moved into Forella's dinning room at the next Seminar meeting. "The words HAD to be tongue in cheek or purposefully overblown," said Brad. "I mean, even back then, people wouldn't claim that Queen Anne's actions were 'divine.' Wouldn't that be blasphemous?" Clara countered, "Oh, they believed in the divine right of kings—and queens. And what is the Ode's repeated Chorus?—'The day that gave great Anna birth, Who fixed a lasting peace on earth.' It's just not something Americans can stomach—the idea of a king or queen being inherently better than everyone else. I remember the first time I was expected to curtsy before the portrait of the Queen in a courtroom in Australia. I was outraged. Clearly an overreaction—but really! That is definitely part of what the American Revolution was all about."

Ross, who had been listening in on the conversation, folded his arms dramatically. "Ah, but this was 1713, and Queen Anne had just signed the treaty that stopped the war to end all wars—with God's help, of course. Handel's old boss, Georg Ludwig, was not happy with the treaty. I wonder what went through Handel's mind as he composed the music praising Queen Anne. He did get a handsome pension from the Queen shortly after writing the 'Ode' as well as a couple pieces celebrating the treaty itself. Music and politics, politics and music—it's not just something from the folknik era. Always, the inescapable power of filthy lucre!"

Peter joined the little assemblage discussing the music Katherine had sent home with them last time. "So, Handel was just playing politics and accepting a royal payoff, eh? Such cynicism! Personally, I think he was secretly in love with Queen Anne and wanted to impress her, no matter what the politics. Why else would he—a foreigner and a German to boot—get involved in British politics? Cherchez la femme, I say. Come, come, my friends, it's always all about sex—or maybe food. I don't know. Speaking of which—Katherine says to grab some lunch and sit down."

As everyone said their hellos, dished up something good from the buffet, and sat down, Ross signaled to Katherine that he had something to say. "Hello, friends, colleagues, and countrypersons—whatever that might mean. It is my lamentable duty to report that our hostess isn't here today. She and Angela are up in Chicago. I am to inform you that it is all in the name of research. They will be enjoying one of Handel's operas—*Xerxes*, I think—put on by the Lyric. And, of course they had to be there a bit early. Ah, the sacrifices we all make for our subject! Anyway, she is counting on Benfey to record our discussion so she can listen to it later—not that you should let that thought intimidate you in any way. And now I turn things back over to Professor Baker. Carry on, Katherine," he said and sat down.

Katherine lifted from the nearby shelf of books one of those edited Cambridge Companions to Music—this one, of course, *The Cambridge Companion to Handel*, edited by Handel expert Donald Burrows. "I thought before we hear from Peter about the next letter he has ready for us," she said, "we might take a look at a short article that describes the social, political, and cultural contexts Handel encountered during his first decade in London. Historian William Weber writes that Handel 'emerged as the leading figure in one of the key cultural activities of the upper classes, and in so doing participated directly in the fast-moving changes that were taking place in English life.'(p. 45) That 'key cultural activity' was of course opera. Weber goes on to explain how opinions about opera came to reflect the differing political attitudes associated with the emerging political parties—Tory and Whig. We are used to this kind of political and ideological division here today, but back then, the whole thing was entirely new—not just in England but in all of Europe. It was the start of two-party politics, and Handel was in the thick of it."

"He's serious?" Wait scoffed. "Opera was important enough to influence politics?! I mean, opera wasn't even in English. I'll admit that most of my wife's friends who like opera are also generally moderate in their politics, but I don't think opera ever comes up as a political issue. I suspect most politicians have never even gone to an opera. I'm trying to imagine some politician from the 1700s—say, Benjamin Franklin—being interested in opera or seeing opera as important in political circles. It just doesn't seem likely."

"Funny you should mention Ben Franklin," said Katherine. "As a matter of fact, Franklin is known to have attended operas in London and Paris, and I've read somewhere that he attended one of Handel's last performances in London. But, back to your point about opera and politics, it IS true—back then, people really did see opera as a kind of signpost indicating one's politics. Throughout the first three decades of Handel's career in London, there was a lot of bickering among the elite who attended opera, and the people, places, and plots of opera often carried political meaning imposed entirely from the outside. It is amazing that Handel managed to somehow float above most of the infighting. He must have been an accomplished diplomat to maneuver so well through those rocky times."

"I wonder," said Alison, "if he perhaps had an advantage in being a foreigner. He didn't become a British citizen until more than a decade later. So, here at the beginning of his time in London, people must have assumed he had no direct interest in British politics—well, other than the fact that his former patron from Hanover soon became Britain's King George, the first."

Rayette ran her finger lightly around the fine wineglass in front of her until a soft resonant tone rang out and grabbed everyone's attention. "Your mention of Benjamin Franklin," she said, "reminded me of his improvement of the glass harmonica. He created a spindle with glass rings that could be turned and touched with wet fingers to produce music much more easily than the tray of water glasses that had comprised the instrument before Franklin modified it. Quite the inventor, Mister

Franklin. But, I wanted to say something about Handel and the political overtones associated with opera in London in the early 1700s. I don't think we can know for sure, but the important thing, it seems to me, is that Handel had strong personal priorities that directed his involvement in musical activities in London, or, in fact wherever he happened to be. He was first and foremost an artist, a musician, a performer, a composer. In any case, his greatest pleasure would likely be in seeing his music move an audience—to tears, to shouts of joy or acclaim, perhaps simply to a gasp of quiet introspection. Music, like poetry, is always a love song. I think Handel tolerated the political and social hullabaloo that surrounded opera because he so fervently valued the opportunity to create and present the music that was his abiding passion. We must not forget that he was, above all, an artist."

"Well said, Rayette," said Ross. "I guess it takes one to know one, as they say. You're a poet, someone immersed in the arts. I'm curious—what makes you say that Handel is primarily an artist rather than, say, a showman and entrepreneur who just happened to be promoting music? What makes someone an artist rather than simply a successful agent of the profession? And of course, Handel WAS a successful entrepreneur. What's the difference?"

"Well," Rayette smiled and moved her hand around to point toward everyone else in the room, "you probably should ask the musicians rather than me. But I can tell you what I think makes a poet or writer an artist rather than simply a reporter or entertainer. To me, an artist reminds us that life is a profound experience, a mysterious privilege we have each been granted. It may at times be painful, silly, comical, or moving—but always profoundly compelling. An artist feels that sense of life's greatness—or even its pain—as a provocation, something that MUST be absorbed and allowed to foment some internal response—which of course must be expressed. I think Handel's music exhibits that same kind of driving expression that all great poets have. It is as if something inside must be released. He is an excellent craftsman as well, of course. But that extra intensity and depth that make his music so exciting even after all these years—those soul-stirring qualities are what make him an artist. And he was an outstanding performer, too. He knew how his best singers felt when they sang with the heart of an artist, and he wanted to give them the music that allowed that compelling expressivity to happen."

Rebecca nodded. "That's something I've wondered about Handel from the very start of our Seminar," she said. "He obviously learned how to play and write music exceptionally well. His teacher, Zachow, must have been very good at guiding Handel's raw talent and inner compulsion into a disciplined skill. I wonder if Zachow knew the young Georg Händel would be a star. As a teacher, over the years, I've had a sense about certain students—a conviction that they would end up as outstanding teachers or writers. Usually it's something in their demeanor, a kind of animation and yet a certain depth as well. They seem more intensely engaged than other students. I imagine that is what Handel was like as a young man—very focused, adept, and eager. I'm sure he DID relish the opportunity to write a piece in praise of the Queen. What a challenge! Of course, Handel didn't write the lyrics—that was someone else—but as composer he had to create the mood and atmosphere of the piece. He needed to make listeners think of stirring deeds and greatness without at the same time promoting idolatry. And, praising a woman as leader rather than a man. He must have found composing that ode a task that demanded all of his skills—musical, emotional, social, intellectual, and I suppose even political."

Katherine looked around the room. She thought again—inexplicably—of Forella's speculation that Ross might be Handel reincarnate. If such a preposterous idea were to be true, then Ross would have that same telltale intensity that marked Handel as an artist. Right? No wonder such ideas are dismissed out of hand. Of course, Ross IS an artist and very devoted to his work. But each person has to grow his own artistic nature. It can't be handed on. Silly idea. Then, with a start, she realized that everyone was looking to her to move things along. "Well," she said, "I think we have some idea of the political and cultural scene that greeted Handel when he moved to London at around age twenty-seven. Despite his young age and foreign birth, he was accepted into the inner circle of London's elite and granted opportunities to compose and perform that no doubt inspired the envy of many local composers. But let us turn to our own hard-working conservator, transcriber, and archivist. Peter, what do you have for us today?"

Peter handed around copies of two letters to each of the people around the table. He left a couple extra copies for Forella and Angela to consider when they returned from Chicago. "Here," he said, "you have the last of the letters written to Handel while he was yet in Germany and the first of the letters Lydia wrote to Handel after he made the move to London. The first is quite long and very interesting. The second is short and mostly informative. Refill your coffee cups and read away."

To: G F Handel, Esqr.
Kapellmeister to the Court
Hanover

18 July 1711

My Dear Mr. Handel,
It seems we both have faced the need of late to negotiate safe boundaries between feuding Whigs and Tories in an England that is more divided with each passing day. I am always eager to visit London, as is the Reverend Mr. Grayston, but we are warned by our friends to speak and move cautiously, lest we incite bitter contests over even the most minor differences. Mary wrote of hearing very uncivil commentary against the opera, and for no other reason than that it is thought to promote foreign tastes and, they say, Catholicism. Who would expect musical theater to be suspect as a disguised political pamphlet? London is certainly not the sleepy town it was when I left eight years ago.

Still, as I said upon seeing you there at the end of the season—I simply cannot believe my good fortune in attending, first, Agrippina in Venice, and then, Rinaldo in London. And in both, in addition to the stirring arias and orchestrations, your brilliant playing extempore on the harpsichord—*ta*, it was a thrilling experience. And you arrived in the city but a short time before! It was a wonderful surprise for me and for Edward. We came on business but were determined to attend at least one opera as the season continued longer than usual. Eggy actually covered my eyes as we alighted from the carriage, to hide from me until we were indoors, the exciting announcement that it was your opera we would be attending. And once inside, what did I see but Maestro Handel preparing to present his excellent new work. It was an amazing piece. The aria Nicolino sang near the end of the first Act—"Cara Sposa"—was so very beautiful. I think, Gif, it is a new kind of music. Dare I say it elicits more feeling, or perhaps guides us to ponder life and human affections more deeply? You have become a musician well beyond your own years. My one disappointment was that I did not have opportunity to talk with you at any length. Ah, my dear Gif, I miss our dilatory afternoons when all met to hear the latest news, poetry, and speculation before the music began in Sir John's parlor.

 And on that note, I must thank you sincerely for the honor you have always extended to me in listening—seriously listening—to my thoughts on music, literature, art, even the newest findings in science and physiology. I recall your reminiscing on how your father loved to talk of the wonders of medical learning—how new treatments were being discovered every day. I, who am so blessed to have my father still alive and well and continuing his good work—I can only offer my heartfelt pity at your losing a parent when you were so young. And yet your mother must surely have been an excellent example for you as well. You have no idea how unusual you are in showing a genuine admiration for the talent and intelligence of women both in your profession and out. I can only assume that in your earlier years your mother commanded your respect for her keen perception and intellect quite beyond her obvious care and affection for her talented son. Whether from her influence or your own generous nature, you *have impressed me with the kind regard you extend to anyone— man, woman, or child. I treasure that quality in you, my friend, and I hope that soon I shall have greater opportunity to enjoy it.*

What do I mean by this, you may wonder. As Edward told you, Sir John had provided him with an enthusiastic letter in support of his seeking a place at Her Majesty's court. He is hopeful that he might soon be offered a position in Westminster. For myself, I have long wished to return to England, and all the more so as it is apparent that you will not be again in Hamburg, nor even for very long in Hanover. Misters Brockes and Telemann are off to other towns, and our erstwhile group of talkative friends will likely never meet up in such a way again. I feel my young and cheerful days slipping away. Did your father ever teach you a cure for such melancholy, my dear Gif? Or am I too easily prone to a sentimental longing for the past?

I met with Dr. Arbuthnot while in London. I could see that he was absolutely delighted to have met you. He is such a sweet and humble man. One would never know that he is physician to the Queen. It was Sir John who arranged for me to meet with him. I would not speak with you on the subject of our meeting except that it has come up before in our conversations, and you have always seemed so knowledgeable about medical issues. Is it your father's influence again? As you know, Edward and I have been disappointed that no children have blessed our marriage. Dr. Arbuthnot asked about my sister's four children—all of them healthy and such a joy to know. I was surprised to hear Dr. Arbuthnot ponder whether the problem might not be mine but rather Eggy's. I've made a study of the subject, and never have I seen a physician question that the fault lies always with the wife, not the husband—if fault you can call it. He offered some herbs I have tried before. Still, he gives some hope. I must admit to being envious that you have been named godfather to your sister's child rather than to one Edward and I would have. But I send along my good wishes. I am sure you will be an excellent godparent to the little one.

I have written at greater length than I intended. I do hope the mail coach does not charge you an additional fee. Once again, it was such a joy to see you. Please do not leave Hanover without sending an address where we may write to you. Stay well, my friend.

I have the honor to be, ever yours,

Mrs. Edward Grayston
Rotth Haus, Hamburg

And the second letter:

To: Mr. G F Handel, Esqr
In care of Mr. Andrews
Barn-Elms, London

20 August 1712

My Dear Mr. Handel,
I write but briefly to inform you, sadly, that your dear old teacher, Herr Zachow, has died in Halle. Custom required that Mr. Grayston and I visit some of the neighboring churches and their long-time clergymen before returning to England at the end of the summer, and that included Halle. We did stop to call upon your mother, and she relayed the sorry news that your teacher had died. Frau H asked Eggy to relay the message to you. She is delighted with your young niece, your godchild, and I agree that she is a dear sweet child—already big enough to crawl upon my lap. I was sorry to leave her.

The funeral for Herr Zachow was a couple weeks ago. I enclose here a few poems that were written by others of his friends and students. I am sure you would have wished to be there. I am so glad you were able to visit him last time you were in Halle.

Edward and I will make the passage from the Hague to London in another month. I feel a chapter of my life closing as I prepare to leave Hamburg. I am so glad that it brought me such fine memories, such dear friends—especially my celebrated friend GF Handel, now the great attraction in London town. I look forward to seeing much more of you. Stay well. There were prayers at the church for your dear teacher, and again for your sister Johanna. They will be missed.

I have the honor to be, ever yours,

Mrs. Edward Grayston
Rotth Haus, Hamburg

Katherine looked around for the tripod and flip chart Angela usually had set up for them, but she didn't see it anywhere. "I don't see our old-fashioned visual aid," she said, "so I guess we will just have to keep ourselves focused on a few topics without its help." Ross volunteered to go in search of the chart, but Katherine said she thought they would be fine without it.

Peter indicated that he had something to add. "Since I had a chance to read the letters before everyone else—AND as I had a little extra time this week, I did a bit of research and brought along a few items you might find interesting. First, I've asked Benfey to stream for us a taste of the aria Lydia mentions—'Cara sposa.' This is from a production of *Rinaldo* recorded more than a decade ago in London. The singer is a countertenor. If you have never heard a countertenor before, you might be surprised. He sings in the range of a mezzo-soprano, but of course the original part was written for a castrato— in this case, for Nicola Grimaldi, or Nicolino. A countertenor is really singing in a falsetto—a well-developed falsetto, to be sure, but the castrato sang in his unnatural natural voice. Here is a picture of Nicolino. He was all the rage in London in the early 1700s, and they say he was also a very talented actor—probably really helped make *Rinaldo* the great success it was."

"And then," he went on, "the other thing I wanted to show you was this picture of the manor house at Barn Elms—the new address Lydia has for Handel in London. This mansion was owned by a Mr. Andrews at the time Handel stayed there, but some few years before that, the place was famous as the setting for meetings of the 'Kit-Kat Club.' It was a literary fraternity of sorts. Several famous Londoners were members. They evidently made a habit of 'toasting' various beautiful women—not really in a lewd way or anything—some of the women were daughters of the members. But in any case, Handel was there, in the Barn Elms mansion, enjoying the company of such frat brothers just a few years later."

At a signal from Peter, Benfey played the recording of "Cara sposa" through Forella's fine audio system. Everyone listened to the surprisingly warm and rich voice singing the words, "cara sposa, amante cara, dove sei?"—my dear love, where are you? Brad frowned. "That's a man singing?" he said. "I've heard men singing in falsetto lots of times. It never sounds like that. I mean, even Roy Orbison sounded, you know, kind of honky up that high. This guy sounds like a woman but, I don't know, maybe bigger. Is he a really big guy with a woman's vocal chords?"

Both CD and Alison laughed and waved a hand to respond. "Go on, Alison," said CD. Alison grinned again. "Well, I could tell just from listening that this is David Daniels, an amazing countertenor whose voice and execution are exceptionally beautiful. Some countertenors do sound—as you said—a little honky, but Daniels doesn't. And he isn't a big man, either. But I suppose he has the advantage of a larger chest cavity than a woman of similar size might have. But, I think he simply had a really good voice to begin with and benefited from a rigorous training program. It will be interesting to see how long he can stay on top of his game. Even Pavorati as a tenor started having problems when he hit sixty. Or maybe he will copy Placido Domingo and switch to baritone. But really a lot people don't realize how much work goes into staying in shape to sing operatic roles. I've often wondered if the castrati who sang for Handel had very long careers as singers. Most of those roles were really demanding."

"Just as an aside," said CD, "and I know we need to get on to discussing the letters—but you might be interested in a book written by Roland Barthes in the early 1970s. The book was titled *S/Z*, and it was a postmodern interpretation of an earlier story by Balzac called *Sarrasine*. Some of you who study literature might know more about it, but the reason I know about it is that it is one of the first works that, in effect, identify the perception of gender as a cultural issue. In Balzac's story, which takes place in the early 1800s, a young man falls in love with a beautiful opera singer and tries to abduct her. He discovers that she is not, in fact, a woman but rather a castrato who sings beautifully and who very convincingly portrays a woman on the stage. The young man—Sarrasine—is killed, and at the end of the story, we see a very old man who is, of course, the once beautiful woman with whom Sarrasine was so infatuated. Barthes used the story to illustrate his interpretive theories, but I remember reading the book as a college student and being blown away by the notion that our perceptions of gender are so dependent on cultural signals. This was about the time that I came out as a gay man—still a risky thing to do back then. I found the story disturbing, and I wasn't even sure why. I think it was kind of like a fable or parable. I thought there was some lesson there for me, but I didn't really know what it was. I just knew that at some level I had been misjudged the same way that the castrato had—as someone other than the person I really was."

Everyone seemed to be letting CD's comment sink in. Katherine thought momentarily of the early discussions she and Ross and Peter had had with Forella, about the Chalice Circles and their practice of letting people speak with no expectation of response or judgment from anyone else. She was glad CD felt comfortable sharing his thoughts, thoughts that must have been troubling at an earlier time in his life. "Yes," she said, "writers like Barthes have helped us recognize that gender is a cultural construct. But it is fascinating to think of the times during which Handel wrote his operas and realize that people worried over the notion of gender then as well. They may not have had the postmodern vocabulary we have now, but they were more aware than we might think of the differences between cultural perceptions and the reality they are assumed to reflect. What questions were they raising through their art? It strikes us today as odd that a male hero would be cast with a high—female range—voice. Why would they do that? And then there were the 'trouser roles' in which women, not castrati, played the role of men. If the genders were so easily mixed on stage, why was it—why IS it—such an issue in day-to-day society?"

Clara indicated with a wave that she had something to say. "As I've mentioned before, I am very interested in the history of science and especially how the period of the Enlightenment affected the evolution of thought and behavior in Western culture. But in the 1700s, people did not really study differences between the sexes. Generally it was assumed that women were simply 'incomplete' males—really, that is what they thought. Girls cannot become 'complete' as men, but boys can. However, if a boy's lovely soprano voice is saved from growing into adulthood, then the castrato can sing with the voice that proclaims his heroic purity. It wasn't until well into the mid-1900s that any real study of gender emerged. As long as women were considered incomplete males and thus inferior and less capable humans, the bias in favor of males was seen as common sense, not prejudice."

Katherine looked at the time on her phone. "Lydia hints at other gender issues in her letters—things besides the role of the castrato, I mean. Neither *Agrippina* nor *Rinaldo* was a romantic opera the way Verdi or Puccini operas are, and yet here was this beautiful aria, 'Cara sposa,' written during the late Baroque era and sung by a castrato portraying a hero of the crusades. I read somewhere that this aria remained throughout his life one of Handel's personal favorites. And clearly Lydia liked it as well. I doubt that she knew Italian, but there must have been word books available at the London operas with translations of the libretti. This aria speaks of a longing for a lover who has been stolen away. I suppose it could be enjoyed as a separate piece in the same way modern audiences enjoy love songs from Broadway musicals. People went about singing 'Cara sposa' instead of 'Some Enchanted Evening.' I read somewhere that some of Handel's most successful arias were published separately as a kind of sheet music even in his own time. But what else do we see in these two letters?"

Rebecca spoke up eagerly, quoting Lydia's lines in which she thanks Handel for listening to her and valuing her ideas. "I find it really interesting that Lydia was aware of Handel's unusualness in this regard. She doesn't SAY that other men seemed to disregard her ideas or treat her as less intelligent than a man, but of course that would be the implication. From what I've read of Handel he was, in general, inclined to be honest and direct with people but probably a bit abstracted since he was absorbed by his work most of the time. I'm sure he did interact with people in what we would consider social situations. After all, he was a performer. But Lydia's comment suggests he was—or at least could be—a good listener and a man who gave some consideration to intellectual concerns beyond his obvious preoccupation with music. From the biographies, we have so little information on Handel's personal life that this glimpse into how he interacted with a woman is especially revealing. Of course, it may be that Lydia was simply unusual herself. It would take a confident, strong woman to voice her opinions in mixed company in the first place. But I get the feeling that Handel liked that kind of woman."

"Well," CD joined in, "*Agrippina* was all about a strong woman, and *Rinaldo* gave us the sorceress Armida, the most powerful character in the opera. I think it is safe to say that Handel found energetic, powerful women attractive. But it seems like his relationship with Lydia is more one of mutual respect rather than the kind of power play his operas present. Personally, what impresses me is her statement that he was kind to everyone—man, woman, or child. You read anecdotes that cast him in a negative light, being sarcastic or temperamental, but I think he knew how to get along with people. It sounds like he and Lydia were good friends, even if it was not customary for men to regard women as equals or simply as friends."

Brad leaned back and scowled. "Ok, I know you are all going to hate this, but I still think there is something more, well, amorous going on here. I think Rebecca told us earlier about how wives were, in effect, owned by their husbands during Handel's time. Why would any husband let his wife write these touchy-feely letters to a young bachelor—and a performer at that? It would be like a man today letting his wife write to Bruce Springsteen or something. Why would Lydia's husband allow it— IF he knew about it? And remember how Handel wrote to her husband, rather than to her, back at the beginning and she promised to destroy his letters? I think she knew she was doing something underhanded. And Handel probably knew he was taking a big risk even in accepting letters from her. But I suppose he was in love with her."

"You mean you wouldn't let your wife write to Bruce Springsteen?" said Ross. "What a tyrant! Of course Springsteen would have an assistant who screens such fan mail: 'Dear Madam, thank you for your recent proclamation of undying love. Your letter will be placed in the huge pile of similar correspondences and tended to by one of our confreres in due course.' Possibly things are simply different now. Or, in fact, the difference here really is that Lydia and Handel were friends. They had interacted many times face-to-face and evidently in the company of others, including Lydia's husband. Granted, friendships can grow into love relationships. Would Lydia's husband have worried about this? Maybe. But it appears that he had confidence in his wife and his friend and expected them to honor Lydia's marriage vow. The more impressive thing is that Handel did seem to treat Lydia as an equal, or at least not as an inferior. It's likely that Handel didn't write to Lydia nearly as often as she wrote to him. It seems he spent little time writing letters to anyone—thus the paucity of information through that medium. But it sounds like he was a good conversationalist in small groups, and that kind of interaction is what Lydia recalls and builds upon in her letters."

Katherine saw a few disgruntled faces and decided to intervene. "If we had our flip chart, I would point—literally—to the differing issues we seem to be mixing together here. On the one hand, we have Handel's supposed love life—or maybe lack of love life, and on the other, we have the mores, the cultural values, of eighteenth century Britain—and maybe some of the cultural values Handel still carried from his Saxon upbringing. It is interesting to me that Lydia herself attributes to the influence of Handel's family—to his father and mother—some of the outward signs of value and attitude Handel displays in his behavior. If we didn't have Lydia's letters, our only sources of information about Handel's values and motivations at this point in his life would come from the operas he chose to compose and the few off-hand remarks of people whose letters from the period survive. And given that he wrote the music but not the libretto of any opera he composed, we have little to go on."

Rayette waved a hesitant hand. "This may not be relevant, but I recall a well-known study of the life and writing of Samuel Taylor Coleridge. I think its title was *The Road to Xanadu*, and it was written by a man named Lowes. The study has fallen out of favor since my grad school days, but I remember being very impressed with what Lowes did to help us understand how Coleridge wrote his poetry. Lowes undertook an extremely thorough examination of the books Coleridge had read previous to writing his great poems 'The Rime of the Ancient Mariner' and 'Kubla Khan.' And he consulted Coleridge's notebooks. Basically he tried to establish connections between the raw materials that were swirling around in Coleridge's head and the texts that became his famous poems. Handel was writing music, of course, rather than poetry, but to some extent, he was like Coleridge—he had various traditional plots and printed libretti offered to him or included among his possible sources, his library if you will. I can imagine Handel sitting at his desk, looking through various libretti or narratives and trying to decide which might make a good opera and how he might make the characters come alive on the stage. In that respect, I think we can read something out of the choices Handel made just as we can interpret something of Coleridge's thoughts by seeing what he valued enough to include in his poetry. What Handel valued and found intriguing reveals itself in the characters and pronouncements, the feelings and motivations that inspired his best arias, his most compelling music."

There was a period of quiet as everyone thought through Rayette's comment. Finally Wait spoke up. "I've spent most of my life around jazz performers. And I kind of see where Rayette is coming from here. A jazz trumpeter will hear a song like, say, 'On the Street Where You Live' and rather than singing the words, he will try to convey something of the song's feeling through the music, how he bends the notes, how he embellishes the melody. I can imagine Handel taking some character's words—especially words that are full of passion or anguish—and creating music that helps the singer express that feeling. The piece Benfey played for us—'Cara sposa'—I can feel the lover's pain in the singing even though I can't understand the Italian. I guess I would concede that anyone who can effectively convey a lover's longing through music knows something about love. If nothing else, Handel has real empathy with the feelings expressed by the characters in his operas."

"Thanks, Rayette, Wait. Real food for thought there," said Katherine. "Unfortunately, we don't have much information even on how Handel chose the libretti he set to music, or perhaps more interesting, which ones he rejected. But we do know that while still a young man, back in Italy, he had understood the heart of a complex woman like Agrippina well enough to write an aria that reveals her worry over her own dark thoughts—'Pensieri.' Chances are he also understood the heart of his friend Lydia, who shared with him her despair at being unable to conceive a child. That she felt free to write to him about something so personal speaks volumes, I think, about their relationship. Lydia knew his background, the knowledge of medicine he carried as a kind of second-hand lore from his father. And she must have heard something of Handel's relationship with his mother as well—her support for his career in music, her encouragement in his desire to travel where the best opportunities lay. Lydia wasn't German and hadn't grown up, as Handel had, under the influence of Saxon values and the teachings of a German gymnasium. But it seems they did share some values—about what makes a good story, about the strength of love, maybe the joy that children bring."

Katherine glanced at the clock. "Our time is getting short again," she said. "I can't say, as Peter did, that I had any extra time lately, but I'll admit that, after hearing the music, I did rent a DVD of Handel's *Agrippina*—the opera he wrote before leaving Italy, the one Lydia heard in Venice. Rayette's comparison of Handel's and Coleridge's composition processes made me think a little more about what Handel might have been hoping to accomplish in composing an opera like *Agrippina*. The lead character is Nero's mother. Her ambition is to put her son on the throne, the throne currently held by her husband, Claudio. Granted, Agrippina has been told that Claudio is downed at sea at the beginning of the opera. She acts immediately to put her son on the throne but soon discovers that Claudio was, after all, saved by a soldier, Ottone, to whom he has now promised the crown. The rest of the plot involves various lies and tricks Agrippina employs in her effort to make sure Nero will be the next emperor rather than Ottone. There are several thwarted love affairs involving both Agrippina herself and Ottone's betrothed, Poppea and all of the male characters, including Claudio. At the end of three acts, all is well as Ottone renounces the throne in favor of marrying his love, Poppea, and Nero accepts the loss of Poppea in exchange for the promise of the throne. Claudio makes a telling observation at the close—that Ottone is right to choose love over kingship because that is where his heart is. And Nero is right to favor his ambition over love because leadership is his true calling. Claudio reconciles with his wife and claims that what is most important for each person is where he invests his heart. The chorus agrees, and the goddess Juno appears, to add her blessing to it all."

"An excellent summary," said Ross. "I wish I had known you wanted to watch a performance of the opera. I saw *Agrippina* in Venice a couple years ago—long before I had any inkling about a Handel Seminar. I thought it was a hoot, and I bought a DVD made by a French opera company. It may be the same one you rented—sparse setting? Restoration era costumes? Anyway, I agree that it raises the question of just what Handel hoped to accomplish in composing *Agrippina*. History is not kind in its reports of the real Agrippina, but somehow in the opera she ends up seeming manipulative, to be sure, but also an exciting woman—wife to one emperor and mother to another. Somehow, Handel was able to make these dusty old characters seem like real people with the kind of real issues real people have. What is more important? Love or ambition? Or is it, as Claudio suggests, more a matter of knowing your own heart and its needs? Maybe that was an important function of the opera for Handel. Help the audience empathize with even a scheming woman like Agrippina or a put-upon lover like Ottone or even a confused emperor like Claudio—and then give them a bit of practical relationship advice to round it out. Maybe Handel understood women—or at least love relationships—better than we thought."

"Maybe, maybe," said Katherine. "Why don't you bring your DVD along next time? I know I would enjoy seeing it again—if you wouldn't mind loaning it out. Meanwhile, Benfey says that Forella left some CDs for us to take home. Some of you will likely already have a copy of this—the famous *Water Music* suite. Thanks, everyone for your comments. I feel like our time today just flew by. See you all next time."

CHAPTER 11

Love Song to a Tree

As Katherine finished watching the DVD of Handel's Agrippina that Ross had loaned her, she thought again of the first time she experienced the thrill an operatic aria can produce. Growing up, Katherine had not heard much opera. In fact, her usual association with opera was the parody record produced by Spike Jones—Pal-Yat-Chee—in which two country bumpkins, Homer and Jethro, sing about going to the opera and being less than entertained. But later in life, after her divorce, she had dated a man who loved opera. Their first romantic interlude was a night of amazing lovemaking to the strains of "Nessun dorma" from Puccini's Turandot. Quite aside from her delight in having found the perfect aphrodisiac, Katherine had been intrigued by the sheer invitation to ecstasy the aria offered. Little wonder that Pavarotti chose it as his signature piece. But why singers, she mused. What is it about the human voice that is so captivating? And why did Handel make the creation of songs for great voices his life-long passion? Something for the Seminar to ponder.

A COUPLE DAYS BEFORE THE next scheduled Seminar gathering, Katherine and Ross met at a coffee shop, and Ross handed over his DVD of *Agrippina*. "I watched it again, just to remind myself of how it went," Ross said. "No need to rush on getting it back to me. The production was recorded in France in 2003 according to the liner notes. It's curious how Handel's operas—virtually ignored for nearly three centuries—are making a comeback. Despite my mother's notions on Handel and reincarnation, I never paid much attention to Handel's music before starting this Seminar. I think I actually bought this DVD several years ago while looking into a production company in Italy. But I'll admit that I really do like some of the music we are hearing piecemeal along with the Seminar. What about you? Was Handel on your iPhone before we started the Seminar meetings?"

Katherine smiled. "Well, I did have the chance excerpt from *Water Music* and of course, like everyone else, I loved hearing *Messiah* every Christmas, but I didn't know much about Handel's operas until some years ago when I started attending productions by the music school here at IU. They are student singers, but really, the operas are done very professionally. It's a great way to hear a variety of operas without spending a fortune. They have presented a few of Handel's operas. And they've always had a fine program in early music with a Baroque orchestra that plays at least once a semester. I hear that a lot of people retire to Bloomington just to enjoy the music."

"Wouldn't surprise me," said Ross. "Since I've moved to Indianapolis, I've attended some of the popular shows that play up there, but, yeah, I think Bloomington has the edge if you want to hear classical music any night of the week. I've always liked Bach—although I get a little tired of the religious themes. It's a pleasant surprise to see that Handel wrote basically secular music for the stage, at least at the beginning of his career. So—how Handel bucked the system and became a secular music sensation—could be our next theme, don't you think?"

"Hmm, Bach wrote some secular material as well—think of the Brandenburg Concertos," said Katherine. "So you are not a fan of religious music? Perhaps it should be obvious, but why is that?"

"So this is how you get all that information for your books on contemporary folk—asking nosey questions,' laughed Ross. "Ok, ok. Let's see. It's not that I don't like the music itself. Bach's cantatas are great, *Messiah* is a masterpiece—I even have some old hymns I can't get out of my head. The truth is, Katherine, I just don't buy the whole religious belief thing. In fact, I think it is dangerous and leads people to do dangerous, unfair, and sometimes cruel things, even now, in the twenty-first century. I guess I resent hearing good music that promotes bad philosophy. And to me, most religious ideas are simply erroneous explanations for what life is about, how it came to be, where it's going. It rankles me that music—good music—can draw you in, make you accept some of the myths and values just because they are associated with the music. Do you see what I mean? It's as though composers have agreed to let their skills serve the needs of some propaganda machine. It's as disappointing to me as it was when Bob Dylan turned away from writing songs like 'Blowing in the Wind' and sang gospel instead. Music can be so ingratiating. It pulls you in and seduces you into thinking that the ideas you associate with the music should not be questioned."

Katherine could see that Ross was sincere. "But think about it," she said. "Why do you suppose a person like Bob Dylan becomes a convert? He is obviously an intelligent, creative man. I don't think he just ran out of subjects for his music. If you can see his other songs, his protest songs, as expressions of his personal philosophy, then why not accept his religious songs as his heartfelt messages as well? These weren't ideas he grew up with. They are part of his adult thinking. Besides, I think he has embraced various other religious ideas since then. Or, do you think songwriters and composers simply need to have a theme or story that interests them? That seemed to be a necessity for Handel."

Ross got up to refill his coffee cup. "More coffee?" he asked. When he came back, he gave Katherine a quizzical look. "I've heard it's best never to discuss politics or religion with anyone unless you've known them for at least five years—or don't mind being dropped from the roster if it's a family member. I think it is amazing how all these people on social networks spill out their political and religious opinions as though everyone who counts is likely to agree with them. Now, much as I find Dylan's switch to gospel music disappointing, I recognize that he was being courageous from the perspective of those who share his beliefs—he was sticking his neck out to praise Jesus. But, from my perspective, he was capitulating to a mythology that feels good rather than looking for a true understanding of how the world works. So I see him as abandoning the hard-edged inquiry that inspired his earlier songs. I don't think he was insincere. I just think he went soft intellectually. He accepted what felt good and stopped questioning it. To me, that's going backwards instead of growing. I'm not sure whether we can compare Dylan and Handel. Handel certainly didn't have the advantage of scientific knowledge we have today. But what about you? Or do folklorists just badger other people about their beliefs and never reveal their own?"

"Badger, badger?" said Katherine. "Most people are eager to share their beliefs. But, yes, actually folklorists are encouraged to sort of stay neutral, if that's possible, in a fieldwork situation. Sometimes you feel hypocritical—as though silence implies consent—especially if someone expresses an idea or belief you find objectionable. Sexist, or racist, or homophobic jokes or comments—it's hard to just let them slide by as though you thought they were ok. But other times I don't know, it's more like you are simply hearing people report experiences and offer interpretations that you know are faulty, misguided, but it isn't your task to correct them, as though you were in a classroom. You are just there to document what they believe. It's ironic that one of the early folklorists—well, actually he would be considered an anthropologist—E. B. Tyler, made it his task to stamp out the folklore he recorded. Basically he felt that most religious views and folk beliefs were survivals from an earlier, primitive cultural period and were no longer needed by modern humans. But folklorists today don't feel comfortable telling the people they work with that their ideas are superstitions and old wives' tales. Tyler thought education would wipe out religion, but obviously he was wrong."

"Education would be part of the solution," said Ross, "but there are some highly educated people out there who profess some sort of religion. Maybe I'm talking to one right now. There is a more insidious factor at work with religion—basically a simple pressure to be part of the herd, especially if the herd has power and tradition backing it up. It's probably just as hard for an atheist to come out of the closet as it is for gays."

"Hmm," Katherine responded, "yes, that's a phenomenon we sometimes call the esoteric-exoteric factor in folklore studies. More often it is about us versus them in ethnic terms or even conflicting religions, but I suppose religious people versus non-religious people would be another example. And atheists seem to be a minority in the US. Or, are you suggesting that it's a matter of discounting and badmouthing a minority belief just because it is a minority? Are people who lack a religion, a faith—are they a repressed minority in the US simply because the majority is Christian?"

"Faith," Ross said, "it's an awkward word. You won't hear me talk much about my father, but I will say this—nothing surprised me more than his becoming a Mormon. He was—at least as I understand it—sort of a lukewarm Baptist when I was a kid. I was long since grown and out of the house when he discovered Mormonism, but the only thing he ever said on the subject was that he felt sorry for me because I lacked faith. My father was an intelligent man. I met some of his Mormon friends, and in the main, they seemed like intelligent people, too—and likable, nice people. I just never understood how anyone could swallow that story about finding golden tablets hidden in America—but, of course, I had already rejected the Christian story as well. So, I suppose he was right. I had no faith. But like your man Tyler, to me 'faith' sounds like a word from another time, something they may have needed before scientific methods and reason were taught in the public schools. I'm still puzzled by it, and I'm sorry to say, I think it really put a wedge between my father and me. As you've seen, my mother is much more tolerant of my errant ways."

"Actually, Forella seems wonderfully open and enlightened," said Katherine. "I wonder how she dealt with your father's conversion. My understanding of Mormonism is that a strong, opinionated woman like your mother wouldn't be particularly welcome—or maybe simply wouldn't be comfortable. But—back to music and its connection to religion. I think even Unitarian churches include religious music in their services—though I hear they change the words accompanying traditional hymns to make them more in line with their humanist thinking. I wonder why people who claim not to believe in, say, Jesus, will nevertheless feel it necessary to sing anthems that praise him or tell his story. I still think there is something about music that people find somehow 'spiritual' even if they don't consider themselves religious. What do you think?"

"Hey, I know that trick—asking me what I think rather than expanding on your own doubts and prejudices," said Ross. "We filmmakers must have a bit of the folklorist in us—always poking around to find out what other people think. Although, I suppose I'm less scrupulous than a folklorist would be about influencing the direction a conversation goes. After all, I want to make an interesting documentary. Now, if I were the interviewee in one of my own films—let's see, I suppose what I would want is a nice juicy story, like Shirley MacLaine and her autobiographical movie *Out on a Limb*. Unfortunately, I've never had any of those supernatural experiences Shirley shares with us—though I suppose I could come up with a few love story plots, just as she did—maybe not with a well-known politician. Have you ever seen the movie?"

"I have," said Katherine, "and you are changing the subject. I can't imagine you, or anyone else for that matter, having the kind of experiences Shirley MacLaine presents in that movie—though I'll admit I thought the movie and the book were fascinating. But, really, my question was much more mundane: basically, do you think there is something 'spiritual' about music? Not just religious music—is there something about music that creates a feeling we usually call 'religious' or inspirational? Think of *Finlandia*, the symphonic piece by Jean Sibelius. It was a celebratory score for the nation, but Christians in the US made it a hymn—'Be Still My Soul.' Or Handel's song about a tree from the opera *Xerxes*—it becomes an anthem, 'Holy Art Thou.' Even blues and gospel overlap. I just wondered if you thought music has a spiritual dimension, even if you don't like the religious subject matter of some if it?"

Ross laughed. "That sounds like one of those questionnaires where they ask 'Are you spiritual but not religious?' as an alternative to admitting you are an atheist. I'll go back to what I said earlier. I resent the fact that songwriters and composers perpetuate an outmoded philosophy and belief system. I don't blame people from Handel's era. The Enlightenment was barely started then. But, yes, I think it is backward thinking for someone in our times to take a fine piece like *Finlandia* and turn it into a hymn that praises God. Isn't life itself praiseworthy enough? Why must we resort to some supernatural being to be inspired enough to perform great music? This notion of 'spiritual' is a loaded concept. There's too much baggage. I think music is exciting, stirring, creative, sometimes soothing or even awe-inspiring, but it doesn't have anything to do with God or even a human 'spirit.' That's my curmudgeonly opinion."

"So, just out of curiosity," said Katherine, "to whom have you felt comfortable expressing this opinion? It's not likely to be very popular. I mean, you live in Indiana. Most people here are Christians—the upper reaches of the Bible belt. Even most of the faculty at IU seem to have some sort of religious identity. Don't you feel you are offending people when you imply that intelligent people should, like you, reject religious ideas as nonsense from an earlier time?"

"I didn't say nonsense," said Ross. "That's a loaded word as well. And, to be honest, no, I don't voice my opinion to most people. I'm only telling you because you asked—and you said it was your professional duty to accept what others say without critique. The truth is, I do empathize with the desire to have some reassuring belief system to fall back on. I just can't make myself believe it. When my father died, I could see how desperately my mother wanted to know that he was still around, still somewhere, still who he was when he was alive. That wouldn't be a good time to say to someone that her beliefs were nonsense. I suppose there is never a good time to confront someone and say that religious beliefs are malarkey, but especially not when the person is hurting. We all wish that we and the people we love could live forever, right? We all like the idea of a heavenly afterlife. But, really, it's a manmade myth, a story people have told for years to help them accept death and other nasty things in life."

"Well, I'm not doing fieldwork today, so I'll just ponder that for a while, if you don't mind," said Katherine. "But the notion that music is somehow a 'spiritual' expression—that idea has been around for some time, quite apart from whether you have a religious outlook or not. Tell you what, I am planning to go to a concert tonight—doing a bit of extra credit homework for our Seminar. It's a chamber music concert, and as part of the program, they are playing Handel's oboe sonata in B flat, something he wrote before leaving Italy. It has no religious connection— just a straight instrumental number. Why don't you join me, and we can decide whether it has any 'spiritual' dimensions or is simply a competently composed piece of music. It's free—as I said before, one of the reasons people move to Bloomington."

"It's been eons since a woman asked me out on a date. How can I refuse?" said Ross. Katherine smirked and shook her head. "You poor dear. I had no idea," said Katherine. "A real date, however, is when I offer to cook my famous Chicken Marsala and ply you with some of Oliver's best wine while watching a steamy video on the TV. And, no, that's not an alternative to the concert. I'll see you at Auer Hall at 8pm. Don't be late. It usually fills up fast. See you there."

Two days later, the Handel Seminar gathered at Forella's townhouse. Benfey had the recording equipment up and running and had set up the flip chart at Forella's request. It had been hiding in an adjacent closet. "Oh, good," said Katherine. "We missed the chart last time. It's probably just an aid to focusing our talk anyway. What happened to the previous sheets of paper?"

Benfey chuckled. "I keep anything and everything that might be considered part of my Seminar archive. You wouldn't believe the files of notes I have so far. My favorite file is the sideline on how often and how attentively Ross watches his co-chair—like now. In my notes: Ross watches Katherine. Seems to have something to say to her but refrains." Katherine grabbed Benfey's laptop, but there was nothing on the screen. "Just kidding," she laughed.

Katherine looked over at Ross. It did in fact seem that he had something to communicate. But Clara, who was asking if he had seen the recent PBS special on Pompeii, diverted his attention. By the time they had finished talking, everyone had moved from the buffet to the table, and Katherine turned instead to Forella and asked if she and Angela would like to say a little about their trip to Chicago and the Handel opera they had seen there.

Waving a hand toward Forella, Angela said, "I'll let Forella give you the informed report I'm sure you really want, but I will say—admit, I guess—that this is the first live opera I have ever seen. It took a while for me to get used to some things—like some of the men singing in really high voices, or the male roles sung by women—but after the first few scenes, I really enjoyed it. We had great seats, and the supertitles—the translation projected above the stage—they were great. I would have been lost without them. I'm eager to attend an opera here in Bloomington now. Of course, it probably won't be as ritzy as the Lyric, but at least I won't think of opera as something I wouldn't enjoy. And to think—I lived in Chicago for two years and never went to the Lyric. It was an awesome experience. But I'll let Forella tell you more about it."

Forella smiled and said, "Before I talk about *Xerxes*, let me offer my thanks to Annie for this excellent Jambalaya—it makes me long to visit New Orleans again. It is delicious. Thanks, Annie." Everyone clapped. Ross, who had opted for a roast beef sandwich, went over to get some of the last of the Jambalaya. Forella continued, "And thanks, Peter, for leaving copies of the last two letters from Lydia—the ones you discussed last time—for me and Angela. I'm most interested to see what you have for us today, but I will say that it was fun to hear an opera Handel wrote later in his career—or at least later than the time period we are looking at right now in our Seminar. I was surprised to see quoted in the *Xerxes* Program notes an introductory comment by Handel himself. Angela brought it to my attention. Why don't you read the quote from Handel, dear?"

Angela took up her program from the opera and read the direct quote: "The contexture of this Drama is so very easy, that it wou'd be troubling the reader to give him a long argument to explain it. Some imbicillities, and the temerity of Xerxes (such as his being deeply enamour'd with a plane tree, and the building a bridge over the Hellespont to unite Asia to Europe) are the basis of the story; the rest is fiction." Angela handed around the Program in which the words were highlighted. "It was really exciting, I thought, to see Handel's own comment on the opera. Forella told me it was unusual for Handel to offer such an introduction, as he said, 'for the reader.' I thought his choice of the word 'imbecilities'—which he misspelled—was especially interesting. I wonder what parts of the story he considered so stupid as to be imbecilities."

"Well," said Forella, "certainly one ridiculous plot element is the line Xerxes uses to describe himself as Romilda's future husband. He speaks of the man she will marry as 'one equal to Xerxes himself.' He, of course in fact meant Xerxes himself, but Romilda's father understood him to mean Xerxes's brother, Arsamene. People who attended opera in Handel's day were used to such silly quandaries—they were a staple of Italian opera—but even informed opera goers were not prepared for a king who would sing of his love for a tree. Clearly, Handel himself saw that as a sign of the king's foolhardiness. I was really pleased that the program notes included this rare instance of Handel commenting on his own production. And yet, it strikes me as curious that Handel would expend the energy to write such a beautiful aria on an idea he scoffed at. As is so often the case, Handel allows himself to side with the character, the singer, and finds a way to express beautifully what the character feels. I think he was a genius. 'Ombra mai fu'—Xerxes's love song to a tree—conveys something good about the king. Xerxes is more complex as a man than the silly plot would suggest. And it is Handel's music that teaches us that lesson. It is a fine work. I'm so glad I heard it. But now, I'm more interested to hear what Peter has for us—the next letter."

Peter stood up. "Your request is my command," he said. "So, I'm sorry to say that I have only one letter today. Other duties have intruded on my time recently. Still, this letter is fairly long and will, I think, occupy us for our allotted time today. Have no fear. As you will see, Lydia has by now moved back to England. Handel has a new address—or at least a different address than the one Lydia used last time. Angela, if you will pass around copies of the letter, I have just one picture to show you today—an engraving of Burlington House as it likely appeared during the time Handel stayed there. As you can see, it was quite a fine mansion—located in Piccadilly. It has been modified some over the years, but if you visit London today, it still stands and parts of it are open to the public. Handel managed to find yet another cushy situation—just as he did in Italy. But on to the letter. It's a long one. Best to get yourself some refreshment."

Here is the letter as Peter transcribed it:

Mr. G F Handel, Esqr
In care of the Right Honorable Lord Burlington
Burlington House
Piccadilly, London

15 September 1713

My Dear Mr. Handel,
Once again our dear Dr. Arbuthnot has proved the perfect host, bringing together many of the friends Edward and I have missed these seven years. And it was such a joy that you were there. I am pleased that you and the good doctor get along so well. He praises your operas at every opportunity. Eggy finds his new post heady but challenging. We are not at all assured that it will keep should Her Majesty's health continue to decline. Nevertheless, our plan is to remain in England now that we have returned. I am so delighted to be back among my family that I shall never return to Hamburg except as a bound prisoner. I hope, my dear Gif, that you, too, will stay here. If the Elector is indeed to be our next king, why would you think of leaving London?

I could see that you have an even more powerful reason for staying in London. Your operatic sorceress has clearly worked her magic on you. I saw that you were taking wine with La Pilotti even as her husband bantered with the Lady Thomas. When, my dear Gif, will you desist from falling in love with married women? Giovanni and Elisabetta struggle much more than you to learn the language, but they are here together. I hope you will keep your passionate regard a secret. She was a wonderful Armida. But, again, it is a false image, a theatrical role. Do not let your heart run off after a dream. Your old university professors may have argued the power of feelings over reason, but you are years and miles away from their tenets. London is not Halle. I urge you to be cautious. Your good sense prevails in your choice of patrons and players. Why let strong feelings dictate your more private affairs?

Before you dismiss me and my letters as from some meddlesome elder sister, let me move instead to a subject you will surely welcome. The young woman sitting next to me at the dinner was Mlle Anastasia Robinson. She has studied with Mr. Croft and knows many of the Italian Londoners. While I know your most ardent desire right now is to create arias that give the floor to Pilotti, you will need a less fiery soprano, I am certain, for some of the operas you spoke of. I have heard Mlle Robinson sing at a house party, and I do believe she is a fine singer. Eggy said you were hoping to find some Italian singers already located in London. He agreed with your argument offered the company at the Queens' Arms Inn that English singers still find the Italian operas too challenging. But here you have an Italian singer who has studied with an English teacher and can take instructions in French. If she accepts work with you, I expect an agent's fee—though I suppose it is the Haymarket's manager who decides upon the singers. Still, you owe at least a fine claret at the next dinner party.

Those of us who had not stayed in town for the season were so fortunate to hear your benefit performance of Teseo, and especially with the harpsichord solo you added for that night. I am reminded again that our very first meeting was at the opera house in Hamburg, where you astounded everyone with your skill and joie de vivre when playing the harpsichord and organ. I have many friends who are musicians, but none is so accomplished as you, nor so successful in pushing the profession of music making to such a new and impressive stage. My dear Gif, at times you make me wish I were a man and could follow in your illustrious footsteps. It must be such a thrill to perform, imagine, and compose music as you do.

I received a letter from your sister Dorothea. She complains that you write but rarely to the family in Halle. Your little niece is walking boldly through the house and chastises her mother for every trifling prohibition. I so envy your sister. She writes that your mother recommends to me an herb called here in England the chasteberry, a remedy your father would prescribe to women who desired to have children. It sounds quite the opposite to me, but I will ask Dr. Arbuthnot about it. She also wrote that your mother fears you are pasturing a few—that was her expression as I translate from the French. I was unsure what she meant by it, but Eggy says it means she fears you have fathered children without the benefit of wedlock. Even your sweet mother is concerned, dear Gif. I, on the other hand, think you spend far too much time closeted away, working on your music. It does not do to have your strongest love scenes only in your mind. Why are you so opposed to taking a bride?

Surely I have now tried your patience to the limit. Yet, I will send this letter—if for no other reason than to let you know that Edward and I are now situated with the Queen's envoy chapel in Westminster. Residents are prepared for duty abroad nearby, and the Reverend Mr. Grayston has sundry tasks associated with their training. I can only hope that none of his acquaintances ask to have him accompany them out of the country. I am eager to stay here near my family and the many delights of London. The new cathedral is magnificent. Please do let us know if you will play the organ there out of season. I can think of no better way to bring the balm of Gilead to my soul. Be well, my dear young maestro.

I have the honor to be, ever yours,

Mrs. Edward Grayston
Carleton House
Westminster

Katherine looked around to see if there were any still reading. As the last readers looked up, she went to the flip chart and asked, "What issues do you see in this letter that you would like to discuss today?"

Wait waved his hand almost at once. "Here it is again—he's what?—nearly thirty years old and still hasn't, as Lydia says, 'taken a bride.' And instead of seeking out a good marriage match himself, he seems to be attracted to other men's wives. I think we have a pattern here, and I'd like to hear what other people think about this repeated scenario in his love life. I still think it is amazing that Lydia feels free to address all this with Handel in a letter, but there you are. I think it has to be a topic on our list."

Katherine wrote HANDEL'S LOVE LIFE in large letters on the blank page. "Ok, Wait, I'll put the topic on our list, but be warned—even Lydia seems to find it an unanswerable question. What else? Yes, Rebecca?"

"I'm attracted to the paragraph in which she praises Handel and reminisces about the first time she heard him play—in Hamburg. She ponders the great accomplishments he has demonstrated in such a short time, and she speaks with some envy about how she, too, might have been able to be a successful musician had she been born a man. I'm not sure what I would identify as the topic here—maybe what cultural and personal strengths and advantages led him to his great success in the London music scene."

"Thanks, Rebecca," said Katherine, and she wrote a second topic on the flip chart: SOURCES THAT LED TO SUCCESS IN LONDON. "Anyone else have a topic?—though I suspect we may have trouble covering even these in the short time we have. Yes, Brad, what do you suggest?"

Brad raised his glass of wine and said, "Well, I'm really interested to learn more about this—I suppose it was tongue-in-cheek—proposition Lydia makes—you know, to serve as his agent in lining up Ms. Robinson as a singer. The whole thing sounds a little suspicious to me, but I'll let it ride. What I will suggest as a topic is sort of related to Rebecca's question, but mostly I'm curious about how he in fact manages to be a success in London—not so much what his personal advantages were but instead what was the situation in London that allowed him to succeed. I mean, he was still relatively young. Why was he such a success in London when he was considered just an also-ran in Hamburg?"

"Hmm," said Katherine. "I guess you are asking about the music scene that he encountered when he arrived in London. What about that situation allowed him to shine? And I know you have said before that you see Handel as a sharp business man, so I'm guessing you would ask why he chose London—because you would see that as a judicious and informed choice." When Brad nodded, Katherine wrote a third topic on the flip chart: WHY DID HANDEL CHOOSE LONDON?

"Ok," said Katherine, "Wait, you introduced our first topic, so is there something you want to say to start the ball rolling?"

"Well," mused Wait, "as I said, I think we have a pattern here. Handel seems to go after women who are—or at least should be—unattainable. Maybe he just likes the challenge? Was adultery illegal back then? I mean, wouldn't he be in trouble if a husband found out Handel was banging his wife? I don't know. I think in this regard anyway, Handel was immature to say the least—maybe even rapacious. It sounds like he didn't respect women enough to marry one but didn't mind stealing favors from women married to other men. He seems like the worst kind of frat boy stereotype. According to Handel's sister, even his mother thinks he is behaving like a jerk."

CD cleared his throat. "Oh, come on Wait. What we have here are rumors and worries voiced by people who have no idea what really goes on in Handel's private life. Even Lydia herself is simply expressing concerns based on her own observations. Maybe she has misinterpreted Handel's supposed secret amours. Or, more likely she has rightly identified his looks and actions as signs of a kind of sophomoric daydreaming. It sounds to me like Handel is infatuated with one of his leading ladies. Lydia basically accuses him of fantasizing about this woman and living in a kind of dream world. In fact, Lydia chastises him for not stepping into the real world and taking a bride. At least then he would have a real sexual relationship, not simply an adolescent wet dream."

Clara said, "Hear, hear. I think you may be onto something, CD. But how does this fit into your earlier theory that Handel was gay? Would he be fantasizing about a woman if he were instead attracted to men? Just curious what you think about that."

"What I actually said," CD replied, "is that many people assume Handel was gay—mostly because he didn't marry but also because some of the men he interacted with were thought to be gay. It's possible that some more recent writers have had some sense of investment in the idea that Handel was gay. It's always good to have a kindred soul from an earlier era. Myself? I'm finding that I am at least partially persuaded by Lydia's observations. Notice that she doesn't say anything about seeing Handel and his lead soprano running off together or in fact doing anything that would be a sign of real intimacy. Instead she comments on Handel's flirting behavior and speaks of his having a 'passionate regard' for the woman called La Pilotti. It sounds to me like he was attracted to these fiery operatic singers but was probably carrying on his romance mostly in his head. I think we have to accept Lydia's remarks as being fairly well-founded."

Rayette waved a hand. "I think it is hard for us, here in the twenty-first century, to grasp what a love relationship would be in the early 1700s. Remember, this is before the word or even the concept of 'romanticism' had emerged in Europe. Granted, there are love scenes, Romeo and Juliet-style dramas, poetry in honor of music, and other signs we often associate with the notion of romance, but really, at that time, the focus on feelings and individual passion characteristic of the Romantics was yet to come. Byron, Keats, Shelley, even Wordsworth—these were all poets who came along after the 'reasonableness' of the Enlightenment has been replaced by the fiery passions of Romanticism."

Alison looked questioningly at Katherine. "This may be a little off the subject, but don't psychologists argue that love is the same emotion whether or not it is experienced in real life or simply celebrated in poetry or music? The movement we call Romanticism is more a way of analyzing the arts starting late in the 1700s and on into the 1800s. Lovers weren't likely to check in with their local literary critic or music reviewer to see if their lovemaking was in keeping with the latest trends. When he was composing, Handel may have had in mind specific musical traditions associated with a lover's anguish, but that wouldn't have influenced his own intimate relationships."

Since Alison had seemed to direct her question toward Katherine, after looking around to see if anyone else wanted to respond, Katherine offered her own slowly formulated answer. "Again, as a folklorist, I try to be aware of how the dominant worldview or Zeitgeist influences individuals and perhaps shows up in their everyday choices. It is still just an interpretation, of course, but you can often identify motifs or patterns that suggest a current cultural convention or behavioral trope—a tradition that unconsciously influences thought and behavior. For example, soon after Goethe published his first novel, *The Sorrows of Young Werther*, there was reportedly a spate of suicides among young European intellectuals, people imitating Werther's sad end. Folklorists speak of ostension in folklore—behavior sparked by hearing a legend perhaps and mimicking the plot in some way. Goethe's Werther ushered in the *Sturm und Drang* movement in Germany, just before Romanticism became the dominant worldview in Europe. But the notion of anguished love relationships leading to suicide was already in the air. Or, perhaps more tellingly, the emerging worldview was accepting of such a drastic response to frustrated feelings of love as somehow a grand, though lamentable, sign that one is human. Unlike the quest for reasonableness during the Enlightenment, this new movement celebrated extreme emotions and valued them over disciplined or even godly behavior."

Peter smiled—as everyone seemed to be looking at him. "There ARE other people in this Seminar who speculate on psychological foibles," he laughed. "Ross, for example, must ponder the unfathomable mystery of human behavior every time he looks in the mirror." He grinned as Ross rolled his eyes. "However," Peter went on, "I have actually looked into this issue of what some might consider the mystique of the overly sensitive suicide. Fortunately, today there are hotlines and therapies specifically aimed at stopping suicides. What's interesting is that, in the past, if the suicide could be construed as martyrdom bravely accepted in opposition to facing a life lived without God, then the individual was regarded as a saint. However, if it were a person who viewed life as not worth living without the love of some human he adored, then people considered him a sinner and a mental misfit—except the Romantics. They were more forgiving."

"But let's bring this back to where we started," Peter went on. "It's true that there were some instances of passion-inspired suicide in real life—long before Goethe wrote his late eighteenth-century novel. In fact, one curious, though roundabout, connection with Handel is the suicide of one Jeremiah Clarke—you know, famous for his trumpet voluntary. It seems Clarke was the original composer of music set to a a poem by the great Restoration poet John Dryden—a poem called 'Alexander's Feast, or, The Power of Music.' How's that for a title? The poem, or ode, really was about how a singer can manipulate even a king's emotions with his music. Dryden had intended the poem to be set to music—something Handel would do some forty years later—and originally London organist and composer Jeremiah Clarke undertook the task. His music has subsequently been lost. Our connection here, however, is that Clarke, a few years after composing the music for Dryden's poem, committed suicide—supposedly as a consequence of his hopeless love for a lady of superior rank. So, why do I bring up this connection? Well, partly because here is an example of a musician well aware of the ties between music and emotions—that was the subject of Dryden's poem. But perhaps more importantly, because Clarke was himself a victim of what self-help writer Dean Delis calls the 'passion paradox.' Delis gave this name to the phenomenon of unequal love matches and the passion the low man on the totem pole feels for the person higher up, or more beautiful, or more talented, etc. You see what I mean. I think Handel may have suffered from a bad case of the 'passion paradox' throughout his life—whether he deserved to or not. That's my theory, for whatever it's worth, and I'm sticking to it."

Everyone seemed to be pondering Peter's lengthy exposition. Finally, Clara spoke up. "Whoa, Peter. That is a lot of information, but I'm not sure it all leads to your theory, as you call it. I'd like to reconsider what Alison was asking. If you think about it, Alison was saying that love is a natural emotion whereas cultural attitudes and conventions are imposed by society. Marriage and sexual mores are manmade, but the emotions we associate with love are part of human nature. So, we can assume that Handel felt the same emotion we feel when we speak of love even though he lived three hundred years ago, before the Romantics or Freud came on the scene. He didn't need poets or psychologists to tell him what he felt."

Ross returned from the buffet with—strangely—a piece of fruit, a ripe Bartlett pear. He frowned and looked at Clara. "I hear what you are saying, Clara, but I think, on this, I agree with Peter. For example, if we have learned nothing else from all of the sad history of homosexuals being persecuted in this country—and across the globe—we should see how clearly assumptions about what is 'natural' and what people accept as true because their culture tells them to—well, we should have learned how faulty these assumptions are. Or, perhaps, what we need to recognize is how complex human behavior is. Every action –from what or how we eat to when, how, or with whom we make love—is influenced by our biological make-up but also by our culture. Today, most psychologists argue that society has placed a powerful burden on anyone who experiences himself or herself as a gay rather than a straight person. Think how hard it would be for such a person to simply ignore what society says and go with what he or she feels. We take in what our culture teaches us—even if it conflicts with our own feelings."

Clara waved her hand and, before Katherine could respond to it, said, "I know I have overused my turn-to-speak card here, but I promise I'll be quiet after this. I typically like playing the devil's advocate, so I suppose my comment on Peter's theory is tinged with a bit of that dye. But let me say a little about some research I've read on sexuality. I admit that I tend to trust the research of people in the hard sciences more than that of social scientists. So, instead of a psychologist like the one Peter mentioned, I would look to a biologist like Frans de Waal, who has studied primates and wrote a provocative book titled *Our Inner Ape*. He has written other books as well, but in this one, he talks about how a recently identified species of primates—the bonobo—sheds new light on human behavior. Most impressive to me—he describes this group of chimp-like primates as female dominant, as inclined to use sex as a means of placating and interacting with each other throughout the day—on average, once every one and a half hours, and as engaging in same-sex interactions as easily as opposite-sex ones. De Waal goes on to say that there are no bonobos that are only heterosexual or only homosexual. All bonobos are bisexual, and all are generally promiscuous. 'So what?' you may say, and I agree, humans are not bonobos. But, as de Waal points out, Kinsey was right: sexual preferences among humans are also naturally on a continuum. It is society, not nature, that insists upon making hard and fast distinctions when it comes to sexual behavior."

With an impatient look at the clock, Brad said, "Do you think we could get back to looking at the letter and talking about what Handel is up to? I don't think we have time to go off on tangents." Clara seemed affronted, but Ross lifted his glass and said, "A pitcher at Nick's later this evening for any who want to continue with these fascinating tangents. But meanwhile, as the man says, back to Lydia and her letter."

Katherine reflected inwardly that it was much easier to direct the flow of talk in a class of graduate students all of whom hoped to get a good grade from the seminar. "Right," she said. "Let's consider Rebecca's question: What kinds of things led to Handel being such a success by the time he arrived in London? Lydia obviously thought he was successful far beyond any other musicians she knew. Rebecca, did you have some thoughts on what some of these advantages might have been?"

"Well," Rebecca began, "I always go back to the fact that Handel managed to find or have thrust upon him the essential elements of a superb musical education. First, he was taught by Zachow, a fine teacher who had accumulated an excellent library of musical compositions from various parts of Europe. There is evidence that Handel copied many of these manuscripts and even used them himself as teaching tools. Then, after his brief forays into work as a church organist in Halle and apprentice composer and harpsichordist in Hamburg, he left for Italy—a kind of graduate program in cantata and opera production. And, by most standards, his crowning achievement at the close of this program of learning was his so-to-speak dissertation—the impressive and energetic opera *Agrippina*. Handel had clearly worked hard and benefited every step of the way from the advantages offered him. Speaking as a teacher, I would characterize him as an enterprising and diligent student, the kind you fully expect to see succeed. Beyond that, he also seemed to have a clear goal for himself. He never faltered, nor was he distracted by offers that would turn him in other directions. I suspect that this is part of the reason he did not marry, at least as a young man. He was unwilling to let anything get in the way of his ambition."

Rayette signaled that she had something to add. "Much is made of Handel's father discouraging his son from playing musical instruments, but in fact what the elder Handel was opposed to was his son taking on the role of musician as a profession. I suspect that he considered musical training to be part of any gentleman's required schooling. The gymnasium that Handel attended in Halle likely included music instruction as well as exposure to poetry and classical literature. We can't really know why music became the compelling focus of Handel's life, but we can assume that his early and all-consuming interest in music contributed to his most obvious personality traits—his intelligence, his ability to focus on a task and concentrate on it until completed, his appreciation for themes and patterns that evoke deep emotional responses, his recognition of depth and feeling in the work of great poets and other musicians. Modern science offers some proof that musical training and intelligence, at least, often go hand in hand. I think Handel's early attraction to music left its mark on his personality for the rest of his life. It profoundly influenced who he became, who he was."

"I've often wondered," said Alison, "what sparked Handel's great love affair with the human voice. Because, even though he started out as an instrumentalist and remained a virtuoso keyboardist throughout his life, and though he contributed greatly to the purely instrumental repertoire, still, his most impressive accomplishment is in writing outstanding music to be sung—either by soloists or by a chorus. That was his great contribution—music that showcased the human voice. He must have delighted in hearing singers bring his music to life. As I've said before, I would love to go back in time and find out what kind of voice Handel himself had. He seemed to know just what a great singer would do with his or her voice to express a given feeling. I expect he was an excellent teacher or coach to the choristers who sang with him. I wonder if he had a singing mentor in Halle, someone who taught him while he was still a young boy. I guess we will never know."

"There is one thing we DO know," said Brad. "Handel figured out that he didn't want to stay in either Germany or Italy but instead to set his sights on London. What was so special about London? From hindsight, we can see that it worked for him, but why is that? I'm guessing it wasn't just wanderlust. I mean, he was serious about his music, so he wanted to be where he could be most successful. How did he figure out it would be London? That's my question."

Ross raised his glass. "I'll take a stab at that, Brad. I've done a lot of film production in Italy, in Germany, and in England and several other European contexts. Every new location, I make it a practice to research the history of the place, especially as it applies to the project at hand. One thing about both Italy and Germany in the late 1600s and early 1700s—they were hotbeds of musical activity. That was why Handel went to Italy. Germany had some outstanding opera, but Italy had even more. However, London had almost no opera at all. If Handel went to London, he would be a big fish in a small pond. Most people find that situation much more conducive to success and creativity than being just another small fish in a large pond. I think Handel knew he would be seen as a kind of wunderkind in London. Or, to put in in modern terms, he made a smart business move that took into account the most likely marketing advantage his skills, age, and background would give him. He chose London with his eyes wide open."

"Sounds reasonable to me," said Brad. "Maybe he thought he would find more women willing to put up with his odd hours and traveling man mentality. I know a lot of musicians who have that problem."

Katherine grimaced a bit at this but smiled as she pointed to the clock. "Ok, my friends, we've come to the end of another session. And despite Forella having been out of town until just recently, she has a recording for each of you to listen to before our next Seminar meeting. This is Handel's *Acis and Galetea*. It is not exactly an opera, but it is opera-like. And, you will be glad to know it is in English. Enjoy. See you all next time."

CHAPTER 12

And Water Music

Ross took the recording of Handel's Acis and Galatea along with him as he drove to a late-afternoon meeting with one of his production collaborators. He was relieved to hear that, in this Handel recording, the male lead—Acis—was singing in the tenor range, as was his friend, Damon. The only other male singer was the bass, Polyphemus. No countertenors this time. Try as he might, Ross just couldn't get the image of a wounded castrato out of his head whenever he heard a man singing in soprano range. And he liked the fact that the piece was in English. The story, he knew, was from Ovid, so he expected there would be some metamorphosis at the end of the story, but he had forgotten the plot. Acis, it seemed, was in love with Galatea—no surprise there, but an intriguing twist was the ardent desire Galatea felt for Acis. In a charming aria, "Love in her eyes," Acis describes to his friend and fellow-shepherd, Damon just how smitten Galatea is. He sings, "Love on her breast sits panting/ And swells with soft desire." Clearly, this is a lusty composition. Even the villain is driven by passion. He sings, "I rage—I melt—I burn!" The short opera was an unusual piece but evidently one of Handel's most popular. Ross wondered if the composer identified with any of the characters—maybe Acis, a man loved passionately by a goddess—or maybe his rival, Polyphemus, the impassioned giant. One thing for sure—Handel knew what fiery love scenes were all about—what they looked like, how they felt, how they could inflame and animate the heart and voice of great singers.

─⸙─

SEVERAL OF THE SEMINAR MEMBERS had taken Ross up on his invitation to gather at a local tavern later in the evening after their last luncheon meeting. Downstairs, Nick's was a pretty noisy place, with jabbering students and townspeople in booths all along the front dining area. But upstairs was a less crowded room with tables and a slower pace. Ross ordered a pitcher and a large basket of fries. And he asked the waiter to bring a hamburger—who can go to Nick's without eating one of their great hamburgers? First to join him was Clara, and shortly after, Peter and Wait. Katherine came as well. She passed along the news that CD would be declining—mostly because he realized that spouses were not really in on the discussion and he had promised to meet his partner for dinner at another restaurant across town.

Katherine looked around to make sure their discussion was not going to be easily overheard by folks sitting nearby. "It's something we still haven't really resolved, isn't it?" she said. "We talked about including spouses early on, but then we let it slip by with no real action. I hope CD doesn't feel excluded."

Peter chuckled. "It's ok. We can tell him if we have any important breakthroughs. Relax, Katherine. This isn't a class," he said. Then he filled a glass with beer and handed it to Katherine, at the same time saying, "So, Ross, my friend, remind me what prompted this visit to my favorite Bloomington watering hole—or was it just to enjoy the beer and burgers?"

"If I remember correctly," Ross said, "the comment that inspired this little gathering was Brad's admonition that we stick to the subject at hand—Lydia's letter. And I believe he accused Clara of going off on a tangent," he said, with a laugh and a tip of his glass to Clara.

"No doubt I overreacted," said Clara. "I suppose some people might see no connection at all between a discussion of Handel's love life and what scientists know about the behavior of various primate groups. But if we are going to invoke words like 'natural' behavior or ideas about what is essentially human, then I think we have to take into account the research that has been done on our closest primate relatives. I can't imagine anyone in our group is still so brainwashed as to deny evolution. But even people who accept evolution may not grasp the implications of a study like de Waal's work with bonobos. To me, it simply shows that at some time in the very distant past, the pre-hominid ancestors who eventually evolved into the human species did, quite possibly, have the option of maintaining a female dominant, bisexual behavior as the norm rather than one with violent male dominance and strong gender divisions. If human evolution had favored bonobo-like hominids, we might have never worried over the notions of homosexual or heterosexual preferences at all. And perceived differences about what is properly male or female behavior might never have emerged. I think a lot of Handel's reluctance to get married probably reflects his dissatisfaction with imposed gender distinctions and duties rather than his own sexual preference or attractions."

Wait shook his head. "Brad isn't here to state his opinion, but I am inclined to agree with him on this. I don't really see the connection. I'm not a Creationist. I get what evolution is all about, but I still don't see what a study of bonobos has to do with how Handel interacted with women back in the 1700s. For most of recorded human history, men and women have gotten married, men have tended to be promiscuous, and men who didn't marry were considered a bit weird—either antisocial or homosexual. To me, it looks like Handel was—I guess—antisocial. He didn't want the responsibility that went with being married, but he liked having sexual relations with women who excited him and who required no commitment from him. I don't think it has anything to do with our evolution as a species. I think it has more to do with Handel's own priorities—in this case, work, music, maybe recognition. Women were somewhere down the chain of necessities. He probably enjoyed women but didn't think they were worth spending a lot of his time and energy pursuing or supporting in a mutual relationship. He would have made a lousy husband. I can promise you, my wife would back me up on that."

Clara smiled at Wait, a bit ruefully. "Actually, that's what I see as part of the problem here. We seem to accept the idea that there is an ideal husband- or wife-type. But individuals differ a lot on what they are looking for in a mate, or even in a friend. The 1950s were notorious for telling people what an ideal husband or wife should be. But most of that was gender stereotyping. I understand what you are saying, Wait—that workaholic men make lousy husbands—but the truth is, anyone who is consumed by his or her work is liable to be seen as hard to live with. I was married for nearly ten years, but my husband and I eventually realized that we had rather different notions on what a spouse is—what it means to be married. We divorced—not because he was a lousy husband—he wasn't—nor because I was a lousy wife—well, I'm sure some would say that I was. But that's the point. Our culture tells us there is some well-defined state called 'marriage,' when in fact, relationships are much more complex than some legally-binding description would suggest. If you asked me, I would say that I still love my former husband—even though he has remarried—but I wouldn't want to be married to him. Obviously, right now I don't want to be married to anyone."

"So, you are arguing that the institution of marriage is the problem—not Handel and his priorities or his personality or his preferences, is that right?" asked Ross. "You think he simply didn't like the idea of being married? That seems possible to me. But I'm still with Wait on wondering why or how this connects with primate studies. After all, even animal species that mate for life don't have marriage as part of their lives. It's a human tradition. What's the connection?"

"Ok," Clara said with a sigh, "maybe I made a big leap here, but let me try to explain. First, even people who accept evolution and acknowledge our ties to past and present primate species will still see the typical alpha male and his harem prototype as the primate pattern most like our own. So, from this perspective, it would make sense that a typical human male would hope that he gets to be like the silverback gorilla and mate with all the females and drive off all the other males. And people consider that somehow natural—male dominance, competition over females, chest-thumping as a sign of virility and power. But gorillas are actually further back on the evolutionary line than are bonobos, and bonobos do not exhibit that pattern but instead a peaceful, female dominant, sexually promiscuous and bisexual behavior. So, why isn't the bonobo behavior pattern held up as what is 'natural' for our later primate species? If bonobos were assumed to reflect the more natural primate pattern, then mothers would be seen as dominant, it would be expected that there would be lots of mating with many different partners, same-sex activity would be par for the course, and sex would be a normal way to express simple affection, apology, reconciliation, or just plain good fun. If we behaved like bonobos, we would not worry over who has the right to have sex with whom nor which babies born are legitimate and which are not. Sex, gender, and reproduction would not define us as individuals. For someone like Handel, his love life would be nobody's business—or, maybe everybody's business and therefore simply ignored. Sex wouldn't be so central to how we define ourselves."

Katherine looked intently at Clara for a moment or two, then said, "I'd like to go back to what Ross said—that marriage is a human tradition. The problem with comparing humans and other primates is that humans have had eons in which to create and pass along traditional practices, ideas, and beliefs. I know there are studies that show other animals do have some practices they pass along to their offspring, but really, tradition, folklore, heritage, worldview—these are primarily human features. We are finding more and more evidence of early burial customs, for example, even among Neanderthals, and we know quite a bit about early hunting and food preparation. Bones and artifacts can tell us something about early customs, but information on marriage and family is something that we have to glean from expressive sources—carvings, hieroglyphs, the earliest forms of writing. I remember when I first read Jean Auel's *Clan of the Cave Bear*—first in her series on

Earth's Children—I was struck by her efforts to account for the rise of traditions among Homo sapiens, especially marriage customs. But even more impressive is, really, the strength and power of tradition once it is established and holds sway. People do challenge and break away, but it is always a struggle. We see that now as people try to challenge laws prohibiting same-sex marriage. Once a favored tradition becomes law, it is hard to change."

Clara jumped back into the discussion. "Society makes sex and intimate touching a scant commodity by insisting that sexual relations be controlled by laws or conventions that entail severe punishments or at least shaming and harassment when broken. And as we all know, scarcity produces want. Imagine, just imagine, if people were free to engage in sexual relations anytime they wanted with whomever they wanted. I don't mean rape or child abuse—unwanted sexual attention—but rather just imagine what it would be like if sex were simply a routine but pleasant way of showing affection or offering an apology or support—like hugs. I'm not saying we should be like the bonobos, but it is interesting to speculate on what human conventions about sexual relations would be like if we accepted and practiced the kind of everyday eroticism we see among bonobos."

"Everyday eroticism," said Ross. "Now there's a concept! But Clara—you'd put the poets out of business. Humans thrive on rejection, denial, painful longing. What would we sing about? Who would dance, paint, or write sonnets if there were no one holding out for the most impressive offer, the most desirable lover? Like the song title says, it's only what we really want when it 'Hurts So Good.' Scarcity or prohibition—that's what makes sex so compelling."

"And there are those," said Peter, "who would argue that marriage destroys the pleasure of sex precisely because those prohibitions are no longer in place. That 'everyday eroticism' is just too tame if there isn't some barrier to overcome, some claim to contradict, some ardent admiration to win. And jealousy! Who hasn't experienced the pangs of jealousy at least some of the time? We may be ashamed of our possessiveness, but we feel it all the same. Humans haven't escaped that aspect of our animal past. I suspect that even bonobos show some signs of selfish ownership."

Wait lifted his glass and stared at it. "Well, I suppose it's true that we can learn something from looking at bonobos or chimps or gorillas—something about human behavior, but I still think humans are different. We at least try to think things through. I wish we knew what Handel was thinking rather than what Lydia thought he was thinking. It sounds to me like he was a man willing to take advantage of his male privilege. I think he saw no reason to tie himself to a woman even if he DID want to have a roll in the hay. We don't seem to have any record of what he thought about any of this. We just know he never married."

"We can keep hoping that we'll learn more," said Katherine. "How's the next letter coming along, Peter? It is so tempting to read between the lines in Lydia's letters. Maybe she will give us more to go on as we move through the stack. Surely once in a while she will quote something back to Handel or question what he has said or written to her. That's my hope. I look forward to our next session. Thanks, Ross, for suggesting we meet here for this little follow-up. I need to run, but I look forward to seeing you all next time. I'll buy a round another time. Bye."

As Katherine left, the rest of the group started gathering things up and heading for the door as well. Wait took out his cell phone to call his wife. Ross smiled a little sadly at Peter and said, "You see how it is with these married men—always under someone's thumb." But he clapped Wait on the shoulder and said, "Have a good night, my friend."

Some time later, when the Handel Seminar met again, Benfey sat unobtrusively in her corner typing in some observations on the behavior of various Seminar members as they came into the room and interacted. *Ross, Katherine, and Wait seem especially attuned to each other as things start up—Peter and Clara as well,* she wrote on her laptop. Katherine looked over Benfey's shoulder, at the notes on her screen. "Whatever does that mean?" she asked. Benfey just laughed and said, "I like to record something about the general atmosphere each time as the meeting starts. Today it strikes me that several of you seem more connected somehow. You know, a little more psychic energy flowing among you. A subjective thing, I know, but, hey, it's my record, and that's what I see."

Katherine looked at Benfey for a moment. "Really, you simply observed that? I mean, you didn't talk to any of us before you wrote that?" Benfey looked a bit concerned. "My mentor back at Cambridge said to record anything that comes to mind when it happens and worry about what it means later. I have pages of notes like this. Most of it probably doesn't mean anything, but who knows? I figure it can't hurt," said Benfey. Katherine smiled and said, "You are amazing! Carry on."

After everyone chose sumptuous edibles from the buffet and sat down at the table, Forella asked Angela to pass around a facsimile of the wordbook from Handel's *Amadigi*. "A contact Ross and Peter met in London," said Forella, "sent this copy of the wordbook from one of Handel's earlier operas. Angela and I discussed it a bit when it arrived. Angela, maybe you could say a little about the copy while it is circulating."

"Certainly," said Angela. "This was the first performance of *Amadigi di Gaula*, presented at the King's Theater on May 25, 1715—about the same timeframe as the letters we are looking at right now. The frontispiece includes the cast for the performance along with an etching suggesting the figures of the four main characters. The script is difficult to read, but I checked to make sure. The castrato Nicolini plays the role of the hero, Amadigi, and the young woman Lydia mentioned last time—Anastasia Robinson—plays the victimized heroine, Oriana. Melissa, the sorceress, is Elisabetta Pilotti-Schiavonetti—the woman Lydia accused Handel of flirting with. There is also an unidentified castrato singing the role of Orgando, Oriana's uncle. Eighteenth-century music critic Charles Burney liked the opera, said it was one of Handel's best that he had heard."

When the circulating wordbook reached Brad, he whistled and said, "Well, no wonder Handel was hankering after his star soprano. Both of the women on this pamphlet look pretty stunning. I guess the sorceress is the one holding the staff. So that would be our Pilotti? The one Handel is in love with?"

Peter laughed and said, "Sorry, Brad, but those are just idealized depictions of the mythological characters. I actually looked for a picture of any sort that would show what Elisabetta Pilotti looked like, but I couldn't find anything. Later in Handel's career, some of the wordbooks, or more likely, the published scores, included a picture of Handel as composer, but the convention of including some standard artwork reflecting the content in some way—that was much more common. Basically, it was a kind of early clip art. So, we can't assume La Pilotti looked anything like the Melissa figure on the wordbook."

Brad poked at his food and said, a bit *sotto voce*, "I still bet she was a looker. Handel's earlier great love—Vittoria—she was supposed to be a beauty, right? I wonder if the music scene in London favored a beautiful woman over a talented woman. I'll have to say, it's always a turn-off for me if the diva is, you know, like the usual Wagnerian soprano—big voice but also physically bigger than her male companions. It just doesn't seem very realistic if the man is supposed to be passionately in love with someone who isn't a beauty. That's why we have gorgeous movie stars, right? If you are in the limelight, you need to be beautiful—at least women do. It may not be fair, but that's showbiz."

Rebecca scowled at Brad. "Really, Brad, that is just sexist. It would have been sexist in 1715, and it's even more sexist now. Singing opera isn't like some beauty contest. The women who sang in Handel's operas had to have talent, musicianship, a great voice, probably some acting ability. They couldn't just stand up there and be beautiful. Besides, if Pilotti were noted for her beauty, Peter should have been able to find pictures of her, don't you think? Artists would have wanted to paint her. Just because YOU can't stand to listen to a woman sing unless she is gorgeous doesn't mean other people make that a first priority."

"Hey, I didn't mean to push anyone's buttons here," said Brad. "I just think it's true that women on the stage or in movies have more pressure

The Handel Letters

on them to be beautiful. I agree it isn't fair, but I still think it's true. My guess is that the really successful women who sang in Handel's operas were good-looking along with being talented—that's all."

"Well," said Ross, "beauty is in the eye of the beholder—especially if beauty is understood as whatever attracts. And in this case, it seems clear that Handel found Pilotti attractive—for whatever reason, but surely because she had a great voice and knew how to interpret his music. So, Peter, when you were looking for pictures of Pilotti, did you find any written records commenting on her looks, one way or the other?"

"No," said Peter, "nothing directly. Some of Handel's contemporaries, such as the music critic Angela mentioned, Charles Burney, did comment on some of Handel's singers—characterizing Margherita Durastanti, for example, as 'course and masculine.' But I didn't find much else. I did, however, run across an interesting comment in a recent documentary in which Handel scholar Donald Burrows mentions Handel's predilection for collecting paintings of naked women—all appropriately mythological figures, of course. If nothing else, he appreciated those womanly features so often celebrated in classical paintings—you know, curvy, not boyish."

Katherine stood and returned the wordbook to Angela. "Thanks, Forella, for sharing the *Amadigi* wordbook with us. It's interesting that, of course, today we have subtitles or supertitles when we watch an opera, and the theater is dark, so wordbooks would be of little use. But in Handel's time, people sat in candle-lit halls and often socialized or played cards while the opera was performed. Usually they already knew the plot—at least in a general way—so their main interest was in how well the singers performed their arias. The wordbook would be useful for the more serious opera-goers, but most probably simply listened when a strong or impressive voice took the stage."

"That's like most jazz venues," said Wait. "People are eating or talking, but they stop and clap when someone plays a solo. I can't imagine an opera production putting up with that kind of audience behavior today, though. Well, the clapping after a great solo does happen at operas, but the talking and socializing would definitely be out. Actually, I'm surprised to hear that's how it was back then. I thought people always took their opera seriously."

Alison spoke up. "In Handel's time, opera was still fairly new, especially in England. Handel was such a success because he gave his singers really good arias to sing. And the singers had to be especially good to impress people who were distracted by other things. I figure most people who went to an opera back then used the production as an excuse to see and be seen. What a challenge for the composer and singers! But Pilotti must have been someone who impressed not just Handel but also the audiences who came to his operas."

"Right you are, Alison," said Ross. "So, Peter, do we have a new letter from Lydia? And does it shed any light on our ongoing solicitude over Handel's love life?"

"I have two letters—two! " said Peter. "Whether they shed light or simply aggravate our worry will be up to all here to decide. Angela, I entrust the copies to you with thanks for passing them around. I must –really MUST—have another of Annie's great meat pies. Nothing this good since I last visited London. The letters are not long. Happy reading."

Here are the transcriptions Angela handed to each of the Seminar members.

Mr. G F Handel, Esqr
In care of the Right Honorable Lord Burlington
Burlington House
Piccadilly, London

10 June 1715

My Dear Mr. Handel,
We had little opportunity to talk at the dinner party last week. I cannot tolerate such an expanse of time without a more satisfying reunion than we were able to achieve then. And so I write.

Once again those years of exile in Hamburg proved a boon to Edward as he petitioned our new monarch for the privilege of continuing his work here at Westminster. Happily we shall be staying in England, and Eggy has already found us a townhouse not far from Marylebone Gardens. I removed to the country while Eggy negotiated his duties here. I did miss attending the music over the past year, but I am now returned and eager to hear what you have for the opera audiences this season. Dr. Arbuthnot was again the consummate host. His house is such a lively place to hear music and gossip. It was no time at all before I was informed of the affair between La Pilotti and our Mr. Handel. And I cannot deny that her eyes and your eyes seemed to follow each other no matter the other distractions in the room.

In truth, my dear Gif, I wish she were free for you to marry. It is such an inspiration to see the two of you working together. I truly believe you each compel the other to greater excellence than you might achieve otherwise. You have written some outstanding arias for her, and she has given you leave to stretch music in new ways simply because you know she can sing it with skill, energy, and compassion for the person she portrays. The new piece she rehearsed for us at the dinner party was beautifully sung. I can see why you find it hard to keep secret your more personal regard. But, dear friend, she is married, and not unhappily. I wonder, if she had an available, unmarried twin, if you would be as smitten with her. But that is unfair. I do pity you. Perhaps it would help to imagine what your father would have advised.

Ah, but you have always been extremely independent. Surely your father would not have advised you to go to Hamburg, or to Italy, and certainly not to London. Perhaps he would have encouraged a safe arrangement in Saxony with our sweet Marie. But just as you could not keep your talent and vigor under a bushel, so could you not tie yourself to anyone whose fervor and character does not match your own. I am sorry to see you thwarted by circumstance, but I smile with

you at the joy you find in composing such stirring music for your lady. I send my good wishes to you and here voice my eager anticipation for the upcoming season and the new opera.
I have the honor to be, ever yours,

Mrs. Edward Grayston
Rowe Estate
Marylebone

And the second letter:

Mr. G F Handel, Esqr
In care of James Brydges
Earl of Carnavon
Cannons Park
Middlesex

25 September 1717

My Dear Mr. Handel,
What a worrisome time this has been for you, my dear young maestro. As you know, Eggy and I joined Dr. Arbuthnot and Margaret to see yet again your wonderful Amadgi. No trump playing at our table. It was such a thrill to hear again the fine arias written for Elisabetta, especially knowing that she would be leaving at the season's close. She did succeed so well in conveying her character's warring thoughts and emotions. Though a sorceress, she could not force Amadgi to love her, but this was no different than Pilotti's other sorceress roles. More telling here was her character's bleak acceptance that her powers were ebbing away along with her blighted love. Your lady did truly stir my woman's heart with pain and dismay at seeing no avenue to happiness—neither power nor love. Her death scene was very touching. She

captured magnificently the deep feelings I could see you intended, my dear Gif. I no longer wonder at your broken heart. Of course it bleeds to see her leaving for Hanover—and without you.

Were you tempted to return to Hanover, even as Giovanni, as he must, led Pilotti back to her former home? Did your friends and family in Halle try to bring you back as well? Herr Schmidt—or as we must now call him—Mr. Smith was reluctant to share any of your news. And I quite understand. Despite the roiling issues surrounding our new king, it is best that you make clear your loyalty and attachment to your new landscape. I thought the series of pieces played upon the Thames –at least what I could hear if it—was wonderful—very fresh. It must surely endear you to our new king in a way returning to Hanover never could. But it is at a heavy price, I am sure.

It pleased me greatly to be included among the guests at your friend's delightful garden party. To hear you, our dear Doctor, Mr. Pope, and so many others discourse amid the flowers—it was almost like our youthful days in Sir John's parlor. I must admit surprise that they would consider the plot of an opera grave enough for their studied converse. It was especially gratifying to hear men speak with such sympathy about a woman's plight and choice to die rather than live without love or magical sway. But Mr. Pope is a poet. Perhaps poets and musicians are indeed more attuned to the humanity women share with men. I enjoyed the discourse immensely, and I could see that you have already instructed your host on the finer points of gardening. Few know their exotic plants so well as you—though perhaps Mr. Telemann challenged you on that, if there were a competition.

Sadly, the opera house will not offer a season this year, it seems. I do hope to hear some of the pieces you will compose while resting from the stage this year. Sir James has done much to restore the lovely chapel, and I do hope the new organ and the choristers there will keep

your mind occupied and rarely haunted by dreams of your lost love. My fond good wishes to you, my dear Gif.
  I have the honor to be, ever yours,

Mrs. Edward Grayston
Rowe Estate
Marylebone

"You may notice," said Peter, coming back from the buffet, "that Handel is still in residence at Burlington House in 1715, when the first letter was written, but has moved to Cannons Park, the home of James Brydges, by the date on the second letter in 1717. Both of these men—the young Lord Burlington and the (eventual) Duke of Chandos—were patrons who, like Ruspoli in Italy, provided the means for an elegant lifestyle while not really hiring Handel as a house musician. It seems that Handel liked being a free agent. But he certainly lived in grand houses at least some of the time during these early years in London."

CD put down his fork and took up his copy of the first letter. "I wonder how Handel was able to find these wealthy patrons—or, more accurately, hosts. I suppose he was something of a celebrity. But think about it, how would such an arrangement come about? You don't just walk up to a rich man and say, 'Hi, wouldn't you love to support me in lavish style while I compose music?' There would have to be something in it for the patron. And if Handel were not under contract, so to speak, well, how would the patron know that he would get something from Handel in exchange for all of his 'friendly' support? I am not trying to bring up the question of Handel's sexual orientation again, but I'll admit that the ever so hospitable situation suggests that these men wanted Handel in their lives—as a friend, not as a paid hireling. Maybe the times were very different, but if you had that situation today, I think people would assume there was some significant, maybe even an intimate, relationship between the two men. Doesn't anyone else see his living arrangements as unusual, or, in fact, significant?"

Katherine stood up and walked over to the flip chart Angela had set up before the meeting. With a wave toward CD, she said, "I think we can consider that our first topic growing out of today's letters. So, the significance of Handel's living arrangements—would that be the topic, then, CD?"

"I don't know if it is worth spending a lot of time on," said CD. "I'm just curious whether anyone else finds it odd that he gets to stay with these wealthy patrons but doesn't have to consider himself an employee. Certainly in today's climate, we would suspect that some sort of benefit accrues to the patron. We talked earlier about the patronage system. I know we said that the patron benefitted, that the musician reflected positively upon him and his household, but that would more likely be the case if the musician were actually in his employ. I just wonder how Handel got away with being a welcome guest rather than a salaried employee. If he had been female rather than male, wouldn't he have been seen as a mistress to the patron? I'm not trying to make a character judgment here, suggesting that Handel was prostituting himself or anything like that. I'm simply curious to know what anyone else thinks."

Katherine smiled over at CD and brought her hand down from the flip chart, leaving it blank. "I appreciate the way you couched your comments in gentle disclaimers, noting that things might be interpreted differently today than they would have been in Handel's day. That is certainly true. And there is no need to apologize for casting Handel's personal relationships or sexual orientation as an issue. Remember, part of the reason we have this Seminar at all is to benefit from each person bringing his or her perspective and interest to the floor. You gave us clear warning that you would voice a perspective that considers unconventional sexual arrangements and their consequences whenever you thought such issues were being overlooked or ignored. And that is important. We all have various culture groups that influence some of our thinking."

CD frowned and looked at Katherine as though seeking further explanation. "Well, I suppose this is slipping into 'professor-speak,' but bear with me," Katherine said. "Scholars recognize that dominant or accepted 'understandings' or paradigms influence the way natural phenomena or scientific data or human behaviors are interpreted or applied in a given time period. Or artists—critics view various artists as working within a given domain or style. And these paradigms or domains shift over time. But what I think they often leave out is the fact that the interpreters—the people writing the historical analyses—are themselves immersed in their own time and worldview as well. For example, you, CD—noted choral conductor, Bernstein scholar, gay rights activist, New York City exile, friend of wild animals taken in by our local animal control group, or so I hear—you have your own culture groups that influence your perspective. Your present situation and set of friends and cohorts must surely affect the way you look at and explain the past. If unchecked, that phenomenon is called 'presentism' among historians. It is usually disparaged as an almost unconscious tendency to impose contemporary values upon an interpretation of the past, and typically the concept is applied to scholars in the fields of history or sociology or literary criticism. But I think you could also imagine any self-identified group—such as the media's favorite 'gay community'—as perhaps employing a kind of 'emic presentism' or shared in-group vision and agenda when it looks to the past as well."

"So, you think I am promoting a GLBTQ perspective when I interpret the past?" said CD. "You think trying to articulate a queer perspective is just another bias rather than an attempt to correct the biased opinions of the majority?"

"Well," said Katherine, "if you are asking what I personally think, then, yes, I guess I do think you are expressing a bias, but I also think 'the majority' have a bias as well. We all do. That is the point. Ideally, conscientious scholars will be aware of their own biases and try to guard against letting them become overbearing obsessions in their own research. I'll admit I haven't read your work on Bernstein, but my guess is that you bent over backwards to make sure that comments on his homosexual affairs were well documented before you published—and not just because that is proper research procedure. You were likely aware that your own involvement in a growing body of avowedly 'queer' scholarship meant that you needed to make it clear that you were not jumping to conclusions, that your position was supported by reliable sources."

"Similarly," she went on, "you were cautious just now in suggesting that Handel's situation might lend itself to an interpretation that favors a homosexual relationship. But in Handel's case, it is even more important that you keep that cautious posture—because there is the added factor of time—a different time, a different set of circumstances. What might look like evidence of an intimate relationship to modern eyes may very well be evidence of quite a different kind of relationship if we could adopt the worldview of people in eighteenth-century London. I think it was, in fact, pretty common for the nobility to open their homes to visiting guests for long periods of time. And Handel was still technically a foreigner. He would have had to rent accommodations as a temporary tenant or rely on friends to provide housing. I guess what I'm saying, CD, is that it is a reasonable thing for you to wonder about Handel's sexual orientation because, as you said, that is a topic of interest to you. But it would be anachronistic to construe Handel's living arrangements as evidence that he was gay. Do you see what I mean?"

Ross stood up and said, "I am now going to play the role of—as, at an earlier meeting, Katherine so ungraciously named me—the heavy. We need to move on to a consideration of the letters. May I suggest that Nick's is a nice venue for continuing this interesting but perhaps less central thread. So, Katherine, I believe you had asked for some topics from today's letters, yes?"

"Yes, yes, thanks, Ross," said Katherine. Ross could tell that she was a bit chagrinned at having let the Seminar bog down in an academic aside. He gave her a quick wink and said, "I have a topic to suggest. I'm interested in what is clearly a reference, in the second letter, to Handel's *Water Music*. Here is music everyone in this Seminar would have heard—whether they recognized it or not—long before we started examining these letters. Lydia doesn't say much about the music, but she does mention it, and I'd like to pick apart the little bit she does say and see where it leads us."

On the flip chart, Katherine wrote: HANDEL'S WATER MUSIC. Then she looked around expectantly and saw Rebecca's hand in the air. "Yes, Rebecca?" she said.

"Notwithstanding CD's suspicions about Handel's patrons—which I wouldn't be opposed to discussing a bit more--. But I am more interested in what Lydia says about his relationship with his lead soprano. He does seem to be searching for some sort of love relationship, even if he does not end up a married man. I guess my question is: What do we make of his obvious interest in this woman? Do we agree with Lydia's hint that her being married is part of the attraction? And, can we assume Handel would act any differently today? Maybe Handel's decision to remain a bachelor but love unattainable married women makes sense to some people, even today."

Katherine added this second topic to their list—the recurrent HANDEL'S LOVE LIFE. Rayette looked at the second letter and said, "I was very excited to see her writing about Alexander Pope—the poet. I would like to explore Handel's ties to these friends he met in London and maybe go back and consider—as Lydia did—how they compare with his friends in Hamburg. So, I guess HANDEL'S FRIENDS would be a third topic."

After writing Rayette's topic on the flip chart, Katherine returned to her seat, saying, "Ross. You suggested our first topic—Handel's *Water Music*. Maybe you could give us a little background and tell us what questions Lydia's remarks sparked in your thinking."

"Happy to do that," said Ross. "Portions of the *Water Music* suite are pretty well known. In fact, certain pieces show up in commercials, movies, or campaigns of various sorts. My favorite use by far was in a video I stumbled across on the IU campus. This was a student project from, I think, the late 1980s, and the two guys who edited it were doing it as a –you'll love this, Katherine—a folklore project. The video is called *Indiana Urinalysis,* and the editors interview a lot of people—mostly men, as you might guess—about 'urinal etiquette.' But the connection here is that as they show examples of various urinals around campus, they play a segment from Handel's *Water Music.* Even non-music majors like me would get it. Anyway, I thought it was very creative."

"But back to Lydia's letter," he went on. "I'm guessing most of you know the story about why Handel wrote the *Water Music.* It's one of those legends that circulate about Handel. They really don't have firm evidence on most of it—other than the fact that the music really was played on a barge on the Thames for King George the first, just as Lydia suggests. Some biographers argue that Handel wrote the *Water Music* in an effort to get back in the King's good graces after deserting his post in Hanover, but more recent scholarship suggests that this wasn't really necessary, that King George was happy to see that Handel was doing well in London and harbored no ill feelings. However, it may well be true—another part of the legend—that the King's right hand man saw an opportunity to bolster the king's popularity among his new subjects by having a water party which everyone could enjoy even if only from the banks of the Thames. I'm sure you would be disappointed if I didn't report that there is a documentary film available that explores the *Water Music* legend. There is indeed. It is a video that documents a 2003 re-creation of the event—the only time the playing of *Water Music* on a barge on the Thames has occurred since the original in 1717—or so says the narrator. The musicians even wear wigs. Check it out."

"However," Ross said, "since I chided Katherine for going off on a tangent, I'll try to reign it in here. *Water Music*—or the collection of pieces now usually played as a three-part suite—was described by Lydia as 'wonderful—very fresh.' Though it wasn't regarded as an issue back in the 1700s, critics in every era since Handel's time have faulted him for obvious and frequent borrowing—usually from himself, but also sometimes from others. So Lydia's comment that this composition was 'very fresh' suggests not only that originality was unusual enough as to be commented upon but also that Lydia was a devoted listener, someone who would know when a piece is new or when a piece is repeated or revamped in a new version. To me, Lydia's comment is evidence that Handel's contemporaries were well aware of his practice of incorporating earlier works into new ones. They seemed to accept that this was one element of his clearly successful method of composition."

Alison signaled that she had something to add. "I was trained by a musicologist who definitely sided with the Handel-as-plagiarist school. He reported with downright glee every one of Handel's borrowings he could find as though they were proof of the man's low character and lack of skill and the reason he should never be listed among the world's greatest composers. I admit that I carried this prejudice with me for most of my early career. I would guess—except for the fact that everyone loves *Messiah*—this view of Handel would have continued up to the present if some scholars hadn't relented and recognized that they had a somewhat different understanding of the compositional process back then. As I understand it, Handel was actually very conscious of every borrowing he initiated. Sometimes he took things directly from earlier works, especially works he knew his current audience wouldn't have heard, and inserted them intact in a new work, and other times he reworked the piece or only used part of it or gave the motif an entirely new encasement. I now see what a genius he was. I wonder what makes a scholar jump on a composer like that, just because he did not choose to always create something new, something 'fresh,' to use Lydia's word."

"Originality," said Wait, "is something most critics expect from a composer, at least today. But I find it interesting—since I deal with jazz artists on a day-to-day basis—that the line between a newly composed piece and a cover of an older piece isn't always clear. You may remember the furor, back in the 1970s, over George Harrison's 'My Sweet Lord.' They found some obvious similarities between the beginning of his song and the same motif in an earlier song called 'He's So Fine' by someone else. Probably no one would have noticed if Harrison hadn't been famous and made a lot of money off of the piece. Tonal sequences are repeated all the time—which isn't to say he wasn't, in fact, borrowing or plagiarizing, to use the harsher term. Songwriters would be too paranoid to compose at all if they had to check every melody or riff to see if it arose from scratch or grew out of some earlier piece. Think of a composer like Gershwin. He tried to create music that sounded like traditional African-American music, for example. 'Summertime' is definitely his own song, but it was influenced by the style and maybe even specific songs he and his brother Ira had heard before they wrote *Porgy and Bess*. Handel probably did just what the Gershwins did—he used what most made sense to him to create the piece he imagined. But if you are a celebrity, you have to be extra careful."

Katherine looked over at Ross and said, with a slightly apologetic smile, "At the risk of falling back into academic mode, let me say a little about the whole notion of borrowing and originality from a folklorist's perspective. As you might guess, some songs, tunes, stories, even proverbs are considered 'traditional' when they were in fact created by an individual and can be traced to their point of origin. More often, however, any given item of folklore shows up in someone's repertoire with no clear path from a single antecedent. Instead, each individual who has sung the song or told the story has created it anew, sometimes remembering something very like what someone else performed, other times changing much, adding pieces from other songs or stories. The process of transmission and variation has been the focus of many folklore studies over the years, and it has been the impetus behind the publication of all the important folklore indexes or collections, such as the *Types of the Folktale* or *The English and Scottish Popular Ballads*."

"But," she continued, "perhaps one of the most interesting studies was an article written shortly after Ralph Stanley won a Grammy for his performance of the song 'Oh, Death' in the Coen Brothers movie *Oh Brother Where Art Thou?* The study was written by folklorist Carl Lindahl, and his challenge in writing the article was exactly this question of who wrote the song 'Oh Death.' In his study, Lindahl offers a painstaking analysis of possible paths of transmission, and he interviews family members of the man most often named as the songwriter—Lloyd Chandler. But for our purposes, it mostly points up how complex is the process by which a song is passed along in tradition but also simply created in the first place. As Lindahl demonstrates, there are many instances of borrowed themes, repeated formulas, 'floating lyrics,' and stylistic patterns that could well have influenced the songwriter as he composed, even as he supposedly created the piece from whole cloth. Folklorists usually view composition as a process reflecting many traceable lines of intertextuality. The songwriter or storyteller is like the bricoleur in artistic parlance. The artist draws from many available sources every time he or she creates a new piece of art or performs a new song. Creativity is never a simple process, and certainly not ever solely the result of individual genius."

Brad smiled, looked at Katherine and shrugged, then said, "I remember all the flak about George Harrison's song. A lot of people were really hostile and blamed him for taking advantage of 'the little guy' who wrote 'He's So Fine.' I think Harrison ended up paying a lot of money for that mistake. But I guess that's my question. Could a really good musician like George Harrison conveniently forget that he had heard some song before? I don't think so. I mean, wouldn't a professional musician—someone like Harrison—have people who could check and make sure his song is entirely original before he put it out on the market? I think he knew but figured he wouldn't get caught. It must be easy enough to check on that kind of thing. Just listen to the two songs. You can hear the similarity."

"I don't know," said Rebecca. "Some cultural traditions value shared conventions more than originality, and even when songs or stories are 'new,' they are expected to incorporate some things familiar to the listeners—as Katherine suggested. Some African epic singers rely upon formulas and themes already a part of the culture when they compose orally. I suppose a popular songwriter is doing something similar when he or she composes a song. Maybe George Harrison thought of that opening pattern as simply a favorite riff but not a whole tune or motif that could be copyrighted."

Brad looked at Rebecca with some surprise. "Well, yeah, I suppose he might have figured it was just a part of the song, that he wasn't ripping off the whole thing. But a song like 'Oh Death'—I remember when all the music from *Oh Brother Where Art Thou?* was so popular in the store. It fit into the plot of the film that the song was a traditional Appalachian folksong. But from what Katherine says, it sounds like another case of someone not getting credit for creating a song that earned someone else a lot of money. Maybe that is what people who blame Handel for his borrowings are complaining about—the fact that he made money at it. Like Wait and CD said, Handel was a celebrity, and celebrities have to be careful. Someone out there is always ready to bring them down."

Katherine came back from the buffet with a cup of coffee, stopping near the flip chart as she came. "We've moved off quite a ways from Ross's inquiry about *Water Music*. I have a feeling the issue of Handel's method of composition will come up again. Our time is getting short, so let's go on to our second topic—the ever-popular problem of HANDEL'S LOVE LIFE.

Rebecca waived her copy of the first letter. "I'm the one who suggested we return to the topic. It continues to amaze me that Lydia feels comfortable bringing up such a personal issue with Handel. She hints that he is simply attracted to Pilotti because she is married—or at least that her being married is part of the attraction. Lydia obviously knew Handel better than we do, and as Katherine said, we need to be aware that our present-day notions on intimate, or especially, adulterous affairs are different than they were back then. Still, I can't help feeling that Lydia is simply imposing society's expectations on Handel, chiding him, as she did in an earlier letter, for not getting married and settling down. She says she understands why he is attracted to Pilotti, but then she turns around and hints that maybe he is naively assuming that real love is the sort of fiery relationship that typically emerges in the plots of operas. I think she feels sorry for him, but she also seems impatient with his tendency to fall in love with divas instead of ordinary women."

No one else seemed eager to take up the topic. Clara finally spoke up. "If we believe what Lydia wrote, we have to concede that it wasn't just Handel who was 'in love.' Elisabetta was evidently flirting right back, or at least so it seemed to Lydia. From what we have read so far, Handel strikes me as—hmm—possibly a bit naïve about relationships with women. He seems to have been pretty comfortable with men, but I can imagine that he found really talented women that he admired a little intimidating. Lydia and Handel got along well because they were friends, but La Pilotti was a star and someone that Handel felt strongly about. The fact that she returned his attention was probably both exciting and challenging. He couldn't necessarily feel superior to Elisabetta. And I think that sense of superiority, of perfectionism, was part of his personality. I suspect he was actually relieved that she was leaving—though pained at the same time. Definitely the old 'Hurts So Good' syndrome."

Katherine looked around. It seemed that everyone was ready to leave that subject. "So," she said, "our third topic—Handel's friends. Rayette, I believe you suggested this one. Could you say a little more about what prompted your interest?"

Rayette looked at her copy of the second letter. "Lydia mentions several of Handel's friends—people she knew as well," Rayette said. "She had written about Dr. Arbuthnot earlier, but this time she adds the poet Alexander Pope—the one who sparked my interest—and of course his new patron, James Brydges, and the German Herr Schmidt, and even his friends from Hamburg days, Georg Philipp Telemann and Sir John—Wyche, I think. But what intrigues me is the fact that Handel doesn't really hang out with other musicians once he moves to London. Instead his friends are poets and writers and playwrights, people like Pope and Arbuthnot and John Gay and likely some of the other writers who were part of what was called the Scriblerians' Club. Some of these writers notoriously disliked opera, but they seemed to like Handel. So, he must have shared some of their sharp wit and interest in literary and artistic topics."

Alison looked over at Rayette. "I'd like to know a little more about Alexander Pope," she said. "I recall maybe one poem he was famous for—was it 'The Rape of the Lock?' The only reason I remember that is because anything with the word 'rape' in it was immediately scandalous back in high school when I first encountered it. But I think Pope was the author, am I right?"

"Yes," answered Rayette, "Pope wrote 'Rape of the Lock' as well as many other poems, usually long ones. He also translated Homer and edited Shakespeare. He was a real scholar. Lots of well-known sayings come from his poetry. He usually wrote in heroic couplets. For example, you've all heard the lines:

A little learning is a dangerous thing.
Drink deep, or taste not the Pierian spring.

There you have the two rhymed lines in iambic pentameter—the heroic couplet. There are many quotes people think are traditional or from the Bible that come instead from Pope's poetry: To err is human, to forgive divine; Fools rush in where angels fear to tread; Hope springs eternal in the human breast—those are from Pope. He was a small and sickly man. Also never married. I can just imagine Handel—who was quite a large man, even when he was young—sitting next to shrimpy little Alexander Pope. But evidently they were very good friends."

"I can't help but add a little something here, too," said Peter. "When I transcribed the second letter, I was pleased, just like Rayette, to see that Handel spent time with the likes of Pope and Arbuthnot. Lydia was quick to commend Pope for empathizing with a woman, and she claims his sensitivity comes from his insights as a poet. I've always thought of Pope as a witty, even a sarcastic, satirist rather than a sensitive romantic, but maybe Lydia saw a side of him we never see. But, that aside, I find it fascinating that Handel hobnobs with literary types. I think his clear interest in the narratives and characterizations that are central to literature is part of the reason he succeeds so well in writing opera—and eventually oratorios.

They are, after all, stories, plots, and they give Handel the outlets he needs for expressing human emotions through music. It makes perfect sense to me that his best friends are poets and writers. I'll bet those coffee shop conversations were something to hear. No wonder Lydia enjoyed the few times she was allowed to join what typically was a men's group. I'm sure she had a real thirst for that kind of camaraderie and intellectual stimulation. Handel must have thrived on it as well." Peter raised his glass: "To great friends—then and now!"

Forella clapped her hands lightly. "Bravo, Peter! You are such a sweetie! I think it is wonderful that Handel was friend to both Pope and Arbuthnot. And here is one of those coincidences that Ross is so quick to disparage. When I thought about what might be a good piece of Handel's music to send with you this time, Angela found instead an ad for a live concert that I hope you can all attend. The premier choral group and Baroque orchestra at IU are presenting Handel's *Esther* this coming weekend. Though there isn't definite proof of this, many scholars believe that Alexander Pope and Dr. Arbuthnot both contributed to the libretto of *Esther*, and it was composed around the time of this letter—in 1718. I had no idea that Pope would be mentioned in our letter this time. Come now, Ross, don't you agree it is a curious coincidence? IU has never presented this oratorio before. I think our Seminar's psychic energy prompted their concert. Isn't this what Jung would call synchronicity?"

Ross smiled over at his mother. "Nice try, Mom, but I think the IU music faculty decide months in advance what their upcoming repertoire will be. The choir has to have time to practice—the orchestra convened, advertisements created, venues reserved. You are the one who sees a coincidence here, but I don't think even Carl Jung would be impressed with the juxtaposition of concert and letter."

"No, no, I think she's right," said Peter. "Let's take a vote—everybody except Clara, who is a notorious skeptic. Doesn't everyone see a significant connection here?"

Katherine laughed and said, "Well, it's a nice concurrence of things that interest all of us, that's for sure. Thank you, Angela and Forella, for letting us know about this upcoming concert. That sounds excellent. Maybe we can talk a bit about this piece next time. I look forward to going to the performance. Maybe we could all sit together. According to this flyer, it is a free concert, supported by the Georgina Joshi Foundation for two nights running. Let's decide on a night we all can go. What fun!"

Even Ross had to smile and grab a copy of the concert announcement. They agreed to attend on Friday night and decided that they wouldn't be giving too much away if spouses or friends were invited to join them. Sometimes Bloomington, Indiana, is the right place to be.

CHAPTER 13

The Esoteric-Exoteric Factor

Katherine had left the last Handel Seminar meeting and driven to Terre Haute for a late afternoon talk she wanted to hear. On the way there, she thought about some of the dialogue emerging from their consideration of the last two letters Peter provided. One of Clara's comments in particular nagged at her. Perfectionism and a sense of superiority—these were part of Handel's personality, according to Clara. Maybe. Certainly Handel was a perfectionist. Katherine recalled with a laugh one anecdote repeated in a number of Handel biographies—the one in which Handel travels by carriage at five in the morning and rouses his librettist, Thomas Morell, from sleep to ask what the word 'billow' meant. Modern psychology might view this as a sure sign of obsessive-compulsive behavior, but after all, such attention to detail is why Handel's music survives to this day. He really did fret over making music and text work together. He would not short-change his art. He would not be second-rate. But, did he think of himself as superior? Are perfectionists inevitably a bit arrogant? Katherine knew that she herself was a perfectionist—most scholars are—but arrogant? No, no, arrogance, a sense of superiority—those are obnoxious traits—well, especially in a woman. Maybe Handel could get away with being a bit arrogant. She wondered if Lydia thought of Handel as arrogant—or maybe simply acutely aware of his own talent. These old missives from Lydia were a painfully slow way to learn about Handel, Katherine mused. Still, she was even more eager than before to read the next letter.

───⸺───

AS THEY GATHERED FOR THE next meeting of the Handel Seminar, several people carried with them copies of the printed program from Handel's *Esther*, the oratorio they had all recently attended on IU's campus. After filling his plate at the buffet, Wait sat down and waved his program around. "Now this is what I thought Handel's music would be like," he said. "Something more along the lines of his *Messiah*. Songs sung in English and choruses mixed in with the solos. I didn't really know the story of Queen Esther, but the printed word sheets they provided made it pretty clear. This was an Old Testament story. Did Handel write this about the same time as the *Messiah*? Has he switched to English oratorios now?"

Katherine tore apart a dinner roll and looked over at Wait. "I don't think so," she said. "If I remember correctly, *Esther* was an anomaly of sorts at this point in Handel's career. Is that right, Alison? Maybe you can fill us in—between bites? She smiled at Alison, who quickly swallowed a forkful of beet salad and picked up her own copy of the program.

"Handel wrote the music for *Esther* while he was staying at the home of James Brydges, Duke of Chandos," Alison explained. "This was early in Handel's career—around 1720—when most of his composing activity was still tied to Italian opera. Oratorios were not a musical form common at all in London at that time, and, in fact, it would be another twenty years before Handel himself would develop the oratorio as a replacement for the operas that had been the focus of his career until then. No one knows why he chose to create this oratorio. Some scholars claim that Handel's friends Arbuthnot, Pope, and John Gay collaborated on the libretto. Late in the 1600s, French playwright Jean Racine had written a tragedy based on the biblical story, and it had recently been performed in

259

translation in London. Perhaps that is what sparked the idea of presenting—in English—a musical interpretation of the story. But why Handel chose to present this plot as an oratorio is not clear. He revised *Esther* several times later in his career. I had never heard it performed before. The version we heard was from 1720. Evidently the later versions were longer and included music from a number of other works. I'm glad we were offered the original, shorter version. To me, it seemed just right. And the singers did a superb job."

"I couldn't agree more," said Forella. "Angela tells me the word sheet identifies the work as a sacred drama—the usual meaning of an oratorio. What I found amusing is that the plot involves the same character—King Xerxes—we met in the opera Angela and I heard in Chicago. But here, in *Esther*, the story is regarded as sacred because its ultimate source is the Bible while in the opera *Xerxes*, the plot is simply secular history. I wonder what Handel was thinking when he decided to create a sacred drama. And why the story of Esther? I'm hoping our Lydia will ask him about it. I look forward to the next letter, Peter. Do you have something for us?"

"Indeed, I do," said Peter. "I have been hard at it while some of our number have seen fit to loll about enjoying the beach at Waikiki." "That was a business trip," interjected Ross, as he sat down with a plate of scaloppini. "Ah, but of course," said Peter. "In any case," he went on, "as I said, I have been assiduous in my efforts to move our project along. I have three—yes, three—letters for you today. I will accept your thanks and applause, along with a ceremonial blowing of the conch shell by our lucky traveler. I assume you can play the pu, Ross." Ross rolled his eyes and went on eating.

Katherine stood and went over to the flip chart Angela had set up for them. "That's excellent, Peter! Three letters. Like Forella, I am hoping Lydia mentions the oratorio *Esther*. I wanted to be sure we come back to the question of why he chose this biblical text. I'll just put the topic up here as one we will likely want to address in our discussion. Are the letters long, Peter? Perhaps we could read them while we are finishing our lunch. What do you think?"

"Here are copies of all three," said Peter. "The second is a bit longer than the other two." Angela jumped up and took the copies. "I'll send them around in order by date," she said. "Go ahead and finish your lunch, Peter. I'm finished."

Here are the three letters Peter had transcribed.

Mr. G F Handel, Esqr
In care of the Most Noble James Duke of Chandos
Cannons Park
Middlesex

10 April 1719

My Dear Mr. Handel,
I do hope this letter reaches you before you leave London for Saxony. I was so very sorry to hear of the passing of your sister. Dora was such an insightful and solicitous correspondent. I welcomed her letters and was concerned when I had not heard from her this past year. Your mother has still her grandchildren and son-in law, of course, but she must be heart broken with her daughters both gone before her and you off in distant London. Please pass along to her my very deepest sympathy when you see her. And condolences as well to Dora's husband and children. So sad to lose such a loving, caring mother and helpmate. And I cannot overlook a brother's sorrow. I grieve along with you, my dearest Gif.

My dear Edward opines that your travels are much more than a family visit, and I detected a hint of evasion in Mr. Smith's response to my query. At first I was hopeful that you went seeking to bring back a long lost love, but no, Eggy says it is likely a mission for the new Music Academy that sends you to the Continent. Both you and Mr Smith seemed like fasting penitents heading to the feast. I surmise that something marvelous is afoot—new singers for the stage, perhaps. I cannot imagine what else would stir such excitement. Travel safely, my friend, and if I have suspected rightly, may you have good fortune in your attempts to win new singers to our English backlands.

Once again, I send my sympathy to your mother. I shall miss hearing from Dora. Meeting her and little Joan—as we English called her—that was one of the great delights of my life. Dora was a dear soul. Your little godchild must be quite the young lady by now. Give her a kiss from me, and her grandmother as well. Return safely

I have the honor to be, ever yours,

Mrs. Edward Grayston
Rowe Estate
Marylebone

The second letter:

Mr. G F Handel, Esqr
In care of Mr. Heidegger
King's Theatre
Haymarket
London

23 February 1723

My Dear Mr. Handel,
I write this day as it is your birthday and I have not written for such a long time. It is a welcome comfort to think of you on your birthday, something I have done every feast day of Saint Serenus these twenty years. How well I remember searching through Sir John's library with you to find the name of the saint who shared your special day—though of course his was a feast day for his martyrdom, not his birth. Serenus the Gardener—it seems so appropriate for you, with your great knowledge and fascination with all things that grow. I suppose your father grew herbs for his medical remedies. I believe you

mentioned that. *I often reflect upon the truth that you are one of my oldest friends, now that Sir John and my father are gone, and most recently my dear sister, my dearest Mary, who kept us all attached to the glory of a life lived every day with a loving smile. I miss her so very much. These past few years have been hard.*

It was so kind of your patron to extend his invitation to the Reverend and Mrs Grayston when their friend Mr. Handel was performing his anthems with the choir and playing his new compositions on the harpsichord or organ. I must say that—in particular—hearing you play, just you alone—was such a balm to my heart as I sat later with my father, watching his life ebb away. There is something so reassuring to me, my dear Gif, as you move through the running melodies with an agile but sure hand until the very end of each piece —when all is known and affirmed, as it should be. Your playing never failed to renew my spirit, no matter how sorrowful I had been before I came to the little chapel. I thank you, dear Gif, for sharing your great gift. Hearing you play is such a comfort. What a loss it would have been to us all if you had turned away from music and instead practiced law. I agree, that is one time it was good to respectfully decline your father's advice.

I was sorry to miss the opera seasons, once the Academy began its productions at KT. The papers were full of comments on the amazing Cuzzoni and the wonderful Senesino. Even Durastanti and Signorina Robinson came in for their share of praise, along with Boschi and Berenstadt. Such excellent singers—and London has you to thank for bringing them here to us. I recall your saying that it was not your favorite task—convincing singers to come and sing for you and other composers who must, of course, recognize that their operas are nothing without the singers' heavenly voices giving vibrancy and power to ordinary words and notes. I admire your patience—not something you are known for—in accommodating these talented but often vain and demanding singers. It must be a challenge. I heard that you did lose your temper and warned Cuzzoni that you were Beelzebub and threatened to toss her out a window. True or not, it makes a good story. But I do pity you. Trying to please people who have such high opinions of themselves must be galling. I know you well enough, Gif, to imagine you considering just how to brook any challenge to your musical taste. Shall I erupt in fury or be playful and cajole? Cuzzoni should have known not to complain of your choice for her opening aria. All of London is charmed with the piece and cannot hear enough of it.

And yet you could do with some of my dear Edward's untiring patience. He has now been made rector at St. Thomas's charitable school in Marylebone. He oversees the teachers and helps prepare the day's lessons for the young boys who attend the school. I do believe he enjoys his work, and of course he delights in guiding children toward a better life than they would have if left on the streets. It keeps his mind from sorrow at having no son of his own to guide and teach. And what of you, Gif? You speak with affection of your godchild back in Saxony, but are you not at times lonesome for the voice of a small one calling out Papa, Papa? You cannot be always writing music or rehearsing operas. You have said that playing the harpsichord or organ all alone as you weave together melodies old or new—that is your creation, your offspring. But there must be times, Gif, when it would be good to have another's hand there along with yours.

Recent losses have left me sad, and I find it hard to write a cheerful letter. I apologize, my friend. I know you will forgive, as you always do. Please do stop by the rectory if you are on the other side of the park. Eggy and I would both love to see you. My period of mourning has kept me from town, but I expect I shall see you at some time later this spring. May Saint Serenus bless you with blooming flowers before Eastertide.

I have the honor to be, ever yours,

Mrs. Edward Grayston
St. Thomas Rectory
Marylebone

And the third letter:

Mr. G F Handel, Esqr
Brook Street, near Hanover Square
London

15 August 1723

My Dear Mr. Handel,
Thank you for stopping by the rectory earlier this month. Edward and I so enjoyed visiting with you, and we are delighted that you are now our neighbor here in the West end. I thought Eggy would fall from his chair laughing when you countered my promise to be quiet as a mouse if I were to visit your parlor when a rehearsal was under way. Through no fault of mine, I assure you, after you left, our friend Mr Hume, whom you met, decided to play the part of Addison's tattler and satirize your comments, thus—Mr Handel: Lydia, ven haft you efer bean kviet as a mouse?! Dat vood be a meeracle—but, ach mein Gott, not a bledsing. Come, unt Herr Schmidt vill learn how Englis vimen schpeak vit sense unt mettle. Mr Hume made much more mockery of your lingering Saxon speech than the language warranted, but in truth, I liked the sense of your words. I find it very flattering to be characterized as outspoken, even if it is unbecoming a lady. You, my friend, are attuned to my true character, and I love you for it. But I do promise—I will try to be quiet as a mouse. I would love to hear you rehearse your singers. Comme c'est merveilleux!

I do fully understand your pleasure in finally having your own house, with no unwritten obligations to concern yourself with the wishes of those around you. Even the Duke's mansion and grounds must have seemed at times confining in its ties to your host's expectations. You are a very independent man. I have known that from the moment I met you. But still, Gif, I wonder if it is always good to have no one whose burdens are yours as well, no one you must answer to. Ah, but for now it is a joy to see you so cheerful at the prospect of playing host after these many years of being the obliging guest. Felicitations to you. May the house ring with your music for a thousand years.

Edward and I are searching the gardens of our friends who travel for just the right plant to bring you as a housewarming gift. You confessed that the grounds behind the house have little room for gardens, but we will find something that can grow in our West End alleyways. It is a quest!

I have the honor to be, ever yours,

Mrs. Edward Grayston
St. Thomas Rectory
Marylebone

Katherine took her plate over to the trolley conveniently placed at the end of the buffet. She thanked Annie for the excellent lunch and returned with a glass of water to her place at the table. "Thanks, again, Peter, for the three letters," she said. "They cover more than four years—a period when Handel seems to have moved around a bit and started his new association with the Academy of Music. Lydia doesn't comment directly on *Esther*, sad to say, but I think we can still keep that topic as one we plan to address. What else do we want to talk about today?"

Brad spoke up—not in his usual brash manner. "I'll have to say, I found this oratorio—*Esther*—very interesting. Well, disturbing, would be more like it. Ok—I think I remember when we started having these meetings, we—our sponsor, Mrs. Wainwright, before underwriting this project—she suggested we agree to some rules about not criticizing other people's ideas, but also upholding a sense of privacy. You know, not letting any of what we talk about go beyond these walls." Brad looked around the table, but no one said anything. "Well, I don't have any big secret or anything. But I have a reaction to this piece *Esther*. It's not the kind of even-handed and brainy comments I usually hear from most of you. So, yeah, I want us to come back to the *Esther* performance, even if it wasn't mentioned in any of the letters."

With a quizzical look at Brad, Katherine went back over to the flip chart and put a star beside the topic listed as simply ESTHER, then asked, "Was there a particular question about the piece, or about Handel, or do you simply want to be sure we come back to the topic?" Brad said, "That's ok. The star works for me. I just wanted to make sure we come back to it."

Rebecca waved her hand toward the chart. "I'm interested in coming back to *Esther* as well, but I was also intrigued by a couple of comments here in Lydia's birthday letter to Handel. First she expresses her own appreciation for the comfort Handel's music has brought her during her recent times of mourning, and then she says something about Handel viewing his own music—both playing and writing—as his offspring, his children, if you will. I guess my question would be one addressing the various roles music plays in Handel's own life and in the lives of his audiences. I am interested in discussing the function or functions of Handel's music back then, and, I suppose, now as well. To some extent, that takes us back to Brad's response to *Esther*, doesn't it?"

Katherine wrote a second topic: FUNCTIONS OF HANDEL'S MUSIC, then and now. She turned to CD, who said with a laugh, "Vell, I vant to tall-ke about heez lankwitch. I thought it was wonderful the way Lydia reported to Handel that his accent was a subject of discussion —well, actually, derision—after he left. Handel and Lydia must have had a pretty comfortable relationship for her to be able to share with him this bit of ridicule at his expense. And what he actually says about her is, as she points out, after all rather flattering. He seems to admire her outspokenness. I suppose it is yet again a look at their relationship that would be the topic. Not a new topic, but I'd like to hear what others have to say on the subject."

"Excellent!" said Katherine, and she wrote the third topic on the chart: HANDEL AND LYDIA'S RELATIONSHIP. Is that enough to be starting with? I think we should go back to Brad, who has been uncommonly patient. Back to *Esthe*r, then. Brad?"

Brad began: "Ok, for reasons that really are not important, in another life I had the name Earon Hochberg. When I went to college, I officially changed my name to Brad Hochensmith. It wasn't all that hard to do. As long as they had my draft number, they didn't care. But guys with obviously Jewish sounding names stood out in southern Indiana, and I wanted to play in a band. Hey, if Robert Zimmerman can become Bob Dylan, why couldn't I pick a more Hoosierish name? Anyway, I wouldn't mind what anyone called me now, but back then it made a difference. So, I stayed with the name Brad. You all thought I seemed like a Brad, right?" Brad did his best Brad Pitt pose and then went on. "But, in my former life, as I said, I was Earon Hochberg, and I even went through my bar mitzvah along with my cousin David. Which leads to my reaction to Handel's *Esther*."

Everyone seemed riveted by Brad's story. He laughed. "I don't think I've ever had this kind of serious attention before the whole time I've been here. This must seem like heavy stuff." He stopped smiling and said, "Yeah, well, I suppose it is. Ok, so my father left while I was still in high school. But my mother still liked to celebrate Purim. It's not a big holiday, but it used to be fun. Sometimes people would put on costumes, and there would be lots of food and drinking. After my dad left, I was the male in the family, so, if we couldn't get to a synagogue—and we usually couldn't—then I was supposed to read the magillah, the Esther scroll. Now you can get a copy online, but back then, we had a printed copy. Anyway, my mother made me do the reading. I could read the Hebrew text, of course, but my sister wanted to know what the story was about. I hadn't paid much attention to the story. I knew it was about an important time that the Jews living in Persia were saved from slaughter by Queen Esther's decision to act on their behalf. Well, the story is pretty much as it was played out in Handel's oratorio. But I remember being bothered by a couple things in the story—especially as I tried to make the story seem reasonable to my sister."

"Any dumbass knows you should never try to make a religious story or ritual seem reasonable," Brad went on. "That isn't the point. But, you know, to a kid the Torah and the sacred writings—they are all absolutely true. This is the history—mostly the history that is hidden from history books—but OUR history, really OLD history. So Sarah—my sister—wanted to know why the bad guy—Haman—was able to talk the king into killing all the Jews living in Persia. Just because Haman didn't like Mordechai that was no reason for the king to agree to kill all of Mordechai's people. But that was the deal Haman had made. That was why Esther had to risk getting put to death in order to ask the king to NOT kill all the Jews. That's why Esther had to reveal to her husband—the king—that she too was a Jew, like her relative, Mordechai. Sarah and I were both incensed and I guess embarrassed the way teenagers are. Why is it so bad to be a Jew? We knew some people didn't like us, but why did it seem like this had been going on for centuries? Mom's only answer was that it is the burden we bear for being God's chosen people. I thought that was a pretty lame excuse. So did Sarah."

Brad looked at his copy of the program from the production of Handel's *Esther*. "What really bothers me about the story—and my memory of that one time I actually tried to make sense of it—is how everyone just accepts the idea that a whole group of people could be killed just because of who they are. The Jews during World War II are the obvious example, but there have been other times and other groups of people. What kind of logic makes that even a possibility? How can you justify killing someone you don't even know just because they are a different religion or race or ethnic group? I mean Esther didn't even LOOK different from other people living in Persia. The king didn't even know she was a Jew. Even Haman didn't know she was a Jew until she said so. How do supposedly smart humans come up with such boneheaded behaviors? I didn't know the answer then, and I don't know it now."

Everyone sat still, letting Brad's comment sink in. Finally, Rayette spoke up. "Yes, I was struck by the evidence of an ancient hate group here. After listening to Handel's oratorio, I thought about just how many literary pieces or musical works start out with some conflict between groups that seem to hate each other. Think of *Romeo and Juliet* or *West Side Story*. I think sociologists and anthropologists talk about how groups play out attitudes about other groups in their day-to-day interactions, but literary critics usually look at how authors represent these conflicts in fiction. That is what Handel's oratorio is doing—and I suppose the biblical source, too. I actually went and pulled out the Bible I was given at my college graduation—back when they still did that. I read the story of *Esther*. It is a short book in the Old Testament—just before the book of Job. When I read the story all the way through, I realized that Handel's version leaves out the last part of the story, the part relating how the Jews countered Haman's threatened slaughter with the slaying of more than five thousand Persians. A lot of the narratives included in the Old Testament recount these extreme retaliations—one group against another. Handel seems to have left it out of his version because it lessens the good effect of the story. But such hatreds of one group against another always betray the endless recycling of warfare from earliest times."

Rayette looked around the group and continued, "I thought, of course, of the racial conflicts that have dominated so much of American history. And many of the religious or political oppositions today. Poets find it hard to avoid thinking things through in the form of a poem. So I hope you'll excuse my sharing a poem I wrote in response to Handel's oratorio." When everyone smiled and Katherine said, "Yes, please do," Rayette shared her short poem.

> We, with good will toward all among us,
> We, who keep safe our dear ones, our own,
> We, the kin who love us and guide us,
> We, who grasp the great truth, heed its laws,
> We, with love for only the good,
> We, marked to be great through god-given worth,
> We, with the code of tradition to cherish and follow,
> We, binding ties that ward off all foes.

They, with enmity first in their thoughts,
They, with hatred for all but their own,
They, the spiteful who mock our good sense,
They, with beliefs that are wrongful and vain,
They, granting love to none but themselves,
They, feared all our days for their drift to the dark,
They, with spirits of sin that harken to lies,
They, hateful other that looms as a foe.

We, who are kindred. They, who are not.
How cross this chasm? Where find an end?
How do we live with such discord and strife?
--Embrace the enemy's soul.

Forella clapped, and the others joined her. "Could you read it again?" Forella asked. Rayette smiled broadly and read the poem a second time. "I like it," Forella said. "I like the ending. If we could all learn to find something to love and cherish in people we dislike—the world would be so much better. I don't think you need to be one religion or another—or any religion at all—to believe that."

Katherine went over to the flip chart, and under the topic identified as ESTHER, she wrote the words ESOTERIC-EXOTERIC FACTOR. "I try not to play 'professor' here very often, but this topic is one that folklorists have thought about for some time. Sociologists and anthropologists have written much about 'us versus them,' too, but usually they are concerned with how various groups are treated by civic institutions or laws. And that's really important because the effect of in-group, out-group situations is often injustice. But how does such injustice come about? How can people who like to see themselves as fair and virtuous behave in ways that are clearly unjust?"

"Folklorists," she continued, "typically assume that tradition has an influence in most human behaviors or expressions. Traditions can be obvious, as in an oft-repeated folktale or legend or superstition, but some deeply held traditions are shared as ideas or beliefs that have no easily classified form. These are the accepted cultural ideas—the prejudices, assumptions, or hatreds—behind or embedded in more obvious examples of folklore or customary behavior. Folklorists have been interested in how people express attitudes about themselves and others through everyday culture—songs, sayings, jokes—anything that reflects a shared notion of 'what we think about them, what they think about us, what we think they think about us, what they think we think about them' and so on. This is what folklorist Hugh Jansen called the 'esoteric-exoteric factor' in folklore. All people grow up identifying with and learning from their own groups—their family, religion, ethnic group, gender, nation or region, class, political party, or even sports fan clubs. They also learn about the other groups that stand in contrast to their own group. They take in many assumptions, both positive and negative, about themselves and about the groups that are different from their own. They incorporate these assumptions into the expressive materials they use every day, the jokes and sayings they share almost without conscious thought. Few people stop and question their own prejudices. Instead, an 'us versus them' mentality seems somehow simply a bit of applied tribal wisdom, a harmless tradition."

"I'm not sure I see the connection," said Brad. "In the Esther story, there were no jokes or songs about the Jews—or about the Persians, for that matter. There was just this proclamation by Haman that all the Jews should be killed. He thought this was a good way to get back at Mordecai, and he had the power to do it. The Jews were enslaved, and they couldn't escape. It seems like a political power play to me."

"We can't really know if there were songs or jokes," said Katherine. "Probably there were, but the people who record history usually ignore lesser genres of folklore, the everyday sayings, legends, or songs and nursery rhymes. They don't seem important. But in the story of Esther, Haman does say that the reason he wants to punish Mordecai is because Mordecai refused to bow down before him, saying that he bowed only before his god, the God of Israel. Haman saw this as an insult, but Mordecai saw it as a righteous behavior required by his religion. This may seem like simply a difference in custom, but to the Jew Mordecai it was an important difference, rather like the American refusal to tip the hat to supposed 'betters' before the American Revolution. It was something that separated one group from another. If it were just one man's anger over another man's behavior, the story would likely not have been remembered through all these centuries. But Haman was able to cast Mordecai as a dangerous representative of all his people because Mordecai's people were already seen as different, unworthy, and despised. Haman was happy to use whatever excuse arose to kill off people he regarded as enemies—even though they had no power and were enslaved. Their difference from the dominant Persians was enough to make them a despised group, and the folklore—the oral materials that incorporate traditional attitudes—this common store of everyday prejudices probably allowed his actions against the Jews to seem somehow justified."

Rebecca waved a hand. "I think it is very interesting that Handel picked this story for this early stab at an oratorio for Londoners" she said. "Handel had quite a bit of personal experience with the in-group, out-group phenomenon. In Lydia's letter he was ridiculed for being a German speaker in English society. He must have felt like on outsider Protestant in mostly Catholic Italy. And even back in Halle, many of his neighbors were French Huguenots. My guess is that he was sensitive to differences between cultures and differences in social class and occupation. But he seemed determined to be his own man, not to be pigeon-holed by any of the characteristics or identities people might thrust upon him—German, musician, Lutheran. I would expect him to have a certain amount of empathy with the Jews in the story of Esther. Granted, the Jews were in Persia against their will, but their experience of being perceived as outsiders was similar to his own. And yet, I think there is more to his choice of this story for his oratorio than even this esoteric-exoteric factor, as Katherine called it. I think he was attracted to Esther's understanding of love—both the love between her husband and herself and the love she felt for her adoptive father and her people. I think Handel saw something in this story that he wanted to express through the music he created to share with his audience. I think he chose the story carefully, not just on a whim."

"So, of course," Rebecca continued, "this leads to my question about function: Why did Handel choose this story, and what did he hope to accomplish by presenting it as an oratorio in early eighteenth century London? In 1720, Handel was thirty-five years old, still fairly young but old enough to be serious about not simply his art but also his moral and ethical contribution to humanity. This was the age of the Enlightenment. I expect Handel was very much aware of the humanistic aims of philosophers like John Locke or his countryman Christian Wolff. There is no evidence that Handel would have been a successful scholar or public intellectual himself—as were some of his friends, such as Alexander Pope or Jonathan Swift. Handel's great talent lay in his ability to wed appropriate music to text in a way that truly enhances the text. Handel understood that the voice makes words and ideas more deeply moving, more profoundly provocative. I am convinced that he would never have allowed his music to convey ideas he did not view as ultimately good and worthy of being embraced by his audience. In fact, I would argue that, through his compositions and public performances, he intentionally taught the human values he revered."

Ross stood and walked slowly over to the buffet. "Well said, Rebecca," he acknowledged, "though I'm sure he made many compromises he would have preferred not to. It's impossible to do otherwise if you are working with others, and over his career, he had many different librettists, singers, musicians, and house managers. But your basic question—what was his objective?—that's a riddle, isn't it? He wanted to make money. He wanted to use his skills, his training. In that respect, he was no different from any other composer of his era. But why create an anomaly like *Esther*? And why did he later abandon the Italian opera and put all his energy into the English oratorio—something that could be appreciated and even performed by amateurs, by the masses? Was it just a response to the market, or did he like the oratorio's effectiveness in entertaining while at the same time conveying a bit of needed wisdom? I suspect it was the latter. I think he found the oratorio a compatible form. It was dramatic and entertaining, but it was also a vehicle for examining how individuals and communities interact. The chorus—the blended voices offering reflection—that was an important new development for Handel. It allowed him to express collectively held thoughts, both good and bad. But at the close, the chorus always gives the audience a welcome affirmation—Hallelujah, Amen, Let Heaven and Earth give praise. The chorus guides the audience. Even in *Esther* the chorus was, at the end, the collective voice of wisdom and good counsel. I agree with Rebecca. Handel found a way to teach his fellow humans to treasure the values he saw in stories like this one of Esther."

"Well, maybe," said Clara. "Someone must have cut out the vengeful, kill-our-enemies part that was in the biblical version. I'd like to think it was Handel who cleaned up the story, made it more acceptable to the audiences of his day, but maybe it was the librettist. I suppose if anyone knew what process Handel went through when deciding on a text for an opera or oratorio, we would have that information available. After all these years, we'd know, wouldn't we?"

Alison waved toward Katherine. "I've been reading some of the biographies of Handel," Alison said. "And Clara is right. If anyone really knew what process Handel used to decide about the libretti he used, it would be published somewhere. But there ARE a few hints here and there. For example, we do have some letters exchanged between Handel and Charles Jennens when Handel was working on *Messiah*. But perhaps more to the point here, I found one writer who made a practice of pulling out quotable quotes relating to Handel's life and highlighting them in little boxes throughout his book titled simply *Handel*. The writer is Christopher Hogwood, a noted Handel scholar but also a celebrated conductor who has made many recordings of Handel's works. Anyway, in Hogwood's Handel biography, he includes a quote from someone named James Beattie, writing in 1780, well after Handel's death. Beattie reports Handel as saying—when complimented on the 'noble entertainment' he provided: 'I should be sorry if I only entertained them, I wish to make them better.' In other words, according to Beattie, Handel was very conscious of the more or less didactic aim of his music. He hoped to improve his audiences through his music."

"There is always an argument over whether some piece of art or literature is meant to be functional or didactic or instead to be expressive and artistic," said CD. "On the other hand, as a choral conductor, I think of the music my choirs and I make as expressive rather than functional. We try to express what we think the composer wanted to express and, in addition, what WE want to express. Since the Romantic era, critics have spoken of this expression as 'feelings'—sentiments or emotions composers hope to evoke in their listeners. But most of Handel's music was functional is some way—honoring the Queen, celebrating a military victory, sometimes simply a musical exercise, and then, of course, often telling a story, in opera or oratorio form. I think of Handel as a very practical man. But I think he also knew that music had significant power, that it could move an audience's emotional response in a particular direction. So in that sense, his desire to make his audience better people required his effective expressivity. My guess is that he took great delight in inspiring people through his music. Music functioned as both inspiration and expression. He succeeded on both fronts."

"And don't forget Lydia," said Wait. "She said she found his music—especially his own keyboard playing—comforting. As Lydia said, nothing against lawyers, but what a loss that would have been, if Handel had not chosen to create music rather than law briefs. And perhaps he did think of his music as his offspring, his progeny. Maybe for him, music making was a substitute for family."

"When I was transcribing the second letter for today," said Peter, "I was struck by that comment, where Lydia seemed to be quoting Handel, saying that he thought of his music as his offspring. That's certainly a cliché often ascribed to poets or writers—that they think of their great oeuvres as their children. I doubt if Handel would have said it quite that way—perhaps something more along the lines of admitting that he invested his time in creating his music just as others might invest in time spent with family. But the truth is, in the eighteenth century many men did not spend much time with their families, certainly not with their children when they were young. No, I think Handel recognized that his music was his legacy. To some people, that might be a substitute for family. But I think Handel was simply expressing his view that his music is what would live on after he was gone. That doesn't mean he prefers his music to real people. It really was just a metaphor."

Clara shot back, "What Lydia actually said was, and I quote: 'You have said that playing the harpsichord or organ all alone as you weave together melodies old or new—that is your creation, your offspring.' Granted that is a metaphor, but I can imagine Handel saying that. I think I've mentioned before that I play the cello—not as a professional by any means, but I play with the community orchestra. And I would say sometimes I do feel, when I'm playing alone, simply practicing a piece, that while playing, I am creating, adding something creative to life—even though no one hears me. Handel's music was his legacy, that's true, but it was also his own personal path to ecstasy and delight. I don't think it had anything to do with his not having a family. And as to men not spending time with their children—some do and some don't. It was probably the same then. Handel seems to have spent time with his own father when Handel was a young boy and his father was still alive. But I'll agree that Handel's comment doesn't mean he prefers his music to real people."

Katherine gestured toward the flip chart. "Maybe we will let this concern with real people be our segue into the third topic: our ever-evolving understanding of the relationship between Handel and Lydia. CD, you suggested the topic. What is your thought?"

"Well, I was amused by the German accent imitation Lydia included in her letter," said CD. "Evidently another guest made fun of Handel's language after he left, and Lydia saw no reason not to share it with Handel. That's the part that intrigues me. Either she knew him well enough to know he would not be offended but rather amused—or she was just sassy enough to risk offending him by passing along her own second hand imitation of his accent. Actually, I think it was the first. I think she knew him pretty well, had known him now for—what did she say?—twenty years. Besides, it seems that people often made fun of his accent. Biographers include lots of anecdotes that depict his heavy accent as well as his tendency to swear. Both must have been considered endearing traits. But it was probably unusual for a woman to relate such a joking scene. More surprising than the friend's imitation of Handel was Lydia's reconstruction of the little skit. She is careful to claim that it is through no fault of hers that the friend decided to repeat Handel's words in his mock German accent. But, after all, it is Lydia's decision to include the report in her letter. It really is her responsibility. And, as I said, I think it says a lot about their relationship. Lydia was clearly confident that Handel would remain her friend no matter what she might say to him."

"Lydia and Handel must have shared an unshakable connection," said Katherine. "We can be certain of that. It seems to me that they started out with the understanding King Lear finally comes to at the end of his life: 'Come, let's away to prison. We two alone will sing like birds i' the cage.' Like Lear and Cordelia, Handel and Lydia were bred in the bone companions—not lovers, not even necessarily soul mates, but clearly two people who would always find each other abiding there, in the heart's deepest sanctum sanctorum. That Handel has chided Lydia about her outspokenness—that in itself speaks to his affectionate regard for her. I think they were two very good friends. The fact that Lydia was a woman makes it all the more telling. Neither of them seemed to let gender attitudes of the day affect their friendship."

"Well, you'll probably never hear me say THIS again, so listen up," said Brad. "There do seem to be some women who relate to men at such a basic human level that the difference in gender is no longer the main issue. That was one thing that impressed me—even as a kid—about Esther. She was not afraid of her husband, the King. And he had made it clear that anyone—ANYONE—who entered into his presence uninvited would be killed. But she was brave enough to approach him, despite knowing that. Same with Lydia. She doesn't seem to be intimidated by Handel or by her society's accepted notions of proper female behavior. She is a gutsy woman without being a bitch. Handel was lucky to know her, I'd say. And she had a good sense of humor. I sort of suspect that Handel wished she wasn't married."

Ross raised his glass. "To our friend Brad and his growing appreciation for the virtues of the fair sex. May he continue to gain the enlightenment he so desperately needs. But, I'll have to say, Brad, that Handel didn't let a woman's married state deter him from more intimate relations earlier in his life. I think our evidence so far suggests that Lydia and Handel are happy to be friends, just as they are—not marriage partners or even lovers. Seriously, what makes you think Handel would have wanted to be married to Lydia rather than simply be her friend?"

Brad smirked. "Man, I try to be honorable, play the game, and what do I get? I'm just saying what I think he would want. Wouldn't you prefer someone like Lydia to, say, the little 'sweet Marie' everyone was trying to fix Handel up with earlier? Doesn't she sound like a more interesting woman?"

"Three points off for Freudian projection," said Peter. "Of course she's a more interesting woman. We wouldn't have these letters to talk about if she weren't a more interesting woman. But painful as it may be, I'll have to agree with Ross. Lydia seems happily married to her Reverend Grayston, and Handel seems content with his bachelorhood. I think the oddity of a married woman writing to an unmarried man—especially back in the early 1700s—tempts us to look for a romantic connection. You're probably not alone in your assumption, Brad—though perhaps alone in being foolish enough to say it out loud. Just kidding, just kidding. Don't worry, Forella, I'm not picking on Brad."

Forella laughed and said, "Ah, you men, you are all foolish Figaros. Always seeking amours for yourself and suspecting it in the schemes of your fellows. But I, too, think that Lydia and Handel are simply very dear friends. That doesn't mean that they do not share a kind of excitement about each other. Lydia obviously liked teasing Handel about his accent. And Handel liked teasing Lydia about her outspokenness. We should all be blessed with such good friends."

"And so, my friends," she went on, "as we come to the close of our session for today, I have for each of you a copy of a wonderful, wonderful DVD—actually it is a two-disc set—and I have never so regretted my poor vision as now, when I would love to see more than moving shadows on the screen. But I have listened to it many times. This is the Met's production of Handel's *Rodelinda*, with Renée Fleming, Andreas Scholl, Joseph Kaiser, Stephanie Blythe, and Iestyn Davies—an outstanding cast. I think you will fall in love with it. It is such an excellent production, and Handel's music is—well, you will see. Enjoy, enjoy. I can hardly wait to hear your reaction."

"Thank you so much, Forella," said Katherine. "How very generous of you! I am sure we are all eager to watch it. I plan to make time this very weekend. Until next time, everyone. Be safe, and stay well."

CHAPTER 14

Mothers

Rather than heading home after teaching her last class for the day, Katherine stopped in at Bear's Place for a salad and went over early to Recital Hall, where she would be hearing a string quartet perform later that evening. The hall was empty except for a young man setting up printed programs on music stands just inside each door. So many new music buildings had been added to the campus since this building—Merrill Hall—had been constructed as the primary site for music classes, practice rooms, and concerts back in the late 1930s. As Katherine looked around the compact hall—no doubt state of the art when it was built—she noticed the bas-relief stone sculptures set into recessed stations along the walls. These half dozen busts depicted famous composers in Western tradition, including Beethoven, Chopin, Tchaikovsky, Mozart, Mendelsohn, even Wagner—but no Handel. The reemergence of Handel's operas, oratorios, and orchestral works began only in the 1950s, well after this Hall was built. Prior to that time, one great work alone—Messiah—was the piece most Americans associated with the name George Frideric Handel. Despite his remarkable popularity during his own lifetime, some two hundred years later, even among those knowledgeable people who advise music-building designers, Handel had slipped out of the top echelon of widely recognized composers.

PETER HAD REQUESTED A SLIGHT delay in the Seminar's next meeting date. It was conference season, and he had had little opportunity to work with even one or two of Lydia's letters to Handel. When they did finally agree upon a date when everyone could attend, most people said they were happy for the later meeting date because it gave them more time to view the three hour DVD of Handel's *Rodelinda* that Forella had sent home with each of them last time. It was a busy time of year for everyone.

As a consequence of the delay, all Seminar members had found time to watch the video, and, at the next meeting, commentary on the opera followed hard on the usual hellos and polite inquiries as people filled plates at the buffet and settled around the table. Even Brad admitted that the story content of *Rodelinda* was really good—not the usual far-fetched plot. "Actually, what I really liked is that they brought a real horse on stage—at the Met! I mean it's not like your usual movie where the camera can stop rolling if something goes wrong. They had a fricken horse on stage. It must have been well trained. Can you imagine if that horse got spooked and decided to jump off into the orchestra pit or race through the audience?"

"Honestly, Brad," said Clara, "if the horse is what impressed you most about this production, you are enamored of the inane. Renée Fleming was outstanding as Rodelinda, and both Andreas Scholl and Joseph Kaiser were excellent. Handel really zeroed in on the depth of feelings in his characters. I sometimes find it hard to realize he wrote this music back before the Romantic period. I could almost envision Frank Sinatra or Barbra Streisand singing the arias Handel composed for his singers, though of course the songs were operatic, not pop—well, and in Italian. Still—very emotional—and long, so they had to find ways to recast the message over and over again for each aria. I thought it was a great production—and NOT because of the horse."

"It's so easy to set you off," said Brad. "I could have complained about the squeaky male voices, but I knew that would just get your knickers in a twist. I DID think the tenor's song about wishing he was a shepherd was good. Do I get points for that?"

Clara snorted. Ross clinked his ring against his water glass for attention. "I'll be sure to report to our esteemed benefactress that everyone found the DVD delightful. Both Angela and my mother are off on yet another trip—this time to the New York City area. But I agree with Clara. This High Def video was excellent. And a few others besides Brad must have been relieved to hear that Andreas Scholl had a typical male speaking voice when they interviewed him backstage during the intermission. Let's hear it for the countertenors. Though I suppose a real castrato might have spoken like a prepubescent boy. What do you think, Alison?"

Alison shrugged. "I have no idea," she said, "but I do know that young men who sing alto or even soprano do not necessarily have high speaking voices. Still, the fact that Handel wrote most of his operas with castratos singing the roles of his leading men has to have contributed to the disappearance of his works from the stage for two hundred years. *Rodelinda* was actually the first of Handel's operas to be presented to a modern audience—in Göttingen in 1920. Then in the 1950s other opera houses in Europe presented a few of Handel's works, but nearly always with a woman singing the part of the hero. Countertenors have hit the stage in a big way only recently. Their growing popularity seems to be part of the 'historically informed performance' practice that has blossomed over the last few decades. Not only does the orchestra use period instruments, but the singers are as close as they can come to the castratos of the Baroque era."

Ross grimaced and said, "I think at least half of us would be glad to leave the subject of Handel's castratos. But there was something I wanted to query the rest of you about. Much is made over Rodelinda's loyalty to her presumed dead husband. She refuses to marry the usurper—Grimaoldo. She relents only when Grimaoldo's henchman threatens to kill her son, Flavio. However, when push comes to shove, Rodelinda says she will marry Grimaoldo only if he—Grimaoldo himself—agrees to kill her son in front of her. The synopsis implies that this was a ploy Rodelinda used, knowing that Grimaoldo would back down, that he would not kill the boy in front of her. Still, I found it a shocking piece of plot. The boy is on stage when she says this—well, sings it. Baroque era or not, I thought this was the worst kind of child abuse to put on stage. How could she know that Grimaoldo was not such a cad as to carry out her ultimatum? And what is the boy to think—even though he is spared? His own mother put him at risk, with no apology. Aren't mothers supposed to sacrifice themselves rather than their children? I can't imagine any of us found that a comfortable scene. And yet Handel seemed to present it as though there were nothing really amiss here. What do you think?"

Katherine looked over at Ross and nodded her head. "Yes, I was disturbed by that scene, too. In fact, it distracted me from the music and the rest of the story the first time I watched it. It was jarring—more like a Greek tragedy or something. I looked up a little background on the opera. The librettist, Nicola Haym, had adapted the libretto from a seventeenth century drama by the French playwright, Pierre Corneille. Corneille's play was based on an historical figure—King Bernardo of Lombardy—but the part about Rodelinda and her son was entirely fictional. The historical record says she was in exile. The marry-me-or-else plot could not have happened. So, it is Corneille's fault, I suppose, that the threat to Rodelinda's son is there at all. But both Haym and Handel must have accepted it as an important part of the plot. I seriously wondered if there was a different worldview—even in Handel's time—that would have failed to see the psychological damage in having the child know his mother was willing to sacrifice him. After all, Freud and modern psychology hadn't yet had an influence on our sensibilities. It was Abraham and Isaac all over again—only without a deity to blame for the idea."

Rebecca leaned forward and said, "The whole notion of how children were treated or viewed before the advent of modern psychology is an interesting subject. It was clearly an issue in Charlotte Brontë's *Jane Eyre* in the mid-1800s, but I wonder what the perspective was in the eighteenth century. I don't suppose it even occurred to people attending *Rodelinda* in Handel's time that the scene was more than simply personally threatening to the characters in the opera. There are some really telling remarks in *Jane Eyre* that reflect the dominant view of that time—basically that children were of good or bad blood. The effects of culture and family weren't taken into account. As Katherine said, Freud hadn't had his impact yet. But still, you would think the notion of a mother sacrificing her child would be disturbing no matter when. Actually, I think as audience we are to assume that Rodelinda resorted to this ploy as a last resort. After all, the threat to kill the boy was already there. It's just that you expect her to be too upset to think of a solution that forces the issue as she does."

"Well, of course," said Wait. "Think of Solomon. Mothers and their children are a predictable theme. The mother who would give up her child rather than sacrifice him is clearly the cultural winner. But maybe we should give Handel and his librettist a break. Maybe Rodelinda had forewarned her son what was going on. They seemed confident that the bad guy would not kill the boy. In fact, the way it develops in the opera, it is as though everyone knows the suggestion to kill the boy is absurd. I don't think the eighteenth century was so far removed from us as we assume—Freud and his influence or not."

Katherine nodded and said, "That's a helpful insight, Wait. I hope the notion of how children are viewed comes up in Lydia's letters. Keep it in mind as we move ahead. What do we have today, Peter? I know you have been busy, but I assume we have a letter to read today?"

"I have two letters for you today," said Peter. "Thanks, everyone, for accommodating my need for a little extra time. So, what I have today are two letters from the period when Handel was in a state of transition with the Royal Academy of Music—or at least that is what I gather. And a couple of important people die—sorry to say. Here are the two letters. A bit grim, I'd say."

The two letters Peter handed out:

Mr. G F Handel, Esqr
Brook Street, near Hanover Square
London

24 November 1727

My Dear Mr. Handel,
Edward and I have missed the lovely strolls through the Park and over to your Lower Brook Street house. But as you know, we were slated to make a visit to the Continent several months ago, and there was

no defying the bishop. In truth it was a fine journey. We have just returned from Hamburg. Sailing up the Elbe and across the channel was most uncomfortable on this return voyage. May you be spared any travels to or from Hamburg as a winter season approaches. And yet this visit over the past month was in the main delightful. We enjoyed several happy evenings with both Mr. Telemann and Mr. Brockes. They each send greetings and chastise you for not writing or visiting. I informed them that they are not alone in wishing you were more often inspired to write, but, still, they forgive and send their good wishes.

We had thought that the bishop might cancel or postpone this trip after the unexpected death of the monarch in June, but once the coronation of George II was accomplished—with your wonderful anthems—he insisted that the journey continue as planned. I am so glad I was there to hear the pieces you composed for the ceremony. Best of all was Zadok. It plays over and over again in my memory. What an amazing piece it is. You are a wonder, my friend.

The cold will keep us from the Park and you will be impossible to find as the season opens, so here I am writing a letter as I have not for many months. But, you need to know that Eggy and I visited your mother in Halle shortly before returning to Hamburg. She seemed a bit downcast. I believe her health is not good, and of course she misses Dora. Johanna is nearly grown and visits her grandmother when she can. They were all ears to hear what I could report of your life in London. I told them first of your music lessons for the young princesses. Princess Anne would be about the same age as Joan. And J's brother was quite jealous when he heard that you were tutoring Mr. Smith's son as well. Your mother did laugh and say that she could not imagine you having the patience to teach anyone. Your mama knows you well.

I described for them the three excellent operas of two years ago—first Giulio Cesare, then Tamerlano, and then the wonderful Rodelinda. I had brought the word book for Rodelinda, but your mother has great trouble seeing now, and of course neither the English nor Italian text would have been of any use to her. Joan knew a little Italian from her studies. And then I told them about how you needed to appease your two singers once Faustina had joined the company. Herr Michaelsen laughed heartily when I told of the precise number of notes allotted each of the two sopranos in Alessandro. At least no one came to blows during your opera. But poor Mr. Bononcini. They all found the newspaper account of the fighting factions at his Astianatte very amusing.

I must apologize, Gif, if I have caused some distress for your mother. I did not know that you had not told her of your petition to the King. She did not know you had become a citizen of England. Of course, I should have thought how that might shock a parent. I am so sorry, Gif, for letting that leak out in our conversation. I think she was reconciled to the idea by the time I left her, but I am so sorry that I did not think how she might hear the news. In the end, I think she saw how very proud we English are to have you choose to stay among us. But, after all, she has a mother's heart and will no doubt always consider you a child of Saxony.

One last bit of homeland news. I saw Marie in Hamburg. I think she still pines for you, my friend, but she has married a fine man—a cook and hautboist. I think you would like him, and I know you would be happy for her. Her brother is also settled in Hamburg. Marie says to tell you Was hots Hertz im ganse Leib? I have no idea what that means, although I do recognize the word for heart. Perhaps you will enlighten me. She was charming and solicitous, as always. All your friends in Hamburg miss you and long to see you again.

You and Mr Haym are, I am sure, hard at work on the next opera. I look forward to visiting your rehearsals when possible. I hear that the King will attend at the theater later in the season. I am glad to be home. Home is where Mr Handel shares his magical music.

I have the honor to be, ever yours,

Mrs. Edward Grayston
St. Thomas Rectory
Marylebone

And the second letter:

Mr. G F Handel, Esqr
Brook Street, near Hanover Square
London

10 January 1731

My Dear Mr. Handel,
Ah, mon cher ami, I was so sorry to hear that we have lost your dear mother. She was a warm hearted soul and truly devoted to you. I am so glad that you were able to visit her at the end of your travels a year ago. She was gracious as always when Edward and I stopped in Halle on our last trip to the Continent. A light has gone out. It pains me even now, knowing that she is no longer there and waiting so patiently for your rare visits or even one from me and Eggy. She was so very dear and welcoming whenever we saw her. You have my deepest sympathy.

My own mother died long ago, before Edward and I went to Hamburg. Eggy's mother, too, died more than twenty years ago. We both felt a tender bond between ourselves and your mother, dear Dorothea. I somehow sensed that I would not see her again when we saw her last. And yet she was so kind and concerned for our comfort. I will always treasure our conversation from that visit. She spoke, almost as though I were a daughter, of the child she had lost, her first born. I did not know you had a brother. Dorothea said he died while yet an infant, not even a year old. She told—in her always eloquent French—of your father's grief, and hers, but especially of your father and his great sorrow that he could not save the baby. How painful that must have been for them. And how grateful they must have been to see you live and thrive. I can only imagine.

And now you are so very busy with the new opera season. I know that things have not gone smoothly ever since the Beggar's Opera took

London by storm. Eggy says that changes were afoot even before that new entertainment came our way. And now Cuzzoni has left, and you have your usual battles with Senesino. Poor Gif, I feel so sorry that you must be ever on the alert lest fate steal away your opportunity to share your wonderful music. The trip to recruit new singers was stressful, I am sure. And now you are without Nicola. It is hard to lose a friend, and Nicola was both friend and collaborator. Watching you work with him reminded me of your work with Elisabetta. Pilotti and Haym, to my mind, they will always be two of your guardian angels, inspiring some of your best work.

Once again, I send my thoughts your way, remembering your mother and hoping that you will find comfort and peace as time passes. I hold you in my heart, dear friend. May solace come.

I have the honor to be, ever yours,

Mrs. Edward Grayston
St. Thomas Rectory
Marylebone

Katherine put down her copies of the letters and walked over to the flip chart. "Sad, isn't it?" said Katherine. "Here is Handel, at age—what is it now?—around forty-five?—and he has already seen so many important people in his life die—his father, his mother, both his sisters, his mentor and teacher, Zachow, his friend and librettist Nicola Haym, even his king. I often forget how our life spans have increased since Handel's day. At least more of us have the luxury of growing old together—among friends and family. And he never knew his brother—the one who died as an infant. Modern medicine has had its effects on both ends of life."

She picked up the marker and looked around at the rather somber faces watching her. "Well," she said, letting a smile ease across her face, "what themes can we draw out of these two letters—besides our ruminations on how frequently death confronted our Mr. Handel?"

"If you don't mind," said Rebecca, "I would like to go back to our discussion of *Rodelinda*—in particular the question of the text, the plot, and what it might say about Handel, even though he did not actually write the words. It seems to me that we can still attach some significance to the content of Handel's operas. After all, he agreed to compose the music, and maybe he had some influence on how the libretto developed, too. I'd like to discuss it a bit more. Could we do that?"

"I don't see why not," said Katherine, and she wrote TEXTUAL CONTENT OF HANDEL'S OPERAS on the flip chart. "What else?"

Brad leaned forward. "I'm intrigued by a few hints we have here about how musicians make a living. Not just a successful composer like Handel, but the off-hand remark about Marie's husband—'a cook and hautboist.' I'm guessing that means he had to have two jobs—a day job as a cook and his performance job playing the oboe. Do you suppose that was par for the course? I'd like to propose the question of HOW MUSICIANS MAKE A LIVING as a theme."

Katherine wrote his suggestion on the flip chart. "Thanks, Brad. That's excellent. Anything else?"

After several seconds passed with no further comment, Katherine started to say that perhaps the two themes would be enough for their discussion but then Ross spoke up. "I would like to pull out a little more information on what is happening in Handel's life at this time—maybe think a little more about some of the things Lydia alludes to in her letters. What is he doing professionally? Why is he travelling to the Continent? What reaction does he have to his mother's death? The king's death? Marie's marriage? Can we know what he is thinking? Not sure what you would call that as a theme—maybe HANDEL: TAKING STOCK AT FORTY-FIVE."

Katherine wrote his suggestion on the chart. "Sounds good to me," she said.

"So, going back to the text of *Rodelinda*—or maybe the texts or subject matter of any of Handel's music," said Katherine. "Rebecca, this was something you wanted to say a little more about, is that right?"

Rebecca looked around and said, "Yes, that's right, and remember, Katherine, how you are always saying you don't want to play professor?

Well, here, just like you, I kept thinking of some of the older theories in my field—anthropology—as we were talking about the differing ways culture views children and how they should be treated. In the 1930s, Ruth Benedict studied Zuni myths and argued that while some story elements or practices in the myths really did represent a 'mirror of culture,' some things that happen in the stories instead reflect an earlier time, or 'cultural lag,' as she called it, or even simply fantasy. In other words, you can't just assume that behaviors in stories from other cultures—or in our case, from earlier times—do in fact represent directly what the culture believed or practiced. Handel's contemporaries would have been troubled—just as we were—by the villain threating to kill the boy. And notice that it is the evil henchman who suggests killing the boy in the first place, not the king, the usurping brother who wants to marry Rodelinda. Later in the opera, that same henchman is shown to be a traitor to his own king and thus seems even more deserving of his death at the hand of the hero, Bernardo, Rodelinda's husband. As in most stories, there is a really evil character—here, the henchman—but also a character—like Grimaoldo—who learns and grows from his experience. I think we can see why Handel chose to set this plot to music."

CD walked back from the buffet with a fresh cup of coffee. "It's true that Handel used librettos created by other people and typically older, often well-known mythical or historical plots for his operas, and I suppose that complicates our response to his body of work. It's a different story if you look at Wagner, for example. Wagner created his own mythology and wrote his own librettos. He didn't want to leave anything in anyone else's hands. Handel seemed more willing to work with other people and their creative ideas—or maybe he felt he had no choice. That was the tradition. The Baroque period wasn't all that far removed from the beginnings of opera, and the earliest operas—from Monteverdi's *Orfeo* on—typically had one person writing the libretto and another composing the score. The genre gave a certain structure to any opera Handel would write, and the librettist, or poet, had to take into account that structure as well. It makes you wonder how different the process was from what, say, Lerner and Lowe or Rogers and Hammerstein went through in creating musicals for the stage."

Across the table, Rayette gave a little smirk. "Poets always get short shrift on play bills. It's always the composer who gets first billing. With operas, hardly anyone ever remembers who wrote the libretto. At least with musicals, they are usually seen as a team. However, I do seem to recall—from my graduate studies—a course on the traditional ballad. Now there we have an instance of people knowing the words but not the music. What was it, Katherine? Weren't the so-called 'Child' ballads collected together by the lyrics only? What's the story there?"

"Well," Katherine replied, turning away from the flip chart and sitting back down at her seat, "the ballads didn't really have known writers—for either the lyrics or the music. And, since they were folksongs that circulated in oral tradition, for a long time no one bothered to set them to paper, either as lyrics or as musical notation. Francis James Child spent some sixteen years gathering and publishing the words to more than three hundred English and Scottish ballads from a great variety of sources and in a great number of different versions, owing to the variation that occurs in oral tradition. But this was at the close of the nineteenth century. There was no recording equipment easily available then and certainly not earlier when many versions were written down. Early in the twentieth century, Cecil Sharp did, in fact, use wax cylinders to record some of the English folksongs still sung in Appalachia. He definitely emphasized the notation of melodies over the recording of words. I suppose it was a matter of what the researcher considered important—and, of course, what technology was available for recording. Now, we have phones that record and software that transcribes. It's a different world."

"But," Katherine went on, "it is interesting that you brought up the example of the Child ballads, Rayette. Long before Child started work on his great collection of ballads—while he was still a student at Harvard—he actually wrote a libretto—in Italian—for a pasticcio opera called *Il Pesceballo*, the Fish-Ball. It was based on a local legend, and Child wrote the piece after picking out music from operas by Rossini, Mozart,

Donizetti, and Bellini. IU professor Mary Ellen Brown edited a performance score of the piece not long ago and arranged to have it presented to an audience here in Bloomington. I can show you the printed score and loan you the CD of the performance if any of you are interested. Child's friend, the poet James Russell Lowell wrote an English version of the libretto. It was an amazingly creative project. I think Handel would have liked it—though the model was more comic opera rather than the more serious kind of opera Handel usually composed. The story revolved around a starving student and his ability to pay for only one fish ball rather than the usual serving of two. But, like most of Handel's operas, it included a love story and a disguised noble identity. Who says librettists don't have their day?"

"So, these pasticcios," said Wait, "was that a common thing? It sounds like cheating, or maybe parody. I know people who, you know, write roasts of friends or colleagues or something and put it to music that everyone knows. Isn't that sort of what's going on here? Nobody is writing anything new—well, at least no new music."

Alison waved her hand. "I'll take this one," she said. "Pasticcio was actually a popular way to fill in the opera season when there was not enough new material around. Then the challenge was more like the one that must have faced Francis James Child when he wrote his libretto. How do you combine various musical numbers into a coherent story? How do you rewrite poetic text so it fits the new story and yet fits the music? It's not as easy as it might seem—though, of course, easier than writing new music from scratch. During Handel's time, it wasn't all that uncommon. Interestingly, just recently the Met premiered a new pasticcio that incorporates arias from several of Handel's operas. The person who compiled the musical selections and wrote the libretto was Jeremy Sams, but the music was all from various Baroque composers, including many arias by Handel. In that case, the creativity of the writer/compiler was to some extent reflected in the choices he made—how he fit the storyline and text to appropriate music that had originally been composed with other text in mind."

Peter joined in. "I think I saw that opera. It was on PBS not long ago. Placido Domingo sang the role of the god Neptune. When he entered, they played Handel's 'Zadok the Priest'—with different words of course. It was perfect! –but also kind of witty, since everyone would recognize it. Wasn't the opera called *Enchanted Island*, or something like that? I think the story was based on Shakespeare—a combination of *The Tempest* and *A Midsummer Night's Dream*? I remember now, they said quite a bit of the music was Handel's. I thought it was good. I'll have to see if I can find a DVD of it."

"It makes you wonder, doesn't it," said Ross, "why Handel didn't pick stories from Shakespeare himself—well, Julius Cesar, I suppose, but none of the other obvious plots. But I suppose that was the point—the texts had to be in Italian. He did use English poets when he composed oratorios—even King James's biblical transcribers—or would that be God?"

"Heathen," said Peter. "But I will say, I recall one anecdote about Handel—when he was asked to write the coronation anthems for George the Second. The story is that the archbishop prepared to tell Handel what texts to use for the anthems, but Handel said he knew his Bible and would pick the texts himself. It caused quite a stir, but he did pick his own texts—although he probably used parts of the Bible that had traditionally been used. But at least we do know 'Zadok' was Handel's own choice. What say you to that, Dr. Pangloss?"

Ross laughed. "Well, it does take us back to our original question. I think we can read something into the choices Handel made, even if he did not himself write the librettos for his operas or oratorios. He had to accept and interpret the storyline. For all we know, he may have made suggestions to the librettists he worked with, maybe even changing the content as well as the language of the texts. And certainly the way he scored each aria revealed his take on the emotional message he thought the character wanted to convey. To me, in *Rodelinda*, one of the most telling arias was actually Grimaoldo's aria in which he longs for the simplicity of life as a shepherd, a commoner rather than a king. What a modern psychological expression that is—and Handel captured it beautifully, I thought.

So, I would say Handel does reveal something about himself through his choice of texts and his musical treatment of them. What do you think, Katherine?"

"The whole thing reminds me of what is often called the 'folklore in literature' debate in folklore studies," said Katherine. "Without my going off on a tangent, suffice it to say that folklorists often recognize traditional plots within authored literature. Then the task is to determine how the author has reconstituted the traditional material, how he or she has reinterpreted it. One of my favorite examples of an author 'using' folklore is the playwright John Millington Synge's reinterpretation of a traditional story he heard when he was making an ethnographic tour of the Aran Islands and other parts of Ireland. He recorded the story—which had been told to him in Gaelic—in his journal and later developed it into the play *In the Shadow of the Glen*. Synge takes a simple, though violent, story of an unfaithful wife and turns it into a commentary on the loneliness of a loveless marriage. In both versions of the story an old man pretends to be dead in order to catch his wife cheating, but in Synge's version the dialogue reveals a much more complex characterization of the woman, who in the end prefers to walk the open road with a visiting tramp rather than live in the lonely glen with her unloving husband. Like Handel, Synge lets us see so much more of the emotional reality of the characters than the bare bones of the story would suggest. Like most artists, Handel and Synge both change or interpret narrative material in ways that capitalize on the dramatic possibility of the story. They show creativity in what they choose and in what they change and expand."

"Along that same line, I could say a little more about that recent pastiche that used so much of Handel's music," said Alison. "In a way, it is the reverse of what your man Synge was doing in creating his play. For Sams and the other collaborators—who as I understand it, also suggested music to be used with the libretto—the important thing would be to find a piece of music that captured something like the feeling the aria or duet calls for. I think that is why so many of Handel's pieces were chosen. For example, the song Miranda and Demetrius sing when they meet and magically fall in love is in fact a love song from Handel's *Ariodante*. Whether in Italian or English, it is clearly a love duet. I think with the English words, it would make a great wedding song. And then toward the end of the opera, Prospero begs forgiveness from the sorceress he has so mistreated—and Sams chose the wonderful 'Ch'io parta' from Handel's *Partenope*. He changes the words to 'Forgive me, please forgive me,' but Handel had already captured that message in his music back in the original opera. The words and music fit together beautifully—and, if I recall, David Daniels sang it wonderfully, and he clearly showed how Prospero had changed as a character. I'm not surprised that Sams chose so many arias or duets from Handel. His songs always really conveyed exactly the kind of emotion the libretto required. Handel allowed his singers to be extraordinarily expressive actors through songs that demanded beautiful, effective singing."

"I can't believe I missed that production," said CD. "I usually at least listen to the Met live on Saturdays on the radio. I just checked online. There's a DVD coming out soon, and as Peter said, it's been on TV. What a great way to keep Handel's music alive and fresh. Wish I had thought of doing it. Maybe we should create our own pasticcio. Hey?"

Katherine grinned. "That WOULD be fun. And it would prompt us to listen to a lot of Handel's music. But, right now we need to move ahead with the letters—though it's a very tempting tangent, CD. Don't put it too far back on the burner. So, our second topic—HOW MUSICIANS MAKE A LIVING. That was your suggestion, Brad. Want to say a little about it?"

"Well, this is more than you probably want to know," said Brad, "but the music business is just as cut-throat as any other. You must all remember the big hubbub over downloading music and making copies for friends. Musicians had to protect themselves, and so did those of us who sell their stuff. We have to make money at it, or we can't stay in business. And I'm guessing it was the same in Handel's day. Although back then they didn't have the problem of easy access, which we have to worry about now. If you wanted to steal someone's music in Handel's day, you had to actually steal a hand-written score. There were no recordings or digital copies, text or otherwise, floating around back then. But that isn't really what I wanted to talk about. What really interests me is how working musicians made a living. It's something that concerns me even today. How can people who really like making music be paid enough in our capitalist society to do what they love on a daily basis? I think it is an issue that has never been solved."

"Oh, man, I know just what you are saying," said Wait. "I have so many friends who hang onto their day jobs so they can pay the bills and have health insurance but really live for the times they can make music. Even worse are the ones who can't piece together any kind of day job and try to make it just by playing whatever gigs they can find. It's a hard world for musicians—even if they manage to be part of a touring band. Then their home life is really a mess. I suspect the sorry life of musicians or anyone in the arts has been with us for centuries. But, Brad, you mentioned the comment in Lydia's letter about the ex-lover's husband—the guy who was, what, a cook by day but played the oboe by night. Was that typical in Handel's day?"

Brad shrugged. "I leave that to someone with more historical knowledge than I have. All I can say is that a person has to be truly committed to being a musician or artist or actor—whatever—if he or she wants to keep artistic expression a part of daily life. Because the odds against being successful enough to really 'make it' are high. My guess is that our oboe player had to make like a short order cook all day just for the privilege of playing his music when he got the chance. Even if he played with a court or church orchestra, he probably wasn't paid enough to support a family and pay his rent. No wonder Handel didn't marry when he was young and just starting out. Fortunately for him, he was eventually able to make music AND money. He was a good business man, no doubt about it."

"Writers and poets have that same problem," said Rayette. "And federal and state support for the arts is shrinking. I sometimes wonder why we can't go back to the WPA program that paid people to create art or build community parks and buildings. Of course that was a tough time for everyone. Still, it would be great to see art, music, and literature regarded as necessary and worth our collective efforts to promote and preserve. I think we have lost that sense of appreciation for the arts earlier generations had. It's hard to compare today's context to Handel's. I guess, as Brad said, it's always hard for artists and musicians—unless they are lucky and make it big."

Peter returned from the buffet, unwrapping a chocolate, which he popped in his mouth before commenting: "When Ross and I were in London, we visited the Handel House Museum, and I noticed they had a facsimile copy of his will. I'm sure we will take up the matter of his will later on, but one thing I noticed when I glanced over its contents was a fairly large sum Handel left to what was called the Society for the Support of Decayed Musicians. According to the short entry in the *Cambridge Handel Encyclopedia*, Handel was one of the founding subscribers to the fund, and in addition to leaving them money in his will, he also played various benefits to raise money for the fund. I would say it speaks well of Handel and also suggests he was very much aware of how difficult the life of a musician was. There was no Social Security to keep them afloat after their music-making days were over."

"There is one of those circulating anecdotes," said Katherine, "in which Handel refers to his cook Waltz, who also sang bass solos in many Handel operas. No one knows for sure whether he really was Handel's cook, but it seems that musicians often took on the role of cook as a day job. I agree with Peter—Handel's support for 'decayed musicians' says much about his concern for the people who performed his music. As someone who came up through the ranks as first a violinist and then a keyboardist before he took on the even chancier role of composer, Handel knew how very problematic life could be for a musician. And yet, despite his father's wish that he become a lawyer, Handel chose to become a professional musician. In fact, it seems that he set some of the terms for what it means to be a professional musician. But even Handel had to accept the fact that the stars—the great Italian singers—were better paid than he was. Still, as Brad said, Handel evidently had a good head for business.

Despite all the ups and downs during his career, he died a wealthy man—wealthy enough to leave a respectable sum to the fund for musicians who did not manage to make enough money to sustain them in old age."

"I guess," Katherine continued, "as Lydia mentioned the two-job situation for Marie's husband without further comment, she must have considered dual occupation livelihoods pretty common. I suppose it makes it all the more impressive that Handel managed to move into a position of relative independence as a composer. Although, he did have a 'pension,' as they called it, from the King, gave lessons to the Royal princesses, and of course worked as a theater music director in addition to composing. Handel managed to escape the church musician or patronage system, but he must have realized how hard it was for the men who played in his orchestras or sang in his choirs to make a living. The few women opera singers, like their male counterparts, were pretty well rewarded, at least while they were in their prime. But even Handel, for most of his career, was always just ahead of his creditors. The life of a musician was never a secure one—probably why Handel senior wanted his son to become a lawyer rather than a musician. So—a nice segue into Ross's topic: Handel taking stock at age forty-five. Want to lead us off, Ross?"

"Yes, I do," said Ross. "I've been thinking about what motivated Handel—what captured his spirit and energy and fueled his lifelong commitment to music. It had to be something that didn't fade with middle age or mounting obstacles. When people talk about talent, they usually contrast the individual who demonstrates analytical skills, diligence, and perfectionism with the person who exudes imagination, passion, and creativity. The first they may think of as a skilled craftsman or maybe a scholar, but the second is the kind of person we usually call an artist. I think Handel was talented in both ways. He knew his craft extremely well, and he performed both as a musician and as a musical director with the high standards of a perfectionist. And yet his composition process demanded creativity and imagination. More than these traits, though, he seems to have carried inside him an inexhaustible reservoir of dramatic scenarios that emerged in music as rich emotional statements. It is as though he daydreamed in music. His inner dialogues were sung rather than spoken. His personal involvement with life around him translated into the language of song or the timbre of an instrument. Because he was both a craftsman and an artist, he was able to create compositions that are timeless contributions. He must have known he was giving the world great music."

"I've often wondered," said Rebecca, "whether Handel might have been a kind of project addict, one of those people who must be engaged in a project at any given time, someone who needs the stimulation of a project or goal to maintain his connection with those around him. I once read a book by a scholar with a nearly unpronounceable name—Mihaly Csikszentmihalyi. The book was called *Finding Flow*. I think he wrote several books on the subject, but this one was short and actually pretty clear. Basically he argued that people thrive on engagement, that they require activities that focus their psychic energy. In other words, most people need to have a project—whether it's winning a new love or writing an opera—if they are going to be happy and engaged in life. But some people—like Handel—seem to require such projects constantly and in the superlative. It certainly sounds like Handel was always working—not necessarily as would a workaholic but rather as an artist who loved his work. I think he substituted the joy of composing for the kind of personal relationship most people would seek out. Music was his love, his closest companion, the object of his devotion and ardor—more than any person."

"It gives a whole new meaning to 'the poet's muse,' doesn't it?" laughed Alison. "It reminds me of that quote from King George the Third that we discussed earlier—where he claims that Handel's love affairs were always within his own profession. It's possible that he really did allow himself to be seduced by his own music when sung by his leading ladies. Music scholars do say that Handel had great empathy with his female characters and gave the women who performed them arias perfectly suited to their voices. What better way to please a lover than to give her wonderfully expressive music to sing. But then, singers came and went, and each new opera brought a new heroine to be celebrated in song. I agree with Ross.

Handel seemed to daydream through his operas. His love life may well have been all in his imagination."

Katherine walked to the buffet to get some iced tea. "We can't seem to pull ourselves away from Handel's disappointing love life. I suppose we feel sorry for him. Still, that isn't really what you meant by your 'taking-stock' topic, is it, Ross? Remind us what you were hoping to examine here. I think you wanted to do a little sleuthing through the letters, didn't you?"

"Yes, yes," said Ross, "I admit it is easy to take a bit of information from the letters and run with it. But, let me see. What I'm really interested in here is getting a sense of how well we have—or maybe have not—gotten to know Handel at this point in our letter-reading venture. I'm starting to have a bit more respect for Handel's biographer—Mainwaring, his first biographer, the one our more recent biographers quote all the time but typically blame for being too dependent on unfounded anecdotes. I suppose this is more up your alley, Katherine. There seems to be a lot of folklore about Handel, but like most folklore, the stories seem to be exaggerated and rhetorical rather than accurate. I find myself asking whether I have gotten to know him better than I did before we started. I'm sure we have learned to know him better, but I feel like we need to stop and consider what we really do know about the man at this point. I wonder what Handel would have thought if he had stepped back and thought about his life at this time, at age forty-five."

Rayette waved a hand. "Ross," she said, "one thing we need to be aware of if we are going to ask what Handel's own perspective might be—we have to recognize his compulsion, his sense of destiny. For whatever reason biographers choose to include that little anecdote about Handel hiding a clavichord in his attic and practicing in secret, we have to admit that it points to a person who knew that creating music was what he must do. Poets, artists, or musicians—they all have to have that drive, that sense of destiny, or they run out of steam and give up the chase. I think we need to ask how Handel is doing in his drive to be—as Lydia said—peerless in his success as a performer and composer."

Ross went over to the shelf that held many of the books and other materials Katherine and Angela had gathered and placed there for the Seminar's use. Taking down a recently revised biography of Handel by Christopher Hogwood, Ross turned the cover toward the table where everyone sat finishing lunch. "Reproduced here on the cover of Hogwood's book is a portrait of Handel at age forty-five. It was painted by a young artist named Phillip Mercier and is one of the few pictures of Handel without his tremendous white wig. It's a really wonderful painting. It shows Handel sitting next to his harpsichord, quill pen in hand, composing. He is wearing what must have been everyday clothes—a simple cloth housecoat and a cap to keep his shaved head warm. The expression is neither jovial nor grim, but he appears to be engaged in his work, perhaps a bit impatient with having to sit still for this portrait. I think Handel probably had as much to say about how this portrait was visualized as did the artist. This is the way Handel saw himself—as a man whose life revolved around the act of composing music. In that respect, he must have been satisfied with the direction his life was going. His 'taking stock' would have been a positive thing—at least so far as his professional life went. I suppose my question is more about his personal life. Even ambitious men start to think a little more deeply about things besides work once they hit middle age. And for Handel's era, he is well into middle age even if he does live another thirty years from the time of this portrait. I wonder how he feels about himself and his life when he isn't composing or playing music."

"Psycho-biographies tend to focus on faults and flaws," said Peter, "but I am pleased to see you are at least interested in Handel's psyche, little as we may ever know about it. I like the mini-critique of the Mercier portrait. It does seem to present Handel as he likely saw himself—eager to work, most himself when he was composing. But then, why did he wear that awful wig? Ah, well, I do think we can surmise he had a practical streak. After all, he contracted to live in his own house as soon as he was able, and he played the market ultimately to his own advantage. He had friends, perhaps mistresses, and his living arrangement was comfortable, with servants and room to work and venues for his operas nearby.

Assuming that he really did not want to be married and have a family, there seems to be little absent from his life here in his forty-fifth year."

Katherine looked over to where Benfey sat taking notes and recording the conversation. "Well, Forella will be pleased that we at least broached the subject of psychological well-being. And Benfey has it all recorded for her. I will admit that the letters so far do not reveal much about Handel himself but rather more about Lydia. It would be so nice if we had even one or two responses he might have written to her. We do have one letter he wrote to his brother-in-law in Germany in which he expresses his great sorrow at his mother's death. It's interesting that the letter is framed in black. Handel was nothing if not dramatic and aware of the power of symbols. But he chose to leave his family in Saxony and take up residence in London, even becoming a British citizen. We have to look at what he did or did not do as a sign of his values and preferences. Personally, I think we can look at little more closely at the stories he chose to honor by setting to music and the characters he allowed to speak through his many arias."

"And so," she went on, "I have for you yet another DVD from Forella. I told Forella we could pass one or two copies around, but she insists that we each need to have our own libraries of Handel videos. This one is of an opera written about the time of the letters we have just read—1730. The opera is *Partenope*, and it is supposedly a comedy. It was filmed in Copenhagen a few years ago, and we see again our friend Andreas Scholl in a leading role. I look forward to watching it and discussing it next time. And, I hope we will hear something of what Forella and Angela have been up to in New York. See you all next time."

CHAPTER 15

Academic Acclaim

Ross drove slowly back to his home in Indianapolis. Earlier in the day, he had rushed to the medical center where Forella had been admitted shortly after landing at the airport when she and Angela returned from New York. Fortunately, the symptoms of confusion and slightly slurred speech quickly disappeared, and the physician at the ER assured Ross that the TIA was minor with no permanent effects. Forella was released yet that evening, and she insisted on going home rather than staying in Indianapolis. Ross drove his mother and Angela to Bloomington, and, after convincing Forella to let Angela or Annie sleep on the couch near her room, he reluctantly headed home himself. He switched off the radio that he typically left on when he stopped the car. Instead, he let his thoughts harken to the deep unease he had felt when he received Angela's call from the hospital. Few things in life had ever shaken him so much as this clear signal that some day he would have to accept Forella's dying. Ross knew his mother was his own timeless link to the world—not simply the physical source of his being but, more importantly, the one other person who loved his life as he did and shared countless memories. He dreaded the day he would have to continue on without that vital connection he had known from birth, from his first sensation of consciousness.

The Handel Letters

FIRST TOPIC OF CONVERSATION AT the next Seminar meeting was Forella's trip to the medical center. She, of course, discounted the whole thing, arguing that she was simply tired from the flight, but frowns greeted this claim all around—though she couldn't see them. Peter handed her a sweet-smelling rose in a bud vase. "You were *à l'hôpital* long enough to earn a flower," he said. "You must allow us all to pour out our concern. It is, dear Forella, the American way. Seriously, seriously, we are glad you came away with the doctor's blessing and positive projection. We WILL worry and fuss. That's what friends are for. Angela says you are feeling much better, and you look wonderful. But, we want to hear it from you—how are you feeling? Can I bring you some wine?"

"Ah, Peter," laughed Forella, "you are such a charmer. I feel fine, and thank you. Thank you all for your concern. I am grateful that it wasn't anything more serious than it was. We nonagenarians have to watch out. I'm so glad Angela was with me. Thank you all. I am feeling much better. Really, I am."

"Thank YOU, Forella, for joining the Seminar today," said Katherine. "We are all relieved to see you looking so well. But, please, if you feel at all tired, don't overdo. Travel is always a draining experience, even without a surprise trip to the ER. Just do whatever feels good to you."

Forella smiled, nodded, and then turned toward Angela. "Shall we tell them what drew us to the City?" Angela grinned and held up a program. "I brought the playbill. My first time at Lincoln Center. It was wonderful. The opera?—Handel's *Giulio Cesare*. Did I pronounce that right?"

"Correct," Ross said with a broad smile. "Your opera tutor has taught you well. But even I did not know that was the goal for this trip. I thought you were going to visit cousin Elizabeth and her family in Dobbs Ferry. When did this opera excursion become a part of the picture?"

Forella laughed. "Well, we did have a nice, long visit with Elizabeth and James. They were very welcoming, and we had a lovely time in their little village, but you know Elizabeth. She loves to surprise people. She bought the tickets when she knew we were coming, and it was just a short train ride into the City. It was purely a coincidence that a Handel opera was on the schedule. Ross, you will have to admit that the universe is conspiring to place you and Handel in close proximity. It is truly a significant phenomenon—a portend, a synchronicity, don't you think?"

Ross chuckled and said, "You remain relentless and misguided on that score. Still, I am glad you were able to attend the opera. Tell us all how it was. Good, I assume." "It was excellent!" Forella said. "With David Daniels in the lead and Natalie Dessay as Cleopatra. Angela says that the dancing was superb as well. I wish you all could have been there. Maybe they will be doing one of those HP showings at the theater."

As plates of food made their way to the table, talk turned to the DVD everyone had taken home from the last meeting—Handel's *Partenope*. CD admitted to viewing it with his partner, Alex. "I think he may suspect that Handel is the topic of our Seminar," CD said. "I haven't said anything directly, but Alex knows I don't usually buy DVDs of operas—even those I like. We talked early on about how the Seminar topic was supposed to remain basically a secret, but I could tell by the way he looked at me that he figured Handel was our man. But he didn't ask. He learned the old 'don't ask, don't tell' routine pretty well, after all."

"I made sure to watch it when my wife wasn't home," said Wait. "Still, I'm sure if she bothers to snoop through the desk drawer where I've put the various DVDs and CDs Forella has given us—and I'm sure she will—she will be suspicious, too. So, how did Alex like it? I actually kind of wished I COULD watch it with my wife. I mean, it's a pretty sexy production—at least I thought so."

"Yeah," said Brad. "Now THAT lady could give the effete excuse of attending the opera a whole new dimension. But I'll acknowledge—much to everyone's surprise I would guess—that even more than the stunning soprano, what I really liked was the humor of the piece. Obviously the director had updated the setting, but the best part, I thought, was the battle scene when they played rock-paper-scissors to decide who won. And musical chairs! Not sure how much to credit Handel with since these were staging decisions, but still, I thought it was great to add a little nonsense to such a serious kind of music."

Alison joined the conversation. "It's true that the director was responsible for many of the decisions that made this such a delightful production, but part of the credit really should go to Handel as well. I was intrigued by this opera because it is actually a kind of parody of the operas Handel usually wrote. And it is clear that he had wanted to have the opportunity to write this piece ever since he first encountered a version of the libretto in Italy back in the early 1700s. He tried to convince the first Academy to let him present it in the 1720s, but the theater agent—Owen Swiney—rejected his proposal, calling it the worst opera story he had ever seen. Handel had to wait until he gained artistic control at King's Theater in 1730. I think this is one time we can safely argue that the story is one Handel really wanted to share with his audience."

"I didn't care for it as much as I did *Rodelinda*," said Rayette. "I suppose I just like tragedies better than comedies—whether it's Shakespeare, Handel, or whoever. And that mustache! How could anyone think Rosmira was a man just because she wore that droopy mustache and men's clothing? Of course the fact that she sang in a high register didn't matter since the men were countertenors. Maybe I'm just not into this genre."

"I don't know," said Peter. "I thought she fit the role pretty well. I can imagine a smallish young man looking like this Norwegian singer who played the role. No worse than female impersonators in drag. But to go back to Alison's comment, I think we should be asking why Handel liked this storyline so much. Basically, you have this woman—Rosmira—who loves a man—our Andreas Scholl—who has abandoned her—loves him enough to follow him to Naples where he is courting the beautiful Queen, Partenope. Rosmira disguises herself as a man but admits to her erstwhile lover that she is his Rosmira. But then she insists that he not tell anyone who she is. Of course you wouldn't have any kind of story if they just got together then and there, so obviously they have to play out the deception. Her excuse is that she doesn't trust him to be loyal to her here on out—even though he says he now realizes he truly loves her. But as we see in the opera, he is pretty easily seduced by the Queen, even after his supposed decision to stay true to Rosmira. A lot of Handel's operas have these fickle lovers. Is it just public taste, or does Handel have a message for us in this recurrent theme? Why DID he insist on bringing this story to the stage?"

Rebecca turned toward Peter. "I've been wondering that, too," she said. "I have a growing impression that our Mr. Handel is an early feminist—anachronistic as that may seem. The eighteenth century—even the Renaissance—was big on masquerade balls. Think of *Romeo and Juliet*. I think back then they didn't have the notion of psychological differences among people, but they did have the rather simple idea of disguise. One could pretend to be someone other than oneself—a poor man rather than a rich man, a shepherd rather than a king, a woman rather than a man—or, in this case, a man rather than a woman. When you don't know who is behind the mask, you are perhaps led to make at least some of the assumptions usually associated with the 'type' of person the mask suggests. There have always been scores of assumptions tied to gender. Maybe Rosmira was not simply trying to win back her lover. Maybe she wanted the experience of being treated as men are usually treated. And maybe Handel supported that lesson—for his character and for his audience."

Clara jumped into the discussion. "Well, I'd say it IS anachronistic to see this opera as an example of Handel taking a feminist stand. As Brad said, it is supposed to be a comedy, maybe even a farce. The audience would have seen the role reversal as funny, not socially significant. It's a man's drama. You'll notice there are no other women besides Queen Partenope and the disguised Rosmira, but there are a good number of other men. I think Handel liked the humor of the plot, and in the end, the seductive queen marries the long-suffering Armindo. It's probably the same incentive that compelled Shakespeare to write *Twelfth Night* rather than yet another *Hamlet*."

"I'm remembering Katherine's word for this," said Ross. "What was it?—'presentism,' or something like that? A filmmaker, or an opera director, doesn't abandon the worldview in his own head. Or, at least I am sure I don't. This was a very effective production of the opera, but try to imagine how it played out in Handel's time. In our Royal Danish Opera production, the un-costuming and re-costuming of the queen certainly got everyone's attention. It has to be the sexiest scene in the whole piece. And Scholl's response is understandable—and pretty funny. Some good acting and directing there. But we can't assume anything like that happened in Handel's production back in 1730. The punch-line ending in which the Scholl character agrees to fight his disguised lover—but only if they fight bare-chested—that scene would be received as bawdy good humor back then just as much as today. But other than that, the words and the music had to carry the day. Handel had to lead his audience to empathize with his flawed characters and go through the sequence of emotions they portray over the course of the three-hour opera. I think his objective was to write music that gave each of his main characters several opportunities to express deep and sometimes conflicted emotions. There were some very beautiful arias in this work, and all together the sequence of songs showed the kind of growth in the opera's characters that we like to see in good dramas."

Katherine carried her empty plate over to the buffet. "I suppose one thing that stands out here is that Handel wrote some very moving arias for this comedy just as he would for a more serious opera like *Rodelinda*. It's as though he regarded the emotional issues that faced his characters as pretty much the same no matter what the situation. He appreciated the turmoil and frustration that love evokes. His best arias always seem to have that painful backstory of love wronged or abandoned. Here in our Danish production, someone made the decision to add the wonderful duet from *Sosarme*—which Handel hadn't composed yet in 1730—'per le porte del tormento,' –through the gate of torment. I have the feeling Handel had a hard time imagining a love relationship that did not involve torment of some kind. A sad thing for him."

"But why he chose this story?" she continued. "Why did he take time to create some twenty-five de capo arias, a good half dozen of which were truly outstanding pieces? De capo arias were a hallmark of *opera seria*—serious opera. *Partenope* took the form of Handel's earlier operas, with three acts and predominantly high voices, but the storyline was hardly heroic. Instead, it reminded me of a folktale. Most people think of what we call magic tales when they speak of fairy tales, but there is a slightly different kind of traditional tale simply called a romantic tale, or *Novelle*, that doesn't have any magic in it at all. 'King Thrushbeard' in the Grimm Brothers' collection would be an example—or the folk version of 'The Taming of the Shrew.' Basically, these are stories about how people learn to be good romantic partners, how to be a good wife or husband. I think that is what is going on in Handel's opera. It's ironic, of course, that he never took this message to heart himself. Which leads, I would guess, to our purpose here today—perhaps yet another letter that makes us ask about poor Handel's love life. What do you have for us today, Peter?"

Peter smiled over at Katherine. "I'd like to hear more about these folktales. King Thrushbeard? Intriguing. I'm sorry to say there is nothing about *Partenope* or even Handel's sorry love life in today's letter. Instead, we are cast into the world of eighteenth century academia—at least in part. Handel travels to Oxford, and Lydia writes in her letter about the goings on there. Here are copies for you. I had time for only this one letter. It is fairly long. I think you will find it interesting. This letter comes some three years after the last one."

Mr. G F Handel, Esqr
Brook Street, near Hanover Square
London

30 July 1733

My Dear Mr. Handel,
Your look of surprise at seeing the Reverend Edward Grayston and his wife in the audience at the Sheldonian in Oxford was truly priceless. I am sure, when we were all in Hamburg, Eggy told you that he had been a tutor at Oxford early in his career. His employment there was as guide to wealthy young men on their grand tour of Europe. He was young and enjoyed the opportunity to travel, and he made

some very good friends, among them the uncle of young Mr Jennens, who showed such a strong interest in your music. And, though he soon left the task of educational tour guide and joined Sir John's retinue instead, still, the kind folks at his old college thought to invite him to the celebratory Act with Mr. Handel. You must know there was no possibility that Edward could come to such an event without allowing me to accompany him.

What a very busy week that was. And everything was sung in English. That must have been a challenge for poor Strada, but it was good of her to join the native English-speakers. The Oxford audiences were clearly pleased with Esther and Deborah, and especially with Acis and Galatea. But best of all to my mind was Athalia—or perhaps it is just because I had not heard it before. What a wonderful oratorio. No need for the elaborate sets and costumes. Your music is enough to make the story shine—and of course the singers and musicians. Mr Waltz was a very good addition I thought. But my dear Mr Handel, what of the honorary doctorate of music you were supposed to receive there? Eggy reported that all—at least among his fellows—expected that honor to be part of the ceremony. Your quip that you would not be another accursed Maurice Greene made no sense. Eggy and I had a long talk about it on the carriage ride back to London. I expect your ears were burning.

A friend of Edward's joined us on the ride back to London. You may know him. His name is Hamilton, a curate with relations who live in Oxford. He knew a bit more about the much discussed refusal to accept an honorary degree. According to Mr Hamilton, you took warning from what transpired three years ago at Cambridge, when Mr Greene was so honored and then immediately was asked to take on the duties of professor at the university. Both Eggy and Mr Hamilton agreed that your stubbornness reflects a great aversion to teaching and to being committed to anyone's employ. They excused your readiness to speak ill of Mr Greene as a simple case of disparaging Maurice Greene's choice to accept a secure position at Cambridge *rather than stay engaged in the rough and tumble world of public musical performance. I disagreed with them and voiced the notion that you found Mr. Greene's friendship with Bononcini irksome. But these are mere guesses. We would love to hear the truth from you, my dear Gif. Or perhaps there is another reason. You rarely act for reasons others assume.*

I suspect you may be responding with your much celebrated competitive spirit and, perhaps, with some unnecessary jealousy and aggression, just as you did those many years ago when poor Johann dared challenge you on who should play the harpsichord. Edward and Mr Hamilton argued strongly against this view. How strange to be in a situation where I am speaking against you and others are supporting your actions. I backed down from that debate—no need to leave a bad impression of me with Eggy's colleague. But I will without qualm share my views with you.

It may well be that Mr. Greene was expected to take on the duties of professor at Cambridge after receiving the honorary degree. But Edward says that this is not always the expectation. I cannot imagine that any one of the colleges at Oxford would expect you to leave your activities in the opera theaters of London and come to Oxford to teach. You have greater renown as a composer than Mr Greene, and your career is in London. The Oxford dons probably wanted to honor you—as well they should. I think you were simply miffed that Mr Greene had been honored with such a degree before you, and perhaps also by his new found affection for being called Doctor Greene. I have heard your hateful names describing him, and I cannot understand why you have started using such terms against the man. Eggy and I agree that he is a decent person. When you first came to London, he was a friend to you and spent hours sitting by as you played the organ at St. Paul's. And yet when he starts having a career that comes up against yours here and there, you feel you must disparage him and lead others to see only the flaws and failings he may have. Gif, you are too great a talent to have such jealousies.

I like Mr Greene, but that is not why I am taking on the role of elder sister again and offering advice. I can see how disturbed you are when you think of him, when you must speak of him. Another person's success should not be so confounding to you. I fear it will simply make you ill, and in the end nothing good comes of it. Remember that your talent will always prevail and you will always find a way to write music and create performances that will win lasting gratitude from your audiences. You do not have to be the only one recognized as a wonder and a gift. Whatever Mr Greene does, he takes nothing away from you. Please, my dear Gif, try to simply enjoy your gift, as we who listen do. There is no need to fight or curse. I worry that it will hurt you somehow to be always so alert to offense. Dr Arbuthnot has warned repeatedly that when one becomes overwrought, nasty illnesses seem to spring up. Wouldn't you rather join Eggy and me for a relaxing walk in Hyde Park? I will promise not to mention Mr Greene. But I do want to hear more about Athalia. What a wonderful piece. Please be good to yourself, dearest Gif. I hope to see you soon.

I have the honor to be, ever yours,

Mrs. Edward Grayston
St. Thomas Rectory
Marylebone

Wait seemed to be first to finish reading the letter. "I can't imagine that Handel much cared for the tone of this letter," he said. "I would say she is overstepping a boundary here. I wonder if he answered her. I'm surprised he didn't write her off just as he did the unfortunate Mr. Greene. Handel is not known for being tolerant or forgiving."

"That was my response, too, when I first read the letter," said Peter. "But then I thought about what Lydia actually said to him—offering her observation on how he reacted negatively to the men who competed with him in any way. I don't think he saw HER as a threat, as someone who could be a rival the way Mattheson or Greene were. I think she knew she could get away with this kind of reprimand. He bristled at professional challengers, men who presumed to play the same game he did. I think she read him right—someone who did not take kindly to recognized rivals in the music profession. He probably didn't like hearing what she wrote in the letter, but I doubt that he let it change the nature of their relationship. Maybe he even responded by walking with the Graystons in Hyde Park and talking it through. These people were friends, not rivals."

"So," said Katherine, writing on the flip chart, "HANDEL'S COMPETITIVENESS would be one theme we will want to discuss. What else did anyone see in this letter? Any other themes?"

"I'm intrigued by this honorary doctorate issue," said Rayette. "I had no idea there even was such a thing that long ago. I thought it was part of modern academic politics to be honest. I'd like to think a little more about what it may or may not have meant to Handel and his contemporaries. It sounds like the information Lydia had was based on rumor rather than anything solid."

Katherine wrote THE HONORARY DOCTORATE ISSUE on the chart. "Anything else?" When no one responded, she said, "I'd like to discuss the hint that Lydia slips in about Handel's health. She suggests he lets himself become too stressed about things. We could call this her Mother Hen letter, I think. Maybe that's what Wait didn't like about its tone, hmm? I know that Handel starts having health issues sometime after this. Maybe Lydia was aware of some of the signs he seemed to be ignoring. So, I guess UNHEALTHY STRESS might be the theme. What do you think?"

"Yeah, stress is definitely a part of it," said CD. "I think all three themes point to the fact that Handel is no longer a young wunderkind but instead a middle-aged professional in a very competitive field. He had to fight to keep his place as the foremost composer in London. Lydia may have decided to play mother hen in her letter, but I suspect she really didn't understand the pressure Handel felt as a man who chose to forge an independent path in a risky profession. And likely she didn't understand the nature of male competitiveness either."

"Male competiveness! Now there's a diagnosis," said Peter. "Our Mister Handel is simply a prime example of the alpha male syndrome. He is really good at what he does, but he bullies and fights and bad-mouths the competition. That's how he stays on top. Sounds reasonable to me. What do you think, Katherine?"

"I'm the one who suggested 'unhealthy stress' as a topic, not male competitiveness," said Katherine. "I leave it to you to say more about this side of Handel's character—if indeed that is your argument."

"I sense a storm in the offing," said Ross. "I'll admit I felt we hadn't really resolved the issue when we were talking about *Partenope*. Gender, that is, not necessarily competiveness. Not that we are supposed to resolve anything in these discussions. But it does seem that views on gender—back then or now—pop up again and again. So, is Handel being the typical male and therefore competitive, or is there something else going on here?"

Clara gave a sigh and entered the fray. "I'm sure you all expect me to bring up my old stand-by, primate research, here—and there is quite a bit of research on competition among males in various primate groups. But actually, I'm taking a cue from Lydia's remark linking Handel's behavior back to his earlier duel with Johann Mattheson. I think she has put her finger on something there—something more peculiar to Handel—not the male gender. And even earlier than that, we learned that Handel tagged along when his father visited the Duke's palace, and he somehow managed to find a way to perform in front of the Duke, supposedly against his father's wishes. I suppose it could still be male competitiveness even at that young age, but to me it seems that this is something in Handel's personality. He is stubborn, aggressive, and single-minded when it comes to his music. Some might call it an artist's temperament—whether in a man or a woman. It seems likely that he was born that way—and not just because he was male. Being male may have made it easier for him to indulge that personality trait, but I don't think we can conclude that he is so competitive just because he is male."

Katherine looked around at the group. No one seemed eager to add to the conversation, so she offered a comment. "I can't imagine that you who are male are any more comfortable with the notion of 'male competitiveness' than we who are female are with, say, the notion of 'female connectedness.' Both are stereotypes, generalizations that may or may not apply to individuals of either gender. On the other hand, cultures everywhere socialize their young people into behaviors the group favors and a worldview the group takes for granted. Alan Dundes was a folklorist who taught for many years at Berkeley, and much of his research was concerned with perspectives individuals learn more or less unconsciously simply by being a part of their culture. He wrote a book about German worldview called *Life Is Like a Chicken Coop Ladder*. Somehow Handel doesn't seem particularly German, given the traits Dundes outlines, but interestingly, Mozart fits those traits very well—at least according to Dundes. Unfortunately, we don't have much background information on Handel—nothing, for example, on how rigorously he was potty trained—data of great concern to Dundes. Ah, well. Maybe we should go on to the next topic."

"Just when it was getting good," said Peter. "I'd like to know what some of these supposed German traits would be. Of course there was a lot of speculation about such things following World War Two. People were desperate to prove that something in the German character would allow the Holocaust, something absent from American or British character. But of course there is no way to support such an assertion. We can only assume people will always find evidence for whatever traits they believe are characteristic of someone from a given culture. I love your field of study, Katherine, but there is just too much stuff and no scientific method for doing the kind of research we need to make reliable statements about something like a national character. Why would someone even try? Why did your Berkeley professor friend try?"

Katherine laughed. "Don't expect me to explain Alan Dundes. He was a wonderfully provocative researcher. With great energy, he would amass countless examples of cultural material—jokes, sayings, songs, customs, stories—whatever supported his thesis. But as you said, he selected the pieces that fit his argument. But he could be very persuasive, and I think that was his objective. He wanted to make people think about the possibility that whatever he was suggesting might actually be true. Maybe Germans really are more anal than other people. Who knows? But I agree with you—there's no scientifically acceptable way to demonstrate something like national character. Dundes was one of the few folklorists who tried to make a case for something like national character. As I said, I think he liked to goad people into thinking about lots of things that most people would rather avoid having an opinion on. He was definitely a colorful figure. AND I think he was the recipient of many honorary degrees—or more likely, he was the one who awarded others such degrees. Shall we go on to that topic?"

Rayette waved her copy of the letter. "Yes, I'm the one who suggested that topic," she said. "I'm surprised to hear it was even a possibility back then. Usually these days the people who receive honorary doctorates are somehow connected with money being donated to the institution awarding the doctorate. That's not to say they are undeserving of the honor, but there are lots of people who COULD be honored with such a degree and only a few well-connected or famous ones seem to be chosen. But if we are talking about Handel back in the 1730s, then it really does seem to be a way of honoring someone whose work in a field is notable and on a par with those contributions someone with a PhD would make. I don't know the history of academic credentialing. I think in that time period it was probably rare to find that even people within the university actually had PhDs. And, of course, there were fewer universities. So, I guess part of my question is just why was Oxford interested in giving Handel an honorary doctorate anyway? What did they hope to gain—if not, as was rumored, to have him join the faculty there?"

"We might want to use the term Doctor of Music rather than PhD here," said Alison. "I'm pretty sure even back then the doctorate offered in recognition of performance or composition of music would be regarded as a DMus rather than a PhD. In any case, Handel was being honored for his work as a musician and composer, not for any scholarly research he had done on, say, the history of music or even music theory. Other people have been known to turn down honorary degrees. Some people see them as tainted by money in some way—either that the person 'bought' the degree by contributing money or perhaps simply by lending his or her name to the university to use to draw in students. I suspect that Handel saw the honorary degree as something akin to the kind of contracted patronage he always tried to avoid. I think he was extremely sensitive to the notion of being beholden to anyone for anything."

CD joined the conversation. "Some of the terms used for academic degrees are different in the UK than in the US. But I think Alison's last point about Handel not liking to accept favors from anyone is a good one. Even today a lot of people with earned PhDs resent someone with an honorary degree calling himself Doctor so and so. I can see where Handel might have viewed his contemporary, Maurice Greene, as a puffed up sparrow parading under false plumage when he accepted the honorary doctorate from Cambridge. We can't know for sure what Handel's thinking on the subject was, but I would guess he saw the whole thing as somehow dishonest. And Handel seems to have been honest—at least in his professional life. I think he would have been uncomfortable with being called Dr. Handel, especially since he had some very good friends—like Arbuthnot and William Croft—who had earned doctorates from Oxford and Cambridge."

Forella touched Angela's arm, indicating that she had something to say. Seeing Angela's signal, Katherine said, "Yes, Forella, did you want to comment as well?" Forella nodded slowly. "Yes, I'm curious—just as you were, Katherine—about whether this was a particularly stressful time for Handel. Why would anyone react negatively to being selected for some sort of honor? I wonder if Handel saw this as another kind of manipulation or attempt to influence his work as a composer. People under stress often seem more paranoid than the situation warrants. Handel was under a lot of pressure, not simply to perform and compose to a very high standard but also to maintain a steady flow of propaganda or advertising that convinced his audiences that he was the greatest thing around. I suppose that is what the life of a musician is all about, but it seems like Handel chose a path that had the least security and the highest level of stress.

People might think that being chosen to receive an honorary doctorate is a positive thing, but I can imagine how Handel might have seen it as yet another instance of having to meet someone else's notion of what is excellent or good. Who wants to be continually pressured by other people's evaluation of your work?"

"No disrespect intended," said Brad, "but that's life in the fast lane. Handel must have liked being a rock star, or he would have dropped out long before this. They didn't have the Pulitzer Prize for Music back then, but there were still reviews in the papers and the ever-important head count at the theaters. He might have had a more stable life if he had chosen to stay in Halle and be the cathedral organist for the rest of his life, but that isn't the life he chose for himself. He chose the life of a successful composer in eighteenth century London—warts and all. I'm more inclined to see Handel as thumbing his nose at the establishment in Oxford. Not literally, of course. I think he was careful not to step on the toes of people in power if he could help it. But I think he felt he had succeeded without the help of academic credentials. So, why should he pretend that they had anything to do with it?"

Rebecca looked over at Brad. "I suppose that's possible," she said. "Handel strikes me as being pretty self-assured. He certainly didn't need that kind of recognition to bolster his own opinion of his work. I'm sure he was happy for the weeklong engagement in Oxford. It was good exposure at a site outside London, and it gave his singers a chance to perform to a new audience. But I think you may have missed Forella's point. The honorary degree issue was just one more example of the kind of pressure Handel encountered day after day. Basically, even though he was confident in his own skills and talent, he had the constant stress of juggling other people's opinions about all sorts of things that were outside his control. And not just their opinions—the practical effects of those opinions, too. As people's tastes changed, Handel's operas became less popular, even though they are now considered excellent compositions. I think Forella was expressing her sympathy for a man who had to endure the daily stress of composing and producing opera in a context that was very unpredictable. It was his choice—that's true. And likely the constant pressure and criticism led to innovations in his music, but all the same, I imagine he noticed the effects of stress, just as we all do."

"Well, Lydia does hint that Handel is under a lot of stress," said Wait. "I guess when I first read the letter, I was reacting to her tone, to her scolding him for being a bit of a jerk about this Mr. Greene. But I suppose she was actually worried about him, about Handel, that is, about the effects of stress on his health. I'm surprised that Handel's friend, Dr. Arbuthnot, had said something about the ill effects of stress. I thought studies of stress and stress-related illnesses represented a fairly recent development in medicine."

"It's true," said Ross, "just like our more recent awareness that depression really does affect physical health. In the past, people simply assumed that stress or depression were signs of weak character. Sufferers were encouraged to have a 'stiff upper lip' or show a bit of pluck and get over it. But observant physicians even in Handel's time must have noticed that prolonged stress or unrelieved depression led to predictable physical ailments. It is obviously something Lydia and Handel's friend Dr. Arbuthnot had talked about at some point. I'm not sure Handel would have taken to heart any advice suggesting he not work so hard and try to relax more, but clearly Lydia knew that was what he needed."

"Of course," Ross went on, "Lydia had voiced many times her wish that Handel would marry and thus have someone who would chase away his stress, perhaps with a nightly massage and other such attractions. Sorry to say, ladies, but research supports the notion that men benefit much more than women from the married state. Maybe there is something to the stereotype that women are more empathetic, comforting, nurturing, etc. Where would Handel be if he didn't have Lydia looking out for him now and then? I think we are back to Handel's sorry love life again after all."

"Promoting the virtues of marriage!" said Forella. "I would never have thought it possible. Was that really Ross speaking, or am I going deaf?" Everyone laughed. Ross shook his head. "Very funny, Mother," he said.

"I've never said I had anything against marriage—just MY marriage. But that's definitely a useless tangent. Instead, I think we should go back to our earlier discussion of *Partenope*. Maybe part of the reason Handel was compelled to put on this opera was that he appreciated the advantage that having a loyal partner could bring. After all, at the close of the opera, the four main characters all seem to have learned something about what makes a marriage relationship good. Maybe Handel was resigned to enjoying such a relationship vicariously—through the lives of his dramatic characters."

Katherine smiled over at Ross. "I can't think of a better way to close out our discussion today. Speaking for myself, I intend to watch *Partenope* again. With all of the insights offered here today, I expect I will get even more out of it this time. Thanks, everyone for coming. Forella, we are all so glad you are doing well. Please take care. No more stressful flights—at least for a while. Besides we missed having you here with us. Until next time, everyone, arrivederci."

CHAPTER 16

In Sickness and in Health

Katherine sat reading through several books and pamphlets she had acquired at the Handel House in London. The previous week, she had traveled to London, then on to Sheffield to present a paper at a small conference there. At the close of the conference, she had purposefully allowed herself a couple days in London before returning to the US. The British Museum, the Handel House, the National Gallery, and the Foundling Museum—each had an abundance of pictures, documents, manuscripts, photographs, sculptures, and period objects relating to Handel and his time. Katherine was especially pleased to see a marble bust of Handel at the Handel House on loan from the Royal Collection. She had seen the impressive terracotta bust of Handel on permanent display at the Foundling Museum, but this bust was different. It was life size, with that warm luminescence that only white marble can give. The bust had an inscription written on its pedestal: By Heaven Inspired. The sculptor had not signed the piece, but the object label stated that it was the work of Louis Francois Roubiliac and that its manufacture was sometime between 1745 and 1755, when Handel was in his sixties. Katherine found the bareheaded, pensive Handel represented by the bust a welcome contrast to the often imposing, bewigged figure found in the many portraits of the man. His curly hair, thick, rumpled eyebrows, and downcast gaze gave him the look of a learned craftsman contemplating his next move. To Katherine the expression seemed entirely likely—a candid shot of the artist at work.

ANNIE ENJOYED MAKING INDIVIDUAL SERVINGS of shepherd's pie for the next Handel Seminar meeting. She had made a few sandwiches too—for anyone reluctant to try this typically English fare. Katherine was delighted, as she had just returned from her trip to the UK and had indulged in the usual fish and chips and then, the next day, a shepherd's pie at a very nice pub in Sheffield. She was quick to tell Annie that her meat and potato pie was even better than the English pub chef's version. Annie admitted to adding a little cream cheese and tomato paste to accommodate American tastes. Even Ross liked it—though he seemed to regard it as a side dish and ate a sandwich as well. People were in a festive mood. Peter walked around complaining, in a British accent, that the beer was too cold.

As luncheon plates were returned to the buffet and talk turned to the subject of today's meeting, Katherine told Alison that she had watched again the wonderful Danish production of Handel's *Partenope*. "I took the DVDs along and watched the opera on my return flight. Whoever did the casting for this production did a great job. I think they all were excellent actors as well as singers. Andreas Scholl has one great aria after another, but I think Handel gave each role at least one really good aria, usually more. I can see how he must have had the idea for this opera just kicking to burst out for all those years."

CD overheard the comment and before Alison could respond, said, "I really liked it, too. Did you know any of these singers before seeing this production, Alison?—I mean besides Andreas Scholl, of course."

"Interesting that you should ask," said Alison. "I actually know the Royal Danish Opera Company primarily because of their outstanding opera chorus. The DVD showed off their new opera house near the water. They have soloists on their roster—people who sing in several productions in a given year—but this production required some outside talent—Andreas Scholl, of course, and Christophe Dumaux, the two countertenors. I knew of them from other productions, but the two women I hadn't seen before. This was a fresh take, one that introduced some fine Scandinavian singers, at least to me. The venue seemed like a great place to present Handel's operas. I wonder if they have done any others since then."

"I like to think Handel would have endorsed the production," said Katherine, "but it's hard to say. Imagine, though, how surprised he would be to discover that *Partenope* still appeals to a modern audience. Handel and his collaborators must have gotten something right."

Ross stood and raised his glass toward Annie, who was just checking the coffee carafe. "To Annie—whose lunches are always a delight and a learning experience. Thanks for whisking us back to an eighteenth century English pub. It's always fun to discover new comfort foods. Shepherd's pie—tastier than it sounds. Jolly good. And now, folks, I believe we may have some letters to read—letters in the plural, at least that is what Dr. Rowe hinted as he came in the door. What's the scoop, Peter?"

"Yes, indeed, I have three letters for you today," said Peter. "If you remember, we last eavesdropped on Lydia telling Handel off for being a jerk about his friend Maurice Greene and for refusing the honorary doctorate from Oxford. That was 1733. These next three letters are written over a four-year period, starting in 1736. I'll pass around copies of all three. And I'd like to hear something from Katherine about her recent trip to England. I wish I had known. We need a blog or FB page—just kidding. Damn shame that we have to be a secret society. Here are the letters. Enjoy."

The three letters Peter passed to the group:

Mr. G F Handel, Esqr
Brook Street, near Hanover Square
London

23 February 1736

My Dear Mr. Handel,
What a delight—to celebrate your birthday a bit early this year with a wonderful concert at your house. Eggy was so pleased to see

you enjoying the wine we brought. His friend M. Reneau transported three cases from Dijon, and we wanted to share a few bottles with you and your guests. You could not have rewarded our effort in any better way than with playing through your new setting of Mr Dryden's poem. I had forgotten, dearest Gif, how very well you sing, how easily you move from one voice to another. I believe you attempted every one of the solo voices—though you would need Strada to properly convey the highest part. Yet, my friend, there is something so expressive about your voice, no matter which part you sing. Thank you again for sharing the new piece with all who were gathered there. May all your future birthdays be so full of friendship. It was clear that you enjoyed the celebration as much as we did.

It has been a while since I have written even one of my customary birthday letters. You are so often in the public eye that it is hardly necessary. And yet I miss our more private moments when I might share some of the observations you alone seem keen to ponder and even cherish. All in attendance were of course pleased to see someone take up again Mr Dryden's famous ode. Mr Pope has always shown great admiration for Dryden's poesy, the fine couplets—and everyone seemed especially taken with the fiery second part as Alexander is awakened to revenge by Timotheus's loud music. It was stirring indeed, but more to my liking were the arias and choruses of the first part. Mr Harris and young John Beard added nicely to the choral parts. The choruses are most like a classical drama, and yet it was clear that each was tied to a different expression—first Alexander's godly stature, then the joyfully drunken Bacchus, then pity for the fallen Darius, and finally the sweet repose of love on the bosom of his lover, Thais. I marveled at every turn at how you showed exactly as the poem argued—that music has the power to move the thoughts and feelings of even so great a king as Alexander. It is a fine piece, Gif. All the saintly spirits of music, both ancient and divine, have surely been honored by your composition and performance.

Spring comes early this year. Edward says he saw you riding horseback near the Park. We both smile to see you enjoying life so energetically. This past year has been a good one. Alcina was a great success and you have offered us so many excellent organ solos. For a musician, that must be a small heaven on earth. Perhaps you have found more time to simply relax and enjoy the coming of the flowers. Stay well, my friend.

I have the honor to be, ever yours,

Mrs. Edward Grayston
St. Thomas Rectory
Marylebone

The second letter:

Mr. G F Handel, Esqr
Brook Street, near Hanover Square
London

23 February 1738

My Dear Mr. Handel,
I write to greet you on your birthday and to repeat my expression of joy and happiness at the speed of your recovery over this past year. Please do listen to the advice your friends offer. The six weeks you were away at Aachen was a most worrisome period for all of us. Mr Hamilton praises your return to health and your strong constitution as near miraculous, yet I am cautious of taking such a view of the matter. I saw that you still favored your left hand upon returning. And you seem to me troubled by abiding afflictions even these several months since your return. Birthdays are a time for all of us to be aware of our mortality. I know the loss of our dear friend Dr Arbuthnot saddened you greatly and has weighed on you these past

months. Please, dear Gif, avoid if you can the very demanding season you performed last year. The nuns and the sulfur waters may not be able to work their miracle a second time. And to add to your sorrow, Her Majesty's passing must give you pause. The Ways of Zion Do Mourn was a very beautiful tribute to her. I know you do truly mourn the passing of our Queen. Life can be a fragile thing. Please take care of yourself.

I have been enjoying the oratorios immensely. Much as I love to hear solo arias, I think I enjoy the choruses even more. Please stay well, my friend.

I have the honor to be, ever yours,

Mrs. Edward Grayston
St. Thomas Rectory
Marylebone

And the third letter:

Mr. G F Handel, Esqr
Brook Street, near Hanover Square
London

10 May 1740

My Dear Mr. Handel,
After this very cold winter it was good to help celebrate your birthday with a welcome first hearing of L'Allegro. Our renowned Mister Milton would be proud, and truth be told, Mr Jennens did very well with the added Moderato. As Steals the Morn is a beautiful duet. The weather since that freezing February has been so much better. Edward and I went to see the newly erected statue in Vauxhall Gardens. It is a good likeness, Gif. You are almost smiling. I was surprised to see you depicted in such casual attire. Happily, I now

have a friend whose life sized statue stands—or rather, sits—near the music stage at Vauxhall Gardens. Eggy says it was Mr Tyers's aim to have you portrayed in a less imposing way than you appear typically in public. You must have agreed—or perhaps M. Roubiliac observed you on the sly. All the little children will want to come sit on your lap. It is a warm, endearing portrait. I like it. When Eggy stopped by M Roubiliac's studio to inquire after the bishop's monument for his nephew, he saw yet another piece in marble—not yet finished—a bust with nary a hat or wig. He said it was even more telling in its depiction of your more pensive moods. Some fortunate friend will have you always looking on with that wise and patient affection that slips out when you think no one is looking. Would that Edward and I could be the happy purchasers. As it is beyond the means of a rector, no matter how thrifty, we will have to make do with visiting the original whenever possible. You must know it is my preference. Stay well, my friend.

I have the honor to be, ever yours,

Mrs. Edward Grayston
St. Thomas Rectory
Marylebone

Katherine looked around to see if most were finished reading. "I'll be happy to talk a bit about my trip to England before our time together slips away, but as the letters are fresh in our minds, let us decide what questions or themes we will talk about today. Yes, Rebecca? You have a topic?"

Rebecca held up the second letter. "I'm remembering Forella's directive early on—that we try to make the Handel letters relevant to our own lives. This second letter seems pretty sobering to me—the one in which we learn about his health problems and Lydia's concern that he isn't taking care of himself. All of us—well, excepting Angela and Benfey—all the rest of us are reaching that point in life when we have to pay attention to signs that time is taking its toll. Clearly, we are fortunate that modern medicine has progressed since Handel's time, but still, Lydia's warning that life can be fragile is timely. I would like us to consider the state of Handel's health and his response to the challenges of life as someone who can no longer count on the health advantages of youth, someone facing life as a senior citizen. Simply the fact that she mentions his health problems and the discussion among his friends—well, it reminds me of so many of my own friends and their now much more frequent complaints of ailments and visits to the doctor. Granted, people live longer today than they did back then, but then as now, fifty, sixty, seventy seems to be the age when health worries enter the picture. What can we learn from looking at Handel's situation?"

Katherine wrote HANDEL'S HEALTH PROBLEMS on the flip chart. "And not only HIS health problems. We'll want to keep in mind how Handel's perspective and possibilities on personal health compare with our own. As Rebecca said—what can we learn from looking at Handel's situation? What else?"

Peter waved his hand and said, "I'll have to admit, as I was preparing copies of these letters for today's meeting, I was most intrigued by the mention of the statue at Vauxhall and the bust by the sculptor Roubiliac. I took time to do a little research on these artifacts, and I'd like to share some of it with you. Don't worry, not a lecture—but I did find some interesting information about Handel and the sculptor who created the most popular three-dimensional representations of our man. So, I guess my topic would be THE HANDEL SCUPTURES."

As Katherine wrote Peter's suggestion on the chart, she looked around for any other signs of interest in posing a topic. After looking around for other responses as well, Brad finally said, "OK, I suppose I am eager to hear more about some of the things our letter writer leaves unsaid, especially about how Handel's career as a musician and entertainer is faring. She hints in the first letter that the year before had been a good one, but then she says—in a defensive way—that she is enjoying the oratorios, as though Handel might be surprised to hear this. I don't know. Maybe I'd just like to know what the backstory is here. What do they know—or assume—that we don't know? IS Handel really under a lot of pressure in his profession? How is he doing as an eighteenth century entrepreneur? And why oratorios—since everyone seems to consider it an important shift in his professional activity?"

"So, HANDEL'S LIFE AS A PROFESSIONAL MUSICIAN IN THE LATE 1730s—is that our topic?" asked Katherine. When Brad shrugged and nodded, she wrote the third topic on the chart. "Rebecca, you wanted us to talk about Handel's health problems. That was our first topic. Would you like to start us off?"

Rebecca pulled a folder out of her handbag. "Actually, if you remember, we talked about Handel's health last time—or at least about Lydia's concern that he was leading a stressful life and suffering some ill effects from it. I was interested, even though I had no idea that one of the letters this time would speak directly to the issue of Handel's health. Often people don't recognize when they are juggling a lot of stress in their lives. I was unaware of the amount of stress I felt while I was still working for the University. You take on more and more duties, say 'yes' too many times, and still try to write and teach—until one day you notice how long it has been since you could sit without hunched shoulders and a headache. I am so glad now to be retired—AND glad my nurse practitioner warned me in time that I was taking on too much stress back when I was still teaching. So, after we mentioned Handel's unhealthy amount of stress last time, I went to the library and checked into the topic of his health. There is quite a bit of research on the subject, but I brought along what I thought was the most interesting article. It speaks pretty directly to the illness Lydia mentions in the second letter. Would you like to hear what the author says?"

"Well, we could all pull it up on our phones and ignore you while we read it along with any random texts we may have received," said Wait. "Isn't that the way lectures are handled these days?"

"This isn't a lecture," said Rebecca, "and, no, you couldn't pull this one up on your phone—at least not easily. The article was published in a British journal—*Eighteenth-Century Music*—and you would likely have to use the old-fashioned interlibrary loan system to get a copy. So, I advise you to listen up, Mr. Thompson." Wait laughed, and Rebecca put on her reading glasses and gave her stapled copy of the article a crisp shake.

"All the biographies mention the attack of paralysis that sent him to Aix-la-Chapelle—or Aachen in the German," Rebecca began. "But as David Hunter, the author of this article, says, most writers seem to accept Handel's quick recovery as 'miraculous' and somehow proof of his excellent constitution and resilient spirit. But as we see in Lydia's letter, Handel was in Germany, in Aachen, recovering for nearly two months, and his symptoms were not entirely gone when he returned to London. According to David Hunter, Handel suffered from lead poisoning—primarily from his heavy wine consumption—and while the spa at Aix-la-Chapelle did relieve the symptoms temporarily, the consequences to his health persisted for the rest of his life, including the onset of blindness some fifteen years after this first attack. I'll leave my copy of the article here for anyone else to read, but let me just point out the two things that impressed me most from the research."

"First, the author draws our attention to the fact that from 1737 on—and maybe sooner—Handel was not a well man. He suffered several more paralytic attacks, small strokes, colic, gout, periods of irritability and confusion—essentially symptoms of a serious and persistent illness that left him in chronic pain. One consequence of this ill health was an inability to direct long performance seasons as he had done previously. In fact, Hunter believes that the gradual turn to oratorio rather than opera was to some extent attributable to this now chronic illness. He argues that most of the great oratorios—with their themes of suffering and death—spring from Handel's own growing awareness of human suffering and the inevitability of death. Here's a great quote you can take with you, from page 266 of the article: 'Handel was forced to come to terms with the solitude of sickness, the pain and suffering of illness and treatments, the humiliation and dependency of incapacity, and his mortality.' I think Hunter's article prompts a greater sense of compassion for Handel. That he kept producing such excellent music despite his chronic pain and affliction speaks volumes. That would be the kind of personal triumph from which we could all take inspiration."

Clara shook her head. "Well, that's a big jump, wouldn't you agree—from a recognition that Handel had health problems to an explanation of why he started writing oratorios. There must be all sorts of other possible causes people could point to—other things that were going on at the time and MIGHT have influenced Handel's decision to write more oratorios and fewer operas. I certainly feel sorry for Handel, and I don't doubt that lead poisoning was behind a lot of his ill health, but why does your author feel it necessary to pose this as an explanation for his move to oratorios? It seems pretty far fetched to me."

Rebecca started to reply, but CD interrupted her. "Let me play referee here," he said. "It happens that I read that article as well—some time ago—and actually BECAUSE the author addresses the question of why the switch to oratorios. I think Rebecca gave us a good précis on the article, but of course she was especially interested in its relevance to the topic of Handel's health. I read it when I was researching the oratorio *Samson* as a piece my choir might perform. We concluded *Samson* was too difficult, but I kept the notes from my research, just in case an opportunity arose. The article Rebecca found so interesting was written more recently than a lot of the other commentary on 'why oratorios.' Usually scholars suggested an economic reason—that is, operas were losing money for the company, or a political reason—the divide between the Opera of the Nobility and Handel's opera project continued even after both companies failed. But a reason that many writers simply take for granted is a religious one—both that Handel wanted to explore religious themes and that the oratorio was a more laudable genre since it drew upon the Scriptures for subject matter rather than pagan myths and ancient history. Hunter reviewed all this research in his article, but his suggestion that Handel's health was important in this switch to oratorio took the discussion in a new direction. I agree with Rebecca. It casts Handel's decision as a more personal one. He found it easier to continue his role as composer AND as impresario if he could present this genre that does not require his search for Italian singers nor require so long a season as he offered in the past. I think Hunter made a good case for Handel's health as at least part of the reason he switched to oratorios. But of course that isn't why we were discussing this article."

Ross signaled Katherine that he had something to say. "It doesn't surprise me that someone made a connection between Handel's health and the switch to oratorios, but CD is right—that isn't why Rebecca brought it up in the first place. Basically we have Handel—starting around age fifty—having to learn to manage what prove to be chronic health problems. Maybe he had symptoms earlier than the dramatic 'paralytic attack' that Lydia mentions. In any case, I'm sure it was frightening. When it became obvious that he was in a bad way, he didn't just go to Tunbridge Wells in the UK. He traveled all the way to Aachen in Germany, and stayed for nearly two months. He was serious about trying to combat whatever was ailing him. I'm sure it DID interfere with his work as composer and especially as performer and impresario—when he had to be leading the orchestra or playing the organ or harpsichord. And, no doubt he didn't need Lydia to remind him that everyone is vulnerable. He grieved for the Queen; he grieved for his friend John Arbuthnot. And, as Gerald Manley Hopkins would say, he grieved for himself when he saw these fallen leaves all around him. I suspect he was very aware of his mortality when he headed to Germany in search of a cure."

"Yes, I think the brevity of life was impressed upon him in a forceful way that year," said Alison. "I've always liked 'The Ways of Zion Do Mourn.' It's quite a long anthem, and, in fact, he reworks it as the opening for *Israel in Egypt* sometime later. But King George had specifically asked Handel to create the music for Queen Caroline's memorial, and Handel gave us one of his best works—in just a week. It's as though the music were there inside just waiting to express the sadness Handel felt in losing his close friends. The Queen was greatly admired by her people. The anthem celebrates her warmth and caring of course, but Handel actually knew her very well. He had been music teacher to her children. She was clever and interested in a variety of intellectual subjects. I can imagine that Handel regarded her as an ideal woman of the Enlightenment—intelligent, interested in the arts, and yet caring and devoted to her husband and children. I'm sure her death weighed upon him and added to his melancholy at that trying time."

As Alison finished speaking, most people sat still, evidently in deep thought. Finally, Peter stood up and started doing jumping jacks. "Ok, everyone. Time to snap out of this gloomy mood," he said. "Get the blood moving, deep breaths—you, too, Ross. No more mopey talk of dying queens and chronic ailments. Wet your whistle, and I'll show you some slides. Well, some photographs anyway. Remember? I said I wanted to talk about the sculptures. You didn't expect me to pass up a show and tell moment did you? I'm all set here with an iced tea. Everyone refreshed and ready? OK. Let the show begin." He flicked on the laptop and brought up a picture of a face seemingly cast from clay.

"You'll remember this, Ross," he said. "We saw it at the Handel House when we were in London negotiating for the letters. It was just there on loan. People used to always refer to it as Handel's 'death mask,' because they thought it was the plaster cast that was made soon after he died. That used to be a pretty common practice, you know, before photography—a way to capture someone's actual facial features. But in Handel's case, it was argued that this cast didn't look much like the portraits of Handel when he was older—like this portrait by Thomas Hudson from the National Portrait Gallery. That one was painted in 1756, just three years before Handel died, and as you can see, Handel's face was heavier and he looked older. So instead, people now seem to feel that the cast of Handel's face is a 'life mask,' one made while he was still alive and then later used by Roubiliac when he sculpted the 'mystery bust' that Lydia refers to in her letter. Let me show you a picture of that sculpture. This is from the article I mentioned by David Wilson, published in *The British Art Journal*. In the notes, Wilson argues that the 'life mask' shows a Handel rather slimmer than he was usually described as being. He thought maybe the mask was cast shortly after Handel returned from Aashen, where he likely lost weight while taking 'the cure' for two months. What do you think?"

Rayette walked up to the picture to examine it more closely. "So you think Roubiliac made a plaster cast of Handel when he returned from Germany—and then used it to model the sculpture in Vauxhall Gardens AND this bust that Wilson is writing about? It DOES look like the face in the picture of the bust—at least to me. I wonder why people thought it was a death mask?"

"Well, there was a later reference," said Peter, "some source that mentioned a death mask, but it would be hasty to conclude that this cast is the one that source is referring to. That's the trouble with doing this kind of research so many years after the fact. But I'll say this—going back to our earlier gloomy discussion about Handel's health—I wouldn't doubt that Handel thought it prudent to have a cast made of his face once he had survived his ordeal and seemed in better health. It may have scared him enough to set him thinking about his legacy. Why else agree to a statue at Vauxhall? Living composers didn't usually have such tributes while they were still alive. Clara will likely object, but it seems connected to me."

Clara lifted her glass of water. "It seems as good a guess as any. And the life mask does look like the bust. I agree with Rayette. I'd really like to see this mystery bust. Where is it, and why is it a mystery?"

Katherine cleared her throat. "I can't think of a better time to report on my little trip to the UK," she said. "It so happens that I actually got to see this mystery bust. It was temporarily on display at the Handel House. I believe it is part of the Royal collection, but it has been shared with the public over this past year. Forella, I'm starting to believe in your synchronicity theory—or maybe sympathetic magic. Honestly, I had no idea we were going to talk about sculptures of Handel today. But I truly feel fortunate that I stopped in London on my way home. The bust is—as Lydia suggested—informal and pensive. You feel almost as though you were peeking in at him at work, as though he were so absorbed that he didn't know you were there. And with his short curly hair, he seems like a person you could meet today. They didn't allow photography, or I would have taken a picture. I feel really lucky to have been there when it was on exhibit. I should have asked if anyone else wanted to make the trip. Sorry."

"Yeah, yeah. NOW you tell us," said Peter. "Damn—I really would have liked seeing it. Any special vibes from it? Did the eyes follow you as you walked around the room? Did it send a psychic message?—'I am really Ross Wainwright, and I want to play jazz piano in America.' Or, did it seem pretty ordinary?"

"Ordinary?!" Katherine countered. "Of course not. But I will say this: Unlike most of the other paintings or sculptures of Handel, this one made me think of him as a real person. He actually kind of reminded me of my Uncle Phil, right down to the slight cleft in his chin. He didn't look particularly happy—but thoughtful, intelligent. It's hard to say, since, thanks to our Seminar, I know so much more about him now, but this bust made Handel seem like a person I would find interesting even today—not a celebrity, which of course, he was—but more like a favorite teacher or eccentric neighbor. I am sorry the rest of you weren't there to see it. I believe it is on display at the Handel House for another month or so, and then it returns to Queen Elizabeth's private collection. At least that is what the guide at the Museum told me."

Forella turned in Katherine's direction. "I've become much more appreciative of three-dimensional art since I can no longer see visual details. I wonder if this new three-D printing everyone is talking about could produce a little replica of the bust. But I suppose that is something yet to come in our ever-growing techno-world. Meanwhile, thank you, Katherine, for the description. I like imagining Handel looking like your uncle—no matter what he looked like. I remember that most pictures of Handel represent him wearing his long, white wig. This bust sounds like a more appealing likeness—at least for our time. I'm glad you were able to see the sculpture while it was on display. You are a lucky lady."

"Indeed, I am," said Katherine. "I'll be happy to talk more about the sculpture with you, Forella. But perhaps we should move on to Brad's topic, as time is again slipping away. I think you wanted to talk about Handel's professional life at this point in his career, is that right, Brad?"

Brad leaned back in his chair. "I'll admit I'm a little lost here. First off, since when do you get lead poisoning from drinking wine? That's a new one on me. And next, what is this Opera of the Nobility and why did it make Handel lose money? As I said, there seem to be some things everyone is supposed to know that I haven't a clue about. I'm interested in what is going on in his professional life, but it seems like there is a lot of background information we need to know before we can talk about how his career is going. Am I the only one who feels like these letters in particular leave a lot things unexplained?"

"I'll take the one about lead poisoning from wine," said Rebecca. "I should have said more about that earlier. Lead poisoning can come from many things. You've probably heard of lead-based paint and the fact that gasoline wasn't lead-free in the past. Those are modern instances of threats from lead. But in Handel's time, lead was often added to wine and also used to seal it in bottles. People just didn't know that it was dangerous. Modern vintners never add lead to wine, and lead usually isn't a part of the bottling process—although I read somewhere that you have to watch out for the band of metallic filament at the top of a wine bottle. It may have some lead in it. But, for our purposes, in Handel's time there was often lead in the wine, and Handel drank a lot of wine. Ergo, lead poisoning. And the symptoms he had do correspond to those associated with lead poisoning. He may have gotten lead from other sources as well, but wine was probably a big contributor for Handel."

CD waved his hand. "Brad, I think your other question was about the Opera of the Nobility. As I said, Rebecca and I both read the article about Handel's health and how it may have influenced his switch to oratorios. In his article, Hunter reviewed some of the reasons Handel scholars offered for why he switched from opera to oratorio, and one prominent reason was economic. That is, Handel's opera company was having trouble because a second and very aggressive opera company was giving him a lot of competition. It was called the Opera of the Nobility, and a lot of the aristocratic people that Handel depended on for support of his company defected and offered their support to this rival company. So—reading between the lines in Lydia's letter—some of the stress Handel was experiencing obviously came from this competitive situation in the world of opera. Some scholars suggest that Handel turned to oratorio because it could be offered during Lent (which makes sense of course) but also because he needed to offer something the other company wasn't offering. There were also some political overtones to the whole thing. King George and his son Frederick were at odds with each other, and while the King sided with Handel, Frederick and many young elites sided with the rival opera company. So, you can see, it was more complicated than you might think."

"Ok," said Brad, "I think I get it. Handel was trying to please his aristocratic economic base, but some of them were being seduced away by this rival company. Sounds like life in the world of public entertainment. The interesting thing to me is that he seems to be introducing the oratorio slowly into the mix. He doesn't just stop doing operas and move to the other genre. So, again, I think he was being pretty cagey about what he should be spending his time and effort on. It sounds like he was busy producing some kind of music all throughout this period. Some of it caught on, and some of it didn't. I guess the point I take away from it is that Handel made a decision to stay productive and try new directions no matter what the response of his supporters. He gets my respect for that. A real professional just keeps working on his craft, his art, and tries not to let popular opinion determine his path. If he did all this while at the same time feeling pretty punk physically, well more power to him."

"Well said, Brad," chimed in Ross. "I think this discussion—and this batch of letters—has finally led us to a closer look at Handel's own priorities. He has suffered some significant personal losses—his friend John Arbuthnot, his Queen—and I think he had great affection for Queen Caroline. And he has had to face his own health issues and try to accommodate what will obviously be an ongoing physical challenge—how to avoid debilitating attacks and how to keep producing despite chronic pain and discomfort. Probably he faced in his own mind the possibility of death and determined to stick with his art no matter what—as Brad said. To me at least, he seems more of a Mensch for having looked into the abyss and moved on. Lydia seems to be aware of what he is going through and offers him the kind of friendship I am sure he appreciates. I like her offhand remark that she would rather visit him in person than own one of the busts that seem to be so popular. But wouldn't it be great if we found out she had one of the mystery busts by Roubiliac after all? Ah, well—maybe next time. So, Katherine, anything else before we close shop?"

Katherine turned away from a quick whispered conversation with Forella. "Angela is just stepping into the next room to get copies of a DVD Forella wants us take with us and enjoy at our leisure before the next meeting. It isn't a Handel opera or oratorio but instead an early biographical film called *The Great Mr. Handel*. Forella, would you like to say a little about the film? This is really a wonderful surprise. I think I remember seeing it years ago, but I had forgotten about it entirely. Can you give us a little preview?"

"Yes, I'm happy to do that," said Forella. "This is a film I saw a long time ago, at a cinema shortly after the War. I asked Angela to watch the DVD version with me just the other day. We had a good discussion, and I am eager to hear what each of you thinks of it. Be warned, it may seem very sentimental, but remember that it was written and filmed years ago. I expect people had a different idea about what a biographical film might be back then. Ross, you probably can say more about the film than I can. I just remember that it influenced my own view of Handel as a person. It seems very unsophisticated now, but back then, it was probably avant-garde. What do you think, Ross?"

Before Ross could respond, Clara jumped in. "What? There is a biopic about Handel that I've never heard of! Granted, I may not be on top of all the composer biography films out there, but, really, I make a practice of watching for them. *Amadeus* and *Immortal Beloved* are two of my favorite films of all times. How could I miss a Handel flick?"

Ross just smiled and said, "Ah, well, don't be too hard on yourself, Clara. This movie would hardly be up there with *Amadeus* and *Immortal Beloved* or even *The Glenn Miller Story*—which was at least closer in time to our Handel film. It is considered an important piece technically, especially for its lighting innovations. But think about it. *The Great Mr. Handel* was made during World War Two—in England—1942, I think. Why would they even choose to do a film about Handel? I recall one scene—actually I need to watch it again, too—but I remember one impressive scene occurs when some bishop or other authority figure complains that Handel isn't even English and shouldn't be composing the coronation anthems for King George the Second. Handel's reply is something like, 'I am more an Englishman than you are, sir, as I chose my country rather than merely being born into it.' We have to assume that some part of the filmmakers' goal was to create effective propaganda in support of the English war effort."

As Angela handed around the DVDs, Katherine looked through the pamphlet and order form that accompanied the disc. She commented, "It appears that the company making the film available to people today sees it as a religious piece—at least judging from the other titles included in their catalogue. As I remember, it is mostly about how Handel came to compose *Messiah*, and I think there was a woman—one of his singers—who was sort of a guardian angel. It may not have been a big hit as a movie, but I'll bet it has had some real influence on how most people view Handel—the inspired creator of the ever popular *Messiah*. Thank you, Forella, for giving us something to dive into before we read our next letter. This should be fun. I intend to sit down with some popcorn and a Margarita and enjoy the show this very evening. See you all next time."

CHAPTER 17

Handel and Mrs. Cibber

Ross and Forella drove west along Interstate 74 toward Indianapolis. They had attended a wedding in Cincinnati, Ohio—one of Forella's nephew's children. With no siblings of his own, Ross had regarded his cousins as brothers and sisters. Their children were the nephews and nieces he would never have. Even when he was married, his ex-wife brought no immediate kin to the family. This wedding in Cincinnati was an especially happy affair. A favorite second cousin had finally decided to marry the man she had lived with for several years. Their two children—ages nine and six—were part of the wedding party. Ross chuckled to think what his father would have thought: "Too little, too late," no doubt. But Ross was pleased that Rosie seemed so happy. He wondered what had prompted her to marry her partner after all.

As the Handel Seminar gathered for their next meeting, Forella told Rayette and Alison about the wedding she had attended in the beautiful Spring Grove cemetery high on a hill overlooking Cincinnati. Forella remembered the cemetery from her childhood—its amazing statuary, its artistically situated trees and rolling hills. She explained, "The wedding was in the small chapel there, of course, but after the ceremony Ross and I walked up to some of the statues I remembered –and the limestone tree stumps. I was happy and even astounded, to find those statues and carvings were all still there, just as they were eighty years ago. Such a rush of memories! I wish you all could visit Spring Grove. It is a remarkable place."

"Cemeteries can be very interesting—almost like a museum," said Rayette. "I like walking in the Rose Hill Cemetery here in Bloomington. It is a beautiful place, and there are quite a few locally famous people buried there—Hoagy Carmichael, for one. If you are African-American or maybe Native American or Jewish or Muslim, some of these historically significant cemeteries can be a little depressing—mostly because of the people who were NOT buried there. The City of Bloomington has a guidebook that lists some of the more famous graves at Rose Hill. I was surprised to learn that one African-American Revolutionary War hero was buried there. The DAR erected a headstone for him in the 1980s. And there is a Negro leagues baseball player there too—died in the 1960s. I heard there is a movement afoot to erect a headstone for him. I think, more than racial discrimination, some cemeteries might reflect class differences. Even low-lying slab headstones cost more than some families could afford."

Clara joined the small group discussing cemeteries. "I couldn't help overhearing," she said. "I've been to Spring Grove in Cincinnati as well, Forella. It is definitely worth visiting if ever you are in the area. It reminds me of the famous Father Lachaise Cemetery in Paris—where Jim Morrison is buried. Well, of course the Paris cemetery has many more famous people, but still, you get that same wonderful sense of being in a park dedicated to the dead. I've often wondered what we will have years hence when people are mostly cremated and their ashes scattered or kept in urns rather than buried. How will we be reminded of all those who went before?"

"Now there's a lively topic—cemeteries!" said Ross. "What have you been doing, Mom? Inviting everyone to make a trip to Spring Grove?"

Forella laughed. "Well, it was a wonderful trip—and a lovely wedding. But visiting the cemetery itself, walking among the weeping statues I remember from when I was a child—that was something I'm not sure I could invite anyone else to experience anyway. We all have things from our pasts—things that are deeply embedded, personal. Maybe it's because I can no longer see them clearly, but those limestone markers and marble statues had a special earthy smell that pulled me back through the decades to the time I first visited the place. It was a little eerie—as though I really had gone back in time."

Ross smiled over at his mother and nodded. Everyone simply sat and thought for a while. Then Katherine broke the spell. "Well, speaking of going back in time," she said, "what did all of you think of our 1940s movie about Handel? I watched it twice. I actually ended up liking the way they portrayed Handel—at least most of the time. The actor didn't overdo the role. My main criticism is that they made everything revolve around *Messiah*. I suppose if it weren't for *Messiah*, the movie would never have been produced at all—there would have been little interest. Still, given what we are learning about Handel's life story, it certainly is a skewed biography."

Peter was just returning from the buffet with a cup of coffee. "It's a film, Katherine, not a piece of scholarship," he said. "I'd say they succeeded in their objective. Your first reaction was that you liked the way they portrayed Handel. Straight biography can be pretty dull. Here the moviemakers focused on the period just before Handel composed *Messiah*, but our attention as viewers was drawn to various little vignettes that hinted at Handel's character. I'm sure there were inaccuracies, and, as you said, much was left out. But still we get a picture of Handel as very human, a compassionate man, someone inspired to write music, and even a pretty reasonable citizen in a class and wealth obsessed London. I liked the scene where he invited his creditors in and persuaded them to serve up a dinner for the two orphan boys. Probably completely bogus, but it got the point across."

"And the lovely soprano just happened to show up and sing 'Ombra mia fu'—I recognized it," said Clara. "How convenient. I agree with Katherine's criticism. It's all about *Messiah*. And the scene where he is actually writing the music—talk about overdone! All those scenes from the life of Christ—the nativity, the crucifixion—and Handel is supposed to be 'seeing' all of this as he is writing out the music. Yes, I know that filmmakers always have an agenda, but in this case, it was mostly an effort to depict Handel as 'inspired.' It is less about Handel and more about how the Christian story inspired a great musician to write music. I thought it was really maudlin. Sorry, any of you who really liked it."

"Forella warned us that it would be sentimental by today's standards," said Rayette. "Personally, I thought the sequence of scenes from the life of Christ worked well in the movie. How else would you represent the ideas going through a composer's head? They wanted viewers to appreciate how inspiring Handel found the Christian story. It's a compelling story—whether you are yourself a Christian or not. What is more impressive to me is that—in effect—the filmmakers found a way to tell the Christian story while seeming to tell the story of Handel's life. It doesn't surprise me that the film is considered a Christian classic."

"Well, I don't want to ruffle any feathers here," said Rebecca, "but I DO agree with Clara that the moviemakers are, in effect, using Handel's decision to write an oratorio based on the life of Christ as a kind of propaganda for Christianity. Granted the story is compelling, as Rayette says, but in fact many of the other stories Handel chose to compose music for were compelling as well. The Christ story isn't unique. Cultures all over the world have very similar stories told about other heroes. I remember the first time I presented an observation along these lines as part of an undergraduate anthropology class. Students in the class had a fit. I suggested they read Lord Ragan's *The Hero* or the ever-popular *Hero with a Thousand Faces* by Joseph Campbell, but they all insisted that Jesus did not match the pattern. Katherine, I even sent them to your friend Alan Dundes and his article on "The Hero Pattern and the Life of Jesus," but they refused to be enlightened on the subject. I think privileging the Christian story above all others is simply part of the American ethos."

"I wouldn't disagree with you on that," said Brad. "What gets me is that the film implies that even Handel getting the libretto for *Messiah* was somehow an 'act of God.' They make Jennens—the librettist—out to be some sort of ignorant dandy who didn't really know the Bible. They suggest it was actually his assistant who selected the texts. It seemed really important to the film's writers that Handel be depicted as being 'used' by God—the Christian God—to bring this inspired message to humanity in an even more impressive way than ever before. The movie wasn't really about Handel. It was about how everything makes sense in life if it leads to an acceptance and adoration of Christ. Spin is not a new thing. It's been going on for years."

"Ruffling feathers, spin," said CD. "It sounds like we are letting our notions of political correctness and rhetorical allowances intrude into our discussion. The film had a bias. There is no denying that. Like it or not, it responded to the dominant sensibilities of the day. As Katherine said earlier, if Handel hadn't composed *Messiah*, we wouldn't have this film about him. Who would have cared? I think we need to ask what the film accomplished in the way of telling viewers something about Handel—quite apart from what it says about Christianity."

"Thanks, CD. I think you are right," said Katherine. "Let's come back to our critique of the movie after we've seen today's letter. Maybe the letter will help us refocus on what we can learn about Handel's life from whatever source. Why don't you tell us what you have for us today, Peter?"

"There is a connection," said Peter. "After all, we have just arrived in our stack of letters at the timeframe highlighted in the film—the very early 1740s, the period just as Handel decides to compose *Messiah*. I have only one letter for you today, but it is a fairly long one."

Here is the letter Peter sent around to the Seminar.

Mr. G F Handel, Esqr
Brook Street, near Hanover Square
London

12 November 1740

My Dear Mr. Handel,
Autumn's rains are fast upon us—'And summer's lease hath all too short a date.' Mrs. Pendarves informs me that you are back from your trip to the continent. I had been in the country for several months

and am fairly ignorant of anyone's comings and goings. And yet, dear Gif, now that I know you are returned, I would like to share some news with you. I recall the talk not over a year ago about the beginnings of the Fund for Decayed Musicians and your very prominent involvement in establishing that much needed charity. Edward was there at the Crown and Anchor when the Fund was first discussed. You are a true Christian and a gentleman in supporting such necessary care for those less fortunate. You may remember meeting Mr Close who was there along with Eggy and your friend Mr Festing. Much has happened in your life since then, but I write to inform you of one benefit your support for that Fund and its concern has already brought to a troubled musician.

You have said before that your greatest solicitude was for the children of musicians who no longer have an income, or for those musicians who have died leaving their children to seek their fortune on the streets of our town. We both know that sometimes it is simply the laws that refuse to acknowledge the needs of children born to those unable to marry. Along with a few other women here in our Upper Brook Street neighborhood, I have started a sewing circle. We call ourselves grands-mères sans petits-enfants. We make blankets and clothing for some of the same children your Fund supports. But that is not my news. Instead I wanted to relate this sad story. You must know already the gossip about Mr Arne's sister, Susannah. My initial worry was not about Mrs Cibber herself but rather about her young daughter, born into another man's household. Eggy asked me to meet with Mrs Cibber and help secure some protections for the child. The father is—most fortunately—a good man and eager to help support the child. The Decayed Musicians Fund gave benefit this time, not so much with needed funds, but rather with simple friendship for a mother and child weighed down with guilt and blame. I believe we were able to help them avoid the worst of society's slings and arrows.

I write remembering our discussions in times past of a theory held by your father and your brother Carl—that troubles in the daily lives of their patients often led to physical ailments, or perhaps were a part of the illness in some way. I have always thought you would have been an excellent surgeon, just as your father was—and not simply because you have a ready mind and nimble hands. No, rather, you have a deep sympathy with the souls of people in pain—whether physical or emotional. I think your nephew Christian shares that insight into troubled souls. I was so happy to meet him. You both prove to me that medicine and music are naturally intertwined. But forgive me, Gif, I shall return to my earlier concern. I am worried for my friend Mrs Cibber. I believe her troubles are bringing her injurious ailments—disturbances in her body and nightly aches that leave her exhausted and frail.

Judgments are harsh in our kingdom of man. Surely heaven will be less quick to condemn those who fall into wrong paths along the way. As do so many women, Susannah married young and to a man who could give her neither kindness nor affection. That she found another who could is counted a sin, but we gain nothing in casting her out of our circle of care—and especially, we fail in God's commands if we punish her child. I applaud your desire to help the children of cast-off musicians—a group often treated as servants without human needs and affections. Susannah is a singer with a rare talent. Not the skill of your Italian sopranos but rather a sad expressiveness that touches the soul. She has won my sympathy. I write in the hope that you will not hear the gossip strewn about her but listen instead to your own generous heart.

I do so wish that we could return once again to those fine evenings in Sir John's parlor. There I could share with you my unconventional misgivings at the treatment of my sex. I recall that you might not always agree with me, but you did listen and take up my opinions with respect and even a sly smile for my independence of mind. But I stray from the topic. You have heard Susannah sing, though I know it was at her brother's work and not your own. Her execution of arias is no less moving because her personal life is flawed—and perhaps more *so for that very reason. Forgive, I pray, her unfortunate misstep and bring her into your fold of English singers. I would delight in hearing her sing your music. She shares your rare sense of music's depth and pathos. And, Gif, you know I have never offered poor advice on singers. On a lighter note, perhaps some day I shall demand my fee, but for now, hearing Susannah sing your wonderful music would be pay enough. I long to hear from you news of your travels. Stay well, my dear friend.*

I have the honor to be, ever yours,

Mrs. Edward Grayston
St. Thomas Rectory
Marylebone

As everyone finished reading the long letter and slipped over to the buffet for a second cup of coffee, Wait turned abruptly toward the rest of the group and said, "This is the woman who actually received this packet of letters! I remember the name—Susannah Cibber. That's right, isn't it? She is the one who ended up accepting the letters because Lydia wasn't at the address in London—the one Handel sent them to. I remember Peter saying this. When we first learned about the letters—isn't that right, Peter?"

Katherine and Peter both looked at Wait in astonishment. "We need to put you on a game show," said Peter. "What a memory! Yes, Susannah Cibber was the person who received the package of letters from Handel and had them sent on to Lydia at the house in West Woodhay. Remind me never to discuss my former colleagues and acquaintances with you, my friend. That's a wicked talent you have there."

Wait laughed. "Yeah, I've always been able to remember bits of trivia better than most people. Sometimes it comes in handy, but usually not. Anyway, so this singer that Lydia is all worried about ends up as her good friend later in life—or at least so it seems. Small world, I guess. AND she is the one the filmmakers cast as a really important friend to Handel. So, this is a name worth remembering, I surmise."

Katherine held up a book as she walked over to the flip chart. At the top of the sheet she wrote the name MRS CIBBER. "I have some very interesting information about Susannah Cibber. Peter gave me a heads up on the content of this letter some few days ago, so I've done a bit of research. I assume you are all fine with having Mrs. Cibber as our first topic of discussion today. Believe it or not, this book I brought along to share with you is all about Susannah Cibber and her complicated life. As we shall see, it wasn't just the producers of *The Great Mr. Handel* who saw Susannah Cibber as a fascinating character from eighteenth-century London. But more of that in a bit. So, besides the topic of Mrs. Cibber, what other themes from the letter grabbed your attention?"

"I suppose it still has to do with Susannah Cibber," said Rebecca, "but I was intrigued by Lydia's mention of the status and treatment of women, especially women who have babies considered illegitimate. Lydia mentions a fund that Handel and some of his colleagues have set up to help out fellow musicians who have fallen on hard times—and their children. I guess I am interested in this theme of how society in Handel's time cared for the poor or outcasts, especially women who had illegitimate children—and I suppose, the attitude toward them."

Katherine wrote: PERSPECTIVE ON POOR AND OUTCASTS IN HANDEL'S TIME. "What else?" she said.

Wait looked around then said, somewhat apologetically, "This would be still about Susannah Cibber, too, but after all, she IS the subject of the letter really. And I wanted to go back to the movie with a question. Is Susannah Cibber an important friend for Handel, as she is depicted in the movie? And what about that servant who stays loyal to Handel even when he isn't paid? I guess my topic would be Handel's friendships—not his love life for once but instead his friendships or other important personal relationships at this point in his life. I'm intrigued by the way Susannah Cibber was portrayed in the movie, but mostly I am curious about the general notion of friendship and how Handel's situation might play out in life today. What do you think?"

"A very interesting question, Wait," said Katherine. "How should we phrase it? HANDEL'S FRIENDS AND WHAT THEY SAY ABOUT FRIENDSHIP. Is that close to what you wanted to say, Wait?" Wait nodded. "Sounds good to me."

"I promised you some helpful information on Susannah Cibber," said Katherine, "so let me tell you about this book." She held aloft, and then passed around, a hardback book with a jacket displaying a portrait of a woman with large eyes, a prominent nose, and otherwise rather slight features. The title of the book: *The Provoked Wife: The Life and Times of Susannah Cibber*, by Mary Nash. "This book is all about the woman presented by our filmmakers as rescuing Handel from his poor skills in self-management and as singing the wonderful aria 'Ombra mia fu,' as Clara pointed out. The movie was clearly playing fast and loose with the truth about Susannah Cibber, but what of this author who acknowledges research contacts at Harvard University and the Victoria and Albert Museum in London? Is she giving us a reliable portrait of our singer and Handel's friend? I am eager to share what I've learned from reading this book, but first I wanted to simply raise the question of sources. In this era of internet and online sources, what are we to make of supposed documentary films and published biographies?"

As the book reached her, Rebecca turned to the title page and flipped over to the edition notice. "The publisher is Little, Brown and Company—a firm out of Boston—and the copyright date is 1977," she said. "Little, Brown isn't a scholarly press, but it is reputable, for both fiction and nonfiction. Actually, I've run across this author before—years ago, when my son was in grade school. He had a favorite book called *Mrs. Coverlet's Detectives*. I see it is mentioned here on the inside flap of the book jacket. I'm not sure what would have drawn this author—Mary Nash—away from children's books to writing a book about an eighteenth-century British singer, but I would guess she is a pretty good writer, if nothing else."

"The kid with the cat!" said Peter. "I remember my older brother and I reading that book more or less together—or maybe another one with Mrs. Coverlet in the title. It was on our bookshelf for years. I liked it because the youngest brother was the hero. I'd forgotten all about it."

CD laughed. "Yes, indeed. Right there with all the Dr. Seuss books, as I remember from my own childhood. But to go back to Rebecca's comment on the publisher of this book about Susannah Cibber—a press like Little, Brown probably indicated more of a popular interest than would a university press or one more noted for weighty scholarship. The publisher must have thought of Mary Nash's book as something the general public would find interesting and maybe even simply entertaining. Did you see the little epigraph after the dedication page? It says: 'The two most fascinating subjects in the universe are sex and the eighteenth century.' Now, there's a teaser for you!"

"Ha, I missed that, CD," said Katherine, "but that does sum up the themes of the book. I want to come back to the question of how much credence to give such popular biographies—and films like *The Great Mr. Handel*—but for now let me quickly review the content of Mary Nash's book, *The Provoked Wife*. As you might guess from the title, Nash argues that Susannah Cibber was persuaded into some sort of action not of her own choosing and that it was her husband who provoked her. And as Rebecca speculated, Nash's book is well written. It reads rather like a detective novel. She relates the story of Susannah's husband Theo Cibber and his scheme to entrap a wealthy landowner, William Sloper, into having an affair with his, that is Theo Cibber's, wife, Susannah. He succeeds and then brings suit against Sloper. Theo actually does this twice, and even hires an accomplice to spy upon the two and describe their lovers' tryst. The very graphic description of the pair's lovemaking becomes a part of court records and is widely spread throughout London, rather like modern gossip sheets at the supermarket. However, the judges were made aware of Theo Cibber's role in bringing about the relationship and awarded him a very paltry sum as the supposed 'aggrieved husband.' Sloper and Susannah found that they did in fact love each other, and they lived together from that point on—though neither was able to divorce his or her partner. The account of Susannah's life is, of course, much more detailed than this short summary, but as you can see, the themes of eighteenth century culture and sex do loom large in the narrative. It is an interesting book. Handel is consistently depicted as a professional colleague and an admirer of Susannah Cibber—despite her fairly undeveloped musical skills. Nash finds evidence that Handel created a few oratorio roles specifically for Susannah. The book is carefully researched, though the author, like any good storyteller, selects the bits of evidence that support her view of the main character. It is definitely worth the time you might take to read it."

Brad shook his head. "The husband sounds like a sleaze ball, but come on, how can a wife be 'provoked' into having an affair with a rich mark like that? Isn't she in on the plan? It sounds like our author is trying to put all the blame on the husband. I AM surprised to hear that the court records were so graphic. You want to pass that book back this way, Ross? Sounds like my kind of research."

"It's Chapter Ten, Brad," said Katherine, with a smirk. "There are a couple paragraphs recounted by the owner of the rooms where Susannah and William Sloper met secretly. Evidently this landlord had drilled a hole in wainscoting of the room so he could observe the goings-on when the lovers were there for their prearranged trysts. I must say, I was surprised that these very scurrilous reports would be made public. Susannah's reputation did suffer because of the trial reports, indeed, but in fact, because she was an actress, she was not in the same social standing as more respected ladies anyway. That was a part of eighteenth century culture—the assumption that actors and musicians were not really a part of the gentry."

"Whoa," said Brad, quickly skimming the pertinent paragraphs in Chapter Ten. "The report doesn't leave much to the imagination, does it? Who would have guessed those Baroque folks were carrying on in such flamboyant fashion? And I quote from page 140: 'he lifted up her clothes and took down his breeches and took his privy member and put it in his hand and put it between her legs.' But I guess sex is sex no matter when."

"Can we move on from this puerile discussion?" said Clara. Katherine took the book back from Brad. Ross clinked his glass to get everyone's attention. "Right you are, Clara," he said. "Let me take on my role as dining room bouncer and steer us back to our discussion of the letter. The truth is, there are lots of biographies and movies that give us glimpses of Handel as seen from some writer or filmmaker's eyes. I remember one made-for-TV video out of the UK in which Handel was depicted as an old man looking back over his life. John Osborne wrote the script—you know, the *Look Back in Anger* man—but it was slanted, just like our *Great Mr. Handel* bio was. This is why I didn't want to have research be a part of our task here. Too easy to get bogged down or off on tangents."

Katherine smiled and put the book down. "Thanks, Ross, for getting us back on track. So, our second topic—the poor and outcast in Handel's time—was sparked in part by Susannah Cibber's illegitimate child. Lydia mentions the child, the daughter Susannah and William Sloper have together, and she tells Handel that she is worried about the child's welfare and about Susannah's health. Rebecca, you are the one who identified the larger topic here. What would you like to say about it?"

Rebecca looked through her copy of this latest letter. "Here toward the end of the letter, Lydia mentions the times, back in Hamburg, when she and Handel discussed the sorry state of women's lives in the society of her day. How does she name her view? Her 'unconventional misgivings at the treatment of my sex.' She doesn't suggest that Handel shared her views, simply that he listened and respected her straightforward articulation, maybe even her courage in stating ideas that were so contrary to the accepted values. Obviously adulterous relationships and illegitimate children were considered moral issues, but even more than that, they were taken as signs of lower class behavior. But Lydia seemed to disagree with the general tendency to judge women caught in such situations so harshly. I think the Victorian era was actually even more judgmental than the eighteenth century, but likely in Handel's day it was still a woman's problem if she got pregnant out of wedlock or through an adulterous affair. Remember Katherine's song from several meetings back—the one about the queen's servant who was pregnant with the King's child—Mary Hamilton? It's never the man's problem. It's the woman who has to bear the social stigma—and that often applies to her illegitimate children as well."

"It IS interesting," said Alison," that Handel met with a group of men at a tavern and created a fund for musicians down on their luck—and their children. This was before welfare states were devised to help take care of the poor. The attitude toward musicians was on the whole pretty negative. Handel's father had been right to worry about his son pursuing music as a career. Often musicians were treated as servants. They rarely rose to the status of 'gentleman' even if they made good money. Handel himself obviously challenged that notion, but I think it is impressive that he must have persuaded some of his friends—who probably WERE gentlemen—to set up a fund in support of musicians who fall on hard times. Basically this was a charity intended to aid people from the 'lower class.' It wasn't so much a concern about whether the people were married or not—if they had children. It was only the upper classes that worried over legitimacy and inheritance. Susannah Cibber's daughter was 'illegitimate' because her father was a wealthy landowner. If he had been a musician like Susannah, no one would have paid much attention to Susannah's spurious pregnancy."

"I don't know that we can make such a generalization," said Rayette. "And we don't know who was doing the persuading—Handel or his friends. Personally, I take some comfort in the fact that it was a group of men—not some individual—who started this charity. Compassion seemed to grow out of some sense of civic duty. The group that met at the tavern represents the kind of community we can applaud yet today—people who shared the values we like to associate with an admirable society. Granted, there were likely a lot of people needing help who were excluded, but it was a start."

Peter stood up and lifted his glass toward Rayette. "Hear, hear," he said. "We rarely get to see how movements or associations that prove to be a part of history actually get started. Obviously, Handel had friends and colleagues among the 'decayed musicians' this charity would help, but in fact, as Rayette said, these men who met at the Crown and Anchor were acting in response to a larger principle rather than simply personal connection—worthy as that might be. God knows, we in the US have had countless debates over the years about whether 'the poor' should or should not be aided by our taxes, our government. A fund that is set up to help some but not others doesn't meet the goal of democratic equality, but it does raise the issue of civic responsibility. Handel and his friends must have been thinking along those lines, even if it was well before the ideals of the American experiment were articulated."

"Before we leave this topic," said Rebecca, "I'd like to go back to Lydia's comments on the help given to Susannah Cibber and her child. She credited the Fund that Handel and his friends had set up, but in fact it was Lydia herself who actually visited Susannah and offered support. Lydia says that she did it on behalf of the Fund for Decayed Musicians, but to me it seems more likely that it was her own—or perhaps her husband's—concern that prompted the show of support. Susannah was not so much destitute as she was outcast. Lydia's husband probably knew about Susannah's situation through some sort of clergy network. But my point here is that Susannah was doubly outcast—not simply because she was an actress or musician and second class but also because she was a woman. As a married woman, she had no rights, and likely society considered her daughter by law the child of her husband, not her lover. No wonder Lydia saw Susannah's situation as yet another instance of the mistreatment of her sex. Society colluded in making Susannah officially a non-person, a property owned by her husband. I can't help but lament the harm patriarchy has done—continues to do. Sorry if this seems special pleading, but every time I hear of such injustices, it makes me sick."

"Outcasts," said CD. "It's an interesting word. Some people suffer because they have no food or shelter. Some suffer because society rejects them and makes life hard for them. We used to think that only the former were really harmed by society's actions. Without food or shelter, you will die. But the harsh judgments of society are harmful, too—especially if they interfere with a personal sense of life's possibilities or happiness. Alex and I have been partners for nearly forty years. When we were younger, we wanted to adopt a child, but society wasn't ready to accept our view of a family. It never happened. There will probably always be people who are afraid to let others have the same rights they have. But as Rayette said, it's good to see where the efforts toward fairness start. Handel and his friends were inching in the right direction."

Katherine walked over to the flip chart. "I'm sorry to hear you and Alex were blocked from becoming parents," she said. "Sadly, society is slow to change. But, to return to Handel—he clearly had a sense of social responsibility, though as Peter pointed out, some of his incentive for becoming involved in a group such as this was tied to his friendship with specific musicians, people he knew personally. I guess this brings us to your topic, Wait—Handel's friends and this intriguing notion of friendship. What would you like to say on the subject?"

Wait stirred his coffee, then looked back through his copy of Lydia's letter. "It's rare of course, but in this case we have the benefit of hindsight. We KNOW that Handel and Susannah Cibber become pretty good friends—maybe not the kind depicted in *The Great Mr. Handel* but certainly professional colleagues who regarded each other with respect, and probably affection. Here is Lydia rather brazenly taking credit for suggesting Susannah as a singer in Handel's English oratorios. Would he have thought to have her sing the alto arias in *Messiah* if Lydia hadn't suggested that Susannah would be a good soloist? I wonder if Lydia didn't simply point out something Handel might have noticed on his own—that Susannah had the kind of dramatic and soulful performance style that he particularly appreciated. Their friendship might have happened without Lydia. Birds of a feather flock together, you know."

"But more than the Handel-Mrs. Cibber connection," Wait continued, "I wanted to consider the general nature of Handel's friendships. Again, from hindsight, we know that Handel never married. As a married man myself, I'll have to admit that I would regard with some dismay the prospect of spending a lifetime without a spouse. Friendships are fine, but to not have that one dependable kind of relationship that comes with marriage—well it seems pretty bleak to me. But Handel must have found his less intimate friendships sufficiently satisfying as to keep him happy. As we have said, he likely would have married if he had wanted to. In the movie, both Susannah Cibber and the Irish man servant were people who cared for Handel—literally, they looked out for him, took care of him. In the movie, Handel was shown to be having a bad patch just before he wrote *Messiah*. And maybe he did rely on some of his friends or servants to help him when he was down, but that one situation doesn't tell us much about his day-to-day friendships. I think his friends must have been people he regarded as equals, people with similar values and interests. I don't think he spent ALL his time writing music. He must have needed some relaxation and camaraderie. What does anyone else think about this?"

"I think you are right, Wait," said CD. "Handel must have had enough supportive friendships to feel comfortable with his life. Earlier when I was looking into the issue of Handel's sexuality, I found several reviews of a book by a scholar named Ellen Harris. Her book *Handel As Orpheus* described in some detail the homoerotic lifestyle and poetic allusions of librettists Handel encountered while a young man in Italy. Harris did not read anything into this herself, but some of her reviewers did. I mention her here because she has also written quite a bit on Handel's friendships. In fact she has a new book out—which I haven't had time to read—called *George Frideric Handel: A Life with Friends*. I've taken a quick look at some of the reviews of the book, and the reviewers say that she does a good job of surveying the lives of several of Handel's friends but is less successful in showing how Handel interacted with them. Chance references to the times and culture these people shared with Handel can only tell us so much. Still, it does suggest that his friendships were a significant part of his life."

Katherine wrote the name of the author and the title of the book at the bottom of the flip chart. "That sounds like a book we should have for our little library here," she said. "I'll see if I can track down a copy." Forella quickly added, "Please let Angela do that, Katherine. I agree that it would be an excellent addition to our collection of books on Handel. Thanks, CD, for telling us about it."

"I'd like to mention another book," said Katherine. "This one isn't about Handel, but it is about friendships. Most sociological studies of friendship look at what we might call primary relationships—spouses, family members, maybe mentors or companions. Handel didn't have any such close, intimate relationships. His family was back in Germany. He wasn't married and, after his mid-twenties, he didn't seem to have a mistress or lover that anyone knew about anyway. However, he did have a good number of more peripheral relationships. I was surprised and pleased a few years back to find a book that examined the importance of these more informal relationships. The authors—Melinda Blau and Karen L. Fingerman—called their study *Consequential Strangers*. The subtitle of the book is telling, I think—'The Power of People Who Don't Seem to Matter—But Really Do.' I know Ross worries about our getting sidetracked by tangents, but let me say just a little about this book and its thesis. It won't be a lecture, I promise."

"One thing the authors emphasized" Katherine continued, "was how increasingly the connections people rely on to feel anchored and in tune with the life around them are in fact not those intense ones we assume are so important but rather more distant ones, such as neighbors, co-workers, the barista at the coffee shop, people you see while jogging, the mailman, the people you see during intermissions at the opera. The authors explain that we don't really have a good vocabulary for such relationships. But I was reminded of this take on social connections while I was watching *The Great Mr. Handel*. Remember the scene where Handel goes into a shop to buy some snuff? The filmmakers wanted to show that he was temporarily low on funds, so they have him say that he had no money with him. The shopkeeper responds that he can pay her later, that she knows him and considers him trustworthy. The scene says something about the shopkeeper, of course, but it also points to

Handel's own circle of supportive but 'non-intimate' social ties. My own sense is that Handel had a rich and diverse group of such casual relationships. Some of them likely grew out of institutions, such as St. George's Church in Hanover Square, which Handel attended regularly, or out of his many professional activities. But the point these two authors would make is that Handel had a unique 'social convoy' or what other scholars might term a personal community that reflected his individual history and peculiar interests and that met his need for social connection and personal valuation."

Ross looked quickly over at Katherine, then back down at his copy of Lydia's letter. "It sounds a little too academic to me—this book," he said. "I don't doubt that the authors researched their subject well and had reasons for offering their thesis, but, to me, it seems like an idea tied to dry statistics rather than real people. Take me, for example. I have plenty of acquaintances, even friends, who make up my social network, but I'll admit, since my divorce, I don't have that one reliable relationship that sort of lies underneath all the others as a kind of solid, unquestioned foundation. I think they were researching something akin to friendship, but not what we think of when we speak of friends, at least close friends, or husbands or wives. When Wait suggested this topic—if you remember—he mentioned the servant in the film—Phineas I think his name was. If you take the movie at face value, Handel is extraordinarily lucky to have this man Phineas as his servant. Not only does he not desert Handel when Handel cannot pay him, but he looks after Handel when he is ill and clearly admires Handel's talent as a composer. The film's writers gave the servant the role of sidekick to Handel's hero—but, in fact, he is a more mature kind of sidekick, in fact, a friend. I thought it was the best thing about the movie, actually."

There were a few moments of awkward silence, and then Forella said, "Katherine, I believe you have inspired the first bit of soul-searching I have heard from that source in many a year. Not that he counted his mother among those who might always support him. Chopped liver, as they say. Jessica would be so pleased to know she is missed."

"Did you ever notice," said Ross, "how after a certain age, people feel they can say whatever they wish—no holds barred? Chopped liver. Right. Ok, mothers are a special case. But, you know, as adults, we don't live with our mothers. To take this discussion back to Handel, where it belongs, he was able to afford a servant, a category our sociological authors don't consider in looking at contemporary Americans. But think about it, Handel had someone who cared about him, wasn't his mother, wasn't his spouse, but was, it seems, truly devoted to him. So, is that a friend? The fact that he stayed on when he wasn't paid suggests that he was a friend—or at least had faith that he would eventually get paid. I don't know. What does anyone else think?"

"Servants are a special case, too," said Peter, "like mothers, I suppose," he added with a laugh. "I lived for a while in Brazil. It was common to have servants, even in middle-class households. I was married then, and I would say both my wife and I relied on Carla as sort of a friend. But there is a difference. Americans don't usually talk about class differences, but I think that is part of what is at issue here. Katherine, this should be your territory—aren't all the fairy tales about the difference between peasants and royalty? Aren't all Cinderella stories about class differences?"

"You really don't want me to get off on that tangent now, do you?" Katherine said with a smile. "But I will say that this line of discussion reminded me of Alison's comment earlier—that in Handel's time musicians were often regarded as servants, not part of the gentry. It is sad but probably true that Handel was not regarded by society as eligible to marry into the gentry. Even though he avoided 'serving' in a patron's household as would many musicians of the time, still Handel was not of the professional class that was starting to slip into the de facto gentry class. He could have friends among the gentry, but marriage in the eighteenth century was not based on friendship. It was an economic arrangement. Handel's friends—whether male or female—had to be maintained outside of the context of alliances tied to marriage. As a bachelor, he was able to have such friendships, but it meant that he could not really have the kind of primary connection we usually think of as a spouse, a partner, a mate."

Brad scowled and said, "It can't have been that much different back then. People either liked Handel or they didn't. Why would it matter whether he was married or not? Most people think of family as people you are obligated to have as part of your life and friends as people you choose. Sometimes it is annoying when a friend marries someone you don't like, but usually you can still find a way to be friends if you really want to. People who liked Handel probably would have accepted his wife if he chose to have one, but he didn't. He probably relied on his friends for some of the chumminess you hope to have with a wife, but as many of us know, sometimes a wife doesn't turn out to be such a good friend after all. Maybe Handel knew this and chose his friends carefully so he wouldn't have to marry just to feel like he had a friend. I vote for accepting Handel's life as being the way he wanted it to be. Why assume that he was unhappy with his lot? He chose as he chose. And that's all, folks."

Ross raised his glass of scotch and said, "Cheers, my friend. Brad gets the gold star for today. Ably summarized commentary I would say. So, what is on tap for our next meeting? I may have to miss—unless we plan to move the date back a bit. Mother, any thoughts?"

Forella whispered something to Angela and then said, "Yes, Angela has found a web address of a recent performance I hope you will all be able to watch in some form or other. She says she will send the link out to you yet today. The performance is of the oratorio *Samson*. Handel wrote *Samson* around the same time as *Messiah*, but of course it isn't nearly as well known. *Samson* has special meaning to me, as I suppose you will guess when you hear it. The Samson we meet at the beginning of the oratorio is not the hero who led the Israelites in battle but rather the blinded captive betrayed by Delilah and shorn of the hair that was his strength. He admits that his loss of sight is his greatest sorrow. His aria, 'Total Eclipse,' expresses perfectly the dismay I remember feeling when I realized that I could do nothing to save my fading vision. It is a very powerful piece. I hope we will be able to talk about the work next time. Perhaps we can delay the meeting, Ross, since you need to be traveling."

Katherine looked over at Forella with a sense of pain and sympathy. "Thank you, Forella. We will watch the performance and talk about it before we look at our next letter. Moving back the date of our next meeting if fine with me. Travel safely, Ross. And thanks, again, Forella for suggesting we all experience Handel's *Samson*. Until next time, my friends."

CHAPTER 18

Getting to Know You

A small plane left the snow-covered hills surrounding Longyearbyen, the major settlement on Svalbard, a group of islands in the Arctic. Ross had traveled there to film some authentic scenes of the midnight sun for a new documentary he was just starting to piece together. As he flew over the expanse of Arctic sea, he thought about the shrinking sea ice and the growing plague of global warming. He wondered how effective his film would be in moving viewers to demand solutions rather than denial of climate change. His Norwegian colleagues would return to Oslo, but Ross had decided that their dialogue could continue electronically. Rather than the short stay he had planned for Oslo, he chose instead to spend a couple days in London before heading back to the US. Despite his many trips to the UK, Ross had never visited the Foundling Museum, another site famously associated with Handel. Peter had sent a brief message suggesting a stop at the Museum, said the next letter for the Handel Seminar made it a relevant visit. A bit cryptic, Ross thought, but he decided to act on the suggestion.

THE NEXT MEETING OF THE Seminar had been postponed a week to accommodate Ross's travel plans. As everyone had already adjusted schedules, Ross felt no guilt whatsoever in taking the time to visit London rather than returning quickly to the US. He always enjoyed London, and this time he spent a few hours wandering through some of the beautiful gardens. St. George's Gardens had tombstones scattered about. Ross indulged his penchant for eccentric, sepulchral photographs and, after finding a cozy pub for a late lunch, headed to the Foundling Museum.

Because Handel had been a major contributor and a governor of the original Foundling Hospital, a fine exhibition of Handel artifacts is a part of the Museum's offering. Ross was surprised to see the range of things on display—not only the fair copy of *Messiah* willed to the charity at Handel's death as well as the manuscript copy of Handel's will, but also an amazing collection of commemorative medals and miniatures associated with various Handel musical productions over the years. And there were listening stations with Handel's music and guidebooks sharing information about the composing and reception of Handel's work over the course of his long career. The Handel room was a treasure house. Ross was eager to tell the Seminar members about the place. He was also surprised to see, as he left the last listening station, that he had spent nearly three hours at the Museum. He headed toward the exit, stopping only briefly to look at the few publications offered for sale across from the entry desk and cloakroom.

One of the publications intrigued him—a thin booklet titled *An Introduction to the Tokens at the Foundling Museum*. On the cover, against a grey background, were more than a dozen images of small trinkets—a heart-shaped medal, a key, a thimble, half of a coin. The authors had only recently published this introductory research on the tokens that had been left as identifiers with children taken into the hospital during the two or three decades after it first opened in 1741. Ross looked through the booklet quickly and decided that it would be something interesting to buy and peruse on the plane. As he moved toward the counter where he would pay for the booklet, along with a couple postcards, he noticed that a woman already at the counter was buying the same book. When the woman turned his way, Ross sputtered in shock. "Damn," he said, "What the hell are you doing here?" It was Katherine—and she looked just as surprised as Ross.

Departing visitors and the woman behind the counter all looked on with some disapproval and curiosity at Ross's outburst. Somewhat chagrinned, he paid for the booklet and postcards and left with Katherine. Ross asked if she had time for an early dinner. As it turned out, they both had flights the next morning, though on different airlines. Katherine explained that she had accepted a last minute invitation to speak at a memorial celebration two days earlier and had stayed on with the aim of visiting a few of the museums she had missed last time she had visited London. She knew that Ross was traveling, but she thought his destination was Norway with little time for anything else. "Don't mention our meeting here to my mother," Ross joked. "She will see all kinds of portends in this morsel of coincidence."

Ross had liked the pub where he had lunch, so he suggested they go there for dinner. "I always like becoming a 'regular' at an alehouse when I'm traveling," he said. "You get to know people, and it feels a little more like home." The waiter waved when he came in, and they headed to a booth toward the back.

"You have to have at least a half pint of bitter—you know, to make your stop over here official," said Ross. "And bangers and mash with peas." Katherine laughed and said, "Do Londoners really eat such things, or will it be obvious that we are tourists?" "Go on," Ross said, "give it a try. I'm sure it's already obvious we are tourists."

The waiter brought a large glass of Uncle Teddy's for Ross and a smaller one for Katherine. "Cheers," said Ross, raising his glass. "So, to our fortuitous meeting—though I suppose it was not exactly a happy excursion for you—if you were here to give a memorial talk. Was this a relative or friend?"

"The memorial was for a former colleague who had moved to the UK a few years back," said Katherine. "We stayed in contact but rarely got to visit. She wasn't much older than I am. Cancer can sometimes take people so quickly. She hardly had time to enjoy her retirement. Her husband was devastated. Life can be harsh. She and her husband ran a small publishing business. I think she really liked the time she spent here in England. I'm not sure I would be able to pick up and move to another country like that. Of course, it helped that her husband was from here. Home is where the heart is, I guess. So, what brought you to London? Last I knew, you were off to Norway and lands further north."

"I saw some amazing landscapes," said Ross. "Some of the islands along the coast of Norway are incredible. And Svalbard is pristine. No trees, just snow and ice. But after I spent several days filming—I don't know—I felt ready to be back in a noisy pub. And London seemed more likely to offer the quintessential bustling pub life, so I headed to London rather than Oslo. I think it was a good choice."

"Well, you are surely right that Forella will make something of our happening to meet here in London—and at the Foundling Museum! It was not something I had planned. But I had spent some time at the Museum earlier in the day and had remembered that I wanted to buy the little book about tokens. I couldn't have been there more than fifteen minutes when I ran into you. I thought the Handel room upstairs was wonderful. Did you get to spend some time there? Besides the artifacts on display, the Museum houses the Gerald Coke Collection—one of the very best resources on Handel. I must have spent twenty minutes staring at the framed manuscript of Handel's will. Just like our letters, it was handwritten. I think we sometimes forget that they didn't have typewriters and copy machines back then."

"Peter's the one who would have noticed lots of details about the artifacts here," Ross said. "I liked the chairs with the audio stations, but you know me, I would have preferred video. In fact I'm surprised no one has made a documentary about the Foundling Hospital. Maybe another project for me somewhere down the line. But, yeah, the manuscript of Handel's will was one of the highlights. 'Considering the uncertainty of human life . . . .' I suppose all wills in the eighteenth century began that way, but I thought it was cool that he bothered to give a reason for writing his will. And then the first people he mentioned and left something to were his servants. I think that says something about Handel. Normally, it would be family first."

"You're right," Katherine replied. "It must have been unusual even then. But think about it. Handel didn't have any immediate family in London. I don't think his remembering his servants first was some sort of social or political statement. More likely, he was simply thanking first the people who were actually in daily contact with him. Handel seems to have been strangely honest and straightforward in his personal relationships, given the high degree of formality and convention that dominated the culture of that time. I'll admit I've never had a real feel for the upstairs-downstairs phenomenon that has always been such a big part of British culture. Maybe Handel was ahead of his time—not the sort to judge people by their station in life."

Ross thanked their waiter for bringing him a second glass of ale. "Well, we have to remember that Handel wasn't born an Englishman," he said. "Not too long ago, I did a little research on the Hanseatic League for one of my films—you know, the mostly German merchants that controlled trade for centuries before the era when Handel was born. The Saxons and other Germanic types were much more inclined to appreciate a man's talent as a merchant over any family heritage or land holdings. Those loose connections that made up the Hanseatic League were built up through years of trade successes. You came to trust and appreciate people who cooperated and helped you carry out your commercial ventures. Capitalism of a different sort than we have today. I think Handel had a bit of the merchant entrepreneur in his blood. So, recognizing a servant's good work would just seem like a smart business practice."

"Where is Clara when we need her?" Katherine laughed. "Talk about a far-fetched connection! The Hanseatic League, indeed! You just don't want to see Handel as someone with a softer side. I think he just wanted to leave something to the people who took care of him on a daily basis. I think it's sweet that he was so appreciative. He even gave his man servant his clothes. And some of those richly brocaded jackets must have been worth quite a bit. So, Ross, have you made out a will? Who would be the people you would remember the way Handel did?"

"That's a rather personal question, don't you think?" said Ross. "Or is that something folklorists can get away with but other people can't?"

"Hmm," said Katherine, "I suppose it is. Sorry, I didn't think about it being a personal question. I know a lot of people don't think about making out a will until they retire. I probably wouldn't have either, but a couple years ago before I went off on a long research trip, I decided that it might be a good idea. Different states have different laws about wills and inheritance. I realized I didn't want the state to decide—in the event of my death—where my money went. Not that I have so much, but still. So, now I know—except for a few charities I would like to support—anything I have when I die will go to my daughter."

With a slight frown, Ross shook his head. "That's disconcerting! How long have we known each other? I didn't even know you had a daughter. There's something wrong with this picture."

"I have a daughter, and a son-in-law. Hold on, I have some photos here on my phone. You know, we don't ever talk about our families or anything like that at our Seminar meetings. There's no reason why you should have known about my daughter. Forella told me you have no children, or I wouldn't have known. Maybe it's time for another social get-together for our group. I know only bits and pieces of the lives of our Seminar friends. I think you are right. There's something wrong about that."

"Well, we ARE the co-chairs, or whatever we agreed to," said Ross. "So, let us hereby institute a socializing event instead of a letter discussion for one of our next meetings. All work and no play, etc. etc. We can blame it all on Handel and his will."

"So, DO you have a will?" said Katherine. "Or am I still being too nosy. As you said earlier, maybe people don't think to make out a will until they are struck by the—what did Handel write?—the 'uncertainty of human life.' I'm just curious whether you have been hit by that worry, the way Handel obviously was—at least enough to make out a will."

"And I just think it's odd," replied Ross, "that folklorists can ask these really personal questions and call it research whereas other people who do the same would be labeled snoopy or intrusive. Lots of 'ethnographic data' could be put to nefarious uses, after all. But, no, actually I don't have will. And, yes, it did come to mind recently—when I realized that my mother is my next of kin and she is likely to slip away sometime in the not too distant future. That trip to the ER hit home. At least Handel had a niece in Germany—and several other relatives he wanted to remember in his will. It's disturbing to admit you have no one to leave anything to. Maybe that's why I haven't thought to make one out. See—folklorists are like confessors. Not something I wanted to talk about."

Katherine looked at Ross, then answered a bit hesitantly, "Well, I wasn't asking as a folklorist—more as a friend. I expect you do have some insights into how Handel felt, and I suppose the researcher in me would like to learn more about that. But, truthfully, Ross, I just wanted to know what YOU think to do when faced with the 'uncertainty of human life.' Making out a will is something society tells us to do. Maybe you have another way of dealing with such uncertainties."

"Another way?" said Ross. "Let's see—what options are out there? Go to the doctor and try to live as long as you can. Avoid dangerous situations. Always wear your goulashes and clean underwear. Maybe go to church if you are so inclined. Don't we just do what our mothers and society tell us to do? What I find scary are people who insist that everyone else do what they choose to do in response to such worries. Give ten percent of your income to the Church, or you will burn in Hell, or at least be denied a proper burial. Maybe that IS why I've avoided making out a will. I was appalled that my father was convinced by someone to leave more to his new-found church than to his own wife. Fortunately, he had plenty of money, so it didn't matter, and I'm happy to say I didn't need anything. But to me, it was a lesson in social values. In a will, you do end up putting your money where your mouth is. You make clear once and for all what your values are."

"Hold that thought," said Katherine. "I want to come back to this at some point with our whole Seminar group. I think Brad would jump right in with your 'money is value' idea. But we'll see. You keep accusing me of playing the folklorist, but actually, a proper ethnographer would follow up on your implied story about your father. I may be wrong, but it sounds like a sore point. The thing about folklore research that most people overlook is that it is always about values. And as you said, we inherit a large percentage of our values from our families or society. But, I like the fact that a lot of people start examining their own values once they hit fifty or sixty. Not everyone, of course, but some people really do try to sort out what they actually believe or value rather than simply holding on to whatever perspective they learned as part of becoming an adult in one cultural context or another. It sounds to me like your father's death, along with his will, brought on some sort of examination of your own thoughts on the subject. I don't think most people would find my asking if they had a will such a personal question."

Ross laughed. "Ok, maybe not. But we laymen have to be on our guard. So, how did you like the bangers and mash?—or is that too personal? It's definitely about values. The bitter even more. Brits are very fond of their local ales. What did you think?"

Katherine held up her empty glass. "It was better than I thought it would be. And bangers and mash—not bad. I like breakfast food at suppertime. So, thanks, Ross, for introducing me to some new tastes—and for picking up the tab. Now there's an old value I'm happy to accept without complaint."

As Ross and Katherine headed out the door, Ross said, "A great evening for a walk. May I escort you, m'lady? Are you staying nearby or riding the Tube?" "My hotel is on Oxford," Katherine answered. "A walk would indeed be nice. Such a nice breeze. Will I be taking you out of your way?" "That would be telling," said Ross. "Come," he continued, "have you been to Foyle's Bookstore?—a nice stop along the way. You don't need to be back right away, do you? Not stuck with an early flight?" Katherine laughed, "That would be telling."

A few days after Ross and Katherine's chance meeting in London, the Seminar met for the group's postponed meeting. Katherine had contacted Peter and shared the plan she and Ross had concocted over dinner at the London pub. Peter said that he did have a couple more letters ready but would be happy to hold them back until the meeting after next. He liked the idea of a more social get-together and perhaps a chance to reflect a bit on what Seminar participants had grasped so far from reading the letters.

As everyone gathered, filled a plate with Annie's wonderful Hungarian goulash, and took a chair at the table, Ross poured into his glass the remaining few ounces of whiskey from a Jameson's flask and placed the empty bottle on its side in the middle of the table. "All right," he said, "this won't be as exciting as it was back in eighth grade, but listen up. Your Seminar co-chairs decided that we needed to take a break from reading the letters and do something more informal and relaxing. Maybe do one or both of the following—share a bit more information about ourselves and then offer a more personal reflection on something we have each taken away from reading and discussing these letters so far. What do you think? And then, it only seemed fair to let an impartial source—such as the spinning bottle—decide who goes first, next, and thereon after. Basically, neither Katherine nor I wanted to go first, and Peter refused. So, the bottle will decide."

"I think you just wanted an excuse to empty that Jameson's bottle," said Clara. "Spin the bottle was ridiculous back in eighth grade, and it is ridiculous now. I'll go first. I think sharing a bit more information about ourselves is a great idea. So, what kind of information do you want to know?"

"Well, we already know you hate spin the bottle," said Ross. "Maybe something more worthy of such a confessional—like do you have family? Where were you born? What is your favorite movie? How long have you had this affair with the cello? And, then, more seriously—really—what have you found personally interesting or thought-provoking in the letters we have read so far? I humbly thank you, Clara, for starting us off. I'll just go find a reserve bottle of Jameson's. Carry on."

Clara rolled her eyes. "Right," she said. "Let's see. I was born in Berkeley, California. My father was a professor, and my mother taught high school French. I loved being a part of the Berkeley scene during my undergraduate years. I had some great teachers, but actually it was

Carl Sagan with his television series *Cosmos* that sparked my interest in science. It was still pretty unusual for women to major in the hard sciences, but I thought physics and the history of science were both fascinating subjects. I went on to MIT after graduation. My mother was the one who insisted I play the cello. Berkeley had a young people's orchestra, and I sort of accepted that playing an instrument was just something you did—like going to college. I let it slide when I went on to graduate school, but I took it up again when I moved to Bloomington. I like playing with the BSO. Practicing cello is satisfying, but also a bit demanding, especially learning new pieces. What else? Family? I have an older brother. He's a heart surgeon in Chicago. I've been dating one of his colleagues for a year or so—so nice to have a brother with interesting friends. I was married once long ago for ten years or so. I don't have any children, but I do have a wonderful Husky named Mike. Mike and I OWN the B-line Trail. Is that about it? What else was it we were supposed to talk about?"

Katherine smiled over at Ross, who was sipping his refreshed beverage. "Thanks, Clara, for volunteering to go first," she said. "Let me say a little about what we were hoping for—beyond the information you shared—which was very succinct and helpful. I think we will all benefit from your modeling such a good bio sketch. This whole notion of a life story is an interesting thing. Here we are—trying to reconstruct something of Handel's life story, and along the way, we are getting bits and pieces of Lydia's life story. But, as Ross pointed out to me earlier, we in this group don't really know each other's life stories in any even partially complete way, either. When people share information about their lives with others, usually it is for some purpose—a job interview, membership in a club, maybe some social network page. But in daily life, the contexts in which we share the 'real stuff' of our personal lives are ones in which we hope to develop a certain amount of intimacy. We meet a new friend, and we tell some story from our life. Usually it is something we think he or she will find interesting or pertinent to the topic at hand, but it also allows that person to know us a little more intimately. It reveals something of our values, our tastes, maybe our sense of humor, and probably our fears and prejudices as well. Humans are social animals. One of our clearest trademarks is our ability and desire to tell stories—about ourselves and about other people we admire, or people we despise. Just watch the political campaigns. But, back to your question, Clara. Whatever you want to share is what we want to hear. It might be especially interesting to hear some personal reflection sparked by the Handel letters—maybe something in the form of a story. Some memory or experience that was brought to mind by Lydia's letters or our discussion—and that you are willing to share with us."

Clara frowned and looked over at Ross, who winked and raised his glass. "Huh," she said, "now I see why Ross didn't want to go first, or maybe at all. You are asking for a story that may reveal more than we might want. Men always like to be in control. Here, some of the control is out of our hands. First we are RESPONDING to something rather than initiating it, and then we are telling a story that others might interpret however they wish. No wonder Ross wanted to play spin the bottle instead."

"Ah, well," said Katherine, "I'm sure Ross isn't the only one with control issues, nor the only gender, for that matter. If you recall, I wasn't eager to be first, either. I think it goes back to our much earlier discussion of the Chalice Circles. Remember, Forella? You talked about how part of the purpose of those gatherings was simply to allow people to share information about themselves without fear of judgment. But any time you have a discussion in a forum or seminar, you risk sliding over into a kind of group therapy. That isn't our intention here. Really, what we would find interesting, and I suppose revealing in a good way, would be some story or memory or simply a private reflection about the Handel letters so far—something that ties the letters and our discussion to your own life."

Before Clara could respond, Forella spoke up. "Excuse me, Katherine," she said. "You mentioned the Chalice Circles. Let me say just a little more about the kind of exchanges that happen in those meetings. I think it would be unlikely that anyone would share anything really compromising or illegal with a Chalice Circle, but people do share stories and information that is revealing and sometimes disturbing. It's not required, of course, and some people never do let down their guard. But at the first group meeting, everyone has to agree NOT to share with others outside the group what is said in the Circle. In other words, anything said in the Circle stays in the Circle. There is no way to enforce this requirement, of course, but it sets the expectation that things are shared in confidence. Usually, as a result, before long, people feel that the members of their Chalice Circle are like friends—people they can trust, and people who know them well. I think this benefit of being known well, or intimately, as Katherine said, is a big part of why people like participating in Chalice Circles. I think they serve a good purpose."

Clara looked to see if Katherine was going to say anything, but Katherine said, "Clara, you have a thought about this?" "Well, yes," Clara said, "I'm not eager to be part of a touchy-feely group. There's a reason people keep their guard up, or their boundaries in place. It's not a matter of not wanting to be friends with people. But who wants to feel like they are part of some reality TV show? A person has a responsibility to solve his or her own problems, not foist them off on other people. And, if you can't manage your own problems, well, that's what psychotherapists are for. I don't mind sharing what I know and a little about my personal history, but I don't see any reason to spill my guts, as they say. What does that have to do with the Handel letters?"

Katherine saw that Peter wanted to say something. She nodded at him, and Peter walked over to the flip chart that usually sat nearby, ready for their list of topics related to the Handel letters. Before writing anything, he said, "I often get razzed by this group for my interest in psychology, so in an effort to not disappoint, let me jump in here. Psychologists, theologians, philosophers, even socio-biologists like E.O. Wilson—all kinds of scholars acknowledge that humans need a balance between autonomy and membership in the tribe." Peter wrote two words on either side of the chart: TRIBALISM and INDEPENDENCE. "There are lots of terms I could use instead of these, but I like these," he said. "I think most intelligent, reflective people—everyone in this group, in other words—are fearful of falling into tribalism and losing their independence. We cling to our independence as a banner of our selfhood, and we all quail at the thought of a life lost to the likes of Alzheimer's or stroke. And anything that threatens our independence and pulls us instead into the connecting, perhaps suffocating, arms of the tribe—is suspect."

"So," he went on, "when we share sensitive or deeply meaningful stories from our lives, we, in effect, invest in the tribe that hears us. We yield a certain amount of power to them because now they know where we are vulnerable. Nothing new here, I know, but I thought I would remind you that researchers have studied this for a long time. But what they have also discovered is that we do benefit from—not baring our souls necessarily—but from sharing something of our self and learning to accept the 'burden' of intimacy. We who prize our independence, our intelligence, our perfectionism—we are the ones who most need a bit of intimacy in our lives. But we've been set up for finding fault with such mushy comforts. And, yes, I know this from experience, not just from books. As Clara suggested, if we can't handle our own problems, we can always go to a psychologist. But most of us don't know that we have a problem. Lack of intimacy in our lives may seem like—well, just a bad patch, something luck and better social skills—or maybe getting married—should remedy. I always thought of an appointment with a psychologist as a measure of last resort, but there was a time in my life when things became pretty desperate. I found going to a psychologist a terribly humbling experience. At my first meeting with her, I tried to distract her with entertaining stories, information from my life I thought she would find impressive. Fortunately, she saw right through me. Long story, short—I learned that I needed to balance my independence with friendship—not what we usually mean by intimacy, but rather more like what Katherine was talking about. I needed to open the curtains a bit, so some other people—not everyone, but a few that I trusted—could see more of who I really am. And I needed to do that on a pretty regular basis."

Rayette waved her hand. "Could we continue with the task at hand? It feels like we are getting bogged down in a side issue. Maybe spinning the bottle would be a good solution after all."

Everyone laughed, but Peter looked a little annoyed. Katherine smiled and said, "Thanks, Rayette. We do need to push on, but let's keep in mind what Peter was saying. Sharing personal information with others is always a two-way street—or maybe a win-win situation would be a better way to look at it. So, Clara, do you have anything to add? You don't have to if you don't want to."

"Ok, ok," said Clara, "I've got something. There was one letter—it seems like it was one of the earlier ones—in which Lydia laments the fact that she couldn't really consider becoming a musician because she was a woman. Even back then there were exceptions, of course. I actually remember one of my teachers talking about a woman named Elizabeth Turner—a composer and performer who lived in the eighteenth century and did become pretty well known. But, as Lydia said, in general, if you were a woman, your choices in life back then were much more limited than they were for men. I could tell that she resented that notion of male privilege. It made me stop and think about my own life—in this supposedly more progressive era. Women are certainly free now to pursue careers they choose and vote and run for political office—whatever. But I still feel there is a pervasive acceptance of male privilege. Women are still second in line—always second, never first. Men's opinions are more highly valued. Men still get away with abusing women. Women are even still denied the right to control their own bodies. Men think they have given women the same rights they have, but they haven't. Women are still not treated as men's equals. It may have been worse in Lydia's day, but it's still not a done deal. Do I have a story from my own life that goes along with this rant? I do, but it's not one I really want to share. And it's not that I don't trust all of you or consider you friends. I just don't think it's anybody else's business."

"True enough," said Katherine, and she smiled at Clara. "Let's hear from someone else and, as Rayette suggested, keep the ball rolling." She saw CD signal that he would say something. "Thanks, CD," she said. "So happy to be saved from Ross's spinning bottle."

"I was born," CD began, "in a tiny little town by the name of Wamego, Kansas. It's not far from the larger town of Manhattan, Kansas, home of Kansas State University. My father taught veterinary medicine at KSU. I started my college years there, but I didn't last long. Oh, and the little town of Wamego is the home of the Oz Museum—everything you've ever wanted to know about the Wizard of Oz. My college experience was not a happy one. Even though Kinsey's research on male sexuality had been out for more than a decade, homosexuality was still completely in the closet for most people. Except for a few people like Cole Porter, there were few examples of how to come out or lead a decent life as a gay man. I left Kansas and moved to New York. Thank God, I met Alex. This was before HIV/AIDS was recognized and affecting so many gay men. Neither Alex nor I were swingers—both pretty introverted, in fact. But we lost a lot of friends over the years. The eighties were a tough time. But I discovered choral conducting and worked my way through graduate school. I'll have to say, my parents were way ahead of the times. They accepted my relationship with Alex. In fact they were the ones who encouraged us to try to adopt. I think they were always sorry that plan didn't work out—maybe even more than Alex and I were. Career-wise—let's see—there aren't many jobs out there for choral conductors—well, in churches, but that wasn't my thing. I was surprised to find that I like teaching, so that's what brought me here. And I expect that's what I'll do until I finally retire. What else?"

"Oh, yes," he continued, "something from the letters or our discussion that connects with my own life. I think several times people mentioned this supposed incident from Handel's childhood—when his father prohibited his playing any musical instruments, and he somehow smuggled a clavichord up into the attic of his house and practiced on it in secret. I remember thinking at the time that it must have been a really big house if his father failed to hear him practicing—although admittedly, the clavichord is a fairly quiet instrument. Anyway, it reminded me of my own childhood keyboard practicing—piano, not clavichord. My parents were happy to have me practice piano, so that is not the connection. It just reminds me of an incident from when I was around nine or ten years old. My older brother, Derek, and I were really into Pop Warner football, and there were practices almost every night of the week. I really liked both football and piano, so I arranged to get up about forty minutes early every morning so I could practice piano before school. One time I must have reset my alarm clock for some reason. I got up at three-thirty in the morning and started practicing. My mom came into the living room—still in her nightgown—and said, 'Chandler, what are you doing? It's the middle of the night!' I looked at the clock, and we both burst out laughing. She never let me forget. Of course, it never led to the kind of success Handel had. But we were both midnight keyboardists."

Alison laughed and said, "That's amazing, CD. I only wish my grandsons would see music practice of any kind as worthwhile as sports—or my granddaughter, for that matter. But at least she does like dance. I might as well be next here. Let's see. I grew up in Louisville, Kentucky. My father played cello with the Louisville Orchestra, so I was encouraged to do something with music early on. I majored in voice in college, and I actually thought about a career in musical theater. I met my husband, Andy, when we both had roles in a production of *Oklahoma!* I was Ado Annie—believe it or not. Andy and I have two sons, both happily married but both, unfortunately, living on either side of the country. I guess one thing from the Handel letters that struck a chord with me was his trip to Oxford and Lydia's comments about how he turned down the honorary doctorate. I see a lot of competition among students and faculty here in Bloomington. It's inevitable when you have a good music school. But I thought it was interesting the way Handel, in effect, thumbed his nose at the academic establishment. I certainly don't see myself opposing what academics are all about, but on the other hand, I do agree with Handel that it is important to perform for the public, too. I made a decision a long time ago to keep my connections with various performing groups in cities around the country. Singing for a variety of audiences has been a really satisfying part of my life all along. I can't imagine giving it up."

"Giving up on music," said Brad, "sometimes it's not a matter of choice. Handel had to overcome a lot of opposition. But, I don't know, maybe the times he lived in were better for a career in music. Maybe it depends on the kind of music. Everyone seems to think it's easy to become a rock star. Ok, what does this have to do with Brad Hochensmith? Well, he never became a household name, did he? Let's see—a short bio, right? I was born in Zionsville, Indiana. I think I told you about having a garage band back in the day. We were pretty good. We called ourselves the Unknown Reason, and we covered most of the Doors' songs. I think we had a few prom gigs and local dances, even though we were all under-age for the bars. Then came Vietnam and the draft. That pretty much broke up the band. You remember the draft lottery? I was all prepared to leave home and go to Canada, but I got some really high number in the draft, so I figured I might not get called up. You still had to go to the selective service office and go through the medical exams and stuff. Would you believe? I was classified as 4-F because I had really, really bad allergies. But most of my buddies were sent to Nam."

"So, I went to business school," Brad continued, "and I became a music store manager and eventually an owner—but not a star, not Jim Morrison, not even close. Of course, he died young. They all die young. But they got to really put across what was inside. I've always envied that. When he was young, Handel was mostly a performer. I like the letters that comment on Handel's playing or even his singing. Maybe he just never had to grow up, huh?"

"No, I don't buy it," said Wait. "Handel is no Peter Pan. Besides, it isn't just young acts that stick with music as a career. Some of the best musicians at my club are pretty old dudes, mostly ones who kept plugging away at it and maybe had a day job. But they obviously really still get their juice from playing for an audience. You should try getting back into it, Brad. I'm serious. If making music was important when you were a kid, it probably still is. Some of those old rock numbers are standards in the jazz repertoire now. I could see 'Light My Fire" coming off as a jazz trio piece, especially if you still have some singing chops. You run a music store, for Pete's sake. There must be lots of guys who would jump at a chance to jam. Ok, I'll get off my soapbox, but I think Handel just kept doing what gave him his kicks—his whole life, no matter what was thrown at him. Everybody's situation is different, but if you want to make music, you should do it."

Brad made a tip of the hat motion toward Wait and said, "Point taken. So what is your story? Isn't running a club as much a cop out as owning a music store?" Wait started to respond, but Ross held aloft his glass and said, "Gentlemen, gentlemen, I believe this is where my role as Seminar bouncer—or maybe umpire would be better—comes up. Perhaps we could move on to Wait's story—without the pejorative aside." "Sorry," said Brad.

"Not a problem," said Wait. "Actually, running a club might have been a cop out IF I had ever had any talent or desire to perform, but I'm not a performer. But I am really good at spotting talent in other people, and even more than talent, I guess determination—a need to perform. I liked the way you said it, Brad—that the Jim Morrisons of the world really found a way to put across what was inside. Those are my favorite acts—people who have something inside that they need to share, something that drives the engine, you know? So, anyway, my story? I was born in Indianapolis—have lived there almost all my life. My folks ran a butcher shop. I have a sister and a brother. They both live in Indiana, too. I'm married and have two kids, both married—a third grandchild on the way. My wife, Patty, does like to sing, and she is pretty good. She performs at nursing homes around town, mostly songs from the thirties, forties—songs the residents remember from their younger days."

"I guess if I were to pick out something from the letters that connects with my life," Wait went on, "it would be the question Lydia posed to Handel about the castrato singers that became so popular in Italy and then in Britain, too. I remember we all joked about it being a really uncomfortable subject, but our discussion reminded me of an incident in my life that left an impression, definitely. Lydia was curious about why everyone liked the super high voices of the castrati. But she didn't say anything about how they got that way. She must have known. Certainly Handel knew. There is a scene in the movie *Farinelli* when Handel confronts the famous castrato with the truth that his castration was not an accident but a deliberate act. As a kid, I didn't know anything about Farinelli or any other castrati, but I do remember my Sunday school teacher skipping hurriedly over a passage about eunuchs in some lesson from the Old Testament. When I asked what the word meant, she said it just meant 'servant,' but that didn't make sense in the context of the story. I looked the word up and then asked my dad about what castration meant. I had actually heard my dad talk about how pork had a bad taste if it was meat from an uncastrated boar—remember my dad was a butcher. Anyway, he thought it would be easiest to just take me out to a farm and let me see what it means to castrate pigs. Maybe if I had grown up on a farm, that would have been ok, but I was just disgusted, horrified. Really, it made me sick. Not just because the pigs squealed, but mostly because it was the first time I really thought about humans—myself—being an animal. It's something that has stuck with me all these years."

No one spoke for a while, then Forella said, "Farm life is a real education most people don't get anymore. I remember being upset when the pigs were castrated, Wait, though I didn't make the kind of connection you did. I just thought it was cruel. Still do. But there were lots of things that were hard to accept on the farm. You didn't dare get too attached to the animals, even the horses. Eventually all the animals were either sold or butchered. I think I have told everyone a little about my background already. Maybe someone else . . ." "No, please, go on," said Katherine. "We want to hear more—whatever you'd like to share."

"Well," Forella began, "I was born on a farm just outside of Dayton, Ohio. The doctors still made house calls back then. My mother said it was a wintry night, and Dad and the Doc had a terrible time getting up the road in time. Anyway, I think you know some of my story from earlier. I grew up there on the farm, and then I went to college in town to get my teaching license, and I and met Ross's father there. He was in the Air Force. Later, after the War, we moved to Tennessee—Kingsport, where my husband's family lived. I think I've told you the rest of my story, but maybe not the part about our move to a new house out along the River. This was after Ross had left home. This is when Stanton had business dealings with a lawyer in town, a man who attended a meetinghouse of the Church of Latter Day Saints nearby. I'm not even sure how it happened that this man invited Stanton to attend a service with him. We had always gone to the Methodist Church—though not very regularly. Somehow the services at the Mormon Church must have impressed him. He tried to get me to go, but I said I didn't see any reason to. I met the man's wife once, but I didn't much care for her. It's not like they were friends or anything. But for some reason, Stanton found the whole thing compelling. In less than a year, he decided that he wanted to join the Mormon Church. He was pretty insistent that I should, too, but I said no. It was the first time we ever really disagreed about something—at least anything important. I don't think our home life was ever quite as agreeable as it had been from then on."

Katherine couldn't help but steal a quick glance at Ross. He was frowning but appeared more concerned than annoyed. He stared into his glass, set it down on the table, and looked up in time to notice Katherine looking his way. He frowned again but looked back over at Forella, who appeared ready to go on, as no one had made a response to her comments. "My generation was never encouraged to talk about our personal lives. Women, especially, were expected to smooth things over and make whatever personal sacrifices were necessary to keep the household running and everybody as happy as possible. Stanton was a good provider and a good man, but he had always relied on other people to help him recognize which path he should take, what he needed to do to lead a good life. At least that is what I saw as the appeal of the Mormon Church. It was almost as though he had slipped back into his life as an officer in the Air Force. I had accepted the idea that a superior officer could tell him what to do, even that his father—as Chairman of the Board of their mining company—could demand certain things from him. But I didn't like the authoritarianism of the Mormon Church, and I especially didn't like their stance on women. Most of my life, I had no strong incentive to become a feminist or even to question the status quo, but somehow Stanton's joining the Mormon church was, as they say, a tipping point. That's when I started getting involved with women's issues."

"As to Lydia's letters to Handel," Forella continued, "I think the ones that intrigued me most so far have been the letters in which Lydia comments directly on Handel's lack of a wife and family. Lydia definitely thought that he would benefit from being married. And probably in practical terms, he would. Even in the case of health—research supports the notion that men benefit more from marriage than women do. But my question about Handel is why did he resist this seeming human need to be married? I would love to know what he said to Lydia after she suggested—for the umpteenth time—that he just needed to get married. It seems he wasn't lonely. And he was evidently often 'in love' with one or another leading lady in his operas. He must have reached some understanding on the issue, at least to his own satisfaction. I do wish he could share that bit of insight with us. But so far the letters are little help on that. It's not that I myself regret getting married—goodness no. That's just what you did back then. Maybe it wasn't quite as important for a man to be married—in Handel's time, or even now. But I remember wondering, every time Lydia remarked on his needing to get married, why it was that he went against the grain like that. It seems to me that Handel valued his independence above anything else. Companionship, children—it's a lot to give up just to keep your independence."

"I wonder," said Rebecca, "how many women go through a painful repudiation of religious ideas before finally recognizing how powerfully sexism or patriarchy affects everything in their lives. Not just Mormons, and not just Muslims and their hijab, but Christians and Jews and their long history of patriarchy and male dominance. Language, stories, rituals, officials, ideologies—everything about religion maintains an assumption that men and boys are more important than women and girls. Why should it be a surprise that men benefit more from marriage than women do? Ok, so where am I going with this? Forella's story reminded me of my own confrontation with religious standards of behavior. I might as well go next. My story is a bit unusual. I was born in Sierra Leone, West Africa. My parents were Methodist missionaries, although Sierra Leone is predominantly Muslim. I liked my life there, but we left when I was around ten and moved to Missouri. One thing that stuck out in my memory of those years in Sierra Leone was the custom of polygamy. Often men had more than one wife. I remember asking my mother about it—sort of like Wait and his question about eunuchs. It was the first time I realized that people could have very different notions about what is proper but still be doing what their culture or religion said was right. When I went on to study anthropology in college, all hell broke loose, so to speak. I woke up—radically—to the fact that everything in culture—my culture and everyone else's culture—was man-made. Nothing was 'ordained by God.' Plain old people—usually men—made up the rules and convinced us that they were God-given. I was basically lost at sea for several years and went into a deep funk. It wasn't just Mormons and Muslims who were misguided. It was my own Protestant friends and family. On top of that, I discovered Jean Paul Sartre and the existentialists. It's a wonder my parents let me finish school. They were not happy."

"I think they were hopeful that my getting married would bring some needed conventionality to my life," Rebecca continued. "But Drew was actually just as much of a nonconformist as I was. We struggled through grad school together, and he is the one who insisted that I finish my PhD. He was an evolutionary biologist. I adored his subject, and he was such a good teacher. We were only married for five years when he developed lung cancer. I know they have much better treatments now than they did then. He died before our son was born. It was a horrible time. I'll always miss Drew. He was one of the few men from my generation who truly rejected the customary privileges of being male. He really tried to be aware of unconscious assumptions about gender. When he died, it was the saddest day of my life. I remarried a few years later, but I just couldn't make it work that time. I think I can empathize with Handel's reluctance to marry. If you haven't found the right person, it just doesn't seem right. I zeroed in on those parts of the letters, too, just like Forella, but I also was struck by Lydia's comments on Handel's health—her concern that he wasn't taking care of himself. It's an irony, I suppose, but at this point in my life I realize that I miss having someone who worries over me the way Lydia worried about Handel. I guess he at least had a servant who accompanied him to the spa in Germany. Not sure if that is male privilege or simply wealth. Maybe just another era."

Katherine stood to return her plate to the buffet. "Thanks, Rebecca," she said, and hesitated. After a pause, she went on, "Anyone else need a short break? Thanks, all of you who jumped in and kept us moving along. What an amazing group of people this is! Forella, you must be thrilled with how these letters to Handel have found resonances with so many people. I'm eager to hear from the rest of you. But before we get started again, maybe Annie could say a little about this wonderful dish you prepared for today—and how you came to be here in Bloomington. These wonderful lunches are a major part of the success of these meetings. We'd love to hear from you."

Annie grinned and looked over at Angela who was sitting beside Forella. Angela waved, and Forella said, "Yes, Annie, tell everyone about your cooking instructor—it's an amazing story." Annie smiled over at Forella. "Well," she said, "I grew up in Bristol, Tennessee, not far from Kingsport. When I was seventeen and finished with high school, I met Randolph, my husband. We both worked for a man who had a job working for Tennessee Ernie Ford, the singer. I was just kitchen help, but the cook at this man's house was a real chef. He went on to have a TV show later on. Anyway, he taught me how to cook lots of fancy foods I had never heard of. He was very easy-going and let me experiment with recipes from far away places. This dish—that I made today—is Hungarian goulash. The secret, he said, was to marinade the beef and to use a special kind of sweet paprika from Hungary. Over the years, I've added a spicier paprika because Mr. Wainwright always liked things a little hotter. And I always leave the skins on the potatoes before I mash them. Randolph and I came here with Forella when she moved up here from Kingsport. Randolph and I both like our new town, but sometimes we miss the mountains. We go down to visit family every now and then. The mountains are pretty in the fall—a good time to visit. That would be my advice. Oh, and you can go to the Birthplace of Country Music Museum, too. It's nearby."

"Thanks, Annie," said Katherine. "It sounds like you love your home place. And you clearly learned to be an outstanding cook while you were there. We are so lucky. So, who would like to continue our belated life story exchange?" Katherine looked around and was surprised to see Peter signaling that he would go next.

"Annie's comments on her hometown make me think of my completely opposite experience growing up," said Peter. "I was born in Fayetteville, North Carolina, near Fort Bragg, but I don't remember anything about that part of the US. My father was connected with the Army as a linguist, and we basically moved around most of my early years, so I don't really have a sense of a home place. My mother finally got tired of all the moves—at least that is what she said was the reason—and she and my father divorced when I was about twelve. But even then my mother and sister and I didn't really settle into any one place. I graduated high school in Athens, Georgia, and went to college there—or at least started college there. I dropped out from UGA and got married. Moving around seemed to be in my blood. I had trouble finding a job I wanted. For a while, I worked as a kind of apprentice park ranger, and I actually liked that. I should probably skip over the next few years. As Clara reminded us, it's best to keep some boundaries intact."

Katherine looked over at Peter with a puzzled frown. "Please, Peter, make that call as you do or do not wish. There aren't any 'shoulds' either way. I'd like to know how you came to be a state historian in Indianapolis—if that is something you are willing to share. I guess you must have completed your studies somewhere other than the University of Georgia. I think I remember you saying something about getting at least one of your degrees from the University of Chicago. I think we had a discussion about one of your professors there—back when we first met."

Peter smiled and shook his head. "You're absolutely right, Katherine," he said. "I shouldn't should, as my therapist would say. Well let's see. I actually didn't go to the U of Chicago until I was nearly forty. A late bloomer, you might say. I managed to avoid the draft during the early 70s—as a student, and then just lucky, I guess. I thought about going back to school to become a teacher, but then my wife discovered that she was pregnant. We weren't ready to be parents. Well, I'll admit that I figured it would be my wife who would have to worry about taking care of a baby. She must have known that was the case, too. She tried to have an abortion—this was before Row vs. Wade. It was a botched operation, and she died. If you ever wonder why I am Pro Choice, that is why. I realize that I was completely irresponsible, but that's no reason why a person—a woman—should have to die. She should have been able to have a safe abortion. I felt so guilty in so many ways. We both messed up, but she is the one who had to die. It affected my life in a lot of ways. Eventually, I went back to school, went on to graduate school, got married again. I moved to Indianapolis only ten years ago. I'm no longer married, but I do love my job at the Historical Museum. And—oh, yes—the thing in the Handel letters that struck a personal chord with me—his constant moving around, at least until he settled down at his home on Brook Street. I'm sure it was exciting when he was younger to move around so much, but I can see why he wanted to have his own place once he was well established in his career. I like my job and my digs in Indy. We're birds of a feather, Handel and I, wouldn't you say?"

"Handel certainly did like his house on Brook Street," said Katherine. "And I hadn't really thought about how he might have felt moving around so much before he settled there. Interesting connection, Peter. –Yes, Alison, you had a question?"

Alison looked around, seeming to want someone else to speak up. "I can't understand," she began, "why you would say you are Pro-Choice after such a horrible incident. Obviously if she had not tried to have an abortion, she wouldn't have died. I can see why you felt awful, of course, but I don't understand your reasoning about the abortion at all."

Ross stood up and said, "I'm going to play my house heavy card here. We don't want to get into a political discussion. Why don't we move on to the next person with an interesting bio?"

Peter turned a bit red and said, "No, Ross. That's what always happens whenever I talk about Stephie's abortion. Someone else gets to feel all smug about being against abortion, and I'm left looking like a monster for saying I believe she should have had access to a safe abortion. If she had needed to have her appendix removed, she would have had a safe operation. I can't believe people are eager to turn back to the days before Roe vs. Wade. We didn't want a baby, and we should have been able to stop the process before the fetus BECAME a baby, but instead some inept fake doctor screwed up and killed my wife. There's no excuse for that kind of callousness in modern America. If a pregnancy is a mistake, we should be able to reverse it. We have the medical procedures to do it safely. I think it is criminal to deny that safe operation to a woman who wants it."

"The late sixties were a hard time for everyone," said Rayette. "I remember hearing about countless black women dying from botched abortions. I guess I was pretty naïve at the time, but I thought it was more of a racial issue. I thought white women could always find a safe way to have an abortion even if it wasn't legal. I'm not in favor of abortions myself. I think they make people irresponsible. But I thought, back then at least, it was more a matter of making it illegal because it was assumed that so many black women were just getting pregnant and then having an abortion. I think laws against abortion were seen as a deterrent. I think that is why people today are questioning Roe vs. Wade. They want to prevent abortions from becoming an easy solution to unwanted pregnancies. Wouldn't that be the best result?"

Peter had closed his eyes during Rayette's comments, but he took a deep breath and said, "Look, I know we don't want to get into this topic, but let me just say two things. First, Stephanie wasn't white; she was a mixed race Creole, and she was wonderful, beautiful. It's possible that she might have found a better doctor if she had been white, but my point is that she should have had access to a safe operation. Of course she didn't WANT to have an abortion. Who would want to have an abortion? She was a twenty-two year old woman, and I loved her. The mass of cells that would have become a fetus didn't constitute a baby; it was just a mass of cells. My wife was a lot more important than that mass of cells. Everybody talks about the 'rights of the unborn.' What about the rights of the living? The woman I married? We make decisions all the time among various actions with negative consequences. That's what humans do. No one will ever convince me that the 'right' of a potential life should take precedence over the rights of someone already alive. It's not an ideal decision, but I think a woman should have the right to decide. It's her body, her life. If you want to read something that might help you see what I am saying, read Susan Wicklund's *This Common Secret*. It helped me come to terms with my own turmoil over this issue. Ok, I'll stop talking."

Katherine looked over toward Ross, but before he could say anything, Rebecca spoke up. "We think of abortion as a modern and American issue, but abortion has been around for centuries, millennia probably. In the past, women usually took some traditional herbal concoction, like pennyroyal, in an attempt to induce a miscarriage if they didn't want to continue with a pregnancy. All too often these attempts resulted in the woman's death. As an anthropologist, and especially as a female anthropologist, I was many times taken into women's confidence and told stories of successful or unsuccessful abortions whenever and wherever I did fieldwork. For American women, since 1973, Roe vs. Wade has made it possible to have an abortion legally and safely, at least in the first or even second trimester. I remember when that decision was made. I was a young activist, and I followed the news. It was controversial then, and it is controversial now. But the lawmakers finally agreed that, for purposes of the law, a fetus was not 'viable' until late in the second trimester— when it could perhaps, with our improved technology, survive outside the womb. The ruling didn't satisfy those who believed that a fertilized egg was a 'person' upon conception, but it was seen as the lesser of two evils and was made the law of the land. My own take, and the reason I agree with Peter's pro-choice stance is that I have seen women struggling with their knowledge that they did not want to be pregnant while at the same time experiencing the condemnation of their own culture. The book Peter mentioned reviews countless cases of women being bullied or prevented from seeking an abortion. My own sympathy is with the woman who must fight through the guilt her own culture thrusts upon her in order to do what she knows is best for her own body, her self. It is not an easy thing to stand up for yourself when your culture tells you that you are being sinful and selfish."

"But that is the point," said Alison. "She is being sinful and selfish. She is ending an innocent life, and everyone would agree that is a sin." Forella thumped her cane to get everyone's attention. "I think we do need to move on," she said, "but, no, Alison, not everyone agrees that abortion is a sin. Most people agree that it is unfortunate, that it would be better if unwanted pregnancies never occurred. From all my years of volunteering and involvement with women's issues, I learned just how desperately some women tried not to get pregnant and how much opposition they encountered when they tried to get an abortion. Once a woman became pregnant—for whatever reason—she found that society demanded the right to tell her what to do with her body. It made me ask myself over and over again—'Would this attitude that basically told a woman what to do with her own body ever have been tolerated if it were men who were the ones who became pregnant?' I know it sounds silly, but I honestly don't think men ever stop to think how they would feel if society told them what they could or could not do with their own bodies. It reminds me of Wait's story he shared earlier. We ARE animals. We reproduce the same way animals do. But we are also humans, and we know how to safely stop a pregnancy. We are appalled at the idea of castrating a man so he retains his beautiful high voice. We should also be appalled at the idea of making a woman continue with a pregnancy if it is not something she wanted or planned. Modern medicine makes it possible for her to have that choice. It shouldn't be anyone else's decision just as no man should have to tolerate someone else deciding that he should be a castrato."

"But what about the baby?!" said Alison. "It has no say about what happens to it. If a woman is pregnant and she doesn't want the baby, she should have the child and put it up for adoption. Killing a baby is wrong! If it were men who carried babies, it would be wrong for them, too. I can't believe people can be so heartless." Alison was as red-faced as Peter had been earlier.

Peter stood up, but he wasn't upset, as he had been when he spoke before. "I said I would stop talking, but I feel I owe everyone an apology. I usually manage to not react when the issue of abortion comes up. I know other people have opposing views on it, and I know that isn't what this exchange was supposed to be about. But here is the thing. I regard Stephie's decision to have an abortion as a brave choice. She knew we would not be good parents. At the time we were too poor and too immature. Rather than bring a child into the world unwanted and probably doomed to an unhappy life, she decided it would be better to stop that pregnancy. I respect her for making that decision. That strength was part of what I loved about her. It hurts to have her disparaged as selfish and sinful. If anything, she was being compassionate toward that potential life. Unfortunately, the person doing the procedure was incompetent. The attempt to induce a miscarriage failed, and they couldn't get her to an emergency room in time. That mass of cells, that embryo, was not a baby. It had no personality, no shared memories. My wife did. She was a person, and I loved her. To put it bluntly, my wife was far more important—to me and to society—than that fetus, no matter how much potential it may have had. My wife was already a person. She is the one whose rights I see as important. It may sound cold-hearted, but a fetus isn't a baby until it is born. That's when 'the breath of life' enters a body and makes it a child of God, if that is your belief."

Katherine stood up and said, "I should have listened to you, Peter, when you said it would be best to skip over those tough years. There are some topics that evoke strong and conflicting feelings. You were wise to suggest we avoid bringing up some subjects. I'm sorry I didn't listen to you. Perhaps we should end our meeting for today and catch up with the last few people next time. If I recall, there were a couple Handel letters already transcribed and ready for us. We can go back to our usual format next time. I apologize for letting the atmosphere become so intense today. I'll try to take my cues a bit better from here on. Thank you to all who shared your stories with us today. It's good to get to know one another better—even if we disagree on some important issues. If nothing else, it is encouraging to see that we can disagree and remain friends. Forella, did you have anything you wanted to add before we finish up?"

Forella turned her head in Katherine's direction and said, "I would hate for us to go off feeling nothing but anger and dismay about our strongly disparate ideas on abortion. That certainly is not what we are here to share and discuss. Given the timeframe of the letters we will be getting back to next time, let me send home with each of you a splendid DVD of Handel's *Messiah*. You will hear and see five young Australian soloists and a choir and an orchestra performing on period instruments. The recording was made for the Australian Broadcasting Corporation, and Angela says it is stunning. I have listened to the DVD several times. I think you will enjoy it immensely. May Handel's masterpiece put us all in a better mood before our next meeting. Enjoy, and stay well, everyone."

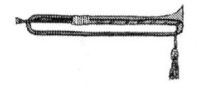

CHAPTER 19

The Trumpet Shall Sound

Peter drove slowly along a county road, heading back toward Indianapolis. He had gone to visit a small rural cemetery a few miles east of one of the state parks in Indiana. The cemetery was well tended, and Peter could tell that it was still serving as a burial spot for families in the area. Some of the older grave markers were nearly unreadable, but the one Peter came to see bore an inscription clearly visible on the small granite stone: Stephanie Michot Rowe, August 23, 1948-April 6, 1971. Peter regularly sent a donation for the maintenance of the cemetery. He was glad to see that it was—as it was whenever he visited--a clean and peaceful place. He left some flowers—nothing fancy, just a simple bouquet. He knew the groundskeeper would just have to clear them away. As though recalling an old movie, he remembered the bitterness he had felt when his wife died. He recalled his futile attempts to find any of her family, anyone else who could share the unspeakable burden of burying that lovely girl. But even these many years later, he still was the only one who knew or cared, the only one who remembered. And even these many years later, it still broke his heart.

As everyone gathered for the Handel Seminar meeting, there was little evidence of any rancor over the abortion issue that arose unexpectedly last time. Instead all of the talk was about Handel's *Messiah*, and especially about the youthful Australian performers on the DVD Forella had sent home with them. "You know," said Katherine to those nearby, "as I was growing up, *Messiah* was really my only association with Handel. Every year around Christmastime, my hometown would hire a director and, usually, several retired soloists, and then invite singers and musicians from throughout the county to perform the first part of the oratorio in the high school gym. I even sang with the chorus a few times myself, when I was in high school. But I didn't care much for the solos, which were usually sung by older singers with really wide vibratos. It was almost a shock to hear these young soloists. They were so expressive, especially the bass. I thought he was amazing. What did you think, Alison? Was this a typical recording?"

Alison smiled and said, "There are so many excellent recordings of *Messiah*—enough for everyone to find a favorite, or even several favorites. I like the London Philharmonic recording, and some of the earlier Robert Shaw CDs, but truthfully, what I thought was impressive about this DVD was the way it was video-recorded. It was pretty simple, but just like the live streaming that happens now at the Met, you could see the expressions on the singers' faces. I think it made the solos in particular come alive. The chorus was a little weak, I thought, but then I'm used to hearing a larger choir perform the piece, and, actually, they left out a few choruses—I'm not sure why. And it's true that the performers—all of them, including the director and orchestra—did seem to be pretty young compared to most amateur groups who put on *Messiah*. I thought the woman who played the trumpet duet with the bass was outstanding. The DVD is a nice addition to my music collection. I need to go over and thank Forella."

Annie's luncheon special this time was a shrimp stir-fry. She provided some chicken salad for those who avoided shellfish. Ross took healthy helpings of both. He asked Katherine if she thought they needed to take up the group biographies again. Other than Ross and Katherine themselves, only Rayette had not talked about herself and her response to the

Handel letters so far. Katherine said she would try to stay on top of things this time. As people one by one returned their plates to the buffet and sat down with cups of coffee or tea, Katherine said, "Before we ask Peter to share the two letters he has for us today, I wondered if we could hear from Rayette—just a little about where you hail from and what you think of the Handel letters thus far. I'm sorry we didn't complete the circle last time. Ross and I both feel we have slipped in bits of our life stories here and there along the way, but we would really like to hear from you, Rayette, if you are willing to share your story."

Rayette said, "I'm eager to get to the letters, and I don't know about letting you and Ross off the hook, but I'll say a little about myself if you wish. Let's see. I was born in St. Louis. My parents owned a restaurant and were pretty successful. My younger brother and I were luckier than most African-American kids growing up in the fifties and sixties. When I say we were luckier, what I really mean is that we escaped, literally, what went on in America during the civil rights era. My family moved to France, and for a musician and restaurateur like my father, being in France was in general a better choice at that time. I still felt out of place in a mostly white world, but I received a good education at a private school. I returned to the US to go to college. I was one of the first women and certainly one of the first black women admitted to a prominent Jesuit school on the east coast—I'll let you guess. I met my wonderful husband, James, at school. He was an English professor for thirty years at the University of Dayton in Ohio. We only recently moved to Bloomington. I work from home—mostly helping with online sites for various NGOs. And, as I've said before, my dearest avocation is writing poetry. Oh, and James and I have two children—two girls. They are both married, and I am the proud grandma of three grandchildren."

"I think you wanted to know what I found most interesting so far about the Handel letters—or maybe most personally relevant," she went on. "Let me preface this by saying how hard it is to express the dismay I felt when I returned to the US as a young woman. You have to realize that I hadn't taken US history or encountered anything like the Ku Klux Klan. My parents tried to warn me about what to expect, but truthfully what really upset me was to learn graphically, truthfully about the history of slavery in the United States and the ongoing effects in terms of racism. It was a shock to know that a significant number of Americans saw me as somehow inferior just because of my skin color—a lesser being, a second-class citizen. As I've been reading the Handel letters, and especially as we have talked about the situations in which Handel repeatedly found himself, I have empathized with his need to avoid being seen as anyone's servant just because he was a musician or even as serving in a patron's employ. I can fully understand how the notion of doing anyone else's bidding could be absolutely repugnant to him. That streak of independence is probably what I most admire about Handel. His was a very different situation than mine, of course, but, like me in many ways, Handel had to decide time and again to follow his own path and stay true to his own sense of self rather than doing what society expected him to do."

"Thank you, Rayette," said Katherine. "Among other things, it seems obvious to me that you have used your experiences to help formulate important insights on how cultures differ. Now we know why you were so adept at spotting the translations from Lydia's earlier letters in French—next best thing to a native speaker. And, as you said, Handel certainly did refuse to be defined by the categories other people would foist upon him. Many thanks for that short bio. And now I believe we have a couple of new letters to read. What do you have for us, Peter?"

Peter handed around copies of two letters, both from the mid-1740s.

Mr. G F Handel, Esqr
Brook Street, near Hanover Square
London

9 April 1743

My Dear Mr. Handel,
Do a gracious host and an unparalleled music salon warrant praise for sparking a friendship between persons who might otherwise drift

apart? This is what I asked myself after the wonderful chamber concert you offered before this winter's season, when my dear Susannah sang, along with Christina, the lovely duets you had so recently composed. You must know, Gif, that your cozy music room and lively entertainment conspired to cast Mrs Cibber and myself again into close proximity. We have become dear friends, and it is all owing to you and your excellent house party. I could not be happier that our paths crossed again and under such improved circumstances. It is a delight to find another who shares with me and with my dear Mr Handel a deep love of music and pleasure in good company. Thank you for inviting us all to your Brook Street gathering.

In the many months since then, Eggy has confessed to Mr Sloper that Susannah's little Molly consumes my excess fretting and doting as the grandchild I will never have. I do not mind their sniggering asides. The child is a sheer delight, and I do so enjoy the time Susannah and I spend together. We have discovered a shared enthusiasm for the plays of our celebrated Mister Shakespeare, and we spend joyous hours studying his words together while Molly and her nurse entertain us on the side. I am so pleased to have found such an excellent friendship. I almost feel as though my sister were returned to me. Susannah is a treasure.

And you, dear Gif—I am so sorry to hear that your longtime friendships with Mr Goupy and Mr. Smith are challenged by the ever-changing fortunes of the opera companies. My opinion is perhaps ill-informed and of no consequence besides, but I believe Lord Middlesex needs to accept your desire to move on to an independent program rather than serve the needs of his enterprise. And your friends should know that this is your character as well. The request and the pressure to comply have caused you great stress I am sure, and it is especially painful to have your friends speaking out against you, against your decision. Once again, it has brought on the afflictions you had hoped to dampen through quiet steady work of your own design. Your health is so much better when you are composing and conducting as you choose rather than as others dictate. You have always been this picture of stubborn talent. Why do your friends not see that you are not likely to change—now or ever?

And yet it is a difficult and sad thing to lose friendships that have sustained you before through trying times. Perhaps their anger will abate. This most recent season was an excellent one. And with both Saul and Samson, you have cast into center stage the important friendships of the heroes—David and Jonathan, Samson and Micah. Susannah gave such a wonderful performance as Samson's fictitious friend Micah. That she can play the loyal male friend rather than the wily lover is proof of her fine dramatic talent. She told me that you and Mr Hamilton contrived of the role to use her dramatic background to good effect. Would that your own friends were as supportive as was this Micah of Samson in his hour of need.

I cannot close this missive without praising the wonder you created in Messiah. Mr Jennens deserves much praise as well. The scriptures are perfectly chosen. I hope you will perform it again next season. Edward and I were able to hear it twice, but that was not nearly enough. The choral pieces were wonderful. I do so like this new oratorio form. But the arias or solos were wonderful as well—with the tenor starting out singing of Every Valley, the beautiful duet He Shall Feed His Flock, the bass and trumpet together in the Trumpet Shall Sound. But best of all is Susannah's solo He Was Despised, just after the choral piece Behold the Lamb of God. That some complained that the oratorio was performed on a stage and by singers who also act in plays—if they but hear it and see how profoundly it does teach the Christian story—well I cannot imagine that they would have a dot to add. It is a masterpiece, Gif. I am so proud of you. And grateful. Rest well, my friend. You have given us your very best.

I have the honor to be, ever yours,

Mrs. Edward Grayston
St. Thomas Rectory
Marylebone

And the second letter:

Mr. G F Handel, Esqr
Brook Street, near Hanover Square
London

23 April 1745

My Dear Mr Handel,
The circle of friends Edward and I brought together to attend the Story of Semele could not have been more varied in their opinions of the piece. I understand Mr. Jennens refused to attend at all, though it was in the oratorio season. To my mind, it is a marvelously entertaining piece, but I must agree with those who ask how we are to name such a work. Is it an English opera? Is it a secular oratorio? Mr Jennens, I hear, called it a bawdy opera. Oh, my, Gif, you are in trouble now. And you gave Francesina that provocative aria in which she warbles of adoring herself. I must admit that I rather liked being able to understand the words as they were sung. Italian has never been an easy language for me. Now all of London can go about singing Myself I Shall Adore. I thought it was witty and had some lovely songs, and yet, Semele herself is hardly a role model.
    But here we are now at St George's day. Eggy and I celebrated with a feast not far from your Brook Street house. I was disappointed that you were not there, but I do know you were at the performance of Belshazzar. I am so glad I was able to hear that piece in rehearsal at your house —before Susannah fell ill. I cannot imagine that any one else would sing the part of Daniel so well as she did. You must tell Mr Jennens that his libretto was excellent. I am not one to speak often of affairs of state, but this work is an inspiration, I believe. Perhaps if people heard the music and saw how these legendary figures came together to promote peace and understanding among nations—perhaps we would have fewer wars. Your music guides us as we listen

to more worthy thoughts than our daily lives show us. And our dear Susannah stirs everyone's heart when she sings. I am so sorry that she was unable to continue in the productions at the KT.

I lift a glass to you on your patron saint's day. May the springtime bring you joy.

I have the honor to be, ever yours,

Mrs. Edward Grayston
St. Thomas Rectory
Marylebone

"The letters don't suggest that *Messiah* was the only thing going on with Handel—or even the most important," said Brad. "I expected to see gushing accolades. Didn't they know this was his masterpiece that would survive for centuries? Lydia just acts like it was another of his usual productions. I'm tempted to say it's like music today. Critics and the public have no idea who will or will not really last and which songs will become classics. It's all just a shot in the dark."

Katherine laughed. "Well, Lydia clearly liked *Messiah*, but you are right—she didn't report any exceptional celebrations or immediate, overwhelming praise. Still, we know that it did catch on with the London audiences and gradually became the perennial favorite it is now. I suppose in that respect her letters seem pretty low-key. However, they do move Handel's story along. After all, he kept composing after *Messiah*. What questions do we have about what she DID say in these two letters?"

"You couldn't ask for a clearer invocation of the theme of friendship," said Wait. "First Lydia talks about her friendship with Susannah, and then she mentions problems in the friendship between Handel and the two gentlemen she names—Goupy and Mr. Smith. And then she even points to the friendships in two of the oratorios recently presented. No doubt about it—friendship has got to be one of our themes."

"Right you are," said Katherine, and she wrote FRIENDSHIP on the flip chart. What else in these two letters? Ross? You have a theme for us?"

"I agree with Wait that friendship is the major theme here," said Ross, "but I'm going to suggest that we need to talk about the elephant in the living room—*Messiah*. What is this piece? Why is it so popular? What was Handel doing with the music he created in response to the texts Jennens chose? And what does it—or does it not—tell us about Handel's own religious views? I think we need to discuss *Messiah*—then and now."

Katherine simply wrote MESSIAH on the flip chart. "That may take all of our time," she said. "Is there anything else we should at least consider as a topic?"

"I'd like to give a little time to this anomaly of a piece she mentions," said CD. "You know, *Semele*—the bawdy opera, as Jennens called it. It sounds like Handel is getting feisty in his old age. What inspired this, I'd like to know?"

With a laugh, Katherine wrote SEMELE on the flip chart and then turned toward Wait. "First up is our consideration of the theme of friendship," she said. "Wait, that was your suggestion. What is your thought?"

"I think it is pretty interesting that Lydia herself named a theme in Handel's most recent oratorios," said Wait. "And she tied it in with her comments on her own friendship with Susannah and Handel's troubles with his two friends. It's almost as though she had joined our little Seminar, don't you think? We don't usually think of people from the 1700s pondering and writing about self-help topics like friendship. But here she is, pointing out to Handel how central the theme is to his own work and how important her own friendship with Susannah is. I don't know either of the two oratorios she mentions—*Saul* or *Samson*, but I do remember from some biblical essay or class years ago that the friendship between Saul's son Jonathan and future king David was supposed to be legendary, right? And then she identifies this Micah in *Samson* as a made-up character, a friend inserted into the story even when there was no evidence for such a person at all. I'd say she is as good as telling us that Handel was obsessed with the notion of friendship at the time. Why else would the theme show up so clearly in his music and in Lydia's letters?"

Clara snorted. "Coincidence does not prove causality," she said. "Lydia is the one zeroing in on friendship as a theme, not Handel. But, you are right—SHE is seemingly obsessed with the theme of friendship. I'm curious about her little segue into a couple of seemingly messy friendships in Handel's life—these two men, Goupy and Smith. Why would she even know about their falling out? I'm assuming Handel wouldn't have written to her about his tiffs with his friends. Maybe, back then, gossip was more easily spread than we assume. Just because they didn't have text messaging or Twitter accounts—what do you suppose?"

Peter stood up and said, "There are so many directions this topic can go, so before we get too immersed in other connections, let me share something I found—well, looked up—after I saw what was in that first letter." He flipped on his laptop and clicked on a file containing a drawing by Joseph Goupy titled *The True Representation and Character*. "This etching—there is also a painting—was created about this same time—1745. Goupy gave the etching another title—*The Charming Brute*—when he circulated copies among friends and nobility in London. It is clearly meant to represent Handel, and it is an obvious insult aimed at his former friend. Not only is Handel depicted as looking like a hog—complete with pig snout—but he is also surrounded by food as he plays the organ. Granted, Handel was obese, but this drawing does more than offer an early example of fat shaming. As you can see, this version of Goupy's caricature includes a ribbon underfoot that reads 'I Am Myself Alone.' In her new book on Handel's friendships, Ellen Harris writes about the background for this bit of ridicule. Clearly Goupy felt that Handel had somehow damaged their longtime friendship. After this etching was circulated among the London upper crust, including the Prince of Wales, Handel never forgave Goupy. I can see why. It's pretty nasty."

As everyone gathered around to look at the copy of the etching on Peter's laptop, Rebecca shook her head. "And we think our modern political cartoons are a sign of the times," she said. "I guess celebrities and political figures have always provoked such insulting graphics. But what a way to treat a friend! It seems almost like the kind of hurtful commentary eighth-graders fling at each other—except the quality of the drawing is more impressive. Do you suppose someone actually paid Goupy to create the painting and then the circulated etchings? It represents a fair amount of artistic effort even if it is ephemeral and shallow. I suspect there is some money behind it in some way or another. I can't help but feel incensed on Handel's behalf."

"Well, it's not like people didn't know he was overweight," said Brad. "I think the real insult or commentary of the piece is the banner under his foot—the one that suggests Handel is self-centered and acts like he doesn't need friends. It's not very nice, of course, but the artist—Goupy—seems to be calling Handel out on his behavior toward his friends, himself in particular. I assume Handel must have somehow really ticked him off for Goupy to go to this kind of effort to get back at him. I'm guessing Handel could be arrogant and rude if he wanted to be."

Peter shut down the laptop and turned toward Brad. "It certainly seems that something must have happened to alienate the two men. As I said, I looked for a little background on the etching in Ellen Harris's new book on Handel and his friendships. Harris suggests that Joseph Goupy had indeed been a friend and neighbor to Handel for several years but that he had, in effect, allowed other interests—both financial and political—to interfere with their friendship. Ellen Harris is, of course, prejudiced in favor of Handel, but she does support the notion that Goupy and Smith together were putting pressure on Handel to commit his time and talents to the Middlesex opera venture rather than his own project. John Smith, Sr. was Handel's primary music copyist. I suppose from one perspective Handel is being uppity and self-serving, but given what we know of Handel's characteristic desire for independence, it isn't surprising that he would resist the kind of pressure Goupy and Smith were bringing to bear. Lydia must have heard about it through some sort of grapevine. She, at least, is on Handel's side. I don't think Handel went about complaining about the situation. He just acted—created his own semi-opera in *Semele* and, yes, I suppose thumbed his nose at Middlesex and his erstwhile friends."

"Clara's comment notwithstanding," said CD, "I agree that Handel did have in mind the subject of friendships at this time. He was clearly exploring the theme of friendship in both *Saul* and *Samson*. We can't know how much input he had into the evolution of those libretti, but given that Milton's *Samson Agonistes* was the source for *Samson*—and Milton offered no Micah character—then we might guess that Handel himself may have negotiated the inclusion of this additional character. His librettist for that oratorio—Newburgh Hamilton—was a friend and collaborator who was used to working with well-known sources such as Dryden and Milton. But Handel is the one who knew how to make a plot come alive as a dramatic piece of music. I imagine he would have insisted there be a character like Micah, a friend to Samson to counter the fickle Delila, even if such a figure wasn't in the biblical story nor in Milton's poem. Handel knew there had to be a Robin for Milton's Batman, someone who could ultimately make obvious Samson's heroic character. And Lydia said that Susannah Cibber sang the role of Micah. Of course—who else could convey the emotional depth Handel reserved for a true friend? Micah was Handel's commentary on the need for friends who support the hero with unwavering loyalty. And maybe for friends who support great artists and composers without question, without challenge to their independent vision. I can see Handel assuming that his own genius demanded his friends simply give him free rein."

Rayette held up her copy of Lydia's letter. "And yet," she said, "Lydia is quick to express her concern that Handel is likely suffering both physically and emotionally as a result of the pressure Middlesex and his company were putting on him and the falling out with his friends. She knew that these things were bothering him—whether because he told her or, more likely, because she was an observant friend and saw his frustration and defensiveness. We need to remember that Handel didn't have a spouse or mistress, no one to offer comfort and listen to his side of the story. And, in fact, the two close friends he might have relied on to support him were instead part of the problem. My own sense is that Handel showed a good bit of integrity and commitment to his art, his creative vision. Once he had turned his back on the opera company and on the two friends who were insisting he work with Middlesex and his rich patrons, it seems that Handel moved very quickly to produce his own work—what was it? *Semele*? I think he recovered pretty well, and I suppose that banner under his foot was in fact accurate—he WAS himself alone. He was composer AND entrepreneur, and that was sufficient."

"I know it is a different time," said Clara, "and the comparison may be far-fetched, but the situation Handel faced with his wealthy would-be funders reminds me of the kind of often subtle constraint that comes with the funding that supports almost any scientific research. Sometimes the pressure is innocuous, more a matter of preference. But other times, the money behind the research really does influence what the scientist is allowed to 'discover' or prove. Have any of you watched the television series that recently aired—a kind of continuation of Carl Sagan's *Cosmos* series from the 1980s? In the new series—with Neil deGrasse Tyson as host—there is one episode in which the scientist who discovered the age of the earth—Clair Patterson—is denied funding for his project because it challenged the use of lead in gasoline and other products. Patterson's research demonstrated that the lead from industry and automobiles was toxic to humans, but it took years for his research to be accepted and acted upon. It is just one of the many instances in which money determines what scientists are allowed to study or how their research is received. Like Handel, a scientist may have a genuine love of knowledge that spurs his or her research interests, but if the companies that support scientific research do not favor that line of research—or in fact directly oppose it, then it may never get off the ground. I agree with Rayette—Handel wins my respect for staying true to his own vision rather than accepting the buy-out offered by the moneyed opera company."

Standing up and taking a glass of iced tea from the buffet, Ross nodded slowly toward Clara. "I suppose that is true," he said. "Money wields power in scientific research, in the arts, in politics, increasingly in how we live our daily lives. It was true then. It's true now. We shouldn't be surprised that a company like the Middlesex Opera was trying to buy

Handel's talent. He was the hottest thing going at the time. Wouldn't it be great if some eighteenth century journalist had asked Handel exactly why he chose to ignore the offer from Middlesex and instead to write and produce his own opera? But, he probably wouldn't have answered truthfully. He still had to be somewhat circumspect about his own motives. After all, he still needed to have the nobility among his audiences. Besides, I think he may have been undergoing a kind of personal transformation, a period of reconsidering his aims with regard to his art and even his own life. To me, that is why he turned his back on the two friends who were trying so hard to convince him to join Middlesex. To Handel, these men were using their friendship, their longtime connection with Handel, to coerce rather than support him and his creativity. They were abusing the privilege of friendship, and Handel was confident enough in his own skill and talent to follow his own path rather than the one they hoped to steer him unto. Lydia was right to see that trait, that stubborn independence, as a solid, maybe even evolving, part of his character."

"So, what are you suggesting here, Ross?" asked Rebecca with a little frown. "Do you think Handel is trying to make more of a personal statement with his music? Is this more than—as Brad might say—Handel simply being the cagey businessman? What makes you think this is some sort of personal transformation? It just looks like a mostly financial decision to me."

"Ok," said, Ross, "I know SOME of you will consider this mere interpretive speculation, but it seems to me that Handel has become even more conscious of the philosophical implications of the stories he tells through his music—more aware than he was when he was younger. He is now—what?—sixty years old—and he has the memory and lingering effects of that health scare that sent him to the Continent just a few years before. I think he knows that the opportunities to create the kind of music he envisions—the music he has inside, if you will—those opportunities are shrinking. I think he feels that the time may be short for him to do what he really still wants to do with his art. So, messing around with what someone else wants him to do seems less appealing. Instead he goes off on his own.

I'm sure he is not ashamed of what he has produced earlier, but he is impatient to move on with ideas that interest him now, personally. He doesn't want to be distracted by others' demands on his time and effort."

Alison waved her hand. "I would agree that Handel has earned the right to do what he wants with his skills as a composer. And maybe he knew that this new, more idiosyncratic direction was also the one that would be best for him financially, too. But, Ross, what do you mean by this supposed 'personal transformation?' The oratorios were on more religious themes—although *Semele* wasn't, unless you believe in Greek myth. But seriously, do you think Handel was becoming more religious? Is that the objective he had in mind—spreading a religious message in the best way possible—through his ever-more splendid music?"

As Ross readied himself to answer, he saw that Forella had signaled that she wanted to speak. "Let us hear what my mother has to say first," he said. "Believe it or not, we've had this conversation before."

"Indeed, we have," said Forella. "Actually, Alison, it was my idea that Handel might be undergoing a personal transformation. Men are always stealing women's ideas and claiming them as their own—even their mothers'." Ross chuckled. Forella went on. "What Ross and I had discussed—not too long ago—was the likely effects of Handel's health, of course, but also his move into late middle-age. By eighteenth century standards, Handel was already an old man. People younger than he died every day. I am delighted that we now have a longer life span, but there is still an interesting change of perspective when one passes through middle age. Some joke about it, of course, but I recall reading a very interesting book on the topic—*Finding Meaning in the Second Half of Life*, by James Hollis. What I liked about Hollis's book is his description of how, at middle age, the soul awakens from its immersion in the demands of culture—or a description, as he says, of how one withdraws from 'compliance with the herd.' James Hollis contends that in the second half of life people give themselves permission to lead their own lives and do what their souls demand they do. I think Handel was finally taking full responsibility for what he did with his amazing talent. That's what I think."

Everyone clapped, and Peter said' "Hear, hear." Ross simply smiled and said, "Touché." And at this, Katherine walked up to the flip chart and said, "I believe we have moved, in our convoluted way, to our second topic—Handel's *Messiah*. Why did he write it? Was it a sign of his personal transformation? What do you have to say, Ross?"

"Let us pause," said Ross, "and remember the film we all saw—*The Great Mr. Handel*—in which the making of *Messiah* loomed so large. There we were led to believe that Handel was rescued from illness and a ruinous financial state by the timely appearance of the libretto for this piece. The film implies that Charles Jennens had little real input even as librettist and that Handel took up the task of composing music for the story of Christ's prophesied birth, death, and resurrection as a kind of religious mission. This implication was both inaccurate and misleading. First off, the libretto was very much Jennens's compilation. He is the one who searched through the Old Testament chapters, mostly Isaiah, to find the words of prophecy associated in Christian theology with the coming of Christ. He is the one who paired them with New Testament verses that—again in Christian theology—gave evidence of Christ's fulfillment of those prophecies as THE MESSIAH. This was a big deal for Jennens, and he had given the libretto to Handel back in 1739 with the hope that Handel would drop everything else and create this very unusual oratorio—without the usual characters, without the usual plot actions. *Messiah* was Jennens's brainchild, not Handel's. If God were directing anyone here, it was the librettist, not the composer."

"Ok," said Ross, "you can see that I was annoyed with the film—but not for reasons you might assume. The truth is I do think Handel created a masterpiece in *Messiah*, but not because he was inspired to tell the Christian story. Actually, Jennens wasn't telling much of a story at all. He lifted verses from the Bible that, in effect, required the audience to fill in the story or guess from the context what was being presented as theological truth. What Handel was able to do was translate those bits of poetry into emotional and musical statements. Think of the way the oratorio begins—'Comfort ye my people.' Handel CREATES a sense of comfort through his music. That is his genius at work. He sat on Jennens's libretto for two years, then composed the whole thing in less than a month, and in 1742 took it with him to Dublin to premiere. I think Handel saw it as an interesting challenge, but his task was to make Jennens's libretto sing. The fact that the piece had no named characters— no Joseph and Mary, no Jesus, no John the Baptist, no Mary Magdalene, no actors singing their heartfelt discourses—well, that was quite a new thing. But—as evidence of Handel's own religious testimony? I don't think so."

"So," Ross continued, "if Handel was indeed experiencing some sort of personal transformation, I don't think it was necessarily a religious one. I imagine Handel was as religious as any other man of his times, but he was certainly not immersed in Anglican theology the way Jennens was. No, what Handel was invested in and intellectually excited about was the composition of great music, especially dramatic music. His personal transformation had more to do with affirming once and for all what he had been striving to demonstrate throughout his career—that skillfully composed music can draw listeners into the human condition in a profoundly moving way. The song that Susannah Cibber sang—the one Lydia commented on—'He Was Despised'—its effect is less a religious appreciation of Christ's sacrifice than a very human sense of compassion for anyone's suffering, grief, and deep sadness. No wonder he chose a dramatic actress to sing it. Handel's empathy with human emotions was sublime. Expressing those emotions magnificently was his aim—not simply composing yet another hit for the opera stage and not, in fact, creating a piece of evangelical celebration."

Wait signaled that he had something to say. "I'm going to have to disagree with you, Ross," he said. "I think Handel was getting tired of the silly mythical or historical plots that were typically the subject of his operas and was instead determined to present more serious oratorios based on stories from the Bible. Nobody made him move in this new direction. He was confident enough in his own abilities and his reputation to finally move almost entirely to biblical material. To my mind, that would indicate that he had a clear agenda. He intended to give praise to God and encourage people to perhaps be better Christians. I would agree that his age and poor health made him more aware of his own mortality. People often become more religious as they get older."

Ross, perhaps feeling that he had already spoken long enough, simply looked down at the floor. Clara, however, seemed ready to jump into the fray. "We would all like to believe that Handel shared our own religious—or secular—view," she said. "I assume Ross was being as amenable as he will allow himself to be in admitting that Handel was—what did you say?—as religious as any other man of his times. But think about it. Handel came of age during the period of the Enlightenment. He had interacted on a daily basis with people of various faiths—German Lutherans, French Huguenots, Italian Catholics, British Anglicans, Methodists, and Calvinists, even London-based Jews. Furthermore, he had read or listened to the libretti of countless stories recounting the exploits of heroes and gods other than those found in the Bible. As a professional composer and musician, he offered his audiences what he thought they would like. He was well aware of the need to accommodate the taste of his wealthy subscribers or ticket buyers. But, he was an artist. He was not a preacher, nor a philosopher, not even a particularly good teacher, they say. I don't think we can read anything into his move to biblical oratorios other than his response to what he saw as an opportunity and a trend. His personal religious belief is only implied through conventional association and lack of any direct challenge. I think we would have to look to his behavior or commentary in other contexts besides his music to gain any sense of his personal religious views."

Katherine left her seat and walked over to the flip chart, where the word MESSIAH drew her eye. "When Handel composed *Messiah*, he had already written two earlier lengthy works on the story of Christ's death and resurrection," she said, "—*La Resurrezione* for an Italian audience and *Brockes Passion* for a German one. Neither work is as well known as *Messiah*, and neither work has an English libretto. I think the reason *Messiah* became so popular is partly because it was in English but also because it told a different story than either the Italian or German oratorio. Jennens chose to call the work *Messiah* because he wanted to tell the story of the biblical prophecy and its fulfillment in the birth, death, and resurrection of Christ. And with the amazing soprano solo 'I Know That My Redeemer Liveth," Jennens and Handel together assured their fellow Christians—and Christians today—that they could expect to gain eternal life. The text of the song comes, surprisingly, from the Old Testament book of Job. That was, of course, Jennens' intent. He wanted to make clear that Christ came to fulfill the idea foreseen in the Old Testament, in Job: 'I know that my redeemer liveth, and that he shall stand at the latter day upon the earth. And though worms destroy this body, yet in my flesh shall I see God.' The redeemer of which Job speaks is not yet born. Job is seeking comfort and hope in the midst of his great suffering. By equating the redeemer Job envisions with the Christ of the New Testament, Jennens proclaims the promise of Christian salvation. Handel, who after all loved to tell dramatic stories in song was happy to compose music for this most epically dramatic story bridging the Old and New Testaments and the lives of people in modern day London."

"What is interesting to me," Katherine went on, "is the 'suspension of disbelief' required by the juxtaposition of biblical texts in this well-known Easter song—the verses from Job lamenting his suffering at God's hand and Saint Paul's New Testament admonition to the people of Corinth, promising salvation. As with any dramatic work, the audience has to believe—at least for the duration of the drama—that the story they are witnessing is true. In this case, they have to believe the Old Testament figure that Job acclaims is indeed some future redeemer who will bring eternal life. The idea is central to Christian theology, but to someone not already convinced of the connection, it seems contrived. Even the language of the song is problematic. It does not, in fact, match the common translations of the verses from Job. Jennens must have made his own selection of which words to set as the song text. And yet, of course, he was guided by his religious tradition, which saw Job and other Old Testament writers as prophesying the coming of Christ. Jewish tradition saw no such connection of course. Still, for Handel, with his love for dramatic musical works, the storytelling that Jennens accomplished in his libretto is just what he wanted. I would have to agree with Clara's warning that we each want to see Handel as sharing our own religious view. And in my case, I see Handel as reveling in the great story he sets to music but also recognizing that it is a story, with all the conventions, flaws, inconsistencies, and reused content that goes into the making of any good story."

Rebecca set down her coffee cup and said, "I'd like to go back to the issue that Wait voiced in a rather direct way—the possibility that Handel had a clear, evangelical purpose in composing *Messiah*. There have always been arguments over the function of art, music, or theater. Is its purpose to instruct and improve the moral understanding and behavior of the audience? Bertolt Brecht, twentieth-century playwright, says that the purpose of 'epic theater' was to stir the audience to action. Handel's friend Alexander Pope was noted for his didactic poetry, poetry that aimed to instruct. Did Handel and Jennens fit into this mold? Did they hope to teach their *Messiah* audiences the fundamental message of the Bible? Did they hope to move them to adopt a Christ-like virtue of compassion and humility? I would agree with Katherine that Charles Jennens did in fact hope to instruct the audiences of *Messiah*—and of *Saul* and *Belshazzar*, certainly the audiences of *L'Allegro ed il Penseroso*—the other librettos Jennens wrote. Did Handel share Jennens's pedagogic and moralistic aim? Well, I'm going to go back to something I think Brad said a long time ago. Handel was a practical man. But he was also a very special kind of artist, one who readily built upon the ideas, compositions, and enthusiasms of others. My guess is that Handel was delighted to bring his talent and skills to the story Jennens offered in his libretto. Still, if the subject matter had been something Handel himself was extraordinarily keen to share, I expect he would not have set the libretto aside for two years and premiered it in Dublin rather than London. I think Ross nailed it when he said that Handel's own objective was to compose beautiful music, music that enhanced whatever story he was asked to tell."

"The notion of didacticism always oversimplifies art of any sort," said Rayette. "It is a given that Handel wanted to create great music, but he may also have wanted to praise God, tell the Christian story, inspire people to better behavior, maybe even simply to show off his skills. Who knows? I really enjoyed the DVD we took home. I am a Christian, so, to no one's surprise I suppose, I found the music particularly uplifting. But I also found the piece a little unsettling, especially as I watched it being performed by these young singers. The bass, especially, made me really listen to the words as though I were hearing them for the first time. Right before that wonderful duet with the trumpet, he sings of a mystery. As I watched his performance, I found a poem writing itself in my head. Would you like to hear it? Feelings always stay with me for a longer time when I write them into a poem."

Everyone said, "Yes, please do." Rayette pulled out a piece of paper and read:

> In his eyes is a fear, a gasp, a melting.
> How do I grasp this mystery?
> Behold, he says.
> But I must turn away. This voice is too strong.
> We shall not sleep, but shall all be changed.
> Changed—in the twinkling of an eye.
> No, stay as I am—change is a mystery.
> He tells of a mystery.
> What trumpet? Whose trumpet?
> Why must we change?
> To what shall we change?
> He is afraid as well.
> He who speaks the mystery is also afraid.
> My comfort is gone.
> He cues the last trumpet.
> The trumpet shall sound.
> I gape and shudder at this mystery.
> Death is a mystery.
> But life—life, too, is a mystery.
> Some solace comes in singing the mystery.

Alison clapped enthusiastically and said, "Yes, I thought the bass was especially impressive, too. And of course the aria that followed just after that recitative was outstanding. Handel gave the bass some wonderful music in *Messiah*. But if I am going to be fair, I will have to admit that many of Handel operas and other oratorios have music just as impressive as that in *Messiah*. We all know *Messiah* better than we know Handel's other works because *Messiah* tells the Christian story. As Katherine suggested earlier, it is a classic narrative of Western culture that still speaks to Christians—and even non-Christians—today. And the music is so familiar. It's hard to imagine how it was, hearing the piece in London back in 1743. I think Handel succeeded so well because he was used to setting poetic expressions of profound emotions to both solo and choral music. He gave his London audiences something they were used to but with a new twist—singers who must look inward and reflect upon their own beliefs, thoughts, and emotions. I think in that respect Handel was well ahead of his time."

"There's no denying that *Messiah* is a unique piece in many ways," said Katherine, "but also a composition building upon Handel's prodigious output before that time. Especially as a composer of operatic arias, Handel knew how to give singers the means for expressing deep and varied emotions. In *Messiah* the emotions may be inspired by religious convictions, but they are still simply human emotions nonetheless. I'm sure we will come back to *Messiah* again and again before we are done, but I believe CD wanted to take a quick look at another of Handel's pieces before we finish up today. What was your thought on Handel's *Semele*, CD?"

"I've never seen *Semele* performed," said CD. "I guess since it is not really an opera, it would be presented more in the manner of an oratorio—at least that is what Handel said it should be. But I have listened to an audio recording. What I find interesting is that *Semele* is like an opera in subject and form but it is in English—unusual for Handel's time. Anyway, what really got my attention—as I suggested earlier—is the fact that Handel thought to present this pagan and very risqué piece right in the midst of his ongoing religious oratorio series. So, I know I will be accused of following in Ross's footsteps and overindulging in interpretation—sorry, Ross—but here is what I think is going on. In *Semele* we have a mortal, Semele, who falls in love with a god, Jupiter. Jupiter's wife, Juno, is jealous and (in disguise, of course) talks Semele into asking Jupiter to make love to her in his true godly form rather than when taking on the appearance of a mortal. Only another immortal would be able to withstand the power of this godly lovemaking, so Semele dies, and all ends happily. Now, to my perhaps irreverent mind, Handel seems to be aligning secular and sacred longings by juxtaposing stories such as *Samson* or even *Messiah* alongside *Semele*. In other words, Handel makes clear the awkward suggestion that sex and religious longing are one and the same. And he highlights the personal riskiness of sex. That's what I see as the subtext in Handel's rush to present *Semele* while everyone else was clamoring for more godly oratorios."

Ross laughed. "Ok, CD," he said. "Even I expect a bit more explanation here. A proof to support this theorem, please."

CD sighed. "It's a fair hypothesis, I would guess, that people in Handel's time—or even today—would scream blasphemy if anyone suggested sex with Jesus or the Judeo-Christian God as a possibility or even a human desire. But sex with a pagan god—that is indeed what those pagans were all about. We are much too civilized. But here we have this human—a woman of course—admitting that she wants to get it on with Jupiter, and Jupiter in his godly form, not some disguised stand-in. I think it raises the age-old question of 'the purpose' of sex. And, believe me, I hear this all the time. Quote: Isn't sex really for the purpose of procreation? Isn't the sex drive an instinctual drive on the part of males to impregnate females? Isn't that the 'natural' purpose of sex? Isn't anything else 'unnatural' and sinful? And with that assumption, females in some African nations are subjected to genital cutting and gay males and lesbians all over the world are threatened with various punishments for their perceived 'unnaturalness.' The view that sex might simply be a conscious choice to pursue pleasure is seen as anathema—unless it is deemed 'natural' as a way to accomplish procreation—and then, really, only for males."

Katherine nodded toward CD. "I'm not sure the juxtaposition of religious oratorios and *Semele* constitute the persuasive proof Ross is looking for," she said, "but I do think *Semele* itself raises the issue of sexual pleasure. Pagan gods were always lusting after mortal women. Think of Yeats's 'Leda and the Swan.' But as I understand the plot of *Semele*, one assumption would be that Semele is presumptuous in thinking that she deserves a god rather than a mere mortal man. Furthermore, she is usurping a man's role in seeking 'endless pleasure' for herself rather than simply being the object that brings pleasure to the man she is supposed to marry—or to Jupiter, for that matter. She gets her comeuppance when she dies and her sister marries the man who was to have been her husband. I would say the story reinforces conventional views of appropriate sexuality—heterosexual male ardor, female restraint and submission, and, as you suggest, CD, no place for homosexual desire. And yet, because the story is regarded as a pagan myth, a fiction, it can serve rather like a joke or fairy tale—with the comic and outrageous actions falling, for a moment at least, into the realm of possibility. I'm intrigued now. I hadn't given much thought to this piece. Maybe it is another one we all should try to listen to or research a bit."

Forella signaled that she had a comment. "Ross won't be eager to do the research, I'm sure," she said. "I'll ask Angela to track down something for us before we meet next time. I had already looked ahead and have DVDs of *Belshazzar* ready for you today. What do you think, Angela?"

Angela looked up from her laptop. "There is a DVD made from a performance of *Semele* in Zurich in 2007. The lead is someone named Cecilia Bartoli. I could get copies to you before the week is over."

"Cecilia Bartoli!" said Alison. "Wonderful! She is outstanding. We may want to take a little longer before we meet again if we have two full Handel productions to watch. But I look forward to both of them. Thanks, Forella. That will be great."

Angela handed out copies of the *Belshazzar* DVD. Ross smiled over at Forella. "Mom, you are always so on top of it. And I appreciate not having to do the research. Now if I just had someone to watch this steamy *Semele* with—well besides you, Mom—no offense."

Katherine gave Ross a thoughtful look and a slight grin. "Ok," she said, somewhat distracted, "we have our work cut out for us. Thanks, again, everyone for a lively discussion. And thanks, Forella, for *Belshazzar* and *Semele* yet to come. Both promise to be really interesting. See you all next time."

CHAPTER 20

Father Confessor

A tightly secured packing crate was delivered to Ross's front door. The deliveryman explained that unpacking the item and placing it where Ross wanted it was part of the service. For a moment Ross couldn't think what it was, but then he saw the address of the sender—a friend from Norway. One of the women who worked with Ross on his climate change project had given him an antique kicksled when he visited her farm above Oslo. Shipping the sled to Indiana had taken quite a while. Together, Ross and the deliveryman unpacked the crate and set the kicksled on the floor of the hallway. The runners continued about two and a half feet behind the sled, and the sled itself consisted of a small chair with handles protruding from the back. Ross said that he could move it to its proper location himself. Carefully he took the sled to his treasure room. He looked forward to writing out the short provenance tag and accompanying story that would record why he had this sled from a tiny village in Norway.

THE HANDEL SEMINAR HAD NOT met for nearly a month. Both Ross and Peter had traveled overseas in the interim—Ross to one of the islands off the western coast of Scotland and Peter to Berne, Switzerland. These travels were not simply pleasure trips. Ross needed to set up some added filming for his documentary on climate change, and Peter wanted to visit an archive he hoped would provide insights into immigrant populations that had settled in the city of Berne, Indiana. Still, both men made use of their travel time to watch the DVDs of Handel's *Semele* and *Belshazzar*—an alternative way to pass a few hours of flying time instead of watching the latest movie the airlines offered.

Everyone else had found time to watch both videos over the intervening weeks as well. As plates of Annie's delicious vegetarian lasagna moved from buffet to table, Brad shared a little background on his own viewing experience. "One of those online dating services finally came through with someone who would go out with a person who admits to being separated rather than divorced," he said. "I may not always play by other people's rules, but I don't lie. So, this gal agrees to watch a video with me, and I thought, 'What could be more impressive than watching an opera! right?' So, I fix us both a drink and put on the DVD of *Semele*. Sure, it wasn't smart to have not watched it first myself, but she said she liked musicals, so I thought I was safe on this one. Turns out, I wasn't. She hated it. But, you know, I actually kind of liked it. So, maybe it was a good test. What do you think?"

"Honestly, Brad!" said Clara. "What were you expecting? That she would fall all over you just because you were sophisticated enough to like opera? For argument's sake, let's say it was a test. What do you think it proved? What advice for the lovelorn can we take away from this little escapade?"

"Smirk smile becomes you," sang Brad to the tune of "Moonlight Becomes You." Before Clara and Brad could continue with their tête-à-tête, Katherine clinked her glass with a spoon to get everyone's attention.

"Annie graciously fixed me a plate of lasagna as an early lunch," Katherine said, "so I am free to offer some background information on our two videos as you enjoy your meal. Peter does have a couple of letters for us, but I thought we could start out with some discussion of these two works—*Semele* and *Belshazzar*—since reports are that everyone had a chance to watch them."

"I particularly enjoyed researching *Semele*," she said. "One source I found especially helpful was a twenty-page Study Guide posted online by the Pacific Opera Company in Victoria, British Columbia. This Guide accompanied their 2009 production of *Semele*, and, like all of their opera Guides, it was intended for students and teachers who would be attending the production. They even included a final response page asking for teachers' comments. *Semele* was definitely intended for an adult audience, so I assume the students in this case would mostly be college students, but maybe not. What I found most interesting about the notes offered by the Director, Wim Trompert, was his assertion that an important 'secret' is often overlooked in presentations of the opera. I certainly didn't make the connection in the DVD we watched. How many of you realized that Semele was pregnant? Granted, we have this concluding scene in which Bacchus rises out of her ashes, but that could just be some gift sent by the gods. But Trompert argues that much of Semele's insistence on gaining immortality was staged in an effort to ensure protection of this now anticipated child. Rather than seeing Semele as a vain, pleasure-seeking and ambitious trollop, the POV production casts her as a worried mother-to-be who seeks the best life possible for the child she carries. The director suggests we should respond with empathy rather than condemning her for, in effect, seeking to rise above her station—the interpretation that usually accompanies productions of this work."

"I was a bit chagrined," Katherine went on, "to realize that I had not recalled my Greek and Roman myths very well. The story of Semele is recounted in Ovid's *Metamorphoses*. Bacchus, or Dionysus in the Greek tradition, is indeed the son of Semele and Zeus, or Jupiter in the Roman tradition. Of course Zeus had many such liaisons with mortal women, and his wife, Hera, or Juno, was notoriously jealous and constantly scheming to end these affairs. In this story, she succeeds by tricking Semele into asking Jupiter to make love to her—Semele—in his godly form. Jupiter knows this will kill her, but he has sworn to do what she asks, so he keeps his promise, and Semele dies. However, he hides the unborn child in his leg—sews the child into his leg—keeping it alive until the baby is born as Bacchus, the god of wine. And, by the way, Bacchus later visits the Underworld to find his mother and takes her to Mount Olympus, whereupon she does, in fact, become immortal. So her crazy desire wasn't so crazy after all."

"Eh bien," Katherine continued, "Handel composed the music for this piece in the summer of 1743. The libretto was based on a text by William Congreve, but it was not originally intended for Handel but rather for the composer John Eccles. Congreve was a well-known Restoration playwright, probably best remembered for the line 'Hell hath no fury like a woman scorned.' Eccles did compose an opera using Congreve's text, but it was never performed. Handel's opera came some thirty years after Eccles's attempt, and again its reception was not very good. I'll be interested to hear what you thought of the performance we watched. Certainly, we did indeed have a talented lead in Cecilia Bartoli. It looks like nearly everyone has finished with lunch. So, what are your thoughts on Handel's *Semele*?"

"Dang! That changes everything," said Brad. "Here I thought she was a hot-blooded wench, so to speak—a lusty match for our horny Jupiter. I like my version better. Who says she was pregnant, anyway? I don't think our DVD gave us that message at all."

Rebecca looked over at Brad. "I'll have to agree with you on that, Brad. I don't think our Cecilia Bartoli version conveyed any hint that Semele was pregnant. On the other hand, I feel a little like Katherine—that I didn't really have my background from classical mythology in mind as I watched the DVD. I would guess that the elite audiences who attended Handel's operas actually did have more familiarity with Greek and Roman myth than most people do today. I suppose that bit of cultural background does change the way we see her behavior—although I would still wonder why she became involved with Jupiter in the first place. She knew he was a god. I think the theme of aiming above your station is still part of the story. It's clear that Semele prefers Jupiter to the man she is supposed to marry."

"Hmm," said Ross, "except for the fact that Semele dies, the piece is actually pretty funny. The Iris character is a sort of female clown—at least in our DVD. And Sommus, the god of sleep, is a comic figure. Even Juno is entertaining, especially as she is played in this version. And the chorus gets to join in the 'endless pleasure, endless love' bit. Semele's song sung to her mirror is a hoot, and our diva really did it justice. I thought Jupiter was underwhelming, but maybe I lack a woman's perspective. What say you, ladies?"

Alison laughed. "Yeah, I wonder how we might have responded if, say, a young Plácido Domingo sang the role of Jupiter. Handel did give the tenor one of the most beautiful songs he has written—'Where 'er You Walk.' Jupiter in our DVD gets a round of applause at the end of the song, but I suspect it was more for the beauty of the aria than for his singing. Cecilia Bartoli was great. But, if I remember from our letter last time, Lydia didn't think the character Semele made a very good role model. No wonder Charles Jennens didn't approve of the piece. Semele was clearly an ambitious, even presumptuous woman. For the times, she must have seemed sinful, completely out of line. British culture was very hierarchical, and women were especially obliged to know their place."

Rayette smiled at Alison. "I liked the way the tenor sang 'Where 'er You Walk.' It IS a beautiful song. Jupiter says he will do for Semele what everyone wishes he or she COULD do for a lover—make the path the lover walks absolutely beautiful, perfect—with cool breezes and fragrant flowers. Actually I've heard the song sung at a funeral. The words are from a longer poem by Alexander Pope—not from Congreve's libretto. If you remember, we talked about Pope being a friend of Handel. Maybe they wrote the song as a separate piece—you know, like Hoagy Carmichael and Johnny Mercer or something. Anyway, I thought it was a lovely piece. It made Jupiter seem more human to me. I liked it."

"But a god as a lover!" said CD. "It reminds me of a song cycle by Benjamin Britten, songs he composed at the close of World War Two. He used poems that John Donne had written early in the seventeenth century, well before Handel's time. I remember I was completely astonished at the words to one song in particular. I still have it memorized. Hold on, give me a minute. The poem was 'Batter My Heart, Three Person'd God.' The last lines were: 'Take me to you, imprison me, for I, Except you enthrall me, never shall be free, Nor ever chaste, except you ravish me.' This was a man speaking to God, the Christian God, not some raunchy Roman deity. It may have been just a metaphor, but it certainly brought a new level of meaning to the notion of one's relationship with God. But, that imagery aside, I'm still mulling over the pregnancy angle. It's possible that—if, as Rebecca said, the audience in Handel's day would have known Semele was pregnant—then they might have really been put off by the whole story, just as Jennens was. Pagan gods lusting after mortal women is one thing, but a god coming to Earth in human form and actually impregnating a woman—a virgin. And the ending—with Jupiter announcing that a new god will arise who will save them all from grief and sorrow. That may be striking a little close to home. After all, Mary was a virgin, and Christ came to save mankind from grief and sorrow. Or, do you think the audience of Handel's time saw Jupiter as being more like a king than a god?"

"It's a fair question," said Katherine. "If I remember right, CD, last time, when we talked briefly about *Semele* in the context of the more religious oratorios Handel was writing, you suggested that some people might even have seen the opera as, perhaps, blasphemous in the midst of the biblical oratorios. If they could politicize it—making Jupiter a king rather than a god—then I suppose it wouldn't risk bringing up religious ideas. But, truthfully, I don't expect that eighteenth century Britons were any more eager to compare Greek or Roman myth to the Christian narrative than are Christian audiences today."

"I don't follow," said Wait. "Are you saying that this story of an affair between Semele and Jupiter has some correlation with the story of Christ being sent to save mankind? I'd say that is pretty far-fetched. It would be sacrilegious now just as much as then to suggest that kind of connection."

Ross looked into his glass of red wine, then held it up. "When Jesus turned water into wine, it was considered a miracle. That kind of magical transformation is a part of many other traditions, not just Christianity. Isn't that right, Katherine? Don't most people just end up ignoring the obvious comparisons between 'pagan' beliefs and stories and Christian ones?"

"Well, yes," Katherine replied, "people do tend to ignore the fact that traditional motifs and storylines are shared throughout the world by various cultures, with various associated religious doctrines. But the real issue, then, is what to make of these similarities. I think that is what Wait is questioning. I may have mentioned this before, but there are several studies of the 'hero pattern' in a variety of cultures, and some of them do, in fact, include Jesus as one of the figures who fall into this widely spread pattern. Pointing that out would be blasphemous only in the context of a very rigid understanding of Christianity. I think most seminarians training for the Christian ministry learn that biblical motifs are not unique to Christianity."

"But a savior born to save mankind, to give them eternal life, that is a unique tenet of Christianity," said Wait. "Belief in Christ means a person will be saved. There may be other stories about gods who have children born to mortal women, but the message of Christianity isn't really about that. Seeing any similarity between the story of *Semele* and Christianity is simply missing the point of Christianity."

Katherine held up her two DVD cases. "*Semele* certainly succeeded in sparking our interest," she said. "What about our other performance—*Belshazzar*? And, yes, the motif of a military victory won by diverting the river IS a traditional motif. It's in Thompson's *Motif-Index of Folk Literature*. Belshazzar is an historical figure, with references in various ancient tablets describing the fall of Babylon but most notably, of course, from the book of Daniel in the Old Testament. It should be no surprise that Charles Jennens wrote the libretto for this oratorio. Like *Messiah*, this work highlights the importance of prophecy in the Judeo-Christian tradition. This time, however, the prophecy is about the fall of Babylon in 539 BCE. And the hero is Cyrus, a Persian ruler who conquers Belshazzar and releases the Jews from bondage. If I remember correctly, even Lydia remarked on the wisdom and tolerance Cyrus demonstrated in simply dispatching the tyrant and not seeking to kill or enslave the people who had been Belshazzar's subjects or captives."

Peter held up a pamphlet from the British Museum. "On one of my many trips to the British Museum," he said, "I examined some clay cylinders with cuneiform inscriptions—artifacts that were found in the mid-1800s by archeologists working in Ur, or present-day Iraq. I was intrigued as I watched *Belshazzar*, wondering if those clay cylinders were connected in any way with this story of the fall of Babylon. So, I checked on the museum's website, and guess what? Those dusty artifacts at the British Museum do indeed tell the same story of Belshazzar and his defeat at the hand of the Persian king, Cyrus. But it is the story as recorded in the book of Daniel that is the real meat of the oratorio. Here we have the famous 'writing on the wall' by the hand of God, no less. I was a little disappointed at how the motif was presented in our version of the piece. Talk about a lost opportunity for special effects and a stunning *deus ex machina*! But I suppose we've all been spoiled by the likes of Peter Jackson and *The Lord of the Rings* or Steven Spielberg and *Jurassic Park*. The interesting thing to me is that this would have been presented as an oratorio in Handel's time—no props—so the imagery of the hand of God writing on the wall would have been in the heads of the audience, so to speak. More like oral storytelling, right Katherine? People really did have to use their imaginations."

"Yes," Katherine said, looking again at the DVD jacket. "Even more than operas, oratorios were straightforward narrative, like oral storytelling, and, of course, in London they were in English, so people could follow the storyline more easily. But this particular oratorio was, I think, almost a kind of exemplum or didactic tale. Even Lydia commented that *Belshazzar* was effective as a lesson in diplomacy and wise government. Probably Jennens should be credited for that, but it was Handel who made the story live. I especially like the way the choruses represented public opinions and the various culture groups involved in the story. In the little bit of research I did on this oratorio, I read that this is the one piece about which we do have letters that were exchanged between Handel and Jennens as Handel worked on the composition. At one point Handel complained that the performance would go on for four hours if he used everything Jennens wrote. So, obviously Handel had the task of selecting, cutting, and making it all fit together. Again, it is Handel's sense of what makes a good dramatic story that is essential. I wonder if he saw Cyrus—the hero—as similar to any of the European kings of his day. Certainly, he was an admirable character, especially in contrast to the drunken, irreverent, and vicious Babylonian king, Belshazzar."

"A man for all seasons," said Ross. "I think we could do with a few Cyruses in the world today. But I promised not to get into politics. So, do we have a letter or two to examine today, Dr. Rowe?"

"Indeed, we do," said Peter. "I'll pass them around now. Some sad news in the second one."

Here are the letters he shared with the Seminar.

Mr. G F Handel, Esqr
Brook Street, near Hanover Square
London

10 November 1745

My Dear Mr Handel,
I am so pleased to hear that your health is better now that you have spent some time in the country. I am sorry to report that my dear Edward too suffered some ill health recently. With great reluctance he has turned over his teaching duties to a younger man. For now we remain here at the rectory. I asked if he had talked at any length with you at the coffeehouse when he saw you at a table nearby just a week ago, but he said that you were engaged and simply waved a greeting. Eggy rarely speaks of his own worries or ailments. I would not be surprised to learn that none at the coffeehouse knew of his malady. He puts a brave face on it among his friends.

It seems that the Stuart uprising was the topic of discussion at Child's. Eggy believes that those gathered round you were hoping to convince you to compose a military piece to counter the Jacobites. Perhaps it is just as well that those of my sex are often unwelcome at such discussions. I would much rather hear a discourse on the planets or on life in the royal colonies than talk of war. And, truth be told, Gif, I like less the rousing militant oratorios with their noble heroes than the more pensive pieces reviewing the life of our Lord or the friendship of Samson and Micah. It may be that my long life is inviting a time of kindness and affection rather than worldly striving. Ah, my friend, you know so well how to plumb the well of attachment in human hearts. For those of us of softer mien, could you not revert again to tales of love and loyal sacrifice? Even wayward Semele was a welcome turn from shouts of war and glorious calls to arms. Think of your friends who never carry the sword. We too savor your brooding tunes, and all the more when they are on the topic of thwarted love.

Please do stop by the rectory if you have a chance. Eggy finds the trip to the coffeehouse tiring. He misses your witty dialogue and extempore playing at the harpsichord. And so do I. Stay well, my friend.

I have the honor to be, ever yours,

Mrs. Edward Grayston
St. Thomas Rectory
Marylebone

The second letter:

Mr. G F Handel, Esqr
Brook Street, near Hanover Square
London

12 August 1747

My Dear Mr Handel,
I appreciated so your friendship and comforting concern as my dear Edward was laid to rest. I have not had the heart nor strength to write these many months, but please know that your tears and warm

embrace were a treasure to me as I have weaned myself away from my life shared with the dearest companion I could ever have hoped to find. You are now one of my oldest remaining friends and one who knew Eggy when we both were young and beginning the great adventure of life together. Keep his memory alive, my friend. He loved you dearly and remembered you nightly in his prayers. We both grew to cherish the great bond that your music gave to us. Your music deepened our lives and our love in ways you cannot imagine. Thank you, my dear Gif, for so willingly sharing your great gift. I hope I will see you in the coming months. For now I am closeted here in West Woodhay, with Susannah's warm friendship when she is able to leave the City. Please stay well, my friend, and thank you again for your abiding care and concern.

I have the honor to be, ever yours,

Mrs. Edward Grayston
Sloper Manor
West Woodhay, Berkshire

Katherine lifted her hand to her throat, which had grown tight as she read the words of Lydia's second letter. "Yes, sad news, indeed—another death," she said, "Lydia's husband, the Reverend Edward Grayston. I am reminded again of the words that serve as preface to Handel's will—the copy I saw at the Foundling Museum. 'Considering the uncertainty of human life,' he wrote—'the uncertainty of human life.' I wonder if Handel had talked of that uncertainty with Lydia's Edward. It seems Edward was reluctant to share information on his illness even among his friends. Handel's sympathy at Lydia's loss and his own sense of grief seem genuine. Even months after the funeral, Lydia recalls with obviously tender gratitude Handel's expression of sorrow, his tears and comforting embrace. I think our first topic of discussion will have to include our thoughts on death and Handel's role in helping Lydia mourn her loss."

On the flip chart, Katherine wrote EDWARD'S DEATH, HANDEL'S RESPONSE. "What other topics do we want to consider? Yes, Rebecca, what do you suggest?"

Rebecca sighed and said, "I, too, think our thoughts on death and the uncertainty of life are most important here, but I was also struck by something Lydia said in the first of these letters. She asks Handel to think of his 'friends who never carry the sword' as he writes his next dramatic work. In other words, she asks him to write something less militaristic and more attentive to the emotions of love and loyalty—sentiments his female audiences find most attractive. I suppose the topic would be LOVE RATHER THAN WAR, OR FEMALE RATHER THAN MALE THEMES. What do you think?"

Katherine wrote the topic on the chart. "Anything else?" she asked. Ross leaned back in his chair. "I don't know about this 'male' versus 'female' subject thing," he said. " Seems a bit reverse sexist to me, but we'll see. I do see another topic tied to Edward Grayston's death and Lydia's letter to Handel. She mentions that Edward had loved Handel dearly, that he had remembered him in his prayers every night. Not to be callous, but why? Why was Edward Grayston remembering Handel in his prayers? Was Handel ill? Did the Reverend Grayston worry over the state of Handel's soul? Should we who read the letter today ponder the meaning of this statement, or is it simply an expression of friendship? We see none of the usual 'He's gone to a better place' idiom that we might expect. Instead, Lydia writes of Edward's concerns about Handel. I'm not sure what I am asking here—maybe if there is some subtext about Handel's health or his likeliness of attaining heaven. Maybe—WHAT IS HANDEL'S OWN CONDITION AND READINESS FOR THE HEREAFTER?"

Katherine added Ross's suggestion to the chart, then said, "Well, our first and third topics seem to be linked to the notion of death, whether Edward's or Handel's own eventual death. But, actually, my own question was more about Handel's response to this very significant loss that Lydia has experienced—the loss of her spouse. We know that Lydia no longer had her parents nor her sister, and she had no children of her own, so Edward was a vital part of her life, even beyond her love and affection for him. Handel had known Edward for years and evidently liked him, so he mourned the loss of a friend just as he had when John Arbuthnot died, or when cellist and librettist Nicola Haym died. But what is striking in Lydia's letter is Handel's great empathy and pain in seeing Lydia's sorrow at losing her husband. Handel's ability to feel what others feel—so apparent in his music—is paramount here. He truly shares Lydia's heartache."

Peter signaled that he had something to say. "When I read this second letter," he began, "I was surprised at Lydia's description of Handel's response—not that he offered his condolences but rather that he offered a hug and tears. I don't want to be accused of xenophobia here, but I've always thought of Germans as being rather cold and standoffish. I DO remember the letter Handel wrote to his brother-in-law when Handel's mother, Dorothea, died—when he said he could not hold back his tears. But that was his MOTHER, and besides it implies that he considered it more proper to in fact hold back his tears. Or, maybe tears and embraces are to be reserved for very, very special situations or people. I don't know. It just seemed odd to me. What do you think, Rebecca? Don't anthropologists agree there are some traits that really are shared by people of a given culture or ethnic group—that maybe Germans really are, umm, overly reserved?"

"Ha," said Rebecca, "I don't think anthropologists agree on much of anything, but, yes, there have been any number of anthropologists who have talked about cultural patterns of behavior or, as Margaret Mead called them, 'temperaments.' It has been typical for ethnographers to look closely at a specific culture rather than offering comparative commentary on how one culture differs from another. That sounds more like what your friend Alan Dundes did, Katherine. Didn't he write about national or ethnic character?"

"Well, yes and no," said Katherine. "Alan Dundes did attempt one lengthy study of German national character. I think I have mentioned it before—*Life Is Like a Chicken-Coop Ladder*—interesting book. But mostly, in several articles, what he researched were examples of how people used folklore to characterize people of culture groups other than their own. In other words, he studied what he called ethnic slurs, jokes and sayings that express stereotypes one group holds about other groups. The jokes usually cast Germans as authoritarian and inclined to warmongering, but of course these are jokes that circulated after World War Two. I'm not sure what the stereotype would have been in the eighteenth century. More useful, I think, are personal narratives that offer individual commentary on family traits, especially if the storyteller believes the family traits are tied in any way to ethnic heritage."

"Oh, my, yes," said Clara. "I remember meeting my great-grandmother on my mother's side when I was a little girl. She actually lived here in the Midwest—Ohio, I think. We were here visiting, and I remember my brother worrying over whether he would have to endure kisses and hugs from strangers—which we usually did when we met friends of my parents in California. But my mother said we wouldn't have to worry about it. Her Grandma was German, and they never kissed or hugged in public, even among family. But the funny thing was—when our visit ended—I had kind of learned to like my great-grandma. She baked us cookies, and she taught me how to do a cat's cradle, with string. When we left, I gave her a kiss on the cheek. She laughed and patted my head. I guess now I would say she was embarrassed, but I thought she was just sweet. I was really sorry I didn't get to see her again."

"People used to be less lovey-dovey," said Brad. "Even grandmas. I don't think it has anything to do with being German. Besides, going back to the letter, maybe Handel expressed his emotional side to Lydia when they were alone. She doesn't say they were out in public. I still think there was something more than just friendship between Handel and Lydia. But I also think Handel would have felt sorry for Lydia, and he would have hated seeing her hurting the way she obviously did on losing her husband. He would be a monster if he didn't feel something. What I find more interesting is her saying that now Handel is one of her oldest remaining friends. As we get older, it starts to be a little disturbing to realize that fewer and fewer people share our early history—fewer people remember us when we were young. I think it is a pretty revealing comment on Lydia's part. She sort of transfers some of her husband's role as long-time friend and keeper of memories over to Handel."

Clara and Ross exchanged a surprised look. Then Clara shrugged. "Brad, you are a mystery," she said. "Startling insights out of the blue! But, back to your question, Katherine. I wonder—did you see Handel's behavior—his hug and tears—as unusual, or do you think this line in Lydia's letter says more about her than about Handel?"

"Well, we certainly know more about Lydia than we do about Handel," said Katherine. "All along, we've had to accept that the choice of subjects, things noticed or not noticed, everything comes from Lydia's head, not Handel's. Would Handel himself have considered it 'out of character' to weep or give Lydia a hug? We'll never know. But we do know that Lydia placed great value on his response. As she said, she viewed Handel's tears and embrace as treasures, behaviors she obviously interprets as signs of deep affection and sympathy. But, I wouldn't disagree with Peter's initial reaction. Perhaps Lydia even knew that Germans didn't usually show outward signs of affection. After all, she lived in Hamburg for seven or eight years. My own question, though, wasn't really about the physical response itself. I was more impressed with her recognition of Handel as a man who could grasp how very painful it might be to lose a spouse—even though he himself had never married. That ability to empathize with such emotional loss is apparent here—and also in many of his most beautiful arias, from 'Cara sposa' on down. I guess I was simply struck by the way Lydia recalled that response to Handel in her letter to him, reminding him that he had allowed that strong response to be shared and to now be savored by someone who truly regards him with the deepest affection."

At the far end of the table, Forella made a slight motion, indicating that she had something to say. "Yes, Forella?" said Katherine. Forella set down her teacup and smiled in Katherine's direction. "Losing a spouse can be daunting," she said. "The hardest thing, I think, is regaining your independent habits of thought—basically learning to think again as a single entity, not a 'we.' As Lydia said, she needed to wean herself away from a life shared with a companion. When Stanton died, I found I no longer knew what I—Forella Wainwright alone—really thought or even liked. I had for so long always felt that any decision needed to be negotiated, even those decisions that I knew would go the way Stanton wanted. It was simply part of being in a relationship. And suddenly that partnership was gone. Despite being a pretty independent woman, I felt lost for a while—as though part of my 'self' had died along with Stanton. I was surprised—not surprised that I felt sad, but surprised that I felt a bit crippled. I hadn't realized how much I depended on Stanton to be there. It was hard to go back to being single, alone, entirely responsible for myself and my life."

Rayette looked again at the letters in her hand. "Lydia was still in mourning, of course," Rayette mused. "But she isn't really writing to Handel about her own sense of loss, or even that feeling of being alone—as Forella said, that feeling of no longer being a 'we.' Instead she asks Handel to remember Edward, to keep him alive in his memory. It is almost as though Lydia is painfully aware of Edward's failure to reach out to his friends before he died. Maybe it came more easily to women to express a desire to be remembered fondly. I've always liked one of Christina Rossetti's poems for just that reason. It starts out 'Remember me when I am gone away, Gone far away into the silent land; When you can no more hold me by the hand.' How sad that Edward did not convey to his friends that longing to be remembered. Lydia must have wanted to communicate that sense of personal connection to Handel—on Edward's behalf. Maybe she, in fact, was the one who initiated the embrace that called forth Handel's tears. Maybe she was the one who nudged Handel toward an emotional response he rarely allowed himself to experience."

"We can speculate all we want about Handel's tears," said Clara, "but the one thing we do have a pretty direct statement on is Lydia's request that Handel write material that is less militaristic and more romantic. I'd like to hear what Rebecca has to say about the LOVE NOT WAR theme.

Don't we have an implication here on our chart that Lydia was invoking a female trope rather than a male one? And I believe Ross tossed out a red flag on this interpretation, n'est-ce pas?"

"This is Rebecca's topic, so I'll let her have her say," said Ross. "I simply wanted it to be known that a preference for stories of love over celebrations of war is, in my humble opinion, NOT a matter of gender differences. But Lydia seemed to think it was, so there you are. But—on to Rebecca's commentary. I'll bide my time."

Rebecca laughed. "Yes, I was accepting Lydia's assessment of life in eighteenth-century London whole cloth, I suppose. Clearly, SHE saw her female compatriots as the ones who appreciated love stories and viewed men as, if nothing else, overly responsive to the glories of war. But, mostly I was struck by the way she described Handel's female audience as those 'who never carry the sword.' Male actors on the stage, even Handel in that famous portrait by Thomas Hudson, all of them had swords dangling from a belt at the side. It was the sign of a gentleman. Lydia was simply perceptive enough to view that custom as a signal of male readiness for the fight. And I suppose she associated that need to have a weapon at the ready with a tendency to see war as more important than love or friendship in the daily scheme of things. Wearing a sword signified an attribute of class, but just like men who parade around with guns in public today, it also proclaims a kind of macho identity. I've often thought that it would have been tragic if that fight that Handel had with Matheson, back when they were both younger—if that fight had involved guns rather than swords, why, we might never have had Handel's beautiful music to listen to, or these letters to read."

"Oh, come on," said Wait. "You can't compare swordplay in Handel's time with the need to be armed in today's world, with terrorists everywhere and drug dealers on every other corner. And it has nothing to do with being male. I know women who always carry a gun, wouldn't go to the mall or grocery without it. I have a license to carry a pistol. It's just part of my uniform, so to speak. If you worked at a club in downtown Indianapolis, you'd know what I mean."

Katherine frowned and looked over at Ross. "Perhaps we should go back to the letter and Rebecca's question about the themes of Handel's music." It was clear that Katherine hoped Ross would step in as "the heavy," as he had agreed to do when the Seminar began. However, it was Forella who spoke up. "Ah, Mr. Thompson, was it?" she said. "I failed to ask if anyone was carrying a gun when we started meeting here. I guess I made the incorrect assumption that no one had a concealed weapon. Are you saying you have a gun with you now?"

Everyone looked over at Wait, who looked a bit discomfited and replied, "Well, yes, I always carry a handgun. But I have a license. And I know how to use it properly. I'm not dangerous." He laughed, but Forella continued. "I don't allow guns in my house," she said, "at least not guns that are not locked up. Randolph keeps some hunting rifles in a cabinet in the back room. It is always locked. Perhaps you would be so good as to let Randolph keep the gun safe for you while you are here. If not, I'm afraid I will have to ask you to leave."

Peter could see that Wait was starting to react, probably defensively. "Let me try to defuse this at bit," he said. "I work in Indianapolis, too. There are reasons to feel threatened sometimes, that's for sure. But we are in relatively safe Bloomington, and I don't think anything is going to happen while you are here, Wait. Think of it this way. You remember that third *Back to the Future* movie—the one where Michael J. Fox and Christopher Lloyd are back in the Wild West? Even then, when EVERYBODY—well, all the men—wore guns, even then at the town party, all the men were required to leave their weapons at the gate, before they joined the festivities. Granted, the bad guy hid a derringer under his hat, but the point is that everyone was supposed to be unarmed while the party was on. The town Marshall was there to see to it that everyone obeyed. The consensus was that guns and gatherings didn't mix."

Wait looked around. "Well, I still don't think you can compare earlier time periods with the situation today. But I'll give Randolph my gun if you prefer it that way, Mrs. Wainwright. Just don't let me leave without it, ok?"

"Thank you, Wait," said Katherine. "Let's go on to the topic Ross suggested. Actually it seems to be a question in two parts—was Handel ill, and did Edward Grayston have reservations about the state of Handel's soul? I think those were the queries you posed for us, weren't they, Ross?"

Ross frowned slightly as he lifted his glass of wine, then set it down. "We know Handel was ill. Likely his friends knew he was ill as well. And they knew he had never heeded their advice—to stop eating so unrestrainedly and drinking so heavily. I am sure that Edward did pray for Handel's good health, just as he would for anyone he knew was not well. That was sort of his job as a clergyman. But, to be honest, I was more interested in the second question. Did the Reverend Grayston have reason to believe that Handel had slipped away from his catechism? Had Edward worried that Handel might not be prepared to meet his Maker—should the need arise? I'm not trying to wring more out of Lydia's words than is warranted, but, after all, Edward was a man of the cloth. It was his duty to see to people's souls. I simply wondered if, perhaps, Edward knew something we don't about Handel's personal behavior or views on religion. I warned you that this was one of my obsessions."

"You, know," said CD, "we have the same glaring lack of information about Handel's own religious views as we have about Handel's sex life. He evidently intended to keep his private life and views private. People make assumptions about his religion on the basis of his composing *Messiah* and the other biblical oratorios, but then, he composed all those mythical and secular operas, too. I think we just have to accept the little bit of circumstantial evidence and go with that. He went to church, and he signed his manuscripts with the phrase *Soli Deo Gloria*—Latin for 'glory to God alone.' He may not have been particularly devout, but he was not an atheist, not even a deist. He was a Lutheran, cum Anglican, as far as I can tell."

"In point of fact, Ross," said Alison, "Lydia's writing that Edward remembered Handel nightly in his prayers would suggest that Handel and Edward Grayston simply shared a common understanding of accepted religious behavior. If she thought Handel would be upset to know that

Edward prayed for him, I assume she would not have mentioned it. On the other hand, especially if Handel had been ill, it would seem unfriendly to NOT say that he was remembered in nightly prayers. That's what people who share a religious tradition do—they pray for each other when anything is amiss. I don't see what you are finding questionable here."

"I think it is possible," said Ross, "that the practice of lay persons—not clergy, but lay persons—saying that they will pray for someone else is actually a more recent tradition, and perhaps one peculiar to American culture. I will admit that my friends who are what I consider to be unrelentingly religious do notice when I fail to state that I am praying for someone who is ill or troubled, when I say instead that I am thinking of them or hoping for a speedy recovery. My über-religious friends typically see it as more than a social gaffe. It is a sign that I have failed to register my allegiance to their God, a sign that I am an ingrate and an infidel, or perhaps simply a stray lamb. Here in the US, it has become a kind of test—are you one of us? But I don't think it was a part of the culture in eighteenth century England. And as a consequence, I see something more significant in Lydia's comment. I believe her words hinted at a deeper concern that, perhaps, Edward had voiced to her—a concern growing out of his role as a priest in the Anglican Church, perhaps a worry over Handel's conduct or theology or maybe his relationship with God."

"This is sounding awfully convoluted to me," said Wait. "Are you saying that it wouldn't have been everyday practice for a religious man like Edward Grayston to pray for his friend who is ill? That doesn't make sense. I don't see where Edward worrying over Handel's spiritual well-being is implied at all. He was just being a devoted Christian and praying for Handel's good health."

"Katherine, help me out here," said Ross. "Isn't this an example of that 'presentism' you mentioned one time? Wouldn't it be projecting our current cultural assumptions back on people of eighteenth century England to say that people back then routinely 'had someone in their prayers?' I mean, it's just like the addition of 'under God' to the Pledge to the Flag in the 1950s. It's more a reflection of recent popular American views of Christian tradition than a sign of the customs from centuries ago in England, right?"

"I think we would probably have to check into some research on customs of the times, and maybe look at some letters from that time period," said Katherine. "But since we are dissecting this sentence so meticulously, I guess I would agree with you, Ross, that there is something odd in Lydia writing that Edward prayed for Handel every night. If Handel had asked Edward to pray for him—as a clergyman—that would be one thing. But an Anglican priest offering an intercessory prayer for someone would have done so in a more formal way. Lydia's report that Edward remembered Handel nightly in his prayers suggests that Edward himself had reason to be concerned on Handel's behalf. Maybe he had confessed something to Edward, or maybe Edward had confronted Handel about some behavior or failing that might keep him from attaining heaven. I guess I would agree that we have a special case here. Edward is a clergyman. His prayers—or at least Lydia's report that he has offered prayers—would be more significant than prayers by the man on the street. So, Ross, just what do you think was behind Lydia's seemingly innocent comment?"

"That's just it, isn't it?" said Ross. "Lydia's comment isn't innocent. She may have known exactly what it was that Edward felt he needed to pray about, but she didn't dare indicate to Handel that she knew—since that would suggest a betrayal of trust. Priests are supposed to hear confessions in confidence—just as psychologists do. Or, if it was simply something Edward had learned from interacting with Handel—maybe an iconoclastic belief or moral lapse—then Edward surely should not have discussed it with Lydia. And maybe he didn't. But she may have guessed something was wrong and felt it best to let Handel know that Edward had hoped to intercede on his behalf, whether he wanted him to or not."

"Out with it, Ross," said Clara. "You've got a bee in your bonnet—or a burr up your butt—sorry for the language, Forella. It's obvious you have some plot already in mind here. What's the story?"

Ross laughed. "Whoa, it's that obvious, is it? All right, all right, I'll admit there is a backstory. So, on my most recent trip overseas, along with watching our two videos on the plane, I actually stopped in London and checked out my favorite bookstore—and found a surprise for us all. A brand new—BRAND NEW—book on Handel had just been released." Ross held up a large hardback book with four pictures of Handel in variously colored wigs on the book's jacket. "My method of research almost never involves reading entire books, especially not huge books like this one. I will admit that I am one of those ne'er-do-wells who skip to the back of a book in hopes of getting the gist of what the writer says. I figured some of you academic types would plough through the whole thing, but I read the Conclusion—a mere fifteen pages. You will be glad to know that the author is our friend David Hunter who wrote the article on Handel's battle with lead poisoning. Remember? Rebecca, you shared that piece with us some time ago. Anyway, his last chapter in this book had a real bombshell. I almost hate to convey the spoiler here. Maybe I shouldn't."

Katherine, who was seated closest, reached for the book. Ross held it up. "Ah, ah," he said, "no grabbing. I'll leave it here on the shelf with our other books. Its title is *The Lives of George Frideric Handel*, by David Hunter. Ok, ok, here's the scoop. This last chapter started off summarizing what he had evidently written about in the preceding four hundred and some pages. He offered nice little headings, and actually it looked like the research must have been pretty good because the summaries were clear and interesting. But the shocker was a section he titled 'Handel in Love: A Final Fantasy.' I have to meet this guy. He took his cue from Marc Norman and Tom Stoppard's *Shakespeare in Love* and created a plausible but still fanciful love story for our long-suffering unmarried Mister Handel. And who do you suppose the love interest was? --No, Brad, it's not some woman named Lydia. No, it is—drum roll, please—Queen Caroline, wife of British King George the Second."

Skeptical frowns appeared on every face. Clara snorted, and Peter folded his arms and chuckled. "No way that could have eluded three centuries worth of research," Peter declared. "Who would include such a far-fetched fantasy in an academic work? Is this a vetted publication? A reputable press?"

Ross grinned at everyone's reaction. "I knew I would face a wall of doubters, so I actually looked up the stats on this guy. Widely respected scholar, excellent press. The book hasn't been reviewed yet, but even I could tell it was well-written and meticulously annotated. Ok, so he doesn't offer incontrovertible proof for the scenario he develops. That's why he calls it a 'fantasy.' But his discussion makes the plot seem entirely plausible. He points to time periods when Handel and Caroline likely first met. He outlines Caroline's marriage arrangements—which, according to Hunter, likely frustrated Handel no end, as Caroline was destined to marry royalty, not a commoner like Handel. And, he even speculates on Handel's sojourn to Italy as an unnecessary choice less reflective of a need for further learning than simply the actions of a man suffering from a broken heart. I'm not doing it justice here, but really it is quite convincing. I leave it to each of you to read it and form your own opinion."

"Dibs on that," said Peter. "You could have at least clued me in on it earlier. I love a good mystery. But I suppose I'll have to fight a few others for the right to read first. Is it online yet? They're usually pretty quick."

"Well, I'll be happy to sit tight and read it later, or maybe even skip it altogether," said CD. "People with all the credentials in the world can still be seduced by their own daydreams. I was as eager as anyone to believe that scholars had determined Handel was gay—maybe more eager than most. But without real evidence, it's all just someone's speculation and very able storytelling finding its way into the realms of scholarship. But, in any case, Ross, what made you connect this fantasy with the good Reverend's praying for Handel? I'll have to echo Wait and say that I don't see the connection."

"It's true," Ross responded, "that a mere unrequited love scenario and lifelong obsession would not qualify as excuses for Edward's worry over Handel's soul. For one thing, Queen Caroline had died years before—a decade before, so Handel could no longer be accused of coveting his neighbor's—or his king's—wife. No, my suspicion is that our Reverend Grayston knew that Handel had in fact acted on his longing and attachment years before, back when he and Caroline were young. And—not done yet—and—I think Handel had confessed to Edward that one of Caroline's children was, in fact, his, not King George's. Princess Anne, to be precise—his favorite."

A general guffaw of disbelief greeted this theory. Brad whistled and said, "Give the man the cup. Best whopper I've heard today!" Katherine simply looked at Ross and smiled. "You actually believe this, don't you?" she said. "What makes you say so? Surely people would have known."

"They had no DNA tests back then," Ross reasoned, "and, besides, there is plenty of evidence for Caroline's fondness for Handel. History tells us that King George had mistresses, and no one seemed to worry much over that. Maybe Caroline thought she deserved a lover as well. I don't know. Read Hunter's book and see if the possibility doesn't seem more likely after you have in mind some of the information the author includes. Granted, Hunter simply argues that Handel was in love with Caroline. He doesn't speculate beyond that. But, for me, a secret affair and a resultant love child make Edward's concerns about Handel—his need to intercede with God on Handel's behalf—more understandable. And Handel takes a real interest in Princess Anne. He even writes the anthem for her wedding to the Prince of Orange and visits Anne and her husband in the Netherlands. I think he loved Queen Caroline and saw in Anne the fruit of their love—as would any father. But, that wouldn't stop him from feeling guilty. I imagine his religious upbringing tore at him as he contemplated the sin of adultery. Could Reverend Grayston grant Handel absolution if he had never confessed publicly? I suppose that is something between a priest and his parishioner. Beyond my expertise."

This time, Peter and Katherine exchanged a look. "Still seems farfetched, to me," said Peter, "but I'll let Katherine fill us in after she peruses your source. I don't have time to read the book right now, anyway. But, hey, stranger things have turned out to be true. And let's admit it. We've all been hoping Handel would have some sort of love life—more than just the fantasies he celebrates on stage. But still, Ross, my friend, you know this scenario probably says more about you than about Handel. Freud isn't always wrong, you know."

Katherine took the book from the shelf where Ross had placed it. "I look forward to reading this. If anyone else wants it before our next meeting, let me know, or let Angela know, and I'll try to hurry along with the reading. Well, quite a new development. Thanks, Ross, for keeping us in mind as you traveled. Forella, do you have any thoughts or comments before we disperse?"

Forella laughed lightly. "My son is such a storyteller. But, I like it, Ross. I like it." She laughed again and then went on, "I have another DVD to send home with each of you. It sounds like everyone is quite busy these days, but I hope you find time to watch this one. The singing was lovely to me when I heard it, but I will have to admit that Angela said it was too long and, well, boring. Still, our talented countertenor David Daniels is in this production. It is one of the last pieces Handel wrote—*Theodora*. Even though it is an oratorio about early Christianity in Roman times, this performance is set in modern America, according to Angela. I will be interested to hear your thoughts on it. And—Katherine, I too will be waiting to hear your response to Ross's bit of guesswork. Our next meeting should surely be a spirited one."

"Indeed, it shall," said Katherine. "Thanks, Forella, for keeping us supplied with Handel performances. This looks intriguing. See you all next time."

CHAPTER 21

Art and Artifacts

Katherine carried *The Lives of George Frideric Handel* with her as she boarded the plane for a folklore conference in Los Angeles. Fortunately, well over a month earlier, she had finished writing the paper she would be presenting at the conference and had long since sent it off to the chair of her paper session. As a consequence, she had had time to read a little of the Handel tome each night and was already three quarters of the way through the book even before arriving at the airport, taking her seat on the direct flight to LA, ordering a glass of wine, and re-immersing herself in the treatise as the plane rose above the clouds. She finished the book before the end of her return flight and sat thinking of Hunter's love story fantasy and Ross's even more fanciful extension of the plot. She was intrigued, but even more, she was impressed with the scholarship that came before the—there's no denying it—well-argued fantasy. She wondered what would inspire a writer to spend more than ten years, as this man had, tracking down scattered obscure resources and minutely examining countless published texts simply to be able to produce yet another Handel biography. And yet, and yet, something inside her resonated with that scholarly passion, that drive to know and share whatever might be learned of a legendary individual's life. It was, after all, a wonderful thing.

A BABBLE OF SCATTERED DISCOURSE challenged Benfey and her recording equipment at the next Seminar meeting. Everyone seemed eager to voice an opinion on Ross's speculation about Handel, Queen Caroline, and her daughter. Finally, as everyone grabbed a plate of food and found a seat, Katherine called the meeting to order and, with an amused smile, suggested that it might be good for all present to get their conflicting theories out on the table. She looked over at Ross and said, "Would you like to remind us what your hypothesis was, Ross—assuming you haven't changed your mind in the interim?"

"No, no," said Ross, stabbing his fork into a meatball, "I still see the likelihood of Handel and Caroline having an affair when they were both young, and Princess Anne being Handel's daughter. Why else would he agree to be Music Master to Anne and her sisters? They say he hated teaching. I'll stick with my story."

Brad chortled, "Why else? For money, moola, filthy lucre. He was PAID to teach the royal princesses—and probably well paid at that. I think both you AND the author of this new biography are dead wrong about who Handel's great love interest is. I still think it is Lydia, and I wouldn't be surprised if Lydia's husband knew about Handel's obsession with his wife and, being the good reverend that he was, he prayed for Handel's soul. Gets him in good with God, you see. Ok, ok, I'm just being cynical. But I still think it is Handel and Lydia sitting in a tree, not Handel and Caroline."

"What's this sitting in a tree thing?" said Clara. Katherine and Brad both laughed. "It's a kid's rhyme," said Brad, "for razzing guys who get interested in girls. You know, 'Brad and Clara, sitting in a tree, K-I-S-S-I-N-G. First comes love, then comes marriage, then comes Clara with a baby carriage.' It was a big hit in the fourth grade. I was a target even way back then. Anyway, I think it is Lydia that Handel is mooning over, not Caroline."

Clara grimaced, shrugged, and shook her head. "I'm staying out of this guessing game, if you don't mind. There is no evidence for any of this," she said. Rayette nodded in agreement. "I think Peter had the right idea," said Rayette. "Our notions on Handel's love life say more about us than about Handel, or Lydia."

"Well," said Alison, "I still think Handel never outgrew his early fascination with opera divas. Even Lydia remarked on his tendency to let his own music work its magic on his emotions. Didn't George the Third say Handel was always carrying on with his female singers? I think he liked being an unattached bachelor with the option to become involved with his latest star—like a lot of Hollywood producers do today, married or not."

"If we are going to toss into the ring whatever strikes our fancy," said CD, "let me go back even further than Handel's supposed love affair with Vittoria Tarquini and his various singers through the years. How about this scenario? Handel was actually in love with Georg Philipp Telemann, whom Handel had met even before leaving Halle. However, Telemann did not return Handel's ardent affection and, in fact, made a career move to Leipzig, perhaps never knowing that Handel secretly pined for something more than a passing friendship with his much-admired friend and fellow musician. It makes as much sense to me as having Handel languishing ever after over Queen Caroline."

Rebecca returned to the table with a cup of coffee. "I'm willing to entertain the idea that Handel had a secret yearning for Queen Caroline," she said, "but I don't think she would have had the freedom to engage in any intimacies with Handel, even if she wanted to. Women were much more restricted in what they could do on their own both before and after marriage, especially women in the upper classes. If we are still fishing for something Handel may have confessed to Edward—some behavior of which he might have been ashamed—well, I would suggest maybe he was inappropriately friendly with Princess Anne during some of those music lessons. It wouldn't surprise me to learn that Anne had a crush on her music teacher. Maybe Handel had a hard time resisting the temptation to encourage her adolescent infatuation."

Wait popped a mint into his mouth and said, "I think Edward Grayston was just remembering his friend Handel in his prayers—because he was ill and maybe, too, because Handel was a man who, for all his success as a musician and composer, never knew the joys and benefits of marriage. I don't think you can read anything more into it than that."

Katherine looked around to see if anyone else wanted to speak up. "Forella, did you want to hypothesize along with the rest of us?" she asked. "Not at all," said Forella. "I will keep hoping the letters might reveal something more solid so we won't have to speculate. It's always possible."

"Yes, we need to move along to whatever Peter has for us today," said Katherine. "Before we do that, however, let me say that I do think David Hunter—our author of this new biography—made a good case for his 'Final Fantasy,' as he called it. Since our last meeting, I actually took the time to read the entire book—all five hundred pages—including the 'Conclusion' Ross skimmed with the aim of informing his own even more robust fantasy. It was an exceptionally well-researched and well-written study. He saves his suppositions for the very end, and he doesn't insist that any of his suggestions have the necessary evidence that solid historical assertions require. But he presents persuasively the bits of information that he used to formulate his theory, and all he really argues is that Handel likely fell in love with the unattainable Caroline of Ansbach from the moment he met her, when he was a visitor to Berlin, at age seventeen. I found Hunter's reasoning convincing. Like him, I see our unlucky Mr. Handel accepting with much sorrow the fact that he would never be able to marry the woman he loved. And he probably resented the power of the class hierarchy that prohibited his even trying to win her hand. He and Caroline did indeed have a warm relationship for the rest of Caroline's life, but it was never the romantic one that Handel probably wanted. He may have confided in Edward Grayston. He may have even told Lydia. Or, they may have guessed. In any case, it seems reasonable to me that Handel may well have chosen to remain a bachelor rather than ever marry anyone other than his beloved, his princess and queen, Caroline."

"So," Katherine went on, "we've all had the chance to fantasize a bit. But back to the task at hand. What do you have for us today, Peter? Anything that quashes our speculations right off the bat?"

"No, I don't think so," said Peter. "I have two letters. Neither speaks to Handel's amours—real or fanciful. It seems Lydia hadn't written for a while. Here is what I have."

The text of Lydia's first letter:

Mr. G F Handel, Esqr
Brook Street, near Hanover Square
London

12 May 1750

My Dear Mr Handel,
The Spring air has inspired a renewed interest in diversions here in the City. I am sorry that my return to customary activities has taken so long. I especially appreciate your inviting me to the Messiah rehearsal at Brook Street and the opportunity to view the wonderful new landscape painting now mounted in your music room. That canvas and so many of the others you have purchased over the last few years—all reflect so well upon your taste and clear enjoyment of beauty, whether natural or created by people of talent and skill. I know the quest for such paintings stirs your sense of adventure and brings a recurring pleasure, not only with each purchase but also as you absorb their deeper messages when viewed in the changing hue of each new day. And yet, you have, I hope, forgiven my chiding comment on the mythical portraiture hidden away in the antechamber. Well I know that fashion allows these scarcely clad figures to be on display with no disgrace, and much acclaim for their striking representation. But, my dear Gif, would not your mother rush from the room, ashamed for her grown-up son? I am not such a prude as to condemn the painting or its beguiling subject, and yet, I cannot help but blush to view it with you or other gentlemen standing by. I must count it a boon, I suppose, that the painting is kept hidden away from company. Your own private delight. Ah, my dear Gif.

Still, I am pleased to see you so absorbed in the pursuit of fine pieces of art, and all the while you are composing an anthem for the Foundling Hospital and a new oratorio on Theodora. You are a wonder, Gif—ever engaged with the world around you. I take courage from your good example. Eggy would have thanked you as well. He was especially proud of your interest in improving the lives of our unfortunate foundlings. Think of my dear Edward when you play that anthem honoring those who care for the disadvantaged. He would have smiled so happily at your generosity.

    I have, in recent days, found more time to spend with Susannah and her young daughters. I make the trip to West Woodhay when they are in the country and when travel is not too difficult. But I must admit that it is lovely to be here in the City with my nephew and his growing family. Samuel extends an invitation and says he would be honored if you find time in the warmer days ahead to stop by the Square. It is not far, and I would so enjoy a visit with you. I was sorry to hear that Theodora was poorly attended. Friends have said they feared to be confined at Covent Garden with the earth quaking so only a month before. The Reverend Mr Morell worked assiduously on the libretto, I know, as did you on the composition. I wish I could have come to hear it, but I wrongly hoped to attend at a later date. Please consider offering it again. I understand from Susannah that the story is one of conscience and self-sacrifice. Such ideas have occupied your mind very much of late. Eggy is no longer here to listen as you ponder these deep thoughts, but I am. I wish you were more given to writing letters, but I know you are not. Please do stop by and enjoy a beaker of wine with Samuel and his family while I am still in town. I miss our fine repartee. Stay well, my friend.

    I have the honor to be, ever yours,

Mrs. Edward Grayston
In care of Mr Samuel Smyth
Berkeley Square, London

And the second letter:

Mr. G F Handel, Esqr
Brook Street, near Hanover Square
London

16 July 1750

My Dear Mr Handel,
I send this short note to convey Susannah's wishes for your good health and to inform you that she now has the dearest little boy. I am so pleased to be here while summer breezes welcome a sweet new little one to this country home and my other surrogate family. We were all hoping you might be traveling to Bath and stop here along the way. But the news is that you are occupied, these few weeks before leaving for the Continent next month, in composing music for a short poetic piece on Hercules and his epic choice between pleasure and virtue—surely a crowded summer. We shall miss you. I did so enjoy seeing you at Samuel's house in the city. I hope your travels go well.

You left me with a most intriguing question as you bid us farewell and returned to Brook Street. Samuel was correct in saying that his mother—my sister, Mary—and I were not alike. She delighted in parties, plays, and dances—a warm and sociable soul. Was I more quiet and bookish simply because I was older? I do not think that is the reason. The truth is, Gif, I was attracted to solitude and learning even as a very young child. My father was early on immersed in philosophy and the writings of John Locke, and, while these ideas were in part the reason he chose to offer classes for boys in addition to his duties at church, he also thought it only fair to teach his daughter right along with his male pupils. I was not allowed to attend Oxford, of course, but my father was such a fine teacher that I acquired a strong habit of study and pleasure in learning well before I married. It was through my father's tutorials that I met Edward. And dear Edward, like you, always accepted my thirst for knowledge and fondness for converse as part of my humanity, not as deplorable stains upon my femininity. I thank you for asking, Gif. I am amused that these many years have passed without your wondering aloud why I am so often outspoken. But, in that respect at least, you are such a gentleman. Please be safe on your travels. It must be hard to visit your home now with nearly all your dear ones gone. My good wishes to your godchild. She must now be grown into a lovely woman and a credit to your sadly departed sister and your brother-in-law.

Awaiting your safe return, I have the honor to be, ever yours,

Mrs. Edward Grayston
Sloper Manor
West Woodhay, Berkshire

Katherine walked over to the flip chart set up near the buffet. "There seem to me a real variety of potential topics here. Who would like to name a subject for discussion today? Yes, Brad, what caught your attention?"

"Caught my attention?" said Brad. "She as good as said Handel had a bit of eighteenth-century pornography hidden away in his back room. Sure, she commented on his tame and proper landscape painting, too, but even she was taken aback by what must have been a voluptuous nude— justified as depicting a goddess. How many people have naked ladies framed on their walls? At least today it's all on internet sites. Anyway, I guess my question is: Why does Handel have this artwork on his walls, especially the mythological nude? Lydia said she found it embarrassing. Was this Handel's attempt at decorating a bachelor pad?"

Ross and Peter laughed. Katherine shook her head and wrote HANDEL'S PAINTINGS on the flip chart. "Any other topics?" she asked.

Rebecca picked up the second letter again and said, "I was pleased to see Lydia commenting directly on her exceptional education and interest in learning. Evidently her comment was in response to a question from

Handel. He, too, must have felt that her affinity for intellectual topics was unusual in a woman—enough so that he finally asked why she differed from other women in that way. I suppose my question has to do with WOMEN AND EDUCATION." Katherine wrote Rebecca's topic on the chart and asked if there were other suggestions.

"Well, it's not as sexy as a topic, I don't suppose," said Wait, "but I'm interested in knowing more about this Foundling Hospital anthem that Handel composed. Lydia hints that this is for some sort of nonprofit or something and that Handel supported it by writing this anthem. I'm not even sure I know what a Foundling Hospital would be. And why was Handel writing an anthem for them? I guess you can just list this as HANDEL'S FOUNDLING HOSPITAL ANTHEM. I think we have mentioned the Foundling Hospital before, but I'm hoping someone will have more information on the subject."

"Thank you, Wait," said Katherine. "We'll be sure to save time for that topic. Meanwhile, back to Brad and his worry over Handel's questionable taste in art. Brad?"

"Nah, nah, Lydia was worried about Handel's art, not me," said Brad. "I'll admit I've never been one to decorate with anything other than photographs of places I've been. Maybe an old show poster or two. But Handel—well, granted this was before photography—but it sounds like he had this painting of a nude woman on his wall. So, of course I've seen lots of nudes in art museums. I'm not some rube who finds this a shocking piece of news. But this was at his home, where he often entertained guests, it seems. I mean, if I had a painting of a nude on MY wall—no matter how artistic or old—well, people would consider me a bit perverse, don't you think? Lydia certainly thought the painting was something to 'chide' him about, as she said. I'm just curious what anyone else thought about her comment."

Peter laughed. "Yep, museums save many people from the shame of being cast as perverts simply because they have a taste for artistically rendered nudes. But what you have to be aware of here is the time period. In the century before Handel's visit to Italy and then his residence in

London, the whole tradition of collecting objects—but particularly art—burgeoned among the European elites. It was a kind of investment, of course, but it was also a statement about the collector's taste and erudition. Several of Handel's friends were noted collectors of art—Lord Burlington, Charles Jennens, and of course the royals. The most prized pieces of art were ones that depicted historical or mythical scenes. I remember reading an article in a British periodical called *Early Music* in which the author listed the works of art that were auctioned off after Handel's death. Most of the pieces were what you might expect, but there were also a few that the author listed as erotica, including one of Venus and Cupid by an Italian painter. That might be the one that brought a blush to the cheeks of our Lydia. I think it was probably expected that revealing paintings like that one would be kept in private rooms or maybe covered with a curtain when guests visit. What do you think, Brad? Was Handel a forerunner of modern day internet porn consumers?"

"I just asked the question," said Brad. "But, since you put it that way, let me say this. We have this notion that earlier time periods were staid and proper and that decency and morals have gone out the window ever since the 1920s—you know, the jazz age, flappers, and all that. Complete nonsense! If I try to imagine myself in Handel's shoes—you know, a man who isn't married but has money to spend on expensive paintings—wouldn't I want to have a couple of pictures of lovely naked women to look at, especially if everyone thought it was ok to have such paintings, maybe even a sign of good taste? And I don't think it is a matter of Handel compensating for not having sex with real women or anything like that. I've liked looking at pictures of naked women ever since I was twelve years old. Besides, I still think Handel had a thing for Lydia. It's no different than sharing an erotic video with a date. Some people really get off on that sort of thing. Why else would Handel have 'let' Lydia see the painting hidden away in the other room? And why would she have commented on it? Sexy pictures make people think of sex—nothing shocking about that."

"I'm inclined to agree with Brad," said CD, "at least with his argument that Handel made the most of eighteenth century views on art. If friends and colleagues consider it a sign that you are one of the sophisticated gentry, then having a few paintings depicting Renaissance-style mythical nudes would be de rigueur. And Handel must have seen Michelangelo's David when he was in Florence. It was Victorian England that turned artistic nudes into pornography. Handel's London was probably more accepting, especially as the subjects were heroic figures or a goddess like Venus. Robert Maplethorpe, in our era, had more trouble with his nudes because they were photographs of real people doing sexy things. But, even in Handel's time, it still was likely a bit naughty to view a nude of either sex in mixed company. Handel's painting of Venus was something he shared with his male friends I would guess. Brad may have a point about his allowing Lydia to see it. He may have wanted to spark an erotic response along with showing off his evolving taste in fine art."

"I don't know," said Ross. "I think we can pull up what we know about Handel's character and let that guide us in our little imaginary tour of his personal art collection. First, think of the things he collected—mostly music, and then later in his life, art. He didn't seem to have a large library of books—beyond the many music manuscripts and libretti. He did, evidently, like to collect good wines—though he consumed them rather than saving them as a kind of investment. So, collecting art was the primary hobby not connected directly with his professional life as a musician. Still, these various collectibles—music, art, wine—and maybe food—he clearly relished good cuisine—these things all reflected his highly developed esthetic sense. You might even argue that he collected languages—particularly the sounds of poetry. So, the works of art that he purchased did, first and foremost, bring him pleasure."

"Second," Ross went on, "Handel was clearly eager to participate in the world of the English gentry, and that involved being knowledgeable about good art and, in fact, supporting the arts by spending money in an obvious and public way. He was eager to show off his new paintings to Lydia and his other guests. In effect, it won him points among the aristocracy. And, finally, try to imagine yourself in that time period—before television, before photography, certainly well before the internet or even the copy machine. You would have to rely upon your imagination for the pictures that accompany the stories you hear. Never forget that Handel was a storyteller. Operas, with their colorful stories and their props and staging, were his first love. I think paintings, lithographs, prints, sculptures—all of the artistic media of the times—all were prized by this man who delighted in stories and relished any well-wrought piece of art that evoked the same feelings he hoped to convey through his music."

Rebecca nodded toward Ross. "I think you are right," she said, "but I wish we knew more about his early education—well, besides his music instruction with Zachow in Halle. I suspect that he did learn the basic history of Western art as a young boy, even before visiting Italy, the cradle of Renaissance art. He surely knew the ancient tradition of Greek art, with their idealized nude art figures. Even though the gymnasium that Handel attended probably was under the Lutheran church, I do not think the stereotype of a more Puritanical view of art—especially the view that art involving naked bodies is somehow sinful—can be associated with his early education. He probably had a fairly sophisticated appreciation for fine art. Wealthy young men on their grand tours of Europe were expected to visit the cathedrals and palaces that housed pieces of fine art. Handel was fortunate, as a young man, to spend four years in Italy, living among the wealthiest patrons of the arts. He must have been immersed in great art—naked or not—from day one."

"I wouldn't mind seeing that article you mentioned, Peter," said Rayette, "the one that listed all the paintings they think Handel had in his house at the time of his death. No doubt some of them were of places or people that figure in his operas or oratorios. But I also think Brad had a good point—especially about the nudes. Maybe the pictures did in fact remind Handel of women or a woman he loved. He was the one who bought the paintings, after all, and he had them mounted on his walls. Art can be a very personal statement—whether you are the creator of the art or the purchaser. And let us be honest—it is quite a different thing to stand alone, looking at a naked human body—quite different than it would be to view that body or painting with a group of people, no matter what the context. Maybe Handel remembered or imagined romantic, erotic scenes as he stood alone, contemplating his painting of Venus. Art and poetry can be very individualized, both in creation and in reception. Our discussion of Handel's pictures reminds me of one of my shorter poems. Would you like to hear it?"

"Yes, as always," said Forella, and several others. Rayette smiled and leaned back in her chair. After a second of quiet, she recited:

"Treasures in my heart—things you have said
Memories, floating in a play, words, thoughts, scenes
Poems without song
They bind us together
Yet, even more, I live again your touch,
I taste your skin
I trail the vein of your dear strong arm.
Nothing so fine, nor thrill compares—
Seeing you there in the doorway
Naked but for that warm smile."

Everyone clapped, but Forella the loudest. "I love your poems," she said. "I love hearing you read them, recite them. We should all follow your example. Every experience should inspire a poem or a song. Thank you so much, Rayette. I'll have to listen to Benfey's recording so I can hear it again."

"Yes, thank you, Rayette," said Katherine. "Handel, the art collector—what an interesting topic. I am curious, though, before we move on to the next question—what did you think about the landscape, the painting he had evidently bought only recently, the one he specifically invited his guests to view and enjoy? My guess is that Handel hoped his guests would find it as pleasing, maybe even as inspiring, as he did. The beauty of nature, awe-inspiring scenes—I can imagine Handel surrounding himself with reminders of the wonders of nature just as much as of the great persons and events of history. Again, it is hard to step back into a time before photography, video, or even museums and art galleries, but to me, the appeal of paintings that recall or recreate beautiful scenes in nature might be even stronger than a liking for portraits or depictions of mythical figures. And Handel really enjoyed the outdoors. Biographers and Lydia often mention his walks in Hyde Park, near his Brook Street home. I wish we could know what scene or place Handel's new landscape represented. Peter, did that article you mentioned say anything more specific about this painting that he had bought about the time of Lydia's letter?"

Peter looked over at Angela. "Maybe we should try to bring up that article and take a look at it," he said. "I'm trying to remember what the author—I think his name was McGeary or something like that—what he said about the landscapes that were a part of the auctioned collection. I do recall that there were quite a few landscapes—maybe half of the paintings were landscapes, and there were something like eighty art works listed at auction. In any case, yes, Handel obviously liked landscape paintings. And I think he had quite a few prints and lithographs depicting places as well—maybe not nature so much as places he had visited, or wanted to visit. I'd say he did what Brad says he does to decorate his walls—displayed pictures of places he had visited or thought of as ideal or beautiful. I'll try to look into it a little more."

"Thanks, Peter," said Katherine. "I'm remembering Clara's comment from many meetings ago, when she said that she needed to envision Handel's life through some sort of cinema. The pictures that decorated Handel's walls would help me in that same way, I think. Now I am trying to remember whether the Handel House in London had many landscapes as a kind of re-creation of his house for visitors today. A reason to visit again, obviously. Ok, on to our next question. Rebecca, I think you suggested the next topic."

"Yes, women and education," said Rebecca. "Actually, my question is about both. I'm interested in how the content and process of education has evolved over the years. But, of course, the truth is that women have often been discouraged—in fact prohibited—from getting an education, or at least one similar to that offered males. I was certainly struck by Lydia's comment about her father—his determination to give his daughter the same education he offered boys. She doesn't say how old she was when she 'sat in' on the lessons intended for the boys her father taught. Even wealthy families assumed that the basic learning provided by governesses was enough for both boys and girls up to a certain age, but before heading to universities, boys were taught by tutors—men, not women, who would prepare them for the kind of advanced learning the world of men required. I would guess it was a breach of the religious code to presume to teach a girl the same curriculum as a boy. On the other hand, it seems that Lydia herself was part of the motivation for doing so. Her father must have recognized that she had a keen mind and wanted to learn more than the usual fundamentals. Lydia's intellectual curiosity must have been readily apparent even as she reached adulthood. Otherwise, why would Handel have asked about her 'outspokenness,' as she called it?"

"Hmm, yes," said Katherine, "that word 'outspokenness' seems to be a euphemism both Handel and Lydia used to describe her presumption in voicing her own opinions or entering into an intellectual dialogue. Clearly, both of them knew such candor and signs of learning were not considered desirable character traits in a proper upper-class lady in eighteenth century England. And yet Lydia was aware of Handel's somewhat amused acceptance of this aspect of her character—her tendency to speak her mind freely, as would a man. He must have commented on it, not as a reproach, but rather as a friendly, even admiring, observation on her behavior."

Peter stood up and walked over to the shelf that held the collection of books the Handel Seminar deemed useful to their enterprise. From it he lifted a large book—*Benjamin Franklin: An American Life*, by Walter Isaacson. "I donated this volume to our little library some time ago," he said. "My thought was that this biography of Franklin might be useful in shedding light on Handel's era. They were contemporaries, though Franklin was twenty years younger than Handel, and Franklin did spend some time in London—was actually there yet in 1759, when Handel died.

I enjoyed reading Isaacson's book, and one of the many bits of information about Franklin that kept haunting me as I have been working with these letters from Lydia to Handel was Franklin's abiding appreciation for charming, witty, intelligent women. According to Isaacson, Franklin, especially while in Europe, had many intimate—though not necessarily sexual—relationships with women, and almost all of these women were clever, charming, and full of good humor. The implication—at least in this biography of Franklin—is that even back then, there were indeed a good number of women who were intelligent and entertaining enough to interest a man like Franklin. Isaacson pulls out for his readers various bits of correspondence between Franklin and some of these women. The women's letters were flirtatious, well written, and brimming with confidence. To me, the letters suggest that Franklin was attracted to women who were bright and independent. Can a person—man or woman—be bright and independent without at least some education--some knowledge and guided inquisitiveness?"

Clara and Rebecca both started to comment. Rebecca waved a hand indicating that Clara should speak first as she hadn't spoken yet. "Thanks," said Clara. "I would be the first to tout the advantages of education, but there were plenty of men in the eighteenth century who had little formal education and yet managed, for example, to make important scientific contributions. To me, the interesting thing about Lydia's remarks is that it was Lydia herself who developed a passion for learning. Her father made it possible for her to get some of the formal training young men did, but she clearly wanted to learn. Evidently her sister did not. I think Lydia's 'outspokenness' was simply a tendency to pursue what she knew she wanted—whether it was an education or a good conversation with friends. She obviously enjoyed her discussions with Susannah Cibber—another independent and bright woman."

Rebecca nodded toward Clara. "Yes, I think Lydia was naturally bright," she said, "and I think we are talking about something more than simply what kinds of education were available to women in eighteenth century England. I will admit that I have always been baffled by the notion that intelligent men would not prefer intelligent women as mates or even paramours. From what Peter has said about this writer's views on Benjamin Franklin, we might conclude that Franklin was someone who wanted to be entertained, intrigued, maybe even challenged by a woman. It is possible that our Mr. Handel was very much like that—though I think Lydia was not so much flirtatious as she was simply straightforwardly friendly and affectionate. But Handel did seem to relish Lydia's pluck. Did she gain that boldness by interacting with the boys her father tutored? Perhaps. Edward, at least, must have found Lydia's ability to hold her own among a bunch of males impressive enough to attract his interest. But, even so, that doesn't speak to my question about women and education. I would still like to know whether Lydia had a general education similar to that Handel himself had acquired—since he did not really pursue a degree. What would she have learned as a young girl, even in this unusual situation? What kind of education did she have?"

"I think we make the mistake of equating education with schooling," said Alison. "Back then, among the elite, learning—especially learning to play an instrument, or read music, or even to write or speak in French—this kind of learning was acquired through private, in-house teaching by a governess. Young women could, in fact, become quite accomplished and know just as much as young men would know if they had a good teacher. The sad thing is, as Lydia wrote, women were not allowed to work with a tutor or go on to college or university. But, if they were sharp and applied themselves, they could be well educated by the time they were ready to 'come out' in society and find a husband. I recall from my studies of early music that there were quite a few women who not only played musical instruments and sang but also composed music and could discourse at length about music theory and counterpoint, just as Handel did. But, these women were, in general, not really allowed to move much beyond the drawing room. Lydia's friend Susannah Cibber is an exception, it seems. In any case, I would argue that some of these bright young women were fairly well educated even if they did not go on to acquire any formal schooling."

"It wasn't fair, of course," said Ross, "that women were not allowed to have formal schooling. But think of it this way—most of the men who were educated at places like Oxford or Cambridge went on to become clergymen of one sort or another. I think the women got the better deal. They had the option of simply learning for learning's sake. Marry a man like Edward Grayston and you can spend your time reading, writing, and conversing with visiting maestros. Lydia's papa probably realized that he could set his daughter up for a life of leisurely learning if he connected her with one of his aspiring young churchmen. I'd say he succeeded."

Katherine looked around to see if anyone else wanted to speak. She hesitated, thinking it might just be better to go on to the next topic, but then she turned to the shelf and the copy of Isaacson's biography of Franklin, which Peter had brought to everyone's attention a short time earlier. "We think of Franklin as a self-made man," she said, "but no one ever speaks of a 'self-made woman.' Why is that? A self-made man starts out poor or lacking in connections or privilege and then, through his own efforts and intelligence, manages to rise in the world and make something of himself. But there is one privilege he is born with that his sisters do not have—male privilege. And male privilege, or the accepted value of the patriarchy, is a subtle part of an individual's personal education that no woman is ever going to be allowed to grow into and benefit from, no matter how much learning and talent she demonstrates. Lydia Grayston probably learned all of the academic subject matter her father taught the boys he tutored. But she also learned the worldview, the unspoken traditions of a patriarchal culture, that she and her fellow scholars were taught inadvertently with every text and every behavior encountered in the classroom and in life."

Placing the Franklin biography back on the shelf, Katherine continued, "I think Rebecca's question about women and education leads to answers much more complex than simply a survey of what kind of learning was available to girls in Handel's time. As Alison reminded us, women could become fairly well educated if they had good teachers, and, after all, Handel himself dropped out of college. It was less a matter of what knowledge an individual had acquired before reaching adulthood than it was a matter of what that individual was allowed to do with that knowledge. In a funny way, both Handel and Lydia knew that women could be smart and talented, knew that a woman being 'outspoken' was simply a sign that the woman chose to use her intelligence and interact in the world just as men did. But perhaps Lydia recognized, in a way that Handel did not, that there was a strong moral proscription against women presuming to be equal to men. The Church, the culture, even governesses and mothers taught little boys and little girls to regard men as superior to women. And Lydia had no Susan B. Anthony or Margaret Fuller or Elizabeth Cady Stanton—or even John Stuart Mill—to inspire her nascent feminism. No, she had only her own internal conviction that she was estimable in the same way that a man would be—even though her culture taught her otherwise. Perhaps her father was, after all, the prod that moved Lydia along the path toward a world in which men and women could converse as equals. And perhaps Handel, unawares, encouraged her as well simply by accepting her as she was. Even Lydia seemed amused that he had taken so long to 'notice' that she was more 'outspoken' than her female compatriots."

As Katherine turned toward the flip chart, preparing to go on to the next topic, Clara cleared her throat and said, "I don't like bringing my own personal history into our discussion, but I will share my thoughts about this particular issue. Actually, I'd like to go back to something I mentioned earlier—that there were plenty of men in eighteenth-century England who managed to become accomplished scientists despite a lack of wealth and connections. We like to think that now even for women those hurdles have been removed. In modern America, anyone—man or woman, rich or poor, black, brown, or white, Christian or not—anyone can pull himself or herself up by the bootstraps, gain an education, and be successful. I was educated through some of the best schools in America, but I was very aware, at every turn, of the greater opportunities afforded my male classmates, especially as I moved into the job market and sought funding and supportive lab benefits."

"Furthermore," she continued, "I have witnessed time and again how my female students have been subjected to any number of subtle and not so subtle prejudices as they have tried to enter the profession. Science is still a man's world. Higher education is still dominated by those who carry a worldview steeped in patriarchal perspectives. The hardest lesson for me to learn was that I myself had grown up accepting the idea that my greater struggles, my need to try twice as hard as the men in my profession—that this idea was somehow simply the way life is, natural. I had come to fully accept the notion that I must 'be as much like a man as I can be' if I hoped to succeed as an academic. The egregiousness of this view finally came home to me when I was sweating the absolutely onerous task of preparing my dossier for promotion to full professor. Review committees are required to view all candidates as if on an equal footing. And yet our culture still imposes so many more obstacles on women, on ethnic minorities, and on the economically disadvantaged. Almost everything is set up with a typical white, middle-class male as the standard. Candidates for promotion are asked to write personal statements as part of their files. As I contemplated this statement, I found myself waging an internal battle between one voice that said I had not been as productive as my male colleagues had been and another voice that argued that there were subtle attitudes, prejudices, differing values that time and again gave the advantage to men, not to me. But even I felt like I was simply making excuses. Writing that statement was one of the hardest things I have ever done—mostly because I could not decide which internal voice was correct. Like Lydia, I felt that I had a sense of my own abilities and talent but that I had never really been allowed to play on the same field as the men or on a field that was particularly suited to me as a woman. It was—has always been—extremely frustrating."

Katherine gave a sadly knowing nod toward Clara. "That is not an uncommon response," she said. "I served on the promotions committee for several years. Many women seemed to share that mixed sense of deficiency and yet unfair disadvantage. For what it is worth, I did discover an explanation I found useful—in a book on politics and language of all things. I was consulting George Lakoff's study *Moral Politics* for his exploration of differing worldviews in American politics, and I ran across one chapter in which he discussed what he called 'conservative feminists'—feminists who, despite their liberal feminism, still accept the conservative notion that the individual, not society, is entirely responsible for a person's success or failure. So often the women who were conflicted about their performance as professors did in fact regard themselves as feminists, yet they adopted a conservative stance on how society had treated them. They blamed themselves, not society for their struggles. The criteria for success were always reflective of a template celebrating behavior males saw as most meritorious—an abundance of books and published articles, substantial funding for research projects, awards, and competing job offers. Women's differing values and understanding of success, often including effective teaching, community and university service, along with much more collaborative research—such contributions were undervalued, ignored, or disparaged as weak and second-rate. At least Lakoff gave a name to the sense of ambivalence among these successful women—conservative feminism."

Peter stood up to get a coffee and dessert from the buffet. "Well, things are still bad—no doubt about it," he said. "But if we want to see how much worse things were back in Handel's time, we should move on to our third topic—the Foundling Hospital and the reason Handel felt he needed to compose an anthem for the opening of its chapel. I am familiar with the history of the Foundling Museum, but I think Wait's question was more about why Handel was even involved, why he decided to compose an anthem for them. Isn't that right, Wait?"

"Yes," said Wait. "I guess I know what a foundling is. It's not a word we hear much today. We would speak of an abandoned child or an orphan, I suppose. But was a hospital for abandoned children a common thing back then? And why would Handel be involved? Those of you who know something about the Museum, maybe you could share a little insight here."

Forella waved lightly from her end of the table. "Yes, Forella," said Katherine, "did you want to speak to Wait's question?"

"Angela and I had wondered the same thing," said Forella. "Actually we had wondered about the Foundling Hospital when we saw the title of the anthem he composed for the opening—*Blessed are they that considereth the poor and needy*. I had asked Angela to look ahead in one of the biographies to see what piece we might send home with you this time. Angela is such a good researcher. She discovered that Handel had indeed composed an anthem in honor of those supporting the Foundling Hospital, and, furthermore, she found that this anthem included part of the Hallelujah chorus from *Messiah*. Evidently, *Messiah* wasn't yet so well known that people would have objected. In any case, we have a recording of the anthem, along with the coronation anthems, performed by the Westminster Choir. But, let me ask Angela to share some of her findings with you. Is that something you could do for us, Dear?"

"I'd be happy to," said Angela. "As Forella said, several of the biographies discuss at length Handel's connection with the Foundling Hospital. But what I found most helpful was a recent article from *The Guardian* written by the current Director of the Foundling Museum, Caro Howell. The article is mostly about how *Messiah* came to be associated with the Foundling Hospital, but Ms. Howell also comments on how the hospital was started. Basically, it was less a hospital and more an orphanage for infants born to unmarried or very poor women. The founder was a British sea captain, Thomas Coram, who had spent nearly two decades trying to even get a charter for the project. Handel became a governor of the Hospital and joined artist William Hogarth in donating his talents to help raise funds for the institution. The Foundling Hospital was actually one of the first art galleries in England, and after the dedication of the chapel with his anthem, Handel gave annual charity concerts of *Messiah* in the chapel. He also donated an organ and an orchestra copy of *Messiah* to the Hospital. The argument in this article is that both Handel and Hogarth did benefit from their connections with the Hospital—Handel gaining a venue for what came to be his most famous oratorio and Hogarth a gallery for his paintings and those of other artists of the period. The article skips over the larger issue of why such an institution was needed, but that

The Handel Letters

wasn't the author's intent. I'm assuming maybe some of you who have visited the Museum have some thoughts on that. I know Ross, for one, has been there."

"Yes, indeed," said Ross. "As has Dr. Baker. A memorable chance meeting. A souvenir of that visit is this pamphlet"—Ross walked over to the bookshelf and took from it a small booklet. "As you can see from the cover, this is a book about little objects—tokens. The authors, Janette Bright and Gillian Clark, created this guidebook or, really, exhibition catalogue of some of the artifacts left with infants admitted to the Foundling Hospital. There are many such tokens archived at the London Metropolitan Archives. Each token was cataloged along with the paperwork admitting the children who were brought to the Hospital. Often they were halved tokens—one piece to stay with the child and the other piece to be retained by the child's mother. These identifiers were to be used if the mother ever returned to reclaim the child. Reclaiming children was rare, and, believe it or not, by the end of the 1700s, some 18,500 children had been admitted to the Foundling Hospital. The more precise name for the Hospital was 'The Hospital for the Education and Maintenance of Exposed and Deserted Young Children.' I'll have to admit that I was dismayed by the number of children admitted—and the many, many mothers and children who were turned away. It was an incredible social disgrace. We are so used to our modern system of welfare or safety nets that are at least intended to care for such unfortunate children, and yet, even now, many fall through the cracks. But imagine London in Handel's time—no government recourse for these desperate mothers and their pitiable children. I found the stories of these abandoned children very moving. Somehow, though, the tokens seem so much more substantial than would simply a written entry in a record book—rather like a lock of hair or favorite toy. I can imagine each of those mothers hoping the child would have a better life than she could provide—like Moses set adrift among the bulrushes."

"Yeah, well," said Brad, "at least we are told Moses was given up by his mother because Pharaoh had ordered all male Hebrew babies killed. But why was London in Handel's time overrun with all these poor and illegitimate children? Not to be callous, but weren't people supposed to be more morally upright and worried about the consequences of promiscuity back then? Where were the fathers of these babies? I'm all for people having a good time, but even fraternity yahoos know that you have to accept responsibility if you get a girl pregnant. We all had to read *The Scarlet Letter* back in high school. Shouldn't there have been some way to make the fathers support these kids even if the parents weren't married?"

No one seemed eager to take up Brad's question. Finally CD said, "This is far from my area of expertise, but I think this question oversimplifies the issue. England had 'poor laws' even in Handel's time, and men were jailed for not supporting their children born out of wedlock. It sounds to me like much of the problem with these poor children was just that—they were poor, or rather their parents were poor, completely indigent and incapable of supporting them. As Ross said, we are used to thinking that some governmental agency will provide for unfortunate children. But, really, the sordidness of *Oliver Twist* or *Les Misérables* was a common situation not all that long ago. Remember Lydia's letter in which she worried over Susannah Cibber? The father in this case was a wealthy man and willing to accept responsibility for his illegitimate child, but obviously that was not often the case. I'm not sure that morality was so much the issue as simply poverty. What kind of message did the Foundling Museum present on the question of why the Hospital was necessary in the first place? Ross? Katherine?"

Katherine picked up the thin pamphlet Ross had returned to the shelf. "Sadly," she said, "the tokens left at the Foundling Hospital each suggest a story of a mother too poor to care for her child. Occasionally there were actual letters or reports that detail some of the circumstances under which children were brought to the Hospital. Besides the sad stories, a couple of points caught my attention. One was that the mothers had to prove that they had only that one child out of wedlock—if that were the case. The understanding was these mothers would lead a blameless life thereafter. So, Brad, I guess there we have the morality issue—but no real attention to the fathers. The other thing I noticed was the practice—strictly adhered to—of renaming the children. All children left at the Foundling Hospital began with a clean slate, so to speak—no family connections at all, unless, of course, they were reclaimed by their parents. Interestingly, there was a child—a three-week-old girl named Maria Augusta Handel—left at the hospital in 1758. Her named was changed, and evidently someone did come to claim her in 1763, but no connection is made between our Mr. Handel and the child. I am sure if there were such a relationship, it would go far toward explaining why Handel would have wanted to support the institution, but there does not seem to be any link—nefarious or otherwise—between Handel and the child. I actually researched it a bit because I was intrigued by the possibility, but I found no support for a claim of connection of any sort."

"So, with no tantalizing mystery to provide a motive," Katherine continued, "I would argue that Handel was simply eager to use his influence—as were other wealthy men of the time—to address the sad situation of so many poor and often abandoned children in London. I do not think he saw the Hospital as a lucrative outlet for his music—though it in fact became that some time later. Rather I am persuaded by his biographers who generally insist that he was appalled by the situation, especially after encountering on the streets two miserable children of a former member of his orchestra. In other words, Handel became an activist for a cause about which he felt strongly. His contribution was to use his influence to draw in others who would support the institution as well. My own admiration for Handel is increased especially in light of the more typical response of the times—which was to condemn unwed mothers and shun any appearance of condoning their behavior by seeking to aid their unfortunate children. Thomas Coram and the governors of the Foundling Hospital were, in my opinion, important pioneers in the long history of charities—of needed social assistance. Handel proved himself a good and generous man."

"Hear, hear," said Forella. "I heartily agree, Katherine. And, as I said, I have a CD for each of you with a performance of Handel's anthem composed for the opening of the chapel at the Hospital. *Blessed are they that considereth the poor and needy*—I think the title says it all. I, too admire our Mr. Handel even more for his sympathy and support for these outcast mothers and their unfortunate children. Would that more people emulated his good example."

"Thank you, Forella," said Katherine. "I look forward to hearing this piece—and the coronation anthems. Until we meet again, everyone. Please be safe."

CHAPTER 22

A Small and Treasured Gift

The slab of limestone jutted into the stream almost as though it had been placed there—a hard bench from which to observe the waterfall and the clear ripples eddying around the rock's base. Katherine had brought her sandwich, fresh peach, and water bottle along for this solitary picnic at her favorite spot in nearby McCormick's Creek State Park. She thought of the years and years of water running over rock that had chiseled out this little canyon—then of the much more impressive gorge she had seen in upper New York state, at Watkins Glen near Ithaca. And of course there was the amazing Grand Canyon. Reflection hints at something primeval about such landscapes, even today with roads and paved trails close by and airplanes overhead. She imagined ancient peoples peering out from shaded overhangs. And she thought of Handel and his relish for the wooded paths of Hyde Park, his habit of walking through that small taste of nature in the heart of London. It was, she felt, a warm and welcome connection with a man she scarcely knew except through story.

RAYETTE CARRIED HER DVD OF Handel's *Theodora* with her as everyone gathered for the next Seminar meeting. Even before most were seated, she held up the plastic case with the picture of Dawn Upshaw and David

Daniels singing their anguish at the climax of Handel's oratorio. "We HAVE to talk about this production," she said. "I hadn't had a chance to watch it before our last meeting, but now I have. I found it extremely disturbing. And I—well, I'm sorry—but I shared it with my husband as well. We both thought it was far more unsettling than the usual Handel material. I'm surprised no one else has asked to talk about it."

"Well, it is definitely an updated production and one treated more like an opera than an oratorio," said CD. "And the director is Peter Sellars, so you can expect it to be out of the ordinary to say the least. The subject was a Christian martyrdom, so it is unusual—given that most of Handel's oratorios were based on stories from the Old Testament. I thought the decision to set the story in modern times and an American context was a little iffy, especially since Christianity is the dominant religion in modern America rather than a persecuted sect as it was in the original setting. But here you have this rather familiar looking tyrant ordering the Christian minority to join in the late antiquity Roman religious celebrations or face serious retribution—in the case of Theodora, rape and prostitution unless she agrees to renounce her Christian belief. It's pretty grim, I admit."

Ross walked back from the buffet with a plate of chicken Marsala. "Peter Sellars is an excellent director," he said. "I thought this production was effective in just the way he probably intended. I'm not surprised that you found it disturbing, Rayette. The original libretto was upsetting enough, and Handel did his best to capitalize on that. I suspect that Handel was remembering his Huguenot neighbors back in Halle. Many were forced to flee France when they refused to convert to Catholicism. But Sellars made it even more real for the audience by setting it in modern America. And, truthfully, I thought the tenor—Richard Croft—was outstanding. I think he really captured Handel's message—the heartbreaking injustice of the plot. But what was it you found so disturbing, Rayette? Anything specific, or just the whole production?"

Rayette looked down at the DVD case. "I was caught up in the plight of this small early Christian sect, of course. And, actually, I really do see how that situation has been reversed in some ways today—with other religious groups, such as Muslims, being singled out for a kind of collective mistreatment. But what disturbed me most was the way they executed the two main characters at the end—by lethal injection, just as they really do perform capitol punishment today in America. I categorically don't believe in the death penalty, and seeing exactly how it is carried out was sickening. It was bad enough that they were being punished for what they believe, but execution—and in that slow, methodical way. I thought it made the whole thing extremely painful to watch. I can't even remember whether I liked the music or not. It was just too disturbing."

"Absolutely, absolutely," said Katherine. "And yet, if we didn't KNOW about our supposedly more 'humane' means of execution, that scene would not be nearly so disturbing as are the many more grisly deaths in modern horror cinema. You have to know that the injection will slowly kill the person strapped to the gurney. I think Ross is right—the director probably intended us to really squirm at the hygienic, detached way we execute people in America—especially knowing that sometimes they may actually be innocent. But *Theodora* was disturbing on so many levels. No wonder it was one of Handel's least popular pieces—even in his own time. The legend on which the oratorio is based is not well known—and wasn't even then. In fact, like much in folklore, the story is a mixture of various traditions, stories that circulated primarily in oral form until someone decided to create a written version. The librettist, Thomas Morell, mostly used as his source a kind of early novelistic work by Robert Boyle, titled *The Martyrdom of Theodora and Didymus*. Evidently, someone had recently published a collection of Boyle's writings about the time that Handel was looking for a new plot to share with his oratorio audiences."

"What?!" exclaimed Clara. "Robert Boyle? The scientist? The one who gave us Boyle's law? Why would he be writing a novel about some obscure Christian martyr? I know some of those early scientists were really into Christian theology—look at Newton. But, really, a novel about some unknown martyr? Maybe it was a different Robert Boyle."

"No, no," said Katherine, laughing. "It really was Robert Boyle of Boyle's law, the famous chemist. I looked up a little about the source that Morell used for the oratorio. Boyle had written a book called *The Christian Virtuoso*, and it was republished about the time Handel was developing the oratorio as his new genre. If you dig a little deeper into Boyle's life, you'll see that he refused to swear an oath as required of one becoming president of the Royal Society—thus refusing the invitation to become President of that institution. The situation in the story of Theodora is much more extreme than a required presidential swearing-in ceremony, of course, but still you can see that Boyle had reason to be attracted by the story of a Christian martyr refusing to deny her own beliefs and swear allegiance to the god of the Roman emperor. As Handel and Morell emphasized in the oratorio, the freedom to hold one's own personal beliefs should be protected as a basic human right."

"Should be," said Rebecca, "but is that a protected right—even in America? The interesting thing about this production of Handel's oratorio is that Sellars deliberately confuses our understanding of the dominant and persecuted groups. In the traditional story, Theodora's group is an early Christian sect worshiping in secret but gaining adherents. The tyrant, who insists they worship as he does, is—as were most Roman citizens—a follower of Jove or Jupiter, the highest and most revered Roman god. By switching the time period, the costumes, the means of execution, even the props of folding chairs, canned soda, and TV cameras, Sellars made clear the notion that the dominant culture gets to impose its practices and its religious worldview, and in modern America, that dominant worldview would be Christianity. Do people watching the modern production see contemporary American culture as aggressively imposing its 'Christian' values and beliefs on everyone—just as the prefect in *Theodora* did with his pagan values in fourth-century Antioch? I doubt it, but the message is definitely there."

"Hold on," said Wait. "There's never been a time that Christian beliefs or tenets have been imposed on the American populace. It's in the Constitution—separation of church and state. The religion demanding compliance here was the old pagan belief system, not Christianity, even if the production was set in modern America. I don't think there is any message about Christians forcing their beliefs on anyone. The director just wanted to update the setting; that's all."

Alison turned toward Wait. "I agree with Wait on this," she said. "Sure, you might be reminded of other 'us versus them' encounters—such as the Nazis and Jews during the Holocaust or war protesters during the Vietnam War—but, really, the oratorio is still about the persecution of early Christians, not about any religious oppression in America today." Rebecca picked up Rayette's copy of the DVD. "I'm still convinced that Sellars, as director, wanted to make the drama more widely relevant, more like a piece of epic theater, a kind of parable about our own culture. It is not really a love story. Instead, it is a representation of how dictators try to impose their will on people, and often religion is a convenient system by which to control and persuade people. In Morell's libretto, we see a culture that requires all citizens—not just office holders, but all citizens—to profess belief in the emperor's god. Theodora and her friends refuse, and Roman law allows Valens—the local ruler—to threaten her with rape and imprisonment unless she disavows her contrary beliefs. Didymus respects her refusal to deny her faith, and he tries to save her. They both end up dying as a result. That was an extreme case of oppression, and Theodora is justly celebrated as an early Christian martyr. But because the director recast the story into a modern American context, we can see that the imposition of ANY religious perspective at the expense of personal freedom is abhorrent. And the 'chorus' is seen as complicit when they raise no objection to the tyrant's use of religion to get what he wants. As Wait said, the American Bill of Rights guarantees that 'Congress shall make no law respecting an establishment of religion, or prohibiting the free exercise thereof.' Handel composed *Theodora* forty years before the new American nation established that individual freedom as part of its Constitution. I think Sellars, in updating the oratorio, wanted to draw attention to the way personal freedoms can be undermined by those in power even today, even when the powerful religious perspective is rooted in Christianity rather than a long-forgotten pagan belief system of ancient Rome."

"I don't see it," said Alison. "The Christians are the ones being oppressed, even in the updated version. Where do you see any commentary on supposed coercive tactics in modern Christianity?"

"Ok, consider this," Rebecca replied. "Modern medicine has made it possible for a woman to safely have an abortion, induce a miscarriage, or take a 'morning after pill' as a means of ending a pregnancy or stop it from even becoming an implanted embryo. From my perspective, a woman should have the right to manage her own body and decide whether she wants to bring a new life into the world, and we should be glad that the procedures available for ending a pregnancy are so very safe and reliable. There are many Christians who support a woman's right to choose, many Christians who recognize that bringing a child into some situations might in fact be cruel. Like most people, they do not like the idea of abortion, but they agree that it is a woman's right to decide whether she wants to continue with an unwanted pregnancy. But there are also some Christians who fight against that right at every turn, claiming the primacy of a religious principle that identifies a human soul as present at conception. They fight to impose that belief on everyone. They fight to rescind Roe versus Wade or make it nearly impossible to fulfill its intended function. In effect, anti-abortion activists feel they should be able to tell others what to do and by implication what to believe. It may not seem as stark as the actions Valens took in *Theodora*, but such religiously motivated legislation is nevertheless an instance of a belief system, an ideology, imposed by those in power. As a drama, *Theodora* makes us question our own culture and its imposition of control over personal decisions. I suspect that is why, even in 1750, it was not a popular oratorio for Handel, though the music was as impressive as usual."

"I'm going to glom onto that line about Handel and segue into today's letter," said Peter. "I have only one letter for you this time. Since our last letter, Handel has moved on from the poor reception of *Theodora* and has made a visit to the Continent. It seems he was injured in a carriage accident while traveling. Even back then, with real horsepower rather than the motorized variety, vehicles invited a certain amount of risk. Here are your copies of the letter.

Mr. G F Handel, Esqr
Brook Street, near Hanover Square
London

5 January 1751

My Dear Mr Handel,
Thank you for accepting Samuel's invitation to dinner so soon after your return. We were all most concerned when we learned of the overturned carriage and your injury. Samuel claims that the roads between Haarlem and The Hague are notoriously poor. I am glad you are recovered. Princess Anne must have tended you like a mama cat her kitten, or perhaps as a gentle Cordelia her chastened father. Nevertheless, now that you are back home, I was disappointed to find opportunity for a private tête-à-tête forestalled by eager guests seeking a word with our famous wanderer. Please do come again, when you and I might talk at greater length. I expect to stay with Samuel's family until late in the Spring, when I shall again visit Susannah and Mr Sloper.
 I did overhear your discussion with Mr Reinhold. He seemed much impressed that you had corresponded with our widely admired Mr Telemann. Perhaps I should move back to Hamburg to gain the prize of a letter from you. But our dear Georg rarely gets to see you. I must not be jealous. I have forgotten now whether I ever told you of Georg's comment to me on first hearing you play the organ in Leipzig. He said he had never before heard anyone play as though a great swell came up from the heart to instruct the fingers. I quite agree. I hope our friend is well. It is more and more saddening as the years go by to realize that we shall likely not meet again the people who were dear from our youth. I remember Dr Arbuthnot speaking of an illness, a nostalgia, that saddens the heart with longing for olden times and early homelands. I believe now in my seventieth year I am allowed to indulge in such sentiments.

And you, my dear Gif. I understand that Mr Harris advised you on the writing of a will just before you left for the Continent. We all are more aware of our mortality as time marches on. I was so grateful that my beloved Edward had arranged for my care and comfort well before his illness threatened to take him from us. Friends and relatives who need not debate what you had wished will appreciate your thoughtfulness in writing out a will. And I, my friend, will always treasure the lovely miniature portrait I have of you as very young man. It is one of my dearest possessions. Edward and I were so honored to be gifted with this reminder of our youthful friendship. I am sure your relatives in Saxony were pleased with the portraits you carried to them as well. I only wish I too could have laid a wreath on the stone of your dear mother and sisters. Our rituals, solitary or shared, connect us to all that have gone before.

You are, I know, eager to begin work on your proposed piece on Jephtha's vow. What a strange choice of story for you. Your customary tireless regimen will prevail, I am sure. But, please do find time to stop by the Square if possible. All good wishes in this new year.

I have the honor to be, ever yours,

Mrs. Edward Grayston
In care of Mr Samuel Smyth
Berkeley Square, London

As everyone finished reading the letter, Katherine looked around and marveled inwardly at how sensibly each Seminar member put aside his or her personal stance on troublesome topics and allowed contrary opinions to be expressed. "A good group," she thought. "Well," she said, "does our letter spark some questions or themes for discussion?"

Brad looked at his copy of the letter. "You know," he said, "I can't honestly say I've ever thought about people from Handel's time having the equivalent of car crashes or other touring accidents. I mean, you think of people like Buddy Holly or Patsy Cline, dying in plane crashes, or James

Dean in a car accident, but Handel was traveling by horse and carriage. I guess I'd like to learn a little more about this accident Lydia mentions."

Katherine wrote HANDEL'S COACH ACCIDENT on the flip chart. "Other questions?" she asked. When no one spoke up, Ross volunteered, "This might be a good time to discuss his will—and I'm curious about the miniature portrait he gave Lydia. Obviously he is thinking about—not so much his legacy as his connections with real people in his life, and what he might want to leave to them when he dies. A somber topic."

Beneath the first topic, Katherine wrote HANDEL'S WILL AND SMALL PORTRAIT. She smiled and started to put down her marker, but Wait waved a hand. "I wouldn't mind taking up the brief mention that Lydia makes of their friend Georg Telemann. I don't know much about Telemann, but I remember that he was one of Handel's friends from his home country, from Germany. I think it's interesting that he evidently wrote a letter to Telemann. Lydia complains here and elsewhere that Handel hardly ever writes letters. Telemann must be a pretty special friend, I would guess."

"Thanks, Wait," said Katherine, and she wrote THE LETTER TO TELEMANN on the chart as the third topic. "So," she said, "our first question was about the accident Handel had while traveling in Holland. Brad, did you want to say something more about that?"

"I've been on a horse maybe three times in my life," Brad laughed. "And I've never been in a horse-drawn carriage, so I have no idea even how such an accident would happen. I'm assuming it wasn't two carriages running into each other. Probably—as Lydia's nephew suggested—the road was bad and the carriage simply got off balance and turned over. But the important thing here is that Handel was injured. I suppose an overturned carriage would give you some bumps and bruises, maybe even a concussion. If he had a broken leg or something, I assume Lydia would have asked specifically about it since it would take a longer time to heal. As I said, I just thought it was a very unusual bit of information on our man Handel. Eighteenth century diseases I would expect, but highway accidents—not so much."

"Interesting that you mention concussion," said Peter. "There has been a lot more research on concussions lately, especially among athletes. They say that repeated incidents involving concussions tend to add up after a while. Back when we were discussing Handel's bouts of paralysis and bizarre behavior that sent him to spas for recovery, I kept thinking that perhaps he—you know—had fallen off his horse one too many times or something. I do believe he had issues with lead poisoning too, but it is possible he also had repeated head injuries that simply weren't recorded. Actually, as Brad suggested, it was odd that this incident was reported among Handel's friends in London. Obviously Handel himself was not the one sharing the information, maybe a newspaper story instead. Recovery from a concussion might be harder to identify and confirm than would be the healing of a cut or bruise. They say, with a concussion, the effect on the brain, vision, and general disposition is cumulative. Some of his characteristic irritability could stem from concussions. In any case, I think the accident should be viewed as a serious event. After all, he wasn't a young man, and he may have lost his natural ability to bounce back after such a blow."

"I think you may be right, Peter," said Clara. "We should keep an eye on what develops with Handel's health from here on out. Any injury that jars the brain has potential for long-term effects even after the person seems to be recovered. A good point to think about, Brad. Thanks for bringing it up."

"You're welcome," said Brad, and he looked a little puzzled. He gave a half smile, shrugged, then turned back to Katherine. For some reason, Katherine smiled as well and looked over to Benfey, who stifled a small chuckle and wrote something in her notebook. Katherine turned back to the flip chart and said, "Our next topic is Handel's will—and that little portrait that Lydia mentions. Ross, you suggested we consider both of these. What is your thought?"

Ross raised his glass toward Katherine in a mock toast. "Ah, Handel's will," he said. "I believe we have conversed on this very topic before, my dear Katherine—on a foggy night in London town. Friends," he said, turning to face the rest of the group, "it was a rendezvous the like of which you ne'er would guess. Poor Handel's final gifts the topic of our furtive tryst. A glass of wine, a solemn goal, our minds entwined to scrutinize his every line. 'Twas the stuff of great drama, I tell you . . . ."

Katherine waved a napkin. " A chance meeting at a museum, Mister Wainwright. And it was some kind of bland ale—not a glass of wine. Ross and I both saw the copy of Handel's will at the Foundling Museum—thus the meeting. So—our esteemed and stupendously silver-tongued devil—do you have you some thoughts on the will, or shall we move on to our next question?"

"No one values good-natured levity anymore," sighed Ross. "Ok—a monochrome report, then—Katherine and I both saw the framed exhibition copy of Handel's will. Actually, I think Peter may have seen it earlier as well, right, Peter? In any case, not only did we view the copy of the will on display at the Foundling Museum, but I—ever on the alert to build up our small but impressive library of materials on Handel—bought a book containing the facsimile of Handel's will, edited by Donald Burrows and published by the Gerald Coke Foundation." Ross walked over to the bookshelf containing the aforementioned small library and removed a paperbound compendium titled *Handel's Will*. "As you can see, this is a British publication," he said. "Notice the large manuscript size pages—just like those annoying off-size letters one gets from British agencies—always too big for normal file folders. Anyway, herein you may all see a facsimile of the original will, written in Handel's own hand and signed by him on June 1, 1750. It includes a couple essays about the will as well. Check it out. I'll pass it around."

"And notice the Signature on page 36," Ross said. "It is his 'signature' signature, so to speak—with the 'd' of both Frideric and Handel curved back in a very charming kind of calligraphy. Sadly, you can see how in later codicils the signature becomes cramped and uneven. But on this first and original statement, Handel's writing is bold and clear. He needed no witnesses on this original document because he had no real estate to be assigned to anyone. He simply made out his will before leaving for the Continent, put it in an envelope and sealed it, and left it in a bureau drawer at his Brook Street home. Fortunately, he returned to London, but no doubt he had considered the wisdom of making a will before traveling abroad. It is an interesting document. Since Handel was a bachelor, he had no wife or children to be the primary beneficiaries. Instead, the first people mentioned in the will are his servants, especially his long-time attendant, Peter le Blond. He remembered a couple close friends with items or money and left the majority of his estate to his niece in Germany. Later, over the three years preceding his death in 1759, he had four separate codicils added to the will. In these later documents—when he could no longer see to write as he had for the original will—he instructed the lawyer to delete the names of people who had died and add the names of others to whom he hoped to leave something. He added a London co-executor for the will to help with getting the substantial inheritance easily transferred to his relatives in Germany, and he indicated that the Foundling Hospital should have fair copy of all parts of *Messiah*. He also left monetary gifts to various musicians who had worked with him over the years and a substantial amount to the Fund for Decayed Musicians. In the end, Handel's estate was worth nearly three million dollars by today's exchange rates, so he clearly had the means to be generous. And he was."

"Three million?!" said Brad. "But I thought he was supposed to be a struggling composer—nearly bankrupt when he decided to switch from operas to oratorios. Remember the creditors hounding him in the movie—the *Great Mr. Handel*, or whatever it was? How did he end up with that much money? Did he have a Swiss bank account or something? I think we've been hoodwinked."

Katherine laughed. "Where was Snopes.com when we needed it?" she said. "The folklore about Handel being bankrupt has stayed with us despite all the research that contradicts it. I imagine people prefer to think of Handel as the proverbial starving artist type, but, as you have said many times yourself, Brad, Handel was a good businessman. His investments were sound, and he did make money on his oratorios—more than he did on the operas. He died a very wealthy man. But, Ross, I think your question was really more about the people and charities he recognized in making out his will. And maybe what motivated him to write it in the first place. Do you want to say a little more about that?"

"Yes indeed," said Ross. "Actually, my friends, Katherine and I DID discuss Handel's will—and, in fact, the whole question of why one makes out a will. I will admit I was not eager to discuss the subject of wills, mostly because Katherine—as seems to be her wont—insisted on making it more personal, as in 'Have you made out a will? Why or why not?' Very nosy questions. However, the conversation did move me to bring up the topic with my lawyer and, more importantly, with my mother. I ask you, who wants to be cajoled into discussing depressing things like wills with one's mother? But, as you might expect, that mother-son dialogue was enlightening. You all should have such a marvel for a mother."

Forella blushed and covered her mouth to hide her big smile. "You may think I pay him to say things like that, but I don't," she said. "What a sweetie. But, seriously, what became clear to me right away was that Ross has always hesitated to think about relationships and money as being in any way connected. He didn't want to think about his own money or, more significantly, my money as having any role in our relationship. I admire that sentiment—but it is very impractical. We had a long talk, and I think we both learned a lot from it. If nothing else, I now know that my bones will not have to bear an eternity hidden away in the dark earth anticipating some long-awaited resurrection. Instead my ashes will gently join the wooded grounds of the beautiful Spring Grove Cemetery above Cincinnati. And after various gifts of money go to friends and family and donations find their way to some of my favorite charities, Ross and his lawyer will have to attend to the rest. I appreciated the remark earlier about Handel's increasingly cramped and illegible signature on the additions to his will. I, too, had to sign—in front of witnesses—a document that was read aloud to me and signed with what I remember as the feel of my signature. I cannot tell whether it resembles the signature I used when I could see. It feels awkward now, and rusty. I can imagine how Handel felt, moving his hand in a signature that he could no longer see. And yet, it does still give one a sense of bringing agreement to the content of the will. Signing a will is a good thing. I can understand why Handel chose to begin the process long before he faced his own imminent passing."

"Thank you, Forella," said Katherine. "Ross was quite right, of course. Asking about someone's will is indeed asking a very personal question. But just as you have demonstrated, we do learn something important about a person's values, likes, hopes, and treasured relationships when we see what is included in that individual's will. It is in some ways the last story we tell—maybe even more revealing than a self-composed obituary. And as you said about Handel, it is especially illuminating to see what a person considers important long before the looming prospect of death rushes things along. We are very fortunate to have this record of Handel's wishes on how his fortune should be dispersed. We have so few written statements from him, so few letters expressing any of his thoughts directly—we must cherish these more formal documents and appreciate the efforts of all who found ways to preserve and make available Handel's will. So, Ross, on to your comments about the will—and the little portrait."

"It seems clear to me," said Ross, "that Handel wanted to do at least three things in writing his will—and the four codicils. He wanted to recognize and leave something to the people who had helped him—personally or professionally—his servants, his copyist, several of his primary musicians and librettists, his apothecary, his legal council, his secretary. He had already gifted his wealthier friends and connections with portraits, paintings, or valuable musical instruments, recognizing that they did not really need monetary bequests. But to some of his neighbors and to several widows of friends who had died, he left generous gifts of money, knowing that many of them certainly could benefit from the gift. And in a similar vein, he remembered various relatives in Germany, including, of course his niece in Saxony, who was his primary beneficiary. He guaranteed the continuing benefits for the Foundling Hospital by leaving a fair copy of *Messiah* for their use, and he left a substantial bequest to the Society for Decayed Musicians. He left his music manuscripts and books to John

Smith Senior, his primary copyist for most of his career. These autograph scores have been preserved for more than 250 years—clearly his greatest gift to future generations. Finally, Handel left a generous sum to be used in creating the monument that marks his burial in Westminster Abbey. To me, one of the interesting things about Handel's will is its progression from a clearly heartfelt appreciation for his 'old servant,' Peter le Blond, who had attended to his personal needs for so many years, to his unapologetic request for a monument and burial in Westminster Abbey. Handel, the ordinary man, grateful for the constant and evidently congenial care given by his servant, contrasted with Handel, the greater-than-life composer celebrated in stone and wearing, even in death, the laurels of a public figure. I think Handel communicated both parts of his personality in his will."

CD paged through the book Ross had sent around and said, "I gather our friend Lydia is not among the widows Handel listed in his will. She did mention in her letter that her husband had provided well for her. I suppose that is why Handel did not include her. But it seems he had given her a portrait—of him, I guess. Actually he had given it to Lydia and her husband some time earlier. I am intrigued by the number of objects Handel gave as gifts to valued friends—mostly portraits or paintings, but also instruments, musical scores, even, I see, his formal wearing apparel. I admit that—when I had reason to do it a couple years ago—I found writing a will a very enlightening exercise. You look around at all of the things you have accumulated over a lifetime and consider whether anyone else would have the same attachment to those objects as you do. It is actually quite humbling. For most things you have collected, it doesn't really matter what happens to them once they are no longer yours. At least that is the way I felt when I tried envisioning who might want any of my things. On the other hand, there are some items I definitely know should go to certain people, and that is a good feeling. Some reminder of you and your life will stay with a person you cared about. I suppose that is why Handel made a point of giving especially the portraits of himself to his closest friends."

"What exactly is a miniature portrait—the one he gave Lydia?" said Clara. "Is this one of the pictures of Handel that is still around—in the National Gallery or at one of the museums?"

Peter cleared his throat. "You have happened upon one of my favorite subjects," he said. "Miniatures were very popular in the eighteenth century. If you visit the Victoria and Albert Museum in London, you will see a fine collection of miniatures, most from the eighteenth and nineteenth centuries—before photography took on the role of easily given portraits. I remember seeing—in the Cambridge Encyclopedia, I think—a photograph of a small portrait of Handel—truly a miniature, maybe two by three inches. According to the Händel-Haus in Halle, the portrait was stolen some time ago from the museum—yes, stolen, very fishy. However, the portrait is considered authentic—or at least it was before it disappeared. It was supposedly painted on vellum in around 1710, when Handel was twenty-five years old. The artist, Christoph Plazer, was a court painter from southern Germany. No one knows why he created the miniature portrait. The tradition of miniatures was in vogue among royalty and the wealthy. Possibly Handel's miniature was connected with his return to Germany and his brief appointment as Kapellmeister to the Elector of Hanover. In any case, it could have been the one that Handel later gave to Lydia and Edward. There is very little in the way of provenance for the portrait, so I suppose we will never know. I for one will hold onto the possibility that this is our Lydia's little portrait. What do you think, Ross?"

"Oh, why not?" said Ross. "It makes a better story. I've developed my own thumbnail philosophy about collectibles—portraits, of course, but also other things that a person might want to save or, conversely, give away. Confession time: I have a room—a treasure room—full of artifacts I have collected over the years. It is like a small museum, I admit. I've always liked museums, but in my case, every artifact is there because it brings with it a story that connects in some way to me. Absolutely egotistical, I know. But here is the saving grace, at least so I hope. In my own perhaps peculiar philosophy about such artifacts, I treasure an object for the story it recalls for me, a story that connects me intimately, uniquely, with someone and some event in my life. A public museum, on the other hand, connects objects with history or shared stories, larger motifs that everyone can treasure. Both kinds of story are valuable, but my treasure room is designed to be a unique and personal repository. I've even created my own label and description for each object—a harmless hobby. But, back to Handel's miniature portrait. I agree it would be wonderful to discover that the missing portrait is indeed the one that Handel gave to Lydia. Imagine the story—some long lost relative of Lydia or Handel seeking to establish a bit of family history by way of this unassuming artifact. No wonder it was stolen. I think you should write it up, Peter. Or, maybe asking the director of the museum in Halle would be a better idea. But their story probably won't be as satisfying as yours. This is why we need literature, right Katherine?"

Katherine smiled and gave Ross a thumbs-up gesture. "Yes, Ross" she said, "I can envision a riveting work of creative nonfiction on the subject—transforming eventually into one of your unconventional documentaries. But, for now, perhaps we should leave Handel's bequests to friends and relatives and take up Wait's question about the letter to Telemann. What was your query on the letter, Wait?"

"Well, as I said," Wait began, "Telemann must have been an especially good friend if Handel still corresponded with him so many years after their actual time together. This is one instance in which I will concede that there might be an advantage to not being married. My wife and I tend to have friends together, that is, friends we interact with as a couple. My own friends from high school or college have pretty much fallen by the way. Handel and Telemann became friends when Handel was, what? Sixteen or seventeen? Granted, they probably interacted quite a bit during those years before Handel left for Italy, but then they went their separate ways. But here in Lydia's letter, we see Handel well up in years still writing to Telemann. I just thought it was interesting and proof of a really important friendship in Handel's life."

"Friendship, yes," said Alison, "but also they remained professional colleagues. Back in graduate school, I remember learning that Telemann was one of the people Handel borrowed from frequently. Along with many of my professors and cohorts in the school of music, I sneered at this supposed proof of Handel's weak compositional skills, but I have since revised that opinion. It is clear that Handel was very creative in adapting such borrowings. I suspect that Telemann rather appreciated the clear tribute evident in such borrowings. During his many years in Hamburg, Telemann presented several of Handel's operas and used some of Handel's compositions as material for lessons with his students. The two men remained friends throughout their lives and obviously respected each other's past and ongoing musical output. My guess is that Handel paid a visit to Telemann while he was in Germany. The letter that Lydia mentions was probably written after Handel returned to London."

"What do you think, Wait?" asked Katherine. "Does Handel remain friends with Telemann because they are musical comrades, or is their friendship more of a fraternal bond than that?"

"Well," said Wait, "given that Handel wrote out his will and visited family and friends on the Continent, I would say he is thinking about his most important connections—the ones he wants to recognize and strengthen as he moves into the later years of his life. Do we know what he wrote to Telemann? Didn't Peter have some book that translated and reprinted all of the few letters Handel wrote? It would be nice to know what Handel had to say to his friend after all those years."

"You DO have a great memory, Wait," said Peter. "I'll bring a copy of that library book next time. Meanwhile, I think Angela has some information Forella wanted us to have as our take-away Handel performance this time. Am I right, Forella?"

"Yes," said Forella. "Angela did her best to find a video of Handel's last major work—his oratorio *Jephtha*. There are a number of very good recordings, and we will send one home with you today. But she found no videos of a live performance. There are, she says, several YouTube video recordings of various singers or choral groups performing individual arias or choruses. She has made out a list for you, but you will have to find them yourself. She included a printout of the libretto as well. I know Ross will have a fit because this seems like a homework assignment, but there you are. Actually, I think you will find it a fun exercise. I know I would. Thanks, Angela, for your hard work."

"My pleasure," said Angela.

"Thank you all for another interesting exchange," said Katherine. "I look forward to reading over the libretto, listening to the recording, and searching out the *Jephtha* clips. See you next time. Be safe."

CHAPTER 23

Whatever First Meets Me

At the local YMCA, Forella moved into the curtained changing area to slip into her bathing suit. Despite her own extremely diminished vision, she maintained a keen sense of privacy about her own body. Still, she was grateful for Angela's helping hand as she made her way to the shower room for a quick rinse and then out into the natatorium. She enjoyed the group exercises in the multipurpose pool and especially the interaction with other members, but her greatest sense of exhilaration came after the class when Angela swam with her in the main pool. Granted, the water was a little colder there than in the other pool, but Forella relished the sense of independence and personal vitality she experienced as her arms cut through the water and propelled her forward like a polar bear seeking out an ice floe, just as she had when she could more clearly see the lanes and tiles all on her own. It was a good day.

As EVERYONE GATHERED AROUND THE table for the next meeting of the Handel Seminar, Ross was delighted to see that Annie had prepared fried chicken for their lunch. She also had some mushroom risotto as a side dish—or as a main dish for anyone who avoided meat. Even Wait declared the fried chicken at least as good as that his grandmother used to make for their summer outings at the state park. A veritable picnic without the ants—they all agreed. However, long before anyone had finished eating, CD offered a comment on the recording of Handel's *Jephtha* Forella had sent home with everyone last time. "Wasn't that an outstanding performance?" he said. "I thought the production, as a whole, was better than any of the many individual arias or choruses on YouTube—although I do thank you, Angela, for finding all those additional recordings. The comparisons were instructive, I thought. But The Sixteen did a great job with the oratorio. I wish they would have made a video while they were at it."

"I didn't find time to actually sit down and listen to the recording," said Rayette, "but I did read through the libretto. I'm not a biblical scholar, but isn't the plot some strange perversion of the Isaac and Abraham story in the Old Testament? Didn't this leader—Jephtha—make a vow, promising God he would sacrifice whatever he first meets on arriving home, if God grants him victory over his enemies? Of course, this time it is a daughter rather than a son that is to be sacrificed, and in the end an angel instructs Jephtha to simply commit his daughter to a life in service to God—as a virgin. I'll admit I had never heard any commentary on this story before. It must not be a popular text for a homily—at least where I have attended church. Somehow the Isaac and Abraham story is more satisfying. I'm not even sure why this Jephtha felt like he had to make such a vow."

"Well, actually that's a good point," said Brad. "One of the things I learned in Hebrew school was that God does not require a sacrifice, and definitely not the sacrifice of a person, especially a child. Abraham was proving his obedience to God, but, if you read the prophet in the case of Jephtha, you will see that Jephtha was worrying about his role as leader against the Ammonites, and he wanted to be sure God would be on his side. He made the decision to offer this vow all on his own. God did not ask him to sacrifice his daughter. It was pretty stupid of Jephtha to try to bribe God. Not all the leaders in ancient Jewish history were people we should emulate, you know. I wonder why Handel picked this story for his last oratorio. Didn't Lydia wonder the same thing in her last letter? It's definitely not what I would call an inspired plot."

Clara frowned and looked over at Brad. "Well, yeah, I suppose we could just dismiss Jephtha as a jerk. After all—at least as I read the libretto—he made the decision to offer this vow while he was alone. It wasn't to impress the soldiers who would be fighting with him or anything like that. So it is just between Jephtha and God. But, of course, later on Jephtha tells everyone that he had made this vow, so he obviously expects everyone to understand why he feels he must keep the promise he made to God. Why does no one question Jephtha's lament that he MUST keep the vow he made to God? Well, actually Storgè—his wife—does object, very forcefully. But generally the understanding seems to be that God would expect him to keep the vow. What kind of god would be that cruel and pedantic? Granted, Jephtha had wanted to make it clear that he needed God's help in conquering the Ammonites, but why make this vow? Why not just ask for God's help? I'm sorry, but this Old Testament notion of God is simply nasty. They may have told you at Hebrew school that God would not expect a sacrifice, but evidently no one told Jephtha and his people. He seemed to think that is what he had to do—promise something to God so he would have God's help in winning the battle."

Brad just shrugged, but Ross took up the question. "I don't think Handel picked the story of Jephtha and his daughter with the aim of showing what a great person Jephtha was—or really even to say anything about the nature of God. Most of the characters in the Old Testament are flawed. That is the point. They need God to guide them, and they are supposedly lucky that God regards them as his chosen people. No matter what they do—we are told—he still loves them and sends them prophets and leaders who will eventually help make them worthy as a chosen people. But Jephtha was one of those imperfect leaders whose story serves to illustrate a lesson. That would be why Handel wanted to turn the plot into an oratorio. Like the old Greek myths, the story of Jephtha highlights the weakness and egotism of our human leaders. In fact, the story has many similarities to the Greek narrative about Agamemnon and his daughter Iphigenia. If it was good enough for Aeschylus and Euripides, why not for Handel?"

"Jephtha's vow is a traditional motif," said Katherine. "In the folktales that have the same story element—the man who promises something to, usually, the devil, in return for an important victory or escape or something similar—in those folktales the man making the vow assumes that his dog or a servant will cross the bridge to meet him when he returns home. But the motif—which Thompson identified as S241—is called Child unwittingly promised. The irony is always that, without knowing it, the man promises not something he considers of little value, such as a dog or servant, but something of great value, his only child. The motif is best known as it is related in the book of Judges in the Bible—the story of Jephtha and his daughter. But it is interesting, I think, that in folk stories, the promise is made not to God but rather to an evil figure—the Devil or a troll or Rumpelstiltskin-like figure. And usually the child will not be sacrificed, as in the story of Jephtha, but rather taken away by the devil or imp to become part of the devil's family. In any case, it is indeed an old story and certainly a tragic one. This dramatic element obviously appealed to Handel. I'm sure he saw a lot of what we would now call existential issues in the plot. Whether he also saw any personal issues—any deeply felt regrets or worries—we likely will never know."

"I expect we will come back to this last important work by Handel," said Katherine, "but let us take a look at what Peter has for us today. A letter or two, maybe?"

"Only one, I'm afraid," said Peter, "and it is short. Nothing more about *Jephtha*. Here is what I have. We ARE getting near the end of the letters. Enjoy while you may."

Mr. G F Handel, Esqr
Brook Street, near Hanover Square
London

15 August 1751

My Dear Mr Handel,
Weeks have passed since we saw you at the Saint James in Bath. I stayed on with Samuel and his family. My favorite features of these summertime excursions are the wonderful lending library and the

lively crowd at the coffeehouse. But you, my dear Gif, were intent upon taking the waters and finding some relief from worry at your ailing eye. All from London noted that the oratorio season was shortened, and perhaps that is a good thing—though, of course, the passing of the Prince was a sad reason for finishing the season so early. Please, please do not push yourself to complete the new piece if it means placing even more of a burden on your troubled vision.

You left for the City long before we did. I do hope the return of the younger Mr Smith from his sojourn in France will prove a boon to the management of your many tasks. I spent several joyful days with Susannah and her children at their country home but am now back in town. Susannah wishes you well and was as sorry as I to hear of your worrisome eye problem. I told her I would write when I have seen you again. Samuel is eager as always to have you visit us in the Square, but if you are immersed in your work as you usually are, I shall find a way to stop by with Samuel's son William and extend our greetings. I am concerned about your health, and it troubles me not to see you hale and walking contentedly in the park. Know that I—that all your friends—hold you in our hearts.

I have the honor to be, ever yours,

Mrs. Edward Grayston
In care of Mr Samuel Smyth
Berkeley Square, London

As everyone finished reading the letter, Peter cast a photograph on the wall opposite the buffet. "I found a picture of the theater Lydia refers to in her letter—the Saint James Theater," said Peter. "It is currently a Masonic Hall in Bath—built of local limestone. Evidently it was brand new when Handel visited Bath in 1751. The famous baths were nearby. Judging from Lydia's letter, I would guess that Handel was more interested in gaining some medical benefits from the mineral waters than in socializing—at least this time. I'm not sure what good he thought 'taking the waters' would do for his eyes, but clearly he was hoping for some of the kind of help he had received from his visit to the spa in Germany some fifteen years earlier. Anyway, FYI—a photo of a building that was around back in Handel's time."

"Thank you, Peter," said Katherine. "Do we have any questions about this rather short letter? What themes do we want to consider? Yes, Rebecca?"

"We've stuck pretty well to our aim of considering what the letters might teach us—about Handel, about Lydia, about life in general," said Rebecca. "Peter says this letter is one of the last ones we have. And yet, forgive me, this one doesn't tell us much. I suppose I wouldn't mind discussing a little about the entertainments that Lydia enjoyed at Bath—the library, the coffeehouse—and maybe more about the medical role of spas in eighteenth century England. But truthfully, I think I am more interested in considering further this last oratorio—*Jephtha*. I will admit I had never heard of it, but it seems that Handel was determined to bring it to life—despite his ailments. Lydia must have known the story—people were better educated in Old Testament stories back then. But even she thought the choice of subject was an odd one for Handel. I think we need to ponder why Handel wanted to create this piece, perhaps knowing it might be the last one he would be able to compose, given his eye problems. Could we go back to the topic of this disturbing oratorio rather than the letter?"

"An absolutely reasonable request," said Katherine. "Perhaps you would like to say a bit more to lead us off, Rebecca. We can always come back to the letter before we finish up if anyone wants to. What are your thoughts on this oratorio *Jephtha*?"

"Over time," said Rebecca, "most anthropologists get used to encountering aspects of other cultures that they find personally disturbing—female genital mutilation, beheading, child-selling, bull fights, child brides, honor killings, maiming as a punishment, human sacrifice. This last one—human sacrifice—isn't something we see anymore. Most modern nations would consider it murder if discovered. But, for me, as I listened to this oratorio and read the libretto, I realized that I felt that same revulsion I have experienced whenever I have seen evidence of some other of these cruel practices, no matter what I might think of the people involved otherwise. Frazer's *Golden Bough* is no longer of much importance in the field, but early on, in 1890, when it was first published, it had the effect of shocking literate society by recording countless examples of such rituals worldwide. What really bothers me is that this story of Jephtha—like so many in the Bible—reflects the religious beliefs and practices of two thousand, even three thousand, years ago but yet continues to be accepted as part of sacred narrative today. People struggle to make this story somehow acceptable when in fact it is horrible and should no longer be treated as somehow sacred or divinely inspired. The cultural understanding that would condone such behavior should have been discarded long ago. That is why I find it disturbing that Handel chose this story to celebrate in a musical production, one that we still listen to today."

"I have heard some commentary on this Old Testament story," said Wait. "Modern scholars argue that God never would have accepted a human sacrifice—just as Brad said. Both Jehptha and his daughter are willing to do whatever is necessary to serve the Lord and the people of Israel. Jephtha's song 'Waft Her Angels' is a beautiful declaration of the larger understanding of heaven Jephtha finally comes to as he contemplates the sacrifice he has promised to make. The Bible says that Jephtha's daughter was offered up to be a burnt sacrifice, but that is the point—she was offered up, but in the end God rewarded Jephtha's devotion by accepting the offered sacrifice but allowing instead the promise that Iphis would serve the Lord as an unmarried handmaid for the rest of her life. The story is important in the same way the Abraham and Isaac story is important. It shows that the people of Israel were repentant of their earlier falling away from worshipping the Lord and were again truly devoted to God and grateful for his protection."

Clara scowled over at Wait and said, "There is so much detestable in what you have just said that I don't know where to begin. First off, the whole thing is completely misogynistic. Iphis is being treated as some object owned by her father—which I suppose she was back then. There is no excuse for accepting that as a good thing now. Furthermore, Jephtha's 'vow' is arrogant and despotic. Why does he not tell God he will sacrifice himself if he wins over the Ammonites? Why should someone else be sacrificed if Jephtha is the one making the vow? The mother's worries before the battle are ignored. Evidently she knows her husband well enough to expect that he will do something rash, something that will endanger the family. I agree with Rebecca. There is nothing sacred about this story—or at least there shouldn't be. It is simply evidence of past beliefs and practices that we should regard as a sad reflection on humanity's slow evolution from its benighted beginnings."

"Oh my, this is where Forella's Chalice Circles would have encouraged much more restraint when we disagree," said Katherine. "Wait is rightly pointing to ways the story has been interpreted as bearing a message for people today. If the reader-response theory scholars in literary studies have taught us nothing else, they have surely convinced us that every reader brings his or her own cultural and personal understanding to any narrative text—whether secular or sacred. Those who view it as a sacred text will want to find messages supportive of their religious worldview, and those who regard it as simply a kind of fable or cautionary tale will try to pull out some sort of lesson for our current social context. The interesting thing to me is that the story is really so simple as to be a folk narrative motif. As I said earlier, the basic plot element shows up worldwide, usually in short folktales. Even in the biblical version, the actual plot action is very limited: Jephtha makes a vow to sacrifice whatever first meets him when he returns home, and his beloved daughter is the one who meets him and must be sacrificed. Together, Handel and his librettist, Thomas Morell, stretch out the plot into a three-hour oratorio. What did Handel and Morell find so compelling about this simple story? I think we need to look at how the story is expanded and emotionally enriched if we are to understand why Handel invested these last fast-dwindling composing opportunities into this piece."

"Well, there is one chorus that is very significant," said Alison. "Once Jephtha realizes that it is his daughter who is implicated in his unholy vow, the chorus sings, 'How dark, O Lord'—a painfully troubled poem set to a stirring and dramatic piece of music. Here, let me read the text:

How dark, O Lord, are thy decrees!
All hid from mortal sight!
All our joys to sorrow turning,
And our triumphs into mourning,
As the night succeeds the day.
No certain bliss,
No solid peace,
We mortals know,
On earth below;
Yet on this maxim still obey:
Whatever is, is right."

"Yes, that is an amazing chorus," said CD. "But it isn't really part of the action—more of a commentary on what the people feel as they witness Jephtha's horror at what he has done. Have you ever seen it performed, Alison? I expect it would be an impressive anthem even out of context—but maybe too negative for most audiences, not your usual 'night of Handel' fare."

Alison nodded. "I think it probably needs to be right where Handel put it—at the close of the climactic second act of this oratorio, just after Iphis accepts her fate and Jephtha is horrified and then overcome by her goodness. I have read somewhere that it was likely Handel himself who changed Morell's original closing line 'What God ordains, is right' to the more all-encompassing line 'Whatever is, is right.' I think this choral piece needs that context to be as effective as it is."

"That line—'Whatever is, is right'—is from a long poem by Alexander Pope," said Rayette. "Remember Pope? --the one who wrote 'The Rape of the Lock?' He wrote several really long poems, mostly in heroic couplets, and this line was from one called 'An Essay on Man.' Pope was one of the people Handel counted as a friend in London, if I remember right. Pope's 'Essay' was a philosophical reflection on man's place in the universe. The 'Whatever is, is right' phrase comes from the last line of Pope's long poem, so we can assume that Handel remembered it as a kind of summary of Pope's view on the relationship between man and God and the role of fate in our daily lives. I can imagine Handel suggesting that Morell substitute this well-known line for the less poetic original. His audience would likely have recognized it and maybe even made the connection between Jephtha and Pope's poem—a kind of eighteenth century sampling. I think it was an effective allusion."

Ross stood up and walked over to the buffet. He poured himself a drink but didn't sit down again. Instead he paced around, frowning. "I don't want to place too much importance on this piece as Handel's last oratorio," he said. "After all, he couldn't know for certain that he would never be able to write music again. He still had some vision, even if his eyes did seem to be weakening. On the other hand, he must have sensed that time was running out for him, that his chances for expressing the thoughts, feelings, maybe regrets or worries—the concerns that dominated his thinking at this point in his life—the chances for expressing those ideas through musical composition were disappearing. So, how would this particular story, with its embodiment of poor judgment, egotism, religious literalism, and a philosophy of fatalism—how would this story figure in Handel's own sense of his creative enterprise, his legacy?"

No one seemed eager to speak to Ross's speculative question, so he continued. "I have two thoughts about this piece. First, as Rayette said, Handel clearly wanted to remind people of Pope's line that advocates accepting whatever happens as being, in fact, what is supposed to happen. Musically, he really plays up that line, over and over again—and very dramatically. Even a musical dabbler like me can hear that. But does Handel highlight this idea because he agrees with it or because he wants to convey the notion that Jephtha and his people accepted that as a maxim and acted on it despite its cruel consequences? I suspect the latter. I suspect

Handel hoped to show in a subtle way that the Enlightenment had it right: sometimes we do need to question our religious assumptions and practices. Sometimes our treasured beliefs are unacceptable and need to be discarded. Whatever is, isn't necessarily right."

"What else?" Ross continued. "A related issue, I think, is that Handel himself was experiencing a lot of existential angst in his own life, and this story allowed him to explore the emotions he perhaps knew all too well. Did he identify with Jephtha—a flawed man trying to lead an oppressed people against a powerful enemy? Did he empathize with Iphis—an innocent young woman who was treated like an object to be traded for victory in battle? Did he sympathize with Storgè—a wife and mother whose wisdom and worries are ignored? Did he identify with the Chorus—the people of Israel desperately hoping that God would save and protect them? Or did he see the story as a kind of parable, a narrative meant to illustrate a point. And what was that point? Did Handel feel that his one source of psychological wisdom—the Church and its teachings—was failing him now as he faced the challenges of disability, old age, and the inevitability of death? I think the story was one Handel found disturbing and at the same time inspiring—a story worthy of his creative fire and skill."

"Well that's a plethora of possibilities, my friend," said Peter. "I rather like the last option you offered—the idea that Handel meant to throw into relief—and perhaps question—the notion that one must simply accept whatever happens as ordained by God. Remember, Handel is a man who lived through the central period of the Enlightenment. He spent time in public coffeehouses where philosophical and scientific issues of the day were discussed. That line in Lydia's letter about the coffeehouse and library in Bath should be noted for its documentation of an important aspect of life in the mid-seventeen hundreds. In public venues, men like Handel, and even educated women like Lydia, debated various ideas and questions that had been bubbling up ever since the Protestant Reformation. Voltaire's *Candide* emerged—though under disguised authorship—about that same time. People were challenging the authority of the Church and the optimistic acceptance of everything the priests told them. So, I see no reason why Handel, as a sophisticated frequenter of coffeehouses, would not see a story such as Jephtha's Vow as ripe for a bit of skeptical interrogation. I think he wanted his audience to experience the same sense of ambivalence he felt about this supposedly sacred bit of scripture."

"You know," said Brad, "I've wondered off and on why Handel kept picking stories from Jewish history—well, after he stopped writing operas and turned to oratorios instead. Believe me, as I was growing up, I heard all about how most of the 'Old Testament' stories were important only because they led to the true gospel of the New Testament and that God had aimed all along to send a savior who would make up for all the suffering people endured before the coming of Christ. As a kid growing up in the Midwest, you heard about the superiority of the New Testament whether you wanted to or not. It was just accepted. They even gave out those nice little pocket-sized New Testaments at school events. I think they have stopped doing that now. But my point is, though it was clear that the Torah and books of Jewish history were considered sacred and part of Christian tradition, it was also obvious that the stories were treated more like legends or stories from some preliterate past. Of course, the stories WERE older, and some of them must have been passed along orally. I don't know what the attitude toward these stories was in Handel's time, but it was clear to me that among the predominantly Christian people I grew up with, that people like Esther or Saul or Samson or Joseph or Joshua or Solomon or our friend Jephtha—all these people were to be pitied because, try as they might, they could not really achieve salvation or the true heaven. For Christians, the stories were really about how everything was one long struggle to survive until Jesus came along and offered himself as a sacrifice—the way Jephtha failed to do. In any case, to me it seems like the stories from Jewish history are treated more like fables than like real religious history. I get the feeling that Handel and his audiences saw the figures in his oratorios as the kind of literary or mythical figures that had shown up in the operas, only they were more respectable because they could be connected to Christian tradition. I may be wrong, but that is how it seems to me."

Katherine nodded slowly in Brad's direction. "Yes," she said, "Other people's stories are regarded as myths while 'our' stories are considered sacred, part of our religious heritage. Old Testament stories have always been a bit problematic in that regard. Christianity seems to want it both ways—the Christian God is the God of Abraham but also the three-personed God of modern Christian theology. To a folklorist, the stories in both the Old and New Testaments clearly emerge from oral tradition, and Jesus was probably one of the best Jewish storytellers of all time. But Brad's comments bring up something else that folklorists try to understand—the pervasive influence of us versus them. First, some three thousand years ago, we have the Israelites and the Ammonites fighting over land along the Jordan River and over whether the pagan gods of Ammon or the God of Israel should be worshiped. As with such conflicts even today, part of the dispute is over economics and part is over simply a clash of cultures. In Handel's day, the conflict may well have been over whether or not England was the New Jerusalem. Ever since the Protestant Reformation, and especially since Henry the Eighth's establishment of the Church of England, the English nobility and gentry have argued back and forth over how to, as Blake said, build 'Jerusalem in England's green and pleasant land.' Much of the military unrest during Handel's time was a continuation of religious and cultural conflicts that characterized the English Reformation. Handel's friend and librettist, Charles Jennens, was prohibited from serving in Parliament because he had the 'wrong' religious and political leanings. And today, we see groups separated by differing beliefs and practices no matter which way we turn. The story of Jephtha will be interpreted according to one's culture and worldview even here in this relatively small and homogeneous group."

"I think you are wrong to say that Christianity wants it both ways," said Wait. "The Old Testament is just as much a part of the Bible as the New Testament. Parts of the Old Testament even predicted the coming of Christ. That's what Handel's *Messiah* is all about. A story like this one about Jephtha is there to show how God's chosen people found it hard to stay faithful and keep God's commandments on their own. That is why they need the Christ. That is why Jesus made the ultimate sacrifice—just as Brad said—because someone like Jephtha was not able to sacrifice himself. Men always fall short. I think this oratorio about Jephtha is Handel's way of making this Old Testament story more memorable and dramatic. People could think about the story more clearly because it was presented in this musical form. That is why we have hymns and anthems at church. They help people appreciate the meaning of the Bible and the blessings their faith gives them."

"I can't believe this!" said Clara. "What hidebound church choir recruitment brochure did you get that from? If Handel wanted to prop up the teachings of the church, he would have stayed in Halle and composed sacred cantatas just like Bach. Honestly, there is no way this horrible story can be twisted into any positive reflection on Jephtha and his supposed interaction with God. Even if I believed in this Judeo-Christian God, I would still see Jephtha's fabrication of the 'vow' as simply that—a made-up excuse for carrying out some ridiculous ritual that has nothing whatsoever to do with whether he did or did not win his battle against his enemies. It's as crazy as the old Son of Sam argument. Just because Jephtha claims he made this vow to God, he expects everyone else to assume that God will hold him to it. You know what I think? I think Jephtha wanted to make himself seem really important—truly God's chosen leader. I read the 'Notes' section in the pamphlet that came with our CDs of the oratorio—the discussion written by the Handel scholar Ruth Smith. She points out that the scriptures indicate that Jephtha did actually sacrifice—that is, kill—his daughter, 'according to his vow.' I think he wanted the people of Israel to realize that he would do anything in service to God, even sacrifice his daughter. And anyone with that level of commitment would have to be a great leader, right? Jephtha was far more ambitious than loving. I don't see any heroism or anything at all admirable in his actions. I agree with those who wonder why Handel even chose to compose a work based on this disgusting story."

"I would hate to see us draw up sides in response to this oratorio," said Katherine. "I don't suppose we can really know why Handel chose this story. And in a way, maybe it doesn't matter. I think we can assume he saw it in the context of his own times—not Old Testament times, and certainly not the quite different context of our global culture today. Try to imagine being alive in Handel's London in 1751, when he was composing *Jephtha*. Very few people were outright atheists. Instead, any dissenters were maybe Deists or early English Unitarians. But the majority of people Handel would have interacted with were probably fairly religious Anglicans. So a story like that of Jephtha and his daughter would have been accepted as simply part of the culture they grew up accepting as a given. This accepting attitude meant avowing a God who had his own unfathomable reasons for doing what he did. Humans just have to accept that. That was the assumption. As Pope said, Whatever is, is right. However, that does not mean that Jephtha's actions cannot be scrutinized as those of a fallible human—a person who comes to understand his sinful pride and appreciate God's mercy. I think that is how the story would have been viewed in Handel's day."

"So you don't think the Enlightenment affected the way Handel understood such stories?" said Peter. "You don't think Handel wanted to make his audience squirm a little bit at how offensive this notion of God was? It may not have been popular even among intellectuals to question whether God was real, but they certainly could have argued when considering the Jephtha story that people in olden times accepted a warped view of God. Clara may have overstated the case, but I can definitely see a similarity between Jephtha's projection—that would be Freud's term for it—that God wanted him to keep this foolish vow and something like the Son of Sam belief that demons have demanded he act a certain way. I think Handel saw Jephtha as an ambitious but foolish man who got caught in his own trap. I don't think the story is about God or even the Jewish people at all. Jephtha had just enough humanity in him to be sorry for the damage he causes, but in the end, he makes the decision to sacrifice others to get what he wants. He is a tyrant."

"Hmm, yes," said Rebecca, "exactly the word I would use. It reminds me of a line Abigail Adams wrote to her husband, John Adams, at the start of the American Revolution. She said, 'Remember, all men would be tyrants if they could.' And she meant MEN, not simply all humans. Neither Iphis nor her mother was treated as a person whose life or intentions were her own to control. That Jephtha could claim 'ownership' of whatever or whoever met him when he returned from battle—that assumption casts him into the role of tyrant. Clearly, women in the seventeen hundreds were making their dissatisfaction with male dominance known. I would guess that Handel had picked up on some of that attitude, even if many in his audience had not."

Katherine saw that Forella wanted to say something. "Yes, Forella? What are your thoughts on this troubling piece?"

"I'm going to take us back to Handel's failing eyesight, if you don't mind," said Forella. "Handel was the son of a physician, and he probably had access to the most sophisticated medical doctors of his time. I suspect that he knew very well that he might be losing his sight, permanently and perhaps sooner rather than later. I think we CAN read more into his selection of this story for his last oratorio than we thought. He had already composed an oratorio about Samson, an Old Testament figure who lost his eyesight. So, I think his decision to compose an oratorio based on the story of Jephtha and his daughter speaks more to a growing sense that his opportunities for doing what he wanted to do with the life he had been given—with his great talent—those opportunities were dwindling. It may be a mistake to assume that Handel identifies with Jephtha—just because Jephtha is a man. I think he feels greater empathy for Iphis, for her willingness to do what is required of her, but mostly for her readiness to forgive her father—who should have done everything to protect her but instead let political ambition and military exigencies win out over human connections, over paternal love. I think Handel was reflecting on his own sacrifices. In a way he has been both Jephtha and Iphis. He has denied himself the very strong kind of connection that a parent-child bond would represent—or even the connection that a husband and wife would share. I think Handel wrote this oratorio as a lament over the power of ambition that so often gets in the way of human love."

Ross looked over at his mother. He could not deny the fleeting image of his father turning his disgruntled face away as, years ago, Forella and Ross joined a protest march for a miner who had died of black lung disease. Ross cherished his mother's values, her warmth and solid sense of justice. He wondered if she sometimes faulted him for failing to be a father or even a successful husband. But he saw that she smiled in his direction. "Yes, instinctively it seems, Handel knew how to make our hearts swell with human emotion," Ross said. "I can see, Mom, why you would view Handel as both Jephtha and Iphis. He regretted the sacrifices he chose to make—his emotional solitude, his immersion in the demands of his musical career. But he also recognized the contributions those sacrifices allowed him to make. I think he was able to forgive himself, just as Iphis forgave her father. Our decisions, not fate, determine whether we have lived well."

Katherine blinked back tears as Ross walked over to grasp his mother's hand and raise it to his lips—a strangely theatrical gesture, and yet poignant. She wished in her deepest heart that she still had her own mother to salute so lovingly. "Well," she said, "I believe we have given Handel's *Jephtha* careful review. Perhaps we can take a look back at today's letter next time. Forella has graciously supplied us with yet another fine CD to take home—this one a 2014 recording of Handel's *Triumph of Time and Truth*. I am sure we will have much to say about this piece next time, and I hope Peter will have another letter for us to consider. Thank you all for coming today. I hope to see each of you next time."

CHAPTER 24

Leave the Thorn

As Katherine sat listening to the final chorus of Handel's Triumph of Time and Truth, she thought back over the inexplicable attraction allegory had held for her, even as a young girl. Abstract notions, like Beauty or Pleasure or Truth, acting and speaking as though they were human—or more than humans, really—as larger-than-life embodiments of human values, yet strangely flat with little of the juice that makes humans melt off the page. And still—that aria just before the Hallelujah—it was truly a comforting poem, a consoling song. What genius can wed advice and insight to music without tramping Truth into a drudge? Perhaps Handel did know how to create self-help music. Beauty's last aria was both lovely and wise.

Ross swirled his glass of whiskey. He had arrived early for the Handel Seminar and rose from his chair to greet Peter, who came into the room, chatting with Randolph. "I'm glad you are here before everyone else, Peter, my friend," said Ross. "I have some sad news. Robert Brown writes that our Mrs. Finch has died after a brief illness. I had always hoped we would be able to make a return trip to her little village and give her a positive report on the content of the letters. Now I feel like a louse for not letting her know how much we appreciated her getting the letters into our hands. I know she just wanted to get them out of her hair, but still. Anyway, Robert says that she gave permission in an affidavit for us to do some limited dissemination, although not the full-blown exhibition you were hoping for—at least not yet."

Peter nodded. "She was a sweet lady," he said. "I'm sorry to hear it. And I didn't really expect to see any change in the arrangements, no matter what the situation. She seemed pretty firm in wanting to keep the originals under wraps for the twenty-five years we agreed on. But, yeah, it would have been fun to visit her again and thank her. I can't believe how the time has zipped by since then. So, did Brown tell us what her name really was?"

"No, he did not," said Ross. "The mystery remains. Ah, here is Katherine. I'll let you fill her in. I need to help Angela with a form Robert had sent with the letter. I think my mother and Angela do plan to be here for the meeting."

Soon all the Seminar members were gathered and eagerly sampling Annie's chicken pad Thai. As they sat down with plates and beverages, Katherine shared the sad tidings about the woman who had rescued the Handel letters from oblivion. Forella lifted a glass of wine that Angela had placed next to her plate. "I'd like to propose a toast," she said, "to the dear lady we know only as Mrs. Finch. She perhaps never really knew how very grateful we are to her for saving the letters, for listening to her instinct that signaled the letters might be of great value to others—to us. I am so sorry I was never able to meet her. To our dear Mrs. Finch—may she rest in peace."

It was a solemn yet warmly sympathetic ritual. Ross stood and put down his glass. "I'd like to say a little more about our Mrs. Finch, if I may," he said. "Peter and I met with her briefly in her small village in the English countryside. She had her reasons for being rather secretive about the whole thing—including keeping her real name out of the picture. Peter and I were both surprised that she chose not to put the letters up for bid at an auction house—something that would have brought her a fair sum of money, I'm sure. Instead, as we talked with her, it became clear that she liked the idea of sharing the letters with people who might learn something valuable from them—not simply biographical information about Handel but rather life lessons, a bit of wisdom from another era. Our Mrs. Finch was not a highly educated person, yet practical and perceptive in her own way. She was, I think, a kind soul who viewed most people as honest and decent folks, whether neighbors or not. She wasn't even put off by our being Americans. And I think she wanted to do her own dab of good in the world. In a curious way, she was actually quite excited to be sending the letters along to us—to people who would learn from them rather than simply making money by selling to the highest bidder. My personal hope is that we have honored her wishes in creating and participating in this Seminar. Having met her, I wanted to share a little of her personality and her vision with you. She, too, is one of our benefactors."

"Hear, hear," said Peter. "And with that reminder of the important artifacts that have brought us together yet again, let me relate another sad bit of news: today's letter is the last of the trove our Mrs. Finch sent us. Today's letter is the last that Lydia wrote to Handel, owing to his fast fading eyesight. Forella has suggested that we meet at least one more time, maybe more, but sadly—at least I find it a sad realization—we will soon be bringing our Seminar to a close. For me, treating and transcribing the letters has truly been a labor of love, and I will sorely miss our dialogues. I am sorry to see this venture end."

Brad was the first to respond to this information. "What? Really?" he said. "I thought there must be at least another dozen or so letters. Didn't Handel live for another six or seven years after the last letter we read? I was finally just getting into the rhythm of this operation. Dang. Now what will I do for fun? There goes my excuse for leaving the shop once in a while. You could have warned us, my man. Maybe we could still get Annie to fix us lunches—you know—until we wean ourselves away. Or, we could drag this last letter out for a while. I figured she would keep writing to Handel until the very end. Someone could have read the letters to him, right?"

Peter laughed. "Well, yes, someone could have read Lydia's letters to him, but evidently that isn't what Handel wanted to have happen. I'm afraid we have to accept—just as Lydia did—Handel's request that no more letters should come to him if he could not read them on his own. It's pretty clear from Lydia's letter. Let me pass your copies around. It does seem rather unceremonious, I admit—each silently reading this last letter just as we have the previous ones. I don't know, Katherine, is there some sort of ritual we could invoke here? Something we could do to underscore the importance of Lydia's last letter? What do you think?"

"Oh, let's see," said Katherine, "I suppose any who have ever attended a church service or something like that will attest to the value of hearing a text read aloud. Peter, you have been our faithful transcriber and archivist. Do you want to read the text aloud for us? Maybe we could burn some incense or sage."

"I think Katherine should read the letter," said Forella. "And we can all imagine her voice as Lydia's. I've enjoyed hearing Angela read out the texts each time for me, but it would be good to hear Katherine recite this last letter. It gives it a certain gravity, don't you think? To have it recited, to have us all hear it the same. I know I would appreciate hearing it read aloud."

Katherine smiled in Forella's direction and reached for a copy of the letter from the small pile Peter had placed on the table. "I will be happy to read the letter," she said, "though I, too, am sorry to know that this will be the last." She took her spoon and gently hit her water glass, which gave off a lovely ringing sound—a little ritual after all. Then she began reading the letter.

Mr. G F Handel, Esqr
Brook Street, near Hanover Square
London

5 March 1752

My Dear Mr Handel,
I have had no opportunity to talk with you since my brief greeting following the first staging of Jephtha at Covent Garden. My dear, dear Gif, I cannot convey how it pains me to witness your struggles to brush aside the dimming eyesight, the bouts of confusion, the impaired arm—so many challenges. Mr Harris tells me that you will

visit another physician later in the summer, but he confessed that you held little hope for improvement, at least for your ailing eyesight.

 I failed to send my customary birthday letter this year. Your request that I no longer send letters that you cannot hope to read in private is a sad petition for me to accept. And yet I understand and with reluctance shall comply. I can scarce see to write this, which must be my last such letter, for tears fill my own eyes. I have treasured this epistolary connection more than you can know. You have been that special audience for my thoughts, someone I could write to with no hesitation. Certainly, I shall speak with you and visit, but my private travels through your reading eyes into your own dear and welcoming heart—that path shall be closed to me. Thank you, dear Gif, for being the caring friend of my youth and of these waning years. I shall miss this pleasure, this quiet joy in writing to you, in imagining your warm or witty thoughts, never written but surely dreamed. Once more I chide you for rarely if ever writing in return, but that is our own private ritual, our shared custom. You compose music while I draft letters to my absorbed and brilliant friend. Whatever is, is right—so it is said, but I wish we could make some matters our own choice rather than the purview of fate.

 I must forgo penning letters to you, and you must end your long seasons of composing glorious music. Yours is the harsher sentence and one the world will lament evermore. But pity me as I agree to your unhappy request. Lascia la spina—leave the thorn but take the rose. Such a beautiful piece—I remember well your first setting of that wonderful sarabande, while we were yet in Hamburg. I will always think of my loving friend and our exchange of words and music when I hear that melody, that air—Lascia la spina, cogli la rosa. May God bless us both and may the years be kind.

 I have the honor to be, ever yours,

Mrs. Edward Grayston
In care of Mr Samuel Smyth
Berkeley Square, London

As Katherine finished reading the letter, she again lifted her free hand to her throat where a knot of sad emotion threatened to betray a mounting ache and welling tears. It was, after all, not such an easy thing to voice Lydia's sorrowful words to Handel, her last very personal admission that this letter would close a treasured kind of communion. "So," she said at last, "what do we want to ask about this last letter to Handel? What will be our themes today?"

The group as a whole was slow to respond. Perhaps everyone felt that same muted melancholy that weighed on Katherine. Finally, Rebecca spoke up. "I think we need to consider once again the many serious consequences of Handel's now inevitable blindness. Clearly it is responsible for the breaking off of this chain of letters, a chain that stretched back more than forty years. And there were other consequences as well. I think we need to talk about Handel's blindness."

Katherine wrote HANDEL'S BLINDNESS on the flip chart. She tried to return an encouraging smile to the rather glum group before her. Rayette—who only rarely offered a theme for discussion—said, "I am drawn to Lydia's forthright statement of the great pleasure she derived from writing to Handel through all those years. I would like us to talk about the peculiar one-sided ritual of letter writing that obviously served an important purpose for Lydia and, I think, for Handel as well."

Below the first topic, Katherine wrote LYDIA'S PLEASURE IN WRITING. She looked expectantly at Ross, hoping he might add a third topic, but to her surprise, it was Peter who offered a suggestion. "I detect a sad nostalgia in Lydia's farewell to their shared tradition," he said. "I think both she and Handel are looking back at their early years and savoring some of the fond memories while at the same time lamenting the falling away of those pieces of their lives that cannot travel with them into the future. I guess the topic might simply be endings and nostalgia for the past."

"We end with endings, then," said Katherine, and she wrote ENDINGS/NOSTALGIA on the flip chart. She put down her marker and turned to Rebecca. "Our first topic was Handel's blindness. Rebecca, what would you like to say to get us started?"

Rebecca reached into her bag and pulled out a printed copy of an article. "You may remember," she said, "that I referenced some time ago an article by David Hunter—the same man who wrote the book that Ross discovered on his trip to London—the book in which the author hypothesizes for Handel a lifelong infatuation with Queen Caroline. But, to our point, Hunter's earlier article had blamed lead poisoning for Handel's various ailments, including his eventual blindness. Hunter repeats that assertion in his book, but he acknowledges commentary that might lead to other explanations. As Katherine said, Hunter is a very thorough researcher. He admits the lead poisoning claim cannot be proved, but he maintains that interpretation as his favored diagnosis. Interestingly, at the same time that Hunter was publishing his most recent research, another article appeared in an international journal of Medical Humanities—this article by an eye doctor who also happens to be a great fan of opera. The man's name is Vincent de Luise, and his suggestion is that Handel suffered an anterior ischemic optic neuropathy—in other words, a small stroke that damages the optic nerve. This is not an uncommon ailment, and it often comes with age and occurs first in one eye and later—though not always—the other. It seems a reasonable alternative explanation to me."

"But," Rebecca went on, "I didn't really want to just talk about how Handel's blindness may have developed—what caused it. More important, I think, are the major changes his blindness brought to his life, to his ability to compose and direct the musical productions that had been his driving project for years—and, of course, the change this blindness brought to Handel's role as the sole and singular reader of Lydia's letters. Lydia recognized the stark finish to a long musical career this failed eyesight would bring—perhaps had already brought. *Jephtha* really was Handel's last composition. He seemed to know it, and so did Lydia. It must have been devastating, knowing that he could no longer compose the music that had been his lifeblood for fifty years."

CD looked again at his copy of Lydia's letter. "I'm sure it was crushing," he said, "not to mention physically painful. I've read about those operations—the ones both Handel and Bach endured. They actually cut directly into the patient's eye—with no anesthesia. But if your source is right, Rebecca, then Handel had no chance of regaining any kind of vision no matter what kind of surgery he had. And he needed to see to compose. Handel's composing methods were dependent on seeing, on writing, on using the intricate codes of musical notation he had always relied on. Perhaps he could play the melodies and counterpoints that were in his head, but were there people trained in musical transcription who could create a score from his playing? I very much doubt it. Musical transcription is a practice that emerged in the 1970s, and it is very difficult to do without the kind of equipment we have today. Musical transcription would come when tape recorders and other devices could slow down the process. In eighteenth-century England, Handel was left without a means to create the written scores his musicians would need. Except for his own memorized or improvisational performances at the keyboard, he was at a dead end."

From her seat at the far end of the table, Forella signaled that she had something to say. "Yes, Forella," said Katherine, "what is your thought?"

Forella held up the sheet of paper that set out a copy of Lydia's last letter. "For someone who has always had the blessing of sight and then, in a relatively short time, been deprived of it, the loss of sight is indeed devastating—depressing, maddening. I know there is writing on this paper, but I cannot read it. I am lucky to have various kinds of technology that can help and, best of all, a wonderful assistant like Angela. I am sure Handel had people able and willing to help him, but the loss of something so central to his sense of who he was must have been traumatic. My own feeling is that he did himself harm in insisting that Lydia stop writing to him. Clearly he was a proud and very private man. Cutting himself off from both his life's work and his friendly source of support in Lydia's letters—to my mind, that was a mistake. You need your friends and you need your projects even if you have to make new kinds of accommodations to continue. I think Handel let his pride get in the way on both counts. I am sorry for him. He might have been happier if he had given up a little of his privacy and perfectionism. Life, especially as one ages, requires adaptation of everyone—more from some than others."

"Handel's request that Lydia stop writing to him," said Katherine, "—that was as damaging for him as it was for Lydia. Is that what you are saying, Forella? It is very likely they were both adversely affected, I would guess. I was struck by CD's comment—that Handel was basically out of luck, except for his continuing ability and opportunities to play the organ or harpsichord. I recall that Charles Burney, writing an account of Handel's performances some years after his death, noted that Handel did continue to practice and often perform organ concertos even after the onset of blindness. But that keyboard skill was not the composing activity that had won him fame. I wonder if he found enough pleasure in playing to make up for the loss of the option to compose."

Alison nodded toward Forella's piano in the adjacent room. "People who play or sing," she said, "often do perform simply for their own enjoyment. It's not that they do not crave engagement with an audience, but there is in addition a personal pleasure in creating music. I suspect that, as Handel became increasingly withdrawn from the world of musical productions and composing, he escaped ever more often into his personal pleasure in making music, in making the keyboard sing the songs he heard in his head. If other people heard and appreciated his playing, that was good as well, but he may have simply enjoyed the thrill of practicing his music making until the very end. He seems the kind of person who had that special quality as a musical performer."

"Thanks, Alison," said Katherine. "That is an important thing to keep in mind. Handel did still have his performance skills to bring him pleasure even as his blindness developed. But he could no longer read Lydia's letters, and rather than inviting a helpful reader into the mix, he gave up that pleasure—and of course denied it henceforth to Lydia as well. More particularly, Rayette was interested in talking about the loss Lydia felt in giving up her long tradition of writing to Handel. Shall we go on to the second topic, Rayette? You wanted us to think a bit more about the value Lydia placed on her experience in writing these many letters to Handel."

"I suppose you could say that Lydia derived a certain amount of vicarious pleasure in writing to Handel," Rayette said. "I'm sure she felt the letters created an intimacy between Handel and herself, an intimacy that—as she said—was her own private path into his heart. She could share his fascinating life while yet simply looking on as a friend. So, from one perspective, Lydia would miss this special connection with the excitement of Handel's richly dynamic life. But from another point of view, we can see that she will perhaps miss even more this creative outlet, this opportunity to express herself in the language of a rarely appreciated art form—the affectionate and informal letter. Essayists, chroniclers, and diarists have come to be regarded as contributing to the pool of literary genres, especially if the writers concerned themselves with timely topics. But letter writers? Perhaps not so much. Still, I believe for eighteenth-century women in particular this may have been a largely unrecognized but popular literary avenue. I think Lydia was sorry to have to give up her own creative project, just as Handel was sorry to give up his."

Peter looked around the room to see if anyone else wanted to join the discussion. "I haven't given much thought to the idea of letters as a kind of literature," he said. "But, of course, letters are essential resources in almost all historical research. It's true that letters were a popular form of communication, especially among ladies of the gentry, but I expect most women in the eighteenth century saw their letter writing as a form of social graciousness, even entertainment. Literature was a male domain until well into the next century. Think of the women novelists in Victorian England who wrote under male pseudonyms. But, I will say, that I recently read a fascinating book about Mrs. John Quincy Adams—Louisa Johnson Adams, wife of America's sixth president. The author of this biography—Louisa Thomson—mentions the challenge Louisa Adams found in trying to write letters to her fiancé, later husband, John Quincy. Evidently elegant letter writing was not a skill taught to young aristocratic women—though many did in fact become quite accomplished at the kind of written repartee that their suitors found appealing. But even so, letters—at least letters from women writers—were seen as domestic endeavors, not expressions intended for the public eye. I don't think Lydia would have thought of her letters to Handel as anything like literature."

Clara scowled over at Peter. "I suppose you are right," she said. "It's only recently that this more intimate, less 'worldly' kind of writing has gained anything like respect—just because it was more often the domain of women. And yet, think of the vast amount of cultural information probably contained in letters like Lydia's. Historians no doubt saw their value, but the gatekeepers of literature probably wanted to reserve the loftier validation of 'literature' for the writings of men. But I think it would be indulging in stereotype to assume that all women viewed their letter writing as simply domestic graciousness, or whatever you called it. Some probably saw their writing as a kind of literature even if it was not destined to become public. Think of Emily Dickinson, writing all those wonderful poems and hiding them under her pillow. She knew they were literature. She probably knew they were really good literature. And I recall from my college classes that she wrote letters, too. But her sister burned all Dickinson's correspondence when she died—just as Emily had asked her to do—though she spared the poems. What if our Mrs. Finch had burned Lydia's letters to Handel, or Susannah Cibber had burned the delivered pack of letters, back in Handel's day? Women's correspondence, no matter how insightful or engaging, was rarely considered worth preserving. Real literature was always a man's game."

With a snort, Brad burst out, "No doubt every bedtime story, every birthday rhyme, every tombstone saying should be recorded as examples of long lost female literary genius just because women have most often been the writers of such things. Letters weren't considered literature because they weren't INTENDED to be literature—whether they were written by men or written by women. Emily Dickinson may have known her poems were literary pieces, but you can bet she didn't think of her letters as anything other than letters. That doesn't mean the letters weren't creative. Lydia's letters were a kind of creative writing, but they weren't literature. I don't doubt that she was sorry to have to give up writing letters to Handel, but I don't think she saw herself as writing literature. Peter is right on that one. Calling Lydia's letters literature is feminist overkill."

"Happily, I get to be the heavy here," said Ross, "as Katherine long ago so unkindly named me. We all seem to be agreed that Lydia relished her letter writing. She clearly experienced a great loss in having to give it up. That was Rayette's point. No need to get into a dry academic argument on the nature of literature. So, after decades of satisfying accomplishment, Lydia and Handel both had to give up the primary expressive activities they enjoyed. Handel could no longer compose—though he could still play the organ or harpsichord. And Lydia could still visit Handel in person, but she seemed to lament losing that greater depth of expression she found in writing. Time was changing the nature of their creative outlets. Sadly, both Handel and Lydia were cast into a state of melancholy by the changes time had wrought, as Peter observed earlier. That would be our third theme, right, Katherine?"

"Yes, indeed," said Katherine. "And thanks, Ross, for being our referee." She cast him a falsely concerned look. "I have no idea what ever you are talking about with this word *heavy*," she mused, as Ross folded his arms and shook his head. "A misunderstanding, no doubt—born from an overburdened imagination. Let us go on, then, to Peter's comment on the sad sense of ending both Handel and Lydia seemed to be facing. Peter?"

"Luckily for Handel," Peter began, "the townhouse on Brook Street where Handel lived was reasonably convenient to pubs, coffeehouses, and musical venues. And Handel had servants to help him with daily tasks, so his life could go on more or less as though he had simply retired from his work as a composer. He didn't have to face moving to a nursing home or trusting to the kindness of a relative to offer a place to live. No, he had the blessing of a home he was used to and servants already well adapted to his habits and wants. Nevertheless, even though he didn't have to endure that unsettling kind of change, he did have to accept the loss of a disciplined creativity that had structured his life ever since he was a teenager. I am sure he looked back on his many accomplishments not so much as grand achievements but rather as constant and even driving sources of pleasure—well, and income."

Peter signaled Benfey to switch on the LCD projector and prepare to show the clip he had set up—a performance by Ann Hallenberg of "Lascia la spina" from Handel's early oratorio, *Il triofo del Tempo e del Disinganno*. Before showing the clip, Peter said, "I thought before we look more closely at Handel and Lydia's descent into wistful nostalgia, I would share this piece of music that Lydia mentions in her letter— 'Lascia la spina'—leave the thorn but take the rose. This performance is from the Polar Prize awards ceremony in Stockholm, Sweden, in June 2016. They were honoring our friend Cecilia Bartoli—remember, from *Semele*? But Ann Hallenberg had sung the aria in a 2004 production of *Il triofo del Tempo*, so she was asked to sing in honor of her colleague at the award ceremony. Cecilia Bartoli had sung the piece as well, but her more famous rendition was of the same tune put to different words in Handel's *Rinaldo*. The version from *Rinaldo* was also famously included in the movie *Farinelli* wherein the castrato—Carlo Broschi, aka Farinelli— sings the aria on stage and sends Handel into a swoon. So, now that you know more about the song than you ever wanted to, let us watch a rather more mature than girlish Ann Hallenberg sing the lovely aria Lydia mentions in her letter."

Everyone listened and watched intently as Ann Hallenberg sang the beautiful aria—accompanied by both the Royal Stockholm Philharmonic and, interestingly, a Swedish folk music trio. Wait exclaimed immediately as the clip finished, "That was beautiful, but wasn't that the Swedish group Väsen with their unusual instruments on stage with her? I remember, back in 2009, they were here in Bloomington for the Lotus Festival, and the city even named a street or alley 'Väsen Street' in honor of them— a really popular group here. I think one of them wrote a song about it afterwards."

"That's true," said Brad. "One of them plays the nyckelharpa—a kind of keyed fiddle or hurdy-gurdy. But I was more interested in the audience shots they included in this clip from the Prize ceremony. I could tell that was Cecilia Bartoli there in the front row, and I would guess maybe her mother next to her, what do you think?"

"It seems a good guess to me," said Peter. "But I want to go back to Wait's first comment—that it was a really beautiful piece. I think it is telling that the producers for the film *Farinelli* picked that tune, out the many beautiful Handel arias, to feature in the story about the famous castrato. What is interesting about the movie is that Handel never does talk Farinelli into singing in one of his opera productions. But clearly the song itself was very popular. I recommend you all watch the movie sometime. Meanwhile, let me say a little more about this aria and its lovely melody. It was the melody that tugged at Lydia's memory. She had heard it back in Hamburg—as an instrumental piece—and had loved it ever since, evidently. In effect, she identifies it as 'their song,' the piece that recalls their relationship whenever she hears it. Handel and Lydia weren't lovers, but they had a kind of mutually recognized song that reminded each of the other—or so Lydia thought, anyway. I suppose maybe she is just projecting this shared notion unto Handel, but who knows? Maybe they had discussed it before. She hints as much. What do you think, Alison? Were these arias regarded as special 'love songs' back in Handel's day?"

"I'm not sure I could answer that," said Alison. "It's true that singers even back then adopted various arias as their signature pieces. But as to what the audience members felt about those pieces, I think we have no way of knowing—unless they wrote about their reactions in letters or reviews. I think we just have to accept the suggestion that Lydia at least saw this piece as having a special place in her heart. Even if Handel didn't have that idea himself before receiving this letter, he surely would ever after. I think it is sweet that she admitted as much to him. What an amazing compliment—the fact that she remembered his melody all those years and watched it transform into a popular song over the years. It seems like a wonderful shared memory to me."

"It's too bad they didn't have radio's top ten back then," said Clara. "But it is interesting that Handel chose to reintroduce that song into works other than that first one that Lydia heard. He must have liked it as well. Or at least he thought it worked well as an expression of some dramatic idea. She says the line she associates with the music is 'leave the thorn but take the rose.' Is that anything like the words put to the same melody in *Rinaldo*? I thought the Italian words in our video clip today were lovely, but I have no idea what they meant. Does anyone have any background on this?"

Katherine looked around the group, but no one spoke up, not even Peter, who had suggested the last theme. She looked over at Ross and smiled. "Despite our promise to not resort to actual research for this Seminar, I did look into a few things Lydia's last letter suggested to me. Peter had shown me the letter a few days ago, and I was intrigued by Lydia's reference to 'Lascia la spina.' The words from that early Italian oratorio have been translated with some variations over the years. Consider the text from the two-CD set from Erato/Warner in 2007, the one with Ann Hallenberg singing the role of Piacere or Pleasure. Speaking to the allegorical Beauty, the heroine of the piece, Pleasure says: *Avoid the thorn, pluck the rose; you are seeking your grief. Hoary frost by a secret way, will arrive when your heart does not expect it.*"

"Perhaps because Londoners were more familiar with the aria's words as they appear in the opera *Rinaldo*," Katherine continued, "Handel did not include the melody for 'Lascia la spina' in the English language reconfiguration of the early oratorio that was performed after Handel had lost his sight—the 1757 version titled *The Triumph of Time and Truth*. In the 1757 English version, the message about avoiding the thorn and plucking the rose is set to a different melody and put into the mouth of Deceit, a new character, rather than Pleasure (who, by the way, becomes a tenor in the English version). But let me share the text of our English version. These are words offered by Handel's friend, Thomas Morell, and they are not exactly a direct translation of the earlier Italian text. Here are Morell's words: *Sharp thorns despising, cull fragrant roses; why seek you treasure mixed with alloy? Old age advancing, soon the scene closes: Life's only pleasure is to enjoy.* To me, the English version, even more than the earlier one, suggests that aging is a burden and indulging in pleasures, its only fitting response."

"Let me get this straight," said Ross. "While he was still in Hamburg, Handel created this melody that Lydia associates with the words about leaving the thorn but plucking the rose, is that right?" Ross walked over and picked up the CD case and the accompanying pamphlet with liner notes Katherine had been quoting. "But," he went on, "the words she remembers are actually from a piece he composed while in Italy—this allegorical oratorio *Il trionfo del Tempo e del Disinganno*. It is the melody itself that stays with her. I find that interesting. But Lydia obviously had an important, maybe even unconscious association with the words of this earlier version of the piece. In the English version, the one that does not include the melody, Deceit, not Pleasure, is the one who suggests one should 'gather ye rosebuds while ye may.' Morell must have known Herrick's poem. His translation of the libretto has that carpe diem ring to it. But I would guess that Lydia had a different take on Pleasure's advice in that earlier Italian piece. 'Avoid the thorn but pluck the rose' could be understood as an admonition to enjoy what you can in life, to not wallow in despair or dwell on the bad times. I think Lydia heard Handel's melody as a positive kind of chorale, something like John Lennon's *Imagine*. I think she clung to the aria as a treasured inspiration, a constant in her entire adult life—and a reminder of her very dear friend, George Frideric Handel. That's my impression."

Clara laughed. "Ah, here we have Ross and his interpretations again. I think Morell had the right reading: old age comes soon enough, best to enjoy youth while you may. Handel accepted Morell's libretto because he, too, was facing old age, just as Beauty did in *The Triumph of Time and Truth*. But it looks like Morell wanted to convince Beauty to turn to God rather than indulge in the pleasures of the world. Don't you think both Handel and Lydia were thinking along those lines by then? Neither of them were spring chickens, you know."

"George Bernard Shaw said that youth is wasted on the young," came from Forella, sitting easily in her chair and lifting a glass of wine. "I think Ross is right. The older one gets, the more likely it is that one recalls with pleasure the music, sayings, and poetry stamped in memory from one's own youth. It is what is personal that resonates with us as we age. Believe me, I know that the silly songs of my youth are more precious to me than the latest compositions from the Music School—much as I appreciate their talent and efforts. Nostalgia is a powerful thing—isn't that what you suggested earlier, Peter? Aren't we all emotionally tied to our own pasts and forever in love with the lingering sights and sounds of our earliest joys and sorrows?"

Peter looked over at Alison, "Could we hear that melody again, the one that haunts Lydia as she writes to Handel?" Alison looked a bit taken aback but looked down at her copy of Lydia's letter. "Lascia la spina, cogli la rosa," she sang. "Yes," said Peter, "think of how significant that melody, those words were to Lydia, and yet they were simple, not really iconic the way, say, the Hallelujah chorus is. No, the power of the song, at least for Lydia, was in the way it sparked a memory of times gone by—when she and Handel were both young, maybe even when she first met Handel and realized that he would be a lifelong friend. Nostalgia has that very positive quality. It is what makes our childhood memories so very precious to us individually—even those memories that may not be good ones. But this one was a good memory, a kind of talisman."

"It is true that early memories often have great emotional appeal," said Katherine. "There is nothing wrong with indulging a nostalgic look backwards, and I do think that Handel and Lydia were each doing that in one way or another. But this last letter—and Handel's recast and last oratorio—these both represented endings to projects started long ago. They were both sorry to let those projects go. Change is always a challenge, but it is especially hard when the past looks better than what the future promises as a replacement. I suppose that is the negative quality of nostalgia. It can tempt us to look back rather than forward. It can lead us away from accepting and moving on to our own necessary and concrete future."

Rayette turned her copy of Lydia's letter over. "I've written out a little stanza," she said, "as is my wont. Would you like to hear it?" "Of course," rang out from all. Rayette recited:

"Constant his melody haunts me,
Recalling a distant day.
Keen was my innocent passion,
On hearing this aria play."

"Ah, that's wonderfully evocative, Rayette," said Katherine. "I'm sure Lydia did indeed remember their earliest meetings most fondly. Endings are always tough. OUR ending of this seminar is, I think, going to be tough as well. During our short break, Forella made a suggestion, one that may help us wean ourselves away a little more easily—as Brad suggested. She wondered if we might each like to reflect on the letters and our discussions in some way—in a more focused and individual statement. I will suggest we agree to meet at least two more times, maybe three, and each time turn the floor over to three or four of us, who will each present a kind of primary summary of what we have personally learned or taken away from our seminar, from our discussions of the letters. What do you think?"

"I don't know," said Brad. "That sounds a little too much like homework—as Ross worried about early on. Would we have to do a Dr. Peter Rowe and come with a PowerPoint lecture fit for a convention? I'm not up for writing a conference paper here."

Peter laughed and said, "Thanks, Brad, for that flattering image of me as a prolific researcher and lecturer. If only my higher-ups at the museum saw me that way. Actually, I think Katherine is asking us to just take the time to prepare whatever kind of presentation we want. Our time to say what we have learned that's new, or what we have found most important, maybe how old ideas have grown or been replaced. Isn't that it, Katherine? It's not really a requirement to suddenly take on the duties of an academic."

"Yes, I would say it is more like thinking back over these past months and maybe creating a long letter to the Editor for the local newspaper," said Katherine. "Since Peter is good at this sort of thing, maybe he would be willing to be our model—a different sort of model than the one we associated with him from earlier discussions. What do you say, Peter?"

"Ok, I'm game," said Peter. "I won't even insist that Ross or Katherine share the burden. I think it would be more fun to see what each of you comes up with, but I don't mind getting my little oral essay out of the way first. Remember, there is no grading going on here. It's supposed to be enlightening and more fun than a cage of monkeys. Bring it on, I say!"

"Such an obliging fellow, our Dr. Rowe," said Ross. "So, any guidelines for this closing confab, Katherine?'

Katherine smiled and looked around the group. "I really am sorry to see this Seminar end," she said. "I have so enjoyed getting to know each of you, and truthfully, I agree with Peter that it will be interesting to see what each of you decides to share as your summary statement to the rest of us. As to guidelines, I would say, do as you wish. Write something out, bring notes, do a PowerPoint if you want to, speak off the top of your head, but we should each make an effort, I think, to express what has been most valuable or personally enlightening about this activity—about reading these letters and discussing them in this group situation. I would expect that you might each spend ten or fifteen minutes, maybe more, sharing what you have found most worthwhile and memorable. I suppose those of us who helped organize this Seminar would find it helpful to hear how you might have changed your mind on some issue or how interacting with others has helped you articulate your own thoughts more clearly—if it has. And if not, then we need to know that as well. Granted, businesses, hotels, and restaurants are always asking for reviews, but it does help to know what people think. Thanks in advance, everyone, for taking time to plan out your short presentation. I'll ask Angela to set up a schedule for us. Look for a message from her. I look forward to what I guess we might call our closing review sessions. See you next time."

CHAPTER 25

Your Humble Servant

―ᔐ―

Peter drove the back roads after visiting yet again that small but well-kept graveyard some forty miles west of his home. He thought about how his first love still lived in his memory, how she came to him in dreams, sweet and unbidden. Why do I treasure this heartache, he wondered. Why do I carry this torch, this sad, unsettling reverie? So much has transpired since that distant time. I have grown. Other loves have come and gone. Why this pull to my first romance? What is the meaning of our dreams and our lingering affections? Is there a tie in this to my immersion in the life of Handel and his letter-writing friend? What has Stephie to do with Lydia? What has Handel to do with me? "What's Hecuba to him or he to Hecuba that he should weep for her?" Or is it Handel's supposed early love for Queen Caroline that stirs my empathy? Perhaps that haunting sense of long lost love is the text I can take from my Handel experience.

―ᔐ―

THE HANDEL SEMINAR GATHERED AT Forella's large table, eager to share the wonderful homemade pizzas Annie had prepared for the day's meeting. Alison and Peter had both followed Annie into the kitchen to hear her comments about (and see) the pizza stone she had used in baking the pizzas. Everyone agreed the crusts were superb, as were the toppings, both meaty and not. As everyone sat down with a slice or two of pizza and a bit of salad, Katherine stood and motioned Ross and Peter to stand as well. "We—the co-chairs of this group," said Katherine, "have decided together on an order of responses, and Angela sent you each a memo with information about this line-up shortly after our last meeting. We wanted you to know that it was indeed a joint decision. We thought it best for each of the three of us to anchor one of the three meetings, thus the placement of Ross and me to subsequent meetings. The rest of you were randomly selected—literally pulled out of a hat. And we included Angela and Benfey as well. They have sat patiently listening through most of our discussions, and it seems right to include them. So, there you have it. Now, on to this delicious pizza party."

Soon after plates were cleared away and everyone settled in once again with beverages in hand and some tangy lemon bars as dessert, Katherine stood and placed a somewhat worn Greek fisherman's cap in front of Peter. "You are now officially our Captain," she said, "at least for the next twenty or thirty minutes. We eagerly await your verbal essay on whatever you have found most personally compelling or valuable or simply provocative about the Handel letters and our many months of discussion here in this Seminar. The floor is yours. We promise not to interrupt, and we all sincerely thank you for volunteering to go first. Bonne chance!"

Peter chuckled and put on the hat, saluting in the direction of Katherine and Ross. Then he rather soberly removed it and placed it on the table again. "I've thought a good bit about what I might say here," he began. "It has been a rare privilege preserving and transcribing these letters, but that is not what I want to talk about today. As you might guess, I have been most attracted by questions these artifacts raise about historical changes, especially how the nearly three hundred years that separate us from Handel have altered the way we live our lives, the way I live my life. There have been innumerable changes but perhaps none so compelling as the change in the role and importance of marriage. Handel did not marry—we know that. You might argue that the topic is therefore not a relevant one. But I have found questions about how our views on marriage have changed since Handel's time very interesting and, shall we say, personally instructive. I promise I will get to this last part—my personal response—before I finish, but let us consider first some of the historical information about marriage that has emerged from our discussion of these letters."

"Early on," he began, "we had a lengthy discussion on the topic of marriage in Handel's time. I actually took some notes on our discussion because I found the exchange so informative. For example, Rebecca mentioned a book titled *Marriage: A History*, by Stephanie Coontz. I tracked down a copy of Coontz's book, and I went back and reread Lydia's letters that had prompted Rebecca to mention that research. Wait mentioned a general consensus that people tended to marry later in Handel's time, and it seems that was true, at least in Western cultures. Alison shared the little anecdote about Buxtehude's daughter and Handel's rejection of the opportunity to marry and take on the position of organist at the church in Lübeck. And Katherine sang the folk ballad about Mary Hamilton, the woman who reportedly sent her illegitimate child—offspring of the king—out to drown at sea. We talked, again at some length, about why people today get married, but we left floating the comparison between marriage in Handel's time and marriage now. I'd like to go back to that juxtaposition of marriage in the two time periods and draw out some significant changes that have occurred over time."

"To some extent, I might be toying with the question: If Handel were alive today, would he choose to marry? And if so, why? But maybe we can come back to that. In the early 1700s, when Handel was a young man, the primary reasons for marrying were social, financial, even political and, of course, religious—though, for Christians, Saint Paul actually advised people to remain single and celibate but admitted in First Corinthians that it is 'better to marry than to burn.' So, generally in Handel's time, it was considered most socially acceptable to be married because, after all, it meant you were a stable adult and thus a responsible citizen. Men who chose not to marry were suspect, mostly because marriage didn't necessarily cut off their chances for sexual adventures outside the marriage since society turned a blind eye to mistresses, and wives were expected to tolerate the practice. Then there was the whole incentive to maintain or even enhance one's social standing, one's place as part of the gentry, by marrying into a high-ranking family. In her recent book on Handel and his many interesting friends, Ellen Harris singles out the life of Mary Granville Delany as especially telling. I took a look at Delany's diaries, and it is true—as Harris argues—that social standing was very significant and marrying well was the primary way to ensure one's place among the gentry. For Mary Delany, marriage—at least her first marriage—was a personal disaster and a clear lesson against the convention of marrying for the sake of monetary or social gain. But even her own family had regarded marrying as more or less her duty—to them, to herself, and to society."

"Handel was unusual, then, in not marrying, but as Ellen Harris points out, many of Handel's closest friends were also either not married or oddly married. It seems that Handel was, if anything, skeptical of the benefits of marriage, at least for himself. If you take the libretti of his many operas at face value, it would appear that he viewed the high drama brought on by obstructed love affairs as absolutely essential to a good opera plot. And those dramatic storylines always led to marriage or a reuniting of married or betrothed lovers at the end. And yet the thing about an opera is that it typically immerses the audience in the drama for three hours and then stops—like the proverbial fairytale—with the 'happily every after' ending. Lydia warned Handel to not follow the fantasies of the stage by falling in love with his singing stars, but in fact, it doesn't appear that Handel needed that advice. He seems to have separated his own life from the fiction of the stage quite well."

"Lydia's worry, it seems to me, stems from her ready acceptance of the generally held, eighteenth century views on marriage—that it was necessary for a good life, that it brought stability and happiness and was preferable to remaining single. But I think, if we give Handel a fair reading, he found a way to be satisfied with his life despite going against the grain. I would say, in fact, that he very likely found the expectation that he would or should marry abhorrent, a restrictive tradition that seemed unnecessary and perhaps even a bit cruel when maintained in the class-conscious way that it was in England of the eighteenth century. It is possible that he did love Queen Caroline—as David Hunter fantasized. And he may well have resented the notion that he could not hope to marry up to her more exalted status. But Handel was a very intelligent and practical man. I would guess that he relished the deep feelings he had for, say, someone like Queen Caroline, but he also recognized that there was little to be gained in pining ever after or even in denying himself other love affairs. He seemed to have found a sane and enjoyable life without being married. I suspect that his own integrity would not allow him to marry simply for the sake of meeting society's expectation that he do so."

"And now," said Peter, signaling Benfey to turn on the projector he had set up beforehand, "I would ask you to sit back and watch a clip from a performance-based film titled *A Night with Handel*. This same duet—'Per le porte del tormento'—was, as you may remember, sung by Inger Dam-Jensen and Cristophe Dumaux in the 2008 Danish Royal Opera production of Handel's *Partenope*, but these are different singers. The duet was actually borrowed from another Handel opera, *Sosarme*, but it perfectly captures Handel's overriding message about love and marriage in *Partenope*, which is likely why the impresario of the Danish production we watched on DVD chose to insert it at the end. In the *Cambridge Handel Encyclopedia*, Handel scholar David Vickers argues that each of the five protagonists in *Partenope* 'experiences a vital lesson of love that makes them wiser.' And I would agree. By the end of this opera, each of the characters seems to have grown in personal understanding and sensitivity. It is telling to me that Handel had wanted to share this story with his audiences for years, ever since he first heard the story back in Venice in 1708. The fact that it involves disguise and cross dressing simply reinforces for me the likelihood that Handel did not see marriage as a necessity so much as a conventional testing ground for depth and sincerity of affections between people, no matter their gender or status."

"And so," Peter said, raising his wineglass in a mock toast as the clip finished, "this leads to our query on whether we might have had a married

Handel if he were living today. I rather doubt it, though he may have tried a brief period of matrimony when he was young. Marriage is still the ideal norm today, and the general consensus is that married people live happier and longer lives. But Handel was contentedly self-sufficient in the 1700s, and I expect he would be similarly independent today. I go back always to that anecdote about a very young Handel running after his father as his father's coach headed to Weissenfels. To me, that is Handel in a nutshell, a stubborn and self-determined person unafraid of going against the rules and expectations that his society (or his mother) placed upon him. Here and now, in the twenty-first century, Handel might live with a woman (or perhaps even a man) that he felt strongly about, but he would not see the necessity to marry. That is my view of his character."

Peter continued. "Does an individual's character or identity determine whether he or she marries? Most people do choose to marry, even if they do not remain married. Many choose to marry several times—either after the death of a spouse or after divorce. But the assumption, even from Handel's time, is that a person wants to marry for love, to marry someone who is compatible, the desired 'other.' In *Partenope*, Arsace loves both Partenope, the Queen, and Rosmira, his betrothed who comes seeking him in disguise as a man. Both of the women are assertive, vigorous, and passionate. Perhaps Arsace needed to see that assertive side of Rosmira before he realized that she is the one he wanted to marry after all. The words to 'Per le porte del tormento' declare what is required of the lovers before they can agree to marry: 'Through the gates of suffering lovers' souls must pass on their way to true joy.' Handel's task as composer was to make that painful suffering and eventual joy come alive in his music. I think he valued marriage as the great incentive it was in his opera scores, but I am not so sure that he personally found the idea attractive."

"How is marriage different today than it was in Handel's time? There is no question that more marriages end in divorce today than did in the 1700s, especially in modern America. Some forty to fifty percent of marriages do not last, and often second and third marriages end in divorce as well. Some people refer to this practice as serial monogamy—one spouse at a time, but several over a lifetime. This same phenomenon might have happened in Handel's time but owing to the death of the spouse rather than divorce. In any case, ex-husbands and ex-wives and step-families are a frequent result today. In Handel's day, families that included half-siblings were fairly common—as was the case in Handel's own family. Handel may even have benefited from having an older father, one no longer concentrating on his own career but instead able to advise and spend time with his son. And, of course today, we have a growing acceptance of same-sex marriage and mixed race marriage—partnerships usually not recognized in any official way in Handel's time. But the ideal psychological connection whereby two people came together out of love and appreciation for the partner's character and compatibility—that bond has become even more important as a reason to marry in the first place. Handel's *Partenope* still speaks to audiences today because it is really a drama about recognizing the role of individual character and personal responsibility in creating a successful marriage."

"Finally, then, what do I, for my part, take away from this meditation on Handel's bachelorhood? Am I likely to emulate Handel's own decision to avoid marriage, or instead to follow the advice his characters sing in *Partenope*? I have been married twice, and I don't rule out the possibility of marrying again. Handel seemed more content with his life as a single person than I am. Perhaps that is because he had servants to take care of him, or maybe he had plenty of non-connubial affairs and saw no need to marry. He does not strike me as the sort to easily accommodate another person's needs or wants, and he was highly competitive—not the easiest kind of person to live with. Maybe he recognized that he would not be a particularly good partner. Yours truly is, however, rather more needy and woebegone than Handel evidently was. Nevertheless, I do find his example reassuring. He survived quite well and seemed not to be horribly depressed. I can only wish the same for myself as the coming years fall away. Or—who knows, maybe I'll get lucky."

Peter picked up the captain's hat, put it on his head, then doffed it as everyone clapped. "Thank you, thank you," he said. "And who is next to get the cap?" Rayette waved. "According to the memo I received, I'm next, but I'll forego the hat," she said with a laugh. Peter placed the hat in front of her, and said, "Just a symbolic icon, then. And a special thank you to Annie, who filled my water glass as I was talking. Carry on, Rayette. We are all ears."

Rayette lifted her own water glass, which she had filled earlier from the pitcher on the buffet. "Your thanking Annie actually makes a nice segue into my topic," she said. "I'd like to talk about people who give service to others, and like you, Peter, I want to compare Handel's time and our time, and maybe Europe and America. We've been blessed to have a wonderful person like Annie preparing our lunches and making sure everything is convenient for us as we hold our meetings. Forella is her employer, but Annie graciously agreed to this arrangement, even welcomed the chance to try her hand at feeding this motley bunch, or so she said. Annie and Randolph are considered household staff. Most people in twenty-first century America do not have such folks on staff in their homes—only the wealthy, and then often not on a full-time basis. But we know that Handel had at least three or four servants in his house on Brook Street, and before that he lived in the homes of various aristocratic patrons, who, of course, had a multitude of servants, many of whom tended to Handel's daily needs. I have a personal reason for being interested in this subject, and again like Peter, I will save it for last. For now, let us consider the group of people identified as servants in our unfolding story of Handel's life."

"There were several things that sparked my interest in servants. They show up in a variety of contexts: for example, we mentioned the young woman, Marie, who accompanied Handel to Hamburg when he left Halle as a teenager. We guessed that she was going there to work as a maid or governess. Then, in an early letter, there was Lydia's remark that she had learned the ballad about Mary and Joseph—the 'Cherry Tree Carol'— from her lady's maid. And several of us commented on how favorably the servant was depicted in the movie about *The Great Mr. Handel*. Then, of course, there was Handel's will, in which he left a substantial sum to his primary manservant and lesser amounts to his other servants. These instances all seem fairly positive, but there is ample evidence that Handel joined his aristocratic friends in viewing servants as a class apart, an underclass. Granted, there was not quite the upstairs/downstairs phenomenon we associate with Victorian England, but servants were still definitely at a lower rung on the social status ladder."

"Several biographers have pointed out Handel's aversion to ever being taken on as a house musician, someone hired to perform for a wealthy household. He gladly accepted a royal pension as music teacher to the royal princesses, and, early in his career, he willingly served without pay or contract in the households of wealthy patrons. But his lifetime goal was to be an independent, self-employed composer, though of course he needed to strike entrepreneurial deals with stage managers, singers, tickets holders, and others. Nevertheless, he wanted always to be seen as a member of the gentry, even when his funds were low. I think he did view work as a servant as suitable to persons of lower status than himself. Does this mean he viewed servants as less worthy as human beings? Did he think of himself as better than they were?"

"I think Handel shared his culture's view of servants as subordinate and, in some ways, inferior to the gentry. But it seems likely that he recognized the role of circumstance as more important than, say, an innate quality in the bloodline. Though a growing middle class was to emerge late in the eighteenth century, during Handel's time, the primary players in European society were a small elite and a large lower class, which included many of the families from which servants were drawn. Handel's own childhood family was part of the emerging professional class. If you remember, we discussed his father's reluctance to have a musician in the family. A doctor or lawyer would, if successful, be deemed part of the professional class while a musician would be regarded as a servant—talented, but a servant nonetheless. And, even though young people from the professional class did often serve for a few years as maids or apprentices, their long-term goals were directed at work and marriage that would move them up the social ladder. Handel, I would guess, never wanted to be seen as even temporarily fitting in with the 'servant class.' When he moved to London, he began signing his letters with the abbreviation for Esquire following his name—a clear sign that he wanted to be viewed as a gentleman, part of the gentry, not as a servant in any capacity."

"There clearly was a conventional view of servants as a lower class of people, and Handel was obviously wary of ever losing his higher status as a gentleman. Handel's audiences were mostly the moneyed elite, the leisure class, and he wanted to be seen as sharing their customs and maybe even their prejudices about the servant class. Several sources report him making a joke about the composer Christoph Gluck knowing less counterpoint than Handel's one-time cook, Waltz. Gustavus Waltz was a bass singer in a number of Handel's operas. The anecdote suggests Handel's sarcastic wit, but it also reveals his shared notion that people of the servant class were a cut below the gentlemen who studied music professionally. Was this truly Handel's view? Or was he just eager to fit in with his socially elite friends? My own feeling is that Handel actually had clear respect and affection for servants who were good at their tasks and eager to offer the support he needed—whether physical or even of the heart."

"This is the crux of my little talk here today. To my mind, what ultimately became clear is that Handel relied heavily upon his servants, not simply to keep him fed and properly dressed each day, but also to be the living connections with his inner human soul, his psyche. The study of psychology isn't my thing. I leave that to Peter. But I have always thought that the care and compassion demonstrated by people who serve others is an overlooked value in just about every human social context. People forget that domestic help is almost always also the source of a comfortable and comforting relationship. And Handel was in special need of this kind of human connection. In his will, he was particularly concerned to show his appreciation for his servants and to give them the means for living a good life after his own death. He left his valet five hundred pounds and all of his linens and wearing apparel. Basically Handel set up his manservant to henceforth live the life of a gentleman if he so chose. John Duburk— the nephew who replaced Handel's old servant, Peter LeBlond—could, because of Handel's generosity, afford to buy the household goods that remained in Handel's Brook Street residence after his death. It seems that Handel wanted to see his servants do well after he was gone."

"Handel had many friends, of course, including Lydia. But the people who saw him every day, stayed with him when he was ill, knew his habits and preferences, welcomed him home after a grueling rehearsal, and probably tried very hard to make his life as cheerful and untroubled as possible—those people were his faithful servants. I think we need to assume that they added immeasurably to Handel's sense of well being. Why was I attracted to this particular theme out of the many we have considered in our seminar? One reason was a very personal connection with care giving. Back in the 1970s, about the time I was ready to go to college, my family moved back to the US because Grand'Mere, my Grandma, who still lived in St. Louis, had suffered a stroke and needed someone to care for her. My parents left their comfortable life in Paris and came back home to be with my Grandma. If you remember, I expressed my dismay at the kind of racism I encountered here in the United States. I was not happy to be back, but I did respect my parents for making that sacrifice. I learned a lot just watching how they made helping my Grandma enjoy her last years their first priority. They did it out of love, of course, not for pay, but still, I could see that it represented the kind of compassion all good caregivers bring to their task. I'm sure they didn't see themselves as servants or anything like that, but in fact they did serve in the best possible way. And I have been impressed with that role ever since—that willingness to be the person that serves another person's needs."

"It has been a big disappointment to me to see a growing loss of respect for what you might call the serving professions—things like teaching, nursing, social work. Even physicians are now micromanaged by insurance agencies. It's as though any line of work that doesn't consider making money it's primary raison d'être doesn't warrant the high respect it used to. I think Handel knew that all the people who served him in some way were in fact very important. In his will he left money to the charity that helped down and out musicians as they aged. He left quite a large sum to a man named James Smyth—a perfumer who lived in Handel's neighborhood. I was intrigued by this and found that a perfumer was a special kind of caregiver in the eighteenth century, someone who used scents to sometimes heal but mostly to soothe and uplift people with chronic illnesses. Smyth was one of the last people to see Handel before he died. I am sure he brought him welcome relief and comfort in his final hours."

Rayette looked around at the other Seminar members. "Blacks in America have almost always been forced to take on the role of giving service, whether they wanted to or not. Slavery is a great blot—a disgrace—on the history of America, well, not just America—wherever slavery was practiced or enabled. And slavery's clearest aftermath has been extreme racism throughout the United States. As I said, I was dismayed by the unabated racism I encountered when I returned to the US as a young woman. I remain dismayed today, and it has become even worse with the added prejudices directed against our Mexican brothers and sisters or anyone, really, who isn't white. But one thing I became aware of as I read these letters and thought about Handel's relationship to his servants back in the 1700s—I realized that he did in fact appreciate the very important way each of them met his need for the services they provided but also for companionship, for a caring support system. Granted, they were paid, and they could have left it they chose to. They weren't slaves. Still, I don't think people here in America have ever recognized the significant contribution black slaves and all the many black or brown service workers have so often made to the psychological health of this country. I think Handel's servants—in whatever capacity they served him—I think they knew that he was grateful for their care, their compassion, and their day-to-day interaction and friendly support. I think we could all learn from this particular of Handel's example. We should all learn to be a little more grateful for the special efforts of caregivers and other people who serve us in so many ways."

"And, as you might expect, I have written a little poem about people who choose to serve others rather than making the acquisition of wealth their only goal. It's not that I am anti-capitalist—though I do think capitalism is largely at fault for the racism in America. Even Handel, through his investments, supported the growing slave trade out of Africa, and the slave trade reinforced the idea that black Africans were less than human—tradable goods, property to be used in gaining a profit. But to return to my theme, I certainly do not think that all African-Americans have a natural capacity to serve or even necessarily a higher level of compassion. I hate that kind of stereotyping. It's just that to my mind, we should all recognize and be grateful for the service we receive. So often these are people who rarely are acknowledged as being so very important to our daily lives, much more important than the people who know very little beyond how to strike deals and make money. I've always liked the way people used to close letters with the words *Your Servant.*"

"So, here is my poem:

My grand-père wore a slave's brand
    You forced him to serve you.
I am a mother
    I serve out of love.
I am an artist
    Art serves out of awe.
I am a teacher
    I serve to inspire.
I am a poet
    Words serve to arouse.
I am a helper
    I serve to be kind.
I take up my calling
    With heart, hand, and soul.
I act as your servant
    But never your slave."

As everyone clapped, Rayette picked up the captain's hat and said, "Thank you for your attention and good fellowship, everyone. I've enjoyed getting to know each of you. And now, I guess this cap is supposed to go to our next speechmaker. Who would that be?"

Forella lifted her walking stick and said, "That would be me. I had hoped to be one of the last to speak, but, as Katherine said, this was a random name-out-of-the-hat selection, so I have no choice but to be the next speaker. I asked Angela to help me find some of the sources I wanted to consult before I spoke. Rayette, you are so right—people like Angela, Annie, and Randolph not only serve in countless essential ways but also make the lives of everyone they work with considerably richer and more agreeable. I am one lucky woman."

Angela smiled and handed Forella a clicker that allowed her to play voice memos from her tablet. These were simple cues in an outline Angela had entered earlier as Forella dictated her thoughts on her chosen topic. "No doubt most of you were expecting me to offer some conclusion about my initial objective," Forella mused, "but I will have to admit that nothing in the letters supported in any way the theory that Ross was a present day reincarnation of George Frideric Handel. I knew that disappointing outcome was a possibility when I first sought out these documents from the past, but I am not sorry at all that we convened our little Seminar. And, to be honest, I still found helpful insights into a closely related question just the same. Ross and Peter reported to me that our Mrs. Finch— back in her home in the English countryside—had toyed with the idea of reincarnation as well. So, it wasn't a misstep at all, just a divergent turn along the way."

"More to the point, then," she continued, "what I remain interested in is the question of what we mean by the word *soul*. Perhaps the soul is not something that can be reincarnated, but is it something that exists before we are born? Does it descend from heaven or emerge from the ether when we take our first breath? Does God give each individual a soul? Is a soul simply part of the larger Oversoul that Ralph Waldo Emerson wrote about? As you can see, I am still pondering the idea of a person having a separate and maybe eternal soul—whether it can be reincarnated or not. I still wonder about the soul of a great man like Handel, or a wonderful person like my son, or even about my own soul. Do we have something in us that defines our self, our personality and existence? That question has stayed with me throughout our time together. I am not sure that I have answered it satisfactorily—for myself or for you, but I can say a bit more about where the question has led me, what I have gained from thinking about Handel and Lydia and the idea of the soul."

"There was a decade or so in Handel's life when he seemed to be thinking rather earnestly about the state of his soul. In 1737, when Handel was fifty-two years old, he suffered a stroke or some kind of paralysis, and soon thereafter he traveled to Aix-la-Chapelle on the far western border of Germany. The goal of this journey was to 'take the waters' of the famous spa there, and he stayed for nearly two months. He did recover and return to London, but his health was not good from that time on, and, interestingly, I thought, he immediately sat for a statue of himself to be placed in the chic Vauxhall Gardens. It seems he was starting to be aware of his own mortality and to consider how he might want to be remembered after his own death. Later that same year, Queen Caroline died, and Handel composed her funeral anthem, *The Ways of Zion Do Mourn*. Soon after, he turned to composing biblical oratorios, including *Messiah*. The state of the human soul certainly was the subject of one of the best-known arias from *Messiah*, 'I Know That My Redeemer Liveth.' In 1750, Handel had that unfortunate coaching accident while travelling in The Netherlands. And, upon returning to London and perhaps while pondering his injuries that were, after all, quite severe, he made the first version of his will."

"The notion of the soul brings up, to me at least, a mishmash of ideas I have thought about throughout my long life—from pre-existence to the survival of the soul after death, from reincarnation to Jung's collective unconscious. Years ago, my cousin thought he had it all figured out. According to his view as a theosophist, the soul was somewhere between the material body and the spiritual self. I was never sure what that meant. With Angela's help, I have been reading some more recent writings about how consciousness emerged in humans. It seems to me that we have to know more about consciousness before we can say whether or not there is a soul. My cousin thought that Handel's soul could have been reborn in my son Ross, but I have come to dislike the idea of anyone having any soul other than his or her own. After all, if you believe in reincarnation, Handel wasn't the start of the line. He inherited someone else's soul, too, and that doesn't seem right. He was a unique and amazing person, just as my son Ross is. I don't think a soul can be shared. Religion—many religions—teach us that we are given a soul when we are born, some people say, even before we are born. Some people say that a soul or person comes into existence only as we live our lives. But if a soul arises as a person lives his or her life, then it is more or less dependent on consciousness. When a person dies, that would be the end."

"I've always liked the old Carter Family song, 'Will the Circle Be Unbroken?' It's about how the singer hopes to meet his mother after death. That's an appealing thought—that we will see the people we have loved when we die. Sometimes my heart breaks all over again when I think about my own mother and other people who have died. But as I have been listening to more books about consciousness and what Daniel Dennett calls 'the science of the soul,' I worry that hopes of reuniting with parents or dear friends in some heaven may just be wishful thinking. When Stanton died, I wanted desperately to know that he was still around, still somehow alive, even if not here, in this world. I have my memories of course, but was there really still a soul, some being somewhere that lives on as a separate person, the person I remember? And, as I've gotten older, I've had to think about my own life. Will I simply stop being when I die? I think Handel was starting to have those thoughts, too, as his health deteriorated and as his friends and relatives died one by one. It is that question of the soul, its source, its possible immortality—that has stayed with me throughout our discussions of Handel. It is the thread I have tried to pick out from reading Lydia's letters and examining Handel's life. It is what I wanted to know from the very beginning."

"Have I succeeded, have I found an answer? I don't think so. But I am still searching, even at my age. I hope that is a good thing. Some of my very dear friends chide me for abandoning the beliefs of my childhood.

They warn that I will long for the comfort of a savior when it is clear that my days must end. But that ending is clear now. I am inches from the end and miles from the beginning. I am less worried at the idea of non-being than I thought I would be. Melting back into the stuff of life, the pool of atoms that made us, does not make me fearful. I have found a new song—a substitute for 'Will the Circle Be Unbroken'—much as I still love that song. My friends at the Unitarian church sing a hymn called 'Spirit of Life.' It is not an old song. Angela looked it up for me in the UU hymnal, *Singing the Living Tradition*. The songwriter, Carolyn McDade, suggests something else, something more inclusive, than the old idea of the soul. I like the notion of Life itself as something I am a part of, something I will continue to inhabit, even after I die. I feel Handel was searching the sources he had available to him back in the 1700s—mostly the Bible of course, but also some of the Enlightenment writers. I wonder what he would find today that would inspire the kind of awe he conveyed through *Messiah*. A part of me does wish that Handel's soul had indeed been reincarnated in my son, or maybe someone else. Then we would have a new kind of *Messiah*—an oratorio that celebrates the wonder of our collective participation in the cosmos—a new kind of Hallelujah."

Angela leaned over and gave Forella a hug. "Forella asked me to share with you the duet we listened to some time ago," she said. "This is 'As Steals the Morn' from Handel's *L'Allegro, Il Penseroso, ed Il Moderato*. If you remember, Ross and Alison performed it for us many meetings ago. This final duet tells us that there is an advantage in letting intellect be our guide. Before you listen, let me read you the text. It was written in English:

> As steals the morn upon the night,
> And melts the shades away:
> So truth does Fancy's charm dissolve,
> And rising reason puts to flight
> The fumes that did the mind involve,
> Restoring intellectual day."

The Handel Letters

Angela brought up the audio clip, and everyone listened as English singers Mark Padmore and Lucy Crowe, along with The English Concert led by Andrew Manze, performed the wonderfully optimistic "As Steals the Morn." Forella clasped her hands together. "I just love that piece—so beautiful."

"And now," said Angela, picking up the Greek captain's hat from in front of Forella, "I guess this cap goes to Benfey—hers was the next name drawn from the hat. Here you go, Benfey. I can watch your recording equipment while you are talking if you want me to. I know you do a lot more than just watch the dials, but I'll do what I can."

"Thanks, Angela," said Benfey, who actually put the hat on her head. "I like the captain's hat. I may have to get myself one. So—my response after these many months of being mostly your recorder, archivist, and IT person: I have followed along. Observing and listening in has been great fun, and I'd say I've learned a lot. Like Peter, I feel this Seminar has been a good opportunity to exercise some of my skills—in this case, as an ethnographer and as an audio engineer. But, yeah, I have also given some thought to what I can personally take away from this Seminar."

"I'd like to go back to the very first meeting I had with all of you. My recording equipment and I have been pretty much in the background throughout most of this Seminar. At our first meeting we learned about the letters we would be examining—the letters that Lydia Grayston sent to Handel. I was actually expecting that Peter would talk about the letters. After all, he is the one who has handled the transcription, translation, printing out—and of course the preservation—of these very important artifacts. But he chose not to talk about his technical management of the letters but to instead talk about marriage in Handel's time and in our time. So, I guess that leaves me free to talk about the letters as artifacts, something I'm very interested in anyway."

"I've grown up with electronic devices being the primary means for sending and receiving messages. I guess I have gotten a few real letters in my life, but not many. Well, documents maybe—like my admission letter to the University or, back in Cambridge, a letter informing me of my qualifications from the sixth form exams. And my Grandmother usually sends me a birthday card with a hand-written note, but mostly I interact with people by texting or sending messages through some social network. So, I was interested in these letters as an earlier and essential means of communicating."

Benfey picked up a small hardbound book. "Peter talked about this book some time ago. It is an edited collection of *The Letters and Writings of George Frideric Handel*, first published in 1935 and reprinted in 1970. I borrowed this copy from the Music Library at IU. The Editor, Erich Müller, rounded up, copied, transcribed, and printed out autographs—letters in Handel's own hand—from various sources, mostly in England and Germany, several in private collections. These would be the equivalent of the letters Lydia wrote to Handel, but of course not conveniently ordered and preserved in a single place as were Lydia's letters. As Müller points out, there weren't a lot of letters out there either to Handel or from him. This collection includes thirty letters written by Handel: seven to his brother-in-law, Michael Michaelsen, nine to one of his librettists, Charles Jennens, a few to his friend Johann Mattheson, two to George Philipp Telemann, and several others, including one written directly to King George the First of England. Imagine that!"

"So, in terms of technology, in the 1700s they had the printing press. It had been around for at least a couple centuries. Books and even sheets of music were printed using movable type. If you visit Independence National Historical Park in Philadelphia, you can see a recreation of Ben Franklin's print shop and see how they set type and created newspapers. I stopped there when I first came to the US, and I thought it was great. But back in the eighteenth century, regular correspondence between individuals was almost entirely through hand written letters. I found it interesting that, in Handel's day, some literary works and quite a few journalistic pieces took the form of personal letters even when printed and made available for public distribution. In other words, some writers mimicked the more personal form of the letter even while they were aiming for some sort of mass communication. Twitter accounts in the eighteenth-century! Well, not really. But I did find one example of this letter-writing representation that seems especially relevant."

"Here at IU, at the Lilly Library, the rare books library," Benfey continued, "there is a collection of Daniel Defoe's political pamphlets—you know, the man who wrote *Robinson Crusoe*. Defoe was writing about the same time that Handel was producing operas in London, the early 1700s. Defoe wrote quite a few pieces under the pseudonym of Andrew Morton, but, despite the fake name, a number of times the law tracked him down and arrested him for expressing subversive views and encouraging dissent. Several of his publications were written as supposed letters between a Frenchman living in England and his brother in France. So at least we can get a sense of the kind of letters that were common in that period. Defoe's materials are pretty interesting—worth a trip to the Lilly."

"But, back to Handel and his letters. Letters were used in place of the telephone or today's texts and emails. If you needed to correspond with someone and couldn't do it in a face-to-face situation, then you sent a letter. But, I think there were probably times when a letter was more appealing than talking directly with someone. It certainly seemed like Lydia often chose to write when she could have instead simply talked with Handel. Handel's letters to his brother-in-law—which continued long after Handel's sister had died—those letters had to go to Germany, so distance was a factor there. Nevertheless, it seemed like Handel used the medium of the letter to say things he might not have said so directly in person. In one letter he tells Michaelsen that he will explain something more clearly in person when he visits—that he was delayed and that some monetary draft would indeed be honored. It appears that his brother-in-law had sent a letter earlier and that Handel had not responded in a timely manner. Handel expresses great regret at this delay—all in very fine French—though Handel and Michelsen both were native German-speakers. In another letter, Handel spoke of his tears at learning of his mother's death. Some such sentiments were probably more easily expressed in a letter than in person. There was a certain almost ritualistic formality about Handel's letters that conveyed a sense of weightiness or honor or a more profound depth of feeling. At least that is how the letters seemed to me."

"Even Handel's letters to Charles Jennens are always extremely polite and formal. Jennens was known to have criticized Handel's composition of—believe it or not—*Messiah*. In one letter sent to Jennens in 1744, some time after Jennens had finally heard the oratorio performed in London, Handel responds without a trace of arrogance, writing, 'Be pleased to point out these passages in the Messiah which you think require altering.' Jennens was a writer and editor—the compiler of the Old and New Testament words of Handel's *Messiah*, but he was not a composer. I am impressed that Handel accepted suggestions from anyone, let alone someone who is not himself a musician and composer. But perhaps, again, that was the advantage in being able to ask in a letter. Body language, eye rolling, and under-the-breath swearing would be absent in a formal and courteous letter—which, in this case, ended with the closing: 'Believe me to be with the greatest Respect, Sir, Your most obedient and most humble Servant, George Frideric Handel.' Handel and Jennens were friends, but the convention of letter writing imposed its own kind of stylistic restraint, it seems to me."

Benfey continued, "Another very interesting letter to Jennens includes Handel's detailed advice on the technical aspects of an organ Jennens was going to have built—evidently for his estate at Gopsall. Handel comments knowledgably on the proposed builder of the organ—a Mr. Richard Bridge—and on the various stops and the materials to be used. Clearly Handel was an expert source for judging the quality of an instrument, and he offered to give his opinion of the organ when the builder finished. Here, Handel's language is direct and includes a long sentence that somehow for me reflects a side of Handel that I can most easily identify with. He writes: 'Yesterday I received Your letter, in answer to which I hereunder specify my Opinion of an Organ which I think will answer the Ends you propose, being every thing that is necessary for a good and grand Organ, without reed Stops, which I have omitted, because they are continually wanting to be tuned, which in the Country is very inconvenient, and should it remain useless on that account, it would still be very expensive althou' that may not be your consideration.' To me, this sentence reveals to us the techy Handel, the engineer he might have been had he not decided to become a musician and composer."

"That organ builder letter also contains a hint of Handel's awareness of his friends' varying levels of wealth. Jennens was independently wealthy. He didn't really need to worry about whether the expense involved in an out-of-tune organ would show up at some point. But obviously Handel knew that such a concern would in fact be significant for some people. I think Handel was very much attuned to the economy of his times. As Brad has said many times, Handel was a cagey businessman. But, to go back to the letters one more time, I would say that Handel—except maybe in this one letter to Jennens and an earlier one written to his banker instructing him to deposit some stock dividends—other than these very practical messages, Handel typically wrote very formal letters to exploit the advantages of this social ritual. By adhering to the established etiquette of the formal letter and its tradition of genteel address and honorifics, Handel was able to present himself as ever the gentleman, never the uncivilized boy from the backwater. Whatever his eccentricities in a face-to-face situation, he was happy to grasp the ritualized language of the patriarchy and the gentry in writing letters. It reassured him that he was indeed a gentleman."

"What do I take away personally from this letter-writing topic? Well, I must admit that I have always been a bit reticent, a bit shy. I am happy to listen to others and record what they say, but I am more comfortable with the medium of writing when it comes to my own thoughts or when it comes to expressing my feelings about something. I am surprised that there are not more letters written by Handel. Maybe they were destroyed. But I do identify with his comfortable reliance on the formality of letters. The process of writing allows me to be a bit more in control of what I say. I think Handel may have been like that to some extent. He may have been entirely at ease playing his music or even sharing technical information with Jennens, but he liked being able to use the tradition of the letter as an aid, maybe a kind of mask, in personal interactions. At least that is how he seems to me, and I feel much the same about my own personal interactions. I am definitely one of those who welcomed the invention of text messaging. I think Handel would have approved."

Benfey removed the captain's cap in a low bow. Everyone clapped. "I suppose I will have to give this up," she said, placing the cap before her. "Well, no one will be claiming it until our next meeting," said Katherine. "Take it with you and see how you like it, but bring it back for our next pro tem captain. Thank you, Benfey, and thank you all for sharing these more personal reflections. I believe Ross will anchor our next meeting, and we will hear from a few more of you. I look forward to our next meeting. Until then, take care, everyone."

CHAPTER 26

Pass the Hat

◦‿◦

Ross walked slowly through his collections room, stopping to read the small cards identifying the sources of various objects and the reasons they were there, their connections with the many adventures, people, and places in Ross's sixty-nine years. He thought of Forella's words about what it means to be a self, a soul. When I am gone, he thought, as he picked up a small carved and hatch-marked crocodile from an early visit to Australia, who will care anything about this collection of memories, all tied to my life, my ephemeral, idiosyncratic story? When my self is no longer the glue that holds this miscellany, this collage together, what will be its purpose? Good God, what is its purpose even now? Why create this archive of identity if the life it records will vanish when I die? Ross put the little carving back on its shelf. Perhaps my mother is not the only one who worries about the soul, he thought. Perhaps I am a seeker as well.

◦‿◦

ANNIE HAD PREPARED A LUNCH of batter-fried fish and chips, complete with mushy peas and malt vinegar for the next meeting of the Handel Seminar. Even Forella was persuaded to drink a bit of pale ale in keeping with the motif of a British workingman's fare. Ross went back for seconds and a large helping of trifle. "Necessary fortification for the demanding task facing me today—starting off our next round of closing comments," he said. "Thanks, Annie, for setting us up so nicely. I wish I could effect some sort of British accent here, but I'll leave that to Peter. And thanks as well to Benfey, who passed along this storied cap, which makes me look like The Skipper on *Gilligan's Island*, so I'll respectfully decline, if you don't mind."

Ross hung the hat on the back of his chair and lifted his glass of ale. "You will all be shocked and amazed," he said, "to know that the truth was revealed to me in a dream: I am, indeed and after all, really George Frideric Handel, and I was desperately in love with Lydia but lost out to that worm of a clergyman, Edward Grayston. Oh, and, soon after, I came back as a lesser known luthier from Latvia in the late 1700s, then a saucy young singer from Singapore in the mid-1800s, and after that a Basin Street bluesman who died an untimely death before I so famously came on the scene in the late 1940s. There you have it, my friends, the whole truth, nothing but the truth, so help me God. And, if you believe that, I have a bridge . . . yadda yadda yadda."

"So, no, I do not want to talk about reincarnation, or the transmigration of souls, or even your garden variety of mystical experiences—well, maybe a little bit this last. First, let me offer my belated apology for skipping out on the exchange of brief bios we shared some time ago. I think Katherine and I both managed to let that opportunity for divulgence slip by. Granted, it was unfair. I will try to make up for it here. Perhaps Katherine will feel chagrined and comply as well—or perhaps remain the sole outlier," he said with a smile in Katherine's direction. She rolled her eyes and said, "Please do carry on. I shall try to muster some sort of chagrin if it seems warranted."

"Ok," Ross went on, "allow me to fill you in on my life in the late sixties, early seventies, mostly because it does, I believe, have some relevance to the Handel theme that draws my attention. As my mother will attest, I was—as were many of my friends—a child of the times, a hippie in the making, a flower child, an idealistic dissenter, a peace-monger, an SDS organizer, a sojourner in Haight-Ashbury, and, yes, a partaker of psychedelic drugs. I was also a sometime student and itinerant keyboardist. I emerged from that counterculture period a bit cynical but also strangely inspired to follow the paths toward expanded awareness promoted by the Timothy Learys and Ram Dasses of the times. I enrolled in film school and learned the basics of—not art film as I had hoped—but documentary filmmaking. It became my life's passion and luckily my career. My parents footed the bill, and I remain forever in their debt. My father and I wrangled over our starkly differing views on just about everything, but he never backed away from paying the bills. I'm not sure I would have ever been that generous with a grown and combative child of mine, but I never had occasion to find out."

"As you can see, I had an advantaged youth and childhood, but you all know Forella Wainwright and her devotion to social justice. I was not allowed to wallow in self-indulgent ignorance of the woes of others—at least not most of the time. I was included in outings to community kitchens, disaster relief fundraisers, clothing drives, and even required to bicycle a paper route and later sack groceries. 'Builds character,' I was told. I'll let you judge. My twenties were somewhat rebellious, but I managed to avoid the worst of the dangers lurking behind the free love, easy roaming, drug-fueled lifestyle of the times. By the time I passed the dreaded over thirty mark, I actually knew what I wanted to do, what turned me on. Not drugs—though as I said—indirectly related. All the Eastern religions and alternate states talk inspired a real interest in some of the new-age thinking, especially philosophy. And I realized that I wanted to document connections between real life and our supposed progress as a human species. To me, the call to documentary filmmaking was as strong as the clichéd call to countless others to be ministers of the gospel. I was hooked, and I have been ever since. I'm pretty sure this obsession with making films has been the downfall of most of my troubled personal relationships, but there you have it. Filmmaking and the lure of philosophy are a seductive duo. What can I say?"

"But let me return to the sixties," he said. "Well, actually the seventies—and I will, I promise, get to the Handel connection. Things were transitioning in the 1970s. The reality of the Vietnam War impinged on a lot of otherwise idealistic thinking. The old counterculture faded away, and while there were many new vaguely religious traditions growing out of the mix of new-age thought, I found the slowly emerging combination of physics and mysticism intriguing—at least for a while. I read the *Tao of Physics* and other such pseudoscience. Then I switched to Bertrand Russell and gave up on anything even slightly dualistic or supernatural. All the while I continued my experiments with documentary film. For me, a film allowed me to tie individuals, history, and a philosophical point of view together in an expressive medium other people could—perhaps—appreciate and debate. With each film I created, I found the process of research, conception and scripting, production of raw footage, editing and even marketing completely absorbing. Academic or even popular writing was not for me. But filmmaking was undisputedly my expression of how I see the world. And it still is. It is my métier, as they say, and it is what, to my mind, actually does tie me to Handel."

Ross walked to the buffet and poured another glass of ale. "So," he continued, "Ever since my mid-thirties I have been making films that, in each instance, demand my undivided attention and commitment. Each film is a momentary addiction. Little can pull me away until it is finished. Nothing satisfies so much as that compelling immersion in this incremental process, each step calling up the next. As I read Lydia's letters to Handel, time and again I heard her admonishing him—in a kindly way—for his devotion to the projects that engaged him. She admired his talent, but, sadly, to my mind at least, she failed to understand how very important it was for him to immerse himself in his composing. Each piece he wrote—especially each opera or oratorio with its drama and human message—each piece affirmed his hold on daily life, his connection to the rest of humanity. Lydia insisted that Handel needed a wife, while Handel gloried in living his musical projects. Who are we to judge that this was a less human way to engage life, a less worthwhile kind of devotion?"

"I do identify with Handel, as you can see—at least in this respect. I can easily imagine Handel viewing each new composing task as a joy for him personally—whether his audiences liked it or not. I also think he recognized his good fortune in being able to do what he did. And Handel certainly was fortunate. He had that royal pension to fall back on, even when his productions were not financial successes. He had the advantage of economic support, and he did not need to feel he had relied upon the church to support this life he found so fulfilling. He was free as an artist to explore the human conundrums that intrigued him. No wonder he pounced on the opportunity to produce *Partenope* for his own company. I think he thrived upon the demands of tying plot or theme to music. It was his way of contemplating the human condition."

"Handel grew up under the influence of the Enlightenment. The skepticism and empiricism of Thomas Hobbes and John Locke were in the air. I expect that Handel heard a lot of talk about new scientific discoveries and humanistic thought right along with discussions of politics and the economy. When I think about these letters we have examined and about Handel's life in general, the thing that draws my attention is this gap, this one neglected topic—Handel's take on religion and the philosophical ideas of the times. I've tried to envision him treating his objectives in composing as I have treated my own objectives in creating films. For me, each film is not just an historical record of something noteworthy but also an interpretation—my own take on what the topic says about life and the many issues facing humanity. And religious or philosophical thought is either obvious or subtly disguised in any creative piece—whether poetic or graphic, musical or cinematic. So, my goal with regard to Handel has been to seek out signs of that contemplative substance."

"Everyone assumes that, for example, *Messiah* is obviously a statement of Handel's religious thinking, but the libretto was written by Jennens. Songs into which Handel poured his heart included ones like 'He Was Despised' or 'Comfort Ye' or 'Worthy Is the Lamb.' Scenes of suffering caused by religious and political hostility were what most often stirred Handel's emotional and creative eloquence. His last oratorio—*Jephtha*—made abundantly clear how harmful religious rigidity could be. I don't think Handel lost his religion as I did, but I do think he questioned the goodness people so blithely associated with anything from the Bible or even ancient history. I think he saw human history as always struggling with the burden of what we now would call existential angst or the troubled human condition. I think he felt compelled to address the reality of a flawed but still admirable human nature."

"What do I take away from my peek into Handel's life? I wish Lydia had asked him more about his beliefs, but obviously that wasn't her druthers. She was wife to a clergyman, after all. We can't make too many assumptions based on the plots of his operas and oratorios. He always had collaborators—though his musical interpretations were his own. More instructive might be a survey of the artwork he collected, though of course that depends on what was available, I admit. Some pieces he bought might have been purchased for the sake of investment or even simply a desire to show off. Who knows? But I would say the fact that his paintings were all of a secular—often even slightly risqué—nature suggests that his worldview was predominantly nonreligious. His Lutheran roots gave him a veneer of religious culture, but he seemed to be attracted to questions of secular politics, misfortune and conflict, and, of course, love. To be slightly anachronistic, I would call Handel a religious humanist. The culture of the church was all around him, but his interests and creativity leaned toward the everyday concerns of human life. I think Handel and I would have had some very lively exchanges. Maybe Lydia really was worried that the Reverend would draw the line at her asking Handel about impious beliefs better kept under wraps. I would love to be transported back and eavesdrop on the conversations he did have in those infamous coffeehouses. Now that would make a superb film! I may have to imagine such a scene and create something like *My Dinner with André* or, better yet, maybe I should find that article on Handel's art collection and have a coffee shop discussion on art between Handel and his friend Goupy before they fell out. What do you think?"

"Well, those are my thoughts for today," Ross said. "Our look at Handel and these letters has left me strangely reverential as I consider how every human life—Handel's life, my life—draws to itself so many connections. There is so much that defines that one person, so much that disappears when that person dies." He took the captain's cap from the back of his chair. "Who is our next speaker? Ah, CD. Hier ist die Zauberkappe. Carry on, my good man."

CD picked up the hat, moved the rim slowly through his fingers, and then set it down again on the table. Looking away from the abandoned hat, he smiled at Katherine and Peter who sat opposite. "I'll not mince words here," he said. "For me the fascinating thing about Handel is how his affections for various people in his life flourished or faded in a kind of *Bildungsroman*. It's as though he took a long time to grow up, or so it seemed to me. No doubt you expect me to say something about Handel's sexual orientation, but I don't think we have convincing evidence on that question, at least from what I have read. And Lydia certainly doesn't give us any hints on the topic. To the contrary, she underscores his presumed heterosexuality in comments she makes in her letters. On the other hand, we have no way of knowing what kind of intimate experiences or sexual desires he may or may not have had. What we do know is that he did not do an especially good job of maintaining the friendships he did have. His eventual clarity on the value of affections and true friendship was slow to emerge. Let me offer a quick survey."

"It seems Handel could be charming when he wanted to be," CD continued. "My guess is that even the famous scene in which a very young Georg Friederich Händel is acclaimed by the Duke at Weissenfels involved not simply the youngster's precocious playing ability but also his winning personality. Handel found it easy to gain the affections of people who helped him on his way. In Hamburg, Johann Mattheson befriended Handel but then quarreled with him over who should direct an opera. They even dueled. Handel never really made up with Mattheson. On the female side, Handel evidently flirted with Vittoria Tarquini while in Italy and Elisabetta Pilotti when in London, but he seemed to regard those as passing romances. Besides both women were already married. He disparaged Maurice Greene and so infuriated Joseph Goupy that Goupy created and circulated an etching of Handel as an organ-playing hog.

Handel did somewhat better with his women friends, but even his longtime friend, secretary, and copyist, John Smith, Senior, fell far out of favor with Handel, to be reconciled with him only a short time before Handel's death. My point is that Handel did little to endear himself to the people who were often his closest friends. He was not—throughout most of his life—what we might call an affectionate man."

"However, with a few very select people he seems to have developed—finally—an abiding attachment that could pass as true affection or love. Queen Caroline and her daughter Anne were two who had unshakable ties to Handel's heart, I would venture to say. Georg Philipp Telemann reemerges toward the end of Handel's life as someone who has perhaps always inspired Handel's deep affection. Handel makes two efforts to send Telemann exotic plants—though the two men had not seen each other in years. Handel develops a friendship with his Brook Street neighbor, the perfumer James Smyth, and leaves him a substantial sum in his will. He also remembers in his will his long-time violinist Matthew Dubourg. Then, of course, he leaves most of his fortune to his godchild, his niece Johanna Friederike Flörcke. And, there is his warm regard for Lydia, our letter-writer. I think it is telling that Handel slowly backed away from the competitive and domineering conduct that characterized his life until his later years. People would say he mellowed, I suppose, but to me it seems that he finally recognized the value of true friendship—something he had been too busy, too absorbed to notice before. I think it took him an awfully long time to grow into his role as—not a prolific artist, which is something he did very well—but rather a loving friend, a kindred spirit who could share others' lives as fully as his own."

"To my mind, for most of his life, Handel exhibited a trait often associated with genius—a seeming impatience with lesser beings. It probably galled him that he had to acquiesce to the conventions of rank, but he typically played on those customs with skill. However, if someone within his own profession dared challenge him, or even simply presumed to match his talent, he was quick to deride them and their efforts. The truth is he was exceptionally gifted, but he suffered from having no one whose talents he regarded as highly as his own. Perhaps he did see Telemann as his equal, or maybe their physical separation allowed Handel to entertain in his mind his own fantasy of the man rather than his real counterpart. Women were less a problem in that regard—society taught him that they were by definition unequal. I think Handel knew from an early age that he was talented and very bright. It was probably the onset of health problems that finally humbled him enough for him to see his common heritage as an ordinary human. Even great geniuses must, in the end, die. Better to do so with a friend or two holding your hand. I think he finally learned that."

CD picked up the venerable—or at least now customary—hat and held it up, looking around for the next speaker. Angela reached for it and placed it on her head with a flourish. "Who knows when I'll ever be invited again to wear a captain's hat?" she said. "It's like those Bishop's hats we used to make out of a folded newspaper printer's hat. Now if I just had a staff to carry around with me! So, anyway, I am the next speaker. Thanks for including me, even though I am not officially part of the Seminar. I've enjoyed being a participant right along with Forella."

"I've thought about what I could consider here," she said, "about what has most impressed me as I've listened in on these discussions. I should probably back up and say that what drew me to joining Forella's enterprise here in the first place was her continuous involvement in social causes, especially women's issues. I admire people who commit themselves to important causes. I was working up in Chicago when they closed down Hull House—the old settlement house that promoted social reform and looked to the needs of the poor. I had been interested in the settlement house movement, especially after I moved to Chicago and learned about Jane Addams and the Hull House. Issues of social justice and inequality have been important to me for most of my life—even in high school. As part of this Seminar, I've enjoyed researching the various DVDs and performances of Handel's music and other issues as they came up, but personally the one bit of research that really caught my attention was background on the Foundling Hospital in London, the institution that received Handel's full copy of *Messiah* as a gift to support the hospital's mission."

"Just to remind you, the Foundling Hospital was actually a home for mostly illegitimate and abandoned children—basically for children of poor unwed mothers who could not afford to take care of their offspring. Handel was made one of the governors of the institution, and it was clear that he wanted to be a part of what was at the time a new kind of almsgiving or support for the poor. Always before, the church had taken responsibility for the poor, but Handel and some of his friends in the emerging professional class wanted to support such charity work as a sign of their enlightened civic engagement. I don't want to seem cynical about Handel's role in establishing and supporting the Foundling Hospital. It's just that I found it very interesting that the beginnings of the whole notion of charitable organizations were actually tied very much to a kind of self-interest or desire for recognition."

"Think about the title Handel gave to the Foundling Hospital Anthem," she continued. "He called it *Blessed are they that considereth the poor and needy*. It isn't one of the Beatitudes from the New Testament. I thought maybe it was because I remember learning those sayings of Jesus that start out 'Blessed are . . .' the meek, or the peacemakers, or the merciful, and so on. But Handel's title is more like a passage from one of the Psalms: Blessed is he who considereth the poor. But my point is that in Handel's piece the person being blessed is the one who does the considering of the poor, not necessarily the poor themselves. In other words, Handel's piece is pronouncing a blessing on those who think about the needs of the poor. And that is fine, but it really is a bit self-congratulatory—as in, 'Isn't it wonderful the way we think of the needs of the poor. We should be blessed because we are so magnanimous.' I do actually think Handel felt compassion for the poor, but I think he was also playing on what he understood about the vanity of the English gentry."

"I don't want to leave you with the idea that I fault Handel for the way he manipulated the words of the Bible and used them to persuade potential contributors to the Foundling Hospital. That's the kind of thing fundraisers always have to do. I'll admit that my real response to this topic is that I personally disagree with the need for charity. I think it is, in most cases, something the government should ensure for everyone—universal health care, adequate housing, sufficient food, public education, the chance to make a good living. The poor and needy shouldn't have to depend on rich people wanting to feel they are being benevolent just to have a decent life. I think it is time for America to be the social democracy it was intended to be—and Great Britain, too. But meanwhile, I will just go on admiring people like Forella who in their quiet way work to help the poor and needy. I suppose Handel did what he could."

Angela whipped off the hat and looked around to a rather stunned group of people. "Sorry for the soapbox speech," she said. "Who's next?" Clara raised her hand. "I'm not sure I can CAP that—LOL. My name was next on the list, so I'll take the ceremonial headgear." Clara placed the hat upside down on the table and threw a coin into it, and said, "That should repurpose it, don't you think?"

"We were encouraged," said Clara, "here at the close of the Seminar, to reflect on what we take away from this experience, maybe some question or topic we have been prompted to think about more deeply or in a new way. You might be surprised to hear that our discussions and Lydia's letters have given me a new appreciation for science and the great wealth of rigorously researched and yet mystifying information I am privileged to deal with on a day-to-day basis. Let me back up and say, first, that, last time, I especially enjoyed Benfey's sharing with us the letter Handel had written to his friend Charles Jennens—the one in which he outlined the technical requirements he would suggest for the house organ Jennens hoped to purchase. Handel really knew the specs on the organ as an instrument. He was a technician as well as a musician. He also knew very well how to teach music—despite his reluctance to actually be a music teacher rather than a composer. Several years ago I came across a wonderful book of exercises Handel wrote for King George's daughters, including Princess Anne, who was evidently quite good on the harpsichord. If you remember, in my second life, I play cello, and Handel wrote many pieces in which the continuo typically called for harpsichord and cello. I was impressed with his clear and useful instructions on how to create the accompanying harmonies. But what, you may ask, does all this have to do with my take-away thoughts on science and Lydia's letters to Handel?"

"All along, as we were reading the letters, I kept waiting for some indication that Handel extended his avid study of music into the wider fields of science and medicine. He was, after all, exposed to medical knowledge through his father, and he had at least started taking university courses in Halle, where such luminaries as Christian Wolff and August Hermann Francke taught. But it seems, instead, that he was driven to learn all he could about musical composition and opera production. Over time, his music came to be regarded as—in the language of the later commentators of the Baroque—the manifestation of 'the sublime.' Many subsequent writers saw this association between Handel's music and the Sublime as a consequence of his writing oratorios—pieces celebrating biblical stories. They thought of Handel's music as stemming directly from Handel's own sense of awe and reverence for God. Handel's music was sublime because he successfully found a way to express his own profound religious fervor. That was the argument. I have not been convinced of this myself. I think Handel did indeed create music that had, as one recent music scholar—Todd Gilman—wrote, a 'powerful emotional effect, and an overpowering impact.' But Handel's powerful response was—at least in my book—to a larger and more general sense of awe, not simply a religious sentiment."

"But, to be honest," she went on, "I think the key point here is that notions of the 'sublime' are perceptions—and maybe not even widely shared perceptions. Handel composed music in support of themes we typically think of as 'grand' in some way—religious jubilation, of course, but also extreme sacrifice, military victory, stirring bravery, martyrdom, unfailing love and devotion, even simply royal acclaim as in *Zadok, the Priest* or the *Ode for the Birthday of Queen Anne*. Why IS Handel's music so often considered sublime? There seemed to be a consensus growing out of the use of the term even in Handel's own time. Gilman—the writer I mentioned earlier—lamented the way Handel was celebrated as writing sublime music while his own biographical subject, Handel's contemporary, Thomas Arne, was regarded as writing merely 'beautiful' music. So the view of Handel's music as sublime came to be something of a shared meme among the critics of the day, as well as among later scholars who repeated the label. I suppose we all share some idea of the sublime as a way of naming our personal sense of awe before aspects of life or nature that are magnificent—the breaching of a whale, the fierceness of a hurricane, the Grand Tetons, the Alps, the Grand Canyon, Niagara Falls, Victoria Falls, Muir Woods—or my personal favorites, Carlsbad Caverns and a dark sky view of the Milky Way. But, back to Handel, was there something about Handel's music that was magnificent—that is still considered magnificent? Does it seem 'larger' or more powerful than other music? Does it use chords or progressions that strike our ears as particularly stirring or grand? I am reminded of Leonard Cohen's song 'Hallelujah' in which he speaks of the 'secret chord' that David played and which pleased the Lord. He goes on to describe the sequence of chords that was so pleasing. Do you suppose Handel found those secret chords and wove them into his music?"

"It is possible, I suppose," she continued. "When I was a teenager, I spent hours listening to Wagner's 'Liebestod' from *Tristan and Isolde*. I don't think you can find a more obviously orgasmic piece of music than that, but of course that was the intention. I'm sure there are certain auditory sensations that stir up the amygdala and release dopamine. Why else would we have music? But think back to Lydia's favorite piece—*Lascia la spina*—leave the thorn but take the rose. Why did Lydia find it so memorable? Partly because of her associations with it, her memories of Handel as a young man, but also because it truly is a beautiful piece of music. But not exactly sublime. Some of Handel's music really was intended for smaller venues—the homes of his friends or his own house on Brook Street. Even so, I think of Handel's music as almost always evoking the magnificence of reality, of life—not the man-made sense of spirituality we call religion. A piece like *Lascia la spina* makes me think of the wonder of evolution, the astounding diversity of life that has emerged so impressively over the eons. And *Messiah* or *Zadok, the Priest*? I am moved to a feeling of awe by these and other of Handel's works, but I am not moved to a personal ecstasy of reverence for a biblical deity or some great king or leader. No, to me Handel's music inspires a feeling of profound appreciation for my own chance to live—and simply for the universe, for the Earth, for the wonder of life as we know it. I can only assume that Handel shared that quiet yet ecstatic regard for nature, for all of life. I think his music celebrates life, not religion. For me, the depth of feeling Handel is able to convey through his music is the same aching spirituality I feel when contemplating the wonder we call the Universe. To my mind he transcends religion and puts us in touch with the awe-inspiring reality of life. Granted, most people will not hear in Handel's music a celebration of the persistence of molecules or the mystery of consciousness or the glory of galaxies, but I certainly do. If nothing else, Handel, the master of musical technology, must have revered life's amazing display of exquisite solutions to the challenges of an ever-emerging universe."

Clara threw another quarter into the captain's cap lying in front of her and then looked around to see who was next. Wait grinned and said, "Well, I obviously picked the right time to claim the hat. Already I've earned a tip and haven't even sung the song." He took the coins, put them on the table in front of him, and, like Ross, placed the cap on the back of his chair.

"I'll admit that Handel's music almost never makes me think of science or the universe or even nature—well, maybe that song about the plane tree, whatever it was," said Wait. "I don't think Handel himself thought about science much—though some of his acquaintances were into that sort of thing. These Enlightenment topics were probably in the air, subjects for speculation at the coffee houses, but I don't think Handel was particularly interested in them. History and politics and religion were the subjects he chose to present or celebrate through his compositions. And I, for one, think he was very concerned to make his own Christian perspective a prominent part of what he offered his audiences. He wasn't a church musician, but he still chose stories from the Bible as plots for his oratorios. Especially toward the end of his life, he seemed to be thinking about how to be a good Christian, how to honor God and Christ's teachings. I think he took his religious topics seriously and personally. There is certainly more evidence that he thought about biblical stories and Christian virtues than any questions that science posed. He attended church, not meetings of the Royal Society of London. That's my take on Handel's spiritual side, but that isn't actually what I wanted to talk about today. Instead, I wanted to go back and say a little more about Handel's connection with the Foundling Hospital in London. Angela introduced the topic, but I want to take it in a different direction."

"I've thought off and on about Handel's decision to support the Foundling Hospital. It was a generous decision. He wrote the anthem *Blessed are they that considereth the poor and needy* and performed it at the Chapel dedication. He had an organ built for the Hospital's chapel, and he offered performances of *Messiah* in support of their mission. And, then, in his will, he left the Hospital a performance copy of *Messiah* as a continuing means of funding through concerts in support of the institution. There may have been other motives involved as well, but I think it is clear that Handel felt a moral obligation to help the people who benefited from these charitable acts. And who were these people? They were mainly women and their illegitimate or impoverished children. I've pondered this fact for a while now, and I'd like to share my thoughts on why he chose this particular charity to support in this very public and powerful way."

"It was interesting that his very last revived piece—*The Triumph of Time and Truth*, in English this time—included a chorus from the Foundling Hospital anthem. The chorus says: 'Comfort them, O Lord, when they are sick, Make Thou their bed in sickness. Keep them alive, let them be blessed upon the earth, And not deliver them unto their foes.' Even here, toward the end of Handel's own life, he was conscious of how dire the situation was for these castoff children—of the necessity of working simply to keep them alive. Why did he see this as his responsibility, his own moral obligation? Handel was a good Christian, and a good Christian accepts the Lord's charge to feed the hungry, clothe the naked, shelter the homeless, and so on. And yet, many if not most of these children were illegitimate. I've tried, in my own mind, to recast the situation as Handel confronted it and imagine how it would be viewed today, maybe how it IS viewed today. It raises several issues, but especially poverty, premarital sex, unwed mothers, starving children—and of course, the related issue of abortion. You might be surprised to know that our discussions have made me rethink some of my opinions on this last troubling topic."

"Unlike Ross, I did share a bit of my personal history some time ago," Wait continued. "But I don't think I told you much about my family. I have two daughters—both grown and off on their own. Two things are probably important here. First, my Christian faith is very important to me, but I accept that everyone else has a right to his or her own faith or belief. I don't try to force my religion on anyone else. And second, my daughters are the most precious gifts God has ever given me. I've never regretted not having a boy, and neither has my wife. So, when I talk about how I view the situation with women and pregnancy, just keep these two things in mind."

"I think Handel felt the kind of responsibility for women that the church usually teaches us to accept—basically that men should lead, provide for, and protect women. I've certainly grown up with that attitude pretty much handed to me as a given. It came as a real surprise to me, as a father, as my daughters were growing up, to find that I started questioning that stance—the idea that women should be treated differently than men. I was especially unhappy with the attitude that girls should expect to be in any way submissive and, well, less important than boys. I'm not sure I would have questioned this whole attitude if I had not had girls, but since I did, I started asking myself more often whether

I believed everything the church and society taught me about the way women should be viewed and treated. I liked the fact that my daughters were creative and feisty, even as young girls. And I remember pretty clearly when my older daughter first started her period and had to face the prospect of being a woman rather than a little girl. I think most men let their wives handle THE TALK with daughters just as men are expected to explain sex to their sons. But my wife and I decided to talk to our girls together—each of them separately well before they entered puberty. It was probably one of the most challenging things I've ever done—talking with my daughters, right along with their mother, about sex and intimate relationships and how society imposes certain responsibilities on women, but I've always been glad I participated the way I did. It's just like my trip to the farm, when I was a kid, to witness the way pigs were castrated—a learning experience about a pretty fundamental part of life. I thought it was important that my daughters understand that sex is a natural human activity and not some shameful dark secret. And I wanted to help prepare them for the prejudices they would encounter. I've always been glad that my daughters could talk with me about anything. I think they could see that I respected them as individuals who happen to be women, and I think they appreciated that."

"So, on to Handel and the Foundling Hospital. Before coming here today, I asked my younger daughter if I could tell you what I will say next. She said it would be ok but asked me not to share her name. Here is the story. Like so many of the young women who came to the Foundling Hospital back in Handel's time, my daughter found herself unexpectedly pregnant. Even today, with easily available birth control, slip-ups occur. I was disappointed, of course, but I didn't see her situation as shameful. I was mostly really sorry for her because it was not the kind of problem you can just walk away from. She wasn't married, and she didn't really want to be pregnant and was definitely not ready to have a baby. She had plans to start college and was excited about her studies and her future. Like Peter said about his wife, the pregnancy was a mistake, and she wanted to stop it as soon as she could. I don't think there is anyone who likes the idea of abortion. My church is strongly opposed to it, even though they will accept birth control so long as it is not the morning after pill. I do think Christ would ask all Christians to help poor mothers who cannot support their children. That is what Handel chose to do. Effective birth control wasn't an option back then, and attempts at abortion in Handel's day most often resulted in the death of the mother right along with the loss of the fetus."

"But I've been trying to imagine what Handel would decide today about young women who find themselves pregnant and unprepared to be mothers—women like my wonderful daughter, who tries always to live by the golden rule and loves Jesus and his teachings. Jesus would try to put himself in the place of that woman, would let himself feel what she feels, fear what she fears. Maybe Handel would have done the same. Maybe he would have empathized with a woman caught in that kind of situation, would have understood why she wanted to just go back and reverse the whole thing. It is not something I, as a man, would have ever had to decide for myself. But I tried to put myself in my daughter's place and think it through. I talked with the pastor at my church, and he recommended having the baby and maybe putting it up for adoption. My daughter decided she would have an abortion. It was a legal option, and she thought the idea of having a baby and then giving it up was too painful. I was torn. I said I would support her no matter what, but I did tell her that I didn't like the idea of abortion. As it turns out, she miscarried naturally before the procedure was actually scheduled. So, a bullet dodged, I suppose. This was several years ago. My daughter is now happily married and has a fine healthy boy that she and her husband very much wanted and that she loves with all her heart. But Handel's concern for the mothers and children who came to the Foundling Hospital made me go back and think about this issue again."

Wait continued, "Remember when we talked about Handel's *Theodora*? I think Rebecca mentioned this some time ago. The heroine in that story was persecuted for her faith, and the tyrant threatened to rape her and force her into a life of prostitution. She refused to abandon her faith, and both she and her friend Didymus were killed. That kind of cruel oppression is terrible whenever and wherever it occurs. But suppose instead that Theodora had been forced to do as the tyrant dictated. Suppose she had been raped and then became pregnant. Both a man and a woman can be killed. And I am sure a man, just like a woman, would be traumatized if he were raped, but only a woman can be raped and then forced to carry her rapist's child until it is born. It raises a difficult ethical question for anyone categorically opposed to abortion. Why would any woman WANT to bring a child into the world under those conditions? My daughter's situation wasn't anything like that, thank God. But still, it was my daughter—not the man whose semen made her pregnant—who had to suddenly face the prospect of other people telling her what to do with her own body. We would be outraged if a man were required to, say, undergo a vasectomy if he had gotten a woman pregnant against her consent or had simply fathered way too many children. When I made that pact with myself years ago to treat my daughter just as I would treat a son, I in effect agreed to acknowledge that she had that right—the right to decide what to do with her own body. Upsetting as I find the idea of abortion, I think—putting myself in my daughter's place—I found the idea that someone else could tell me what to do with my own body even more disturbing. Handel showed respect for the women AND the children who needed the support of an institution like the Foundling Hospital. He followed the most important of the New Testament commandments: Be ye kind one to another, tenderhearted, forgiving one another, even as God for Christ's sake hath forgiven you."

As Wait took the hat from the back of his chair and put it down on the table, he added, "I think we have a population explosion problem. Every day children are born without our having nearly enough resources to care for them all as we should. I don't like the idea of abortion, and I have a lot of friends who are adamantly opposed, but I think it is time we start forgiving the women who decide to end their pregnancies, just as we obviously forgive the men who got them pregnant. As to calling abortion murder and acting all self righteous about saving innocent children—no, a fetus is not a baby. It could become one, but it isn't one yet. People who look back and say what a pity it would be if some child had never been born—those people are using a faulty argument and appealing to emotions tied to a life already here, a child already born and sharing experiences with others. As a Christian, I feel it is my responsibility to accept the imperfections of life and try to do what seems best, even if the choice isn't an ideal one. There are lots of times we have to make decisions that we don't like—placing an aging parent in a nursing home, for example, or finally leaving a marriage that makes us miserable. I've watched friends make hard choices, and I've had to make a few myself. Seeking an abortion would be a complicated decision for any woman, but bringing an unwanted child into the world would not necessarily be a better decision. You would probably be surprised to learn that I find cruelty to animals a much greater wrong than abortion. I've been to some so-called farms that produce the animals we slaughter for food. I am a hunter, and I think humans are meant to eat meat, but I have never really liked the way most American producers grow our meat and chickens. And I've seen it first hand. My parents were butchers, after all. There are worse things than stopping a potential human life from ever seeing the light of day. I think we need to beef up our efforts at making birth control easily available BEFORE children are conceived. I know that a lot of Christians believe that it is always God's will when a baby is conceived, but I don't agree, and I've never seen a Bible verse that really says that. I agree with Handel that the Christian thing to do—the kind thing to do—is to help people who need help and not judge others. Young women caught in unwanted pregnancies are all too often the ones who need our help, and legal, safe abortion is sometimes the best way to help them. As Angela said, when it came to women who needed help, Handel did what he could, and I respect him for that."

Katherine walked over and put her hand on Wait's shoulder. "Thanks, Wait," she said. "You have obviously pondered this issue for some time. Your reasoning reminds me of a recent book by an OB/GYN, Dr. Willie Parker. He is a devoted and caring Christian, just like you. In his book, he argues that women should have the choice to have an abortion without judgment and should be supported rather than thwarted if they have made that decision. His story and commentary are worth reading—an insightful book." She looked at him thoughtfully for a moment and then picked up the cap lying on the table in front of him. "I believe I am the next one to inherit this hat," she said. "I'll start us off next time, and we'll have—what?—three more after that and be finished with our wrap-up sessions. I still find a final session a sad thing to think about. But time marches on. See you all when we meet again. Stay well."

CHAPTER 27

Us versus Them

Katherine pulled her eyes away from the photograph of the small Syrian child, drowned and washed ashore on the Mediterranean. She turned the magazine over and slid it under some other reading matter on her desk. The refugee crisis is disheartening, a horrible sign of the times—families trying to escape in flimsy, overcrowded boats. A child dying—that is the hardest thing—under any circumstances. She remembered the day—years ago--when she learned of her nephew's accident, of his death—so young, so eager for the future he thought would be his. At his funeral she sang "He Shall Feed His Flock" from Handel's Messiah. It offers a comforting image—the shepherd who gathers all the lambs with his arm, who carries all the young ones in his bosom. And yet, now, for her it simply brought a painful lump to her throat whenever she heard the song. "Ye shall find rest onto your souls," says the second part of the song. But the idea of a child's soul rocking in the bosom of Christ or Abraham or some other far-removed deity is not the same as encircling with your own arms that precious child, alive and safe and looking into your eyes.

THE FINAL MEETING OF THE Handel Seminar started a little earlier than usual. Forella wanted to give everyone a chance to relax and chat over lunch before beginning the last session, a chance to reflect. Annie had prepared individual meat pasties, along with a few vegetarian ones. Just for fun, she had carved in initials on one end of each pasty. Forella explained that the tradition of adding initials had carried over from much earlier British mining customs—the idea was that a half-finished pasty could still be identified later if work meant it was left uneaten for a while. Clara laughed when she noticed that there were four pasties with the initials RW—just in case Ross wanted seconds, or thirds, or fourths. Everyone enjoyed the meal and the dessert that followed—Spotted Dick. After Brad nearly choked, Annie explained—with a slight blush—that, yes, Spotted Dick is the name of the steamed pudding. She knew it simply as suet pudding, but she was trying to be authentically British. In short, as this final meeting got under way, a convivial and yet contemplative mood prevailed. All were pleased to be there.

With dishes cleared away and coffees or teas in hand, the members of the Handel Seminar looked toward Katherine—mostly to see if she would actually wear the captain's cap. She did not, though she did give a quick tip of the hat before setting it down. "Thanks, Annie, for that wonderful meal," she said. "I thought the pudding was great—despite the disgusting name. Ah, those Brits."

"So, I get to lead off this last session," she said, "and then we have three other speakers and are done. I had so many topics I wanted to talk about. It was hard to select just one, but this is it: I want to consider the instances of bullying, coercion, or intimidation in Handel's life and in our lives today."

"Bullying," Katherine continued, "is a term we usually associate with children. And it is possible that Handel was bullied as a child. We know almost nothing about his childhood. What we do know about Handel's early years we learn from John Mainwaring's *Memoirs of the Late George Frederic Handel*, published in 1760, a year after Handel's death. I always think of Mainwaring as a kind of early folklorist, ferreting out the anecdotes that various ones of Handel's friends recalled from conversations with the great man. Biographers since then have lamented the lack of information on Handel's childhood, claiming that Handel, in talking with his friends, must have skipped over those years except for the one famous story of hiding a clavichord in the attic against his father's wishes. Perhaps that is a telling anecdote. Perhaps his father was extremely domineering, strict, and, yes, bullying. More likely, however, if the young Handel was bullied, it was probably something that happened at school—just as is so sadly common today. In any case, I was surprised to find a recent article from the *London Daily Telegraph* reporting that childhood bullying leads to a high number of adults who suffer from obesity by age forty or so. It makes me wonder whether Handel's obesity could have resulted from early instances of bullying while he was a schoolboy in Halle. We have no real way of knowing, but I find myself intrigued by the possibility. It may also be why he neglected to talk with any of his friends about his childhood. Being the victim of bullying is a humiliating experience. The *Telegraph* article was pretty straightforward in claiming a strong correlation between bullying and later obesity. Not all bullied children become obese as adults, of course, and certainly not all obese individuals were bullied as children. Still, the research may suggest a likely reason why Handel could not control his eating."

"I can only guess at what may or may not have happened at the gymnasium Handel attended in Halle. College preparatory schools had only very recently been established by the time Handel was of an age to attend. I would guess that his father enrolled him in such an academy with the aim of preparing him to enroll some years later at the university. Germany—actually Handel's homeland, Saxony—was a leader in establishing such educational institutions, but they were intended for the sons of upper class families. Handel likely did qualify to attend, but he may have been viewed as a nouveau riche. Just as an aside, there is a 1998 DVD intended for grade school classrooms—*Handel's Last Chance*—an almost completely fictional piece about the first performance of *Messiah* in Dublin. The young boy who is the hero and the golden-voiced singer Handel supposedly needs for his performance is depicted as suffering the bullying behavior of his parish school classmates primarily because his family is not of the upper class. I expect there was a lot of class-based bullying in schools back then. Handel's own experience as a boy may have been similar, and furthermore his peers may have seen him as less manly because he preferred studying music to the more typical enthusiasms of hunting and fox tossing."

"Without any clues from Handel himself or any of his friends," Katherine explained, "we cannot know what details of his early life may or may not have influenced his character. By age eighteen he had already rejected the idea of staying in Halle as organist at the main cathedral. Typically, job security would be something used as a carrot to force a bit of compliance, but Handel felt compelled to leave his post and his home and move to Hamburg. It may have been a spirit of adventure and desire to further his career, or he may have been running away from something rather than to something. Again, Handel says little about his experience as organist in Halle. It is possible that he felt that he was being constrained to fit into a mold he did not welcome. One of the few anecdotal memories Mainwaring does record from Handel's early life is the Duke of Saxe-Weissenfels telling Handel's father that his son would more likely succeed if he followed his natural inclination rather than being forced to pursue a career for which he felt no enthusiasm. The advice reminds me of the highly acclaimed film *Dead Poets Society*, in which a young man so strongly despises the way his father tries to force his career choice that he, sadly, commits suicide rather than comply. Fortunately, Handel escaped that kind of family pressure."

"As a folklorist," Katherine continued, "I can't resist seeing Handel's decision to leave Halle and go to Hamburg as one of the essential actions or plot elements of the typical fairytale—in this case, the eleventh function which Russian folklore scholar Vladimir Propp called, appropriately enough, The Hero Leaves Home. In analyzing the structure of fairytales, Propp saw this action as characteristic of the genre. European folktales required that the hero set off from home and encounter the many challenges (usually three) he must overcome. Most folktale scholars agree that the traditional tales were told with a young adult audience in mind—not little children. Folktale heroes or heroines were intended to serve as role models for young adults—adolescents, really—who needed to leave their childhood homes and enter the larger world of work. And, once in Hamburg, Handel played the role of folktale protagonist rather well, even fighting a duel with a 'false hero' much as would any worthy folktale hero. But, folktales are fiction and don't really tell us much about individual character. What I actually find more persuasive is the idea that Handel demonstrated even in his earliest reported behaviors a tendency toward perfectionism, obsessiveness, and demand resistance—traits often associated with high achievement and the kind of brilliance we so accurately ascribe to Handel. I admit that I myself am a bit of a perfectionist—I think most academics are. However, I especially started seeing associated instances of demand resistance in Handel mostly because I am used to recognizing that trait in myself. No, I don't presume to share Handel's brilliance, but some of his reactions to the expectations placed upon him seem all too familiar."

"Let me back up a little," Katherine continued. "Ross badgered me to share a short bio just as everyone else had done. You could say that my reluctance to comply with that minor request is indeed part of my story. As part of a research project some years ago, I read a book titled *Too Perfect*, a popular study of obsessive personality. What I found interesting about the book was the argument that many successful people suffer the burden of expectations or demands that may not have been placed upon them in the first place. I recognized my own tendency to be overly conscientious, to perceive expectations where there were none, or where there were at least less onerous ones than those I imagined. It occurred to me that Handel very likely displayed that same tendency. In fact, I expect some of the damaged friendships that CD discussed last time may have resulted from Handel's resistance to 'demands' he perceived as coercive or extreme. It may well be that people did ask too much of Handel or that they were unfair in their treatment of him, or it may simply be that they opposed his artistic judgments. On the other hand, Handel may have been quick to see a demand or rigid expectation where his supposed adversary might have been flexible or even unaware that Handel saw a conflict. I have always had a strong resistance to being told what to do. I can see Handel having a similar inclination and finding it a troublesome trait when others—especially those in positions of power—were asking or, worse yet, requiring something of him."

"It is never a good idea to psychoanalyze from a distance, with little real information on the individual's life, and when the person died two and a half centuries ago. So, I am not prepared to describe Handel categorically as a demand-sensitive, obsessive personality. However, he did seem to experience notable stress when he came up against people who had the power to thwart his plans. I think he expected excellence from himself and was angered and frustrated when he was opposed. I believe he had supreme confidence in his own abilities, but he often found himself facing a well-established hierarchical social context that required his accommodation of others' demands. Handel had an impressive ability to immerse himself in a project once he started it. In fact, he became obsessed, I would argue, finishing projects in record time and pushing anyone else involved to supply relevant information immediately when needed. According to Allan Mallinger, in *Too Perfect*, obsessive personalities tend to see or even create obligations for themselves and often allow those obligations to ruin any joy or happiness that might have otherwise accompanied any activity. I see Handel as someone who carried with him a strong sense of duty, loyalty, and responsibility throughout his life. It made him a man very responsive to others' demands and yet perhaps stubbornly resentful at the same time. Little wonder that his health was affected by the high level of stress in his life."

"What do I take away from our discussions of Handel and Lydia's letters?" she concluded. "I empathize with what I see as a significant and troublesome—yet hidden—ailment. I believe Handel may have been what Mallinger identifies as an obsessive personality—someone often 'controlling or cerebral or distrustful or secretive or emotionally constricted or resistant to change or all of the above.' (p. xiii) I believe Handel was, like me, averse to being told what to do. His fight with Goupy, Smith Senior, and the Middlesex Opera Company is evidence of that. His stress-related illnesses were likely tied at least in part to his sensitivity to the pressures—real or imagined—that accompanied him in his professional and perhaps even his personal life. I see a glimmer of hope in the choices he made toward the end of his life. He seemed to start asking himself what he WANTED to do rather than what he should do. I sincerely hope that he experienced some true pleasure in his life—that he learned to leave the thorn and pluck the rose. For myself, that is what I take away from learning about his life. Learn to love your own life, enjoy what you can, stop worrying about the many 'shoulds' you think you hear. Listen to your own inner voice rather the people from your past or present who would tell you what you must do. That's my story." And with that, she picked up the hat and looked around for the next speaker.

"Oh, Captain! My Captain!" said Rebecca as she took the ship captain's hat from Katherine. She placed the cap on the table. "*Dead Poets Society*--such a fine movie. So sad that we lost Robin Williams that same way. I guess we in this Seminar have started a Dead Composers Society—or at least a society celebrating one dead composer. I am the next speaker. I thought perhaps Katherine would address the topic I have been thinking about—the issue of us versus them. It is related, of course. Bias, bullying, injustice—nearly all such social evils stem from some instance of us versus them. Why is the world full of this kind of conflict? The professional turn to ethnography—typically the study of other cultures—was initially intended to expose academic anthropologists to cultural practices that differ from their own. In other words, anthropologists needed to be nudged into discarding their ethnocentrism if they were to study other cultures with any kind of objectivity. It is surprising how easy it is to overlook the assumptions a person makes about what is 'normal' based on his or her own culture."

"If I am looking at Handel and his era," Rebecca continued, "there were no psychologists or anthropologists or sociologists around to examine critically the inequalities in class or gender or religion that constricted the lives of so many people. Even as is true today, those in power then saw themselves as simply in the right. At least today we in the US announce in our Constitution that all persons should be treated as equals—though of course we all too often continue to ignore that important wisdom, with prejudices tied to race or gender or religion or ethnicity or sexual orientation sparking violence and conflict at every turn. But in Handel's time, class differences were generally seen as innate. Religious belief was often mandated by the state—for example, Handel was required to sign on as an Anglican when he became a British citizen. Political differences divided many nation states. And the subjugation of women was part of the law of the land. There were many other inequalities, but these are the ones I would like to consider here—the ones that seemed most significant in Handel's time and continue to be a problem in ours."

"Thanks to Charles Dickens," Rebecca continued, "we think of the Victorian era as the poster child for class divisions and the miserable effects of poverty in England. But London, in particular, had its problems in the eighteenth century as well. The city was growing. Children were orphaned and living on the streets. Many men and women were sent to debtors' prison. And the hereditary elite controlled most of the money and political power. Handel's support for the Foundling Hospital was triggered in part by his seeing the children of a former orchestra member roaming the streets in search of food. While it was commonly held to be a Christian virtue to care for the poor, the British elite often treated people of lower social status as inferior by nature and essentially undeserving. Just as today, the wealthy were quick to view people in poverty as simply of bad character, lazy, and unwilling to pull themselves up by the bootstraps. Despite the progressive economic reforms of the last century, many people–even middle-class people today—regard the poor as ungodly and burdensome, a class of people who conspire to force 'their betters' to support them through taxes. As is usual, those in power find ways to justify, at least in their own eyes, their continuing dominance and subjugation of others."

"The important issue here," Rebecca explained, "is something Katherine hinted at earlier. When group-based ties—what some call tribalism—dominate in social interactions, then there will inevitably be winners and losers, those who impose their will upon others and those who find themselves being manipulated, bullied, or terrorized. The sad truth about most instances of us versus them is that the group with the greater power sincerely believes that its biased behavior is justified, even morally required. Most religious texts can be twisted to support a favored worldview. Other times, no twisting is necessary—the texts are biased and outdated. But the real issue is that the dominant culture has the privilege of imposing its beliefs, worldview, and often its laws on others. That privilege is maintained by a bizarre kind of rationalization. The more powerful group in the us versus them equation goes to great lengths to protect its favorable status—if necessary casting 'the other' as evil, inhuman, or naturally inferior and naming any attempts to gain equal status as attacks on their own rights, beliefs, and values."

"Again," said Rebecca, "why is this such a common phenomenon? There is a lot of research supporting the notion that people respond unquestioningly to values or fears they already share. Politicians are quick to capitalize on this tendency—casting their campaigns in language that seems to invoke traditional virtues—whether they truly do or not. Partly it is a matter of people favoring their own identities, but it is also a matter of human emotional attachment. We are drawn to our own people more strongly than to others. As the song says, 'Blest be the tie that binds.' In-crowds are made up of individuals liking their own kin, their own kind."

"My personal interest in all of the us versus them issues that were obvious in Handel's day is easily wrapped up in one glaring schism—inequality in how the world treats men and women. In the 1700s, patriarchal values meant that women were dependent on men economically, politically, even religiously, and rarely if ever were women allowed to further themselves academically or professionally. I think that is why I so enjoyed Handel's *Partenope*—especially the version we watched. As a comic opera, it did little to actually challenge the plight of women in Handel's day, or even of an earlier time—the period of Naples' legendary founder, Partenope, in Italy's late Iron Age. The story of Queen Partenope and her suitors is fairly ordinary, but the character Rosmira, who pretends to be a man and, in disguise, taunts her lover Arsace, is a forceful exploration of how culture confines women and denies them opportunities to live as independently as men. It is so apparent throughout the opera that Rosmira (as the supposed shipwrecked prince, Eurimene) has exciting opportunities to participate in important activities that would have been denied her as a woman. And when the other suitors denigrate Arsace for his apparent cowardice in tolerating 'Eurimene's' insults, Rosmira defends him, saying to the others that Arsace 'clearly sees what you cannot, a hidden flame, that blazes in me and frightens' him. Arsace is reluctant to combat Rosmira because he knows who she really is, but he may also be frightened of her presumption of equality, her successful impersonation of a man."

"So many instances of conflict, hatefulness, and constraint are, in the end, a result of one group feeling they have the right to tell others what to do, what to believe, who is most important, what the hierarchical pecking order should be. Our cultures teach us this—as the song from *South Pacific* says, 'You've got to be taught to be afraid of people' who are not like you. And you need to look down on those your culture sees as beneath you lest they take away your privilege and right to see yourself as better than they are. Handel was not in the business of protesting the political or religious inequalities of his day, but some of his works do give us fodder for such challenges today. That is what I take away from our Seminar—incentive to find creative ways to combat habitual and treasured sources of bias and conflict, especially the staunchly preserved patriarchy."

Rebecca picked the hat up and looked around. "Who's next?" she said. "That would be me," said Brad. He took the hat, turned it inside out, and said, "It would take some work to turn this into a yarmulke. Now if you want to talk about a cap with some real potential for ritualistic significance, we should have a *kippah*, the traditional Jewish skullcap—a yarmulke—not this unimpressive captain's topper. But, I'm only observant during the holidays, so we'll just let it slide—no hat of any sort." He put the cap aside.

"Have you all seen the movie *Thoroughly Modern Millie?*" Brad asked. "I think I was just starting college when I first saw it—a great date flick. Anyway, the reason I bring it up—there is a scene in which Julie Andrews, who plays Millie, sings at a Jewish wedding. She sings this song in Yiddish—Trinkt Le Chaim—drink to life, and her friend, played by Mary Tyler Moore, says to a wedding guest, 'It's Jewish.' It really cracked me up, but the girl I was with said, 'What's so funny?' I said something like 'Can you imagine going to a Methodist wedding and someone saying in a kind of naïve but hush-hush way, 'It's Christian?' She didn't get it—said it would just be dumb. But, to me it was another, maybe subtle, instance of the mainstream culture being the standard and anything else being seen as odd, an outlier."

"We've talked some about how Handel was the odd man out in the London of his time, and I'll admit I finally did a little reading about Handel so I could sound more highbrow in my spiel here today. Handel was not your typical Londoner. He had a German accent, he was—until forced to swear otherwise—a Lutheran rather than an Anglican, he wasn't married, he decided to make music composition his career, and he was content to rent a house rather than own it. By most norms of the times, Handel did not fit in, but still he was probably more savvy about customs from other places than most of his friends. I think it is interesting how he came to be that way—a kind of cultural polyglot. Partly it was just that he lived in several different places—first in Halle, then Hamburg, then various large cities in Italy, and finally London. But I think it was more than that. Handel was always actively curious about the materials he worked with as a composer. He learned the languages his singers would use. He asked about what specific words meant in the context of the texts he would set. Supposedly he even suggested changes to texts that would make more sense or be better received. But you said I should connect these thoughts to something significant in my own life, so I'll say a little more about Handel's use of stories from the Hebrew Bible, or as most here will call it—the Old Testament."

"There is no point in my getting all bent out of shape about it," Brad continued, "but even the common use of the words Old Testament is a kind of backhanded insult. Would most Americans know anything about the Hebrew Bible if the men who decided what would constitute the Bible of Christendom had not included the books of the Jewish canon, the Tanakh? I'm no anthropologist, but I've heard about the concept of cultural appropriation—you know, where one culture takes something from another culture and changes it to suit the pilfering culture's own purposes. When I first heard about cultural appropriation, I thought about all the stories I learned from my culture's books—the Torah, the Prophets, the Writings—and how those sacred books were taken up and used by Christianity. It's true that there were prophecies about a messiah in the books of the prophets, but the Jewish people did not see Jesus as that messiah. It was earlier Christian leaders who decided that the Hebrew Bible could be incorporated into the Christian Bible, but only if everything in the OLD testament was revamped as a prequel leading to the main figure in the NEW testament. I know that skips over a lot of history, but what really bothers me is that Handel's most celebrated work—*Messiah*—is actually a validation of this theft and repurposing of Jewish stories."

"Ok," Brad continued, "I know theologians, even some Jewish ones, will argue that it is reasonable to include the Hebrew Bible in the Christian one. I'm not even going to try to go there. What irks me is the way everyone in America knows the books of the Tanakh through a kind of 'cultural literacy,' but most—other than Jews—know them only as they have been reinterpreted into a Christian belief system, a Christian perspective. Let me explain. First, *cultural literacy*—it's a useful concept I learned about recently. Actually a man named E. D. Hirsch introduced the term maybe thirty years ago, and then there were a lot of dictionaries and other books expanding the idea. What he argued in his book was that all Americans needed to know, or at least recognize, a lot of information—specific words and phrases—that would prove they were educated citizens, that they were smart enough to get certain allusions that only smart people get. His book included long lists of words, and some twenty or thirty of them referred to people or events from the Hebrew Bible. Now—thirty years later—all we need to do is check on our smart phones, no need to remember. But there is another side to his argument—one he didn't really articulate. He—or someone like him—gets to decide what is worth knowing AND maybe how it is understood. In other words, the person in power—whether it is a teacher or a politician or a priest— is the one who informs the rest of us what and how we need to know. Ok, I know I have overstated the case, but it bothers me that the average American is supposed to know about, say the book of Isaiah, as an ancient text that foretells the coming of Jesus rather than as words of one of the latter prophets of Israel, sufficient and sacred in its own right. To me, the books of the 'Old Testament' were not simply borrowed and put to a new use but were ultimately turned around and used to denigrate the culture that originally owned them. Jews have always been blamed for not accepting the Christian interpretation of Jesus as the messiah. And the cultural deciders get to dictate that this Christian perspective is correct and Jews are wrong. It is blatant cultural appropriation and pretty nasty appropriation at that."

"I can see all kinds of metaphorical flares going off here. Actually—to use a Christian turn of phrase—among this group I am probably preaching to the choir. What I really want to leave you with is my own sense of disgruntlement. It can't be anything stronger than that. After all, I have to live in the world I'm in. What I would really like to convey is how bad I felt for my mother, who was really much more bothered by this than I am. It is some years since my mother died. At the beginning of World War Two, she was young and really glad to be living in America. She lost relatives in the Holocaust. Growing up in Indiana, she tried to fit in as well as any Jewish girl living in the Protestant heartland could. She even participated in the community singing of Handel's *Messiah*—something that happened every Christmas in her hometown. She was smart—a much better student than I ever was. And she was interested and listened carefully to the way Handel's *Messiah* quoted material from the Prophets, from the Holy Books she had studied in Hebrew school. But she was unhappy with the way words were changed or left out or conflated into ideas not in the texts she knew. And she didn't like the way words that spoke of Adonai became words that spoke of a Christian God, one that for most Americans identified a divine trinity and included a messiah, a savior called Jesus Christ. To her, that meant the text was changed. It was no longer the Holy Books of her people but something that was taken and used without permission—like an Ojibwe dream catcher or a feathered headdress worn at some white guys' charity ball—even if it is for a good cause. It's just not right. My mother knew about Handel's other oratorios—*Solomon, Saul, Samson, Judas Maccabaeus, Joshua*, even *Israel in Egypt*. She hadn't heard them performed, but she knew Handel had composed music for all of those stories and more. She thought they were all—at least to her mind—changed into something different by their association with *Messiah* and the way that ever-popular piece reflected on the older stories, the stories that should have been seen as Jewish stories, stories from the Hebrew Bible, not stories simply leading to the coming of Christ."

"I will say I found a book that vindicated my mother and her attitude toward *Messiah*—a book titled *Tainted Glory in Handel's Messiah*, by Michael Marissen. Marissen—he is not Jewish, by the way—points to the many instances in which the text of *Messiah* exhibits what he calls Christian triumphalism, the tendency to assume that, from a Christian perspective, Jews deserve contempt, an attitude present in Handel's day and still around in ours. Certainly not all or even most Christians feel contempt for Jews. I remember my mother telling of how, when she was young, her synagogue in Fort Wayne was graffitied with Nazi swastikas, and, right away, her Christian neighbors came to help wash off the offensive symbols. Still, I am glad I didn't have to live through that kind of abuse or the selectively closed clubs, hotels, and schools my mother encountered, but I've had my share of hassles, especially when I was younger. My mother did not approve of my name change. She thought I should show more pride in my heritage. But she loved me anyway. She was a wonderful woman. I should have tried harder to make her happy and proud—should have taken up the cause, I suppose. Actually you people are the first ones to hear this story about my mother—well, other than my family. That must be a good thing, right? Handel had his worthwhile impact after all."

Alison turned the hat Brad had set aside right side out again. She smiled at Brad. "I am sorry to hear that your mother had such unhappy things as part of her life. I'm sure she was proud of you even if you did change your name. Mothers are usually wonderfully forgiving. Mine was. Now here is something MY mother did when times were hard." Alison put the captain's hat on and started doing a noisy little stiff-legged dance. "Back in Handel's day, this would have been dubbed a sailor's hornpipe," said Alison, "but today it's usually called *clogging*, and folks from Kentucky do it at the proverbial drop of a hat. Needs some harder shoes, but you get the idea."

"Ok, my wrap-up comments on Handel. You may remember that I had been taught to deride Handel because earlier, in the mid-1900s, he was regarded as something of a plagiarist. It is true that he borrowed from others and from himself, recasting some pieces into new works, reusing old material often several times. But as we have examined some of his works for our discussions and as I have actually gone back and listened to quite a bit of his music, I have gained a real respect for the way he composed, often building on earlier material but tweaking it or taking it in a new direction. I have not studied composition. My area is voice and choral conducting, but I appreciate what I have come to see as Handel's objective. He wanted to give singers and musicians a chance to shine, to be really impressive and moving during performance. And he wanted to really grab his audience. If that meant reusing something he had used before, he would work with the melody or piece until it conveyed the new idea he wanted to present. I think he truly relished transforming the vast traditions that he knew into new arias, new choruses, new operas. I think he was more interested in having an excellent end product than in worrying about whether he had reused bits that had been used before. And he had to adapt things to the singers and orchestras he had available. He was a much more interactive composer than later critics maybe wanted him to be. But now, in retrospect, I am really glad that he chose to compose the way he did. It reminds me of how I absolutely loved hearing Elvis Presley sing *I Can't Help Falling in Love with You*. Remember that? It was actually an old French love song called *Plaisir d'amour*. Kathleen Battle sings the French original if you want to listen. But most people know it because a more recent songwriter reconfigured it, and Elvis sang it. It IS a beautiful melody."

"And actually, as I was listening to Brad earlier, I realized that the issue here is something like the practice of using other people's ideas or traditions or stories. Anything that gets played or sung or spoken or acted—any performance—is going to change a little bit each time someone else uses it in a performance. It is true that Christian theologians borrowed the books of the Old Testament from the Hebrew Bible, but I suspect it was actually a gradual kind of thing. A lot of those old stories were oral and were widely shared by people who may or may not have been Jewish or Christian or Roman or Turkish. Who knows? Anyway, I like Handel's operas—which were mostly based on heroic tales from ancient history or mythology. And I like Handel's oratorios, too, and they are, as Brad said, based mainly on Old Testament stories. Handel was a man of his times. His Lord or God was the Christian God, even if the stories involving that God were borrowed from the Hebrew Bible. Personally, I thought Handel's ending to *Jephtha* was better than the Old Testament narrative. I think most modern Christians—and maybe many modern Jews—accept that the stories were part of an older culture and need to be seen with new eyes. It's always better to notice what we share rather than dwelling on what makes us different from each other. I think Handel's music is ultimately good for bringing people together rather than keeping them apart. I am really glad to see that there is a resurgence of interest in Handel's music—his operas and oratorios, especially. I for one plan to make *Lascia la spina* a permanent part of my repertoire."

Alison handed the Captain's hat over to Katherine. "Thanks, everyone," said Katherine. "I think, unless anyone objects, I will hand this hat on to Benfey for all her hard work recording our discussions. No doubt Ross would have liked to add it to his collection of memorabilia, but I think Benfey earned it." Ross said, "I agree, definitely. Don't worry about my collections. I always find something—and not always what everyone else would guess should serve that purpose."

"Now," Ross continued, "I believe we have finished our formal obligations here. However, our esteemed convener—Forella Wainwright—has asked that we meet one more time. I, too, hope everyone will agree to one additional get-together. Hey, how can you not want to sample Annie's great cooking one more time? But it will be a short meeting, and soon—maybe two weeks from now. Mother, I will let you explain the purpose."

"Thank you, Ross," said Forella. "Yes, I do indeed hope each of you can join us for this last meeting. We have recently been in contact with the lawyer handling our dear Mrs. Finch's affairs. I have some important news to share with you on what may or may not be done with the letters and with our collective discussion of them. I need to make sure everything is in order before I pass this information along to you. And, truthfully, I simply want to visit with you all one more time. This ongoing seminar has been such a delight. I will miss each of you and our wonderful discussions. And I am sure I will miss having Handel so prominently a part of my life. I have asked Angela to contact each of you with the time and date. Until then, enjoy this changeable Indiana weather."

CHAPTER 28
Personal Proverbs

Forella held the small penknife she had received from the lawyer's office in Newbury, Berkshire. The woman who had sold her the Handel letters wanted her to have it. The knife had been a family heirloom, or so the woman had been told. As far as she knew, it had nothing to do with Handel or the letters she had found, but it was, according to family stories, a knife her great-great grandfather used to trim feather quills, back before metal nibs were invented. Forella thought of the many artifacts, the many customs, surrounding our need to communicate beyond our easy, everyday verbal exchanges. For centuries, writing was a primary means of communicating, a way to move our thoughts into the future, when someone else would see them written in ink or printed on vellum, and, reading, would understand. Yet now, with her vision fading to a handicap, Forella recognized the value of new technology, new ways of using alternate senses to learn what others were thinking moments or even years before. She smiled and put the small knife to the side, thinking that perhaps Ross would want it for his eccentric collection of memorable objects. It was certainly part of the Handel saga.

Annie had searched out the typical luncheon fare for Saxony during Handel's time. She saw a lot of possibilities but decided on bratwurst with sauerkraut, potato soup, white asparagus, and of course Black Forest cake to top it all off. She had some beer on hand, but nearly everyone wanted coffee to complement the cake. Peter gave a small lecture on how coffee houses became so popular throughout Europe during the eighteenth century. The gathering was clearly convivial, and, to Forella's delight, everyone was able to attend.

As food disappeared and second cups of coffee were welcomed, Ross stood up and clinked his water glass for attention. "As they say in the political arena, our people have talked with her people—that is, mother's lawyer has corresponded with our Mrs. Finch's lawyer about the Handel letters. There is nothing really new on the public display front. The twenty-five year wait is still in place on that score. However, we were told that an alternative, perhaps more unorthodox, means of sharing the information is possible. And, as we shall see, Benfey has certainly earned her pay (and her cap) in this instance. It has been agreed that we can use the letters in a project that might be dubbed a biographical conversation, a kind of creative nonfiction. As you might guess, this is the sort of thing dear to my heart—although, sadly, making a documentary film is not an option at this time. However, if all of you agree to the terms of the project proposal, we could see something at least informative and fun arise from our months of dialogue. We could see a book that modestly avers to share our discussions and thoughts about the letters, along with printed transcriptions of the letters, even if the letters themselves remain unavailable for display for another twenty years. What do you say? I have a paper with information on the proposal for each of you."

Everyone read the document carefully, and after a short discussion, everyone agreed to sign on. Ross smiled and said, "One more thing—remember our flip chart—the one that has been our makeshift blackboard for nearly every meeting? Benfey has documented each page as a digital photo, so I feel at least somewhat justified in asking to place the chart in my infamous collections room—with one modification: I'd like each of you to sign this last page. I can think of few things I would treasure more than this record of our seminar, and having each of your signatures is way better than even a team-signed baseball. I'd really appreciate the favor. And if any of you want to come visit the chart in its new habitat, you are more than welcome."

Ross flipped to the last page of the chart, and everyone came forward and signed. "I'll take a photo of this page once each of us has signed," said Benfey. "Annie, could you track down Randolph? We need to have everyone on here. Actually, I was wondering if you would each like a t-shirt with this page reproduced on the back—and maybe a picture of Handel on the front. I know someone who can do that for us pretty quickly. What do you think?"

"A t-shirt! Of course," said Peter. "Great idea. Years hence—when we finally get to display the letters, the shirt will be a marketing wonder. Thanks, everyone, for making this Seminar such an enjoyable project. I will miss our interactions. Please do stop by the history museum if you are up in Indianapolis. I'd love to give you a tour."

"I echo those sentiments," said Katherine. "I can't think of a time I have had so much fun simply talking with a group of people. Thanks to each of you for participating. And now I believe Forella would like to say a few words."

Forella smiled broadly and fingered her cat-topped walking stick. "I do indeed want to thank you all for staying the course through these many months. I am sure some of you thought my original reasons for starting this seminar were completely daft, or perhaps simply a waste of time. But you persisted, and I am grateful. I found little in the letters to support my query on reincarnation, but I did find evidence that Handel can still teach us something about music and about life here in the twenty-first century. And now I am rather excited to move in this new direction with all of our ideas and discussions channeled into a book. Ross and Katherine have scouted out an author who will help us, and Benfey has agreed to work with her to create a manuscript. Our little library of resources will be available to her, and Angela will be our editing expert. I couldn't be happier with the prospects for in fact doing what our Mrs. Finch wanted to do in the first place—making this little addition to the record of Handel's life and work more easily available as an inspiration and touchstone for readers in our time, in our world."

"And now," Forella continued, "before I reluctantly let you all go your separate ways, I would like to thank Peter and Katherine and Ross for being our chairs of this Seminar. You may remember that I had originally thought I might simply listen to the recorded discussion and not participate much. Oh, my, was I wrong! I soon found that with everyone's thought-provoking commentary and the leadership of our three chairs, I wanted to be present nearly every time we met. There is nothing quite so enjoyable as sitting back and letting other people be the ones who take responsibility for keeping all on course. I was free to participate only as it struck my fancy, and it was a delight! I'll ask only one other thing from each of our three leaders. I wonder if you would each offer a maxim, an aphorism, that you feel summarizes what you take away from our examination of Handel, his life, and these letters. I think our Mrs. Finch would be gratified. She wanted these letters to have an effect beyond simply biographical particulars."

"Ah, Forella, you are such a shining star," said Peter. "What a lovely way to end our sojourn together. Ok, I will go first. As I have thought about Handel and his many talents and his many foibles, here is what I take away from contemplating his life: Everyone is as self-centered as I am. To me, Handel was nothing if not a self-centered man, and yet I do not see that as necessarily a bad thing. If one is constantly aware of the fact that other people are thinking of their own needs rather than what we ourselves may want or find interesting, then one is more likely to understand that other person and maybe even empathize with that person's perspective. I think Handel did that—at least some of the time. He was able to recognize when his own ideas and plans were simply not what other people wanted. He learned to accept the truth that other people's desires will sometimes prevail and that he might be wise to work with them. Remember his patient query to Jennens on what changes might be needed in *Messiah*? Sometimes Handel let another person's wants be more important than his own. So, that is my little maxim: Everyone is as self-centered as I am. Make of it what you will."

The Handel Letters

Everyone clapped appreciatively. Katherine looked a little disquieted. "Oh, dear, let me think. Peter is much quicker on his feet than I am. Well, I would agree that Handel was in the main self-centered, but he was also, I think, very strongly attached to the perhaps few people he let into his personal world. I think he recognized an important interconnection with many of the people in his life, and I think he basically viewed most people as the same under their skin. We have perhaps seen Handel as primarily a cerebral and talented, left-brain kind of person. But I think he was also deeply emotional and compassionate. His music was in many ways his means of reaching into the hearts of people in his life, as well as ours—his love songs to humanity. I think his desire to connect with others was what drove his career, not simply the competitiveness we so often attribute to him. So, my little proverb would simply be: We are all interconnected. In an odd way, I see it as a necessary complement to Peter's words. I think they are both something I take away from this look at Handel and his life."

As everyone acknowledged Katherine's remarks, Ross stood and walked over to the bookshelf holding the various Handel materials and picked up Christopher Hogwood's biography of Handel. He turned to page 191 and held it up for everyone to see. "This photo," Ross explained, "is labeled 'Cast of death mask, by Roubiliac. Now lost.' I find it a very moving picture, whether the cast really is Handel's death mask or simply one fashioned from a clay overlay while he was still living. I think, in any case, we can agree that it is the purest representation of Handel to come down to us—the closest thing to a photograph, a true likeness. Handel asked Lydia to stop writing to him once his vision started to fail so badly that he could no longer read her letters on his own. We, in effect, left him contemplating the last remaining years of his life. We read parts of his will. We learned who was likely to be in his thoughts as he died—his friends, servants, and relatives—and perhaps his perception of God. My own words to the wise are tied to this image of a fading Handel, a man contemplating his own death after such a full and amazing life. My maxim would be: The universe will take care of me. As you might guess,

I do not myself have visions of a heaven or an anthropomorphic god, but I expect maybe Handel did. Nevertheless, I have something of the same confidence that—in the end—my atoms will reenter what we might call the realm of the infinite and that my life will have been a unique and excellent part of what we relish as existence in our great universe. I feel I will be unafraid to die and grateful for being a part of it all. That is my motto: The universe will take care of me. I hope it complements the other two as well."

Forella shed a few tears as everyone applauded. "Thank you all, my friends," she said. What a wonderful experience this has been. May your days be rich and joyful. Stay safe, and be well. I cherish each and every one of you. I hope our paths cross many more times. Farewell and good fortune to all."

EPILOGUE

The omniscient author sat at her desk, thinking of how she might present the material on Handel that had been entrusted to her. It should not be a typical biography but, then, not a biographical novel either. Perhaps an epic—the Epic of Handel, hero of Halle, Orpheus of London, beloved Saxon, composer of Messiah and creator of Water Music. Perhaps a fairy tale, but, no, the materials were, after all, recorded in the form of an ethnography, a sequence of dialogues. Still, it would be good if the piece would draw in the reader, as does a story, just as did the many stories that enticed Handel, with the subtle power of a Burgundy wine. She opened her laptop and began to type: Katherine took up the letter in her white-gloved hand. Yes—whether fairy tale or ethnography, there must be a hero, some loyal friends, and an omniscient author.

Ross was pleased that Katherine had taken him up on his offer to show anyone from the Handel Seminar his now infamous collections room. So far she was the only one to visit—besides Peter, and of course Forella and Angela, who had been there countless times before. Katherine was a bit intimidated by the grandeur of the place, Ross's large home on the north side of Indianapolis. Really wealthy folks were not usually among her everyday friends—and Ross had definitely become a very good friend. Katherine was a little more relaxed when Ross steered her toward the veranda and the small table with the makings of a lunch set out along with a bottle of chilled wine.

"I usually eat at a cafe with some of my collaborators" said Ross, "but I make a pretty good ham and cheese sandwich, if do say so myself. And the Jewish deli a couple blocks from here makes a great potato salad—in the blue dish there. I could rustle up some steamed broccoli if you would like. I know you like to eat healthy. Sorry, I have no Annie on staff. I'm usually not home enough to make it worth anyone's time."

Katherine laughed and said, "Ross, this is just fine, and the sandwich looks great—and the potato salad. Really, you didn't need to feed me, but thank you. I like your little table out here on the porch. But, I wonder, don't you find the house awfully large, knocking about here all by yourself? It is beautiful, and I can't wait to see this notorious collections room, but this is a home fit for a huge family, or at least several large dogs. Do you entertain a lot?--Ok, I know, more of my nosy questions."

Ross smiled. "I'm not home regularly enough to have pets. I think it would be cruel, given my erratic schedule. Yes, you are good at those nosy questions. Sometimes the house DOES seem too large, but as I say, I'm usually not here long enough for it to become a problem. Mostly I needed a place for all the furniture and artwork from my parents' home in Tennessee. In some ways I envy my mother's smaller condo down in Bloomington, but, on the other hand, I love the grounds here—great for walking. There's a pond, and I get quite a few water birds and other things that like the wet. I even saw a beaver out by the beech trees. But let's finish up this humble repast, and I'll show you the Ross Wainwright collection room. You can bring your wine."

As they walked back through the main part of the house, Katherine noticed the many fine pieces of furniture and the paintings and bronzes. She wondered if Ross's special collection was more of the same—not that more of the same would in any way be shoddy. Every piece she saw was beautiful, interesting, and in good taste. But Ross had said that his special room contained things that had specific personal meanings for him. That was what intrigued Katherine—the promise of a clearer view into this engaging and yet puzzling man's inner life. Rather like her curiosity about Handel—another fascinating man.

Off the second floor balustrade, a large oak door led into the collections room. Katherine was not disappointed. It was indeed like a small museum, with a great variety of objects, each labeled with a card, in fine calligraphy, describing the circumstances and the person responsible for the item's inclusion in the collection. "Did you create these labels yourself? Did you do the calligraphy? They are really wonderful!" Katherine exclaimed. Ross grinned. "It's been my favorite hobby for years. Yes, I like having a use for that calligraphy I learned back in school. I'm glad you like them."

Katherine continued to move around the room, reading each card. Ross disappeared and quickly returned with the wine bottle, filled Katherine's glass, and stood back, clearly enjoying showing off his little collection of memorabilia. Katherine spent a good hour walking around the room, asking occasionally about specific objects or the places mentioned on the cards. Finally, she said, "What a marvelous room, Ross! Everyone in our Seminar needs to see this. It is just wonderful, and I feel, indeed, that I know you even so much better after seeing all of this. Thank you for sharing it with me. What a treasure!"

Ross stopped in front of the flip chart from their Handel Seminar meetings. "It would be nice to share my collection room with everyone else in the group, but, you know, Katherine, you and I shared some good times the others didn't. So, in commemoration of our co-chairmanship, our chance meeting in London, our extra consultations on the Handel letters, whatever—let me make this unprecedented offer. You, my dear Katherine, may take with you any object—well, one you can carry, of course—and I promise I will tell you the full story behind that piece. It can become a kind of touchstone for you, just as it has been for me. That is what these things are for me—reminders of parts of my life I never want to forget. What will it be? Anything. Even the Handel flip chart. If you can carry it, it is yours."

Katherine looked around the room. There were several large pieces of furniture—beautiful and interesting with impressive stories attached to them—but too big for her to lift, obviously. She examined the kicksled from Norway and a puppet from France. Then there was an abundance of smaller items on shelves—all compelling in their own way. "Have you ever heard of the Grimm tale called *The Clever Peasant Girl*?" she asked. Ross shook his head. "It's a great story," Katherine continued. "The heroine gets to choose an object, too. I may have to take a cue from her—pick something like the treasure she chose."

She walked over near the door. Ross followed. Katherine stopped in front of a small object on a shelf near the door. "Come here, if you would, for a minute," she said to Ross. He stood next to her. "Did I ever tell you my father was a fireman?" she asked. "No," said Ross, "does this silver watch have something to do with firemen?" "I have no idea," said Katherine, "but this does." And she backed up until she was right in front of him with her back to his front, took his arms and draped them over her shoulders, and leaned over. With great effort she lifted him up long enough to move—bearlike and with shaking limbs—through the door and unto the second floor landing.

Ross sputtered and stood upright while Katherine turned around, put her arms around his neck, and smiled. Ross exclaimed, "I guess I'll have to read that story. I'm pretty sure I like it already. But here's one for you. Do you know who William Goldman is?" Katherine shook her head. "He wrote the story that gave us the amazing movie *The Princess Bride*. Goldman wrote—at the end of the his book—'There have been five great kisses since 1642 BC . . . .' To take nothing away from Wesley and Buttercup, but methinks it is time to bring this saga up to date."

And they did.

Finished: July 14, 2017

George Frideric Handel

ACKNOWLEDGMENTS

My parents and the people of my hometown, Huntington, Indiana, introduced me to Handel's music—in particular, to Handel's *Messiah*—because that it what people in small Midwestern towns did back then. Every year, at Christmastime, the community came together to sing *Messiah*, with orchestra and choir conducted by the high school choir director, Cloyde Slater. In high school and college, I happily joined whatever choirs were available, and I have continued to seek out a church choir or community choir every year since then—with the confident understanding that I would, at some point, get to sing again some of the choral masterpieces of George Frideric Handel. I was not disappointed.

I am grateful to all of the people who, like Cloyde Slater, have ensured that Handel's music remains an important part of our cultural heritage. And I am grateful to my educational mentors, especially professors and scholars in the field of folklore studies, who gave me the theories and tools to appreciate and examine human creativity and expression. Indiana University granted me an MA and a PHD in Folklore and later hired me to teach in the renowned Department of Folklore and Ethnomusicology. I thank my colleagues and students for sharing their stimulating ideas, performances, and research. And I thank the University and the town of Bloomington for its commitment to abundant and excellent music—the Jacobs School of Music, the Lotus Festival, the Archives of Traditional Music. Bloomington is a special place.

For this project, I am especially grateful for the many biographers, scholars, opera houses and video producers, singers, and Handel enthusiasts who have made their research and commentary and performances available to the public. Every piece of research has been a pleasure to read, and every production I have been able to view or attend has been moving and instructive in turn. The Bibliography that closes this book is the list of sources without which I could not have imagined my subject nor compiled this collage of ideas, biography, and performance. They are the essential resources in my treasure house, my inanimate yet ever vitally present instructors.

And also for this project, the purest personal delight came in being able to call upon my daughter, Alexis Stahl, to create the cover and the chapter images throughout this work. I remember her designing and fabricating small books as part of her MFA training. I knew she would create the perfect icons to go with each chapter and capitalize on her artist's understanding of what goes into the physical presentation we call a book. Again, I was not disappointed, but elated, and of course, proud and grateful.

Finally, I would like to thank my friends and neighbors and family, many of whom have listened patiently to my effusive comments on Handel and his long-ago life. Many gifted me with books, videos, or articles on my subject. I especially thank the various discussion groups at the Bloomington UU Church for modeling the seminar I present here—the UU Humanist Forum, The Free Thinkers, the Chalice Circles, the Walkers, the Choir, the Fellowship Dinners. It has been my good fortune to be surrounded by so many articulate and deep-thinking friends. I thank you all.

BIBLIOGRAPHY

A Night with Handel: Great Handel Arias Set in Contemporary London by Night. 2007. Dir. Alex Marengo. DVD. Kultur. Warner Music Group.

Altemeyer, Robert. 2009. *The Authoritarians.* Ramona, CA: Cherry Hill Publishing.

André, Naomi. 2006. *Voicing Gender.* Bloomington: Indiana University Press.

Barockstar: George Frideric Handel. 2009. Dir. Ulrich Meyszies. DVD. ArtHaus Musik.

Bayles, David and Ted Orland. 1993. *Art and Fear.* Santa Cruz, CA: The Image Continuum.

Bennett, Gillian. 1987. *Traditions of Belief.* London: Penguin Books.

Blau, Melinda and Karen L. Fingerman. 2009. *Consequential Strangers.* New York: W.W. Norton.

Bright, Janette and Gillian Clark. 2011. *An Introduction to the Tokens at the Foundling Museum.* London: The Foundling Museum.

Brookfield, Stephen D. and Stephen Preskill. 2005. *Discussion as a Way of Teaching*. 2nd Ed. San Francisco: Jossey-Bass.

Brooks, Helen. 2008. "'Your Sincere Friend and Humble Servant': Evidence of Managerial Aspirations in Susannah Cibber's Letters." *Studies in Theatre and Performance* 28: 147-59.

Brown, Mary Ellen, ed. 2008. Performance score for *Il Pesceballo (The Fish-Ball)*, A Twenty-First Century Revival, August 2008.

Burrows, Donald, ed. 1997. *The Cambridge Companion to Handel*. Cambridge: Cambridge University Press.

Burrows, Donald. 1994. *Handel*. Oxford: Oxford University Press.

Burrows, Donald. 1991. *Handel: Messiah*. Cambridge: Cambridge University Press.

Burrows, Donald, ed. 2008. *Handel's Will: Facsimiles and Commentary*. London: The Gerald Coke Handel Foundation.

Burrows, Donald and Peter Ward Jones. 2004. "Musicians and Music Copyists in Mid-Eighteenth-Century Oxford." In *Concert Life in Eighteenth-Century Britain*, ed. Susan Wollenberg and Simon McVeigh. Burlington, VT: Ashgate Publishing. Pp. 115-39.

Chrissochoides, Ilias. 2007. "A Handel Relative in Britain?" *The Musical Times* 148: 49-58.

Clegg, Jeanne. 2015. "Good to Think with: Domestic Servants, England 1660-1750."*Journal of Modern Studies* 4:43-66.

Coontz, Stephanie. 2005. *Marriage, a History*. New York: Viking.

Cosmos: A Spacetime Odyssey. 2014. Host: Neil deGrasse Tyson. DVD Series. Twentieth Century Fox.

Coxe, William. 1979. *Anecdotes of George Frederick Handel and John Christopher Smith.* New York: Da Capo Press.

Daniel Defoe: The Collection of the Lilly Library. 2008. Curator, Denise Griggs. Online exhibitions. http://www.indiana.edu/~liblilly/defoe/index.html

De Luise, Vincent P. 2015. "The Eyes of Bach and Handel." *Hektoen International: A Journal of Medical Humanities.* Vol. 7: No. 4 (Fall 2015).

Dolby (Stahl), Sandra K. 1989. "Family Settlement Stories and Personal Values." In *The Old Traditional Way of Life*, ed. Robert E Walls and George H. Schoemaker. Bloomington, IN: Trickster Press. Pp. 362-66.

Dolby, Sandra K. 2005. *Self-Help Books: Why Americans Keep Reading Them.* Urbana: University of Illinois Press.

Dolby, Sandra K. 2008. *Literary Folkloristics and the Personal Narrative.* Bloomington, IN: Trickster Press.

Dundes, Alan. 1971. "A Study of Ethnic Slurs: The Jew and the Polack in the United States." *Journal of American Folklore.* Vol. 84. Pp. 186-203.

Dundes, Alan. 1975. "Slurs International: Folk Comparisons of Ethnicity and National Character." *Southern Folklore Quarterly.* Vol. 39. Pp. 15-38.

Dundes, Alan. 1980. "The Hero Pattern and the Life of Jesus." In *Interpreting Folklore*, by Alan Dundes. Bloomington: Indiana University Press. Pp. 223-61.

Dundes, Alan. 1984. *Life Is Like a Chicken Coop Ladder: A Study of German National Character through Folklore*. New York: Columbia University Press.

Flower, Newman. 1923. *George Frideric Handel: His Personality and His Times*. London: Waverley Book Co.

Gardner, Howard. 1993. *Creating Minds*. New York: Basic Books.

Geehern, Gregory Jon. 2012. *It Must Be So: Reconsidering the Dramatic Agencies in George Frideric Handel's Jephtha*. Bloomington: Indiana University.

Gilman, Todd. 2009. "Arne, Handel, the Beautiful, and the Sublime." *Eighteenth-Century Studies*. 42 (4): 529-55.

God Rot Tunbridge Wells: The Life of Georg Frederic Handel. 1985. Dir. Tony Palmer. DVD. Isolde Films.

Handel: *Alcina*. 2015. Warner DVD. Aix en Provence: Festival d'Aix-en-Provence.

Handel: *Messiah, A Sacred Oratorio*. 2006. Cantillation and Australian Broadcasting Corp. DVD. Kultur Studios.

Handel: *Partenope*. 2008. Decca DVD. Copenhagen: Royal Danish Opera.

Handel: *Semele*. 2007. Decca DVD. Zurich: Opernhaus.

Handel: *Serse*. 2000. EuroArts DVD. Dresden: Semperoper.

Handel: *Theodora*. 1996. Kultur DVD. Lewes, UK: Glyndebourne.

Handel's Water Music: Recreating a Royal Spectacular. 2003. Dir. Andrew Manze. BBC. Pdr. DVD James Whitbourn. Opus Arte.

Handel's Last Chance. 1996. Dir. Milan Cheylov. DVD. Devine Entertainment.

Harris, Ellen T. 2001. *Handel as Orpheus: Voice and Desire in the Chamber Cantatas.* Cambridge, MA: Harvard University Press.

Harris, Ellen T. 2008. "Joseph Goupy and George Frideric Handel: From Professional Triumphs to Personal Estrangement." *Huntington Library Quarterly* 71: 397-452.

Harris, Ellen T. 2014. *George Frideric Handel: A Life with Friends.* New York: W.W. Norton and Co.

Harris, Mark W. 2011. *Elite: Uncovering Classism in Unitarian Universalist History.* Boston: Skinner House Books.

Hirsch, E.D., Jr. 1987. *Cultural Literacy.* Boston: Houghton Mifflin.

Hogan, Margaret A. and C. James Taylor, eds. 2007. *My Dearest Friend: Letters of Abigail and John Adams.* Cambridge, MA: Harvard University Press.

Hogwood, Christopher. 2007. *Handel.* Rev ed. London: Thames & Hudson.

Hollis, James. 2005. *Finding Meaning in the Second Half of Life.* New York: Gotham Books.

Howell, Caro. 2014. "How Handel's Messiah helped London's orphans—and vice versa." *The Guardian.* March 13, 2014.

Hunter, David. 2006. "Miraculous Recovery? Handel's Illnesses, the Narrative Tradition of Heroic Strength and the Oratorio Turn." *Eighteenth-Century Music* 3: 253-67.

Hunter, David. 2015. *The Lives of George Frideric Handel*. Woodbridge, Suffolk: The Boydell Press.

Indiana Urinalysis. 1988. Dir. Bart Everson and Brian Jones. DVD. B.rox.

Isaacson, Walter. 2003. *Benjamin Franklin: An American Life*. New York: Simon and Schuster.

James, Kirsten. 2014. "What Was Perfume in the Eighteenth Century?" Retrieved from https://recipes.hypotheses.org/tag/kirsten-james

Jansen, William Hugh. 1959. "The Esoteric-Exoteric Factor in Folklore." *Fabula* 2:205-11.

Keates, Jonathan. 2008. *Handel: The Man and His Music*. London: Pimlico.

Knapton, Sarah. 2015. "Bullying in Childhood to Blame for One Million Obese Britons." *The Telegraph*. May 20, 2015.

Lakoff, George. 2002. *Moral Politics: How Liberals and Conservatives Think*. 2nd ed. Chicago: University of Chicago Press.

Landgraf, Annette and David Vickers, eds. 2009. *The Cambridge Handel Encyclopedia*. Cambridge: Cambridge University Press.

LaRue, C. Steven. 1995. *Handel and His Singers*. Oxford: Clarendon Press.

Ledbetter, David, ed. 1990. *Continuo Playing According to Handel*. Oxford: Oxford University Press.

Lindahl, Carl. 2004. "Thrills and Miracles: Legends of Lloyd Chandler." *Journal of Folklore Research* 14: 133-71.

Mallinger, Allan E. and Jeannette DeWyze. 1992. *Too Perfect*. New York: Clarkson Potter.

Man from Earth. 2007. DVD. Starz. Movie: *Jerome Bixby's Man from Earth*. Dir. Richard Schenkman.

Marissen, Michael. 2014. *Tainted Glory in Handel's Messiah*. New Haven: Yale University Press.

Marshall, Emma. 1896. *The Master of Musicians: A Story of Handel's Days*. London: Seeley and Company.

Martinec, Radan. 2003. "Concept Evaluation in Focus Groups: Semantic Fields and Evaluative Strategies." *Semiotica* 147: 357-388.

McGeary, Thomas. 2009. "Handel as Art Collector: Art, Connoisseurship and Taste in Hanoverian Britain." *Early Music* 37: 533-574.

Melchert, Norman. 1994. *Who's to Say? A Dialogue on Relativism*. Indianapolis: Hackett Publishing Company.

Müller, Erich H., ed. 1970. *The Letters and Writings of George Frideric Handel*. New York: Arno Press.

Nash, Mary. 1977. *The Provoked Wife: The Life and Times of Susannah Cibber*. Boston: Little, Brown and Co.

Nunez, Paul L. 2016. *The New Science of Consciousness: Exploring the Complexity of Brain, Mind and Self.* New York: Prometheus Books.

Owen, David. 1995. *Getting There from Here: Meditations for the Journey.* Bloomington IN: St. Mark's Methodist Church.

Owen, David. 2002. *Wending Our Way: Reflections on the Journey.* Indianapolis: North United Methodist Church.

Parker, Willie, MD. 2017. *Life's Work: From the Trenches, A Moral Argument for Choice.* New York: Atria.

Pool, Daniel. 1993. *What Jane Austen Ate and Charles Dickens Knew.* New York: Simon & Schuster.

Porter, Roy. 1994. *London: A Social History.* Cambridge: Harvard University Press.

Propp, Vladimir. 1968. *Morphology of the Folktale.* 2nd Ed. Trans. Laurence Scott. Austin: University of Texas Press.

Riding, Jacqueline. 2010. *Mid-Georgian Britain.* Oxford: Shire Publications.

Rothman, Joshua. 2017. "Daniel Dennett's Science of the Soul." *The New Yorker.* March 27, 2017.

Rufus, Anneli. 2003. *Party of One.* Cambridge, MA: Da Capo Press.

Sapolsky, Robert M. 2017. *Behave: The Biology of Humans at Our Best and Worst.* New York: Penguin Press.

Singing the Living Tradition. 1993. Unitarian Universalist Association. Boston: UUA.

Smith, Ruth. 1995. *Handel's Oratorios and Eighteenth-Century Thought.* Cambridge: Cambridge University Press.

Smith, Ruth. 2014. Liner Notes to *Jephtha.* The Sixteen. Coro. COR16121. CD.

Symonds, Emily Morse (George Paston, pseudonym), compiler. 1900. *Mrs. Delany (Mary Granville) A Memoir, 1700-1788.* London: Grant Richards.

The Great Mr. Handel, Movie. 1942. Dir. Norman Walker. Perfs. Wilfrid Lawson, Elizabeth Allan. DVD. 2004. Vision Video.

Thompson, Stith. 1955. *Motif-Index of Folk Literature.* 6 vols. Bloomington: Indiana University Press.

Trompert, Wim. 2009. "Director's Notes." In *Study Guide to Semele.* Pacific Opera Victoria. Archived at http://www.pov.bc.ca.

Waal, Frans de. 2005. *Our Inner Ape.* New York: Penguin Books.

Weinstock, Herbert. 1959. *Handel.* 2nd Ed. New York: Alfred A. Knopf.

Wilson, David. 2009. "'By Heaven Inspired': A Marble Bust of Handel by Roubiliac Rediscovered." *The British Art Journal* 10 (No. 1): 14-29.

Wollenberg, Susan and Simon McVeigh, eds. 2004. *Concert Life in Eighteenth-Century Britain.* Burlington, VT: Ashgate Publishing.

Yelloly, Margaret. 2005. "'The Ingenious Miss Turner': Elizabeth Turner (d 1756), Singer, Harpsichordist and Composer." *Early Music* 33: 65-79.

Zumkeller, W. 2001. "The University of Halle through the Centuries." *Molecular Pathology* 54(1): 36-37.

Made in the USA
Columbia, SC
22 November 2017